CW01619979

ACCRINGTON STANLEY

A Complete Record
1894-1962

Dedications

'For my parents'
Mike Jackman

'For Angela, Craig and Nigel'
Garth Dykes

ACCRINGTON STANLEY

A Complete Record 1894-1962

MIKE JACKMAN & GARTH DYKES

BREEDON
BOOKS
SPORT

First published in Great Britain by
The Breedon Books Publishing Company Limited
44 Friar Gate, Derby DE1 1DA
1991

© Mike Jackman & Garth Dykes 1991

All Rights Reserved. No part of this publication may be reproduced, stored in a retrieval system, or transmitted in any form, or by any means, electronic, mechanical, photocopying, recording or otherwise without the prior permission in writing of the Copyright holders, nor be otherwise circulated in any form or binding or cover other than in which it is published and without a similar condition including this condition being imposed on the subsequent publisher.

ISBN 0 907969 89 5

Printed and bound in Great Britain by Bath Press, Bath and London.
Jacket printed by The Nuffield Press, Cowley, Oxford.

Contents

Introduction

IF IT'S possible for a small provincial football club to acquire cult status, then Accrington Stanley is probably that club. Sadly, as with many cults, it took the death of the club to bring it a fame which had eluded it whilst it was active. Other clubs have left the Football League, but none have found quite the same niche in history as Accrington Stanley. Perhaps it was the unusual name or the drama surrounding the final hours in the Football League which has given Stanley such a unique status in football folklore. Whatever the reason, the name of Accrington Stanley still has a magic which continues to this day.

A generation has grown up since Stanley died and yet the club still holds a place close to the hearts of most football followers. Surpisingly, very little has been written about he club or its history. Indeed, Accrington Stanley are often wrongly credited with being founder members of the Football League. In fact Stanley were the second football club from Accrington to enter the Football League. The original League pioneers from the town were the old Accrington Football Club. Sadly, 'Th 'Owd Reds', as they were known, survived only five seasons before leaving the League and passing into the pages of history. It was in 1921 that Stanley entered the Third Division North and brought League football back to the town.

The story of both clubs is contained within the pages of this book. It is a story of perpetual struggle and one which is a million miles removed from the glamorous game we know today. True, a few well-known players in the twilight of their careers graced Peel Park. Similarly, a handful of promising youngsters found Stanley to be a launching pad to higher things. But for the most part, Peel Park was remarkably deviod of 'stars'. The men who wore the famous old red shirts were honest journeymen, who were cheered by a small but loyal band of followers. Their names might not rank amongst the greatest in the game, but they left a legacy which has never been forgotten in the town.

Geographically situated between Blackburn and Burnley, Accrington was not well placed to support a Football League club. That it did so for 40 years is a testimony to the men involved with Accrington Stanley. Sadly, however, not even they could overcome the obstacle of having First Division football five miles on either side of the town.

As with all good stories, the history of Accrington and Accrington Stanley has its fair share of heroes and villians. The final days of the club's League life threw up plenty of both, either real or imagined. Sadly, most of the key men involved in Stanley's demise are now dead and the truth behind the club's final fall may never be told.

Whatever the truth behind the final demise of the club, the geographical location and the club's continual history of struggle were probably the key factors in the death of Accrington Stanley. The need to keep Stanley financially stable saw a procession of players leave the club. Eventually a position was reached when the club had little left to sell as the debts mounted. Whether the sale of Mike Ferguson or Alex Smith would have saved the club is open to question. In truth, North-East Lancashire couldn't support three Football League clubs and sadly, it was Stanley, the weakest of the three, who went to the wall.

As can be seen from the sources listed below, every effort has been made to ensure that the information contained in this book is correct. However, those who know the problems of collating football statistics will realize that it would be foolish to claim that every statistic in this work is indisputable. However, the authors believe that this work is as near complete as it is possible to achieve.

Work on the history and statistics was already underway when Anton Rippon at Breedon Books put me in contact with Garth Dykes. The result was that Garth undertook the daunting task to contribute a complete Who's Who of Accrington Stanley between 1921 and 1961. It should be noted that as the 1961-2 season appearances were erased from League records, it was decided not to include this season in the Who's Who section.

Mike Jackman
Blackburn
June, 1991

Notes on sources

The main sources used in researching this book have been the records of the Football League and the pages of the local Press. In particular, the *Accrington Observer & Times,* the *Accrington Gazette, Accrington Times, Accrington Advertiser, Northern Daily Telegraph* (later the *Lancashire Evening Telegraph*) and the *Lancashire Daily Post* (later the *Lancashire Evening Post*) have provided the basis of the work which follows. To these must be added innumerable newspapers which Garth consulted at Colindale for the Who's Who section. Dates of registrations are those given in the official League records.

Attendances for the period from 1924-5 onwards are those obtained from the records at the Football League offices at Lytham St Annes. It should be noted that the Football League did not keep attendance records before 1924-5. Prior to this season, approximate attendances given by newspapers have been used whenever possible.

Acknowledgements

THE authors would like to place on record their sincere appreciation of the many organizations and individuals who have co-operated so readily in the compilation of this book. From the Accrington district, particular thanks are due to the staff of the Accrington Reference Library for their kindness and co-operation at all times. In particular, Mrs J.Green, Mr A.Duckworth and Mr M.Clarke provided many leads which may otherwise have gone undetected. Bill Palmer, a lifelong supporter and reporter of the club's matches, was kind enough to loan his early notebooks which proved invaluable. Our thanks also go to Mrs Joan Croasdale, daughter of Jack Wrigglesworth, the late Secretary of Accrington Stanley FC who received the Football League's long-service medal, for her practical help and the loan of many team photographs which appear in this book. Thanks, too, to Mrs Ann Plachta, daughter of the late Chris Dodds who played over 150 matches for Stanley before the war, for her interest and support.

Our thanks to former players Jack Ash, Joe Devlin, Jimmy Forrest, Jack Hacking, Tommy Henderson, Charlie Sneddon, Joe Slattery and John Waddington, who were kind enough to relate first-hand information and in many cases loaned treasured photographs and memorabilia. Our gratitude also to the secretary and staff of the Football League, with a particular thank you to Mrs Lorna Parnell, for her unfailing help and efficiency.

The authors would like to thank the Editor of the *Lancashire Evening Telegraph* for granting access to their extensive library of back-numbers. The help of sports writer Peter White in this respect was also much appreciated.

For invaluable help with the 'Who's Who' section our thanks, as ever, go to Michael Braham, Jim Creasy, Mike Davage, Ian Garland, Brian H.Hobbs, Douglas Lamming and Peter Windle. Many correspondents and friends from the Association of Football Statisticans have supplied details of players and loaned photographs. Our thanks go to Ray Goble, Malcolm Hartley, Bryan Phillips, Ray Spiller and Roger J.Triggs. Thanks must also go to W.H. and A.Jackman for many hours spent proof-reading.

Finally, our thanks to Anton Rippon at Breedon Books for his willingness to support a project on one of the so-called 'minnows' of professional football.

Mike Jackman and Garth Dykes
June 1991

Photographic acknowledgements

Other than the sources mentioned above, photographs in this book have been supplied by Colorsport Ltd, Garth Dawson Ltd and Popperfoto Ltd.

THE ACCRINGTON STORY

ALTHOUGH there is some evidence to suggest that Accrington Cricket Club decided to form a football club as early as 1876, it is doubtful whether they played anything other than a mixture of Rugby and Association rules. The real roots of Accrington Football Club would appear to go back to a fine summer evening in 1878. It was on that evening that a meeting was convened in the Black Horse, Abbey Street, with the aim of forming a football club to bear the town's name.

Football, of course, was no stranger to East Lancashire. At a senior level Blackburn, Darwen, Clitheroe, Church and Enfield could all boast senior teams, whilst a myriad of smaller clubs had been formed throughout the area.

The men who met at the Black Horse, appointed Colonel John Hargreaves as president of the newly-formed club. This was a wise choice considering that Hargreaves was a well-known local philanthropist. A member of a wealthy local family, Hargreaves had been educated for a commercial career in banking. However, he found commerce not to his liking and had returned to Accrington to look after the considerable family estates and to oversee the operations of other local family interests.

Hargreaves was well known as a benefactor of local clubs and organizations in the town. As well as being president of Accrington Football Club, he also enjoyed spells as president of the cricket and athletic clubs. Indeed, it was Hargreaves who found Accrington Cricket Club its Thorneyholme Road ground and then charged them only a nominal rent of one shilling per year for its use.

Having installed Hargreaves as president, the meeting elected J.W.Cunliffe as treasurer and W.Eaton as secretary. The committee was made up of Messrs Talbot, Yates, Horne, Heald, Hartley,

Colonel John Hargreaves, a local philanthropist and the first president of Accrington FC.

Lightfoot and Whittaker — all men who would play an active part in the early Accrington teams. The committee decided that the club colours should be scarlet shirts and black shorts and 'Th' Owd Reds' — as they were fondly known — were born.

The newly-formed club saw its first action on 28 September 1878, when they entertained Church Rovers. In hindsight, it is perhaps hardly surprising that Accrington's first match should end in controversy. During the next decade and a half, Accrington appeared to stumble from controversy to controversy. The die, it would appear, was cast from the first match. The *Accrington Times* of 5 October carried the following report of this momentous occasion:

Football match – Accrington v Church Rovers

A match between the above clubs was played on the Accrington Cricket ground on Saturday last, in the midst of drizzling rain, and the consequence was that only a few spectators assembled. The Rovers played well together throughout, but only scored one goal, and that a rather lucky one. At the commencement the Accrington team played rather loosely, but improved as the game got more lively, and scored one goal at half-time, and then the ball was struck from the goal and hit the tape of the Church goal. The umpire of Accrington (Mr R. Calverley of Church) gave it as a goal, but the Church umpire (Mr C. West) disputed it. This caused a little unpleasantness. The Church umpire called time and the match was drawn.

A surviving score-card from the club's first season shows that Accrington played 26 matches. Although the score-card occasionally differs from results reported in the local Press, the club were able to look back on 14 victories in their inaugral season. Apart from an early reversal against St Mark's, the remaining defeats came at the hands of the stronger outfits of Blackburn Rovers, Darwen and Enfield.

However, not everyone was appreciative of Accrington's enthusiastic style of play. Reporting their defeat by Blackburn Rovers in March, 1879, the *Lancashire Cricket & Football Times* remarked: 'If Accrington would only play football more scientifically, they would show a better figure before the public; but until they drop their long kicking and mad rushing about, they must expect nothing but a good beating from such clubs as the Rovers and Darwen'. The direct approach, it would appear, had its critics over 100 years ago!

Two outstanding events during the 1878-9 season were matches played under artificial light, against Blackburn Rovers and Church. In the circumstances the Accrington club could look back with some satisfaction on their first season.

The 1879-80 campaign saw the club beginning to establish itself as one of the major teams in the area. As a result, stronger opposition was able to be found. The players remained largely the same as in the first season with William Eaton, Jim Hindle, William John Whittaker, Dennis Talbot, Jim Yates, Joe Hartley, Johnny Lonsdale and Dick Horne turning out on a fairly regular basis.

This season saw the introduction of the Lancashire Association Cup competition and on 18 October 1879, Accrington played their first 'competitive' match when they entertained Halliwell in the first round. With a sharp eye for financial gain the club decided to raise the admission charges for the game and the Accrington public promptly boycotted the match!

The 1880-81 season saw the club enjoy 21 victories in the 28 matches which were played. They had continued to improve the quality of their opposition as they made a determined bid to reach the same level as Darwen and Blackburn Rovers. It was at Alexandra Meadows, Blackburn, on 2 October 1880 that Accrington nearly lost the services of Joe Hartley, one of its most faithful servants. The correspondent of *The Blackburn Times* described one of the strangest accidents to befall a footballer on a football field in the following way:

'Immediately before the commencement of the game a most unfortunate accident occured to one of the Accrington players, Mr J.P.Hartley, who should have taken a position on the right wing. Whilst in the act of cutting a piece of leather from off the heel of the right foot and whilst it was resting on the left thigh, the knife he was using slipped and running across the left thigh, inflicted a wound four inches in length and three-quarters of an inch deep. Dr James Higson happened to be on the ground at the time and he was quickly in attendance upon the injured player. He stitched up the wound and afterwards Hartley, who suffered keenly, was removed home.'

Fortunately Hartley recovered to reappear in 'Th' Owd Reds' colours and went on to become the Accrington secretary.

Joe Hartley, one of Accrington FC's most faithful servants, who was injured in a freak accident at Blackburn in 1880.

Accrington FC, winners of the Lancashire Cup in 1880-81. Back row (left to right): S.Ormerod, D.Talbot (captain), J.Lonsdale, W.Latham, J.P.Hartley, J.Yates, J.Riley. Middle row: R.Howorth, J.Hindle. Front row: R.Horne, W.J.Whittaker, T.French, W.Eastham. Sam Ormerod later made his name as secretary-manager of Manchester City.

That season culminated in the club winning their first honour when the Lancashire Association Cup was won against Park Road at Barley Bank, Darwen. A dispute between Darwen and Blackburn Rovers had seen both teams ejected from the competition and with the two strongest teams eliminated, Accrington enjoyed a comfortable passage to the Final.

The game against Park Road of Blackburn provided yet another turbulant page in Accrington's history. Accrington had led at half-time by two goals to one, but Park Road equalized soon after the resumpton. Accrington again forged ahead, but the Blackburn side again drew level. The men from Accrington responded with another two goals and looked to be heading for a comfortable victory. However, eight minutes from the end, Park Road pulled a goal back and the Accrington team looked distinctly vulnerable.

With only two minutes left, Accrington managed to score another goal which effectively settled the tie. However, Park Road immediately protested against the goal on the grounds of offside. When the referee refused to disallow the goal, the Park Road team marched off the field clearly dissatisfied with the referee's decision. Accrington were thus declared the winners by six goals to four and the first trophy was brought back to the town by 'Th' Owd Reds'.

Twelve months later the team narrowly failed to defend the trophy when they were beaten by Blackburn Rovers in the Final. However, the 1882-3 season unearthed a real jewel in the shape of George Haworth. Haworth, who was affectionately known to everyone as 'Jud', quickly caught the eye as a player of great promise. After an outstanding performance against Great Harwood in the first round of the Lancashire Cup in October 1882, the *Accrington Times* stated that in George Haworth 'the Accrington club has discovered a rattling good back player'. The prediction proved to be wholly justified when Haworth went on to win five caps for England and became the backbone of the Accrington team for the next decade. He was so highly regarded in Lancashire that both Preston North End and Blackburn Rovers called upon his services from time to time. Indeed, he gained an FA Cup winners' medal during a brief spell with Blackburn Rovers in 1885.

Unfortunately, increasing success on the field would soon be overshadowed by events off it. Relationships with their landlords at the Cricket Club continued to be difficult and the storm clouds of professionalism were to envelop the Accrington club for two seasons.

The 1883-4 season began disappointingly with a heavy home defeat at the hands of Blackburn Rovers. However, when Accrington defeated Rossendale 5-1 in the second match of the season, few could have predicted the traumatic consequences that the match would bring. Accrington had given James Beresford of the Church club a trial run and he had responded by scoring a couple of goals. However, competition for places was keen and Beresford did not reappear in the team but returned to Church.

In November 1883, the Football Association met to discuss a representation by Darwen accusing both Accrington and Church of employing a professional player — one James Beresford. The FA committee felt that there was sufficient proof against Accrington to pass a resolution asking them to show good cause why they should not be ejected from the FA Cup under Rule 15, regarding the employment of professionals.

The resolution rocked the Accrington club to its very foundations. On 26 November, the club disposed of Blackburn Park Road by 3-2 in the second round of the FA Cup and two days later representatives of the club had to travel to London to defend its right to appear in the next round. Three men represented the Accrington club, including John Grimshaw, the treasurer, and Mr C.F.Critchley, the secretary.

From the statements made by the Church representative, it appeared that Beresford who had arrived at Church from Staveley, had offered his services to the Accrington club. After some hesitation on the part of Accrington, Beresford was made a member of the club and appeared in the team in the match against Rossendale on 15 September. This was his one and only appearance for the club. However, Beresford was later paid a sum of money by a gentleman not connected with the club, but who was anxious that his services should be retained by Accrington. Although Beresford was not selected for any further matches, his name remained on the club's books as a member.

Subsequent events showed that the payment of money to Beresford had been brought to the attention of both Critchley and Grimshaw, but that the committee had been kept in the dark as to what had happened. The Accrington officials hoped that this would be sufficient to keep the club in the competition. However, the FA took a different view. The fact that the officials were aware of the circumstances and took no steps to have Beresford struck off the rolls, or condemn the payment of money meant that the club was in breach of the rule. As a result the Accrington club were disqualified from the competition and from taking part in matches involving any other member of the English Association.

Incredibly, no proof could be found against Church and although they were censured for playing Beresford when they knew he had played for another town, they were allowed to continue in the FA Cup.

The next day saw the resignations of Grimshaw and Critchley. Although many of their Lancashire neighbours felt that the Accrington club had been harshly treated, other associations followed the line of the parent association. The Birmingham Association, for example, moved quickly to prohibit any of their clubs from playing Accrington under penalty of expulsion.

Fortunately, faced with growing unrest in Lancashire at the treatment handed out to Accrington, the English FA took another look at the matter. In December it was decided that Accrington should once again be accepted into the fold of the English Football

Association, but that they should not continue in the cup for that season, but take on the position of a defeated club.

In the wake of the problems with the Football Association, the Accrington public provided even greater backing for the club. At the start of the 1883-4 campaign the club had 553 members on the books, but the end of the season had seen this grow to 761 members. The improvements on the field were noted by the *Athletic News* when reporting on the match against Church in November 1884:

'The winners when they got warmed to their work, displayed excellent combination and proved that they are yet in the front rank and I should think they will still further improve.'

The start of the 1884-5 season had seen the election of Eli Higham jnr as one of the two honorary secretaries of Accrington Football Club. Higham's co-secretary was Joseph Pickup Hartley, who had been a teammate of Higham in the early Accrington teams.

The appointment of Higham further strengthened the club's financial position as he was the second son of Eli Higham, who owned the Woodnook spinning and weaving mill in the town. The link between the Highams and the club had been in evidence before when the Scottish forward, Friel, was brought from Vale of Leven in 1883 and had been fixed up with employment at the Woodnook Mill.

Sadly, the leadership of Hartley and Higham ended in November 1884 when the latter was tragically struck down with illness and died at the age of 26.

The man chosen to replace Higham as co-secretary was Bethel Robinson of Preston North End. Robinson had applied for the position at Accrington and had fulfilled a similar role at Preston during the 1883-4 season, whilst still playing with the club. Indeed, he had also found time during the 1883-4 season to be secretary and captain of Preston Zingari.

In the weeks before Higham's death, the club had once again become embroiled in the professionalism debate. The first round of the FA Cup had given Accrington a home tie with Southport. Conscious of the difficulties that had occurred barely 12 months earlier, the committee omitted a number of regular first-team men from the side. Unfortunately it was only after the club had recorded a victory by 3-0 that it was discovered that Accrington had fielded non-registered players. For the second season in succession the club were ejected from the national competition.

Locally, there was a great deal of sympathy for Accrington FC and no little animosity towards the Football Association. The *Accrington Gazette* argued on 18 October 1884: 'If the limitation to local talent means poor football, we say let us have professionalism. Besides, what are called 'good gates' can only be got with good matches . . .the conduct of the spectators towards second-team men, who filled the places of regular players, was not encouraging, but it shows that they will not be content with poor play.'

However, professionalism was not the only problem to beset the club during the mid-1880s. The growing friction between the cricket and football clubs at Thorneyholme Road caused further difficulties for the Accrington committee.

Throughout their existence, relationships between Accrington Football Club and their hosts at the cricket club had been abrasive. In May 1884, matters took an intriguing turn when the cricket club announced an ambitious proposal to amalgamate with the football club. Many of those who had watched both sports at Thorneyholme Road may have been puzzled by this proposal. After all, a flag flew over the ground on match days emblazoned with the letters 'AC and FC'. Did this not signify a cricket *and* football club?

Apparently not, as far as the cricketers were concerned. They claimed that the maintenance costs of the ground increased because of the demands of football. The footballers countered by saying that they already made a substantial contribution to the cricket club. Fearing that the cricket club wanted to exert more influence over the football club, the footballers opposed all attempts to merge on the cricketers terms. In the end matters became deadlocked and the whole problem was shelved. In truth, the cricket club needed the revenue which the football club brought and the football club needed the use of the finest ground in the town.

Throughout the 1880s success continued on the field and in 1888, Accrington FC lifted the Lancashire Cup for a second time. However, once again, the cup was brought to Accrington in controversial circumstances. The semi-final against Witton had gone to a replay and Accrington scraped home by the narrowest of margins in a 2-1 victory. The winning goal by Bob Conway

Accrington FC in 1886. The identity of the players, alas, long disappeared.

was a controversial one and after the match, Witton appealed to the Lancashire FA that the goal should have been overruled because of offside. An enquiry upheld the result and Accrington passed into the Final. If the semi-final had proved controversial, the Final was to dissolve into complete farce.

The club were due to meet Preston North End in the Final which was to be held in Blackburn. The Preston club immediately complained that this was too close to Accrington and that the Blackburn public were unduly hostile to North End. The Preston officials informed the Lancashire Association that they would not take part in the Final if it remained in Blackburn. The Lancashire Football Association were in no mood to allow one club to dictate the venue of the Final and insisted that the game would be played at Blackburn.

A crowd of some 2,000 people turned up on 21 April 1888 to see if Preston would carry out their threat not to turn up. At 3.30pm the Accrington side took the field and the referee duly tossed up. The toss was apparently won by George Haworth and Accrington kicked-off. With only the Accrington players on the field, the spectators witnessed a sweeping passing movement which resulted in Haworth scoring a goal. The match immediately ended and Accrington were presented with the trophy.

Aware that Preston North End would not appear, it had been arranged beforehand that a match would be played between Accrington and Witton, the defeated semi-finalists. Needless to say Witton triumphed by 4-0.

The 1887-8 season had seen the Accrington club try to rebuild the strength of their playing squad. This had led to Joseph Lofthouse and Harry Fecitt joining them from Blackburn Rovers. Both were highly experienced men who had gained FA Cup winners' medals whilst with Blackburn; Lofthouse had also been capped by England.

The club tried to bring a third Blackburn Rovers player to Accrington when they reached agreement with Herbie Arthur, an England international goalkeeper, to sign for the club. However, Arthur had a change of heart and declined the offer to join Accrington, thus leaving the club without an experienced custodian.

Fortunately the problem was solved when Johnny Horne returned to the club from Burslem Port Vale. The defence had been improved with the inclusion of John McLellan, from Heart of Midlothian, and John Stevenson, from Arthurlie. The two Scottish full-backs had joined Accrington in 1884 and immediately became the first-choice pairing in that position.

George Haworth continued to dominate the half-back positions along with Peter Chippendale from Church, who had first appeared with the club in 1882. The forwards were strengthened by the inclusion of Lofthouse and Fecitt, who were added to Jim Bonar, Bob Conway and Jack Yates, all of whom had given good service to the club and scored numerous goals.

By 1888 the Accrington Football Club was sufficently well-established to be one of the 12 clubs invited to form the Football League. However, the selection of Accrington was not universally popular and the *Athletic News* noted that Accrington were 'not particular whether they win or lose matches with clubs admittedly inferior to them'.

Popular or not, Accrington began their League campaign on 8 September 1888, when they travelled to Everton. Punctuality had never been a strong point with the Accrington club and, true to form, they arrived 20 minutes late. The match proved a great disappointment and the loss of goalkeeper John Horne with a fractured rib did not help the Accrington cause as they went down 2-1.

Putting an unpromising start behind them the club finished seventh in the League and lifted the Lancashire Cup for the third time. Many of the men who had served Accrington so well in previous seasons were retained for the inaugral League campaign. Thus, John Kay Horne kept goal in all the League matches, whilst Stevenson, McLellan, and Haworth were the backbone of the defence together with newcomer Luther Pemberton. The forwards had been infused with new blood by the introduction of John Kirkham, Robert Brand and Alex Barbour, whilst Jim Bonar continued to retain his position in the front line..

The 1889-90 season saw Accrington finish one place higher in the League, but hopes that this improvement could be maintained were ill-founded. In an attempt to build on their improved placing, they strengthened their playing resources by bringing the former Wolves forward, Sam Thompson, from Everton.

An attempt was also made to bring old favourite Bob Macbeth back to the club. Initially, Macbeth agreed to play for the club as an amateur until the end of October 1890. However, after appearing in the first match of the season, he received an attractive offer from Burton Swifts to become player-coach and the Accrington committee felt unable to stand in his way. The club slipped to tenth position at the end of the 1890-91 season, as fortunes both on and off the field began to wane.

The 1891-2 season saw Accrington struggle to compete with many of the teams in the League. Although their form at home was respectable if unspectacular, away from Thorneyholme Road they suffered some humiliating reversals, including a 12-2 defeat at the hands of Aston Villa. Having finished in 11th position the club were forced to apply for re-election. This was complicated by the fact that the Football League were intending to create a Second Division and increase the First Division by four clubs. Fortunately, the seven votes Accrington received proved sufficient to keep them in the top flight.

Having gained re-election, the Accrington club faced what has now become the classic scenario for struggling clubs. If they were to succeed, they needed more support from the public and that support would only be forthcoming if the club was successful

As the *Accrington Observer & Times* pointed out when previewing

Accrington FC in 1891. Back row (left to right): Mr J.W.Brown, Mr T.Sefton, McVickers, Hay, McLellan, Mr J.Hindle, Mr J.Coe (secretary), Mr Foster (groundsman). Middle row: Mr J.Wilkinson, Faulds, Barr, Haworth, Tattersall, Kirkham, McKay. Front row: Whitehead, Irvine, Elliott.

the 1892-3 season: 'Accrington people are not the worst of sportsmen, but they like to see their team win'.

Unfortunately the Accrington public saw their team win very few games during the 1892-3 campaign. The season began ominously with a 6-0 home defeat at the hands of Sunderland. By early December only two wins had been achieved, despite some good performances. A mini-revival of four consecutive victories in December brought renewed hope that the club could avoid the bottom places. Sadly, those victories proved to be the last that Accrington FC enjoyed in the Football League and five draws and seven defeats condemned them to the end-of-season Test Matches.

Incredibly, the season which had been so disappointing on the field had been unexpectedly successful financially. The money was used to pay off old debts and on 15 April 1893 the *Accrington Observer & Times* concluded that 'it had often been said that football would not pay in Accrington, but season 1892-3 has demonstrated the fallacy of this'.

Ominously, the newspaper added that future success would be dependent on being able to 'find their way into the League'.

Alas, seven days later Accrington were no longer members of the First Division. The play-off match with Sheffield United proved to be typical of a disappointing season. After having shown themselves to be the better side against Sheffield they contrived to lose by the odd goal. Accrington wasted numerous chances — Kirkham as early as the opening minutes — then could only watch as the old Preston North End player, Drummond, hit a splendid shot past Mason.

At the annual general meeting it was agreed that Accrington should seek entry into the Second Division and in June the fixture list was released. Having had time to study the implications of Second Division football, a special meeting was called in the last week of July. Members of the club were informed that the financial situation called into question their ability to fulfill a season in the Second Division which would involve matches at clubs as far apart as Woolwich Arsenal and Newcastle United.

Apart from the expense of travelling to these matches, past experience had shown that the Accrington public did not support matches against teams from outside the district. It was argued that the Accrington public would support matches against Lancashire League clubs in greater numbers than against those in the Second Division.

Another factor to be considered was the cost of admittance to matches. In the First Division, Accrington had been able to charge sixpence. However, former secretary J.P.Hartley pointed out that they all knew from past experience that Accrington folk would not pay sixpence for anything that was not first-class. A drop into the Second Division meant dropping admission to fourpence — the same as could be charged in the Lancashire League. Having projected that remaining in the Second Division could lose the club somewhere in the region of £1,000, it was unanimously agreed to leave the Second Division and apply to join the Lancashire League.

The major problem facing the club was how to leave the Second Division without antagonizing the members of the Football League. It was felt that if the matter was explained to the League, then they would understand the predicament in which Accrington found themselves. By coincidence, the Football League had only elected its first management committee in May and so Accrington became its first major crisis case.

The resignation of Accrington FC was discussed by the League committee on 3 August 1893. Those Accringtonians who felt that the League would understand their difficulties were in for a rude awakening. The committee immediately demanded that the club pay seven guineas in expenses incurred at the last two meetings. They went on to instruct all members of the Football League that matches could not be played against Accrington until the dispute was settled. It was not the reaction Accrington had hoped for and the debt was not paid until 16 November, by which time valuable friendly fixtures had been lost.

Furthermore, the fact that the fixture list was curtailed led to a number of players leaving the club.

The inaugural season in the Lancashire League brought a complete change to the club's playing personnel. Being blacklisted by the Football League had not helped to retain players and most of those who appeared during the League years now departed. In their place, the club committee recruited a number of new men from Scotland. The first home match, against Blackpool on 2 September 1893, attracted an attendance of 3,000. Accrington fielded the following team: Mason; Hodge, Ditchfield, Shuttleworth, Matthews, Frame, Foulds, Lawrie, McKay, Dickson, Barlow.

It was not an auspicious beginning as Blackpool ran out 3-1 winners. However, Accrington finally finished in fourth position, although in truth, the Lancashire League proved a poor substitute for the Football League.

Hopes of a return to the Football League rapidly faded during the 1894-5 season as the club slumped to 12th position in the Lancashire League. With the club now playing at Moorhead, the opening of the 1895-6 campaign brought little enthusiasm to the followers of 'Th' Owd Reds'.

The club had dropped into the Lancashire Combination and the correspondent of *The Accrington Observer & Times* wrote the following prophetic words at the start of the season: 'If a poor beginning is indicative of an indifferent season, then Accrington Football Club have indeed a bad time before them. Time was when I might have written of the unbounded enthusiasm of the opening game and the hopeful prospects for the season, but now all this is changed and the football horizon is black as night.'

The opening four League matches brought only three points and increasing difficulties in raising a team. On 12 October 1895, Accrington travelled to Oswaldtwistle Rovers for what proved to be their last-ever league match. The Accrington club had experienced difficulty in finding 11 men but eventually fielded the following team: Walmsley; Livesey, Nuttall, Crabtree, Smith, Duffield, Richards, Rawcliffe, Alexander, Hargreaves, Wilmington. Goals by Wilmington and Smith were little consolation as the Accrington side crashed to a 7-2 defeat.

To all intents and purposes this was the end of the Accrington Football Club. They failed to fulfill any more league fixtures and most people assumed that the club had folded.

However, there was still one last chapter in the story of Accrington Football Club. On 18 January 1896, much to everyone's surprise, they undertook to fulfill their first-round match in the Lancashire Senior Cup, against Second Division Darwen at Barley Bank. Once again the club struggled to find 11 men, but eventually they were represented for the very last time by the following team: Walmsley; Hodgson, Smith, Crabtree, Frame, Duffield, Johnson, J.Smith, Shepherd, Dawson, Greenrod.

Their opponents were able to include two former England internationals from Blackburn Rovers, Billy Townley and Jim Forrest. The gulf between the teams was obvious and the Reds seldom got over the half-way line. Yet despite his side losing by a score of 12-0, Walmsley turned in the best performance for the visitors and the Darwen club were so impressed that they signed him for their reserve team.

The humiliation at the hands of their old rivals marked the end of the Accrington Football Club. No more matches were played and, sadly, few appeared to mourn the passing of 'Th' Owd Reds'. Footballing interest switched to the junior clubs in the area, of which Accrington Stanley was but one of many trying to fill the void left by the former Football League club.

THE ACCRINGTON STANLEY STORY

THE death of Accrington Stanley in March 1962 was an event that was well chronicled by both local and national media. The last rites were given under the glare of the television cameras, whilst news reporters scribbled furiously as each intimate detail of the club's demise was revealed. Its end was in marked contrast to its beginning; an event regarded as so unremarkable that no documentary evidence has survived the ravages of time to tell the tale. This, of course, was hardly surprising, for in the early 1890s, football in Accrington was dominated by 'Th' Owd Reds'.

However, a number of smaller clubs managed to thrive in the shadow of the town's League team. It is believed that around 1892 these teams were joined by a club named Stanley Villa. The club apparently gained its name because it was made up of local lads from the Stanley Street area of Accrington. In March, 1962, the *Accrington Observer* interviewed 92-year-old Fred Carr who '. . .was one of the gang of young boys from the Peel Park district who became the original Stanley.'

According to Fred Carr, two men associated with the Stanley Arms in Stanley Street came along and suggested that they should form a football team to play other local teams. In 1893, as 'Th' Owd Reds' were falling on hard times, Stanley Villa underwent a metamorphosis and emerged as Accrington Stanley. In fact, all that had changed was the name; the club did not compete in a league until the 1894-5 season, when they joined the Accrington & District League.

Unfortunately for the modern chronicler, matches in the Accrington & District League were rarely commented upon by the local Press. It is therefore somewhat ironic, considering the volatile history of 'Th' Owd Reds', that probably the earliest report of a Stanley match should be one dealing with controversy. The *Accrington Advertiser* carried the following report of Accrington Stanley's encounter with Knuzden on 3 November 1894:

'There was an unpleasant ending to the Accrington & District League match between Accrington Stanley and Knuzden at Moorhead on Saturday. The match was well advanced in the second-half and Knuzden were leading 2-1, when the Stanley allege that Tattersall scored a legitimate goal for them, and that the referee gave it as a goal, but on the Knuzden players protesting he altered his decision and gave a goal-kick to Knuzden. At this time the crowd broke in the field and rendered it impossible to finish the match. When Knuzden were leading, the Stanley state that the former's players deliberately kicked the ball out of play to waste time.'

The referee claimed that he had never allowed the goal. "I gave Knuzden a goal-kick on the ground that I could not tell whether the ball passed between the posts owing to its being too dark." The referee explained that he had wanted to play 35 minutes instead of 45 and was quick to point out that if the captains had agreed the 'trouble would not have cropped up'.

Accrington Stanley met Knuzden again at Moorhead Park in the final match of the season. Stanley needed two points for the championship and Knuzden needed only a draw to win the title. A 2-1 victory for Knuzden meant that Stanley had to settle for the runners-up spot in their inaugural season of league football. The team included Billy Barnes, Albert Snape, Billy Hopkins, Jack Tattersall and Tommy Duerden; all men whom Fred Carr remembered as being members of the first Accrington Stanley team.

Success in the Accrington & District League encouraged the club to move to a higher lever of football and for the 1895-6 season they joined the North East Lancashire Combination. It was during this season that their exploits were reported on in some detail for the first time. As 'Th' Owd Reds' quietly died, Accrington Stanley began the long hard climb which would eventually see them inherit the Reds' old Football League status.

The 1890s were largely unremarkable in the story of Accrington

Stanley. They established themselves as one of the stronger outfits in the North East Lancashire Combination and won the title in 1897-8. However, the club found it difficult to repeat the success despite a number of prominent names appearing in their team. By December 1899, the team could boast three of the famous 'Owd Reds' line up in Tom Pendergast, Jimmy Whitehead and Arthur Wilkinson. The latter two had both enjoyed League experience with Blackburn Rovers and Bury respectively after their time with Accrington.

In February 1900, moves were made to join the Lancashire Combination, despite the fact that the team were struggling in their minor league competition. The infusion of older, more experienced players had not worked. The correspondent of the *Accrington Gazette* was succinct in his criticism of this policy when he wrote, 'Poor Accrington Stanley. They don't seem to be realizing the expectations formed by the committee when the season opened. A good many men have been tried — some of them with good old reputations. In some cases the reputations were too old — reputations of other days.' It was a criticism which would surface again from time to time during their period in the Football League.

Only a few months after joining the Lancashire Combination, Accrington Stanley found themselves in trouble due to financial irregularities. At a meeting of the Executive of the Lancashire Association held on 1 March 1909, Accrington Stanley and its players were suspended until those involved in the irregularities had been identified by the club. The problem had arisen in connection with gate receipts of the second-round Junior Cup match against Heywood. The Lancashire Association had proved that at least £5 19s 0d had been improperly retained.

Within a week the Lancashire Association were reconvened to hear that the Accrington Stanley treasurer had resigned. Furthermore, it was revealed that four ticket sellers, who included three members of the committee, had signed a declaration to the effect that they had sold tickets which had not been accounted for to the Heywood club. It was further stated that the money had been handed over to the Stanley treasurer. As a result the treasurer received a five-year suspension and the ticket sellers were suspended for two years each. Fortunately, this incident did not restrict the progress the club was clearly making.

The 1902-03 season saw Stanley challenging at the top of the

Accrington Stanley's highly successful 1902-03 side which won the Lancashire Combination championship. Back row (left to right): W.Chadwick (committee), Finney, Coupe, Boulton, S.Emmet (trainer). Middle row: Morgan, Golding, J.Bradshaw, W.Bradshaw, Gardner. Front row: Watkins, Brunton, Hargreaves. The photograph was taken by Harry Bergan of the King's Hotel, Accrington.

table. The club did not suffer their first defeat in the league until 13 December 1902, when they lost to Manchester City Reserves who were also title contenders. Manchester was proving a stumbling block to Stanley's ambitions, as City had knocked them out of the Lancashire Senior Cup and United had knocked them out of the FA Cup. However, Stanley had the last laugh when they pipped City to become the first non-reserve team to lift the Lancashire Combination title.

Ably led by captain and full-back Jack Finney, the team included the hard-working Jack Bradshaw and his younger brother Billy, who joined Blackburn Rovers for the start of the 1903-04 campaign and went on to be capped by England. The attack was led by 40-goal Matt Brunton, whose other clubs included Leicester Fosse and Oldham Athletic before he returned to Accrington as trainer-coach to the team which entered the Football League in 1921.

Stanley almost clinched the title in the 1903-04 season but finally had to settle for second place. However, two years later the club had captured the 1905-06 title and in 1912-13 they were runners-up once more. It was a remarkable achievement considering that

Accrington Stanley in 1906-07. Back row (left to right): Mr T.Prendergast (chairman), Sheridan, McGuigan, Carter, Turner, Randall, Kenyon, Unknown, Mr T.J.Whittaker (treasurer). Front row: Wilson, Chadwick, Jack Bradshaw, Brindle, Stott, Garside.

until the creation of the Central League in 1911, the Lancashire Combination contained the reserve teams of top First Division clubs. The only other non-reserve teams to lift the title during this period were Rochdale (1910-11), Oldham Athletic (1906-07), and Stockport County (1904-05).

The 1914-15 season was the last in peacetime football and Stanley finished in sixth position. The outbreak of World War One saw the men of Accrington answer their country's call. The formation of the East Lancashire Regiment which became known as the Accrington Pals and the fate they met has been well documented. Little wonder that in the midst of such carnage, Accrington Stanley should slip into the relative oblivion of wartime Lancashire Combination football. Although they claimed the title, few in the town had an appetite for football and at the end of the 1915-16 season, the club called a halt to activities until the war was won.

When peace returned and football began to be resurrected, Accrington Stanley were in severe debt. Only the tireless efforts of a loyal band of supporters prevented the club from going under and, to all intents and purposes, the Stanley club was re-formed

Scene from one of Stanley's first games at Peel Park.

during the early part of 1919. This dedicated group who revived the club's fortunes included a former player called Sam Pilkington. Pilkington went on to hold office as secretary, director, chairman and president of his beloved Stanley. For the next 40 years and more his name would be synonymous with Accrington Stanley Football Club.

The start of the 1919-20 season saw Stanley move to a new ground at Peel Park. This was a convenient site for the town centre and the cost was a mere £2,500. Although money was in short supply, it was viewed as a better option than remaining at Moorhead Park and paying the increased rental charges.

Although the early sides were made up of local amateurs, there was one notable exception in George Chapman, the former Blackburn Rovers stalwart who made 138 League appearances for the Ewood Park club. Despite a 7-0 trouncing at the hands of Tranmere Rovers in the opening match, Stanley managed to finish in a respectable mid-table position.

The 1920-21 season was to prove the last for Stanley as a non-League outfit. The club eventually finished in a disappointing sixth position, but did not hesitate to accept the invitation to become part of the new Third Division North. However, the club did leave the non-League scene on a high point when they beat Chorley in the Lancashire Junior Cup Final in front of around 20,000 spectators at Ewood Park, Blackburn.

Accrington Stanley embarked on their 'great adventure' into the Football League with a determination to make good. Guided by secretary, Sam Pilkington, the club signed over 20 players for the

ACCRINGTON

STANLEY F.C.

WINNERS LANCASHIRE JUNIOR CUP, 1920-1921.
Winners Rossendale & District Cup, 1913-14, 1914-15. Winners Lancashire Combination, 1902-3, 1905-6. Winners Best Non-Reserve Medals, 1901-2, 1903-4.

1d. **OFFICIAL PROGRAMME.** 1d.

Smoke "Old Bob's" Mixture

—— **11½d. per Oz.** ——

WOOD & Co. Opposite TOWN HALL **Accrington**

BAZAAR JOTTINGS.

Our Bazaar will definitely take place in the Town Hall, last week in April which is now about three months off.

So far we have done splendidly, we hope to raise at least £2,000 towards the ground extensions.

The Bazaar Club has now reached the handsome total of £700, and through the efforts of our committee we have raised over £300 in concerts, whist drives, etc.

It is only eight months since we decided on this method of swelling the Club's Funds, and up to now it has been very successful.

If you have not already got a ticket for the Gent.'s Suit or Lady's Costume do so.

We have a workroom in Woodnook P.S.A. Institute. We want many workers (not forgetting the donors) so come along and put your shoulder to the wheel. If you can't come let us know, we shall only be too pleased if you will take some home.

Persons being members of our Club are asked to let their collector know if any special article is required so that we may obtain what they want.

Make a note of March 9th—we are having another Whist Drive and Dance in the Conservative Club. The last one being a great success.

We hope to give you all the items of interest about the Bazaar which is sure to be a big success. Keep your eye on this page, and order your copy of the Programme so that you will be sure of having one next week.

FOR FULL REPORTS

—OF—

STANLEY'S MATCHES

READ

Tuesday's "Observer."

The first programme produced by Accrington Stanley, for a Lancashire Combination fixture against Morecambe in 1920-21, the season before Stanley were elected members of the new Third Division North.

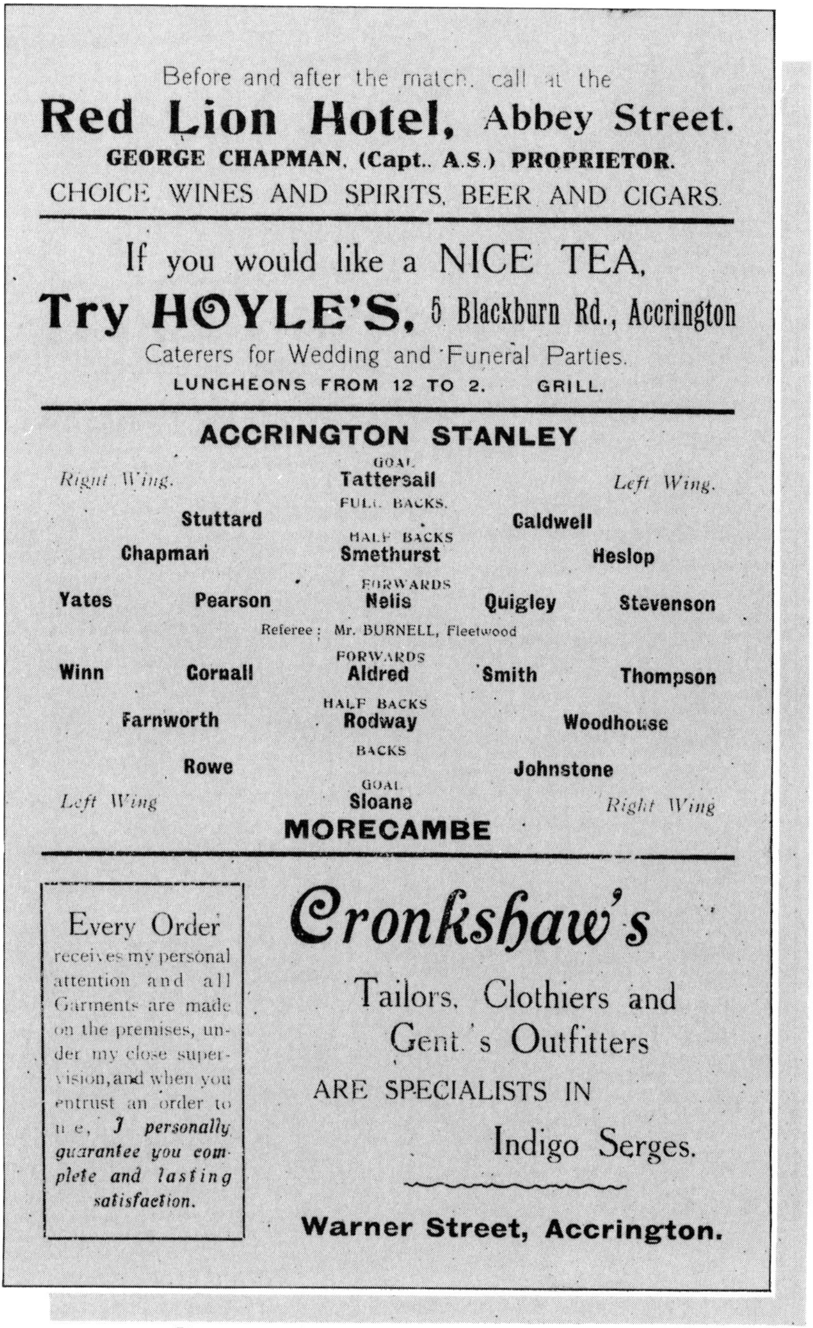

Before and after the match, call at the

Red Lion Hotel, Abbey Street.

GEORGE CHAPMAN, (Capt., A.S.) PROPRIETOR.

CHOICE WINES AND SPIRITS, BEER AND CIGARS.

If you would like a NICE TEA,

Try HOYLE'S, 5 Blackburn Rd., Accrington

Caterers for Wedding and Funeral Parties.

LUNCHEONS FROM 12 TO 2. GRILL.

ACCRINGTON STANLEY

Right Wing. GOAL **Tattersall** *Left Wing.*

FULL BACKS.

Stuttard **Caldwell**

HALF BACKS

Chapman **Smethurst** **Heslop**

FORWARDS

Yates **Pearson** **Nelis** **Quigley** **Stevenson**

Referee: Mr. BURNELL, Fleetwood

FORWARDS

Winn **Gornall** **Aldred** **Smith** **Thompson**

HALF BACKS

Farnworth **Rodway** **Woodhouse**

BACKS

Rowe **Johnstone**

Left Wing GOAL **Sloane** *Right Wing*

MORECAMBE

Every Order receives my personal attention and all Garments are made on the premises, under my close supervision, and when you entrust an order to me, *I personally guarantee you complete and lasting satisfaction.*

Cronkshaw's

Tailors, Clothiers and Gent.'s Outfitters

ARE SPECIALISTS IN

Indigo Serges.

Warner Street, Accrington.

Line-up page from the first match-day programme.

new venture, but included a number of the men who had served them well during the previous season. The new players included John Burkinshaw, who had experience with Bradford and Sheffield Wednesday, Stanley Popplewell who had appeared with Blackpool and Bolton Wanderers, and Aaron Crawshaw and James Makin, both of whom had appeared in the first team at Exeter City. All four were to be the backbone of the team, in the formative years in the Football League.

As Accrington prepared to take their first tentative steps in the Football League, moves were underway to form the club into a limited liability company. On 31 August, only three days before their first League match, the club formally became a limited company with a share capital of £5,000.

The attendance of 11,500 for the first home match suggested that the new venture would be a tremendous success. The season proved to live up to expectations. Although there was disappointment with an early exit from the FA Cup at the hands of Nelson, the club finished in a very satisfactory fifth position. However, it was during their first campaign in the Football League that the harsh realities of their limited financial resources were brought home. In March the club lost the services of the highly talented Patrick Nelis to Nottingham Forest. The 14 goals which Nelis scored in only 11 matches included three hat-tricks. In the close season, a fee of £200 took leading goalscorer Tommy Green to Stockport County.

The summer of 1922 saw not only a number of players leave Peel Park, but also a influx of new blood. These end-of-season comings and goings were going to be a regular feature of life at Peel Park. Amongst the new players signed was Andrew Walker who had played for Chelsea in the 1915 FA Cup Final and had captained Newport County in the 1921-2 season. Another new arrival was Arthur Metcalf the former Swindon Town, Sunderland, Norwich City and Liverpool inside-forward.

Although they were hit by injuries during November and December, the 1922-3 season saw Stanley finish in a respectable eighth position. However, the senior team achieved some local success when they wrested the East Lancashire Charity Shield from Darwen, the holders in the two previous years. The reserve team finished as champions of the West Lancashire League and won the Richardson Cup, a feat which helped them become elected to the Lancashire

Accrington Stanley in 1920-21, winners of the Lancashire Junior Cup. Standing (left to right): J.Jacques, E.Chadwick, F.Heyes, G.E.Holman, R.Cragg, C.Smithies, G.Chapman, G.Wilson, J.Yates, J.Tattersall, H.Smethurst, A.Colwell, T.Heslop, J.Richardson, T.Prendergast, J.Sutcliffe, A.Stoddard, E.Hargreaves. Seated: J.Brown, J.Holland, J.Miller, C.Pearson, P.Nelis, P.Quigley, A.Stevenson, S.T.Pilkington (secretary), F.Brennand (trainer), J.Parramore. Front: Unknown, W.H.Pilkington (mascot).

Combination. It was hoped that admission into the Lancashire Combination would swell the income generated from reserve-team matches, as well as provide a sterner test for the second-team men.

Off the field, the season saw the club complete the taking up of the £5,000 share capital, due in part to the efforts of the supporters and the generosity of local firms. However, the club still lost £1,581 on the season, largely owing to the unemployment in the district and to serious accidents to several of the players.

The close season brought a major innovation with the appointment of Curtis Booth to the position of player-manager. It was planned that Booth would take charge of the team and become its captain, whilst Sam Pilkington would continue to act

as the secretary. In a bid to make the team more successful, the directors made a conscious effort to reduce the age of the playing staff by releasing a number of the older players.

The season began tragically when Booth received a serious injury in the opening match at Darlington. It was an injury which would keep him away from Peel Park until the final weeks of the season and thus end Stanley's brave experiment of employing a manager.

Despite the injury to Booth the opening day's defeat at Darlington was the only loss suffered in the first seven matches. During this period the club took the Irish international McCandless from Bradford, but his engagement with the club ended after only two matches. The bright start quickly faded and Stanley finished in

13th place. There was some consolation in the FA Cup, the first round was reached and Charlton Athletic were taken to two matches before Accrington bowed out.

Before the season was over, the board announced that Booth would leave the club at the end of the season, due to financial reasons. Once again, the close season brought another flurry of activity as work was done to improve the playing surface of Peel Park and new players were signed.

With the season barely two months old, Sam Pilkington expressed a wish to step down from the position of secretary. After moves to appoint a successor had fallen through, the directors asked Ernest Blackburn to become secretary-manager. Blackburn, who had been appointed as trainer at the start of the season, accepted, and immediately appointed the former Barnsley full-back Tindall to the trainer's position. Tindall had been one of the few experienced players that the club had signed during the close season. Aware of the value of Pilkington to the club, the directors invited their former secretary to join the board.

Although the first round of the FA Cup was again reached, the 1924-5 season was another tale of disappointment with the club finishing in 17th position in the League.

The end of the 1924-5 season saw the directors engaged in a massive clear out of playing personnel. Only Billy Rooks and two or three of the junior players were kept whilst the rest all departed. In their place came a host of new faces including Tom Whittaker (Darwen), Edward Gregory (Oldham Athletic), Joe Kasher (Stoke), Dick Field (Grimsby), Edgar Powell (Stoke), and Walter Gummery (Wolves).

Sadly, the influx of new faces did little to improve results. The team never found the right blend and finished in a disappointing 18th position; one place worse than before the large-scale rebuilding programme. However, the season had one bright spot with the introduction of Johnny Jepson to the forward line in October 1925. A tallish, balding, gawky figure with round shoulders, Jepson looked anything but a footballer. His first home appearance had brought howls of derision from the Peel Park fans, who had been promised a new signing instead of promotion for a little-known reserve.

Jepson had made little impact in his first-team debut at Nelson a week earlier. However, after his first 90 minutes at Peel Park,

Accrington Stanley in 1924-5, the season Stanley finished 17th in the table, although they reached the first round of the FA Cup.

he was hailed as a hero after hitting a hat-trick in a 3-1 win over Coventry City. Jepson's fearsome left-foot shot helped him to notch 30 goals in as many League games, whilst in the FA Cup he scored six goals in 4 games. These 36 goals included no less than seven hat-tricks.

However, if the 1925-6 season was disappointing, the following campaign was even more traumatic. Not even an FA Cup appearance at Stamford Bridge in front of 30,142 spectators could compensate for Stanley's worst campaign in the League up to that point.

Fears at the start of the season about the capabilities of the men signed were soon proved correct. After several defeats the directors were forced to pay fees to bring Norman Wilson from Bury and Len Hughes from Burnley. Whilst the team found it difficult to keep a clean sheet, Jepson found it difficult to recapture his form of the previous season and his total of 11 goals in 26 League games was a huge disappointment. The main goalscoring roles were now filled by Jimmy Gee and Richard Clarkson. Gee,

Accrington Stanley line-up taken before the game at home to Wigan Borough on 17 April 1926. Players only, back row (left to right): Field, Kasher, Bell, Holden, Armitt, Gregory. Front row: Wyper, Gee, Jepson, Powell, Gummery.

a former Blackburn Rovers reserve had been with the club since the summer of 1924 and had scored 21 goals in 52 League matches prior to the 1926-7 campaign.

Although Clarkson had not been signed as a first-team player, he kept Jepson out of the side at various times during the season. Clarkson ended the season with 17 League and Cup goals, whilst Gee claimed 16 in both competitions. Only they and Tom Whittaker emerged with any credit from the season. However, not even his clever resourcefulness was able to hold a defence together in which Wilson and Hughes did little to add to their considerable reputations. It came as no surprise when the team finished next to bottom and were forced to apply for re-election.

Obviously keen to avoid applying for re-election a second time, the Stanley board once again cleared the decks. Only Tom Whittaker, Andrew Curran, John Martin, Frank Slater and Richard Clarkson survived the purge. The departure of Jepson, however, was extemely controversial. Although the Accrington board had put a fee of £250 on his head, the Football League reduced this to £150. In July, Jepson signed for Carlisle United, a club outside the Football League and therefore not liable to pay the fee. The loss of a player of such calibre without recompense was a bitter blow to the Accrington club.

The newcomers to Peel Park included George McLoughlin and Patrick Lee from Hull City, John Parkin from Durham City, John Barclay from Liverpool and Frank Parry from Grimsby Town.

A group of Stanley players from the 1927-8 season, probably photographed before a trial match since several did not appear in the first team. Back row (left to right): S.Popplewell (assistant trainer), R.Haworth, A.Tootill, J.Tomlinson, R.Hall, H.Haworth, M.Shutt (linesman), J.Mellor. Front row: J.Parramore (assistant trainer), J.Haworth, R.Clarkson, P.Brooke, B.Aspin, J.Chadwick, J.Martin.

One signing that was to prove of great importance was that of Jimmy Armstrong from Bournemouth, a full-back who would make 260 appearances between 1927 and 1934. This was a remarkable record considering the constant chopping and changing which took place during each close season.

To the relief of everyone at Peel Park this bold experiment in team building proved extremely successful as the club climbed to ninth position in the League. Only Tom Whittaker, Andrew Curran and John Parkin of the old team played on a regular basis, but the team had a more settled look than in previous seasons. Richard Finnigan proved a reliable custodian, whilst Armstrong, Whittaker, and Curran provided the backbone of the defence. The season saw the introduction of Chris Dodds, a young wing-half of immense promise who retained his place after making his debut on 17

December 1927. Fears that the attack would be impotent without Jepson and Gee proved unfounded as Parkin hit 27 goals in 38 matches. However, Parkin had often had to shoulder the goalscoring burden alone. Clarkson made only spasmodic appearances and the need for another goalscorer was an obvious priority.

The chief close season acquisition turned out to be a major surprise, for few could have expected to see the return of Johnny Jepson to Accrington colours. The prospects of Jepson and Parkin in partnership, together with an improved defence behind them, led to a growing feeling of optimism at Peel Park.

Unfortunately, Jepson took time to settle in and Parkin completely lost his goalscoring touch. In fact, the two men partnered each other on only 13 occasions during the season.

The club was rocked early in the season when they lost the services of Finnigan after only two matches. His contract was cancelled by mutual consent after he clashed with a director and he joined Wrexham. Fortunately, Stanley found an excellent replacement in young Alf Tootill.

Once again, Whittaker, Armstrong and Curran were consistent in defence with Albert Latham and Lee the regular wing-halves. Unfortunately, the need to supplement the money taken at the 'gate' saw the departure of the promising Chris Dodds to Sheffield Wednesday in October 1928. In March 1929 the club accepted an offer from Wolverhampton Wanderers for Alf Tootill. The combined fees brought in £1,150 and this combined with a good Cup run enabled Stanley to show a profit of £394 on the season. However, a slump to 18th position in the League was reflected in fewer people coming through the turnstiles. If the sale of young talent helped to keep the club afloat, it did little to entice the Accrington public to Peel Park.

Satisfied that the defence was sufficiently sound, the directors signed four new forwards in a bid to solve their goalscoring problems. Once again responsibility for leading the attack would fall on the shoulders of Johnny Jepson. However, Arthur Hawes (Bradford), John Pears (Rotherham United), Billy Hamilton and Jacob Parsons (both from Barrow) were signed to provide him with the ammunition and support he had so sadly lacked during the previous campaign. Two other new forwards were signed in Daniel Ferguson of Reading and George Whyte, a Scot who joined the club from Rhyl. Surprisingly, the directors decided to part company with Parry, McLoughlin and Parkin.

The 1929-30 campaign proved an anxious one for the directors of the club. Their hopes of a windfall from either transfer fees or a Cup run were not realized. Furthermore, receipts from the majority of home gates fell below £200 and the last home match against Southport produced only £54. However, considering that prior to the Southport fixture — Stanley had lost five and drawn one of the previous six home matches — it was hardly surprising that Accrington folk were reluctant visitors to Peel Park.

After losing only one match in the opening nine fixtures, the team failed to find any level of consistency and finally finished in 16th position. Although Jepson weighed in with another 20 goals, he no longer looked the force he had once been. His mantle looked to have been picked up by a young reserve called John Parsons. In only his second game of the season he scored four goals against Halifax Town and a week later scored another four against Rotherham United. Although Parsons could not maintain this strike rate, he finished the season with a creditable 12 goals from 15 matches.

The summer of 1930 finally saw the departure of Jepson to Wigan Borough, whilst young Parsons left to join Exeter City. Jepson left Peel Park with an impressive scoring record to his name. During his four seasons with Stanley he had scored 82 goals in 117 League matches, whilst ten FA Cup games had brought him 12 goals. To replace Jepson and Parsons, Stanley signed Samuel Abel from Bury, William Broome from Crewe Alexandra and Harold Riley from Oldham. The season also found former Stanley favourite, Stanley Popplewell appointed assistant trainer.

The new forwards proved to be extremely consistent in front of goal. Alf Agar scored 14 goals from the outside-right position, whilst Riley and Abel notched 18 goals apiece. Early in January 1931, the directors signed Sydney Johnson of Barnoldswick, a talented young centre-forward. However, he did not realize expectations and after seven appearances, in which he scored three goals, he was relegated to the Reserves and later transferred back to his former club.

Although Accrington Stanley finished in a mid-table position, they fared badly in the FA Cup and made an early exit at the hands of Torquay United at Peel Park. Defensively the team looked extremely suspect and conceded 108 goals — the worst defensive record in the club's League history at that point. On tour they lost 7-3 at Carlisle United and Chesterfield, 8-1 at Rotherham United and 8-0 at Tranmere Rovers.

Curiously, the appalling record was not the result of continual changes in players used. Armstrong and Whittaker continued in the full-back positions, whilst Ferguson, Viner and Whyte were regulars in the three half-back positions. When injury forced Armstrong out of the team on 30 September 1930, it ended a sequence of 130 successive appearances in League games with Stanley at right-back. In addition he had also figured in seven FA Cup ties and seven Lancashire Senior Cup matches as well as a few East Lancashire Charity Cup games. To achieve such a record in the continual ebb and flow of playing staff showed why the Peel Park faithful rated this whole-hearted player so highly.

The 1931-2 season saw the introduction of new goalkeeper John Bell, together with Norman Price and Stanley High to the defence. As the season developed, the club introduced Sam McCulloch into the half-back line on a regular basis. McCulloch had been signed in the close season from Thames but had previously played League football with Blackburn Rovers. During the next five seasons he was to prove to be the cornerstone of the Accrington defence and became one of the club's greatest servants.

Although the club finished one position lower than the previous campaign, the 1931-2 season saw a tightening up in defence. Once again Alf Agar was a consistent scorer, but only he and Thomas Williamson got into double figures with 14 goals apiece.

Accrington Stanley suffered a setback in January 1932, when Ernest Blackburn accepted the managerial seat at Wrexham. Stanley quickly appointed former director Amos Wade as his replacement. With financial storm clouds hovering threateningly over Peel Park, the appointment of a businessman to the post of secretary-manager was probably a shrewd move.

The 1932-3 season saw the club in deep financial difficulties. The summer of 1932 had once again witnessed a procession of new faces into Peel Park. Amongst the better known names to arrive were Thomas Allen, the experienced Coventry City goalkeeper, and Joe Eddleston, the former Swindon Town, Nelson and Blackburn Rovers forward. The close season also saw the return of Chris Dodds from Sheffield Wednesday.

Accrington Stanley, 1932-3. Back row (left to right): Brennand (trainer), Price, Dodds, McCulloch, Allen, Corcoran, Bentley, Walton. Front row: Hachett, Fitton, Armstrong, Eddleston, Johnson, Wright.

Three wins and a draw in the opening four matches suggested that better times might be on the horizon. Yet the Accrington public remained to be convinced and they continued to stay away from Peel Park. On 22 October, only 2,927 spectators watched the team demolish Hartlepools United 7-1. In the wake of such attendances, Sam Pilkington declared, 'We are the worst-supported club in the League and we think it is very unfair the way the public are treating us'.

Stanley were in fourth position, only one point behind top-placed Chester at the time. Pilkington went on: 'The directors are absolutely disgusted with the support given in view of the fact that we are nearly at the top of the League.' He also warned that 'if better support is not forthcoming, we shall have to withdraw from the League'.

The financial pressures saw the departure of Roy Viner, the centre-half and captain to Chester, whilst the promising George

Walton left for Bolton Wanderers. Unable to maintain their early season form, the club eventually finished in 15th position.

Having faced criticism over the average age of the playing staff, the close season saw the departure of a number of the older faces, including Allen and Eddleston.

The opening match of the 1933-4 season saw eight changes compared with the last line-up of the previous campaign. The former Millwall and Notts County goalkeeper, Jim Maidment was introduced in place of Allen, whilst Bill Stoddart of Southampton replaced Viner at the heart of the defence.

Having strengthened the team, it was unfortunate that an abnormally dry winter was in favour of youthful runners and against the players of weight and experience that Accrington had secured for their ordinarily heavy ground.

The team suffered some embarrassing reversals, but none more so than a humiliating record 9-0 home defeat at the hands of Barnsley. Curiously, the season also produced a record-breaking 8-0 home victory over New Brighton, only weeks after the Barnsley match.

However, even this record victory could not hide the deficiencies in the Stanley attack. In 42 League matches the team had failed to score on 14 occasions, whilst they had managed only a solitary goal in another 12 games. Only John Cheetham reached double figures and his 15 goals could not prevent Stanley finishing with their worst scoring record since 1926-7.

With an equally appalling defensive record it was no surprise that the club should finish in 20th position.

An early exit from the 1934-5 FA Cup competition meant that much-needed revenue had once again to be raised from transfers. Thus the followers of Stanley were forced to witness the departure of more talented youngsters. Joe Clare, a young outside-left, was sold to Arsenal, whilst Wolves speculated on the inexperienced pair of Fred Marsden (five appearances) and James Aspin (one appearance).

The season also saw the departure of the experienced Fred Leedham to Oldham Athletic. These transfers meant that the club were able to show a profit of £182 on the season, but the overall balance still showed a loss of £1,750.

The 1934-5 campaign had seen the appointment of the former Blackburn Rovers, Everton and England international, Joe Clennell

Accrington Stanley, 1933-4. Back row (left to right): F.Fitton, J.Meakin, J.Maidment, J.Dulson, B.McCulloch. Middle row: Councillor Arnett (director), M.J.Briggs (director), W.E.Bradshaw (director), J.Kenyon, J.Parkinson (director), W.Lennox, W.Stoddart, C.Dodds, N.Price, W.Bentley, H.Travis, J.Armstrong, F.Brennand (trainer), H.Watts (director), Councillor A.Wade (secretary-manager), W.W.Cocker (director). Front row: J.Holland (director), H.T.Wyper, F.Leedham, W.Jeavons, G.Hayhurst JP (president), A.Hughes, J.Cheetham, W.Watson.

Accrington Stanley, 1934-5. Back row (left to right): F.Marsden, C.Dodds, J.Gill, T.Lockie, S.McCulloch, A.Hunter. Front row: J.Cull, W.Harker, F.Brown, F.Leedham, J.Clare.

as team coach. Whilst Wade concentrated on the crippling financial situation, Clennell was left to look after playing matters. However, nothing he could do could prevent the club from finishing in 18th position and at the end of the season he left the club.

The work of Clennell during the season may well have convinced the directors of the need to divide administrative responsibilities from those of looking after the team. In May 1935, the directors took the decision to appoint John Hacking as player-manager. The former Oldham Athletic, Manchester United and England goalkeeper was given responsibility for all playing affairs, whilst Amos Wade remained as the club secretary.

A busy close season saw Hacking assemble a number of new faces at Peel Park. Although the season opened disappointingly with two defeats, Hacking quickly turned things around. In Willie Harker and Bob Mortimer, Stanley finally had two men capable of destroying the best defences in the division.

However, Hacking's masterstroke was to sign the veteran outside-left George Mee to supply the crosses on which a player like Mortimer thrived.

After losing at Crewe on Christmas Day, they were undefeated and dropped only three points in eight games up to 22 February. Sadly, February saw the departure of Harker and Mortimer to Portsmouth and only three matches were won out of the 14 played after their sale. Despite this disappointing finale, Stanley finished in a highly respectable ninth position. This was their highest placing since the 1927-8 season and only the fourth time they had finished in the top ten.

In a bid to replace Mortimer and add much-needed punch to the attack, Hacking signed George Pateman from Reading during the close season. This was something of a gamble on Hacking's part. Before moving to Reading, Pateman had been on the books of Bradford City and Clapton Orient, but had failed to establish himself at any of his three previous clubs.

Stanley began the season poorly and in mid-September were at the bottom of the table and without a win in their opening four matches. Although Pateman had scored Stanley's two League goals, it was clear that they were woefully lacking in the forward line.

The fifth game of the season was at Gateshead and brought the return of Bob Mortimer to Accrington colours. Unable to win a place in the first team at Fratton Park, Mortimer readily agreed to return to Peel Park when the opportunity arose. He quickly demonstrated that he had not lost his touch when he scored Stanley's goal in a 1-1 draw at Gateshead.

Accrington Stanley Reserves 1936-7. Players only, back row (left to right): E.Ivill, J.Leigh, J.Ash, A.Robertson, H.Andrews, T.Yates. Front row: J.Young, A.Rimmer, J.Blakeney, W.Tyson, J.Martin. At the end of the season, the shirts with the white 'V' were changed to all-red.

In fact, Mortimer enjoyed a highly successful season and scored 33 goals in 37 League appearances. As the form of Pateman began to wane, the club found a new partner for Mortimer in the shape of Billy Tyson. Hacking then arranged a deal with Southport which saw Pateman move in a straight swop for forward Frank Curran, the younger brother of Andrew Curran who had played for Stanley in the 1920s.

Although the final League position showed a slight slip, 13th as opposed to ninth, the FA Cup offered major compensation. After overcoming two non-League clubs, Stanley were paired with neighbouring Blackburn Rovers in the third round. A thrilling 2-2 draw in front of a 31,080 cowd at Ewood Park was followed by a sensational victory at Peel Park in front of a record 11,636 spectators.

In both matches Bob Mortimer grabbed a brace of goals, a fact which did not go unnoticed by the Blackburn directors. Although Stanley crashed 2-0 in a fourth-round tie at Manchester City, the crowd of 39,135 provided ample financial consolation.

Players training for the FA Cup game against Crystal Palace in the 1937-8 season. The stand in the background is the old Burnley Road side stand, which was replaced at the end of that season. Its common name was the 'Scratting Shed', Lancashire slang for 'Scratching Shed'.

Although the club had reaped a financial bonanza from the FA Cup, the directors still felt unable to resist offers for their players. Thus in April 1937, full-back Willis Gregg and promising young goalkeeper, John Robinson moved to Manchester City. The sale of these two players, together with the earlier sales of Treanor to Hull City and Maurice Reeday to Leicester City, brought a windfall of £3,000.

In the wake of the previous season's exploits, the 1937-8 campaign saw a remarkable decline in the club's fortunes. At a time when attendances were averaging 6,000 and Stanley was financially sound for the first time in years, the directors astounded supporters and sanctioned the sale of Mortimer and Tyson to Blackburn Rovers.

Mortimer had scored 49 of the 85 goals scored by Stanley whilst he was at the club. It was little wonder that the supporters were bewildered by the decision to sell.

After the sale of Mortimer and Tyson, the team's inability to score goals became a major problem. In a bid to rectify the situation,

Accrington Stanley, 1937-8. Back row (left to right): F.Brennand (trainer), H.Randle, W.Pickering, J.Bowles, S.Simpson, J.Ash, H.Andrews, A.Ellison (mascot). Front row: W.Reynolds, W.Rivers, J.Moir, H.O'Grady, G.Mee.

Hacking bought Albert Valentine from Stockport County for a substantial fee.

Sadly, Valentine never looked like adding to an impressive reputation as a goalscorer which he had gained with Halifax Town. In his seven appearances he hit the target only once. This was a stark contrast to his 98 goals from 115 games at The Shay and in marked contrast to Mortimer's opening salvo of four goals in eight games before his departure.

Between 2 October and 13 November, the team lost seven games in succession. This was followed by three consecutive victories but the rot set in again and Stanley were soon anchored in the basement of the table.

The introduction of James Blakeney in the New Year helped ease the scoring problems and Dick Webster was turned into a promising half-back during the latter part of the season.

However, only George Mee, whose career had begun in the 1919-20 season, supplied any real quality on a consistent basis.

Ten defeats at Peel Park and a tally of 45 goals scored in 42 matches sealed the club's fate. Accrington Stanley finished bottom

Manager Jack Hacking and his players, plotting an opponents' downfall in 1937-8. Alas, Stanley finished bottom of the Third Division North for the first time.

of the table for the first time since entering the Football League in 1921.

Although re-election proved a formality the 1938-9 season began inauspiciously with the team losing their first four matches. The close season had seen the departure of the promising youngster Blakeney to Arsenal. The need for a consistent marksman was reflected in the fact that no Stanley player reached double figures in the scoring lists during 1938-9.

After winning at Barrow on 10 September, Accrington had to wait until 7 January, for their next victory. The intervening 18 games supplied a mere four points. By the evening of 18 February, Accrington had collected only eight points from 30 matches. Fortuntely, the remaining dozen games produced 12 points to give their final tally an air of respectability.

But a total of 20 points was insufficient to lift them off bottom spot and, indeed, they finished some 11 points behind the next club. Few players came out of the season with much credit, but one was the former Aston Villa and England player, 'Pongo' Waring, who brought some power to the forward line. Stanley had paid a fee of about £700 for Waring, which was easily the largest the club had forked out.

Unfortunately, the veteran Waring, was one of the few signings who proved successful. A classic example of Stanley's misfortunes in the transfer market was Sam Hunt. He arrived at Peel Park after experience with Rochdale and Stockport County and brought with him a fine reputation as a marksman.

Sadly, at Accrington he struggled to find his form and scored only one League goal — and that from a penalty — before being transferred to Carlisle United. With the Cumbrian club he was an instant success and ended the season as the Northern Section's leading goalscorer.

The 1938-9 campaign proved an unmitigated disaster. Only 49 goals were scored whilst 103 were conceded. One contemporary reviewer made the following damning condemnation of the team: 'If there was no weakness that stood out it was because the whole side was weak.'

Having had to apply for re-election two years running, the start of the 1939-40 season was a complete revelation. Three wins in three matches saw Accrington Stanley sit proudly at the top of the Third Division North. However, the outbreak of war saw the Football League close down normal operations and introduce a system of regional football.

Stanley played out the remainder of the season in the Regional League North West Division and finished 12th. However, the football had become increasingly meaningless with an endless number of guest players and a steady decline in spectators.

The annual meeting of shareholders on 26 August 1940 had to be abandoned for 24 hours owing to the fact that there was not a quorum of 30 members present. Grave doubts were now expressed as to what the future held for Accrington Stanley FC. Jack Hacking had left the club on war work and Jack Wigglesworth stepped into the breach as secretary-manager.

The 1940-41 season was played in the unlikely surroundings of the Blackburn & District Combination. Financially unable to continue in the Regional League, the directors felt that it was important to try to maintain some interest in football in the area; hence the decision to play in the Combination.

Officially the team was called Stanley 'A', although it was the only team the club fielded and included a number of men who had played during the previous season and a handful of men who had played League football. Even so the club could only finish fourth, although they did win the Birtwistle Cup, a local knock-out competition.

The following season saw the club step up to the Lancashire Combination. A large number of local players were utilized, but there was a distinct lack of interest amongst the Accrington public. At the end of the season the directors decided to close down operations until there was a better climate in which to revive activities.

In June 1944 the directors announced their decision to re-enter League football for the 1944-5 season. With the restoration of the Football League in sight, it was felt that a season in wartime football would enable them to experiment with local players.

When Stanley ceased their activities in 1942, they had agreed to allow Howard & Bullough's Sports and Recreation Club to use Peel Park for the duration of the war. When the club announced their intention of returning to wartime football, the Howard & Bullough Club offered to return the ground for Stanley's use for their home matches.

With Jack Hacking back at the helm, Stanley embarked on the new season with a mixture of guest players and local youngsters. Although the 1944-5 season had seen the rebirth of the club, few could have predicted that Stanley were on the verge of lifting their first championship trophy since 1905-06. However, a 4-0 victory at Barrow on 29 December 1945 gave them the 1945-6 championship of the Third Division North West Region. Not a major achievement perhaps, but one which would provide a platform on which to build when peacetime football returned in 1946.

The return to League football in 1946 brought renewed optimism for the followers of Accrington Stanley. Sadly, a season which began on such an optimistic note ended disappointingly. Indeed, the team only escaped having to apply for re-election by the skin of their teeth. More significantly, this was due mainly to the failures of Southport and Halifax Town rather than as a result of their own efforts.

Whilst individual players performed as well as many had

John Malcolm, Jack Hacking junior and Dick Webster, pictured in 1945-6, the last season before the Football League proper got underway again.

expected, team work was signally lacking. Hacking tried a total of 33 players without ever finding a successful blend.

The nucleus of players around which Hacking could build a new team was fairly small. The reserve team had finished 1946-7 next to bottom of the Lancashire Combination after using no less than 84 players.

It was from this unpromising base that Hacking produced a team which enjoyed Stanley's best season in the Third Division North up to that point. The peak of this success was reached at Christmas 1947 with Stanley challenging for promotion. Two holiday victories over eventual promotion winners, Lincoln City, gave cause for real optimisim.

Sadly, a rapid decline in playing fortunes followed. After victory over Lincoln three of the next four matches at Peel Park were lost. Weeks before the season ended, hope had vanished and the only consolation left were the club records which had been broken. These were for the most away points, the most wins in a season and the highest number of points ever gained.

Raich Carter, player-manager of Hull City, flanked by Accrington Stanley players Walter Keeley (who had rejoined Stanley) and Reg Edwards, after the Tigers' 2-1 win at Peel Park in September 1948 smashed a 45-year-old Football League record with nine consecutive wins from the start of a season.

The constant struggle to keep the club financially stable meant Hacking was unable to strengthen his team. The continual need to raise money meant good players departed on a regular basis and were rarely replaced.

In October 1947, Stanley had sold Walter Keeley to Bury for what was reported to be a record fee. Yet only a few weeks before Keeley left, the club had emphatically stated that Stanley were buying not selling players. However, the directors promised that if one did go another would be secured equal or better in ability. Needless to say Keeley's place was not filled and his match-winning bursts were sadly missed.

The 1948-9 campaign was a bitter disappointment to all concerned at Peel Park. The first victory was not achieved until their 13th outing, when they disposed of New Brighton on 16 October by 5-1. The match proved a triumph for Johnny Wilson, who had been signed a fortnight earlier from Oldham Athletic for £650. He made four goals in a brilliant display.

The beaten goalkeeper is Accrington Stanley's Bill Harris, who let in four goals during this game at Oldham on New Year's Day 1949.

Unfortunately such displays were rare, and the New Year saw Stanley striving to avoid re-election. A first away win, also against New Brighton, on 12 March helped the club to finish in 20th position.

In May 1949, the directors decided that a change of direction in Accrington Stanley's affairs meant a change of manager. Hacking took the decision diplomatically and was soon installed as the secretary-manager of Barrow. The new man at Peel Park was Jimmy Porter, the former Bury player and assistant manager. Porter found that he had inherited a club that was struggling both on and off the field.

By Christmas 1949, Stanley found themselves in a precarious position. Two home games against Darlington and Carlisle United saw attendances fall below 3,000. Fortunately, not everything was bleak. Immediately following Christmas, 21-year-old Eric Lovett stepped into the senior team and showed real promise. In only his third game he faced former Scottish international Jock Dodds and completely subdued him as Stanley beat Lincoln by 2-0.

Top: Cyril Briggs (5) heads clear from an Oldham Athletic attack at Boundary Park in September 1949. Bottom: Walter Keeley (10) is beaten to the ball by Oldham defenders Fred Ogden and Bill Hayes. Stanley won 1-0.

Accrington Stanley, 1950-51. Back row (left to right): D.Smith, J.Wilson, W.Mellor, D.Daniels. F.Martin, R.Webster. Front row: W.Keeley, T.Butler, G.Rothwell, J.Slattery, W.Robinson.

Although Stanley were at the foot of the League on 21 January 1950, a run of five out of six matches at home gave them the opportunity to claw their way to safety. Indeed, a final League placing of 13th was looked upon as quite respectable.

Considering the financial plight, Porter had done a miraculous job to lift Stanley to a mid-table position. So grave was the financial position that the club appeared to be in real danger of going under.

In December 1949, Newcastle United had made an offer for Stan Lynn which Accrington were prepared to accept. However, the promising young full-back was employed as a stripper and grinder in the cotton industry and came under the Control of Employment Order which had been brought in during the war. As a result he had to remain in his occupation and play part-time football. Newcastle were not prepared to sign him on a part-time basis and the deal fell through.

At the time of his eventual sale to Aston Villa, the Birmingham club were trying to find him a similar job within the city, when the Employment Order was relaxed, thus enabling Lynn to join Villa without any problems. Indeed, only the sale of Stan Lynn to Aston Villa on 15 March, for a much-needed £5,000 saved Accrington Stanley from going out of existence there and then.

Top: Accrington Stanley goalkeeper Doug Daniels under pressure against Southport during the 1950-51 season. Bottom: Stanley on the attack during the same match.

At the time the seriousness of the situation was not truly revealed for the good of the club.

The patience of supporters was tested again the following season when, on 10 November 1950, the club announced that Sam Parker and Don Travis had been sold to Crewe Alexandra. This was a major shock to the fans who thought that the club might have held on until after their fate in the FA Cup was known.

The public were furious at what they saw as panic measures and the attendance against Bradford City dropped to 4,662, of whom about 1,000 came from Bradford.

As part of the deal which took Travis and Parker to Gresty Road, Porter took Billy Woods from Crewe in a bid to solve the problem inside-right position. Sadly, the much-travelled forward failed to make any impact and lost his place after only three matches.

Needless to say, the signing did little to appease the Accrington supporters. Travis in particular was sorely missed. The former West Ham United and Southend United centre-forward had scored 36 goals in his 71 League matches with the Peel Park club. Although the directors had managed to put the club on an even keel financially; they were in grave danger of losing their comfortable League position.

In January 1951, the club announced a 'new players' loan scheme. Supporters were asked to contribute block loans of £10 to a fund to be used exclusively for buying new players, the target being not less than £3,000. The Supporters' Club immediately stepped in with a cheque for £500. The need for new players was obvious. After the departure of Travis and Parker the team went 12 matches without a win and by 13 January they were once again at the foot of the League.

On 18 January, a beleaguered Jimmy Porter spent a record £3,000 to bring Billy Watkinson from Liverpool, where he was understudy to the prolific Albert Stubbins. Two days after signing, Watkinson scored on his debut against Oldham Athletic, but could not prevent the team going down to their seventh successive defeat.

Matters came to a head for Porter when the team suffered a crushing 9-1 defeat at Lincoln. A disagreement over club policy two days after this humilating defeat brought Porter's resignation along with that of trainer-coach Alick Robinson.

The directors acted swiftly to find a replacement and 24 hours later, Walter Crook, the former Blackburn Rovers and Bolton

Director Charlie Kilby, groundsman Charlie Smith and trainer Fred Brennand with workman as alterations are made to the Peel Park teraces in the early 1950s.

Wanderers full-back was appointed trainer-coach. The team was now selected by the directors in consultation with Crook.

Although the club were forced to apply for re-election for the fourth time in their history, Crook made a sufficient impression to be appointed manager. Fortunately re-election proved a formality with Accrington gaining 46 votes. However, New Brighton (18 votes), who had finished in bottom position, found themselves replaced by Workignton (28 votes). It was a clear warning to Stanley of the dangers of continually propping up the League.

The difficulties under which Crook would have to work were revealed when it was announced that Stanley had suffered a loss of £6,244, during the 1950-51 season. This was more than double that suffered during the previous year.

Despite the financial difficulties, Crook set about building his own team. In an attempt to strengthen the defence he brought goalkeeper George Turnbull from Grimsby Town, a young full-back from West Bromwich Albion called Sam Cox and centre-half Colin Senior from Huddersfield Town.

The signings of Doug Roberts from Brighton and John Spencer

Sam Pilkington (extreme right) in discussion with manager Walter Crook just before Crook's resignation in January 1953.

from Burnley increased competition for the forward positions. In September 1951, Crook went to Halifax Town to sign George Glaister, with whom he had played at Blackburn Rovers.

Unfortunately, the introduction of new players produced the same old results and Stanley ended the 1951-2 season in 22nd position.

Once again, Crook responded with a frenzy of transfer activity. A new goalkeeper was signed in John Meadows, and Ken Holliday was brought from Blackburn Rovers to bolster the defence. In a bid to add experience to the team, Crook signed Sid Goodfellow, a wing-half from Oldham Athletic who was approaching his 37th birthday.

However, no matter how Crook shuffled the pack, a winning combination continued to elude him. This was all a far cry from the success he had enjoyed whilst coaching Ajax in Holland. As the 1952-3 season continued in the same monotously depressing vein as previous campaigns, Crook grew increasingly disenchanted with life in football's bargain basement.

Rumours persisted that Stanley's manager yearned for a return to the Continent and was on the brink of accepting a move back to Holland. On 17 February 1953 it was announced that Crook had handed in his resignation which would take affect from 26 February. The directors tried to change his mind, but Crook remained unmoved to the overtures and left the club at the end of the month.

The departure of Crook once again saw the directors having to take charge. The result was that Accrington had to apply for re-election. Already reeling from finishing at the foot of the Northern Division and without a manager, the club suffered a further blow in May 1953. In the early hours of Saturday 16 May, popular full-back Billy Robinson was murdered in Salford. Robinson had been shot, along with a lady friend, by the woman's estranged husband. It was a tragic end to the life of one of Stanley's most popular players. Robinson had appeared in 96 League games since his signing from Stockport County in December 1950.

Another disappointing season was reflected in the balance sheets which once again showed the seriousness of the financial position. A loss of £4,037 was recorded and only the efforts of supporters and directors had reduced the actual loss to £2,599.

It was this seemingly impossible position which Walter Galbraith inherited when he accepted the position of player-manager in June 1953. Galbraith had experienced this type of situation before when he had been player-manager at New Brighton. He had seen his club ejected from the Football League and few would have backed him to prevent a similar fate befalling Accrington Stanley.

However against all predictions, there was great cause for satisfaction at the end of Walter Galbraith's first campaign at Peel Park. Stanley finished in a respectable 15th position, having gained 15 points more than the previous season. In the process they had managed to score 27 goals more and conceded 15 fewer than during 1952-3.

Only 12 months after seemingly being down and almost out, this marked a tremendous turn around. Furthermore, the Accrington public had responded and including floodlit games, the average home attendance had soared to 8,000 and takings were 50 per cent up. This achievement was all the more remarkable considering that Galbraith had found himself having to build a team to start the season and then reassemble it as the season progressed.

However, amidst the various transfer deals, the Accrington public

The first of Millwall's three FA Cup goals against Accrington Stanley at The Den in December 1954. The Lions winger Ken Prior shoots past Stanley right-back Fred Pirie as defenders Jimmy Jones and John Ryden flounder. The other Millwall player is Fred Ramscar.

were given a hint of the future when Galbraith brought Armour Ashe from St Mirren and Charlie Sneddon from Stenhousemuir. The Scottish twang was to be a familiar sound at Peel Park during Galbraith's reign.

Galbraith continued his rebuilding the following season after selling Billy Watkinson to Halifax Town for £3,000, a fee reported to be a record for the Yorkshire club. On the field, Stanley got off to a tremendous start by winning eight out their opening nine games. On 1 October 1953, Galbraith moved to replace Watkinson and signed George Stewart from St Mirren. This was to prove an inspirational signing as the big, bustling centre-forward went on to become the most prolific goal-machine in Stanley's League history. Other Scottish players journeyed south to join the growing contingent at Peel Park. These included Jimmy Harrower from Third Lanark, Tom McQueen and Tom McKeown who both came from Queen of the South, and Eddie Hunter from Falkirk.

The new look was proving refreshingly successful. New Year victories over Barrow and Chesterfield put Stanley in second position, despite increasing concern over defensive frailties. In a bid to strengthen his defence, Galbraith paid a fee of £270 to bring Bill Heggie from Winsford United. However, the former New Brighton, Wrexham and Leeds United full-back made only one appearance during the season.

The success of the Stanley outfit was recognized when Jimmy Harrower and George Stewart were selected to play for the Third Division North against the Third Division South at Reading. Both gave outstanding displays, although the South won by 2-0.

By defeating Bradford at Peel Park on 12 March 1955, Stanley broke a club record by securing their 21st win of the season. By

26 March, Stanley held a five-point lead over Barnsley, although the Yorkshire side had two games in hand. Both sides were drawing away from the chasing pack, and as the Easter programme dawned, the championship seemed to rest with these two clubs.

On Good Friday, a crowd of 19,843 watched Stanley gain a 1-1 draw at York City. The result was a great disappointment as the Accrington team had given a truly championship performance and ought to have won.

Typical blockbuster from Accrington Stanley centre-forward George Stewart, who netted 136 League goals in 182 appearances for the Peel Park club between 1954 and 1958. Gateshead goalkeeper Bobby Gray and two defenders look on helplessly as Stewart smashes in Stanley's second goal in a 3-0 victory on 23 November 1957.

Alas, 24 hours later they turned in a nightmare performance and were crushed 5-2 by Hartlepools United at Peel Park.

As Stanley stumbled, Barnsley marched on relentlessly. However, when the Colliers slipped at Chesterfield, Stanley leap-frogged to the top with a win at Hartlepool; but Barnsley still had two games

Liverpool goalkeeper Dave Underwood under pressure during an Accrington Stanley raid in the FA Cup third-round tie at Anfield in January 1956. A crowd of 48,385 saw Stanley go down 2-0.

in hand and were only a point behind. A crushing 6-1 defeat at Chesterfield finally put paid to Stanley's promotion hopes.

Although failure to achieve promotion was a bitter blow, the club had, nonetheless, enjoyed its most successful season ever. Not only had the first team come close to winning the title, but the reserve team had lifted the Lancashire Combination title for the first time and then gone on to win the Combination Cup.

On the 29 August 1955, Galbraith created a small piece of football history when he selected the following side to face Rochdale at Spotland Road: McQueen, Ashe, Harrower, Hunter, Ryden, Sneddon, Scott, Stewart, Dick, McCreadie.

Although there was nothing remarkable about a 1-1 draw, this was the first time since 1902 that an English League club had fielded 11 Scottish players.

The 1955-6 campaign saw Stanley again fighting for promotion. Unfortunately they found that they simply hadn't got the reserve power of their main rivals, Derby County and Grimsby Town. The season finally saw the departure of the highly-rated John Ryden to Tottenham Hotspur, although Jimmy Harrower proved a more than reliable replacement. Unfortunately, League attendances were hit by a clash with Blackburn Rovers' matches and averaged 8,967, a drop of about 1,000 from the previous season. The fall in 'gates' meant a loss of revenue of about £3,000. Fortunately, an FA Cup run had brought in over £8,000 and Stanley had received a record fee in the region of £10,000 for Ryden.

The 1956-7 campaign saw Stanley finish in third place on goal-average over Workington. Disappointment in failing to gain promotion was compounded by a continuing decline in attendances which fell to an average of 8,486.

Thus, over two highly successful seasons the average home attendance had dropped by some 1,500. Home form had been disappointing during the season and the loss of 12 points at Peel Park had proved too great a handicap to be made up away from home.

However, Stanley continued to be prolific goalscorers, with George Stewart hitting another 33 League goals. The past three League campaigns had produced a staggering 283 goals in only 138 matches.

Once again, 1957-8 saw the Accrington club chasing promotion despite taking only nine points from the opening 11 matches. Under the astute guidance of Galbraith, the team was once again evolving as new players continued to be introduced.

In June 1957, Galbraith brought Harry Anders from Port Vale to play on the opposite wing to brother Jimmy, who had arrived from Bradford in January. Galbraith also signed Terry Tighe from Dunfermline Atheltic in June and in the early part of the season brought Willie Kelly from Blackburn Rovers and Sid Storey from Barnsley.

Once again the main goalscoring threat was George Stewart, who notched another 27 League goals. Indeed, but for a loss of form towards the end of the season Stewart might well have beaten his record tally at Peel Park.

Unfortunately only 19-goal Jimmy Mulkerrin provided support for Stewart and for the first time since 1953-4, Stanley failed to register 90 or more League goals. The team failed once more at the final hurdle, leaving the Accrington public to accuse the club of not wanting promotion.

A drop of 1,641 in the average home attendance suggested that the Accrington public were none too keen on promotion either.

Galbraith retained his entire squad of 21 full-time professionals and five part-timers and promised a renewed effort to capture the elusive promotion spot.

The 1958-9 season was to be an historical landmark in the history of both the Football League and Accrington Stanley. The old Third Divisions North and South were to be replaced with a national Third and Fourth Division. Accrington now found themselves in the new Third Division, playing with the combined élite of the former north and south Third Division clubs.

The reorganization posed several questions for Accrington. Could Stanley compete on the field with the top southern clubs as well as the leading northern teams? Would they be able to cope financially with the increased costs of travelling to away matches in the south?

A new ingredient in the melting pot was that Blackburn Rovers had gained promotion to the First Division; so could Accrington really prosper with a First Division side just five miles either side of them?

Manager Walter Galbraith had no hestitation in believing that the team could do well: "The new league will undoubtedly be a tough competiton, but of a high standard with attractive new opponents from the south. Because of the quality of the football and better grounds than in the north, I believe our players will do well."

Tragically, an eve-of-season sensation was to rock Accrington Stanley to its very foundations before a ball was kicked in the new Third Division.

At the shareholders meeting in July, 1958, Bob Moore, the Stanley chairman, highlighted the stark statistics which threatened

Accrington's continuing revival. Another successful season had resulted in a loss of £4,568. Although the directors had resisted the temptation to wipe out this loss by resisting offers for some of the players, the Accrington public continued to give luke-warm support to the club.

Moore stated, "We tried to keep faith with the Accrington public. But have they kept faith with Stanley? Not when you look at the gates."

Once again the Accrington public stood acused of failing to support their team, and a winning team at that. The figures certainly supported Moore's argument. Gate receipts had fallen by about £3,600 as the average home attendance dropped by 1,600. Yet in the face of these grim statistics, the Accrington board, under the leadership of Bob Moore, had gone ahead with additions to the playing staff and ground improvements, including the purchase of a new stand for the Burnley Road side of the ground.

Less than 72 hours before the start of the 1958-9 season, Walter Galbraith sensationally tendered his resignation as manager at an eve-of-season board meeting. After the meeting it was stated on behalf of the board that the move 'followed differences between the manager and directors, arising out of economy measures the board felt bound to take, in view of the substantial losses incurred in the past two years'.

Although Galbraith had been linked with top managerial posts on both sides of the border, it was a complete surprise that he should leave in such a way.

Playing affairs were put in the hands of trainer-coach Harry Hubbick, whilst the directors decided upon a successor. A short list of six men was drawn up which included, Hubbick, Harold Bodle (the former Stanley captain), and former England internationals George Eastham and Stan Rickaby.

On 7 October, Eastham was appointed manager, although he was unable to leave Ards, his current club, until the end of the month.

Stanley found life in the new Third Division a tougher proposition than in the old Northern section. However, five straight wins at the end of year kept them in touch with the promotion race. Eastham found himself with a number of promising youngsters who were emerging in the first team.

However, he felt the need to strengthen the team if promotion was going to be a viable proposition. Unfortunately, the financial situation was rapidly deteriorating. It was this, coupled with Eastham's desire to bring in new players which led to the sale of record goalscorer George Stewart in November 1958, to Coventry City for a fee of £3,700.

The move came only a fortnight after the 31-year-old Scot had rejected a move to Chesterfield and the fee was the third highest that Stanley had ever received. The leading goalscorer in each of the previous four seasons, Stewart had amassed a total of 136 League goals in 182 appearances. In the FA Cup he had scored seven goals in ten matches, thus making him the most prolific goalscorer in the club's history.

Needless to say his departure was difficult for the Accrington public to understand. For a time, the gap was adequately filled when Mulkerrin took over as a deep-lying schemer. However, long before the season ended, it was clear that Stewart would have to be replaced.

Having finished in 19th place, Stanley retained 15 professionals, of which three were still in the Forces. These were supplemented by two amateurs, two part-timers and three members of the groundstaff. Clearly the economies which the directors had demanded were reducing the size of one of the largest playing staffs in the lower divisions.

Less than 12 months after the departure of Walter Galbriath, the club suffered another bombshell when George Eastham resigned on 15 June 1959. After only eight months in the Peel Park hot seat, Eastham left to accept the manager's job with Distillery in the Irish League.

The recent departure of Bob McNicol to Brighton may well have proved the final straw for Eastham. Financial difficulties during Eastham's brief reign at Peel Park had forced the sale of five players, including key men like Stewart, Dick and finally McNicol. In a bid to replace them and build for the future, Eastham had put his faith in the slow process of bringing on the club's own young players. However, he felt frustrated that he had not been able to use some of the money he had generated to bring in new blood; although the board always insisted he had enjoyed a free hand in finding the players he wanted.

Within days of Eastham's departure, former Stanley favourite, Harold Bodle was installed as manager. Having been pipped at the post for the appointment the previous October, Bodle won the unanimous support of the board to take over from Eastham.

Bodle arrived at Peel Park with two factors in his favour. First, he had been hugely popular as captain of the side; indeed, many of the Peel Park faithful had longed for his on-the-field leadership during the crucial stages of recent campaigns. The Accrington public retained their faith in Bodle and genuinely believed he would get the best out of the team in the same way he had done when captain. Second, Bodle inherited the nucleus of a strong squad.

The summer of 1959 had also seen the departure of Ian Gibson to Bradford. The loss of the talented youngster left Stanley rather threadbare in the forward department and in a bid to solve this problem, Bodle signed Jackie Keeley from Everton and Eric Jones from Doncaster Rovers.

During a hectic close season, Bodle brought 11 new faces to Peel Park. However, the financial restraints meant that six of the new men could only be signed on a part-time basis. On 17 August, Bodle narrowed his forward options by selling Jimmy Mulkerrin to Tranmere Rovers for a fee said to be just under £3,000.

When the team took the field for the first match of the season, Keeley and Jones were the only new faces in the line-up. A meagre haul of four points from the first eight matches set the trend for the season. Neither Keeley nor Jones, who had been appointed captain, proved a success. Keeley managed only one goal in ten appearances and Jones failed to score in his 18 outings.

Only the form of young Harvey McCreadie brightened the gloom during the first half of the season. However, the arrival of Blackburn Rovers' reserve centre-forward, Jackie Swindells brought about a brief revival when he teamed up with McCreadie. Alas, serious financial problems forced the sale of McCreadie to Luton Town for £5,500. With the departure of the talented youngster, Stanley's hopes of avoiding relegation began to fade.

A depressing campaign took a surprising twist on 21 April 1960, when it was announced that Harold Bodle's engagement had been terminated and that skipper Jimmy Harrower was to take over immediately as player-manager. Although the club were heading for the Fourth Division, chairman Edwin Slinger made it clear that the reason for the change was the need to economize.

The end of the 1959-60 season saw Stanley relegated to the Fourth Division. Quite simply, it was their worst campaign for 21 years.

They collected fewer points than any season since 1938-9 and their 30 defeats created a new but unwanted club record. In conceding 123 goals they also broke the previous record for goals against. The 126 team changes made during the season was yet another unwanted statistic. As the team slipped into the Fourth Division, attendances at Peel Park continued to fall. The average dropped from 6,322 during the previous campaign to only 4,116.

Consignment to the basement of the Football League brought with it hopes of some respite from the crippling financial situation. The Fourth Division contained more northern and midlands teams than the Third Division, so expenses would hopefully be reduced. Furthermore, Stanley had fewer full-time professionals as a result of the considerable pruning which had taken place at the end of the previous season.

Although economies were essential, Jimmy Harrower was still able to bring in nine new signings for the start of the 1960-61 season. After his appointment as successor to Harold Bodle, Harrower covered a vast amount of ground, particularly in the cheaper Scottish market looking for new players. Considering that he had been left with only eight players at the end of the previous season, Harrower did a remarkable job in signing new recruits.

The club retained Willie McInnes, George Forrester, Graham Lord, Terry Tighe, Alex Hamilton, Charlie Sneddon, Ian McCrae (part-timer), Lawson Bennett and Jackie Swindells. In addition to these, Gordon Stones, Brian Bades and John Marshall were still in the Services.

Harrower proved undaunted by his task and moved quickly to bring in new men. These included Sam Logue, a sturdily-built, ball-playing forward from Scotland, George Hudson, a centre-forward from Blackburn Rovers, and Willie Devine, an outside-left from Partick Thistle.

Another newcomer who made a surprisingly early impact was 18-year-old Michael Ferguson. A native of Burnley, Ferguson had gained County FA honours during his two seasons with Plymouth Argyle. The southern club had wanted to sign him as a professional, but Ferguson was keen to return to his native Lancashire. Although not expected to feature prominently in the first team, injuries gave Ferguson the opportunity to break into the side.

As well as looking to strengthen the playing squad, Harrower was careful to hand-pick his backroom team. First, Harry Hubbick

Accrington Stanley, 1960. Back row (left to right): W.Smith, T.Tighe, G.Forrester, W.McInnes, J.Swindells, C.Sneddon. Front row: G.Hudson, S.Logue, J.Harrower, L.Bennett, W.Devine.

returned to the club as trainer after a short spell with Bury. He was quickly followed by Bill Smith from Blackburn Rovers, who was appointed player-coach.

Sadly, the only successful spell during the season was between the end of October and November, when five games were won in succession. The club then suffered a spate of injuries which totally upset the balance of the side.

The injury crisis did give Harrower the opportunity to thrust Ferguson into the first team and the youngster proved what an excellent capture he had been.

However, it was the arrival of Joe Walton from Preston North End in February 1961 which finally saw the side settle down to show better form. Walton, Harrower and the remarkably consistent Forrester helped to keep Stanley away from the bottom of the table and lift them to 18th position.

In the third round of the FA Cup there was a magnificent draw at Deepdale against Preston North End before Stanley crashed out in the replay. However, the two ties provided much needed cash for the Stanley club.

Throughout the 1960-61 campaign the club had become reliant,

Stanley players preparing for what proved to be the club's last season of League football. From left to right are A.Hamilton, R.Gordon, L.Bennett, G.Forrester, H.Hubbick (trainer), M.Ferguson and P.Vipham.

perhaps over reliant, on the goalscoring attributes of George Hudson and Jackie Swindells. Hudson hit 35 League goals, thus equalling Stewart's record, in 44 appearances, whilst Swindells finished second in the scoring charts with 17 League goals.

However, the fact that 52 of the club's 74 goals were scored by two men ought to have been a cause for some concern.

The departure of Jackie Swindells to Barnsley in July 1961, coupled with the sale of George Hudson to Peterborough United in October 1961, ripped the heart out of the Stanley attack. The 1961-2 campaign was going to be dominated by Accrington Stanley's inability to put the ball in the back of the net.

Although some concern must have been felt during the close season, with the departure of Swindells, this was balanced with the arrival of three key men. In Bob Wilson, Garbutt Richardson and Alex Smith, Harrower had managed to strengthen defensive positions without any major outlay.

Smith was quick to establish himself as one of the best goalkeepers in the division, whilst Wilson came with a sound reputation after spells with Gillingham and Norwich City. Although Richardson, a former colleague of Joe Walton, had played mainly Central League football with Preston North End, he was still highly rated.

Defeat in both the pre-season friendlies against Stockport County proved an ominous start to the campaign. The opening League fixture at Tranmere resulted in a three-hour nightmare journey which saw Stanley stuck in traffic jams in Preston.

Having changed on the coach whilst going through the Mersey Tunnel, the team arrived only two minutes before the kick-off and suffered a 2-0 defeat.

After seven matches the team had six points and six goals to their credit, with three of the goals coming from Hudson. The visit of Carlisle United to Peel Park on 9 September saw Hudson score the only goal of the match. This was Hudson's last for the club, as he was transferred to Peterborough United before the month was out.

Hudson was not the only player Stanley lost in September. In the match at Barrow on 18 September, Garbutt Richardson badly injured his knee ligaments, an injury which meant he never played again for Stanley. The loss of Richardson came only days after Harrower had spent what little money was available on Jim Milner. Milner was an experienced inside-forward from Darlington and Harrower hoped he would help take the burden off Hudson up front.

The loss of Richardson and Hudson proved too great a handicap for Stanley to bear. Between 18 September 1961 and 2 March 1962, Accrington Stanley picked up a mere ten points from 25 matches.

In the middle of this sequence the club lost the services of Jimmy Harrower as manager. The directors had requested that Harrower make a comeback after retiring at the end of the 1960-61 season. Harrower tentatively agreed to see if he could reach match fitness.

The directors took this as a signal that Harrower would play again and announced his return for the match against Millwall on 9 December. Although the directors were intent on a player-manager, Harrower was reluctant to make a comeback. Two days before the visit of Millwall, the board announced the departure of Jimmy Harrower.

Accrington Stanley, 1961-2. Back row (left to right): A.Hamilton, W.Smith (player-coach), G.Richardson, M.Pickup, J.Walton. Middle row: Mr C.G.Kirby (director), J.Harrower (manager), G.Forrester, A.Smith, P.Vipham, R.Wilson, Mr.J.Wigglesworth (secretary), R.Walton (director), H.Hubbick (trainer). Front row: R.Gordon, L.Bennett, P.Irving, M.Ferguson, D.Sturrock, G.Hudson, P.Mulvey, W.Devine.

Playing affairs were put in the hands of Bill Smith and Harry Hubbick, whilst the directors looked for a new player-manager. In January 1962, the directors were thought to have enquired about the availability of Ronnie Allen, the former West Bromwich Albion and England centre-forward. Allen was playing with Crystal Palace and the London club's insistence on a £5,000 fee ended Stanley's interest. Similarly, when Manchester City quoted a fee of £9,000 for George Hannah, any interest Stanley might have had quickly evaporated.

The New Year brought a general feeling of depression around Peel Park. Attendances had fallen rapidly after the first few home matches. The weather meant that Christmas and New Year holiday matches had to be postponed, thus depriving the club of urgently needed revenue. Between 21 October and 3 February, the team had managed only two goals in 1,080 minutes of League football. Little wonder that attendance at Peel Park was reduced to the diehards.

If the position on the field was bleak, the position in the

boardroom was becoming critical. In December 1961, the club had been prohibited from further transfer deals as they already owed £3,000 to other clubs.

Not for the first time in their history a 'Save Stanley' appeal was launched. However, having been to the well so often, it was perhaps hardly surprising that only £450 was raised out of a target of £20,000.

Hopes of raising money from the transfer of Mike Ferguson were dashed when the young inside-forward turned down the opportunity of joining Workington for £3,000. Whilst Alex Smith was supposedly attracting the interest of other clubs, no firm offers were forthcoming.

On 20 February, the Football League wrote to Accrington Stanley expressing concern at the club's financial position and asking them to clarify it. The directors immediately called in former chairman Sam Pilkington to help them out of the crisis.

Pilkington decided to ask Bob Lord, the Burnley chairman for assistance. Lord was prepared to help his lifelong friend, but only if the six directors of the Accrington club agreed to resign.

Although Lord had great respect for Pilkington's ability, he was quoted as saying that he felt the six directors were incapable of running a football club. This was a harsh indictment on the men who had provided the cash to keep Stanley alive for many months and who now were expected to 'sack' themselves.

The directors' view was summed up by Mr R.Walton when he commented, "We have decided to resign because we consider the club is bigger than any individual, and if Mr Lord can do any better, we won't stand in his way."

On 23 February, Sam Pilkington met Alan Hardaker at the Football League in a bid to ease the club's plight. After the meeting, Hardaker remained uncommitted, merely stating that Pilkington had supplied him with all the information the League required and that he would be making a report to the Management Committee. However, the feeling in Accrington was that the club had survived the immediate crisis.

Although it appeared that Stanley would be able to escape the embarrassment of not fulfilling the season's commitments, doubts remained as to their long-term future.

Lord was quoted in the *Accrington Observer* on 24 February 1962, as stating that "I would like to see Stanley carrying on in

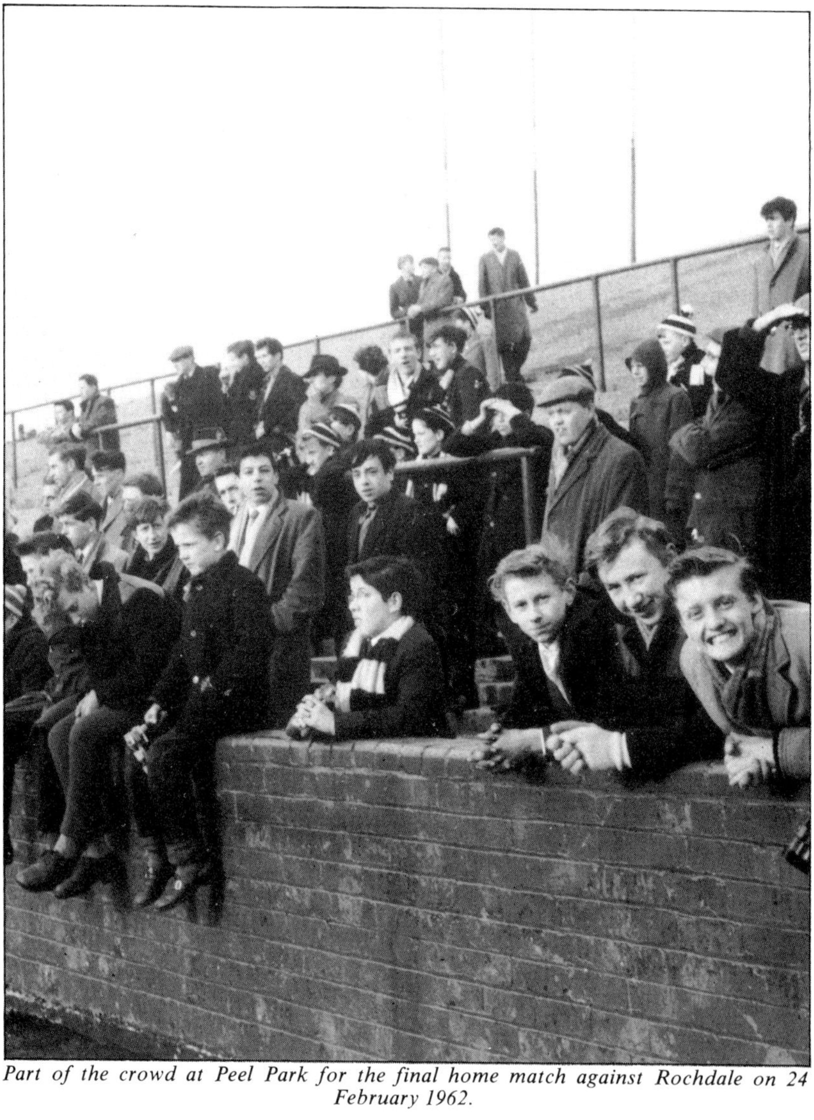

Part of the crowd at Peel Park for the final home match against Rochdale on 24 February 1962.

the League. It would be a shame if they went out. But I cannot guarantee that they will."

The only financial committment given by Lord was to buy sufficient shares to qualify as a director. However, he made it perfectly clear that it was not his intention to take over Accrington Stanley. In fact, Lord wanted to see Pilkington installed as chairman

Veteran winger Joe Devine (left) makes his only appearance of the season in Stanley's last-ever home game in the Football League.

once more, but Pilkington had doubts about taking up the reigns of office.

He preferred the option of a third person as chairman, but someone who was agreeable to both Lord and himself. More importantly, Lord admitted that at the time of his offer he had not seen any documents relating to the club's assets and liabilities.

Sam Pilkington was quick to deny suggestions that Accrington Stanley would become a 'nursery' for Burnley. The Football League would obviously not allow Stanley to continue in the League under those circumstances.

On 24 February 1962, a crowd of 2,727 watched Accrington

lose what was to be their last-ever home match in the Football League. Pilkington had asked the town to rally round the club and this was Stanley's largest home attendance since the end of October.

On the same afternoon that Stanley played their last home match,

Two young Stanleyites cheer on their team for the last time in a Football League match at Peel Park.

some 33,914 spectators watched Blackburn Rovers defeat Burnley at Ewood Park. The gulf in attendance figures put into perspective the problems facing Stanley. Whatever financial solutions could be found, there was simply no answer to the geographical location of being sandwiched so closely between two First Division clubs.

Three days later, Stanley picked up a point at Doncaster and then travelled to Gresty Road on Friday 2 March. A 4-0 hammering on the snow-covered pitch at Crewe was to be Accrington Stanley's last outing in the Football League.

On 5 March, a creditors' meeting heard a grim statement of Stanley's financial affairs from Mr John Haworth of Messrs Hopkinson & Pollard, the club accountants. He reported that during the year ending on 31 May 1961, there had been a loss of £5,500.

Since then there had been a further loss of about £5,000 up to 23 February 1962. The meeting was also told of further debts which the club had incurred. The total amount owing unsecured creditors was £43,566. The amount owing the Ministry of Pensions for players' insurance stamps was £458. In addition, about £9,000 was guaranteed to a number of people against the bank overdraft.

Furthermore, there was still more than £3,000 owing to other clubs in transfer fees; including £1,000 which was owed to Bob Lord's Burnley as the fee for Michael Pickup, who had been signed at the start of the season. To meet the players' wages until their contracts ended in June, the club would require more than £7,000.

The meeting was told that the balance sheet showed that the assets were worth £35,600, although it was anybody's guess what they would realize. A stunned meeting heard Bob Lord state, "I didn't think that the position was anything like as bad as we have heard. I had thought that if the position had not been as dark as it is, there may have been some hope to restore some life into the club, but looking at it carefully and seriously, I just cannot see any hope of attempting to carry on."

It was Lord who bluntly spelt out the options for the club: "My recommendations, as a creditor, is that there is only one course of action any reasonable, businesslike person could take, and that is to fold up."

Of pressing concern was the fact that unless £400 was found immediately, it looked as if the club would find telephone, electricity, gas and water supplies cut off from Peel Park. The first casualty was to be a Lancashire Senior Cup tie against Burnley, due to be played at Peel Park on 6 March 1962.

Accrington Stanley were now national news and in the national

March 1962 and a gas board official leaves Peel Park after turning off the club's supply.

Press, Sam Pilkington criticized the recent administration of the club's affairs. He was quoted as saying: "The balance sheet was not produced last June when it was due. It was only at last night's creditors meeting that we learned the whole truth. If we had known of the desperate position last June, a few enthusiasts might have been moved to make a last bid for survival."

He added, "I, for one, was not aware until recently that players' insurance stamps had not been bought by the club. Bob Lord and I shied off at once when we heard that. You can't tolerate that kind of thing."

The withdrawal of Pilkington and Lord left the directors with few options. Within 24 hours of the creditors' meeting, the Football League received a letter from the directors offering Accrington's resignation. Reaction to the resignation within the town was predictable and in the wake of public uproar, the Accrington directors had a change of heart.

In fact, not all the club's directors had been told of the letter of resignation and on 8 March, the club president, Sir William Cocker, sent another letter asking the League to disregard the first one.

There now followed three days in which Accrington Stanley found themselves in limbo. The matter was to be discussed by the Management Committee at a meeting in London on 11 March. In the meantime, Sir William Cocker attempted to put together another rescue package with the aid of other local businessmen.

It was hoped that the club would be able to fulfill their fixture with Exeter City at Peel Park on Saturday 10 March. However, the Football League refused to let the game go ahead. Director George Clarkson told the Press that 'Exeter were willing but the League have refused permission'.

On the afternoon of Monday, 12 March, the news the whole town had dreaded duly arrived. A letter from Alan Hardaker was received which informed the club that the Management Committee had decided to accept the first letter which the club had sent.

The Football League had sought legal advice before making their decision and were told that, according to established legal precedent, the League had to accept the first letter of resignation.

Although the club vowed to fight on, the end was seen as something of a blessing by some. George Forrester was quoted in the Press as saying: "As far as I am concerned the close-down is a good thing. We know, at last, just where we stand. The writing was on the wall for Stanley when the few spectators who turned up at home matches began to jeer."

Within days of the club's exit from the Football League, the chase for their players began. On Wednesday, 14 March, two managers arrived in Accrington hoping to sign Mike Ferguson. However, Jimmy Milne of Preston North End and Jack Marshall of Blackburn Rovers were disappointed to find that Ferugson was not at Peel Park.

Marshall learned that the player was training with the Burnley reserve squad at Gawthorpe and made the short journey to discuss terms with him. The next day the Stanley directors agreed to sign the documents which made Ferguson a Blackburn player for a modest fee, thought to be about £2,000.

On the same day, Alex Smith joined Bolton Wanderers to become understudy to former England goalkeeper Eddie Hopkinson. Another 24 hours brought the departure of Alex Hamilton to York

City and Willie Devine to Cambridge City of the Southern League.

The bitterness felt by those closest to Stanley was well expressed by director Stan Armitage when he said, "People have converged on Peel Park like vultures swooping to pick the remains of a dead body. Alex Smith was sold for £750. This figure is farcical. Smith was worth at least £6,500 in any football market."

He told the *Accrington Observer*: "If the clubs who are so interested in the players had been as interested a month or two ago, the club would not be where it is today."

Although no longer in the Football League, Accrington Stanley continued to survive. At a sparsely attended meeting of the creditors on the 17 August 1962, the club's creditors gave the go-ahead for Stanley to carry on in the Lancashire Combination for at least a year.

The meeting was told that it would take about £100 a week to run the club in the Combination and that if it was possible to make a surplus it would be applied to the payment of creditors.

Sir William Cocker, president of the club, urged the public to support Stanley and watch 'local lads playing in the town's own team'.

During the summer the club had attempted to appoint Bill Eckersley, the former Blackburn Rovers and England full-back, as manager. However, work committments meant Eckersley had to give up the idea of entering Football management with Stanley.

Nevertheless, the 1962-3 season saw Accrington Stanley enter the Second Division of the Lancashire Combination with home matches continuing to be played at Peel Park. A crowd of 995 turned out to watch the first home match of season against Rolls-Royce FC.

Unfortunately, the first season of non-League football proved to be a major disappointment. With high hopes early on in the season of gaining promotion, the team faded after the long winter lay-off due to the arctic weather conditions.

As a result of the club's serious financial situation, Stanley were unable to retain any of the 40 players who were on their books. Quite simply, Accrington Stanley could not afford to pay summer wages and the chairman expressed the hope that some of the players would be prepared to re-sign for the start of the 1963-4 season.

The 1963-4 campaign brought brighter performances on the field under player-manager Jimmy Hinksman. However, the financial

Forlorn if not entirely forgotten: Peel Park is already showing signs of neglect only a few weeks after Accrington Stanley left the League.

position continued to be grim and in December 1963, a petition was presented by the Commissioners of Inland Revenue in the High Court, to have Accrington Stanley (1921) Limited wound-up.

With the fate of the old company sealed, steps were taken to form a new club to carry on football at Peel Park. On 7 December 1963, the new Accrington FC took the field at Peel Park against Great Harwood. Under the astute leadership of Jimmy Hinksman, the new club ended the season as Second Division champions.

Unfortunately, life in the First Division of the Lancashire Combination proved a great anticlimax and Stanley were relegated within a year and with little or no money available, the club made the decision to become an all-amateur side.

Sadly, fortunes slumped and so did attendances. The beginning of 1966 found the club bottom of the table with only one point from 16 games. On 8 January 1966, a crowd of around 50 people watched what was to be the final game played by Accrington FC.

Ironically, the team beat Glossop 3-2 at Peel Park to record the first win of the season. With their ground about to be sold to Lancashire County Council and interest at an all-time low, few mourned the death of Accrington Football Club.

However, the name of Accrington Stanley was not to be consigned to the pages of football history. In 1968, a public meeting was held in the town with a view to forming a new Accrington Stanley. And after two years of hard work, Accrington Stanley (1968) entered the Second Division of the Lancashire Combination for the start of the 1970-71 season.

On 15 August 1970, a crowd of over 800 gave the new Stanley a great send-off to their first season in the Lancashire Combination at their Crown Inn ground.

The team of six semi-professionals and five amateurs which had been assembled by player-manager Jimmy Hinksman, beat Formby Town by 2-1. Thus another team was born to inherit the legacy of 'Th' Owd Reds' and Accrington Stanley.

The Accrington Grounds

The Cricket Field, Thorneyholme Road

CONSIDERING the origins of Accrington Football Club, it was hardly surprising that their first home should be the Thorneyholme Road cricket ground. The Cricket Club had moved there from Peel Park in 1877 and Accrington Football Club made their first appearance on the ground in September of the following year.

The new ground was soon the centre of attention when a match between Accrington and Church was played under electric lights on 13 November 1878. The excitement caused is well recorded by the correspondent of *The Accrington Times*, who stated that 'about 3,000 spectators assembled on the field to witness the light, whilst every point of vantage ground outside was crowded with people who contented themselves by witnessing the glare from the lights without paying for admission into the field'.

Proceedings were not without a hitch, however, and only the last-minute loan of a steam-engine from the Gas Company allowed the Accrington public its first view of football under artificial light. The lights were somewhat primitive in nature, consisting of two lamps fixed on a post at opposite corners of the field. Fortunately, a moonlit night and the surrounding snow, which acted as a reflector, helped to make the lights an impressive spectacle.

Unfortunately, the match was interrupted for half an hour whilst one of the lamps was repaired. In the meantime, the crowd were entertained by the Accrington Band and the sight of Accrington players playing leap-frog. The game finally ended at 9.30pm with the playing of the *National Anthem* and an honourable score-line of three goals each.

The sharing of a ground used for cricket presented obvious problems for the Football Club. In late summer and early spring, the cricketers had priority on use of the ground. This meant that the footballers had to wait until the last week of September to open their home programme and had to complete their home fixtures by mid to late April.

In July 1882, the Cricket Committee agreed to allow the Football Club to play Bolton Wanderers on the south-west side of the ground on 10 September. It was in that month that the Football Club was granted permission to build a stand as long as it did not encroach upon the cricket field. At the same time it was decided that the football season should commence on the first Saturday in October and end on the last day of March. In September 1883, further restrictions were put on the Football Club when they were informed that the stand had to be removed after every match.

The uneasy relations between the two clubs rumbled on for over a decade. In August 1888 it was agreed that the Football Club would be charged £40 for the use of the ground and on 6 October the visit of Wolverhampton Wanderers saw the first Football League match at the Cricket Field.

On leaving the Football League in 1893, Accrington FC managed to play a further season at Thorneyholme Road before their desperate financial plight forced them to leave the ground. The cricketers remained and today Thorneyholme Road is still the home of Accrington Cricket Club.

Moorhead Park

MOORHEAD Park was the site where the histories of Accrington and Accrington Stanley converge. Built in the 1890s, this rather attractive venue provided the opportunity for Accrington to share expenses with an up-and-coming junior side called Accrington Stanley. Located off Whalley Road, at the ends of Cromwell Street and Orange Street, the Moorhead Ground was some distance from the town centre. However, the facilites more than made up for the less than desirable location as the ground had been enclosed and a grandstand built for the use of supporters.

After the Accrington club folded, Moorhead continued to be the home of Accrington Stanley until the end of the 1896-7 season. However, for the following campaign, Stanley were forced to find a new home as they could no longer afford the rental at Moorhead.

In 1901, encouraged by the support which they had received during their inaugral season in the Lancashire Combination, the Committee gambled on returning to the plusher surroundings of Moorhead Park. Any fears that the Committee may have had about attendances dispelled. A crowd of 2,000 supporters turned up on a glorious afternoon to watch the first practice match of the 1901-02 campaign.

The club suffered a crippling financial set-back in Feburary 1910, when the ground suffered severe storm damage. Gale-force winds overturned and wrecked what was known as the 'new' stand and about 100 yards of hordings fell victim to the storm. Although the repairs proved to be a serious drain on resources, the ground continued to be Stanley's home venue until World War One ended the footballing activities of the Stanley club.

No trace remains of the ground today, for by the 1930s it had disappeared to be replaced by a Girls' High School and playing fields.

Bell's Ground, Woodnook

ACCRINGTON Stanley moved to the former home of the Bell's Temperance Club for the start of the 1897-8 season. Compared with their previous home at Moorhead Park, the facilites which their new home offered were spartan to say the least. However, at Woodnook, they shared a ground with the amateur team, Accrington Villa, and thus costs were drastically reduced.

Another important factor in the move was that the ground was more centrally situated, and it was hoped that Stanley would be able to attract larger crowds than at Moorhead. Certainly, the attendance of 1,500 for the opening game against Trawden Forest suggested that the move might be more successful than was eventually the case. The ground was situated in the west end of Robert Nuttall Street (now Belfield Road) on its junction with Hudson Street. The west side of the ground was enclosed by a railway line which has now been dismantled. Although probably enclosed, the pitch had a pronounced slope and, despite its more central location, the move back to Moorhead was viewed with some relief by most of those connected with the club. The Woodnook ground suffered a similar fate to that of Moorhead and had ceased to exist as a football ground by the early 1930s.

Peel Park

OF the quartet of grounds used by the town's two premier soccer clubs, it is Peel Park which is synonymous with senior football in Accrington. The stadium was within the formerly large grounds of the Peel Park Hotel, in an area which had previously been well known for sporting activities. The Peel Park area of Accrington had previously been the home of Accrington Cricket Club and 'Th'Owd Reds' had played two matches against Baxenden in this area in 1884.

Accrington Stanley moved to Peel Park in 1919, when the newly-resurrected club was looking for a new base. Although the £2,500 purchase price was a considerable

Peel Park, probably pictured during Accrington Stanley's first home game in the Football League, against Rochdale in 1921-2.

sum for a club in Stanley's position, it provided them with a chance to own their own ground instead of paying the increasing rental for Moorhead Park.

On 20 September 1919, the visit of Stalybridge Celtic saw the official opening of Peel Park (see *Matches to Remember*). Conditions were fairly spartan and the

teams had to change in the neighbouring school. The pitch ran parallel alongside the school from the Peel Park Hotel towards Manor Street. However, the following season it was decided to have the pitch from the Huncoat end to the school.

The move required a huge amount of voluntary labour in order for the work to be completed on time. The pitch resembled a spider's web as drains, 6ft deep and 3ft wide, were dug across the playing field. However, time was at a premium and in order for the pitch to be ready for the start of the season, the final turfing had to be done in a hurry. The result was that the playing pitch was left with a huge slope of 17ft from the top corner-flag at the cottice side to the bottom corner-flag at Manor Street.

By the start of the first campaign in the Football League, the club had managed to make considerable improvements to the ground but, even so, standards were still spartan. A small seated stand provided the only real form of comfort for spectators on a small and compact ground. By 1930 narrow strips of concrete terracing had been introduced on all four sides, although this was restricted to the lower areas of the ground.

This piecemeal approach to ground improvements continued after World War Two. However, in August 1953, Accrington Stanley shocked many neighbouring clubs by announcing their intention to introduce floodlights. The club hoped to invite teams which people in the district rarely got a chance of watching, to play friendly exhibition games. Despite the initial costs, it was thought that in the long term this would prove to be a good source of revenue for the club. They planned to use eight 40ft pylons on which ten 500-watt floodlights would be placed.

In January 1954, a crowd of 4,794 paid more than £250 to watch Accrington Stanley Reserves play Nelson in the Lancashire Combination Cup under floodlights. The only hitch was a brief one when play was held up for five minutes when lights on the Burnley Road side fused and part of the pitch was in shadow. As a memento of the occasion, the Stanley club presented each team and trainer with ties in their club colours. The value of the floodlights was proven the following November, when a record crowd of 17,634 watched the floodlit friendly against Blackburn Rovers.

Ground improvements had continued throughout the early 1950s, so that the Peel Park capacity stood at 24,692 in September 1954. The summer of 1955 saw continued activity at Peel Park under the direction of Mr C.G.Kilby, a director of Accrington Stanley. Kilby became architect, engineer, steel-erector and labourer as terracing was improved, toilets installed and offices and walls erected.

However, despite continuing improvements to the terraces, Peel Park was desperately short of seating accommodation with less than 800 seats available. It was to rectify this problem that the club agreed to purchase the Aldershot Military Tattoo Grandstand in April 1958.

The cost of the stand was a bargain £1,450 and it was believed that an additional £12,000 would cover the cost of transporting and erecting the structure. The 60yd-long timber and galvanized steel clad stand could provide seating for 2,300 spectators. The cost eventually rose to between £14,000 and £15,000 and was completed at the time when Peel Park attendances were starting to fall. Accrington Stanley was an early example of how a new stand could prove to be something of a 'white elephant'.

When Accrington Stanley eventually became defunct, Peel Park passed to a businessman from Wigan and then, in turn, to the local authority. Although the ground showed signs of decay and vandalism, Lancashire County Council planned to use it as a sporting venue for local schools and they improved spectator facilities there.

Alas, hopes for a revival in the fortunes of Peel Park came to an end in the early hours of Sunday, 23 April 1972. The original timber framework of the club's old stand was gutted by fire and, after only 20 minutes, all that remained were a few metal girders among the charred debris.

Today, little remains of the Peel Park ground. Parts of the perimeter wall and dressing-rooms can still be seen and a grass bank now covers the site of part of the old terracing. However, football continues to thrive at Peel Park as it is used for schoolboy football, including the Hyndburn Under-11 representative team. As a point of interest, the orientation of the pitch has changed to that used by Accrington Stanley in their 1919-20 season.

Peel Park in the late 1950s, showing the Main Stand backing on to Manor Street and the open terracing at the Huncoat End.

The Aldershot Military Tattoo Grandstand which was erected at Peel Park in 1958, at a cost reported to be around £15,000.

Accrington Stanley's Managers

Samuel Pilkington
1921-1924

IT is perhaps something of an anomaly to classify Samuel Turneil Pilkington as a manager. Throughout an association with the Accrington Stanley club which lasted for over half a century, Pilkington was never officially given the title of manager. However, when Accrington were elected to the Third Division North in 1921, Pilkington it was who fulfilled the role of the traditional secretary-manager, although he only ever bore the first half of that title.

Born in Accrington in 1890, Pilkington had first joined Accrington Stanley as a player in 1906. He later enjoyed spells with Haslingden and Oldham Athletic before returning to Accrington Stanley's colours in July 1913. During World War One he had played a great deal of football with the Army before returning to Accrington when hostilities ended. On his return he found that the Stanley club had fallen on hard times and he was instrumental in reviving its flagging fortunes.

When Stanley made their debut in the newly formed Third Division North, Pilkington held the post of secretary. He was responsible for the day-to-day running of the club as well as signing new players. However, on the eve of the 1921-2 season, the club had appointed Matthew Brunton as trainer-coach to look after the players. This appointment allowed Pilkington to devote more time to finding new players as well as trying to keep the club on a financially sound footing.

In June 1923, Stanley appointed Curtis Booth as player-manager and Pilkington's role became totally administrative. The secretary's main task at this time was to try to solve the crippling financial problems which dogged the club. However, when Booth was seriously injured in the first match of the 1923-4 campaign, Pilkington was once again left at the helm until the manager was sufficiently recovered to resume his duties. When financial economies meant Booth was released at the end of the 1923-4 season, Pilkington was again left to shoulder the full burden of management responsibilites. In October 1924, Pilkington announced his intention to resign as secretary. However, his services were too valuable to lose and he was invited to join the board of directors.

Always a keen advocate of the Third Division North, Pilkington later served for a spell as chairman of the Northern Section of the Third Division and then had a lengthy period as honorary secretary. In 1946, Pilkington became president of the Lancashire Football Combination and at the same time he was elected chairman of Accrington Stanley, a post he held until July 1953. On leaving the chairmanship, Pilkington was appointed honorary vice-president and adopted the role of elder statesman at the club. It was perhaps therefore fitting that when Bob Lord mounted a rescue plan to save Stanley in 1962 he should want Pilkington by his side.

Although Pilkington will forever be regarded as 'Mr Accrington Stanley', he also gave over 50 years service to

Accrington Cricket Club as player, secretary, chairman and president. A successful businessman in Accrington, Pilkington was an independent member of the town council for some 14 years and became mayor in 1942. He died on 29 June 1970, aged 80.

Curtis Booth
1923-1924

CURTIS Booth had the distinction of being Accrington Stanley's first official manager in the Football League. Booth had enjoyed a moderately successful playing career which had been severely interrupted by World War One (see *Who's Who* section). In June 1923, the Accrington club announced that they had appointed Booth to the new position of player-manager. The adminstrative work would remain in the hands of Sam Pilkington, whilst Booth would play in the team and act as captain as well as manager.

It was an innovative experiment for Accrington Stanley and one which deserved a better fate than it enjoyed. In the first match of the 1923-4 campaign, at Darlington, Booth suffered a serious injury which kept him away from the club for several months. He eventually returned to take up his managerial duties for the last two months of the campaign. No longer able to play, Booth none the less won the confidence of players and directors alike by the workmanlike way he got down to the job. Certainly he did enough during those two months to suggest that he had a promising career in management.

Unfortunately, Accrington Stanley were not able to reap the rewards of their ingenuity. As the season drew to a close, the financial position made it clear that a manager was simply a luxury the club could not afford. The board announced that they could not continue with the experiment of engaging a manager and Booth was released.

After leaving Accrington, Booth went on

to carve out a successful career coaching on the Continent before his death in Amsterdam in October 1947.

Ernest Blackburn
1924-1932

ERNEST Blackburn was thrust into the position of secretary-manager almost by accident. He had arrived at Peel Park in August 1924 to succeed Matt Brunton as trainer, and when Sam Pilkington resigned in October, few expected Blackburn to take over. However, negotiations to bring Harry Hadley to Accrington foundered and in late November, Blackburn was announced as Pilkington's successor.

In appointing Ernest Blackburn, the board had chosen a man who was well experienced in football. Born in Crawshaw Booth in April 1892, he played for Loveclough in the Burnley & District League before World War One. However, it was in Army football that Blackburn first

Accrington Stanley's team that met Rotherham County at Peel Park on 30 August 1924. Back row (left to right): Richardson, Watson (captain), Salt, McIntosh, Crawley, Ernest Blackburn (team manager). Front row: J. Thompson, Bedford, Mutch, Rooks, R. Thompson, Skillen.

came to prominence. When the war broke out he had volunteered for the Medical Corps and served in France for almost five years. He played for the Corps teams, being able to fill either full-back position. When he was moved to the GHQ he made the acquaintance of Harry Hampton, the famous Aston Villa centre-forward, who introduced Blackburn to the club.

Blackburn spent three years with Aston Villa before moving to Bradford City. During his two years with the Yorkshire club he suffered a series of injuries which evenutally ended his career. It was on leaving Bradford that he arrived at Peel Park as trainer in August 1924. On his appointment as secretary-manager, he immediately appointed the veteran full-back Thomas Tindall as his player-trainer.

Throughout his reign at Peel Park, Blackburn worked under the burden of serious financial problems. These difficulties made it impossible for him to build a settled team. Each season saw numerous changes to the playing personnel and this was ultimately reflected in the club's final League placings. During his eight and a half seasons in charge, Stanley finished in the top ten only once but, whilst Blackburn maintained charge of the day-to-day running of the club, team selection rested with a committee of directors. Although Blackburn could advise, he was never given sole responsibility for team selection.

In January 1932, Blackburn's potential was recognized when he was appointed manager of Wrexham. Although the Welsh club were in the Third Division North, Blackburn's move was seen as a promotion and at the Racecourse Ground he enjoyed the financial resources which were never available during his time at Peel Park.

In December 1936, he moved to take over the managership of Hull City, where his financial astuteness helped build a team which almost gained promotion in 1938. In January 1946, Blackburn made his final managerial move when he was appointed secretary-manager of Tranmere Rovers. Once again he developed some successful and entertaining sides on a limited budget. In 1955 he handed over playing matters to Noel Kelly and concentrated on the club's administrative affairs before finally retiring at the end of the 1958-9 season. Ernest Blackburn spent his remaining years in Birkenhead before his death in July 1964.

Amos Wade
1932-1935

THE departure of Ernest Blackburn brought a most unlikely successor to the manager's office in the shape of Amos Wade. Although a native of Accrington and a former director, at the time of his appointment Wade was living in retirement in the seaside resort of Morecambe.

Unlike his predecessors who had experience of playing professional football, Amos Wade was an administrator first and foremost. He had started a confectionary business in Nelson in 1907 and two years later had returned to Accrington to pursue his business interests. He became a director of Accrington Stanley in 1922 and remained in the town until 1929. He then retired from the confectionary business and moved to Morecambe to keep a boarding-house.

Within days of Ernest Blackburn moving to Wrexham in January, 1932, Wade was offered the position of secretary-manager. In spite of the severe financial difficulties which the club found itself in, he immediately accepted the invitation to take the Peel Park hot seat.

Throughout his time in charge at Peel Park, finance — or to be more accurate the lack of it — dominated the agenda. Training was generally left in the hands of Fred Brennand, whilst Wade turned his attention to keeping the club afloat. In December 1933, long-serving full-back, James Armstrong was appointed player-coach but results continued to be disappointing and the team finished in 20th position in the Third Division North at the end of the 1932-3 campaign.

The dawn of the 1934-5 season saw the club appoint the former Blackburn Rovers and Everton, England international Joe Clennell as coach. At times he was described by the local Press as team manager, but the team was still picked by committee as it always had been. Wade was now totally preoccupied with the financial problems of the club and it is doubtful if he had much input into what went on with regard to players and tactics.

At the end of a dismal season which saw the club struggle to climb to 18th position, Clennell departed. The directors decided to appoint a manager and give him sole responsibility for the playing affairs. At the same time Amos Wade retained the position of secretary, a role he would keep until the end of the decade.

After the war, Wade continued to reside in Accrington. He had become a Liberal councillor in 1932 and was the mayor of Accrington in 1941. After losing his seat in 1949 he became an alderman in the town until 1952 and in 1955 regained a seat on the council which he kept until his death on 15 December 1961, at the age of 76.

John Hacking
1935-1949

ARGUABLY Accrington Stanley's first manager in the modern sense of the word, John Hacking — who was known as 'Jack' — also proved to be the longest serving. A product of junior football in his native Blackburn, Hacking had joined Blackpool as a young goalkeeper in 1919. Unfortunately he failed to win a regular first-team place and after 33 appearances he moved to neighbouring Fleetwood. A brief and successful spell with the Lancashire Combination outfit ended with a move to Oldham Athletic in May 1926. At Boundary Park he proved to be a consistent and able custodian who won three England caps and represented the Football League team on two occasions. After 223 League appearances for the Latics, he made the short move to Manchester United in March 1934. After a further 32 League games he moved to Peel Park as player-manager in May 1935.

At the time of Hacking's appointment it was announced by the Accrington club that he would be placed in sole charge of team selection. Certainly none of his predecessors had enjoyed such freedom and there is evidence to suggest that Hacking himself had to bow to 'committee' decisions during his later years with the club.

Hacking made an immediate impact on the club and raised them to their highest League position since the 1927-8 season. It was an achievement made all the more remarkable by the fact that he had lost the services of two outstanding forwards — Harker and Mortimer — to Portsmouth in February 1936. Hacking had retired from playing in December 1935 to concentrate on managing and weekly tactical talks became a feature of his reign.

After an impressive first 12 months at Peel Park, Hacking shocked the directors and fans when he declined the terms offered him for the 1936-7 season. Fortunately for Stanley, he quickly reconsidered and decided to stay. Although League performances were not quite as good as the previous season, the FA Cup brought a memorable victory over neighbouring Blackburn Rovers.

Hopes of reviving Stanley began to fade as Hacking found that he was continually losing the club's better players in order to balance the books. Hacking's hard work could not compensate for the loss of good players and Accrington finished the 1937-8 and 1938-9 seasons bottom of the Third Division North. Ironically, when League football was brought to a halt in 1939, Accrington Stanley sat proudly at the top of the table. The outbreak of hostilities saw Hacking leave Peel Park because of his war work. However, the 1944-5 season brought Hacking's return and the following campaign saw him lead the club to the Third Division North (West Region) championship. It was the first title the club had won since their days in the Lancashire Combination, before World War One.

When Accrington Stanley returned to Football League action in 1946, Hacking had been given the old role of secretary-manager. Like so many managers, Hacking found that the first season after the war was to be a time of rebuilding. No fewer than 33 players were used as Stanley struggled to 20th position in the table. The following campaign proved to be one of the most successful in Accrington's history as the club climbed to sixth position.

Having finally achieved a fairly settled squad, Hacking hoped to build on this success during the 1948-9 campaign. Unfortunately, injuries ravaged the squad from the very start and Stanley did not win any of their first 12 matches. After such a terrible start, Hacking did well to lift the club from the bottom of the table to finish the season in 20th position.

In May 1949, the directors decided that the club needed a change of direction. As a result Hacking parted company with Stanley on amicable terms. He was reported as saying that he had resigned 'because the directors had intimated that they desired a change and that was all there was to the matter'. Within days of the announcement that Hacking was leaving Accrington he was appointed secretary-manager of Barrow. He remained at Holker Street until his death in 1955.

James Porter
1949-1951

THE man chosen to succeed the long-serving John Hacking was Bury assistant manager James Porter. Born in Hamilton, Scotland, in 1903, Porter arrived at Bury in 1922 from Wishaw YMCA, a Scottish junior club. He made over 500 League and FA Cup appearances for the Shakers before being appointed assistant manager and chief scout at Gigg Lane. He remained in that capacity until November 1938, when he became team manager of Manchester United. Porter remained in this post until the outbreak of war, during which he held an important administrative position with the Air Ministry until 1944. In that year he returned to look after Bury's wartime team and when Norman Bullock resumed the managership at Gigg Lane, Porter became assistant manager once more.

In June 1949, the Accrington board managed to negotiate Porter's release from his contract at Bury and installed him as manager. Having a deep regard for his knowledge of the game, and particularly his ability to spot young talent, the directors gave him a completely free hand. Within a fortnight Porter had taken Alick Robinson from Gigg Lane to become his trainer-coach.

Unfortunately, the new manager at Peel Park faced old problems. By Christmas 1949, the club was in serious trouble both financially and in a playing sense. Porter put his trust in youth and a defence which included promising youngsters like Stan Lynn and Eric Lovett gradually began to steady the ship. Although the club finished in a respectable mid-table position, the financial position remained critical. Once again Stanley had no option but to sell to survive and Porter reluctantly allowed Lynn to move to Aston Villa in order to keep the club afloat.

The 1950-51 campaign saw the team struggling once more at the foot of the table. Despite the results, Porter worked tirelessly to turn the situation around without ever having the resources which were obviously required. His efforts had not gone unnoticed elsewhere and in the first week of November 1950, he was offered the managership of Wrexham. Porter surprised many supporters when he rejected the offer, insisting that he would see the job through at Peel Park. Within days of pledging his future to the club the financial pressures once again forced the sale of good players. The transfer of Don Travis and Samuel Parker to Crewe Alexandra brought bitter criticism from the supporters. As a result, attendances dropped and Porter found the loss of Travis in particular to be a severe blow.

During the period from 11 November 1950 to 20 January 1951, only one point was gained from ten matches as the club slumped to the bottom of the table. Such a drastic situation required drastic measures and Porter shocked many supporters when he splashed out a club record fee — said to be in the region of £3,000 — to sign William Watkinson from Liverpool. At Anfield, Watkinson had understudied Albert Stubbins and Porter banked on him adding the punch which had been so clearly missing since the departure of Travis.

Unfortunately, Porter did not remain at Peel Park long enough to reap the dividends of his enterprise. On 3 March 1951 the team lost 9-1 at Lincoln and two days later the club issued the following statement:

'Owing to disagreement on club policy, Mr J.Porter, manager and Mr A.Robinson, trainer-coach, have tendered their resignations to the club today. These have been reluctantly accepted by the board.'

The twin aims of achieving success on the pitch and financial stability off it were to bring about the fall of six managers between 1951-1961. Porter was simply the first who found the twin objectives impossible to achieve.

Walter Crook
1951-1953

A DAY after the announcement of James Porter's resignation, Walter Crook was engaged as trainer-coach. Whilst the directors carried on team selection in consultation with Crook, the new man again had day-to-day responsibility for playing affairs. His appointment was seen as something of a major coup for struggling Accrington Stanley. Crook was well known to the Accrington board, having

Walter Crook (left) and chairman Sam Pilkington, who was Stanley's first manager, in the dressing-room at Peel Park.

spent the majority of his playing career with neighbouring Blackburn Rovers. He had made his debut for Blackburn in 1932 and from December 1934 until the outbreak of war, had remained an ever-present in the team. In 1947, Crook moved to Bolton Wanderers but injury forced him into premature retirement. He then enjoyed a successful period coaching abroad, taking the struggling Ajax club of Amsterdam to the Dutch Championship within two years of his arrival.

However, the team he took charge of at Peel Park provided a stark contrast to the team of seven internationals he had left in Holland. Although there was no dramatic improvement in results, Crook sufficiently impressed the directors to be appointed manager-coach in June 1951.

Crook's first full season in charge proved an uphill battle. Stanley finished 22nd in the Third Division North and a first-round exit in the FA Cup denied them much-needed funds. However, considering the appalling financial plight of the club, few, if any, laid the blame for a disappointing season at the manager's door. In July 1952, Crook was appointed to the post of secretary-manager in a bid to give him greater freedom in signing new players. Almost immediately Crook appointed the former Wolves and Manchester United player, Billy Wrigglesworth, as his trainer-coach.

Despite the new moves the team

continued to struggle. Furthermore, the financial situation meant that the manager was unable to sign the type of players he wanted. Early in February 1953, Mellor and Robinson rocked the club when they handed in transfer requests. On 17 February, Crook tendered his resignation which was to take effect on 26 February. The manager gave 'differences with some of the directors' as the reason for his departure. He emphasized that his decision had nothing to do with the club's position at the foot of the Third Division North.

In truth, Crook had been disenchanted with life at Peel Park for some time. A clash with the directors at the end of January, following a match at Mansfield and the transfer requests from Mellor and Robinson, simply brought matters to a head. The dire position of the club led Sam Pilkington to make strenuous efforts to keep Crook at Peel Park. Although some directors were less than happy with his management, there were others who believed that he would eventually turn the situation around. However, all attempts to get him to change his mind proved futile.

After leaving Accrington, Crook returned to Holland for a spell and was then out of football until being appointed manager of Wigan Athletic in October 1954. He then joined the coaching staff of Preston North End, where he remained for some 18 years. After leaving Deepdale he became disillusioned with the modern game and was reported as saying that he did not watch football any more. He died at his home in Mellor, near Blackburn, in December 1988.

Walter Galbraith
1953-1958

WALTER McMurray Galbraith proved to be the most successful manager in Accrington Stanley's history. He was appointed player-manager in June 1953, following a spell with Grimsby Town. However, Galbraith had already gained experience of management from his spell as player-manager with New Brighton from June 1950 until leaving for Blundell Park in August 1951 (see *Who's Who* section).

In his first season, Galbraith built not one, but in effect two teams. The first had to be hurriedly assembled at a time when most clubs had completed their signings. Then, as the inevitable weaknesses showed he shrewdly recruited talented young players with remarkably little outlay, often from his native Scotland. A final position of 15th and the nucleus of a strong squad was a good start. However, the 1954-5 campaign proved even better as Accrington Stanley experienced their best ever season.

Success on the field brought the fans flocking in — an average home attendance of 9,965 could only be bettered by championship-winning Barnsley. Improved attendances meant that the financial burdens eased and Galbraith was given more scope than his predecessors in the transfer market. Even so, Galbraith was content to journey to his native Scotland and pluck men from 'B' Division clubs. The strength of the squad was reflected in the fact that the Reserves won the Lancashire Combination and the Combination Cup, whilst the 'A' team finished third in the Lancashire League. The first team experienced their best season in the Third Division North challenging for promotion until almost the last match before finally finishing second.

Galbraith continued to strengthen his squad over the next three seasons, but the promotion prize remained tantilizingly out of reach. Galbraith led the club to two third-place spots and in 1957-8 he again took them to the runners-up spot. During this time there was continual speculation linking Galbraith to more attractive clubs. In April 1956, he was awarded an improved contract to keep him at Peel Park for a further three years. However, in March 1957 he was short-listed for the vacant position at Blackpool and in June, he was offered the managership of Kilmarnock. Although many thought the lure of Scotland would appeal to Galbraith, he turned the offer down because he felt

confident about the future at Accrington. A little over 12 months later that confidence was to prove ill-founded.

Throughout the period from 1956 to 1958 success on the field had not produced the healthy bank balance which had accompanied Galbraith's earlier campaigns with the club. As a result the directors felt that the time had come to take some economy measures. Galbraith disagreed and on the evening of 20 August 1958 he tendered his resignation, less than 72 hours before the start of the season. Thus, in the most dramatic of circumstances the most successful reign of any Accrington Stanley manager came to an end.

Obviously a man of Galbraith's calibre was not out of work for long. In November 1958 he became manager of Bradford and continued his Accrington policy of signing his fellow countrymen. He remained with the Yorkshire club until January 1961, when he joined Tranmere Rovers. At Tranmere he followed his tried and trusted method of recruiting low-priced Scotsmen to lift the club into a challenging position in the Fourth Division. In November 1961 he returned to Scotland to become manager of Hibernian. His last managerial appointment was with Stockport County, whom he had joined in July 1968 as chief scout. However, following the departure of Jimmy Meadows, Galbraith took charge between August 1969 and April 1970.

George Eastham
1958-1959

ALTHOUGH on a short-list of six, George Eastham was in a different country when the interviews for the Stanley managership took place on 7 October 1958. Even so, it did not prevent the former England international from succeeding Walter Galbraith at Peel Park.

Like his predecessor, the new manager had sampled life in football's bargain basement, but Eastham had also tasted the champagne end of professional football. Born in Blackpool in September 1913, he had played in local football before joining Bolton Wanderers in 1932. During a successful spell with the Trotters, as a skilful inside-forward, he had been awarded an England cap in 1935. He moved to Brentford in June 1937 and in November 1938 returned to his native Blackpool. After World War Two he had brief spells with Swansea Town, Rochdale and Lincoln City before dropping out of the League to join Hyde United in 1950. In July 1953, he 'crossed the water' initially as player-coach and then manager with Ards.

In Ireland, Eastham had taken a club which was languishing in the doldrums to European Cup status within five years. Indeed, European Cup commitments were the reason for his absence during the interviews for the Stanley position. However, Eastham was given the opportunity to visit Accrington on the Sunday before the interviews, *en route* to France where Ards were playing Reims. His track record for developing young talent in Ireland — including his son George Eastham, who was sold to Newcastle United for £9,000, and Billy Humphries, who moved to Leeds United for £5,000 — obviously impressed the Stanley board. Even though he could not take over until later in the month, the directors had no hesitation in offering him a contract said to be worth over £1,000 a year.

When he arrived at Peel Park in late October, Eastham found a team which was struggling to achieve the consistency of previous seasons. Eastham managed to engineer five straight wins during the final weeks of 1958 to lift the club back into the promotion race. Despite the upturn in results, though, Eastham believed that the team were not good enough to win promotion from the Third Division — arguing that the newly-created section was a far tougher proposition than the old Third Division North.

Although Eastham believed that the club possessed a number of promising youngsters, he also wanted to bring in one or two new players. In order to do this he was forced to sell to obtain the resources he required. Thus, George Stewart, Peter Dick and Ray Byrom were allowed to leave in the wake of stern criticism from the supporters. However, with Lord, Hamilton, Nightingale, Garrity, McCreadie and Gibson ready to take their chance in the first team, Eastham saw the sale of popular players as part of his policy for introducing young blood. Unfortunately, Eastham's plans never had the opportunity to flourish, as the club's debts voraciously swallowed the money raised from transfers.

Promotion hopes faded over the second part of the 1958-9 campaign as a meagre four victories were gained from the final 21 matches. A crippling injury list, which saw five goalkeepers used in March alone, finally sabotaged Eastham's reconstruction plans. None the less his first campaign had been very satisfactory considering the crippling injuries and lack of funds with which to strengthen the squad. Indeed, in January 1959, Eastham became the third Stanley manager in the 1950s to reject a move to another club when he turned down an offer to manage Distillery.

The club and supporters were therefore rocked in June 1959, when Eastham resigned from the club to accept Distillery's offer. At the time of his resignation, Eastham complained that the lack of encouragement from the directors with regard to bringing in new players was the issue which finally made up his mind to leave. Although the directors strenuously denied his claims, Eastham left the club with these prophetic words: "Any further transfers would be disastrous for the club. It is now up to the supporters to decide whether they want better football or see Accrington Stanley slide into the Fourth Division."

After leaving Accrington, Eastham managed Distillery until March 1964. Later in that year he returned to the managerial position at Ards, where he remained until 1970. Eastham had a further spell in management with Glentoran in 1972.

Harold Bodle
1959-1960

HAROLD Bodle obtained the manager's chair at Peel Park some eight months after he applied for the post! Having been short-listed in October 1958, following the resignation of Walter Galbraith, he had been narrowly pipped for the job by George Eastham. However, with Eastham's departure in June 1959, Bodle won the unanimous approval of the directors to try to solve the seemingly insurmountable problems which faced Accrington Stanley.

Bodle's return to Peel Park was genuinely welcomed in most quarters. Regarded by many as the most inspiring captain ever to lead the Accrington club, Bodle had a wide experience of the game at all levels (see *Who's Who* section).

Unfortunately, not even someone as well versed in Stanley's problems as Bodle could stop the rot. The club experienced an horrific opening spell which saw only four wins from 19 games. In November 1958 further disruption was caused by the loss of first-team coach Harry Hubbick to Bury. Bodle immediately promoted reserve-team coach Harry Whitworth, who had joined the club as recently as August, but by the turn of the year Stanley were deep in relegation trouble. The arrival of Jack Swindells from Blackburn Rovers Reserves briefly sparked something of a rival. With six goals in his first four League matches, Swindells began to form an exciting partnership with the highly-rated Harvey McCreadie. It was this partnership which provided Stanley with their best hope of avoiding the drop to the Fourth Division.

Unfortunately, the crippling financial situation meant that the club could not refuse an offer of £5,500 for McCreadie from Luton Town in January 1960. Bodle desperately tried to fill the gap with other youngsters, but without success. Throughout his reign Bodle had tried to utilize the promising youngsters by whom Eastham had put such great store. Unfortunately they were unequal to the task and the Fourth Division loomed ever nearer as attendances at Peel Park continued to fall.

By the end of April 1960, with the team doomed to the Fourth Division, the directors held two special meetings. The outcome was that Bodle was informed that his contract would not be renewed when it expired at the end of June. The chairman, Edwin Slinger, stated that financial reasons were the cause of Bodle's departure and that he would be replaced immediately by first-team captain Jimmy Harrower in the capacity of player-manager.

After leaving Stanley, Bodle left football to take up a grocery shop in Manchester and then took over a sub-post office in Derby. Whilst in Derby he ran a successful boy's team in the Derby Sunday League. He then had a spell as trainer and later manager of Burton Albion.

James Harrower
1960-1961

JAMES Swanson Harrower became Accrington Stanley's seventh manager since the war when he inherited the Peel Park hot seat in April 1960. More tellingly perhaps, he was the fourth manager in less than two years. The task facing Stanley's new player-manager was an immense one as he inherited a team which was already doomed to relegation to the Fourth Division.

The appointment of the quietly-spoken Scot was a popular one with players and supporters alike. Harrower had joined Accrington Stanley from Third Lanark in December 1954 and had proved to be a sound and cultured defender (see *Who's Who* section).

The end of the disastrous 1959-60 campaign saw what was obviously an all-out economy drive by the board as they began to prune one of the largest squads in the Third Division. When they had finished, Harrower found himself with a staff of only eight full-time professionals, one part-timer and three men still in the Forces. Such was the daunting task facing a new and inexperienced manager.

During the close season, Harrower quickly assembled a new playing staff and appointed two new backroom boys. The former Blackburn Rovers utility player Bill Smith was appointed as player-coach and ex-Stanley coach Harry Hubbick returned to become trainer.

Harrower worked hard, both on and off the pitch, to rebuild Stanley and 18th position in the Fourth Division was no mean achievement considering the circumstances. There had also been a good FA Cup run which had provided much-needed cash thanks to two matches against neighbouring Preston North End. Gradually, Harrower had begun to build his own team, but one which would not include his own ageing legs. The last match of the season saw Harrower make his last appearance before hanging up his boots.

With no money to spend, Harrower worked wonders in persuading Alex Smith, Gerry Richardson and Bob Wilson to Peel Park during the summer of 1961. Unfortunately Richardson received an early injury which cut short his season and Harrower simply did not have the funds to buy a replacement. The loss of a key defender had to be compensated for by moving other players around; the small amount of money Harrower had available was required to buy a much-needed forward. In truth, Harrower needed more than one, but he managed to sign Jim Milner from Darlington who provided some much needed guile and punch to the Stanley attack. Unfortunately, just as the new man began to form a partnership with George Hudson, the latter was transferred to Peterborough United. The sale of Hudson proved a tremendous blow as the team was always woefully short up front. From 29 September to 8 February, Stanley managed only four goals in the Football League, although Harrower was no longer in control when this miserable run came to an end.

In early December, with the club struggling at the foot of the table, the directors announced that Harrower would put his boots on again and turn out for the club. In fact he claimed that all he had promised was to try and get himself fit enough to be able to play. With the club due to meet Tranmere Rovers at Peel Park on 16 December, the board fully expected Harrower to play. After various discussions it was announced that Harrower had tended his resignation and that this had been accepted by the club. Harrower claimed that it had been impossible to get fit in time for the match and that he would 'only be risking making a fool of himself' if he played. The chairman, Edwin Slinger, insisted that it was essential to have a player-manager in the existing financial climate. An amicable settlement was reached and Harrower became the last manager to leave the club.

Harry Hubbick, joint caretaker manager when Stanley left the Football League in March 1962.

ACCRINGTON STANLEY
Who's Who

This section contains biographies of every player who has appeared in a Football League match for Accrington Stanley. Each entry shows (where known) the player's date of birth and death and dates of signing for his respective clubs. Where only the year of a player's birth or death is known, the period of year registered at St Catherine's appears in brackets, ie: (April quarter). Where brackets show in a player's christian name, ie: W(illiam), this signifies the name was not the dominant one used. cs = close season. The appearances and goals totals are for Football League games only.

ABEL, Samuel **1930-31**
Centre-forward. 5ft 11in; 12st.
Born: Peel Park, Neston, 30 December 1908.
Debut v Crewe Alex (h) 30 August 1930 (scored two goals).
Appearances: 26; Goals: 18.

Career: Neston Brickworks FC; Bury amateur 6 June, signing professional 21 October 1929; STANLEY 10 July 1930; Chesterfield 20 February 1931 (fee £100); Fulham 3 June 1933 (fee £500); Queen's Park Rangers 29 May 1934 (fee £400); Wartime guest player with Brighton & Hove Albion; Chelsea, Crystal Palace and Fulham.

A tall, thrustful centre-forward, Sam Abel marked his debut in the Football League by scoring two goals for Stanley on the opening Saturday of season 1930-31. He duly became leading goalscorer for the season with 19 goals in League and Cup, this despite leaving Peel Park in February 1931. Although the fee received for his transfer was almost negligible, Stanley were obliged to part with him, in order to steer clear of bankruptcy. Abel assisted Chesterfield to promotion in his first season and recorded 73 appearances and 39 goals before moving to Fulham. During a lengthy spell with QPR, he was converted into a full-back. Abel was a keen golfer, and also played cricket for Neston CC.

AGAR, Alfred **1930-32**
Outside-right. 5ft 8in; 10st 12lb.
Born: Esh Winning, 28 August 1904.
Debut: v Crewe Alexandra (h) 30 August 1930 (scored one goal).
Appearances: 73; Goals: 27.
Career: Shildon; West Stanley; Dundee cs 1926; Barrow 5 July 1927; Carlisle United 14 June 1928; STANLEY 21 June 1930; Oldham Athletic 18 May 1932 (fee £200); York City 16 June 1936; Scarborough Town 10 July 1937.
'Tricky, helpful, and no mean goalscorer himself' was the *Lancashire Daily Post's* verdict on Alf Agar in 1931. He scored on his debut for Stanley and continued to make a significant contribution to the team's goal-scoring during his two seasons at Peel Park. After leaving Stanley, Agar enjoyed a lengthy spell with Oldham Athletic. In his first season at Boundary Park, he joined another ex-Stanley wingman, Jack Pears (*qv*) in the Latics' attack. The two ex-Reds contributed 25 of the 67 goals scored by Oldham during the season. When Stanley opened the season with a visit to Carlisle United in August 1949, Alf Agar was a welcome visitor to Stanley's dressing-room. At that time, he was living in Carlisle and was employed at a local electricity station.

ALEXANDER, Stanley **1938-40**
Inside-forward. 5ft 8½in; 11st 4lb.
Born: Percy Main, 17 September 1905.
Died: Anlaby, Hull, 5 June 1961.
Debut v Halifax Town (a) 27 August 1938.
Appearances: 22; Goals: 2.
Career: Percy Main Amateurs; Hull City 19 June 1926;

Bradford City 21 November 1931 (In exchange for Jack Hill, plus a fee); Millwall 5 October 1933; Tottenham Hotspur 12 June 1936; STANLEY 19 July 1938. Joined Royal Navy in 1940 and retired from playing during the war. Was coach to Hull City juniors during the 1950s.
International honour: England Schoolboys.
Representative honour: FA Tour to Canada in 1931.
An ex-collier and noted sprinter, Stan Alexander occupied a variety of forward positions during Stanley's final season before World War Two. He was one of 32 players utilized during the campaign, which ended with a second, consecutive, application for re-election. At the outset of his career, Alexander spent a little over five years with Hull City, where he recorded 98 appearances and scored 41 goals. His final aggregate career figures were 278 appearances, 84 goals. A brother, John William C.Alexander, was also on the books of Hull City, Ashington, Workington and Bury.

ALLEN, Thomas **1932-33**
Goalkeeper. 6ft; 11st 6lb.
Born: Moxley, Staffs, 1 May 1897.
Died: Solihull, 1968 (April quarter).
Debut v Halifax Town (h) 27 August 1932.

Career: Wednesday Old Park Works; Bilston United; Hickman's Institute; Wolverhampton Wanderers during World War One; Sunderland 13 May 1919; Southampton May 1920; Coventry City amateur 23, professional 26 June 1928; STANLEY 4 July 1932; Northampton Town 30 September 1933; Kidderminster Harriers August 1934.
International honour: England Schoolboys.
Club honour: Southampton, Third Division South champions season 1921-2.
A vastly experienced goalkeeper, Tom Allen recorded his 500th Football League appearance during his season at Peel Park. Experienced in all four divisions of the League, Allen spent eight seasons at Southampton, making 291 appearances. During the Saints' Third Division South championship of 1921-2, Allen was ever-present, conceding only 21 goals in the 42-match programme.

ALLINSON, Charles **1922-23**
Centre-forward.
Born: Accrington, 24 November 1901.
Died: Cuckfield, Sussex, 1975 (October quarter).
Debut v Lincoln City (h) 5 May 1923.
Appearances: 1.
Career: St Mary's RC (Oswaldtwistle); Stanley amateur 23 September 1922 to 15 June 1923; Darwen season 1924-5.
Consistently on the mark for the Reserves, Charlie Allinson's tally included five against Chorley Motors in the 10-0 win at Peel Park in November 1922. Given a run out in the first team in the final fixture of season 1922-3, he appeared to lack fitness for League football. The *Accrington Observer* commented: 'Allinson gave a very satisfactory first-half display, but he fell off considerably after the interval'.

ANDERS, Henry **1957-60**
Wing-forward. 5ft 6in; 10st 8lb.
Born: St Helens, 28 November 1926.
Debut v Rochdale (a) 28 August 1957.
Appearances: 114; Goals: 18.
Career: St Helens; Preston North End amateur 12 professional 26 March 1945; Manchester City 6 March 1953; Port Vale 28 July 1956; STANLEY 26 June 1957; Workington 25 July 1960; Runcorn cs 1961.
Harry Anders, a former St Helens miner, joined his brother Jimmy, also a winger, at Peel Park some 12 years after they had commenced their careers with Preston. A former understudy to the great Tom Finney at Deepdale, on his day Anders was one of the most devastating wingers in the Northern Section. In season 1957-8 he was selected to represent the Third Division North at Carlisle, in the last of the representative matches before the Third Division reorganization. Unfortunately, he had to withdraw due to a pulled muscle injury.

ANDERS, James **1957-60**
Wing-forward. 5ft 6in; 10st 11lb.
Born: St Helens, 8 March 1928.
Debut v Carlisle United (h) 26 January 1957.
Appearances: 129; Goals: 29.
Career: Preston North End amateur 3 April, professional 28 August 1945; Brentford 1 September 1948; Bradford City 2 June 1951; Rochdale 2 July 1953; Bradford 10 September 1956; STANLEY 25 January 1957; Buxton August 1960; Bradford 5 September 1960; Tranmere Rovers November 1961 to June 1962.
Small but stockily built, Jimmy Anders was a fast moving and tricky winger with an excellent shot. In season 1958-9 he became the highest scoring winger

in Stanley's history with 20 League and Cup goals. The previous highest total in a season was recorded by Alf Agar, who scored 15 League and Cup goals in consecutive seasons 1930-31 and 1931-2. Elder brother of Harry (*qv*), the wingers formed part of a quite remarkable off-the-field 'hat-trick', by Stanley players in 1959. In late January, twins Gillian and Jimmy were born to Jimmy Anders and his wife Joan. A little over three months later, Christopher and Mark were born to brother Harry and his wife Vera. Bert Scott and his wife Patricia completed the 'hat-trick' of 'doubles' in early April!

ANDREWS, Harold **1936-38**
Inside-forward or half-back. 5ft 9½in; 10st 10lb.
Born: Lincoln, 13 August 1903.
Debut v Harlepools United (a) 2 September 1936.
Appearances: 65; Goals: 2.
Career: St Botolph's (Lincoln); Lincoln City 22 August 1925; Notts County 17 March 1928; Barnsley 4 July 1932; Luton Town 11 May 1935; STANLEY 27 May 1936 to June 1938.
Club honours: Notts County, Third Division South champions season 1930-31. Barnsley, Third Division North champions season 1933-4.
With championship medals from both Northern and Southern sections of the Third Division and over 300 Football League appearances, Andrews brought sound experience to bear in his final two seasons of League football at Peel Park. Good aerial ability and a fine left-foot drive had brought the Lincolnshire schoolmaster a career total of 130 goals, but he was mainly to be found at wing-half with Stanley. He proved to be a fine prompter, particularly effective in the 1936-7 season when the team scored 85 goals in League and Cup, and reached the fourth round of the FA Cup. After leaving Stanley in the summer of 1938, he was reported to be working for a large cigarette manufacturing company in Nottingham.

ARMITT, Thomas **1926-27**
Centre-half. 5ft 11½in; 12st 4lb.
Born: Pendleton, Manchester, 1 April 1904. Died: Salford, Manchester, 15 October 1972.
Debut v Wigan Borough (h) 15 October 1926.
Appearances: 1.
Career: Pendleton FC; STANLEY 15 February 1926 to 10 January 1927.
A reserve half-back whose single senior appearance, as deputy for the injured Billy Rookes, saw him introduced at centre-half against Wigan Borough at Peel Park. On a waterlogged pitch and before an attendance of only 2,028 spectators, Stanley won 4-0 to record their most clear-cut victory of the season. It was also a rare 'clean-sheet' for the Stanley defence, which had conceded over a century of League goals during the course of the season. Tom Armitt's solitary Football League outing brought the following verdict from the *Accrington Observer*: 'A big fellow and a trifle slow, but with a cool and collected style. and a good idea of the duties of a centre-half back'.

ARMSTRONG, James D. **1927-34**
Full-back. 5ft 8in; 12st 3lb.
Born: Chester-le-Street, 12 June 1899.
Debut v Doncaster Rovers (a) 10 September 1927.
Appearances: 260; Goals: 7.

Career: Chester-le-Street (North Eastern League); Barnsley 30 April 1921; Bournemouth & Boscombe Athletic 5 June 1925; STANLEY 12 July 1927; Stalybridge Celtic 13 August 1934, later scouted for Barnsley.
A Stanley stalwart and fixture at right-back for seven seasons, Jimmy Armstrong combined hard work with speedy defence and a powerful clearance. A fine foil to Tom Whittaker (*qv*) in the last line of Stanley's defence, the pair were full-back partners in 89 consecutive Football League games from the inception of their association in September 1927. Armstrong's run of consecutive appearances stretched to 150 before an injury broke the sequence. Briefly Stanley's player-coach — from December 1933 — Armstrong departed Peel Park in the summer of 1934 with a career total of 335 Football League appearances. In 1938 he was reported to be working as a commissionaire at a large Barnsley works.

ARNOLD, Harold Stanley **1929**
Outside-left. 5ft 7in; 9st 12lb.
Born: St Helens, 1904 (July quarter).
Debut v New Brighton (a) 6 Feburary 1929.
Appearances: 1.
Career: Davies Athletic (Runcorn); STANLEY amateur 5 February to June 1929.
A lightly-build winger who was pressed into service at senior level only one day after signing amateur forms. His debut, at Rake Lane, saw Stanley beaten 2-1 after they had taken the lead within two minutes of the kick-off. Arnold's debut prompted the following Press comment: 'A trier all the way who occasionally did smart bits of work'.

ASH, John William **1935-38 & 1939-46**
Half-back. 5ft 10½in; 11st 12lb.
Born: Hebburn-on-Tyne, 31 December 1911.
Debut v Mansfield Town (a) 10 April 1936.
Appearances: 29.
Career: Hebburn St Cuthbert's; Norwich City amateur (trial) 4 July 1935; Carlisle United (trial) October 1935; STANLEY 12 November 1935; Southport 28 July 1938; STANLEY 9 August 1939 to 1946.
Jack Ash saw little senior action in his first two seasons at Peel Park, being understudy to Sam McCulloch and later to Joe Craven. Considered by many sound judges to be one of the Lancashire Combination's outstanding pivots, he took a major share of the credit when Stanley Reserves finished Combination runners-up (one point behind South Liverpool) in season 1936-7. He took over the senior centre-half role in November 1937 and his fearless and tireless style soon attracted the scouts. After a season with Southport, Ash returned to Stanley just before World War Two. It was during a wartime Cup tie, against Chorley in November 1945, that he suffered a broken leg injury which ended his career. An engineer by trade, Jack Ash was foreman of an Accrington engineering works, until his retirement in 1976.

ASHE, Armour Donald **1953-57**
Full-back. 5ft 10in; 11st 6lb.
Born: Paisley, 14 October 1925.
Died: Accrington, 15 June 1968.
Debut v Barnsley (h) 24 October 1953.
Appearances: 162.

Career: Dalry Thistle; Aberdeen 1949; St Mirren cs 1950; Stockport County 20 June 1953; STANLEY 26 September 1953; Gateshead 29 November 1957; Southport 2 July 1959; Horwich RMI cs 1960.
After three seasons with St Mirren, Armour Ashe first crossed the border to undertake trials with Stockport County. One of his appearances for Stockport was against Stanley and when Ashe declined County's offer of terms, he was quickly snapped up by Walter Galbraith. He proved to be a fine capture, whose tenacious tackling and positional flair played a big part in Stanley's glorious era of the 1950s. Raised in a footballing family, his father was a player and his uncle played for St Mirren. Ashe's only regret in moving to Lancashire was said to be the lack of facilities for his favourite sport outside of football — ice skating.

ASPIN, James Cressy **1933-35 & 1935-36**
Inside-forward. 5ft 6½in; 10st 7lb.
Born: Blackburn, 13 September 1914. Died: Blackburn, 10 June 1963.
Debut v Darlington (a) 1 January 1935.
Appearances: 3.
Career: STANLEY amateur 24 May 1933, signing professional 5 December 1934; Wolverhampton Wanderers 31 January 1935 (with F.Marsden, for a combined fee of £750); STANLEY 14 May 1935; Jiffy FC (Accrington & District Combination) season 1936-37.
Jim Aspin had played only once for Stanley's League side, but in the month of his debut he was snapped up by First Division Wolves. Along with Fred Marsden (*qv*), the two young hopefuls were recruited by Wolves' manager Major Buckley, as ever in search of fresh talent. Sadly, neither player progressed at Molineux, Aspin declining terms for 1935-6 and returning to Stanley. One of several brothers who became well known in Lancashire Combination circles, Jim Aspin's lightweight build proved a handicap at senior level.

AVEYARD, Walter **1952-53**
Inside-forward. 5ft 11in; 11st.
Born: Hemsworth, Yorkshire, 11 June 1918.
Debut v York City (h) 15 March 1952 (scored one goal).
Appearances: 24; Goals: 4.
Career: Denaby United; Sheffield Wednesday amateur 25 August, signing professional 17 October 1938; Birmingham City 14 April 1947; Port Vale 17 June 1948; STANLEY 1 March 1952 to 1 May 1953.
Largely in reserve with both Sheffield Wednesday and Birmingham City, Walter Aveyard scored three goals in seven appearances for the Blues in their Second Division championship side of 1947-8. In four seasons with Port Vale, he made 103 appearances and scored 26 goals, being club leading goalscorer in 1948-9 with 13 in 34 appearances. Signed by Stanley for what was decribed as a 'fairly big fee' 27 hours before the 'deadline' for transfers in March 1952, Aveyard scored the winning goal on his debut with a stunning 30-yard drive. In 1952-3 he struggled in a poor side, occupying every forward position whilst totalling only 13 appearances. He was transfer-listed at the close of the season which had finished with Stanley in 24th place, having registered only 39 goals in 46 League matches.

BAILEY, Malcolm **1960-61**
Outside-right.
Born: Halifax, 7 May 1937.
Debut v Hartlepools United (a) 8 October 1960.
Appearances: 2.
Career: Luddenfoot FC; Bradford amateur 7, signing professional 26 April 1958; Leeds United 8 August

1960; STANLEY 5 October 1960; Barnsley (One month's trial) 27 October 1961.
Player-manager Jimmy Harrower used six different players at outside-right in less than two months at the start of season 1960-61. Malcolm Bailey was discarded after playing in two consecutive matches in October, which proved to be his last in the Football League. Earlier in his career, he began at outside-left with Bradford. He appeared in their last five matches in the Third Division North in 1957-8. He also appeared in five of the opening six matches of the following season, Bradford's inaugural term in the new Fourth Division.

BAINES, Frederick **1921-22**
Full-back. 5ft 8in; 12st 1lb.
Born: Leeds, 1898.
Debut v Rochdale (a) 27 August 1921.
Appearances: 2.
Career: Leeds City September 1917; Rochdale February 1919; Rotherham County June 1919; Rochdale cs 1920; STANLEY 8 June 1921, released on a free transfer 6 March 1922.
In Stanley's first season in the Third Division North, eight different full-backs were used in League matches. The original pairing of Newton and Baines did not survive beyond the opening fixture, a 6-3 defeat at Rochdale. Playing against his former club, Fred Baines had a particularly unhappy afternoon, prompting the *Accrington Observer* to comment: 'Baines seemed unable to do the right thing and surely it was one of those days when everything goes agley'. The former Rochdale captain made only one more senior appearance prior to his release in early March.

BARCLAY, John Birrell **1927-29**
Outside-left. 5ft 8in; 11st 5lb.
Born: Thornton, Fifeshire, 22 January 1904.
Debut v Nelson (a) 27 August 1927.
Appearances: 76; Goals: 11.
Career: Dundee season 1924-5; Reading 6 August 1926; STANLEY 8 July 1927; Yeovil & Petters United August 1929.
Stanley's pre-season trials in August 1927 featured a high proportion of new recruits. In an entirely new first-team forward line, John Barclay created an excellent impression. He had good command of the ball, the ability to beat an opponent, and accuracy in centering. Considering his lack of previous senior experience, he proved to be an excellent signing, missing only eight League matches in two seasons at Peel Park. Although not a big goalscorer, Barclay was a reliable man from the penalty-spot. He was successful in converting five such awards in season 1927-8.

BARNES, Kossuth Seed **1923**
Goalkeeper. 5ft 9½in; 11st 7lb.
Born: Preston, 1892. Died: Sunderland, 12 October 1965.
Debut v Barrow (h) 17 February 1923.
Appearances: 2.
Career: Durham City; Bristol Rovers 16 November 1921; Houghton FC (Sunderland) cs 1922; STANLEY (trial) 15 February 1923.
Signed on trial with a view to providing extra goalkeeping cover, Barnes featured in two high scoring matches against Barrow. Stanley lost 4-3 at home and 5-2 at Barrow a week later. Barnes had been out of senior football for nine months, having failed to secure a new League club after leaving Bristol Rovers in the close season of 1922. At Eastville he made 17 appearances in season 1921-2, being one of three goalkeepers used by the Rovers in their second season as a Football League club.

BEDFORD, Fred **1924-25**
Outside-right. 5ft 8in; 10st 7lb.
Born: Blackburn, 25 June 1902. Died: Morecambe, 18 January 1972.
Debut v Rotherham County (h) 30 August 1924.
Appearances: 25; Goals: 5.
Career: Blackburn junior football; Blackburn Rovers 26 November 1923; STANLEY 9 June 1924; Barnsley 19 May 1925; Lancaster Town September 1926; Tranmere Rovers 13 October 1927; Morecambe; Bradford City 9 October 1928; Morecambe August 1929.
Fred Bedford's first season of League action — he had not appeared at senior level with Blackburn Rovers — was interrupted by a lengthy lay-off, due to a torn ligament injury sustained in the Portsmouth FA Cup tie. Nevertheless, his 25 appearances proved to be his highest seasonal return in League circles. Billed as a 'speed merchant' on his arrival at Peel Park, the *Accrington Observer* commented in September 1924: 'Bedford's speed was very servicable, but he needs to develop football craft and the artfulness which enables a forward to beat a full-back.' In season 1928-9 Bedford scored a 'hat-trick' on his debut for Bradford City at Ashington. The Valley Paraders won 8-2 and went on to take the championship of the Third Division North, but Fred Bedford was restricted to only nine appearances, despite scoring eight goals.

BELL, Albert **1925-27**
Full-back. 5ft 10½in; 12st 7lb.
Born: Sunderland, 8 February 1898. Died: Annfield Plain, 1973 (July quarter).
Debut v Walsall (a) 29 August 1925.

Appearances: 70.
Career: Annfield Plain; West Stanley; Leeds United 21 December 1922; STANLEY 17 June 1925; Durham City 23 August 1927.
One of four players from County Durham in Stanley's ranks for season 1925-6, Albert Bell had an uncertain start at Peel Park, failing to adapt to the new type of football or do himself justice. After a period in the Reserves he returned to League action in early November and was much more successful. Of hefty build, Bell proved a formidable opponent to forwards and seemed particularly at home on the rather heavy Stanley ground. A homeward move in the summer of 1927 took him to Durham City, but after finishing season 1927-8 in 21st place in the Third Division North, they failed to gain re-election in favour of Carlisle United.

BELL, John Cuthbert **1931-32**
Goalkeeper. 6ft ½in; 12st 7lb.
Born: Seaham Harbour, 24 October 1905.
Debut v Rochdale (a) 29 August 1931.
Appearances: 28.
Career: Seaham Colliery; Sunderland amateur 4 September, signing professional 28 November 1924; Walsall 28 November 1930; STANLEY 23 July 1931; Bradford 16 March 1932 (fee £250) to cs 1936.
Rather unusually for a goalkeeper, Jack Bell was ordered off the field in the second-round FA Cup tie at Halifax Town on 12 December 1931 and missed three games due to suspension. That apart, he was ever-present in Stanley's goal until his transfer to Second Division Bradford, just prior to the 'deadline' in March 1932. Bell gained his initial experience at Roker Park, but in seven seasons was restricted to a total of 42 League appearances, spending several seasons as understudy to the consistent English international goalkeeper, Albert McInroy.

BENNETT, Lawson Henry **1958-62**
Outside-right. 5ft 9½in; 10st 7lb.
Born: Darwen, 28 August 1938.
Debut v Stockport County (h) 11 April 1959.
Appearances: 29; Goals: 2.
Career: Darwen; STANLEY 24 May 1958 to March 1962.
During Lawson Bennett's stay of almost four years at Peel Park, he served under four different managers and two 'caretakers'. Some indication of the unsettled times at Accrington in the late 1950s and early 1960s. When first signed, Bennett was employed at a wallpaper manufacturing firm in Darwen. He showed early promise, but his progress was hampered by a knee injury in his first season as a full-time professional. This restricted him to only 11 appearances in season 1959-60. Bennett was still on Stanley's books when the club was put into liquidation in March 1962. He played in Stanley's last match, at Crewe Alexandra on 2 March, and had made 17 appearancs plus one in the FA Cup in the unfinished 1961-2 season which was expunged from the Football League's records.

BENSON, John **1932**
Goalkeeper.
Debut v Carlisle United (a) 7 May 1932.
Appearances: 1.
Career: Storey Brothers (North Lancashire League); Lancaster Town 1925; STANLEY 29 March to May 1932.
Signed to provide cover for Bob Foster, following the sale of Jack Bell to Bradford in March 1932, John Benson appeared in only one League fixture during his sojourn at Peel Park. In a lengthy spell as Lancaster Town's reserve goalkeeper, Benson had assisted the Dollies'* second string to a Richardson Cup victory and two West Lancashire League championships.
**Lancaster Town's unusual nickname derived from the colour of their shirts, 'Dolly' Blue – a washday accessory perhaps unfamiliar to younger readers.*

BENTLEY, Walter B. **1932-34**
Half-back. 5ft 9½in; 11st 4lb.
Born: Accrington, summer of 1907.
Debut v Gateshead (h) 3 December 1932.
Appearances: 22; Goals: 1.
Career: Barnoldswick Town; Manchester Central July 1931; STANLEY 13 June 1932; Nelson September 1934.
Walter Bentley was promoted from the Reserves to the League team on the transfer of Ron Viner to Chester in February 1933. Somewhat lacking in the final points of the game, but wholehearted and a trier to the last, Bentley's game advanced notably after his promotion. He scored the final goal of season 1932-3 in the 3-0 defeat of Tranmere Rovers at Peel Park, but he lost his first-team place in the following season in the face of stiff competition from new signings Stoddart and Crawshaw.

BENYON, Joseph **1926-27**
Outside-left.
Debut v Halifax Town (h) 9 October 1926 (scored one goal).
Appearances: 4; Goals: 1.
Career: Atherton; Chorley; Norwich City (trial); Runcorn; Chorley August 1926 (trial); STANLEY 29 September to 7 March 1927.
Joe Benyon joined Stanley, initially on a months's trial, after he had declined Chorley's terms, following a month at Victory Park. During his trial with Chorley, he had given an excellent display against Stanley's Reserve team, which doubtless prompted his move to Peel Park. Fast and with a penchant for nipping inside to score, he was on the mark on his debut at Peel Park, but was unable to dislodge Jack Martin, Stanley's established outside-left.

BIRCH, Wallace **1931**
Outside-right. 5ft 9½in; 11st.
Born: Wortley, Sheffield, 1910.
Debut v Doncaster Rovers (h) 5 September 1931 (scored one goal).
Appearances: 2; Goals: 1.
Career: Grenoside Sports; Luton Town 11 March 1929; Sheffield Wednesday 31 July 1930; STANLEY 24 July 1931; Blackpool 29 September to 6 November 1931.
Despite having been on the books of three different League clubs before his 21st birthday, Wallace Birch failed to establish himself in top-grade football. With Stanley, he scored on his debut for the Reserve team and repeated the feat when he made his first-team debut. Nevertheless, his two League appearances with Stanley proved to be his last. His previous experience at senior level came in season 1929-30, when he played

in 15 League matches for Luton Town and scored three goals. A brother, Arnold Birch, played for Sheffield Wednesday and Chesterfield as a penalty-taking goalkeeper.

BIRKETT, Ronald **1949-50**
Wing-forward. 5ft 9in; 10st 8lb.
Born: Warrington, 21 July 1927.
Debut v Rotheham United (h) 27 August 1949.
Appearance: 14; Goals: 2.
Career: Garswood St Andrew's; Cromptons Recs, Manchester City amateur 2 May 1945, signing professional 29 January 1946; New Brighton 21 January 1947; Oldham Athletic 10 August 1948; STANLEY 11 July 1949; New Brighton season 1950-51.
During his first spell with New Brighton, Ronnie Birkett was given the nickname 'Jet', effectively describing his major asset, an electrifying burst of speed. Two-footed, he could occupy either flank, but he did not establish a regular first-team berth at Peel Park. His total of 14 League appearances was, however, his highest seasonal return in League circles. Footballing brothers were Wilf Birkett, a goalkeeper who made 162 League appearances for Southport, and Cliff Birkett, an English Schoolboy international and also a winger with Manchester United and Southport.

BLACK, John Ross **1924**
Centre-forward. 5ft 7½in; 10st 12lb.
Born: Denny, 26 May 1900.
Debut v Tranmere Rovers (h) 9 February 1924.
Appearances: 14; Goals: 5.
Career: Gordon Highlanders; Denny Hibs.; Sunderland amateur 12 April, signing professional 30 August 1921; Nelson 23 August 1922; STANLEY 9 February 1924; Chesterfield 13 June 1924; Luton Town 6 August 1926; Bristol Rovers 22 October 1930 to 1932.
International honour: Scottish Junior.
Club honour: Nelson, Third Division North champions season 1922-3.
Red-haired John Black appeared in all four divisions of the Football League, and during his career occupied most outfield positions. The young Scotsman was a valuable utility man in Nelson's team in 1922-3, when they won promotion to the Second Division. During the campaign he appeared in four different forward positions, also at half-back. With Stanley, he took over at centre-forward from Fred Cooke with some success in a brief stay before Chesterfield signed him. In his second season at Saltergate a broken leg side-lined him for most of the 1925-6 campaign but he made a complete recovery and enjoyed a lengthy spell with Luton Town.

BLACKADDER, William **1924-25**
Half-back. 5ft 8½in; 11st 2lb.
Born: Padiham, Lancashire, 9 January 1899. Died: St Annes-on-Sea, Lancashire, 11 January 1977.
Debut v Nelson (a) 17 January 1925.
Appearances: 17.
Career: Local Sunday School League football; Burnley amateur 3 February, signing professional 14 December 1922; STANLEY 5 September 1924; Chorley cs 1925; Clitheroe cs 1926; Lancaster Town cs 1927 to 1929.
Initially recruited from local junior football into Burnley's North East Lancashire Combination team, Bill Blackadder graduated through the 'A' team and into the Central League side at Turf Moor. He was without League experience when Stanley recruited him, and he had some time to wait for a senior outing with the Reds. Once into the side, however, he held his place — usually at left-half — for most of the second half of the season. At the close of what had been a disappointing campaign, with Stanley finishing 17th in the table, Blackadder was released and moved into Lancashire Combination circles. In 1928 he was captain of Lancaster Town's reserve team and also coach to their junior players.

BLACKWOOD, John Syme Duncan **1958-59**
Inside-forward. 5ft 8½in; 11st 2lb.
Born: Cronberry, Ayr, 25 January 1935.
Debut v Halifax Town (h) 26 December 1958.
Appearances: 4; Goals: 1.
Career: Girvan Juniors; STANLEY 2 October 1958, re-registering as an amateur on 5 May 1959; York City 19 November to 8 December 1959.
An apprentice printer when signed by Stanley, John Blackwood was recommended to the club by Peter Devlin, Stanley's 'A' team manager. He made his Football League debut over the Christmas period in 1958, following the sale of Ray Byrom and Wattie Dick to Bradford. Blackwood scored in his final League match for Stanley, against Norwich City in October 1959. Shortly afterwards he was signed as a professional by York City, along with David Toward, another of Stanley's amateur forwards. Neither player appeared in League football with York City.

BLAKE, John **1925**

Goalkeeper. 5ft 10½in; 11st.
Born: Stoneclough, near Manchester, 1899.
Debut v Rochdale (a) 21 February 1925.
Appearances: 5.
Career: Farnworth Town; STANLEY amateur 23 January, signing professional 12 February 1925 to 9 November 1925; Herrington Swifts; Durham City July 1928; Ballymena (Ireland) February 1931.
On his debut for Stanley, John Blake gave a wonderful display of goalkeeping at Rochdale, who were beaten 1-0 — their first home defeat for almost two years. Blake also kept a 'clean sheet' on his second appearance against Durham City, a club he was later to join after they had failed to gain re-election to the Third Division North at the close of season 1927-8. Blake's season at Peel Park ended in March 1925 when he suffered an attack of pneumonia. A month later, Stanley, who had not paid a fee for him, met Farnworth Town in a friendly match and donated the proceeds to the Farnworth club.

BLAKENEY, James **1936-38**

Centre-forward. 5ft 7½in; 10st 4lb.
Born: Crawcrook, Co Durham, 26 September 1919.
Debut v Wrexham (h) 3 January 1938 (scored one goal).
Appearances: 20; Goals 11.
Career: Ryton Intermediate School; Bladon Boys; Spen Juniors; STANLEY amateur 25 August signing professional 2 October 1936; Arsenal 16 June 1938 (fee £500); post war with Annfield Plain, Throckley and Crawcrook Albion *c.*1946-7, then retiring.
Jim Blakeney gave up his work as a clerk at Clara Vale Colliery when Stanley took him on to their groundstaff in August 1936. Signed as a professional when just past his 17th birthday, in the same month he scored successive hat-tricks in three matches for Stanley Reserves, totalling 12 goals in his first five appearances. Lightning darts and a natural body swerve were his outstanding assets, whilst his headwork and left foot improved with coaching. Once into the first team, although indifferently supported, Blakeney scored four goals in his first three League appearances and finished the season as joint leading goalscorer with Frank Curran, with 11 goals in 20 appearances. A dream move to Highbury in the summer of 1938 was sadly curtailed by the outbreak of World War Two and a bad leg injury ended his first-class career. Despite having a metal plate inserted in his leg, he was able to play in junior football in the North East after the war. Latterly an office manager in Newcastle upon Tyne, Jim Blakeney today lives in retirement at Kibblesworth, Gateshead.

BLUNT, Edwin **1949-50**

Wing-half or inside-forward. 5ft 8in; 11st 2lb.
Born: Tunstall, Staffordshire, 21 May 1918.
Debut v Carlisle United (a) 20 August 1949.
Appearances: 9; Goals: 1.
Career: Lichfield Town: Port Vale amateur 17 March 1937; Northampton Town 5 May 1937; Bury (wartime guest player) October 1944; STANLEY 11 July 1949 to 21 February 1950.
Eddie Blunt was one of many unfortunates whose footballing careers were blighted by the outbreak of World War Two. In the final peacetime season he was only 20 years old but had established himself in Northampton Town's first team. After guesting for Bury during the war, he returned to the Cobblers and had made 59 post-war appearances when Stanley signed him, for what was described as a 'substantial fee'. In the pre-season trials he was outstanding, but at League level he failed to do himself justice and in nine first-team appearances he collected only one winning bonus. When he left Stanley in February 1950, he was reported to be considering offers from two Cheshire League clubs.

BODLE, Harold **1953-57**

Inside-forward or wing-half. 5ft 10in; 11st 10lb.
Born: Woodlands, near Doncaster, 4 October 1920.
Debut v Stockport County (h) 22 August 1953 (scored one goal).

Appearances: 94; Goals: 13.
Career: Doncaster Schoolboys; Silverwood Colliery; Ridgehill Athletic; Rotherham United 13 May 1938; Birmingham 2 December 1938 (fee £2,000); Rotherham United and Doncaster Rovers (wartime guest player); Bury 17 March 1949; Stockport County 17 October 1952; STANLEY 13 August 1953 to 1 May 1957; appointed STANLEY manager June 1959 to April 1960; later managed Burton Albion.
Harold Bodle announced his arrival at Peel Park by scoring three goals in his first two games. In his second match, against Workington, he scored twice from the penalty-spot. Best remembered as Stanley's finest captain, Bodle was an inspiring personality and an astute tactician. He had two excellent seasons before injury and then ill health ended his playing career at the age of 37 years. He gave noted service to all of

his clubs and during wartime football assisted Birmingham City to the championship of the League South and to the semi-final of the FA Cup in season 1945-6. He was appointed manager of Stanley in June 1959, having been pipped for the post in the previous October by George Eastham. Unfortunately, his excursion into management proved an unrewarding experience. With the team already booked for the Fourth Division and with attendances averaging a little over 2,000, his appointment was terminated in April 1960.

BOLTON, Fred **1921-22**
Outside-left.
Debut v Wrexham (h) 22 October 1921.
Appearances: 1.
Career: Great Harwood; STANLEY amateur 30 September 1921 to May 1922.
One of seven different outside-lefts used by Stanley in their initial Third Division North campaign, amateur winger Fred Bolton was promoted to League action after only two reserve-team appearances. Although Stanley maintained their 100 per cent home record on his debut with a 1-0 victory, the *Accrington Observer* reported that Bolton 'had a lot to learn, despite sending across several splendid centres'.

BOND, Anthony **1946-47**
Outside-right.
Born: Preston, 27 December 1913.
Debut v Bradford City (a) 31 August 1946.
Appearances: 29; Goals: 4.
Career: Junior with Preston North End; Dick Kerr's FC; Blackburn Rovers 1 April 1932; Dick Kerr's FC; Chorley; Wolverhampton Wanderers 6 November 1936; Torquay United 21 June 1937; Wartime guest player for Everton, Barrow and Preston North End; Southport 24 August 1945; STANLEY 29 May 1946; Fleetwood 7 June 1947.
An experienced performer, Tony Bond was with Torquay United when war broke out and he joined Southport for the last season of wartime football. He scored five goals in his first five appearances for the Sandgrounders and was their second highest goalscorer for the season with 12 in 29 appearances. In a season with Stanley he had little serious competition for the outside-right berth. He left to join Fleetwood and in a return visit to Peel Park in December 1948, scored against Stanley Reserves in a Lancashire Combination fixture. He was the nephew of Dicky Bond, the former Preston North End, Bradford City and Blackburn Rovers star winger, eight times capped by England.

BOOTH, Curtis **1923-24**
Inside-forward. 5ft 11in; 12st 7lb.
Born: Gateshead, 12 October 1891. Died: Amsterdam, 29 October 1949.
Debut v Darlington (a) 25 August 1923.
Appearances: 1.
Career: Wallsend Elm Villa; Newcastle United 7 November 1913; Leeds City (wartime guest player); Norwich City 29 September 1920 (fee £800); STANLEY player-manager 28 June 1923 to May 1924; Erfurt FC (Germany) coach June 1925; subsequent coaching appointments held in Germany, France (with Racing Club de Paris), Holland, Egypt and Turkey, where he was head coach to Turkish FA.

Stanley's appointment of a player-manager for season 1923-4 was a new departure and a forward-looking step. Unfortunately, however, Curtis Booth was injured at Darlington, 20 minutes into his debut and was hospitalized with knee ligament damage. He did not play again and sadly the Accrington public were restricted to the briefest glimpse of his talent in the pre-season trials. In these matches he had shown himself to be an unselfish player and just the sort of inside-forward to hold a team together by sound advice and example on the field.

BOWLES, John Charles **1937-38**
Goalkeeper. 5ft 11in; 12st.
Born: Cheltenham, 4 August 1914.
Debut v Lincoln City (a) 16 October 1937.
Appearances: 12.
Career: Cheltenham Town; Newport County 23 May 1936; STANLEY 16 June 1937; Stockport County 12 July 1938 (In exchange for S.W.Hunt and J.F.Daniels); Winsford United July 1953.
Daring dives into the tracks of onrushing forwards were a colourful feature of Jack Bowles' play. On his debut for Stanley he sustained concussion and kept goal automatically for most of the game, with only a vague idea of what was happening. In the immediate post-war years 'Tiger' Bowles, as he was popularly known, was one of the outstanding goalkeepers in the Northern Section with over 200 appearances for Stockport County. Whilst on Stanley's books, Bowles had a few games for Accrington Cricket Club as a fast bowler. Bowles' father, an Evesham fruit farmer, was professional for Enfield Cricket Club in the Lancashire League, from 1919 to 1921.

BRADBURN, Richard **1921-23**
Outside-right. 5ft 8in; 10st 3lb.
Born: Hapton, Lancashire, 1903 (January quarter).
Debut v Halifax Town (h) 30 December 1922 (scored one goal).
Appearances: 14; Goals: 1.
Career: STANLEY amateur 30 March 1921, signing professional 11 January 1923; Great Harwood during season 1923-4.
'A speedy winger who centres with judgement' was the *Lancashire Daily Post Annual's* verdict on Bradburn in 1923. He had first attracted Stanley's attention in 1921, being a discovery of the season's medal competitions. A scorer on his Football League debut, Bradburn had an extended run in the first team during 1922-3, but finished the season in the Reserves. On 5 May 1923 he scored one of the goals in a 2-0 win against Lytham at Deepdale, Preston, when Stanley Reserves won the Richardson Cup.

BRETHERTON, Thomas **1947-48**
Inside-forward. 5ft 6½in; 10st 10lb.
Born: Chorley, 9 April 1920.
Debut v Doncaster Rovers (h) 1 February 1947.
Appearances: 4.
Career: Leyland Motors; STANLEY 1 February 1947; Nelson August 1948; Leyland Motors January 1949; Wigan Athletic season 1949-50.
A former RAF air-gunnery instructor, Tom Bretherton's Accrington career was beset by injuries. Good ball-control and a strong shot combined to net him 13 goals in 18 games for Leyland Motors in season 1946-7 and Stanley's manager Jack Hacking beat several interested parties when he obtained Bretherton's signature. Sadly, on his fourth appearance in Stanley's colours, he suffered a broken right leg in a collision with Rotherham United's goalkeeper at Peel Park on 22 March 1947. His first-class career was effectively terminated when he cracked the same bone in a training accident in October 1947.

BRIGGS, John Cyril **1945-50**
Centre-half. 5ft 9in; 12st 3lb.

Born: Lower Broughton, Manchester, 24 November 1918.
Debut v Bradford City (a) 31 August 1946.
Appearances: 135; Goals: 1.
Career: Lancashire Schoolboys; Adelphi Lads' Club; Darwen; Manchester United 2 October 1944; STANLEY 20 August 1945 (after guest appearances in 1944-5); Southport 17 March 1950; Hyde United cs 1950; Altrincham.
International honour: England Schoolboys v Scotland at Hampden Park in 1933.
A stocky, fair-haired centre-half whose wholehearted, never-say-die efforts introduced solidarity into Stanley's defence. As quiet and modest off the field as he was militant on it, Cyril Briggs marshalled a fine defence in Stanley's 1945-6 side, championship winners in the Third Division North (West Region). He was a regular in Stanley's rearguard until December 1949, when he lost his place to Eric Lovett. He was transferred to Southport, for a small fee, on 17 March 1950. On the previous day, Stanley had collected £5,000, then a record fee, when Stan Lynn was transferred to Aston Villa. A part-time professional, Briggs was employed in the engineering trade in Manchester. Later he emigrated with his family to Australia.

BRITTON, Francis G. **1935**
Centre-forward. 5ft 7in; 10st 8lb.
Born: Bristol, 1910 (April quarter).
Debut v Crewe Alexandra (h) 9 February 1935 (scored one goal).
Appearances: 11; Goals: 9.
Career: Bristol St George; Bristol Rovers 17 September 1927; Blackburn Rovers 12 June 1930; Oldham Athletic 30 June 1934; STANLEY 8 February 1935 (In part exchange for Fred Leedham); Reading (one month's trial) 23 August 1935; Aldershot 29 October 1935; Worcester City November 1935; Hereford United 20 August 1936.
Frank Britton was the younger brother of Clifford S.Britton, the Bristol Rovers and Everton wing-half who played nine times for England. The brothers were together at Bristol Rovers and left Eastville at the same time, Cliff to Everton and Frank to Blackburn Rovers. Described in the 1932 edition of the *Lancashire Daily Post Annual* as: 'a stocky player, full of grit and determination to succeed'. He had to fight hard for recognition at Ewood Park, where he proved to be a fine utility man. Generally at left-half but also at centre-forward on occasions, he totalled 45 First Division appearances and scored eight goals. In a brief but eventful spell with Stanley, he did particularly well at Peel Park, failing to score only once in seven home matches.

BROCKLEHURST, John Fletcher **1952-53**
Half-back. 5ft 11in; 12st 7lb.
Born: Horwich, Lancashire, 15 December 1927.
Debut v Halifax Town (a) 15 September 1952.
Appearances: 34.
Career: Oldham Athletic amateur August 1947; Stalybridge Celtic 1949; STANLEY 21 May 1952; Stalybridge Celtic cs 1953; Bradford 21 August 1954 to cs 1956.
John Brocklehurst was manager Walter Crook's first new signing for season 1952-3. A tall, strongly-build

wing-half with a prematurely receding hairline, he soon established himself in the middle line after two early outings at inside-right. A painter and decorator in his father's business in Bolton, Brocklehurst began as a 19-year-old amateur with Oldham Athletic Reserves. He became a professional with Stalybridge Celtic and returned to play for them after his season at Peel Park. He was brought back into League football by Bradford, where he made 47 appearances in two seasons. He left Park Avenue in the close season of 1956, after Bradford had finished 23rd in the Third Division North and had been obliged to apply for re-election for the first time in their historv.

BROOKE, Percy **1927-28**
Full-back. 5ft 10in; 12st 2lb.
Born: Kidsgrove, Staffordshire, 1893 (April quarter).
Debut v Nelson (a) 27 August 1927.
Appearances: 2.
Career: Kidsgrove Wellington FC; Stoke 25 December 1919; Aberdare Athletic 7 July 1921; Swindon Town

19 August 1926; STANLEY 22 July 1927 to cs 1928.
Representative honour: Welsh League v Southern League at Aberdare 29 September 1921.
Club honour: Aberdare Athletic, Welsh Cup runners-up v Cardiff City 3 May 1923.
A seasoned defender, Percy Brooke had spent five seasons with Aberdare Athletic, being their captain for two seasons. With Stanley he lost his place to Jimmy Armstrong after appearing in the first two matches of the season 1927-8. Of Brooke's career total of 138 Football League appearances, all but 16 were made in Aberdare's colours.

BROOME, W(illiam) Henry **1930-31**
Inside-forward. 5ft 7½in; 11st 3lb.
Born: Chorlton, 1904 (April quarter).
Debut v Crewe Alexandra (h) 30 August 1930.
Appearances: 33; Goals 9.
Career: Altrincham; Bury 5 May 1926; Colwyn Bay United July 1927; Bangor (Welsh National League) 24 August 1928; Caernarfon Town 14 November 1928; Crewe Alexandra 29 June 1929; STANLEY 12 July 1930; Mansfield Town 8 July 1931 to June 1933.
Stanley's heavy pitch with its pronounced slope did not suit Harry Broome's style of football. A 'box of tricks' inside-forward who made judicious use of the ball, he seemed to reserve his best displays for away matches. His most memorable game in Stanley's colours came at Rochdale on 3 April 1931. Stanley had not won an away match all season, yet they demolished Rochdale 6-1, Broome scoring four of Stanley's goals. With his final League club, Mansfield Town, Broome scored twice in the Stags' first-ever Football League fixture, a 3-2 win against Swindon Town on 29 August 1931.

BROWN, Ernest **1949-50**
Half-back. 5ft 8½in; 11st.
Born: Stockport, 30 May 1923.
Debut v Mansfield Town (a) 29 August 1949.
Appearances: 2.
Career: Manchester City during wartime season 1943-4; Aldershot 18 June 1946; STANLEY 31 August 1949 to June 1950.
In an early-season defensive reshuffle, Ernie Brown was paired with Stan Lynn in a new full-back combination. Before the season was out, Lynn had moved to Aston Villa for a record fee, whilst Brown was back in the Lancashire Combination side, which he captained from left-half. Described as a 'dour and industrious flank man', Brown began in wartime football with Manchester City. His Football League debut was made with Aldershot during the 1946-7 season, when he totalled 12 appearances.

BROWN, Frederick Walter **1934-36**
Inside-forward. 5ft 11in; 11st 4lb.
Born: Birmingham, 1911.
Debut v Mansfield Town (h) 19 September 1934.
Appearances: 76; Goals: 25.
Career: Hinckley Juniors; Sunderland 9 April 1931; Rochdale 21 November 1931; Halifax Town, 30 July 1932; STANLEY 23 July 1934; Torquay United 30 May 1936 to June 1937.
'An attractive player, adaptable to any forward position' was the verdict of the 1935 issue of the *Lancashire Daily Post Annual.* Club leading goalscorer in his first season with 12 in 37 League appearances, Fred Brown began the following season in sparkling form, scoring 11 League goals before the end of November 1935. A switch from centre-forward to inside-right effectively cut off his personal goalscoring, but he retained his place in the side as a provider, keeping a very potent front line on the move. The loss of both Mortimer and Harker to Portsmouth in February 1936 broke up one of Stanley's best-ever forward lines, Reynolds, Brown, Mortimer, Harker and Mee. In 1947 he was reported to be living in Torquay and working as a painter and decorator.

BROWN, Robert G. **1922**

Outside-right. 5ft 7in; 11st.
Born: Probably in the Middlesbrough area.
Debut v Grimsby Town (a) 15 April 1922.
Appearances: 5; Goals 1.
Career: Hathersage FC; Bradford City 8 February 1921; STANLEY 7 April to May 1922; Rotherham County August 1923.
Signed as Stanley's first-ever Third Division North campaign entered its final weeks, Bob Brown appeared at outside-right in the final five matches of the 1921-2 season. He scored the only goal of the game on 22 April, against Grimsby Town, but his overall form was dissappointing. 'Lacks skill in beating an opponent,' was the *Accrington Observer's* verdict. A teacher of physical culture, Brown had not appeared in League football with his previous club, Bradford City.

BROWN, Thomas **1923-24**

Outside-right. 5ft 11in; 11st 6lb.
Born: Middlesbrough, summer of 1898.
Debut v Darlington (a) 25 August 1923.
Appearances: 16; Goals 1.

Career: Middlesbrough amateur March 1920, signing professional 23 April 1921; STANLEY 13 June 1923 to May 1924.
In August 1923 the *Sports Telegraph* commented: 'Brown is trickiness itself when cornered by opponents'. The ex-Middlesbrough winger made a bright start with Stanley, but the team's indifferent form resulted in a number of forward changes and Brown was one of the players who lost his first-team place. After a long spell in the Reserves, he reappeared in the seniors at the season's close, scoring Stanley's last goal of the season, at Rochdale.

BROWN, William **1953**

Centre-forward. 5ft 6in; 11st 2lb.
Born: Scotland, 1928.
Debut v Stockport County (h) 22 August 1953 (scored one goal).
Appearances: 6; Goals 2.
Career: Falkirk; Forfar Athletic; STANLEY 4 August 1953; Nelson, 30 October 1953.
Willie Brown, an early Scottish signing by Stanley's new player-manager Walter Galbraith, scored on his first two appearances in the number-nine shirt. The new season opened with two home wins, but the next four matches were all lost and Brown was replaced at centre-forward by Les Cocker. He had originally been signed for a month's trial and was signed for the season on 27 August. In the event, he departed Peel Park two months later to join Nelson. He assisted his new club to third place in the Lancashire Combination in season 1953-4.

BROWN, William Inglis **1959-60**

Goalkeeper. 6ft 1in; 12st 8lb.
Born: Clydebank, 25 November 1938.
Debut v Shrewsbury Town (a) 31 August 1959.
Appearances: 29.
Career: St Mirren; STANLEY 18 August 1959; Chester, 7 June 1960 to May 1961.
Bill Brown successfully contested the senior goalkeeping position with Willie McInnes in season 1959-60. Unfortunately, he was operating behind one of Stanley's worst-ever defences, 123 goals being conceded in the 46-match programme. Brown left Stanley to join Chester, but fared little better at Sealand Road. He made 41 appearances in season 1960-61 when Chester finished 24th in Division Four with the worst defensive record in the Division.

BRYDON, Ian Forrester **1953-55**

Centre-forward. 5ft 9½in; 11st 6lb.
Born: Edinburgh, 22 March 1927. Died: Spain, *c.*1973.
Debut v Port Vale (h) 7 November 1953 (scored one goal).
Appearances: 27; Goals: 19.
Career: Armadale Thistle; Leith Athletic 1946-7; Tranent Juniors 1948; St Johnstone 1950; Darlington (trial) 19 September 1953; Bradford 16 June 1955 (fee £500) to May 1956; Netherfield October 1956; Accrington FC team manager 1965-6.
Ian Brydon had two trial games in Stanley's Reserve team at the beginning of season 1953-4. He then had a month's trial with Darlington but declined their terms and, shortly afterwards, signed for Stanley. A former sergeant in the Army Physical Training Corps and a noted sprinter, he made an immediate impact with Stanley. he scored eight goals in his first four appearances, but after only six matches was badly injured at Halifax Town on Christmas Day 1953. He was out of the team until April 1954, but still managed to end the season with 15 goals in as many appearances. Season 1954-5 had hardly got underway when he was injured again, and with the arrival of George Stewart, he was restricted mainly to reserve-team football. A younger son, born whilst Ian Brydon was at Accrington was named 'Stanley'.

BURKINSHAW, John Dean Lewis **1921-22**

Half-back. 5ft 8in; 12st 7lb.

Born: Kilnhurst, 12 May 1890. Died: Wortley, Sheffield, 1947.
Debut v Rochdale (a) 27 August 1921.
Appearances: 31; Goals: 1.
Career: Rotherham Town cs 1909; Swindon Town cs 1910; Sheffield Wednesday 30 May 1913; Bradford 28 June 1920; STANLEY 16 June 1921 to May 1922. He was reported to be playing in Chicago in 1924.
Club honour: Swindon Town, Southern League Champions season 1910-11.
Jack Burkinshaw began his career as a centre-forward and he scored eight goals in only 13 appearances for Swindon Town when they won the Southern League championship in 1910-11. In the two seasons immediately following World War One, Burkinshaw had the unenviable experience of sampling relegation from Division One with Sheffield Wednesday (in 1919-20) and Bradford (in 1920-21). In Stanley's first Third Division North campaign, Burkinshaw exhibited deft footwork in the middle line, often lending material aid to the attack. In the early stages of his career, he was invited by Swindon Town to appear for them in an exhibition match against Barnsley, played in Paris. This rather unusual trial led to his permanent move to Swindon Town.

BURROWS, Arthur **1948-50**
Half-back. 5ft 8in; 11st 1lb.
Born: Stockport, 4 December 1919.
Debut v Rotherham United (a) 30 August 1948.
Appearances: 9.
Career: Stockport County amateur 2 October signing professional 11 November 1937; STANLEY (wartime guest) season 1944-5; Ashton United cs 1947; STANLEY 15 March 1948 to 6 May 1950.
A late-season signing in 1947-8, Arthur Burrows did not appear in Stanley's first team, and two months after signing, was placed on the transfer list. It was then decided that he should be retained, and during 1948-9 he proved a useful stand-in. He appeared on both flanks as wing-half and at inside-forward in the seniors, but was mainly employed in the reserve team. He had a long association with Stockport County either side of World War Two. In wartime football at Edgeley Park he made 116 appearances (8 goals). In season 1944-5 he guested for Stanley in two matches against Bolton Wanderers, in the League War Cup. He was allowed to go to Ashton United in 1947, after injury had kept him out of Stockport's first team.

BUSHELL, Alan **1952-53**
Outside-right.
Born: Burnley, 4 September 1932.
Debut v Rochdale (h) 29 November 1952 (scored one goal).
Appearances: 8; Goals: 1.
Career: Wood Top FC; STANLEY 14 May 1952, released on a free transfer, 29 April 1953.
Alan Bushell made his senior bow for Stanley in late November 1952. He was the third outside-right tried in as many matches, and whilst obviously in need of considerably more experience, he obliged by scoring the winning goal against Rochdale. It was only Stanley's third win of the season, after 19 matches. In a campaign only remarkable for the number of different team permutations tried, Bushell was typically next fielded on the opposite wing. He played in five consecutive matches, but then lost his place.

BUTLER, Malcolm P. **1947-48**
Full-back. 5ft 9in; 11st 10lb.
Born: Belfast, 6 August 1913.
Debut v Hartlepools United (h) 23 August 1947.
Appearances: 32.
Career: Elmgrove FC; Belfast Celtic; Blackpool, 18 January 1935; Wartime guest with Brighton & Hove Albion and Chelsea; STANLEY 8 July 1947; retired cs 1948.
International honour: 1 cap for Ireland v Wales at Wrexham 15 March 1939.
Representative honour: (Wartime) Irish FA v The Army at Belfast 12 September 1942.
Malcolm Butler's career peaked just at the time when World War Two broke out. He had represented his country in their last peacetime international and was just becoming established at Bloomfield Road. When the ill-fated 1939-40 season opened, Butler was at left-back for the Seasiders. They won their first three fixtures and were top of the First Division when the competition had to be abandoned. After the war, in which he served as a Flt-Lt navigator in the RAF, he joined Stanley. A polished performer with a sound knowledge of play and an unflurried approach, he captained Stanley to sixth place in the table before announcing his intention to retire, in order to become a licensee in Blackpool.

BUTLER, Reuben **1927-28**
Inside-forward. 5ft 10in; 11st 5lb.
Born: Stillington, Co Durham, 10 October 1890. Died: Heworth, Co Durham, 15 July 1958.
Debut v Nelson (a) 27 August 1927.
Appearances: 28; Goals 9.
Career: Stillington St John's; Stockton Amateurs season 1910-11; Spennymoor Athletic season 1911-12; Middlesbrough amateur 31 May, signing professional 20 October 1912; Hartlepools United (wartime guest) January 1919; Oldham Atheltic 10 May 1920 (fee £1,850); Bury 17 July 1923 (fee £375); Bradford City 21 October 1924; Crewe Alexandra 12 March 1926; Rochdale 25 May 1926; STANLEY 23 May 1927; Great Harwood, 17 August 1929; Bacup Borough February 1930. Reverted to amateur status September 1932, then became player-coach to Rossendale United's Reserve Team; Bacup Borough manager cs 1933 to 6 April 1935.
Two days prior to his 37th birthday, Reuben Butler netted for Stanley at Halifax Town. When signed, Accrington's manager, Ernest Blackburn, admitted that Butler was 'getting on a bit' and also commented that 'he has worn as many colours as Joseph had in his coat'. Nevertheless, the veteran forward proved a shrewd signing, as he held the Stanley forward line well together and helped bring out the younger players. Earlier in his career, Oldham Athletic parted with a large fee to recruit him in 1920 and he became the Latics' leading goalscorer, by a wide margin, in seasons 1920-21 and 1921-2.

BUTLER, Thomas **1947-53**
Outside-right. 5ft 7½in; 10st 6lb.
Born: Atherton, 28 April 1918.
Debut v Hartlepools United (h) 23 August 1947.
Appearances: 218; Goals: 26.
Career: Astley and Tyldesley Colliers; Bolton Wanderers 5 September 1936; Macclesfield cs 1937; Oldham

Athletic 25 February 1938; Middlesbrough, 8 March 1939 (fee £1,500); Oldham Athletic, after wartime appearances as a guest player, 17 August 1946 (fee £500); STANLEY 12 July 1947; Wigan Athletic cs 1953.
Younger brother of Billy Butler, the famous Bolton Wanderer, who won three FA Cup medals and played for England. Tommy Butler also began at Burnden Park but broke his left leg and began season 1937-8 with Macclesfield. He gave good service to Oldham Athletic on either side of World War Two, after a move to Middlesbrough was restricted to only two First Division appearances before the outbreak of hostilities. Butler stayed long enough at Peel Park at qualify for a benefit. In six seasons he was rarely absent and occupied every front-line position except centre-forward in the course of his 218 appearances. A crowd of approximately 7,000 attended his benefit match in March 1954 (by which time he had joined Wigan Athletic).

BYROM, Raymond **1954-58**
Outside-left. 5ft 6in; 10st 8lb.
Born: Blackburn, 2 January 1935.
Debut v Crewe Alexandra (h) 26 December 1957 (scored one goal).
Appearances: 9; Goals: 1.
Career: Blackburn Rovers amateur; STANLEY amateur season 1954-5, signing professional 28 January 1956; Bradford 27 December 1958 (along with P.W.Dick for a combined fee of £2,750) to June 1962.
One of Stanley's promising youngsters who was developed in the 'A' team and in Lancashire Combination football. Byrom became a full-time professional on being 'demobbed' after Army service in January 1958. He first came into prominence during season 1957-8 with sparkling displays in the third round FA Cup matches against Bristol City. Injuries and a subsequent loss of form restricted him to only five appearances in 1958-9, before he was transferred, along with Wattie Dick, to Bradford where he joined up again with Walter Galbriath, Stanley's ex manager. At Park Avenue, Bryom was ever-present in season 1959-60 and totalled 70 appearances and scored 14 goals.

CADDEN, Joseph Y. **1953-54**
Centre-half. 6ft; 12st 10lb.
Born: Glasgow, 13 April 1920.
Debut v Stockport County (h) 22 August 1953.
Appearances: 17.
Career: Brooklyn Wanderers (USA); Liverpool 12 June 1948; Grimsby Town 2 July 1952; STANLEY 30 June 1953, released on a free transfer 29 April 1954; New Brighton 1955.
A Scot who left Glasgow to play in New York football, in which Liverpool saw him in an opposing team during their 1948 tour. They brought him back to Anfield and retained him for four seasons before Grimsby Town signed him in 1952. Cadden was the first player sought by Stanley's new player-manager, Walter Galbraith, a former Blundell Park clubmate. After appearing in the first 17 games of 1953-4, Cadden broke down in training with back trouble, and he did not appear in the first team again.

CALVERT, James **1938-39**
Half-back. 5ft 8in; 11st.
Born: Blackburn, 1917 (April quarter).
Debut v York City (a) 3 December 1938.
Appearances: 8.
Career: Local junior football; Blackburn Rovrs amateur 8 May 1936, signing professional 12 January 1937; STANLEY 6 June 1938 to June 1939.
A junior with Blackburn Rovers, Jim Calvert graduated to Central League football, making 23 appearances with Rovers Reserves in 1937-8. He was one of a welter of new signings made by Stanley in the summer of 1938, the side selected for the opening fixture contained no less than eight debutants. Calvert did not get a run in the League side until December, but then featured in the final six fixtures of the season. These games brought a 'mini-revival' of three wins and one draw, seven points out of the final abysmal total of 20. Stanley finished bottom of the table, 11 points adrift of Hartlepools United in 23rd place.

CAPSTICK, Albert Lewin **1945-46 & 1948-49**
Inside-forward. 5ft 9½in; 10st 12lb.
Born: South Kirkby, 2 January 1928.
Debut v Halifax Town (h) 26 February 1949.
Appearances: 1.
Career: STANLEY amateur 17 March 1945; Fleetwood cs 1946; STANLEY on professional forms 31 July 1948 to May 1949.
Albert Capstick first played for Stanley during the war. He was then called to the pits as a 'Bevin Boy' and later returned to his home in Blackpool, subsequently signing for Fleetwood. He had several games as an amateur in Stanley's reserve team in the season before he was signed on as a full-time professional. Regarded as a promising forward, his Football Legue debut was made at wing half-back. Despite the unaccustomed role he gave a sound performance, assisting Stanley to win 1-0 and record what was only their second win in two months.

CARRICK, James H. **1927-28 & 1929-30**
Half-back. 5ft 10½in; 11st 6lb.

Debut v Nelson (a) 27 August 1927.
Appearances: 33; Goals: 1.
Career: Blackburn Wanderers; Astley Wanderers; Plank Lane FC November 1919; Airdrieonians (trial); Exeter City 23 August 1920; Oldham Athletic 6 June 1921 (fee £650); Stockport County 25 June 1923 (fee £150); Barrow 5 July 1924; Bradford 20 August 1925; STANLEY 23 May 1927; Torquay United 31 May 1928; STANLEY 27 May 1929; Burton Town July 1930; Stalybridge Celtic August 1930.
Jim Carrick's first club of note was Blackburn Wanderers of the Leigh and District League. He first encountered Stanley in 1920, when he played against their reserve team whilst assisting Plank Lane (Leigh), a Lancashire Combination team. In Exeter City's initial Football League campaign, he made 41 appearances and scored three goals. In his first spell with Stanley, he lost his first-team place to Chris Dodds in mid-term. After a season with Torquay, Ernest Blackburn brought Carrick back to Peel Park for a second time, but he made only six first-team appearances in 1929-30.

CHADWICK, John **1926-30**
Inside-forward. 5ft 8½in; 11st 3lb.
Born: Burnley, 25 August 1905.
Debut v Rochdale (h) 28 August 1926.
Appearnces: 46; Goals: 12.
Career: Hapton Valley Miners; Burnley Amateur 16 January, signing professional 30 May 1925; STANLEY 18 June 1926; Stalybridge Celtic June 1930; Chorley July 1933; Nelson January 1934; Clitheroe September 1934; Frickley Colliery August 1936; Lancaster Town.
John Chadwick first drew attention when he assisted Hapton Valley Miners to win the Burnley Hospital Cup. Burnley recruited him shortly afterwards and he made 26 Central league appearances for the Clarets in 1925-6. With Stanley, he scored 13 goals for the Reserves in season 1926-7, but it was not until 1928-9 that he figured regularly in the first team. In this season he appeared in 26 matches and scored nine goals. A glimpse of his playing style was revealed in the *Lancashire Daily Post Annual* for 1929, which stated that Chadwick 'trapped neatly and distributed smartly'.

CHALLINOR, Samuel **1922-23**
Half-back. 5ft 11in; 12st 4lb.
Born: Middlewich, 2 April 1900.
Debut v Darlington (h) 26 August 1922.
Appearances: 23; Goals: 1.
Career: Witton Albion; Everton September 1917; Brentford 28 August 1920; Halifax Town 26 July 1921; STANLEY 8 June 1922; New Brighton 14 June 1923; Mold 23 August 1924.
Club honour: Mold, Welsh League champions 1924-5.
Captain of Halifax Town in their first season as a Football League club, Sam Challinor had a particularly good game against Stanley at Halifax, scoring in the Town's 2-1 win. When he became available in the summer of 1922, Stanley were quick to secure his signature. A versatile performer, Challinor occupied the three half-back positions and also turned out at centre-forward for Stanley, all of this within the space of his first four appearances! In a season with New Brighton, the Rakers' first in the Football League, he made 40 appearances. He was also the scorer of the first League goal to be recorded at Rake Lane, on 1 September 1923 against Bradford. It gave the Rakers the points in a 1-0 victory.

CHAPMAN, Edwin **1938-39**
Inside-forward. 5ft 11in; 12st 8lb.
Born: Blackburn, 2 May 1919. Died: Blackburn, 4 December 1976.
Debut v Bradford City (a) 24 September 1938 (scored one goal).
Appearances: 4; Goals: 1.
Career: Darwen; Blackburn Rovers 5 May 1936;

STANLEY 1 July 1938; Oldham Athletic 27 June 1939; Stockport County 28 August 1946 to June 1947.
Eddie Chapman was only 19 years old when he joined Stanley and, after a season spent mainly in the Reserves, he was signed by Oldham Athletic. His move to Boundary Park coincided with the outbreak of World War Two, and in wartime regional football he did well, scoring 50 goals in 89 appearances. A move to Stockport County for the first peacetime season was cruelly cut short on 12 October 1946. Playing against Southport at Edgeley Park he sustained the injury which ended his career.

CHEETHAM, John **1933-34**
Centre-forward. 5ft 10in; 11st 6lb.
Born: Wishaw, Strath, 1907.
Debut v Stockport County (a) 26 August 1933.
Appearances: 39; Goals: 15.
Career: Broxburn FC; Brighton & Hove Albion October 1925; West Ham United (trial); Eccles Borough; Hurst FC August 1928; Swansea Town 22 January 1929; Connah's Quay & Shotton 4 August 1930; Ashton National 7 November 1930; Hyde United 1931; STANLEY 20 May 1933; Stalybridge Celtic 7 September 1934; Witton Albion June 1936.

When signed by Stanley in May 1933, Jackie Cheetham was said to have scored 160 goals in two and a half seasons for his previous club, Hyde United. Despite being Stanley's leading goalscorer in 1933-4 with 15 League and three FA Cup goals, he never quite lived up to the reputation he had gained in Cheshire League circles. One glimpse of his goalscoring potential came on 17 March 1934. Cheetham scored four of Stanley's goals against New Brighton, who were beaten 8-0 at Peel Park. In a match played for the most part in a blinding hailstorm, only 1,429 spectators witnessed Cheetham's 'finest hour'.

CHILDS, Walter **1919-25**
Full-back. 5ft 5in; 10st 3lb.
Born: Hapton, 1900 (October quarter).
Debut v Wigan Borough (h) 7 October 1922.
Appearances: 22.
Career: Hapton FC; STANLEY amateur August 1919, re-registered 30 March 1922, signed professional 14 September 1922; Clitheroe June 1925.
There can have been few full-backs in senior football as slightly-built as Walter Childs, who was first associated with Stanley before they gained admission to the Third Division North. Although small, Childs tackled gamely and his cool play and forceful kicking was much admired. He also lasted the pace of a hard game better than many bigger men. In a lengthy spell at Peel Park, he made 12 appearances in 1922-3 season, but a knee injury side-lined him for much of 1923-4. He left Stanley to join Clitheroe for their first season in the Lancashire Combination, 1925-6.

CLARE, Joseph **1933-34**
Outside-left. 5ft 11in; 11st 8lb.
Born: Westhoughton, 4 February 1910. Died: Christchurch, Hamshire, 23 September 1987.
Debut v Barrow (a) 16 December 1933.
Appearances: 25; Goals: 1.
Career: Sacred Heart (Westhoughton); Westhoughton Town; Manchester City amateur 8 August signing professional 5 September 1930; Wigan Borough 11 August 1931; Westhoughton Town October 1931; STANLEY 3 November 1933; Arsenal 6 December 1934 (fee £700); Margate Town (loan) season 1935-6; Norwich City 8 May 1936; Lincoln City 1 July 1937 to season 1939-40. Subsequently Bournemouth and Boscombe Athletic coach-trainer until 1960, then trainer to Bournemouth & District Water Company until 1968.
Joe Clare's introduction into the Stanley team certainly had the desired effect. The previous two matches had resulted in heavy defeats (5-0 at Walsall and 7-0 at Chester). Clare's debut was at Barrow and Stanley won 6-2 to record one of their best-ever away victories. Taller than the average winger and with a natural inward swerve and good pace, he soon attracted the scouts. He earned Stanley a very useful fee when Arsenal signed him in December 1934. Loaned out to Margate, Arsenal's nursery team, in 1935-6, he took part in one of the season's surprises when Margate won through to the third round of the FA Cup, at which stage Blackpool beat them 3-1.

CLARKE, William Vincent **1938**
Half-back., 5ft 7½in; 11st 1lb.
Born: Newport, Gwent, 17 January 1911. Died: Newport, Gwent, 16 September 1970.
Debut v Halifax Town (a) 27 August 1938.
Appearances: 3; Goals: 1.
Career: Corporation Road School (Pontymister); Newport County 5 November 1930; Charlton Athletic 7 April 1932; Portsmouth 1 July 1934; Brighton & Hove Albion 16 May 1935; Aldershot 12 August 1936; Crewe Alexandra 13 August 1937; Hereford Town November 1937; STANLEY 16 August 1938; Rhyl October 1938; Ebbw Vale.
Signed for a month's trial in August 1938, Bill Clarke played at inside-left in the opening three fixtures of the season. He was the scorer of the team's first goal of the new campaign against New Brighton at Peel Park on 3 September. At this point, however, three games had been lost and Clarke was not offered an extension to his trial. Described by the *Accrington Observer* as having a 'bustling style of play and an impressive left-foot shot', he had left Crewe Alexandra in the previous season, for domestic reasons, after only six appearances.

CLARKSON, Richard **1926-28**
Inside-forward. 5ft 7½in; 11st 6lb.
Born: Lytham, Lancashire, 1898.
Debut v Lincoln City (a) 13 September 1926.
Appearances: 38; Goals: 17.
Career: Lytham FC; STANLEY 2 June 1926; Darwen June 1928; Lytham 1929.

In the season prior to his joining Stanley, Richard Clarkson scored 38 goals for Lytham in the West Lancashire League. He enjoyed a good first season with Stanley, despite lacking quality support in a poor side which ended the season in 21st place. His 17 goals included four in the FA Cup, and he also netted four in one match, against Hartlepools United on 5 February 1927. He was one of only five players retained, but failed to break into the first team in 1927-8, when an entirely new forward line formed a good understanding from the outset and helped the team to ninth place in the table.

COATES, Frank **1948**
Outside-right. 5ft 9in; 10st 10lb.
Born: Farrington, 16 April 1922.
Debut v Stockport County (a) 17 January 1948.
Appearances: 4.
Career: Leyland Motors; Blackburn Rovers amateur 5 September 1942, professional 18 January 1943; Leyland Motors cs 1947; STANLEY 14 January to May 1948.
In mid-season 1947-8, Stanley recruited a new right-wing pairing, Frank Coates from Leyland Motors and Geoff Dyson from Bradford City. Of the two, Coates was the least successful, disappointing by his lack of speed. Of his debut, the *Accrington Observer* commented: 'Coates beats his man deliciously, but he will have to speed up in the sprint if he is to be fully effective'. After a run of four matches he lost his first-team place and his sojourn at Peel Park ended when he was granted a free transfer in May 1948.

COCKER, Leslie **1953-59**
Utility forward. 5ft 8½in; 11st 4lb.
Born: Stockport, 13 March 1924. Died: 4 October 1979.
Debut v Stockport County (h) 22 August 1953.
Appearances: 122; Goals: 48.
Career: Army football; Stockport County amateur 2 September 1946, signing professional 7 August 1947; STANLEY 29 August 1953, appointed assistant trainer May 1957 but was then re-signed as a player in September 1957 to help out in an injury crisis; Luton Town assistant trainer 10 August 1959; Leeds United trainer cs 1960; England coach and assistant manager 30 July 1975 to 27 August 1977. After a spell abroad was appointed Doncaster Rovers trainer, and was that club's assistant manager when he died, during a training session, in October 1979.
A painter and decorator by trade, Les Cocker served in the Reconnaissance Regiment of the 53rd Division in France in 1944, and his initial outings with Stockport County were made whilst he was still a soldier. At this time he made a round trip of 250 miles from his unit in Dorset, every time he played for the club. With Stanley he was one of very few Englishmen to appear regularly in the side during Walter Galbraith's term as manager. Formerly an outside-right, but a most versatile performer, Cocker appeared in most positions during his stay at Peel Park. He even took over the goalkeeper's jersey for Stanley Reserves at Lancaster in August 1955. He deputized for Jimmy Jones, who had been taken to hospital with a shoulder injury, but he was sent off the field himself, shortly afterwards! As one of the 'twins' in Stanley's double centre-forward game, he had an outstanding season in 1954-5, scoring 21 goals in 41 appearances. This included his scoring hat-tricks in successive matches in January 1955. He was appointed assistant trainer to Stanley in May 1957 and it was in this field that he reached the highest rank. His association with the England team, initially at Under-23 level, first being made in November 1961.

COLL, Liam Sean **1949-51**
Outside-right.
Born: Carrick Macross, Ireland, 16 December 1929.
Debut v Carlisle United (a) 20 August 1949.
Appearances: 13.
Career: Irish Junior football; STANLEY (trial) April 1949, signing professional 25 June 1949, released on a free transfer 14 April 1951 and joined Ballymena United; Doncaster Rovers 14 December 1954 to 31 March 1955.
In a stay of just under two years at Peel Park, 'Paddy' Coll showed occasional glimpses of genius. He appeared in the first two matches of season 1949-50 but was then injured and finished the season in the Reserves. He was retained for 1950-51 and had several first-team outings. He did not, however, develop as had been hoped and was one of several players released towards the close of a very disappointing season which saw Stanley finish in 23rd place. They were only two points clear of New Brighton, who failed to gain re-election.

COLLINS, Albert Desmond **1952-53**
Outside-right. 5ft 7in; 11st 4lb.
Born: Chesterfield, 15 April 1923.
Debut v Hartlepools United (a) 23 August 1952.
Appearances: 17; Goals: 2.
Career: Local junior football to Chesterfield October 1941; Halifax Town 15 November 1946; Carlisle United 1 March 1948; Barrow 24 December 1948; Bournemouth & Boscombe Athletic 7 August 1950; Shrewsbury Town 31 August 1951; STANLEY 2 July 1952; Boston United cs 1953.
Albert Collins began in wartime football with Chesterfield, and was one of five forwards who all scored when Chesterfield beat Blackburn Rovers 7-0 at Blackburn on 17 September 1945. His senior career ended at Peel Park, Stanley being his seventh League club in a career which spanned Division Two and both Sections of Division Three. He totalled 158 League appearances and scored 25 goals, and had often been prominent in opposition to Stanley, during his Barrow spell. He appeared on both wings for Stanley but failed to establish a regular place in the first team, who finished the season in 24th place, having scored only 39 League goals, much the lowest by any League club that season.

CONGDON, James **1922-23**
Outside-left. 5ft 8½in; 11st 9lb.
Born: Plymouth.
Debut v Tranmere Rovers (a) 9 September 1922.
Appearances: 5.
Career: Millbrook Rangers; Second Battalion of the Devon Regiment; Exeter City 12 July 1921; STANLEY 9 June 1922, released 17 February 1923; Torquay United (Southern League) 10 March 1923.
Prior to joining Exeter City, Jim Congdon represented Cornwall County and the Plymouth & District League in all their matches during season 1920-21. As understudy to the Grecians' star outside-left, John Dockray, Congdon found little opportunity and he took the long journey north to join Stanley in June 1922. In only a handful of senior appearances Congdon failed to impress. He was unable to capitalize on the misfortune of Syd Harrold, whose broken ankle left the senior outside-left berth vacant. Congdon's

unhappy northern sojourn ended in February 1923, when he was released from his contract.

CONROY R(ichard) Maurice **1944-49**
Half-back or wing-forward. 5ft 9in; 11st 10lb.
Born: Bradford, 26 April 1919.
Debut v Bradford City (a) 31 August 1946.
Appearances: 87; Goals: 1.
Career: Fulham 17 May 1937; Bradford City and Aldershot (wartime guest); STANLEY 9 September 1944; Scunthorpe United as player-coach cs 1949, continuing as trainer-coach during season 1950-51 after an injury had ended his playing career.
A fine utility player, Maurice Conroy began with Stanley during wartime football as an outside-right and scored 12 goals in 36 appearances in season 1944-5. In the following term he was switched from winger to right-back in mid-season. When League football resumed in 1946-7, he occupied five different outfield positions, finally settling at right-back for the remainder of his stay at Peel Park. A former Army sergeant-major physical training instructor, Conroy qualifed as an FA coach in January 1949 and joined Scunthorpe United shortly afterwards. He was also appointed football coach to the Scunthorpe Education Authority.

COOKE, Frederick Robert **1923-24**
Centre-forward. 5ft 10in; 12st 6lb.
Born: Kirkby-in-Ashfield, 5 July 1896.
Debut v Darlington (a) 25 August 1923.
Appearances: 25; Goals: 5.
Career: East Kirkby FC; Sunderland 26 July 1919; Swindon Town 14 May 1921; STANLEY 15 August 1923 (fee £40) to May 1924.
Fred Cooke appeared in most of Stanley's matches until early February in 1924, when new signing J.R.Black, the Scottish junior international from Nelson, took over the centre-forward berth. Cooke's return of five goals from 25 appearances was disappointing, even in a season when Stanley barely averaged a goal a game. Without a great deal of senior experience when he arrived at Peel Park, Cooke had managed to average a reasonable striking rate, scoring 20 goals in 45 appearances with Sunderland and Swindon Town.

COOPER, Fred **1921-22**
Outside-right.
Born: Bolton, 1900.
Debut v Barrow (a) 7 January 1922.
Appearances: 1.
Career: Bolton St Mary's; STANLEY amateur 24 December 1921 to June 1922.
After impressing in a trial with Stanley Reserves against Horwich Central in early December 1921, Fred Cooper was signed up on amateur forms. He made his Football League debut as one of six changes for the visit to Barrow, a game which resulted in Stanley's third away defeat within the space of one week. Cooper's solitary Football League outing exposed his lack of experience, despite the fact that he 'laid on' Stanley's goal in a 3-1 defeat.

COOPER, James Else **1952-53**
Inside-right. 5ft 9½in; 11st.
Born: Blackpool, 13 January 1928.
Debut v Stockport County (h) 15 November 1952.
Appearances: 7; Goals: 1.
Career: Blackpool junior football; Fleetwood cs 1949; STANLEY 18 June 1952, released on a free transfer 1 May 1953.
Jim Cooper was a regular member of Fleetwood's first team in the Lancashire Combination for three years before he joined Stanley. He was a part-time professional, employed as an engineer in Blackpool, where he lived. Probably unfortunate to arrive on the Peel Park scene when the club's fortunes were at their lowest ebb, he failed to impress in a poor team, who sought re-election in the close season.

CORCORAN, Thomas **1932-36**
Full-back. 5ft 10in; 11st 3lb.
Born: Earlestown, 1907 (July quarter)
Debut v Walsall (a) 3 December 1932.
Appearances: 64; Goals: 1.
Career: Junior with Bolton Wanderers; Horwich RMI; Atherton; Bradford City 30 August 1929; Rochdale 26 July 1930; Guildford City cs 1931; STANLEY 15 September 1932 to May 1935; Prescot Cables season 1936-7.
Injury to Norman Price in December 1932 gave Tommy Corcoran his chance, and he played so well that he became a fixture at left-back for the remainder of the season. Two seasons later, he was deposed by George Fieldsend, leading to his eventual release in May 1935. He failed to secure a new club and in October 1935 he was re-signed by Stanley, with a view to strengthening the ranks of the reserve team.

CORNWELL, Ellis **1945-47**
Full-back. 5ft 8in; 10st 12lb.
Born: Coppull, 14 November 1913.
Debut v Stockport County (a) 14 September 1946.
Appearances: 5.
Career: Heskin Parish Church; Chorley August 1938; Rochdale (wartime guest player); STANLEY 30 November 1945; Rossendale United 2 August 1947.
When Stanley's Jack Ash suffered a broken leg in the first round FA Cup tie against Chorley in November 1945, Ellis Cornwell was signed as an emergency replacement defender. By coincidence, Cornwell had Chorley connections, having commenced his career at Victory Park as a utility forward, before joining

Rochdale as a wartime guest player. Stationed at Kirkham, he was 'demobbed' just after Christmas 1945. He made 24 appearances in the final wartime season, but then was one of seven different full-backs fielded by Stanley in 1946-7. Some idea of the kind of team changes indulged in during this season was illustrated in Cornwell's final appearance in Stanley's colours. For the Tranmere Rovers fixture on 7 December 1946, eight team changes were made, one positional. The 'shake-up' on this occasion had the desired effect, as Stanley won 2-1.

COUPE, John C. **1938-39**
Wing-half. 5ft 9in; 11st 7lb.
Born: Walton-le-Dale, 1913 (July quarter).
Debut v Hull City (a) 4 February 1939.
Appearnces: 1.
Career: Preston North End Amateur, signing professional 22 March 1934; Fleetwood midway through season 1937-8; STANLEY 3 August 1938 to May 1939.
Jack Coupe was developed at Deepdale, where he was mainly used as a utility man. This was not always to advantage, as he seemed most at home at left-half. He had some Central League experience when he joined Fleetwood, where he soon attracted Stanley's attention. In a season when the Reds conceded over a century of goals and finished the season as re-election candidates for the second year in succession, Jack Coupe's only League outing resulted in a 6-1 defeat at Hull City.

COX, Samuel **1951-52**
Full-back or centre-half. 5ft 10½in; 12st 6lb.
Born: Mexborough, 30 October 1920.
Debut v Gateshead (h) 18 August 1951.
Appearances: 43.
Career: Mexborough & Wath upon Dearne Schools; Denaby United; West Bromwich Albion 4 May 1948 (fee £750); STANLEY 20 July 1951 (fee £1,250); Scunthorpe United 14 July 1952, retiring due to injury in 1954.
A submariner during World War Two, Sam Cox joined Stanley after three years and over 100 Central League appearances for West Brom. In a season at Peel Park he made 27 appearances at left-back before being switched to centre-half on 23 February. From that point on, Stanley's defence became a different proposition and the team were able, by a single point, to avoid a re-election application.

CRABTREE, James Joseph MC **1924-25**
Goalkeeper. 6ft 1in; 11st 5lb.
Born: Clitheroe, February 1895. Died: Clitheroe, 1 December 1965.
Debut v Chesterfield (a) 1 March 1924.
Appearances: 7.
Career: Clitheroe FC; Blackburn Rovers amateur 30 April 1913, signing professional 11 March 1914; Rochdale September 1920 to May 1923; STANLEY 27 February 1924 to May 1925.
International honour: England Amateur v Wales at Plymouth 7 February 1914 (This followed his appearance for the North v South, England amateur trial at Oxford on 24 January 1914).
A clerk in a local cotton mill, Jimmy Crabtee was only 19 years old when he made his debut for Blackburn Rovers. In the same month, he was capped by England

Amateurs. His height gave him a fine reach which, coupled with his natural agility, earned him promotion into the Rovers first team in their run-in to the League Championship in season 1913-14. Crabtree served with distinction during World War One, rising from the ranks to a commission and being decorated with the Military Cross for gallantry. After the war he joined Rochdale and in a feat of some versatility, once appeared at inside-left and scored two goals. Stanley also tried him at centre-forward in the Reserves in January 1925, but he failed to get on to the score-sheet in a 3-3 draw against Eccles Borough. After retiring from playing, he kept in close touch with the game when he qualified as a Lancashire Combination referee and also ran the line at League level.

CRAGG, Richard Hartley **1921-22**
Inside-forward. 5ft 7½in; 11st.
Born: Burnley, 1892 (January quarter).
Debut v Chesterfield (h) 24 September 1921.
Appearances: 6.
Career: Army football; Burnley May 1919; Stockport County 4 September 1920; STANLEY 23 August 1921 to June 1922.
Richard Cragg, an aggressive hard-running inside-forward, saw his fortunes diminish in three seasons of senior football following World War One. In 1919-20 he made 15 appearances and scored five goals for Burnley, who were runners-up for the Football League Championship. For Stockport County in 1920-21 he appeared in 21 matches and scored three goals in a season which saw County relegated from

the Second Division. Joining Stanley for their debut in the Third Division North, he failed to break into the first team. On one of his infrequent senior outings the *Sports Telegraph* commented: 'Cragg did well in approach play but was erratic as a marksman'.

CRAVEN, Joseph Gerrard **1936-38**
Centre-half. 5ft 11in; 11st 12lb.
Born: Preston, 28 December 1903. Died: Chorley, 1972 (July quarter).
Debut v Lincoln City (h) 29 August 1936.
Appearances: 57.
Career: St Augustine's FC; Stockport County amateur 9 December 1922, signing professional 5 February 1923; Preston North End 30 October 1925; Swansea Town 7 July 1931; Port Vale 15 June 1934; Newport County 22 June 1935; STANLEY 16 June 1936; Leyland Motors August 1938.
Club honour: Swansea Town, Welsh Cup winners v Wrexham 6 May 1932 (after a 1-1 draw on 5 May).
Although into the veteran stage when he joined Stanley, Joe Craven had an excellent first season, playing in 42 League games and five FA Cup ties. He began 1937-8 as senior pivot but in November, following a 5-1 home defeat by Gateshead, he was deposed by Jack Ash. Craven gave good value to all his clubs and enjoyed a spell of almost six years at Deepdale, after he had been given a free transfer by Stockport County. In the summer of 1929 he was a member of Preston's touring party to the USA and Canada. In a career which totalled over 200 Football League appearances, he scored only one goal, this on his debut for Preston North End.

CRAWLEY, Felix Patrick 'Frank' **1924-25**
Full-back. 5ft 10in; 12st 13lb.
Born: Paisley, 22 May 1894. Died: Detroit, USA, April 1945.
Debut v Rotherham County (h) 30 August 1924.
Appearances: 11.
Career: Croy Celtic; Kirkintilloch Rob Roy; Blackburn Rovers 28 October 1921; Lincoln City 15 September 1923; STANLEY 11 August 1924 to 12 January 1925; Toronto Bell Telephone 1926; Toronto Dunlops; coach to Detroit All Stars.
International honours: 3 caps for Canada in 1927, during tour of New Zealand.
Frank Crawley was brought into League football by Blackburn Rovers from Kikintilloch Rob Roy, one of the most productive Scottish nurseries. A versatile defender, usually seen at left-back, Crawley made 24 First Division appearances for the Rovers, scoring once. He spent the summer of 1922 in Canada and was later to return there, after spells with Lincoln City and Stanley. An obituary in April 1945 revealed that he had captained a Canadian touring team to New Zealand and he had also toured America. Of his brief stay with Stanley, the *Accrington Observer* commented: 'A little more pace would have greatly added to Crawley's value to the team'.

CRAWSHAW, A(aron) William **1921-23**
Wing-half. 5ft 9½in; 10st 10lb.
Born: Darwen, 11 August 1895.
Debut v Rochdale (a) 27 August 1921.
Appearances: 59.
Career: Royal Artillery (Topsham Barracks); Exeter City June 1919; STANLEY 17 June 1921; Exeter City 3 August 1923; Taunton United cs 1925, retired May 1927.
Billy Crawshaw's neat play and gentlemanly conduct made him a great Peel Park favourite. A steady and effective half-back, he was generally to be found in

the right place at the right moment. Popularly known as 'Spider' Crawshaw, probably due to his lightweight build, he had two spells with Exeter City. His second period with the Grecians being hampered by knee ligament damage. He settled in Exeter and later became a director of Exeter City FC.

CRAWSHAW, Raymond **1933-34**
Half-back. 6ft; 11st 3lb.
Born: Padiham, Lancashire, 1908 (July quarter).
Debut v Hartlepools United (a) 7 October 1933.
Appearances: 19.
Career: Great Harwood; Southport amateur July 1929; Great Harwood; Burnley 30 July 1931; Great Harwood season 1932-3; STANLEY 9 June 1933; Birmingham 12 April 1934 (fee £600); Bromsgrove Rovers 1935; Burton Town August 1936.
Ray Crawshaw joined Stanley as a wing-half but it was a centre-half that he made his mark. A whole-hearted player, his lack of polish was more than compensated for by his spirit and enthusiasm. His displays in the centre of Stanley's defence soon attracted the scouts, and it was First Division Birmingham who signed him, near to the end of the 1933-4 season. He found few opportunities at St Andrew's, making only four League appearances before moving into the Birmingham Combination with Bromsgrove Rovers.

CROCKFORD, Harold Arthur **1925**
Centre-forward. 5ft 10½in; 12st.
Born: Derby, 25 September 1893. Died: Tunbridge Wells, 15 December 1983.
Debut v Walsall (a) 29 August 1925 (scored two goals).
Appearances: 11; Goals: 5.
Career: Chatham; Fulham during wartime season 1917-18; Exeter City 23 May 1922; Port Vale 23 May 1923; Chesterfield 5 October 1923; Gillingham 6 March 1925; STANLEY 26 May 1925; Walsall 16 November 1925; Darlington 31 May 1926; Norwich City 13 May to June 1927; Bedford Town October 1928; Tunbridge Wells Rangers December 1929.

An energetic and hard-working centre-forward who did most of his shooting with his left foot, Crockford scored twice on his debut at Walsall. This was obviously noted by the Fellows Park directorate, for only a matter of weeks later Walsall signed him from Stanley. In the same season he led the Saddlers' goalscoring charts with 17 goals in 24 appearances, his total including two against his former teammates, when Walsall came to Peel Park in January 1926. In a career which spanned nine different Football League clubs, Crockford's career figures were 175 appearances, 85 goals. Later, he worked as a turf accountant at Stamford Bridge.

CUDDIHEY, Russell Francis **1960-62**
Half-back.
Born: Rawtenstall, Lancashire, 8 September 1939.
Debut v Rochdale (h) 29 October 1960.
Appearances: 10.
Career: Local amateur football to STANLEY, signing professional 15 September 1960 to March 1962, but continued to assist Stanley in season 1962-3, after they had resigned from the Football League.
In January 1963, Russell Cuddihey was reported to be the only one of the previous season's Football League players left at Peel Park, playing for the club in the Second Division of the Lancashire Combination. When he began with Stanley, they were in their first season of Fourth Division football. Cuddihey's introduction into the League side at left-half resulted in the team taking maximum points from each of his first three matches. When he made his debut against Rochdale he emulated the record of the Finney brothers, Jack and Bill, both of whom played senior football and cricket for their home-town team.

CULL, John Ernest **1934-35**
Outside-right. 5ft 7½in; 10st 10lb.
Born: Aston, Birmingham, 18 November 1900.
Debut v New Brighton (h) 25 August 1934.
Appearances: 38; Goals: 6.
Career: Shrewsbury Town; Stoke 18 September 1925 (fee £1,000); Coventry City 11 August 1931; Shrewsbury Town August 1932; Crewe Alexandra 10 August 1933; STANLEY 16 June 1934; Gateshead 23 July 1935; Aldershot 4 January to May 1936.
After six seasons with Stoke, Jack Cull embarked on a wandering path which took in six clubs in the course of the next five seasons. With Stoke he played in ten matches in season 1926-7, when the Potters won the championship of the Third Division North. A good season with Crewe Alexandra preceded his move to Stanley, where he began the season at outside-right. He later switched wings, following Joe Clare's transfer to Arsenal. Cull's 38 appearances for Stanley constituted his highest seasonal return in a League career which totalled 182 appearances and 32 goals.

CUMMINGS, Daniel **1922-23**
Inside-forward.
Debut v Wrexham (a) 28 October 1922.
Appearances: 1.
Career: STANLEY during season 1920-21, re-registering 8 September 1922 until 4 November 1922.
Some polished and artistic displays in Stanley's Reserve team, which included a hat-trick against Chorley in late September, brought Cummings into contention for a League outing. An injury delayed his senior debut, but having been 'rarely in the picture,' he was, nevertheless, selected to play against Chesterfield on the following Saturday, but failed to turn up and was suspended *sine die* by the club. He was still on Stanley's retained list in May 1923, but by this time he had emigrated to USA.

CURRAN, Andrew Eltringham **1927-31**
Centre-half. 5ft 10½in; 11st 5lb.
Born: Ryton-on-Tyne, 5 July 1898.
Debut v Ashington (h) 19 March 1927.
Appearances: 136; Goals: 5.
Career: Mickley FC; Sunderland 7 May 1920; Blackpool 10 May 1921; STANLEY 17 March 1927; Lytham August 1931 to 1934.
At the outset of his career Andy Curran, when a Sunderland reserve-team player, was selected as reserve

for the North-Eastern League v the Central League at Newcastle in January 1921. About a year later, by which time he had moved to Blackpool, the *Lancashire Daily Post Annual* described him as 'an industrious centre-half who is rapidly acquiring polish'. He spent almost six seasons at Bloomfield Road and had appeared in almost 100 Second Division matches when he joined Stanley. He proved a tower of strength at Peel Park, being keen, energetic, and an inspiring captain. A younger brother, Frank Curran (*qv*) was with Stanley in season 1937-8.

CURRAN, Frank **1936-38**
Inside-forward. 5ft 8½in; 10st 10lb.
Born: Ryton-on-Tyne, 31 May 1917.
Debut v Southport (h) 20 February 1936.
Appearances: 34; Goals: 14.
Career: Spen Black & White Juniors; Blaydon & District Boys; Washington Colliery; Southport 8 August 1935; STANLEY 18 February 1937 (in exchange for G.E.Pateman); Bristol Rovers 14 June 1938; Bristol City 17 May 1939; Southport, Everton & STANLEY (wartime guest player); Bristol Rovers 29 May 1946; Shrewsbury Town later in the same season; Tranmere Rovers 17 June 1947; Shrewsbury Town March 1948; Ashton United during season 1948-9; Hyde United 1950; Darwen cs 1952.
Frank Curran's League career was launched at Southport when he was only 18 years of age. He was from a famous footballing family, for aside from Andrew (*qv*), another brother played for Barnsley. A smart dribbler with an eye for an opening, he joined Stanley from Southport and two days later made his debut, against Southport. Curran's feelings can be imagined, as Stanley won 6-3. In his second appearance in Stanley's colours he scored two goals in a 3-2 win against Halifax Town. Frank Curran's career spanned World War Two and threw up an unusual statistic. When he joined Tranmere Rovers, the local Press noted that brother, Andrew, had been a Football League professional over a quarter of a century ago, when he signed for Sunderland in 1920.

CURRIE, John **1953-57**
Inside-forward. 5ft 8in; 10st 8lb.
Born: Motherwell, 19 March 1935.
Debut v Southport (a) 28 November 1953.
Appearances: 16; Goals: 3.
Career: Clelland Juniors; STANLEY 24 November 1953, retiring due to a knee injury in January 1957.
Jack Currie, recruited from a village club in Scotland, made his Football League debut as an 18-year-old. He scored twice against Halifax Town on Boxing Day 1953, on his fourth League appearance, and totalled 15 appearances in his first season. He also played for the Lancashire League team against the Intermediate League at Maine Road, Manchester, under floodlights on 9 December 1953. In the 1954-5 season, he played only once in the League, scoring the equalizing goal against fellow promotion contenders York City at Peel Park in April 1955. National Service call-up interrupted his career in February 1956 and less than a year later he was advised to quit the game because of an unusual knee condition. At 21 years of age, Currie applied for compensation and continued with his job as an electrician, on a full-time basis.

CUTHBERT, Westgarth **1937-38**
Full-back. 5ft 10in; 12st 4lb.
Born: Morpeth, 1913 (October quarter).
Debut v Rochdale (a) 25 December 1937.
Appearances: 6.
Career: South Elmsall; Rotherham United amateur 29 January, signing professional 21 March 1934; Hull City 23 May 1935; Carlisle United 11 July 1936; STANLEY 27 May 1937; Frickley Colliery July 1938; Grantham Town July 1939.
'Wes' Cuthbert was the first new player signed by Stanley's manager Jack Hacking for season 1937-8. He spent most of his season at Peel Park in the reserve team, making 33 Lancashire Combination appearances. He had a run of six matches in the League side at left-back in December-January, but lost his place after the team had conceded four goals in consecutive matches against Port Vale and Halifax Town. When he was signed by Hull City in May 1935, the local Press commented: 'Cuthbert is described as a defender of much promise. Possessed of plenty of dash, he knows how to act in a difficult situation and tackles with promptitude.' Cuthbert's father, also W.Cuthbert, was said to have been on the books of Newcastle United.

CUTTING, Jack Andrew **1948-50**
Inside-forward. 5ft 9in; 11st 10lb.
Born: Fleetwood, 15 April 1924.
Debut v Darlington (a) 21 August 1948.
Appearances: 23; Goals: 5.
Career: RAF football; Oldham Athletic amateur 13 June, signing professional 20 November 1946;

Fleetwood September 1947; STANLEY 24 June 1948 to 21 January 1950; Fleetwood 27 September 1950; Northwich Victoria; Winsford United.
A former RAF pilot officer, Jack Cutting was recommended to Oldham Athletic by one of their players who had been a teammate in Services football. He was largely in reserve at Boundary Park (four appearances, one goal) and left after one season to join Fleetwood, where he scored 18 goals in 38 appearances in season 1947-8. Easily spotted on the field due to his blond hair and all-action style, Cutting did not find his best form until late in the season, appearing in the final 13 fixtures, which yielded six wins and three draws. A bout of kidney trouble ended his first-class career but he was later able to resume in non-League football. In 1978 he was reported to be running his own photography business in Cleveleys.

DALE, F(rederick) William **1954**
Wing-forward. 5ft 7in; 10st 10lb.
Born: Balby near Doncaster, 26 October 1925.
Debut v Crewe Alexandra (h) 18 September 1954.
Appearances: 1.
Career: Elmfield House FC; Doncaster Rovers (trial); Frickley Colliery 1947-8; Denaby United; Scunthorpe United (Midland League) late season 1948-9; Halifax Town 22 August 1949; Southport 22 July 1952; STANLEY (two month's trial) 27 August 1954; Crewe Alexandra (trial) 5 October to 30 November 1954; Cheltenham Town later in season 1954-5; Denaby United; Retford 1955-6.
A lightweight winger, Billy Dale gave good service to both Halifax Town and Southport, before a broken leg intervened. This was sustained in training at Haigh Avenue in December 1953. He was signed by Stanley for a month's trial and, whilst this was subsequently extended by a further month, he did not win a permanent contract. A trial with Crewe Alexandra followed, and despite his scoring three goals in four appearances, he had gravitated to Southern League football by the end of the season. A great follower of the 'Health & Strength' movement, Billy Dale was a vegetarian whose hobbies included wieght-lifting and table tennis. In 1982 he was reported to be living in Sydney, New South Wales.

DANIELS, Douglas **1949-53**
Goalkeeper. 5ft 10½in; 12st.
Born: Salford, Lancashire, 21 August 1924.
Debut v Hartlepools United (a) 5 November 1949.
Appearances: 112.
Career: RAF football; Manchester City amateur (trial) 18 August 1945; New Brighton 26 August 1947; Chesterfield 29 July 1948 (In part exchange for T.K.Lyon); STANLEY 10 October 1949 to 12 May 1953.
A former RAF corporal drill-instructor, Doug Daniels took over from Bill Harris in Stanley's goal. He was immediately impressive, being unbeaten in his first two matches. Sound anticipation, clean handling and speed off his line combined to make Daniels a reliable last line of defence and he was a popular performer throughout his four-year stay at Peel Park. His League career began with New Brighton and when Chesterfield signed him, they gave a fee and a player in part-exchange.

DANIELS, John Francis G. **1938-39**
Goalkeeper. 5ft 10½in; 12st.
Born: Bramley, near Leeds, 1906 (October quarter).
Debut v Crewe Alexandra (a) 22 October 1938.
Appearances: 10.
Career: Stockport County amateur 25 August 1932; Manchester North End; Ashton National; Leeds United amateur 2 October 1933, signing professional 19 April 1934; Stockport County 14 June 1935; STANLEY 8 July 1938; Tranmere Rovers 9 June 1939; Leeds United (wartime guest).
A good all-round sportsman, Daniels spent his summers playing cricket in the High Peak League. He was a versatile footballer too, as he gave a more than competent display as a winger at Gateshead on 19 November 1938. This followed a hand injury during the game which necessitated his moving on to the wing. One correspondent noted that Daniels found little difficulty in avoiding his marker and he supplied several inviting centres. It was almost three months before he was able to reappear in goal and he did not feature regularly in the first team again. As a guest player for Leeds United during the war he made 121 appearances. A qualified FA coach, he was a sportsmaster at a school in Boston Spa, Yorkshire, in the 1950s.

D'ARCY, Arnold Joseph **1952-53**
Outside-left. 5ft 6in; 10st.
Born: Blackburn, 13 January 1933.
Debut v Southport (h) 1 December 1951.
Appearances: 39; Goals: 9.
Career: St Aidan's School (Blackburn); Mill Hill Rangers; St Matthew's (Blackburn and District Combination) cs 1951; STANLEY amateur, signing professional 15 March 1952; Wigan Athletic September 1953; Swindon Town 2 November 1956 to June 1964; Cheltenham Town.
One of the bright spots of season 1951-2 was the discovery of 18-year-old Arnold D'Arcy, who broke into League football only a matter of weeks after playing in Blackburn junior football. The pocket-sized outside left was a Blackburn painter and decorator's apprentice when he came to Peel Park. After three games in the 'A' team and three in the Reserves, he made his Football League debut and scored six goals in 12 appearances in his first season. On leaving Stanley he had a spell of non-League football but subsequently gave excellent service to Swindon Town, assisting them in season 1962-3 to promotion to Division Two as runners-up to Northampton Town. His figures with the Wiltshire club were 223 appearances and 29 goals. A younger brother, Gordon D'Arcy, was on the Peel Park staff in 1952-3 as a 16-year-old, but he did not graduate into League football.

DAVIS, Samuel Storey **1926**
Full-back. 5ft 9in; 11st.
Born: Whitburn Colliery, 25 May 1900.
Debut v Rochdale (h) 28 August 1926.
Appearances: 2.
Career: Marsden School; Whitburn; Stoke amateur 13 November 1923, signing professional 1 January 1924; Tranmere Rovers 26 May 1925; STANLEY 14 August to 29 September 1926.
Sam Davis was a member of the Marsden School XI which also featured three other youngsters who made

their mark in the game — Thompson (Workington), Wilson (South Shields and Blackpool) and Grimwood (Manchester United and Blackpool). A serious knee injury blighted Davis' career, after he had shown outstanding form as a junior. Only briefly at Peel Park, he appeared in the opening two fixtures of season 1926-7, but was reported as being 'shaky at times'. It took some time for Stanley's selectors to resolve the left-back position, which eventually fell to Tom Whittaker, who clocked up 131 consecutive appearances.

DEACON, Henry **1934-35**
Inside-forward. 5ft 9in; 10st 7lb.
Born: Sheffield, 25 April 1900. Died: Rotherham, 5 January 1946.
Debut v Chesterfield (h) 8 December 1934.
Appearances: 25; Goals: 11.
Career: Sheffield Schoolboys; Hallam FC; Birmingham 12 May 1920; Swansea Town 31 July 1922; Crewe Alexandra 21 August 1931; Southport 18 June 1934; STANLEY 3 December 1934; Rotherham United 1 June 1935 to May 1936.

Club honour: Swansea Town, Third Division South champions season 1924-5.
Representative honour: Welsh League v Free State League at Dalymount Park, Dublin, 2 May 1931.
In half a season with Stanley towards the end of his first-class career, Harry Deacon revealed clever constructive ability at inside-right. He made his first League appearance with Birmingham, but it was with Swansea that he forged his reputation, materially assisting the Swans to secure promotion to the Second Division in 1924-5. In his nine years with Swansea, Deacon proved a most consistent performer, totalling 318 Football League appearances and scoring 89 goals. His total career figures were 476 appearances and 151 goals.

DEVINE, William **1960-62**
Outside-left. 5ft 8in; 11st 6lb.
Born: Whitletts, Ayr, 22 August 1933.
Debut v Crystal Palace (a) 20 August 1960.
Appearances: 46; Goals: 6.
Career: St Mirren; Watford 7 March 1958 (fee £6,000); Partick Thistle 20 November 1959; STANLEY 23 May 1960; Cambridge City 16 March 1962.
Willie Devine's second appearance for Stanley came on his 27th birthday and the team won a good point from a visit to Millwall. Two days earlier, he had made his debut at Selhurst Park, where Stanley lost their first-ever Division Four match by 9-2. Despite the traumatic start, Devlin settled well and did not miss a single first-team match in his initial season at Peel Park. In the unfinished campaign of 1961-2 he had played in 20 matches, including the final fixture at Crewe Alexandra on 4 March 1962. His previous experience in English League football was with Watford in season 1957-8. Devine scored six goals in 30 matches in what was the final season of the Third Division South. Watford's final League position, 16th, was below the half-way mark and condemned them to Division Four, as founder-members.

DEVLIN, Joseph **1953-56 & 1962**
Outside-right. 5ft 6½in; 11st 1lb.
Born: Cleland, Lanarkshire, 12 March 1931.
Debut v Stockport County (h) 22 August 1953.
Appearances: 114; Goals: 18.
Career: Albion Rovers 1947; Falkirk 1950; STANLEY 23 July 1953; Rochdale 22 September 1956 (fee £2,000); Bradford 4 November 1957; Carlisle United 18 July 1959; Nelson cs 1960; Northwich Victoria; STANLEY 9 February to 16 March 1962; Northwich Victoria; Netherfield.
A strong, sturdy little winger with a powerful shot, Joe Devlin was one of a number of fellow Scots recruited by player-manager Galbraith, shortly after his appointment in the summer of 1953. Despite initially combining football with colliery work at Huncoat Pit, as part of his National Service, Devlin quickly won a reputation for the quality of his pace, accuracy and footcraft. He returned to Stanley just before the club was wound-up in 1962 and his career ended, after half a season with Netherfield, due to a knee injury. Joe Devlin is a self-employed electrical engineer in Accrington.

DEWSNAP, George Henry **1932-33**
Outside-right. 5ft 7in; 10st 7lb.
Born: Bolton, 13 December 1905. Died: Blackpool, 2 March 1974.
Debut v Wrexham (h) 17 December 1932.
Appearances: 18; Goals: 3.
Career: Rossendale United; Bacup Borough; Rhyl; Runcorn; STANLEY 11 June 1932; Rossendale United cs 1933.
Club honour: Rhyl, Welsh Cup runners-up v Cardiff City, season 1929-30.

George Dewsnap was something of a latecomer into League football, as he was 27 years old when he made his debut for Stanley. Less than 2,000 spectators witnessed his first appearance, on the last Saturday before Christmas 1932. The faithful few were rewarded as Stanley won an entertaining match 5-3. As the following two matches were won 6-0 and 5-4, Dewsnap was proving to be a lucky mascot and he remained first choice outside-right for the remainder of the season. During the close season he returned to Rossendale United, the club which had first introduced him into Lancashire Combination football.

DICK, P(eter) Watt **1955-58**
Inside-forward, later half-back. 5ft 10in; 11st 7lb.
Born: Newmains, Lanarkshire, 20 August 1927.
Debut v Gateshead (h) 20 August 1955.
Appearances: 125; Goals: 37.
Career: Third Lanark 1950; STANLEY 15 June 1955; Bradford 27 December 1958 (With Ray Byrom for a combined fee of £2,750) to June 1963.

In five seasons with Third Lanark, Wattie Dick was well amongst the goals, recording 84 which included 26 in only 28 appearances in season 1954-5. He quickly settled into English football and initially helped to take some of the onus of goalscoring off George Stewart's shoulders. A fine inside-left, he later became one of the most accomplished wing half-backs in the Northern Section, strong in both attack and defence. He was kept out of the team for over five months of season 1957-8 with a broken arm, but was back to form and fitness in the following season. In mid-term, former Stanley manager Walter Galbriath took him and Ray Byrom to Park Avenue. Dick made 44 appearances in season 1960-61, when Bradford won promotion to Division Three.

DODDS, Christopher **1926-28 & 1932-36**
Inside-forward or half-back. 5ft 9½in; 11st 9lb.

Born: Gateshead, 24 March 1904. Died: Gateshead, 24 June 1990.
Debut v Durham City (a) 27 December 1926.
Appearances: 157; Goals: 9.
Career: Greenfield Locomotive Athletic (Gateshead); Middlesbrough amateur 1 December 1925, signing professional 5 February 1926; STANLEY 23 July 1926; Sheffield Wednesday 24 October 1928 (fee £700); Colwyn Bay United August 1931; STANLEY 11 June 1932; Great Harwood September 1936.
Chris Dodds spent much of his first season at Peel Park in the Reserves. Normally at inside-forward, he exhibited neat footwork, excellent ball-control and scored 20 goals in the Combination. A move to wing-half in 1927-8 seemed to improve his overall game, and he won promotion to the first team midway through the season. A move to Sheffield Wednesday brought Stanley a welcome fee and six years later they were pleased to have him back. For three seasons he was a regular in Stanley's middle line, until his move to Great Harwood in 1936. In late season 1946-7 he was still playing, for Charter Street in the Accrington Combination, when past his 43rd birthday.

DOLAN, Andrew **1949-50**
Inside-forward. 5ft 7½in; 11st.
Born: Glasgow, 2 August 1920.
Debut v Wrexham (h) 26 December 1949.
Appearances: 19; Goals: 4.
Career: Raith Rovers; Bury 16 August 1948; STANLEY 15 September 1949; Albion Rovers 15 December 1950.
Andy Dolan was one of several former Bury players in Stanley's ranks during Jimmy Porter's period as manager at Peel Park. Dolan began with Raith Rovers and joined Stanley after a season at Gigg Lane, when he played in ten League matches and score two goals. First introduced into Stanley's League side on Boxing Day 1949, he was one of seven team changes made in the wake of a 6-0 defeat at Rotherham United on Christmas Eve. The reshuffle certainly had the desired effect, as the best spell of the season followed, seven

wins and four draws being obtained in a run of 12 consecutive fixtures. In ball-control and distribution, the sturdy little Scot left no room for complaint, but his finishing was less impressive.

DONE, Robert **1938**
Full-back. 5ft 9in; 11st 3lb.
Born: Runcorn, 27 April 1904. Died: Chester, September 1982.
Debut v Halifax Town (a) 27 August 1938.
Appearances: 6.
Career: Runcorn FC; Liverpool amateur 18 February, signing professional 13 April 1926; Reading 17 May 1935; Chester 14 June 1937; STANLEY 6 June 1938; Bangor City November 1938.
Stanley proved to be the end of the line for former railway worker Bob Done. He had appeared in nine seasons of First Division football with Liverpool, making 147 appearances and scoring nine goals, these coming mainly from the penalty-spot. He arrived at Peel Park for the last peacetime season and lost his place after appearing in half a dozen games which yielded one point. He left Stanley to join Bangor City and assisted them to the runners-up position for the Lancashire Combination championship.

DONNELLY, James **1922-24**
Full-back. 5ft 11in; 12st 6lb.
Born: Mayo, 18 December 1899.
Debut v Durham City (h) 30 September 1922.
Appearances: 54.
Career: Army football; Blackburn Rovers November 1919; STANLEY 18 May 1922; Southend United 19 May 1924; Brentford 14 August 1925; Thames Association July 1928 to May 1932; Grajanski (Yugoslavia); Gunes (Turkey).
An Irish full-back, initially recommended to Blackburn Rovers by one of their players, A.McGhie, who served with Donnelly in the Royal Artillery in France during World War One. After three seasons at Ewood, he joined Stanley on a free transfer. Only three months into his contract he asked for a transfer, but he remained at Peel Park and eventually established himself in the first team. A powerful and dashing back, his one drawback was said to be a tendency to get too far up the field with the ball. Obviously, overlapping full-backs were not appreciated in the 1920s! He dropped out of League football when he joined Thames Association, but stayed with them long enough to figure in their two seasons of League football, when they were known simply as 'Thames', the 'Association' having been dropped from their title.

DONNELLY, James **1951-52**
Wing-half or inside-forward. 5ft 6½in; 11st 2lb.
Born: Cork, 6 May 1919.
Debut v Halifax Town (h) 25 September 1951.
Appearances: 4; Goals: 1.
Career: Cork; Sligo Rovers; STANLEY 17 August 1951; released on a free transfer 2 May 1952.
International honour: Irish Amateur, 5 caps.
Jim Donnelly was employed as a foreman engineer at Huncoat Power Station. When Stanley's manager Walter Crook obtained his signature on the main building, he probably became the only Stanley player to have been signed 100 feet above the ground! A gifted amateur footballer and reserve for the League of Ireland team in 1946, he nevertheless failed to establish himself at senior level with Stanley. This despite a very promising start, when he scored on his second appearance, a 4-2 win against Wrexham.

DOOLEY, Thomas Edward **1938-39**
Half-back or inside-forward. 5ft 9in; 11st.
Born: Accrington, 15 December 1914. Died: Hyndburn, 25 April 1975.
Debut v Southport (h) 15 October 1938.
Appearances: 28; Goals: 2.
Career: Accrington Schoolboys; Bacup Borough; Blackpool 11 October 1934; Bacup Borough; STANLEY 9 June 1938 to September 1939; Rochdale (wartime guest) season 1942-3.
A product of local football who showed considerable promise when assisting Accrington Schoolboys. Dooley gained useful Central League experience during his Blackpool spell, after first coming into prominence with Bacup Borough. He was one of the few bright spots in a depressing season in 1938-9, being one of only six players to be retained. The outbreak of World War Two and subsequent call-up curtailed his League career, his final Stanley appearances coming in 1945-6, when he was on leave from India.

DUCKWORTH, Allan **1934-35**
Centre-forward. 5ft 10in; 11st 4lb.
Born: Darwen, 1914 (October quarter).
Debut v Barrow (a) 4 May 1935 (scored one goal).
Appearances: 1; Goals: 1.
Career: Darwen Juniors; STANLEY 21 November 1934, retiring due to knee injury October 1935.
A consistent goalscoring record in the Lancashire Combination gave young Allan Duckworth a merited promotion on the last day of season 1934-5. In scoring a vital goal, which saved Stanley from having to apply for re-election, he suffered a knee injury. Some four months later, his knee was not completely recovered and he had, in the meantime, badly dislocated a shoulder. The two set-backs combined, tragically ended his promising career.

DUFF, William Francis Andrew **1960-61**
Outside-left. 5ft 8in; 10st 7lb.
Born: Littleborough, Lancashire, 16 December 1938.
Debut v Rochdale (a) 29 October 1960.
Appearances: 14; Goals: 3.
Career: Rochdale amateur season 1955-6, signing professional 7 May 1956; Scunthorpe United 17 October 1958; Grimsby Town 13 October 1959; Toronto White Eagles (Canada) July 1960; STANLEY 20 October 1960; Runcorn July 1961; Stalybridge Celtic February 1962; Rossendale United 1963-4; Eastlands United (Johannesburg) May 1964.
Son of Joe Duff, Rochdale's long-serving wing-half, trainer and later groundsman. Billy Duff followed in his father's footsteps when he signed on as a professional with Rochdale when only 17 years of age. He did not graduate into League action at Spotland, or with Scunthorpe United, but made a scoring Football League debut with Grimsby Town in October 1959. His final League outing with the Mariners, later in the same season, was in a 4-2 victory against Stanley at Peel Park. Nine months later, and with a spell in Canada between, he was signed by Stanley's manager, Jimmy Harrower. Duff made a bright start, scoring

in his second match, a 4-1 win against Stockport County. He also did well in the season's FA Cup ties, his goal in the 1-1 draw at Deepdale in the third round brought the First Division side back to Peel Park. The replay proved to be a disappointment, however, as Preston North End won quite easily by 4-0.

DUFFUS, Robert Morrice Duncan **1923-24**
Half-back. 5ft 10in; 12st.
Born: Aberdeen, 28 February 1891. Died: Aberdeen, 19 March 1949.
Debut v Darlington (a) 25 August 1923.
Appearances: 29.
Career: Aberdeen; Dundee; Dumbarton (fee £50); Scunthorpe United July 1920; Millwall 15 May 1921 (fee £200); Clapton Orient 9 Septmeber 1922; STANLEY 28 July 1923; Bangor City player-manager August 1924.
A cool and calculating half-back whose studied play earned him the following Press verdict, shortly after his arrival at Peel Park: 'He distributes the ball as neatly and correctly as if there was nobody on the field to stop him'. Elder brother of J.M.Duffus, whose clubs included Clapton Orient, Tottenham Hotspur and Norwich City. Bob Duffus died suddenly in 1949, whilst he was watching a football match.

DULSON, Joseph **1933-34**
Inside-forward. 5ft 9in; 11st.
Born: Basford, Notts, 31 January 1913.
Debut v Southport (a) 29 August 1933.
Appearances: 11; Goals: 1.
Career: Newstead Colliery; STANLEY (trial); Nottingham Forest (amateur) 4 March 1932; STANLEY 15 August 1933 to cs 1934; Bournemouth and Boscombe Athletic (trial) August 1935.
A fractured ankle sustained in a reserve-team match against Rochdale in December 1933 brought a premature end to Joe Dulson's season at Peel Park. He had earlier seized his opportunity when first-team inside-left Fred Leedham was injured on the opening Saturday of the season. Dulson was flanked by veteran winger W.T.Watson (*qv*) and the blend of youth and experience assisted the team to an impressive start to the campaign. In Dulson's first five matches, three wins and two draws were obtained. After leaving Stanley, he had a trial with Bournemouth but was not signed on a regular basis. Rather surprisingly, Dulson's only other League outing with Nottingham Forest saw him score twice in a match against Swansea Town on 23 April 1932. Forest won 6-2 but did not give Dulson another chance at senior level.

DYSON, Geoffrey **1948-49**
Inside-forward. 5ft 6½in; 10st 10lb.
Born: Huddersfield, 16 March 1923.
Debut v Stockport County (a) 17 January 1948.
Appearances: 20; Goals: 1.
Career: Junior football to Huddersfield Town 12 March 1946; Bradford City 12 June 1947; STANLEY 17 January 1948 to May 1949.
A hard-working inside-forward with a keen sense of duty in both defence and attack. Geoff Dyson was a mid-season signing in 1947-8 and, whilst he held the inside-right berth to the season's close, the Stanley attack in general had lacked thrust. Their final placing of sixth in the table was achieved by a much improved defensive performance. Close-season recruiting was mainly concentrated on the signing of new forwards and Dyson was restricted to only two first-team appearances in his final season. In August 1949 he was reported to have set up in business as a painter and decorator in Huddersfield. It was thought unlikely that he would resume in football.

EASTHAM, Henry **1953-55**
Inside-forward. 5ft 9in; 11st 6lb.
Born: Blackpool, 30 June 1917.
Debut v Stockport County (h) 22 August 1953.
Appearances: 42; Goals: 3.
Career: Blackpool amateur 23 September 1933, signing professional 4 July 1934; Liverpool 29 February 1936; Southport, New Brighton, Brighton & Hove Albion, Bolton Wanderers, Leeds United, Newcastle United and Blackpool (wartime guest); Tranmere Rovers 19 May 1948; STANLEY 20 July 1953; Netherfield cs 1955; Rolls-Royce FC (Lancashire Combination).
Club honour: Liverpool, Football League Champions season 1946-7.
Harry Eastham did an excellent job in two seasons at Peel Park. In 1953-4 he ran the midfield area in the first team and in 1954-5 guided the Reserves to a Lancashire Combination League and Cup 'double'. Never a free scorer but a craftsman who impressed by his skill on the ball, Eastham was a professional with Blackpool at 17 years of age. He assisted Liverpool at either side of World War Two and made 19 appearances in 1946-7 when the League Championship came to Anfield. He played in 154 League matches for Tranmere Rovers in a five-year spell, prior to joining Stanley. Brother to George R.Eastham, briefly Stanley's manager in 1958-9 (see *Accrington Stanley's Managers*), and uncle to George E.Eastham, the English international inside-forward who took the football 'establishment' to court over the retain-and-transfer system. After retiring from football, Harry Eastham became a Bolton licensee.

EASTWOOD, Raymond **1944-46**
Full-back. 5ft 11in; 11st 12lb.
Born: Moston, Manchester, 1 January 1913.
Debut v Bradford City (a) 31 August 1946.
Appearances: 3.
Career: Bacup Borough; Oldham Athletic 7 May 1935; Altrincham cs 1936; Aldershot 25 June 1938; STANLEY 20 July 1946 (after wartime guest appearances from December 1944); Nelson 21 September 1946.
After trials at Boundary Park in the closing stages of the 1934-5 season, Ray Eastwood was signed by Oldham Athletic for their first season in the Third Division North. He spent a season in the Latics' reserve team and then drifted back into non-League football. Aldershot took him south in 1938 and in the final season before World War Two he made his Football League debut. He joined Stanley after initially appearing as a wartime guest player, but his stay was brief. He left Peel Park two months after signing, having lost his first-team place after appearing in the first three fixtures of season 1946-7. Ironically, his final Football League appearance was against Oldham Athletic, the club where his professional career had begun, 11 years earlier.

EDDLESTON, Joseph **1932-33**
Inside-forward. 5ft 6½in; 10st 6lb.
Born: Oswaldtwistle, Lancashire, 29 December 1896.
Debut v Halifax Town (h) 27 August 1932 (scored one goal).
Appearances: 40; Goals: 12.
Career: St Mary's RC (Oswaldtwistle); Blackburn Rovers May 1919; Nelson April 1921; Swindon Town 17 August 1926; STANLEY 4 July 1932; Fleetwood 11 August 1933.
Club honour: Nelson, Third Division North champions season 1922-3.

An experienced utility forward, Joe Eddleston was a prolific goalscorer for Nelson, leading their scoring charts for five consecutive seasons, accumulating 99 goals in 183 appearances. A product of St Mary's RC, the outstanding Oswaldtwistle junior club who, over the years, supplied several players to Stanley. Eddleston began with Blackburn Rovers but blossomed with Nelson. He spent six seasons with Swindon Town (203 appearances, 64 goals) and ended his first-class career with a season at Peel Park. During this campaign he recorded his 400th Football League appearance.

EDWARDS, Reginald Charles **1946-49**
Outside-left. 5ft 6in; 10st.
Born: Newton-le-Willows, 24 July 1919.
Debut v Bradford City (a) 31 August 1946.
Appearances: 66; Goals: 10.
Career: Alloa Athletic; Luton Town amateur 21 August, signing professional 27 November 1945; STANLEY 3 August 1946 (fee £500) to May 1949.

An elusive and resourceful little winger with a deceptive body-swerve who impressed in partnership with Walter Keeley (*qv*) in the first peacetime season. Reg Edwards first turned professional with Luton Town, who were keen to retain him after the war, but he preferred a club nearer to his home. Stanley transfer-listed him in May 1948, but two months into the new season they re-signed him, after three different outside-lefts had failed to impress. Edwards linked up again with his old inside partner, Walter Keeley, who Stanley had re-signed from Port Vale. After retiring from the game, Edwards had a guest house in Llandudno.

EGAN, John **1960-61**
Outside-right.
Born: Kilsyth, Stirling, 19 August 1937.
Debut v Chester (h) 10 September 1960.
Appearances: 1.
Career: Stenhousemuir; Halifax Town 24 November 1959; STANLEY (trial) 19 August 1960; Nelson 27 September 1960.
In Stanley's official match programme for the 24 September 1960 visit of Oldham Athletic, the editor commented that John Egan had been one of three reserve-team players who had 'stood in' for the injured Lawson Bennett in successive games, earlier in the month. The *Accrington Observer* noted that Egan had 'never settled' on his debut and in the same month he left Peel Park. In joining Nelson, he linked up with two other former Stanley players, Bert Scott and Joe Devlin.

EGERTON, Frank **1947-48**
Half-back. 5ft 8½in; 10st 12lb.
Born: Atherton, 5 April 1926.
Debut v Mansfield Town (a) 15 November 1947.
Appearances: 8.
Career: Atherton Colliery; Blackburn Rovers amateur

17 April 1944; STANLEY 21 June 1947 to May 1948.
Frank Egerton began in wartime football with Blackburn Rovers, making his debut in the final fixture of season 1943-4. In the following two terms he played in 55 matches, generally in the wing half-back position. When normal League football resumed he did not feature at senior level with the Rovers. His Football League debut came with Stanley in the relatively unaccustomed role of full-back. Few opportunities came his way, however, in his normal position, as the team's middle line of Rothwell, Briggs and Webster was very well established.

ENTWISTLE, Robert Peter **1960-61**
Wing-forward.
Born: Bury, 6 October 1938.
Debut v Aldershot (a) 1 October 1960.
Appearances: 2.
Career: Macclesfield Town; Rochdale amateur 7 February 1959; STANLEY September 1960; Llandudno; Hartlepools United 17 October 1964; Chesterfield (trial) 3 August to 2 October 1965.
In two consecutive League matches, Bob Entwistle appeared at outside-right and outside-left, winning an early promotion after scoring twice on his debut for the Reserves against Bradford Reserves. During the 1960-61 season, manager Harrower's permutations featured seven different outside-rights and five outside-lefts, so Entwistle was not alone in experiencing a sojourn on Stanley's wing. In a League career of modest proportions, all but three of his Football League appearances were made with Hartlepools United in the 1964-5 season, when he played in 14 games and scored three goals.

ENTWISTLE, William **1923-25**
Half-back. 5ft 6½in; 11st 6lb.
Born: Leeds, 21 March (year unknown).
Debut v Southport (h) 24 March 1923.
Appearances: 29; Goals: 2.
Career: West Riding Amateurs; STANLEY amateur 17 January 1923, signing professional 15 May 1923 to June 1925.
One of three players signed on amateur forms after they had appeared for West Riding Amateurs v Staffordshire Amateurs on 13 January 1923. Entwistle was the only one of the three to graduate to professional status, joining the paid ranks at the close of his first season at Peel Park. Following one of his early appearances in Stanley's colours, the *Accrington Observer* commented: 'He is sturdy and watchful, showed good discrimination in tackling and, best of all, pushed the ball along the ground to his forwards'.

FARRELL, Francis **1932-33**
Centre-half. 5ft 10in; 13st.
Born: Salford, Lancashire, 1908.
Debut v Barnsley (a) 29 October 1932.
Appearances: 2.
Career: Mossley FC; Aston Villa 10 May 1930; Sunderland February 1931; Mossley FC; STANLEY 3 June 1932; Altrincham June 1933; Northwich Victoria May 1934.
A solid, sturdy centre-half with a powerful kick and with 13st to throw usefully into the tussle, Frank Farrell's Football League experience was limited to his two appearances with Stanley. His season at Peel Park was spent as understudy to senior pivot, Ron Viner. According to Press reports on his two senior outings, Farrell's form fluctuated to a marked degree. Of his debut, the *Accrington Observer* noted: 'He tackled effectively and was not lacking in resourcefulness and anticipation'. One week later, the same correspondent noted that Farrell was 'ineffective and the weak link in the chain'.

FARRELL, John **1954-55**
Outside-left. 5ft 9½in; 11st.
Born: Clunie, Perth, 22 June 1933
Debut v Barrow (a) 28 August 1954.
Appearances: 2.
Career: Perth Celtic; STANLEY 20 August 1954 (fee £100), released on a free transfer May 1955.
A part-time professional and apprentice electrician at a local colliery, Jackie Farrell scored two goals in an impressive debut for Stanley Reserves. Immediately promoted into League action, he featured in consecutive wins, at Barrow and at home against Carlisle United. He then lost his place, never to reappear, as the outside-left spot was taken over by new signing Bob Scott (*qv*), who was an immediate success.

FARRINGTON, Robert **1922**
Outside-right. 5ft 8½in; 10st 5lb.
Born: Radcliffe, Lancashire, 1902 (January quarter).
Debut v Grimsby Town (h) 22 April 1922.
Appearances: 1.
Career: Little Lever; STANLEY amateur 22 April 1922; Bolton Wanderers 25 May 1922 to June 1923.
An amateur winger who, despite appearing in the unacustomed position of inside-right, managed to create a favourable impression. He showed good ball-control, skill in avoiding opponents and good constructive ideas. About a month following his debut at Peel Park, Bolton Wanderers signed him as a professional but he did not appear at senior level during his season at Burnden Park.

FERGUSON, A(rchibald) Daniel **1929-32**
Inside-forward, later half-back. 5ft 8in; 11st 2lb.
Born: Flint, 25 January (year unknown).
Debut v Doncaster Rovers (a) 31 August 1929.
Appearances: 113; Goals: 12.
Career: Rhyl Athletic; Manchester United amateur 22, signing professional 29 March 1926; Reading 17 March 1928; STANLEY 11 June 1929; Chester 14 March 1932; Halifax Town 3 July 1933; Stockport County July 1935; Macclesfield July 1936.
Danny Ferguson had no more than half a dozen Football League outings to his credit when he joined Stanley, but he proved ideally suited to Northern Section football. The most wholehearted player on the club's books, Ferguson did not pretend to possess polish, but he was worth his place in the side, if only for his untiring vigour. In just short of three seasons with Stanley he missed just two first team matches. In season 1934-5, he assisted Halifax Town to the runners-up position in the Third Division North. He was later a Macclesfield landlord and lived at Connah's Quay in retirement.

FERGUSON, Charles **1954-55**
Full-back or centre-half. 5ft 11in; 11st 10lb.
Born: Glasgow, 22 April 1930.

Debut v Southport (h) 21 August 1954.
Appearances: 1.
Career: Glasgow YMCA; Heart of Midlothian 1948; Hamilton Academical cs 1953; STANLEY 19 May 1954; Rochdale 19 September 1955 (fee £500); Oldham Athletic 8 July 1959; Rossendale United player-coach August 1961.
Charlie Ferguson began season 1954-5 as Stanley's first-team right-back, but immediately lost his place to Ken Holliday. In the Lancashire Combination side he was developed into a strong, two-footed centre-half and he led the Reserves to a League and Cup 'double'. As understudy to John Ryden for the senior centre-half berth there seemed little prospect of advancement, and Ferguson asked for a transfer at the end of the season. he moved to Rochdale, who also took Stanley's goalkeeper, Jimmy Jones (*qv*), to stiffen a leaky defence. Both players gave excellent service at Spotland, Ferguson recording 150 appearances before making the short journey to Oldham Athletic in July 1959. At Boundary Park, he missed only one match in 1959-60, but lost his place in the following season after playing in the first 12 League matches.

FERGUSON, Michael K. 1960-62
Inside-forward. 5ft 10in; 11st 2lb.
Born: Burnley, 9 March 1943.
Debut v Gillingham (h) 12 September 1960.
Appearances: 23; Goals: 1.
Career: Burnley Schools; Plymouth Argyle amateur 16 March 1959; STANLEY 4 July 1960; Blackburn Rovers 15 March 1962 (fee £2,500); Aston Villa May 1968 (fee £50,000); Queen's Park Rangers November 1969 (fee £15,000); Cambridge United July 1973; Rochdale July 1974; IA Akranes (Iceland) 1975-6; Halifax Town December 1976; briefly Rochdale's manager in the early months of season 1977-8. Subsequently held coaching appointments world-wide, but particularly in the Middle East. Was briefly manager of Enfield in the early weeks of season 1989-90.
Signed by Stanley as a 17-year-old, Mike Ferguson had previous experience as an amateur with Plymouth Argyle. He had also represented the FA Youth team, played in the FA Youth Cup for Plymouth and played for the Devon FA at Youth level. A move back to his native parts saw him a Football League debutant with Stanley at 17 years and 187 days old, the youngest since Harvey McCreadie (*qv*). Despite operating in a poor side, Ferguson's raw talent was immediately apparent. He appeared 23 times in the League team in 1960-61 and in the following, unfinished season, he scored Stanley's last goal in a League match, a point later nullified when the League expunged the season's record. Ferguson's professional career took in seven League clubs, he appeared in every Division, and his aggregate career figures were 458 appearances, 42 goals.

FIELD, Richard 1925-27
Half-back. 5ft 10in; 12st 7lb.
Born: Sunderland, 2 August 1891. Died: Sunderland, 15 July 1963.
Debut v Walsall (a) 29 August 1925.
Appearances: 52; Goals: 1.
Career: Lambton Stars; Sunderland (Victory League); Willington FC; Barry FC; Aberdare Athletic 8 December 1923; Norwich City 2 June 1923; Grimsby Town 16 May 1924; STANLEY 20 June 1925; Boston Town July 1927.
Club honour: Aberdare Athletic, Welsh Cup runners-up v Cardiff City 3 May 1923.
Ever-present in season 1925-6, Dick Field lost out in the following term when only victory in the first seven League matches brought radical team changes. A sturdily-built player with sandy hair, Field renewed acquaintance with two former Willington teammates at Peel Park, Billy Rooks and Joe Kasher. During Stanley's FA Cup run in 1925-6, Field was involved in the incident which led to the sending-off of Ted Vizard, in the third-round tie at Burnden Park. Bolton's famous inside-right, without a stain on his soccer character during 16 years in the game, was later completely exonerated by the FA. Vizard's actions were ruled to 'constitute a legitimate attempt to free himself from Field's grasp'. The Wanderers player had 'handed-off' Field, who immediately buried his face in his hands and bent double. As Stanley players rushed to his assistance, referee Mr Watson, after consulting with a linesman, ordered Vizard off the field.

FIELDSEND, George Henry 1934-36
Full-back. 5ft 9in; 11st 7lb.
Born: Ecclesall Bierley, Sheffield, 1908 (January quarter).
Debut v New Brighton (h) 25 August 1934.
Appearances: 57.
Career: Chorley; Burnley 8 December 1933; STANLEY 18 July 1934; Rotherham United 11 June 1936; Scarborough Town cs 1937 to 1939.
Apart from a solitary outing with Rotherham United, all of George Fieldsend's League experience was gained with Stanley. Tenacity and determination were the chief characteristics of his play and he was unfortunate to lose his place in February 1926. This followed a severe bout of tonsilitis, which let in veteran deputy Teddy Ivill, thus ending Fieldsend's run of 28 consecutive appearances.

FINN, John 1930-32
Full-back.
Born: Accrington, 18 April 1907. Died: Accrington, 29 January 1984.
Debut v Hartlepools United (a) 21 February 1931.
Appearances: 5.
Career: St Anne's FC (A local junior team): STANLEY amateur 24 December 1930, signing professional 10 August 1931 to 15 February 1932; Barnoldswick Town 1932-34; Rossendale United 1934-5.
First spotted when playing in an end of season Medal Competition for junior teams at Peel Park, Jack Finn eventually progressed to become a professional with Stanley. As a full-back, he was unfortunate to be on the books at the same time as Jimmy Armstrong, Tom Whittaker and Norman Price, a seasoned trio of defenders who, between them, totalled 569 appearances for Stanley. Finn made his Football League debut as an amateur and gave a creditable performance, despite having the misfortune to concede a penalty in a game which was drawn 3-3.

FINNIGAN, Richard Prytherch 1927-28
Goalkeeper. 6ft; 11st 4lb.
Born: Wrexham, 16 May 1904. Died: Halton, 1979 (October quarter).

Debut v Nelson (a) 27 August 1927.
Appearances: 42.
Career: Oswestry; Holyhead Town; Connah's Quay & Shotton; Wrexham August 1922; Holyhead Town September 1924; Connah's Quay & Shotton August 1925; Manchester City 4 May 1926; STANLEY 23 May 1927; Connah's Quay 5 September 1928; Wrexham 30 May 1929; Colwyn Bay United August 1932; Chester 17 February 1933; Stockport County 17 March 1934 to June 1935; Winsford United 1936.
Kept out of Manchester City's team by fellow Welshman, international goalkeeper Albert Gray, Finnigan was able to hold off the challenge of the emerging Alf Tootill in recording 40 appearances for Stanley in 1927-8. Operating behind Armstrong and Whittaker in the last line of the Reds' defence, Finnigan had an excellent season as Stanley improved beyond measure to finish ninth in the table. Season 1928-9 had hardly commenced, however, when his contract was cancelled following a clash with a Stanley director. This occured on the return journey from the game at Rotherham on Saturday, 1 September 1928.

FITTON, Frederick **1932-33**
Inside-forward. 5ft 11in; 10st 7lb.
Born: Bury.
Debut v Halifax Town (h) 27 August 1932 (scored one goal).
Appearances: 45; Goals: 24.
Career: Adlington; Bolton Wanderers (trial); Darwen; Stoke (trial) 26 August 1927; Adlington September 1927; Burnley 9 May 1928; Oldham Athletic June 1930; Southend United 5 November 1931 (fee £150); STANLEY 30 July 1932; Rochdale 11 November 1933; Nelson August 1934; Runcorn.
In November 1933 the *Lancashire Daily Post* noted that Fred Fitton 'distributed well and kept the line well together'. He had also proved to be a dangerous man in the penalty area in 1932-3, when he headed Stanley's scoring lists with 24 League goals. He scored five in his first four appearances, helping Stanley to what was then their best-ever start to a Northern Section campaign. Formerly employed in a Bury boot and shoe factory, Fitton proved to be a regular marksman throughout his career. In season 1938-9 he was with Runcorn, champions of the Cheshire County League, and one of the 'surprise packets' of the season's FA Cup competition. They fought through to the third round, where they won high praise in defeat, by 4-2, against the Cup holders, Preston North End.

FLETCHER, Jack **1930**
Outside-right. 5ft 8in; 11st 7lb.
Born: Burnley, 1909.
Debut v Hull City (h) 1 November 1930.
Appearances: 1.
Career: Nelson amateur 29 October 1927, re-registering, again on amateur forms, 14 May 1929; STANLEY amateur 30 October 1930 Burnley amateur 7 February 1932; Fleetwood season 1933-4.
Jack Fletcher's initial trial in Stanley's reserve team against Darwen on 18 October 1930 prompted the *Accrington Observer* to comment that the newcomer was 'clever and tricky and altogether gave promise of being something of a find'. His Football League debut came within a matter of weeks, when he was a late deputy for Alf Agar at outside-right in the 3-1 home defeat by Hull City. It was Stanley's fifth consecutive League defeat and one is left to assume that Jack Fletcher had a quiet debut, as he was not mentioned at all in the *Accrington Observer's* report of the match!

FLOYD, Peter **1922-24**
Goalkeeper. 6ft 1in; 12st 10lb.
Born: Burnley, 8 July 1899.
Debut v Grimsby Town (a) 15 April 1922.
Appearances: 34.
Career: Huncoat Baptists FC; STANLEY amateur 18 April, signing professional 25 April 1921; Clitheroe cs 1925; Lancaster Town 1926-28; Oldham Athletic 8 May 1928; Lancaster Town cs 1929 retiring later in the same year.
A local collier, Peter Floyd had all the necessary physical attributes for a goalkeeper. Nevertheless, he made an uncertain start and some credit was due to Stanley's selection committee who continued to persevere with him. Floyd was to replay their persistance by developing into a sound and dependable custodian. He appeared on the score-sheet in a reserve-team match against Atherton in Sepember 1923. Entrusted with a penalty-kick, he began his run-up in his own goalmouth. His resultant and rather tame shot, deceived both spectators and the Atherton goalkeeper, who dived the wrong way. In a season with Oldham Athletic, he was understudy to England's current goalkeeper, Jack Hacking (*qv*), later to play for and manage Stanley. Floyd was a miner at Calder and Huncoat Collieries for 50 years.

FORREST, James **1951-52**
Inside-forward. 6ft 1in; 12st 2lb.
Born: Dalkeith, 14 November 1929.
Debut v Chester (h) 3 November 1951.
Appearances: 5; Goals: 2.
Career: Carricean Hearts; Winchburgh Albion; RAF football; Musselburgh Athletic; Leeds United 28 November 1950; STANLEY 1 November 1951 to May 1952 when he retired to join Edinburgh City Police.
Jimmy Forrest was signed by Stanley in an effort to add strength to the attack. He had joined Leeds United as a junior about a year earlier and had appeared in more than 30 Central League games. He had a quiet debut against Chester, who were defeated 4-2, but then scored two goals at Lincoln City a week later. After four matches, which had yielded five points and eight goals, he was rather surprisingly deposed. He made only one more senior appearance, in a 1-0 win at York City. In a season when Stanley lost over half of their fixtures, Forrest did not appear in a losing side. On leaving Stanley he returned to Scotland and in 1953 represented the Scottish Police against the English Police at Preston. He retired with the rank of inspector in 1978 and took over the Anchor Tavern in Bo'ness, where he remains today. His former father-in-law was Chris Dodds (*qv*), a pre-war Stanley footballer.

FORRESTER, George Hogg **1960-62**
Full-back. 6ft; 12st 7lb.
Born: Glasgow, 28 August 1934.
Debut v Bury (a) 19 March 1960.
Appearances: 54.
Career: Raith Rovers; Sunderland 2 March 1953 to 30 June 1954; Eyemouth United; STANLEY 16 March 1960; Sankey's (Wellington) 23 March 1962; Maccles-

field Town 1968-9.
George Forrester's transfer beat the 'deadline' by a matter of hours and it came after his previous club, Eyemouth United, a Scottish non-League side, had been knocked out of the fourth round of the Scottish Cup by Kilmarnock. Stanley's defence was in need of bolstering, as their record of 93 goals against in 35 matches was, at that time, the worst in the Football League. An ideally-built defender who was resourceful in the tackle and a loyal wholehearted performer, Forrester was ever-present in season 1960-61 and had not missed a game in the abandoned season 1961-2, a run of 87 consecutive League and Cup appearances.

FOSTER, Joseph **1921-23**
Half-back. 5ft 7in; 10st 5lb.
Born: Church, Lancashire.
Debut v Ashington (h) 27 December 1921.
Appearances: 6.
Career: Local junior football to STANLEY prior to League entry, re-registering in August 1921; Great Harwood March 1923; Barnoldswick Town 1924-5.
As understudy to Jack Burkinshaw for the left-half berth in Stanley's first season in the Third Division North, Joe Foster found little opportunity. A September 1924 match report gave a clue as to Foster's lack of success in League circles. Playing for Barnoldswick Town in a Lancashire Combination fixture against Stanley Reserves, his display brought the following comment from the local correspondent: 'Foster played just the same neat football as when he was tried by Stanley, but he has not increased his pace'.

FOSTER, Robert **1932**
Goalkeeper. 5ft 11in; 12st.
Born: Dean, near Bolton, 1911 (April quarter).
Debut v Doncaster Rovers (a) 16 January 1932.
Appearances: 11.
Career: Farnworth Standard; STANLEY amateur 6 January 1932; Southampton 24 June 1932; Wrexham 9 June 1933; Bury 23 August 1935; Oldham Athletic 15 September 1936; Mossley season 1937-8.
Bob Foster first appeared in Stanley's goal as deputy for Jack Bell, after the senior goalkeeper had been suspended following his sending-off at Halifax in December 1931. When Bell left to join Bradford in March 1932, Foster took over for the remainder of the season. Despite his association with five different Football League clubs, Foster's career total was a relatively modest 62 appearances. His best season in League football was in 1933-4, when he appeared in 29 matches for Wrexham. During his spell with Oldham Athletic, he also ran a newsagency business in the Bolton district.

GALBRAITH, Walter McMurray **1953-54**
Left-back. 5ft 10½in; 11st 8lb.
Born: Glasgow, 26 May 1918.
Debut v Stockport County (h) 22 August 1953.
Appearances: 21.
Career: Strath Bungo School; Strathclyde Juniors; Clyde FC 1939; Queen's Park 1941; Clyde FC 1946; New Brighton 15 September 1948 (fee approx £1,000); appointed player-manager 19 June 1950; Grimsby Town 29 August 1951 (fee £660); STANLEY player-manager 30 June 1953, retiring as a player May 1954; Bradford manager 7 November 1958; Tranmere Rovers manager 7 January 1961; Hibernian manager 25 November 1961; Stockport County chief scout July 1968, appointed manager August 1969 to April 1970.
Whilst Walter Galbraith is probably best remembered for his long and successful career in football management, he was also a very fine player with over 200 Football League appearances to his credit. His career began when he joined his father's old team, Strathclyde Juniors. With both Clyde and Queen's Park he was a Glasgow Cup winner. He made 109 appearances for New Brighton, captaining the Rakers in 1949-50 and being appointed player-manager for season 1950-51. When New Brighton failed to gain re-election in the summer of 1951, he signed for Grimsby Town as a player and made 77 appearances in two seasons. He was then appointed Stanley's player-manager in succession to Walter Crook, but stepped down as a player after 21 appearancs. He formally announced his retirement as a player in May 1954, in order to concentrate his efforts on management (see *Accrington Stanley's Managers*).

GARBUTT, Henry Penty **1931-32**
Inside-forward. 5ft 10in; 10st 10lb.
Born: Pontefract, Yorkshire, 12 November 1907.
Debut v Halifax Town (a) 14 November 1931.
Appearances: 12; Goals: 7.
Career: Castleford Town; Tottenham Hotspur 18 March 1927; Clapton Orient 11 June 1930; STANLEY 4 September 1931, released on a free transfer May 1932.
Harry Garbutt began with Spurs as a 19-year-old, but he did not graduate into League action at White Hart

Lane. His Football League debut was made with Clapton Orient and this came on the occasion of Orient's first-ever home game on their new ground at Lea Bridge Road. In his season at Peel Park, Garbutt had appeared only four times in the first team by mid-March, when he then had a run of eight consecutive matches at the end of the campaign. His final return of seven goals in only a dozen appearances suggested that he had something to offer, but he was not retained, being one of six players to be given a free transfer in the close season.

GARRITY, Kenneth **1956-60**
Inside-forward. 5ft 11in; 11st 10lb.
Born: Blackburn, 6 August 1935
Debut v Rochdale (a) 8 November 1958.
Appearances: 37; Goals: 5.
Career: Local junior football; STANLEY 4 February 1956 to June 1960; Chorley; Darwen 1962-64.
Ken Garrity had some time to wait for his Football League debut after signing as a part-time professional when 20 years of age. A go-ahead forward who packed a strong shot, he was the most consistent marksman in the reserve team in 1957-8, when he was also given his first run-out with the first team, in a Lancashire Senior Cup tie against Preston North End. His first League action came in the following season and in an early appearance he scored in Stanley's 'coupon-busting' 4-2 victory at Home Park in March 1959 against the eventual champions, Plymouth Argyle. Under new manager Harold Bodle in 1959-60, Garrity's first two appearances of the season were made in both full-back berths. Later he appeared in all three inside-forward positions. He was not retained at the end of a season which saw Stanley relegated from Division Three after finishing bottom of the table with only 27 points and a goal difference of 57-123.

GASTALL, John William Holden **1938-39**
Centre-forward. 5ft 8½in; 11st 7lb.
Born: Oswaldtwistle, 25 May 1913.
Debut v Oldham Athletic (a) 5 September 1938.
Appearances: 8; Goals: 2.
Career: Accrington Grammar School; Blackburn Rovers amateur 30 August 1930; Burscough Rangers; St Luke's College; Darwen; Oldham Athletic (trial) 24 August to 6 November 1934; Bacup Borough; Aston Villa (trial); Burnley 12 May 1936; STANLEY 26 May 1938; Rochdale 28 January 1939 (in exchange for G.W.Mee) to June 1939.
John Gastall's duties as a Bacup schoolmaster prevented him from accepting a contract with Aston Villa. Strangely enough, when he made his Football League debut with Burnley, the opponents were the Villa and Gastall scored within four minutes of the kick-off. A prolific goalscorer for Bacup Borough, his 41 goals in 1935-6 paved the way for his move to Turf Moor. He spent little time at Peel Park, moving to Rochdale after eight months in an exchange transfer which brought verteran winger George Mee back to Stanley for a second spell.

GEE, James **1922-23 & 1924-27**
Inside-forward. 5ft 6½in; 10st 12lb.
Born: Wigan, 30 September 1898.
Debut v Chesterfield (a) 6 September 1924.
Appearances: 86; Goals: 35.
Career: Kirk Bobbin Works (Oswaldtwistle and District Amateur Football League); Blackburn Rovers amateur 13 May 1922; STANLEY amateur December 1922; Blackburn Rovers January 1923; STANLEY as professional 9 August 1924; Clitheroe cs 1927; Rossendale United.
Controversy surrounded Jimmy Gee's first spell at Peel Park. A hard-shooting inside-forward with brainy methods, he was discovered playing in the local Medal Competitions which Stanley used to run. In the month of his signing amateur forms, Gee scored four goals for Stanley Reserves against Leyland Motors and five against Chorley Motors on Christmas Day. At about this point it transpired that Blackburn Rovers had an option on his services. In view of his success at Peel Park, the Rovers were anxious to reclaim him. The position was put before the Football League in January 1923 and Stanley were fined £5 and Gee returned to Ewood Park. He eventually returned, as a professional and became a great favourite, occupying the inside-right berth with flair, dash and a dangerous shot from all angles.

GIBSON, Ian Stewart **1958-59**
Inside-forward. 5ft 7in; 10st 4lb.
Born: Newton Stewart, 30 March 1943.
Debut v Norwich City (h) 23 March 1959.
Appearances: 9; Goals: 3.
Career: Stranraer; STANLEY amateur 2 July 1958; Bradford amateur 24 July 1959, signing professional 1 April 1960; Middlesbrough 15 March 1962 (fee £20,000); Coventry City July 1966 (fee £40,000); Cardiff City July 1970 (fee £35,000); Bournemouth & Boscombe Athletic October 1972 (with B.Clark for a combined fee of £100,000) to June 1973.
International honours: Scotland Schoolboys. Scotland Under-23, 2 caps.
Club honour: Coventry City, Division Two champions season 1966-7.
Ian Gibson was Stanley's youngest Football League player, making his debut at the age of 15 years and 358 days. Predictably, it was not long before he was attracting attention. In his stay of just less than a year on Stanley's groundstaff, there were many rumblings of 'back-door' methods being used to tempt him away. When he was on the point of signing for Bradford, the Football League at first held up the move to allow time for a meeting to be held to consider all the implications of Stanley's protest against the move. In the event, the League Management Committee decided that the move could proceed. It was an awful irony that Bradford eventually sold Gibson to Middlesbrough for a fee of £20,000 in March 1962. This was just at the time when Stanley were wound-up and the Gibson fee, which Stanley felt was rightly theirs, would have wiped off at least a third of the club's debts. Gibson was an untiring worker and an accomplished initiator who enjoyed a lengthy career. He totalled 461 appearances (plus seven as sub) and scored 89 goals.

GILL, James Joshua Allison **1934-36**
Goalkeeper. 5ft 10½in; 11st 4lb.
Born: Crook, 21 July 1903. Died: 1985.
Debut v Carlisle United (a) 30 August 1934.
Appearances: 62.
Career: Crook Town; Bear Park Welfare; Bolton Wanderers amateur 25, signing professional 28 August

1926; Bradford City 13 June 1930; Clapton Orient 18 July 1933; STANLEY 26 June 1934; Great Harwood September 1936 to cs 1938.

A shoulder injury sustained in the pre-season trial games was an unlucky start for Jimmy Gill, but he made a speedy recovery. With experience in all four Divisions, Gill was a sound and skilful goalkeeper who gave Stanley excellent service. He lost his first-team place at the start of season 1935-6, when new player-manager Jack Hacking arrived at Peel Park. When the former English international decided to hang up his boots to concentrate fully on management, Gill was reinstated.

GLAISTER, George **1951-52**

Outside-left. 5ft 8½in; 10st 12lb.

Born: Bywell, Northumberland, 18 May 1918.

Debut v Stockport County (h) 1 September 1951.

Appearances: 24; Goals: 1.

Career: North Shields; Blackburn Rovers 10 May 1937; Stockport County 21 May 1947; Halifax Town 25 August 1950; STANLEY 1 September 1951; Bangor City cs 1952.

George Glaister's Football League debut was made in the First Division with Blackburn Rovers in season 1946-7. He scored once in eight appearances before losing his place and moving on to Stockport County, late in the same season. He spent an eventful three years at Edgeley Park, where he recorded 92 appearances and scored 21 goals. Whilst Stockport County at that time were basically a mid-table team, they were renowned Cup fighters and won through to rounds four, three and five in successive seasons. Glaister was brought to Peel Park from Halifax by Stanley's manager Walter Crook, a former teammate at Blackburn Rovers. It was hoped that his signing would solve a problem position at outside-left. Three different players had occupied the number-11 jersey in four matches prior to Glaister's arrival. By the end of the season, the number of left-wingers tried had risen to seven. The *Accrington Observer* were not alone in wishing for another George Mee.

GLAZZARD, Malcolm **1951**

Outside-left. 5ft 10½in; 11st.

Born: Eastham, Cheshire, 1 July 1931.

Debut v Mansfield Town (a) 27 August 1951.

Appearances: 1.

Career: Junior football to Liverpool 28 May 1949; STANLEY (trial) 4 August to 3 November 1951.

At the time of his signing, Malcolm Glazzard was said to have been a regular member of Liverpool's Central League side. In a very brief stay at Peel Park, the 21-year-old Manchester University student had a solitary League outing. He deputized at outside-left for Walter Keeley and was one of three team changes for Stanley's visit to Field Mill, Mansfield, which resulted in defeat by 3-0.

GOLDIE, John **1922**

Inside-forward.

Born: Scotland.

Debut v Walsall (h) 29 April 1922.

Appearances: 1.

Career: Ayr Juniors; Preston North End (trial) April 1922; STANLEY amateur (trial) 29 April 1922.

Although John Goldie flitted but briefly across the Peel Park scene, he nevertheless established something of a record. Although his Football League debut came late in the campaign, he was the first Scotsman to appear for Stanley that season. This meant, of course, that he was also the first Scot to appear for the club in a Third Division North fixture. He was certainly the forerunner of many, as in 1955 Stanley fielded an entire team of Scotsmen, during Walter Galbraith's managership.

GOODFELLOW, Sydney **1952-53**

Half-back. 5ft 9in; 11st 7lb.

Born: Woolstanton, Staffs, 6 July 1915.

Debut v Hartlepools United (a) 23 August 1952 (scored one goal).

Appearances: 28; Goals: 3.

Career: North Staffordshire Boys; Hanley FC; Port Vale amateur, signing professional 12 November 1936; Glentoran 14 July 1937; Rochdale 19 May 1938; Chesterfield 29 April 1939; Doncaster Rovers 10 May 1948; Oldham Athletic 16 September 1950 (fee £750); STANLEY 27 June 1952; Wellington Town August 1953.

Club honour: Doncaster Rovers, Third Division North champions 1949-50 season.

Syd Goodfellow was 37 years of age when he first appeared in Stanley's colours, but he marked his debut by scoring at Hartlepools. In what proved to be his final season of League football, he appeared in all three half-back positions and at inside-left. Curly-haired and of rather gaunt appearance, he was a well-known figure on Northern Section grounds. He made over 100 consecutive appearances during his spell with Chesterfield and played in 39 matches in Doncaster Rovers' championship team of 1949-50. He had two good seasons with Oldham Athletic prior to joining Stanley, making 72 appearances and scoring twice for the Latics.

GRAHAM, A. **1922-23**

Outside-left.

Born: Possibly in Belfast.

Debut v Wrexham (h) 21 October 1922 (scored one goal).

Appearances: 1; Goals: 1.

Career: Irish football; STANLEY August 1922 to May 1923.

A tall and nicely-built player, Graham appeared in Stanley's first public trial match of season 1922-3 at outside-left. A week later, he was centre-forward for the 'Whites' in the final trial, but sustained an injury early in the game. He returned to action in the reserve team during September and was selected for his Football League debut a month later. Probably due to nervousness, he did not enjoy the best of debuts, although he did succeed in scoring the only goal of the game, five minutes from time.

Note: This player does not appear in the registration records of the Football League and much research has unfortunately failed to reveal Graham's forename(s) or his previous club(s).

GRAY, Edward **1959-60**

Forward. 5ft 9in; 10st 10lb.

Born: Bellshill, Lanarkshire, 19 October 1934.

Debut v Wrexham (h) 29 August 1959.

Appearances: 6.

Career: Hibernian; Yeovil Town; Barrow 14 December

1957; STANLEY 16 July 1959 to May 1960.
International honour: Scotland Schoolboys.
Eddie Gray joined Barrow in mid-season 1957-8, but his introduction into the team failed to lift them into the top half of the table. It was the final season of regionalized Third Division football and by finishing in 18th place, Barrow became founder-members of Division Four. He left Holker Street at the end of the following season, after Barrow had finished 23rd in the table, and faced a re-election application. He fared little better in a season at Peel Park, being unable to establish himself at senior level in a team which finished at the foot of Division Three.

GREEN, Donald **1952-54**
Full-back. 5ft 8in; 11st.
Born: Blackburn, 13 May 1932.
Debut v Chester (h) 1 November 1952.
Appearances: 12.
Career: Blackburn junior football (with some earlier experience with Blackburn Rovers 'A' team); STANLEY trialist late season 1951-2, signing amateur forms 14 May 1952 to May 1954.
Don Green had initial trials in Stanley's 'A' team as a 19-year-old and swiftly graduated via the Lancashire Combination side into League action. As deputy to Billy Robinson he had two early outings and then played in the final ten matches of the season. A spirited, fast-moving defender who could well have progressed with further experience. He did not, however, feature in the plans of Walter Galbraith, whose appointment came at the mid-point of Green's spell at Peel Park.

GREEN, James Huntley **1935-36**
Inside-forward. 5ft 5in; 10st 2lb.
Born: Shilbottle, 1915 (July quarter).
Debut v Rochdale (a) 4 January 1936.
Appearances: 15; Goals: 2.
Career: Gateshead amateur; STANLEY amateur 3 December 1935, signing professional 11 March 1936; Walsall 2 June 1936; Queen of the South September 1937.
'Although a midget, he is a delightful trickster' said the *Accrington Observer* in February 1936. At this time, Green had been recalled from the North-East, with a view to his signing professional forms. He had earlier shown promise as an amateur, but Stanley had found difficulty in paying his travelling expenses from the northerly side of Newcastle where he lived and worked as a collier. When the sale of Mortimer and Harker to Portsmouth left Stanley short of forward cover, Green was brought to Accrington for full-time training. He did not stay for long, however, Walsall signing him in the summer. Injury blighted his season with the Saddlers, and he was one of 13 players released by Walsall's new manager, Tommy Lowes, in April 1937.

GREEN, John **1938-39**
Full-back. 5ft 9in; 11st 7lb.
Born: Atherton, Lancashire, 1919.
Debut v Lincoln City (a) 8 October 1938.
Appearances: 13.
Career: Plymouth Argyle; Manchester City 7 May 1936; Altrincham (loan) December 1937 to April 1938; STANLEY 26 July 1938 to May 1939.
John Green was one of the newcomers who took the eye in Stanley's pre-season trials in August 1938. On the small side, but sturdy, he was terrier-like and sure-footed and often looked above his class in the Combination side. This was despite his very limited experience with Plymouth Argyle and with Manchester City, for whom he appeared in only four Central League matches, all at wing-half. The departure of Robert Done, the former Liverpool full-back, gave Green an early first-team opportunity with Accrington but he failed to establish a regular place in a season when 32 players were used in League matches as Stanley finished bottom of the table, having conceded over 100 League goals.

GREEN, Thomas **1920-22**
Centre-forward. 5ft 8½in; 11st 8lb.
Born: Liverpool, 25 November 1893. Died: Liverpool, 1975 (October quarter).
Debut v Rochdale (a) 27 August 1921.
Appearances: 30; Goals: 23.
Career: Liverpool and Stockport County during the World War One period; West Ham United May 1919; Southport Central October 1919; South Liverpool;

STANLEY during season 1920-21; Stockport County 27 May 1922 (fee £200); Clapton Orient May 1923; Heart of Midlothian 27 February 1924; Third Lanark cs 1925.
Representative honour: Lancashire Combination v Central League at Tranmere, 25 April 1921.
'Green would be a capital centre-forward if he were not always in such a desperate hurry to shoot,' said the *Athletic News* in 1923. There seemed little doubt that Green, who joined Stanley before they gained entry into the Third Division North, had a fair share of the selfishness that often marks a good goalscorer. For Stanley he proved a dangerous leader, whose left foot was the trusty one. His return of 23 goals in 30 matches, under the old offside law, was a commendable effort. He would doubtless have done even better but for a knee ligament injury which side-lined him for about two months in mid-season. Green's debut for West Ham United was memorable, for all the wrong reasons. It was the Hammers' first season as a Football League club and, although they conceded only 40 goals in the 42-match campaign, they lost 7-0 at Oakwell, Barnsley, in their first away match.

GREENHALGH, John Stanley **1925-26**
Inside-forward. 5ft 8½in; 11st 3lb.
Born: Bolton, 1898 (July quarter).
Debut v Walsall (a) 29 August 1925.
Appearances: 13; Goals: 3.
Career: St Augustine's (Bolton League); Bolton St Mark's; Leyland cs 1920; Burnley 14 October 1921 (fee £500); STANLEY 5 August 1925, released on a free transfer 2 July 1936.
Leading scorer for Leyland in season 1920-21, John Greenhalgh was partnered on the wing by his brother, Robert. John joined Burnley, and in season 1922-3 he appeared in all four of Burnley's teams, ending a season of progress by making his Football League debut on the last Saturday of the season. In a season at Peel Park he did not establish a regular berth, actually appearing in four different forward positions, within his total of 13 League appearances. During one early-season match, when the Stanley front line did not impress either individually or collectively, he was criticized by the local correspondent: 'Greenhalgh was smart at times, but in his eagerness to help he often rambled, and his wandering did not tend to unity'.

GREGG, Willis **1936-37**
Full-back. 5ft 8in; 11st 4lb.
Born: Woodhouse, Sheffield, 21 July 1908.
Debut v Hull City (h) 12 September 1936.
Appearances: 33.
Career: Mexborough Town; Chesterfield 13 May 1932; Torquay United 21 June 1934; STANLEY 13 June 1936; Manchester City 17 April 1937 (with J.J.Robinson, for a combined fee of £1,350); Chester 11 November 1938 to September 1939.
In March 1937 the *Athletic News* reported that Willis Gregg 'is fast, kicks well with either foot, positions himself intelligently and places the ball directly'. One month later, Willis Gregg, in company with goalkeeper Jack Robinson, departed Peel Park for First Division Manchester City. An amateur international trialist in season 1930-31, Gregg prospered in his spell with Stanley, despite being called upon to occupy both flanks as full-back and half-back. Stanley actually transferred a complete rearguard in season 1936-7, Robinson and Gregg plus Maurice Reeday, who joined Leicester City. A 1935 publication revealed that Gregg, then a Torquay player, was a keen walker and swimmer, whose hobby was pigeon racing.

GREGORY, Edward **1925-27**
Full-back. 5ft 10in; 11st.
Born: Radcliffe, Lancashire, 1902.
Debut v Crewe Alexandra (h) 3 April 1926.
Appearances: 10.
Career: Little Lever St Mark's; Rossendale United (trial) April 1923; Oldham Athletic amateur 14 April, signing professional 25 July 1923; STANLEY 25 July 1925; Hurst FC 1927; Manchester Central 1928-9.
Ted Gregory began with Oldham Athletic after playing for Little Lever St Mark's, who won their way into three local cup finals in season 1922-3. Rossendale United gave him a trial before the Latics stepped in and, following an impressive display for Oldham's reserve side against Wolverhampton Wanderers Reserves at Boundary Park, he was signed on. A fine display for the Latics against Stanley in a Lancashire Senior Cup tie in 1924-5 season paved the way for his eventual move to Peel Park. Manager Ernest Blackburn recruiting him after he had been given a free transfer from Boundary Park. As deputy to long-serving full-back Tom Whittaker, Gregory found only limited openings. He failed to do himself justice, however, in two early senior appearances in season 1926-7, on both occasions, the team suffered heavy defeats.

GRUMMETT, James **1952-53**
Half-back. 5ft 7in; 12st.
Born: Birdwell, near Barnsley, 3 July 1921.
Debut v Carlisle United (a) 4 September 1952.
Appearances: 40; Goals: 1.
Career: Ruston Sports; Lincoln City amateur 30 August, signing professional 17 September 1943; STANLEY 4 September 1952; Boston United cs 1953.
Club honour: Lincoln City, Third Division North champions season 1947-8.
A former Yorkshire miner, Jim Grummett was a dour, determined player, who made up for lack of inches by an immense capacity for work. He began as an inside-left but was converted into a wing half-back by Lincoln City. He appeared in two of their promotion sides. In addition to the 1947-8 team, he also made 11 appearances in the 1951-2 championship side. He was a consistent performer during his time at Peel Park, missing only three first-team matches after signing in early September. Grummett made 205 League appearances in his career, a total well exceeded by his son, Jim (junior). The younger Grummett was also a half-back and an England Youth international. He totalled 374 appearances in a career which took in Lincoln City, Aldershot, Chester and Rochdale.

GUMMERY, Walter Harry **1925-26**
Outside-left. 5ft 9½in; 11st 4lb.
Born: Worcester, 1 May 1900. Died: Sutton, Surrey, 18 October 1974.
Debut v Walsall (a) 29 August 1925 (scored one goal).
Appearances: 31; Goals: 3.
Career: Army football; Worcester City; Wolverhampton Wanderers 27 May 1924; STANLEY 19 June 1925 to June 1926.

Walter Gummery learned his football in the Army, which he joined when only 15 years of age. Playing with the 3rd Battalion of the Worcestershire Regiment during a four-year spell of service in India, he assisted them to win the Calcutta Cup. After 'demob' in 1922 he joined Worcester City and contributed materially to his team's success in winning the championship of the Birmingham League. He joined Stanley after a season with the Wolves (ten appearances, one goal). It was Gummery's goal, scored direct from a corner-kick, which set Stanley on their way to a 5-0 victory over Blyth Spartans. This was in the second round of the FA Cup and Stanley's reward was a lucrative visit to Burnden Park, which drew a crowd of over 32,000. Apart from a spell on the injury list, Gummery held the outside-left position for Stanley in 1925-6. He formed part of a virile front line which scored 90 goals in League and Cup during the season.

HACKETT, Christopher Edward **1932-33**

Outside-right. 5ft 7½in; 11st 1lb.
Born: Mansfield, 9 February 1903. Died: Leicester, 1983 (January quarter).
Debut v Halifax Town (h) 27 August 1932.
Appearances: 7.
Career: Junior with Mansfield Town; Langwith Colliery; Newark Town; Grantham Town; Leicester City 6 December 1924; Caernarfon Town cs 1928; Bury 8 November 1928; Scunthorpe United July 1929; Bristol Rovers 23 May 1930; Loughborough Corinthians September 1931; STANLEY 11 June 1932 to June 1933.

After a lengthy spell with Leicester City, Chris Hackett moved from Football League clubs to non-League soccer three times in as many years. Along the way, he failed to graduate beyond reserve-team football in League circles and his seven appearances with Stanley were his only Football League outings. He began brightly at Peel Park, assisting the team to an impressive start to the 1932-3 season. Three wins and one draw from the first four fixtures with a goal-difference of 14-6 constituted the team's best-ever start to a Northern Section campaign. Two matches later, and following heavy defeats at home and away, Hackett lost his place to Joe Eddleston.

HACKING, John (Junior) **1945-46**

Goalkeeper. 5ft 9½in; 11st 2lb.
Born: Blackpool, 24 August 1925.
Debut v Bradford City (a) 31 August 1946.
Appearances: 8.
Career: Woodnook Council School; Accrington Schoolboys; Lancashire Schoolboys (trial); Howard & Bullough FC; Manchester United (wartime guest) season 1943-4; Blackburn Rovers 'A' team; STANLEY amateur 9 August, signing professional 22 September 1945; Stockport County 29 November 1946; Macclesfield 1950; Nelson 1955-59.

Jack Hacking showed early goalkeeping promise when he assisted Howard & Bullough's to win the Lancashire Junior Shield and the Lancashire Junior Cup in 1944-5, a unique 'double'. He took over in Stanley's goal from Harry Holdcroft, the English international, who had been a guest player at Peel Park in season 1944-5. When Stanley won the championship of the Third Division North (West Region) in 1945-6, Hacking conceded only 19 goals in the 18-match programme and was dubbed by the local Press as 'a true son of his father'. His father was, of course, Stanley's manager and former England international goalkeeper, Jack Hacking (senior). In the first season of peacetime football, father rather surprisingly transferred son to Stockport County, where he was unfortunately overshadowed by another ex-Stanley custodian, Jack Bowles (*qv*). Employed in the woodworking trade, Jack Hacking played most sports but today enjoys golf and bowls. A son, John, played in goal for the new Accrington Stanley, and one of his sons has played for the Accrington Schoolboys team at Under-13 level.

HACKING, John (Senior) **1935**

Goalkeeper. 5ft 11in; 13st.
Born: Blackburn, 22 December 1897. Died: Accrington, 1 June 1955.
Debut v Lincoln City (a) 31 August 1935.
Appearances: 17.
Career: Grimshaw Park Co-operative (Blackburn); Blackpool January 1919; Fleetwood cs 1925; Oldham Athletic 4 May 1926; Manchester United 15 March

1934; STANLEY player-manager 31 May 1935, retiring as a player December 1935; Barrow manager May 1949 until his death.
International honour: 3 caps England 1928-9.
Representative honour: 2 appearances for the Football League in 1928.
A former grocer's assistant, Jack Hacking joined Blackpool after Army service with the RGA during World War One. His potential was not realized at Bloomfield Road and he was given a free transfer after six seasons of mainly reserve-team football. After a season with Fleetwood, his career blossomed with Oldham Athletic, where he won League and international recognition during an eight-year stay. After a year at Old Trafford, during which time his inspired goalkeeping helped Manchester United retain their Second Division status, he joined Stanley as player-manager. He could hardly have had a more unpleasant initiation into the realms of management. Consecutive defeats of 6-0, 3-0, 4-2 and 4-0 must have been a bitter disappointment to him, more so since he was in goal. He retired as a player after 17 appearances in Stanley's goal, but in an emergency included himself in the Reserves at right-back in February 1936 and gave a sound display, revealing no inclination to use his hands! Father of John (junior), also a Stanley goalkeeper (*qv*).

HAIGH, Charles **1923-25**
Centre-half. 5ft 10in; 10st 10lb.
Born: Leicester, August 1903.
Debut v Doncaster Rovers (a) 12 April 1924.
Appearances: 12.
Career: Lapage Street School (Bradford); Fairweather Green FC; Calverley FC; Yorkshire Amateurs; STANLEY amateur 17 January, signing professional 27 June 1923; Bradford City (trial) 28 October 1925; Selby Town; Lancaster Town 1928-9.
International honour: Captained England Schoolboys v Scotland Schoolboys at Valley Parade, Bradford in April 1917.
An ex-schoolboy prodigy and Leicester native, whose early football career was closely associated with the Bradford district. Speedier than he appeared with his cool, incisive style, Haigh assisted Stanley Reserves to the championship of the West Lancashire League in his first season. From centre-half, he scored the only goal of the game against Horwich Central which clinched the championship in late April 1923. An appearance for Yorkshire Amateurs against the Corinthians in London had first brought him to Stanley's notice and he became a professional at Peel Park before his 19th birthday. With such a start, it was surprising that his career spanned no more than a dozen Third Division appearances. Some hint of reason was given in the *Accrington Observer* of September 1924 which revealed that Haigh had moved to live in Accrington for a month 'in order to have the benefits of special stamina training'.

HALL, John **1924-25**
Inside or wing-forward. 5ft 9in; 10st 12lb.
Born: Bolton, 1905.
Debut v Walsall (a) 6 December 1924.
Appearances: 5; Goals: 1.
Career: Junior football; Lincoln City 22 August 1923; STANLEY 28 July 1924; Manchester United 6 May 1925 to May 1927.
Despite association with three League clubs, Jack Hall totalled only nine Football League appearances. After a single outing with Lincoln City he joined Stanley. In his season at Peel Park he had a four-match run at outside-right as deputy for the injured Fred Bedford. Later in the season he appeared at inside-left against Ashington and scored what proved to be his only goal in the Football League. He had done enough in the reserve team, however, to find his name on the retained list in April 1925. Subsequently, due to financial considerations, he was given a free transfer. He moved to Old Trafford where he was rather unfortuante to be cast as understudy to Joe Spence, a player whose 481 Football League appearances constituted a club record until season 1966-7, when Billy Foulkes passed his total.

HALL, John **1933-39**
Full-back. 5ft 8½in; 10st 12lb.
Born: Accrington, 1916.
Debut v Carlisle United (h) 28 August 1937.
Appearances: 43; Goals: 3.
Career: Clarendon Villa; STANLEY amateur 24 May 1933, signing professional 14 May 1935; Hull City 13 May 1939.
A classic example of 'the local boy who made good', Jack Hall began as a half-back and first signed amateur forms with Stanley when only 17 years old. He had been a prominent schoolboy footballer before joining a well-known local junior club, Clarendon Villa. He spent a long time in reserve, but finally broke through into League action during the 1937-8 season. In the following term, the Bradford City programme for Stanley's visit to Valley Parade on 24 September 1938 revealed an interesting statistic. The programme editor had quite correctly noted that despite Hall being little more than a youngster, he had been longer with the club than any other current player. In the summer of 1939, Ernest Blackburn the former Stanley manager, at that time in charge of Hull City, included Jack Hall in his 14 new signings for that coming season.

HALL, Robert **1925-29**
Centre-half. 5ft 11½in; 11st 9lb.
Born: Preston.
Debut v Doncaster Rovers (a) 24 April 1926.
Appearances: 7.
Career: Leyland; Burnley amateur 12 October 1923; STANLEY amateur 1 December 1925, signing professional 11 May 1926 to May 1929.
A nicely proportioned centre-half whose debut, whilst he was still an amateur, came towards the end of a season in which over a century of goals had been conceded. At the time of his signing professional, the *Lancashire Daily Post* described him as 'a centre-half quite in the Martin tradition, whose height ensures that he intercepts most high balls'. Hall began season 1926-7 as first-team pivot but he was injured in September and was out of action for three months. In a season when the 'goals against' column again recorded over 100 in League and Cup, he was one of eight different centre-halves tried during the course of the season.

HALLARD, William **1947**
Wing-half. 5ft 10in; 11st 2lb.
Born: St Helens, 28 August 1913. Died: Rochdale, 21

January 1979.
Debut v Southport (a) 15 March 1947.
Appearances: 3.
Career: Junior football; Bury 19 August 1935; Bradford 12 June 1937; Rochdale June 1946; STANLEY 15 March to May 1947.
Stanley used 33 players in season 1946-7 and one who figured briefly was Bill Hallard, who had begun the season with Rochdale. In a career interrupted by the war years, Hallard established himself with Bradford after spending his earliest days in reserve with Bury. In two seasons before the war he totalled 69 appearances and scored five goals in Second Division football. In season 1937-8 he appeared in the fifth round of the FA Cup at Sunderland, a game which attracted an attendance of 59,326. In 1945-6, when the FA Cup was contested on a two-legged basis, Hallard scored in the first leg of the quarter-final against Birmingham. In an earlier round, he appeared in the Avenue team which shocked the football world by winning 8-2 at Maine Road against Manchester City, to win the fourth-round tie by an aggregate score of 9-5.

HALSHAW, John Thomas **1923-24**
Inside-forward. 5ft 7in; 11st.
Born: Preston, 1896 (July quarter).
Debut v Halifax Town (h) 5 January 1924.
Appearances: 1.
Career: Croston FC (West Lancashire League); STANLEY 21 June 1923 to June 1923 to June 1924; Dick Kerr's FC 1925-27.
A collision with goalkeeper Floyd in the final pre-season trial left Jack Halshaw with sprained knee ligaments. Some weeks later, when on his way to what should have been his 'comeback' match at Darwen, his injured knee gave way again. It was not until the end of October that he played his first game for the Reserves. A hardworking, clever forward with refreshing dash, he proved a good man in the reserve team, he nevertheless had only one senior outing. He returned to non-League football in his native town with Dick Kerr's FC.

HAMILTON, Alexander McGregor **1957-62**
Wing-half. 5ft 7in; 10st 9lb.
Born: Kirkcolm, Wigtown, 21 November 1937.
Debut v Reading (h) 13 December 1958.
Appearances: 82.
Career: Drumore Juniors; STANLEY 20 August 1957; York City 16 March 1962; Nelson season 1962-3; Clayton FC (West Lancashire League); Poplar FC (Accrington & District Combination).
Once decribed in an opposing team's programme as 'the mighty atom of Stanley's middle line', Alex Hamilton was one of the most consistent performers in the club's final seasons of League football. In his first season he was a reserve-team player, when the seniors finished as runners-up for the Third Division North championship. He became an established first-team player about half-way through season 1959-60, and thereafter missed only a handful of matches. In addition to the 82 appearances quoted above, he had a further 32 matches in the unfinished final season, 1961-2. A significant statistic in Hamilton's career was the fact that in just short of five seasons with Stanley, he played for five different managers, plus one 'caretaker' boss.

HAMILTON, Herbert Harold **1938-39**
Full-back. 5ft 9½in; 12st 7lb.
Born: Wallasey, 27 March 1906. Died: In the Ontario district of Canada, June 1951.
Debut v Hartlepools United (h) 12 November 1938.
Appearances: 10.
Career: New Brighton Baptists; Harrowby; Poulton Rovers; New Brighton 19 December 1923; Everton 1 October 1924; Preston North End 17 May 1927; Chesterfield 4 June 1931 (fee £250); Tranmere Rovers 12 May 1937; STANLEY 10 November 1938 (with T.Waring for a combined fee of £700); Bangor City cs 1939; Marine FC during season 1939-40.
International honour: England Junior.
Club honour: Chesterfield, Division Three North champions season 1935-6. Tranmere Rovers, Division Three North champions season 1937-8.
'Duke' Hamilton began with New Brighton as a 17-year-old, but he was a seasoned campaigner by the time he arrived at Peel Park. He was part of a double signing, with former English international 'Pongo' Waring, as Stanley strived to lift themselves from the foot of the table. Their first appearance in Stanley's colours boosted the Peel Park attendance to over 5,000 for the first time that season, but the 0-0 scoreline was a typical disappointment. Earlier in his career, Hamilton won two Third Division championship medals, one with Chesterfield, where he was a beneficiary during a stay of six years. In March 1948 he was reported to be in Amsterdam, working as a football coach.

HAMILTON, William **1929-30**
Outside-right. 5ft 8in; 11st 4lb.
Born: Mussleburgh, 24 October 1904. Died: Glasgow, 19 July 1984.
Debut v Doncaster Rovers (a) 31 August 1929.
Appearances: 41; Goals: 14.
Career: Vale of Clyde; Shettleston; Bellshill Athletic; Bradford City 29 August 1925; Southport 12 July 1927; Barrow 18 July 1928; STANLEY 11 June 1929; Notts County 9 June 1930; Alloa Athletic cs 1931 to cs 1934. In 1942 he joined Shettleston where, over a period of 40 years, he served as trainer, groundsman, secretary, vice-chairman and chairman.
Billy Hamilton played in every first team match but one in his season at Peel Park. He played a vital role in a forward line which recorded 84 League goals, at that time the club's highest return in the Third Division North. A winger who could show his heels to most full-backs, Hamilton was not afraid to cut in for a shot at goal. He recorded a hat-trick from the wing on Christmas Day 1929, when Stanley pulled off one of the day's shock results by beating Darlington, at Feethams, by 4-2.

HANN, Leslie **1937-39**
Inside-forward. 5ft 8in; 10st 10lb.
Born: Tynemouth, 1915 (January quarter).
Debut v York City (a) 14 April 1937.
Appearances: 29; Goals: 1.
Career: Felling Red Star; STANLEY amateur 1 March, signing professional 11 March 1937; Clapton Orient 13 July 1939.
'A clever dribbler and a cute distributor' was an early Press verdict on Leslie Hann. He was signed as a professional when less than two weeks into a month's

trial. On his senior debut at Peel Park, the *Accrington Observer* noted that he 'greatly impressed in a sparkling partnership with George Mee. He also celebrated by scoring his first Football League goal.' In the last peacetime season Hann proved his versatility by successfully taking over the left-half berth, following Dick Webster's transfer to Sheffield United.

HARKER, William **1934-36**
Inside-forward. 5ft 8in; 11st 2lb.
Born: Briefield, Lancashire, 1911 (January quarter).
Debut v New Brighton (h) 25 August 1934.
Appearances: 62; Goals: 23.
Career: West Lancashire League junior football; Nelson amateur 9 August 1930; Burnley 21 May 1931; Torquay United 2 June 1933; STANLEY 9 June 1934; Portsmouth 13 February 1936 (with R.A.Mortimer for a combined fee of £1,450); Stockport County 18 September 1936; Rochdale 7 June 1939.
On 16 November 1935, Billy Harker broke the club's individual goalscoring record by netting five goals in the 6-1 defeat of Gateshead at Peel Park. He scored three in six minutes and four in ten minutes, and the club presented him with the match ball. It was an 'out of the blue' occasion in many ways, as Stanley had lost 6-0 on the previous Saturday and Billy Harker had scored only once in his previous 14 games. Some three months later, following a stunning 3-0 victory at Chesterfield (the eventual champions), Billy Harker and Bob Mortimer were transferred to First Division Portsmouth. Some years later, an own-goal by Harker helped Stanley to a 3-2 victory in the last Football League match before World War Two, against Stockport County. After retiring from football, Billy Harker became an Oswaldtwistle licensee.

HARRIS, William **1947-50**
Goalkeeper. 6ft ½in; 12st.
Born: Oakham, Dudley, Staffs, 1 December 1918.
Debut v Hartlepools United (h) 23 August 1947.
Appearances: 99.
Career: Rowley Regis Boys; Oakham Juniors; Whiteheath 1934; West Bromwich Albion amateur 29 October 1936, signing professional 27 February 1937; Wartime guest player with Newport County, Norwich City and Shrewsbury Town; Oldham Athletic 19 June 1946 (fee £150); STANLEY 6 August 1947; Dudley Town player-coach July 1950; Bilston United player-manager 1953-55. Scouted for West Bromwich Albion on retirement.
Bill Harris made his Football League debut as a 19-year-old with West Bromwich Albion in season 1937-8. After military service, during which he was wounded in Normandy, he resumed his football career with Oldham Athletic, after an Army posting had taken him to Lancashire. With good height and reach, Harris was a cool and confident goalkeeper who gave Stanley excellent service. He came within a dozen matches of making 100 consecutive appearances in League and Cup, before losing his place to Doug Daniels.

HARRISON, Herbert K.G. **1947-48**
Outside-right.
Born: Burnley, 23 January 1916.
Debut v Lincoln City (a) 25 December 1947.
Appearances: 3.
Career: Morecambe amateur; STANLEY amateur October 1947 to May 1948.
Herbert Harrison had experience as an amateur player with Morecambe, one of the leading teams in the Lancashire Combination at that time. He had declined to sign for them as a professional, as he was living in the Burnley area. On joining Stanley as an amateur, he impressed in the reserve side and quickly won promotion to the League team, playing in three matches over the Christmas holiday period. His first two games were against Lincoln City, Stanley winning both matches to become the only team to take four points from the eventual champions of the Division. Harrison had a fine debut, prompting the *Accrington Observer* to comment: 'To Harrison goes credit to a large extent for two goals while his general play augers well for both club and player'.

HARROLD, Sidney **1922-23**
Wing-forward. 5ft 8in; 10st 12lb.
Born: Dudley, Staffs, 5 June 1895.
Debut v Darlington (h) 26 August 1922.
Appearances: 6; Goals: 1.
Career: Willenhall FC; Stourbridge season 1914-15; Wednesbury; Leicester Fosse February 1919; Nottingham Forest 7 May 1920; STANLEY 14 June 1922, retiring due to injury in January 1923.

Recommended to Accrington's directors by Pat Nelis, the former Stanley and Nottingham Forest centre-forward, Sid Harrold was a fine winger whose career was tragically cut short by injury. He suffered a badly broken and dislocated ankle in a game against Durham City in September 1922. It was, incidentally, a game which Stanley managed to win 3-1, despite the fact that they also lost their other winger, Ernest Pinkney, who was carried off the field five minutes before Harrold's injury. Sid Harrold was subsequently pronounced unfit to resume his football career and a benefit match was played for him in May 1922. About 3,000 spectators attended the game which featured a Lancashire-Yorkshire XI versus a Nottingham Forest-Leicester City XI. Harrold was able to resume his cricket career as professional with Newtown Wednesbury and was later a licensee in Wednesbury.

HARROWER, James Swanson **1954-61**
Full-back or centre-half. 5ft 10½in; 11st 7lb.
Born: Crossgates, Fife, 19 June 1924.
Debut v Southport (a) 18 December 1954.
Appearances: 246; Goals: 2.
Career: Dunfermline 1943; Third Lanark 1945; STANLEY 13 December 1954 (fee £1,750), appointed player-manager 21 April 1960, resigning 14 December 1961.
Representative honour: Third Division North v Third Division South 16 March 1955, at Reading.
Jim Harrower settled so well into English League football that he was selected to represent the Northern Section, in the season following his arrival at Peel Park. Signed as a left full-back, he later appeared at centre-half, following John Ryden's transfer to Tottenham Hotspur. He had begun his career as an outside-left during wartime Scottish football. Whilst with Third

Lanark he was twice a medal winner in the Glasgow Cup competition and was twice selected as reserve for the Scottish League. He was appointed Stanley's player-manager in April 1960, taking over a team already doomed to relegation. He was unable to halt the downward spiral before his resignation in December 1961. In the following year he became licensee of the Castle Hotel in Accrington and later worked as a heating engineer (see *Accrington Stanley's Managers*).

HARTLES, Wilfred **1921-22**
Outside-left. 5ft 9in; 12st 8lb.
Born: Warrington, 1890 (October quarter).
Debut v Rochdale (a) 27 August 1921.
Appearances: 14.
Career: Runcorn; Bradford 18 September 1920; STANLEY 7 July 1921 to May 1922.
Wilf Hartles began as a wing half-back with Runcorn, but he was at outside-left when he made his Football League debut for Bradford against Burnley in season 1920-21. Despite scoring on his initial outing, Hartles played only twice, as he was understudy to McCandless (*qv*) the Irish international who was briefly with Stanley in season 1923-4. Prematurely balding, Hartles had an exceptional turn of speed, being a professional sprinter with many successes, notably over the 100 yards distance. He was Stanley's first outside-left in the Third Division North, but his final matches saw him at left-half, after he had lost his place on the wing to Pat Quigley, the Irish junior international.

HAWES, Arthur Robert **1929-30**
Inside-forward. 5ft 9in; 11st 4lb.
Born: Swanton Morley, Norfolk, 2 October 1895. Died: Norwich, 11 October 1963.
Appearances: 39; Goals: 9.
Career: Thorpe Hamlet School; Junior Institute; CEYMS; Boulton & Paul; Norwich Schoolboys; Norwich City 16 September 1915; Boulton & Paul 1918; Norwich City 21 April 1919; South Shields 8 May 1920; Sunderland 23 December 1921 (fee £1,750); Bradford 26 August 1927; STANLEY 5 July 1929 (fee

£100); Nelson 15 July 1930 (fee £50); Hyde United September 1931; Wombwell later in same season; Rochdale 22 February 1932 to May 1932; Goole Town August 1932; Frost's Athletic; Gothic FC trainer to 1958.

Representative honours: Norfolk County Colours 1919-20. FA XI v Cambridge University 20 November 1919. The Rest v England at Maine Road, Manchester 9 February 1925.

Former England trialist Arthur Hawes exhibited a sure touch and a sound knowledge of the game during his season at Peel Park. In earlier days, his transfer from Norwich City to South Shields involved an inquiry, but he proved a bargain for the Horsley Hill team, scoring 17 goals in 38 appearances in his first season. He moved to Sunderland and was a regular first-team player for four seasons, assisting them to the runners-up position for the League Championship in 1922-3. In Bradford's Third Division North championship winning side he scored 14 goals in 41 matches. With Stanley he was the star in a dangerous forward line. In a high-scoring season, one run of five consecutive fixtures saw 21 goals scored. Arthur Hawes' father, Arthur Thomas Hawes, was for 21 years assistant trainer to Norwich City. He died in 1951 aged 87 years.

HAWORTH, Harry **1926-30**

Full-back or half-back. 5ft 9½in; 11st 3lb.
Born: Ramsbottom, Lancashire.
Debut v Walsall (h) 5 March 1927.
Appearances: 4.
Career: Local junior football to STANLEY on amateur forms 28 December 1926 to June 1930.

Harry Haworth was a reserve defender whose senior opportunities were few and far between. His initial two-match baptism into League action proved traumatic, as Stanley went down 5-3 at home to Walsall on his debut and at Nelson a week later were well beaten by 7-0. He had to wait almost two years for another senior outing and on this occasion Stanley took an unexpected point from a 1-1 draw at Tranmere Rovers.

HAWORTH, Herbert **1946-47**

Inside-forward.
Born: Accrington, 5 May 1920.
Debut v Hartlepools United (a) 19 October 1946.
Appearances: 2.
Career: Woodnook Amateurs; STANLEY amateur 18 October 1946; Rossendale Unted May 1947.

A hard-working and enthusiastic local inside-forward whose promotion from amateur to League football came hard upon his third appearance in Stanley's Reserve team. He was a goalscorer, 'hit beautifully from 25 yards,' according to one match report, in the 5-1 win against Rochdale Reserves. On his League debut, Stanley won 2-0 at Hartlepools. At home, one week later, Crewe Alexandra took the points in a 3-2 victory. This proved to be his last game at senior level.

HAWORTH, James **1928-32**

Outside-left. 5ft 7in; 10st 2lb.
Born: Accrington.
Debut v Rochdale (h) 1 December 1928.
Appearances: 20; Goals: 4.
Career: STANLEY amateur 3 April 1928; Stalybridge Celtic 1931-2; Nelson 1932-35; Bacup Borough 1935-37; Great Harwood 1937-8; during World War Two assisted STANLEY and Howard & Bullough FC.

Despite Jimmy Haworth's long association with Stanley, it was as a cricketer that he was best known locally. He was one of the Lancashire League's outstanding amateur batsmen with the Church club. Amongst many fine performances were his fourth place finish in the League batting averages for 1929 and his 552 runs in 18 completed innings in 1937. From 1961 to 1979 he spent each summer as a cricket coach in Holland, which included his coaching the Dutch national team. In 1935 he took over his family's plumbing business and retired in 1973.

HAWORTH, John **1925**

Goalkeeper.
Born: Huncoat, near Accrington.
Debut v Hartlepools United (a) 16 September 1925.
Appearances: 1.
Career: Local junior football; STANLEY amateur 22 July to 9 November 1925.

Although John Haworth did not sign amateur forms for Stanley until 1925, he had appeared at Peel Park a year earlier. On this occasion he appeared in one of the pre-season trial games as deputy for Jimmy Crabtree, who was unavailable due to prior cricketing commitments. Tom Holden was regarded as the first choice goalkeeper in 1925-6 and Haworth was one of three other goalkeepers on the books during the season. His debut at Hartlepools proved to be a severe initiation into League football, as Stanley went down 5-1.

HAWORTH, Ralph **1926-31**

Half-back. 5ft 9½in; 11st 8lb.
Born: Crawshawbooth, Lancashire, 1907 (April quarter).
Debut v Barrow (a) 8 March 1930.
Appearances: 3.
Career: Local junior football; STANLEY amateur 14 October 1926 to May 1931.

Ralph Haworth, a useful reserve-team utility defender, seemed unable to do himself justice in his infrequent senior outings. His final appearance in a League match, when he was preferred to George Law at right-back, was against Rotherham United at Millmoor in October 1930. Stanley lost 8-1 and the *Accrington Observer* commented: 'Haworth was invariably beaten for possession of the ball and often when he had quite a decent start'.

HAWORTH, Robert **1932-33**

Full-back. 5ft 8in; 11st 12lb.
Born: Atherton, Lancashire, 26 June 1897. Died: March 1962.
Appearances: 3.
Career: Howe Bridge; Atherton Collieries; Bolton Wanderers 6 August 1920; STANLEY as player-coach 25 May 1932 to June 1933.

Club honours: Bolton Wanderers, FA Cup winners 1923, 1926 and 1929.

A former captain of Bolton Wanderers and a dependable stalwart at right-back for ten years, Bob Haworth was a member of all three of Bolton's FA Cup winning teams in the 1920s. In his final season at Burnden Park, a broken leg brought to an end a wonderful record of 332 Football League and 35 FA

Cup appearances. Haworth was signed by Stanley as player-coach, but at nearly 35 years of age, his playing days were virtually finished. After retiring from the game he became a newsagent.

HAYES, Samuel **1946-47**
Goalkeeper.
Born: Accrington, 21 June 1920. Died: 1959.
Debut v New Brighton (a) 12 October 1946.
Appearances: 13.
Career: Accrington Schoolboys; Blackburn Rovers amateur; STANLEY amateur 8 October 1946; Rossendale United February 1947; Clitheroe November 1947; Mossley August 1948.
Sam Hayes made many confident saves on his Football League debut, but his mastery of the goal area and thereabouts could not prevent New Brighton from recording a 4-0 victory. Strangely enough, one week earlier he had performed similar heroics on the same Tower Ground for Stanley Reserves, which led to his promotion. 'Hayes was in fine fettle' said the local correspondent, in true Lancashire style! Hayes left Peel Park before the end of the season during which Stanley used five different goalkeepers in League matches. One of the 'keepers, Walter Keeley, was really an inside-left, but he managed to keep a clean sheet in his one appearance under the crossbar, at Haigh Avenue, Southport. Son of William Edward Hayes (*qv*) a pre-war Stanley goalkeeper.

HAYES, William Edward **1926-27**
Goalkeeper. 5ft 11in; 13st.
Born: Croston, 8 November 1895.
Debut v Rochdale (h) 28 August 1926.
Appearances: 41.
Career: Halton Juniors; Eccleston FC; Preston North End amateur 30 November, signing professional 22 December 1912; Chorley (loan) season 1913-14; Brighton & Hove Albion August 1919; Southend United 16 June 1924; STANLEY 22 June 1926; Stockport County May 1927 to May 1928; Winsford United October 1928; Burscough Rangers; Stalybridge Celtic March 1930; Bacup Borough September 1931.
On Preston North End's books at 16 years of age, Bill Hayes enjoyed a long career. He set up a remarkable record of appearances in the seasons immediately following World War One. With Brighton & Hove Albion he missed only one first-team game between 1919 and 1924, a total of 209 out of a possible 210 appearances. In the following season he joined

Southend United and was an ever-present. A hefty goalkeeper who presented a formidable barrier to opposing forwards, Hayes typically appeared in all but one of Stanley's League and Cup matches in 1926-7. His career figures were 285 Football League appearances and 42 Southern League appearances. Father of Samuel Hayes (*qv*).

HAZZLETON, James **1952-53**
Inside-forward. 5ft 9½in; 11st.
Born: Bolton, 29 September 1930.
Debut v Hartlepools United (a) 23 August 1952.
Appearances: 4.
Career: Atherton Collieries; Bury 14 May 1950 to 14 March 1951; Rochdale 14 August 1951; STANLEY 12 July 1952, released on a free transfer 1 May 1953.
Jim Hazzleton began with Bury, but first appeared at League level with Rochdale. He was one of 30 players used by the Dale in 1951-2, making 11 appearances and scoring once. Signed by Walter Crook, Hazzleton began as first-choice inside-right for Stanley. He was soon deposed, however, in a season when goals were at a premium, only 39 being scored in 46 matches.

HEAP, Clifford **1932**
Full-back. 5ft 11in; 11st 8lb.
Born: Burnley, 14 February 1906. Died: Torbay, 7 September 1984.
Debut v Doncaster Rovers (a) 16 January 1932.
Appearances: 4.
Career: Burnley amateur, signing professional August 1925; Thames July 1930; Clitheroe; Manchester Central June 1931; Millwall October 1931; STANLEY 13 January 1932; Southend United (one month's trial) February 1932; Stalybridge Celtic March 1932; Tunbridge Wells Rangers June 1933.
Peel Park was only one of Clifford Heap's stop-overs in the 1931-2 season. He additionally passed swiftly through Manchester Central, Millwall, Southend

United and Stalybridge Celtic. During the same season he was also married to Miss Hilda Bromley, the elder daughter of Mr John Bromley, a director of Burnley FC. Heap's career had begun at Turf Moor, where he started Burnley's 'A' team in early 1925. He became a regular in the Central League side from 1925-6 onwards but had a long wait before making his Football League debut against Leeds United in February 1929, some four years after he had first joined the Clarets.

HEAP, Dennis **1924-25**
Inside-forward. 5ft 6in; 9st 10lb.
Born: Padiham, Lancashire, 2 March 1902.
Debut v Lincoln City (a) 19 January 1924.
Appearances: 10; Goals: 4.
Career: Padiham junior football; STANLEY amateur 9 January, signing professional 2 February 1924 to May 1925.
At 9st 10lb, Dennis Heap seemed to be seriously lacking in pounds avoirdupois for the rigours of Third Division football. He nevertheless made a good showing as deputy to John Hosker in mid-season. He scored two goals in a run of seven matches which yielded three wins and three draws. Despite scoring twice at Halifax in a 2-2 draw in January 1925, he found few opportunities in his second season, making only three senior appearances.

HEGGIE, William Campbell **1955**
Full-back. 6ft; 12st 8lb.
Born: Scone, Perth, 7 June 1927.
Debut v Wrexham (a) 12 February 1955.
Appearances: 1.
Career: Perth City Boy's Club; Earngrove FC; Jeanfield Swifts (fee £75); New Brighton 9 February 1951; Leeds United 15 June 1951 (in a joint transfer with J.Finlay, for a combined fee of £6,000); Wrexham 31 July 1952; Winsford United 30 November 1954; STANLEY 10 February 1955 (fee £270); New Brighton August 1955.
Born in the Scottish district famous for its 'Stone', Bill Heggie was first introduced to League football by Walter Galbraith, at that time player-manager of New Brighton. Some four years later, Galbraith brought Heggie out of non-League football to join Stanley. As full-back cover, he made only one senior appearance, against Wrexham, one of his previous clubs. For the Welsh club he scored 13 goals in 33 appearances. He had earlier scored five goals in ten appearances for New Brighton, after being tried at centre-forward in the last months of League football in Wallasey. A coal merchant by trade, Heggie returned to New Brighton and played a key role in their FA Cup exploits in 1956-7, when the Rakers reached the fourth round, beating three Football League sides on the way.

HELLIWELL, Tim **1923-24**
Outside-left. 5ft 6in; 11st.
Born: Sowerby Bridge, near Halifax, 1897 (January quarter).
Debut v Rochdale (h) 3 February 1923.
Appearances: 18; Goals: 1.
Career: West Riding Amateurs; STANLEY amateur 26 January 1923 to 4 February 1924; Darwen season 1924-5.
Scintillating runs crowned by accurate centres were Tim Helliwell's forte. A match report of his debut was lavish in praise of his display and rather amusingly concluded: 'He tripped off the field with his pants unsullied, an indisputable testimonial to his elusiveness'. After a bright opening, a series of misfortunes hampered his progress. An ankle injury sustained in a reserve-team game was subject to additional damage in an accident. He was injured whilst alighting from a tram-car.

HENDERSON, Joseph **1953-54**
Goalkeeper. 5ft 10in; 11st 7lb.
Born: Cleland, 21 December 1924.
Debut v Stockport County (h) 22 August 1953.
Appearances: 14.
Career: Albion Rovers; Northampton Town 4 June 1949; Stenhousemuir; STANLEY 17 July 1953; Alloa Athletic 26 February 1954; Canterbury City 18 May 1955.
Joe Henderson shuttled rapidly between Scotland and England, thrice crossing the border during the course of his career. He was unfortunate during his Stanley spell to break a bone in his hand at Valley Parade, Bradford in September 1953. This came after he had appeared in the first 11 matches of the season. In early November he was back into the first team, but he appeared to have lost confidence. After a three-match run he was succeeded in goal by Bill White. Henderson remained in the Reserve team, but when Jimmy Jones was signed from Lincoln City, he requested a transfer. This was granted and he was almost immediately signed by Alloa Athletic.

HENDERSON, William **1932**
Full-back.
Born: Probably in the Accrington area.
Debut v Carlisle United (a) 7 May 1932.
Appearances: 1.
Career: Stanhill FC; STANLEY amateur 30 April 1932.
A local player with the Stanhill Club, Bill Henderson signed amateur forms for Stanley after appearing in a handful of reserve-team games towards the close of season 1931-2. As he normally appeared at right-back in the Combination team, his selection at inside-right for the season's final League match seemed an odd move. Stanley lost 3-0 at Carlisle, but the *Accrington Observer* had kind words for the debutant: 'Henderson aquitted himself with distinct credit, especially considering that he was playing in an unaccustomed position'.

HEYS, Richard **1924-25**
Inside-right. 5ft 7½in; 10st 2lb.
Born: Clitheroe.
Debut v Tranmere Rovers (h) 9 Feburary 1924.
Appearances: 15; Goals: 3.
Career: Blackburn Olympic; STANLEY amateur 7 February, signing professional 17 March 1924; Clitheroe early in season 1925-6; Chorley 1929-30.
Richard Heys signed amateur forms following trials with Stanley Reserves and quickly won a professional contract. A young player, quick in thought and action, his only drawback was a lack of weight and an occasional inclination to run the ball too far. He managed to hold on to the first-team inside-right spot for much of the final three months of his debut season and was retained for 1924-5. A change of management in the close season led to much activity on the transfer

market. On the opening Saturday of season 1924-5, a brand-new forward line was included within the total of eight players who were making their debuts for the club. Heys was restricted to a single League appearance during the season, in which he scored against Chesterfield. When he joined Clitheroe, his home-town club, for their first season in the Lancashire Combination, he became one of five former Stanley players on the club's books. In season 1928-9 he won a Lancashire Combination championship medal with Chorley, Heys' contribution being 26 goals in only 21 matches.

HIGH, Stanley **1931-32**
Half-back. 5ft 8in; 10st 8lb.
Born: Hetton, 18 February 1908. Died: Horden, 13 April 1982.
Debut v Rochdale (a) 29 August 1931.
Appearances: 28; Goals: 1.

Career: Easington Colliery; Leicester City 4 July 1928; Torquay United 24 June 1929; STANLEY 11 August 1931; Gillingham 4 August 1932 to June 1933.
Stanley High left the pit to become a professional footballer with Leicester City, but his League debut was made with Torquay United in season 1929-30. He joined Stanley after two years at Plainmoor (44 appearances, one goal). In a season with Stanley he proved a quick and forceful defender who, although on the light side, tackled with great determination. Stanley's half-back line in 1931-2 centered around Viner, in the pivotal role, whilst the wing-halves were any two from High, Ferguson and McCulloch.

HOBSON, Ernest **1933**
Centre-forward.
Debut v Tranmere Rovers (h) 6 May 1933. (scored one goal).
Appearances: 1; Goals: 1.
Career: Bolton Wanderers amateur August 1932; STANLEY amateur 25 March 1933.
Ernest Hobson came to Peel Park in an exchange transfer which took Wade, Stanley's reserve centre-forward, to Burnden Park. On his debut for Stanley Reserves, Hobson scored twice against Rossendale United in an 8-1 win. Given a run-out in the first team on the last Saturday of the season, he made an impressive debut, despite being handicapped by the heavy ground. The match was played in a heavy rainstorm and thunder and lightning, and the pitch soon became a sea of mud. Hobson scored Stanley's second goal after 30 minutes, beating Tranmere's Welsh international goalkeeper, Albert Gray, with a fine shot. There were few spectators present to witness his scoring debut, only 1,079 braved the elements, and the 'gate' receipts amounted to only £27.

HOGAN, Charles **1949-51**
Outside-right. 5ft 6in; 11st 6lb.
Born: Bury, 23 April 1926.
Debut v Carlisle United (a) 20 August 1949.
Appearances: 56; Goals: 4.
Career: Spartan Athletic; Bury 2 June 1948; STANLEY 5 August 1949; Southport August 1951; Rochdale 15 August 1952; Nelson cs 1953; Wigan Athletic September 1953.
Charlie Hogan's League career began with Bury, but he had made only one senior appearance with the Shakers before he joined Stanley's new manager, Jimmy Porter, at Peel Park. Speedy and adept on either wing, Hogan scored in his first game at Peel Park. Subsequently, however, he was disappointing as a marksman, although his spirited play and clever ball-control made him a dangerous opponent. He departed Stanley after two seasons to join Southport, but in only his second game he sustained a knee injury which necessitated a cartilage operation. The bulk of Hogan's career figures of 69 appearances and five goals were made with Stanley, despite his association with three other League clubs in his native county.

HOLDEN, Thomas **1925-28**
Goalkeeper. 5ft 8in; 11st 4lb.
Born: Leyland, Lancashire.
Debut v Walsall (a) 29 August 1925.
Appearances: 34.
Career: Leyland; Fleetwood; STANLEY 28 May 1925; Hurst 10 February 1928.
At 5ft 8in Tom Holden was on the short side for his position, but he possessed unusual agility and excellent anticipation. Recruited from Lancashire Combination circles, he spent almost three years with Stanley, but the bulk of his senior appearances came in his first season at Peel Park. After one particularly fine display of goalkeeping in September 1925, the *Athletic News* reported: 'Holden dealt with shots high or low with equal celerity and his judgment was unerring'.

HOLLIDAY, Kenneth Joseph **1952-55**
Centre-half. 6ft 1½in; 12st 8lb.
Born: Darwen, 19 August 1925.
Debut v Hartlepools United (a) 23 August 1952.
Appearances: 96; Goals: 5.
Career: Darwen Juniors; Blackburn Rovers amateur 13 June, signing professional 17 October 1946; STANLEY 12 July 1952; Barrow 21 May 1955; Nelson cs 1956; Darwen; Padiham.

Ken Holliday served in the Royal Navy before joining Blackburn Rovers, who were reported to have placed a fee of £4,000 on him in 1952. In three seasons at Peel Park he proved to be one of Stanley's most servicable defenders. He was equally effective as a full-back or a half-back and he even scored three goals in two outings as an emergency centre-forward in October 1953. A player whose height and ginger hair made him a prominent figure on the field, he was a tower of strength in Stanley's defence and always reliable.

HOSKER, John **1921-24**
Inside-forward. 5ft 5½in; 10st 12lb.
Born: Preston, 15 February 1894.
Debut v Rochdale (a) 27 August 1921 (scored two goals).
Appearances: 104; Goals: 29.
Career: Lancaster Town; Preston North End September 1915; STANLEY 15 June 1921; Morecambe December 1924 to 1926.
A dashing, energetic inside-forward, Preston railwayman John Hosker was invariably the hardest worker in the Stanley attack. His all-action style meant that he was often in the wars, yet he was seldom on the casualty list. He was the only Stanley forward to be retained for a third season in the close season of 1923. 'Hustler' Hosker, as the local Press liked to call him, took his total appearances to over 100. On leaving Peel Park he joined Morecambe and in two seasons assisted them to win the Lancashire Combination Championship in season 1924-5 and to the runners-up position the following term.

HOWELL, Harry **1922**
Centre-forward: 5ft 8in; 11st 6lb.
Born: Birmingham, 29 November 1890. Died: Birmingham, 9 July 1932.
Debut v Wrexham (h) 21 October 1922.
Appearances: 3.
Career: Associated with both Port Vale and Stoke, whilst both clubs were operating outside of the Football League; Wolverhampton Wanderers 5 March 1913; Southampton season 1920-21; Northfleet FC; STANLEY (trial) 20 October to 11 November 1922.
Cricketer-footballer Harry Howell made his debut for Stanley against Wrexham. It was the ninth match of season 1922-3 and he was the sixth different centre-forward fielded. His inclusion failed to strengthen the attack and he departed after a trial spanning three matches. He was far more famous as a cricketer than as a footballer. A fast bowler with Warwickshire from 1913 to 1929, he had twice toured Australia and played four times for England. Amongst many notable bowling feats, he took ten wickets for 51 runs against Yorkshire at Edgbaston in 1923. A year later, on the same ground, he took six Hampshire wickets for seven runs in 4.5 overs. Hampshire, incidentally, were dismissed for 15 runs but still managed to win! After following-on 208 runs behind they then hit up 521 and in the end won by 155 runs. Howell returned to Accrington, as cricket professional, in 1926. He departed just before the end of the season having taken 87 wickets at 8.10 runs each, to finish third in the League bowling averages. His replacement for 1927 was a young spin bowler who subsequently reached the highest rank, Hedley Verity.

HOWSHALL, John Henry **1938**
Half-back. 5ft 9in; 11st 8lb.
Born: Normacote, Longton, Staffs, 12 July 1912. Died: Shelton, Hanley, 24 December 1962.
Debut v Halifax Town (a) 27 August 1938.
Appearances: 8.
Career: Dresden Juniors; Stoke amateur October, signing professional 23 November 1931; Chesterfield 4 June 1934; Southport 14 June 1935; Bristol Rovers 25 June 1937 (fee £350); STANLEY 26 July 1938; Carlisle United 21 October 1938 to September 1939. Post war assisted Northwich Victoria cs 1946; Wigan Athletic cs 1947.
A red-haired son of the Potteries, Jack Howshall graduated from Dresden Juniors to Stoke, but his first League experience came with Chesterfield in the 1934-5 season. He arrived at Peel Park after spells with Southport (51 appearances) and Bristol Rovers (20 appearances). He did not remain for very long with Stanley, leaving to join Carlisle United after appearing in the opening eight fixtures, seven of which ended in defeat. Howshall served in the RAF during the war and subsequently reappeared in non-League football in 1946. A brother, Tony Howshall, was on Southport's books in 1938-9.

HUDSON, Charles A. **1945-46**
Centre-forward.
Born: Bytham, 3 April 1920.
Debut v Wrexham (h) 21 September 1946.
Appearances: 11; Goals: 3.
Career: Guisley FC; STANLEY amateur 18 October 1945 to late December 1946.
Charlie Hudson first appeared for Stanley in wartime football, totalling 18 League and Cup appearances and scoring 11 goals in 1945-6. In one of his early appearances, he was involved in a car crash on his way to Peel Park for the game against Chester on 3 November. Despite having received a severe shaking, he continued his journey by taxi, arriving a few minutes before the kick-off. Within half an hour he had scored two fine goals which helped to set up a 5-2 victory. He continued to assist Stanley as an amateur when normal League football resumed in 1946-7, but he left in mid-season after playing at centre-forward, right-half and inside-right, all within the space of 11 matches. A draughtsman with the Rolls-Royce company, Hudson's transfer from Barnoldswick to the main works at Derby in December 1946 prevented him from continuing with Stanley.

HUDSON, George Anthony **1960-61**
Centre-forward. 5ft 11in; 11st 7lb.
Born: Manchester, 14 March 1937.
Debut v Crystal Palace (a) 20 August 1960 (scored one goal).
Appearances: 55; Goals: 39.
Career: Manchester junior football; Blackburn Rovers amateur, signing professional 29 January 1958; STANLEY 4 July 1960; Peterborough United 2 October 1961 (fee £5,000); Coventry City 6 April 1963 (fee £20,000); Northampton Town 4 March 1966; Tranmere Rovers January 1967 (fee £15,000) to cs 1969.
Club honour: Coventry City, Third Division champions season 1963-4.
Signed from Blackburn Rovers on a free transfer, George Hudson had been a reserve centre-forward at

Ewood and had made only four First Division appearances. He was an immediate 'hit' with Stanley and equalled George Stewart's earlier record of 35 League goals in season 1960-61. After 11 appearances in the following term, Stanley reluctantly transferred him to Peterborough United. In a little under two seasons with the Posh he scored 38 goals. In 1963-4, his 25 goals in 32 appearances for Coventry City spearheaded the Sky Blues' championship of the Third Division. Two seasons later, a move to Northampton Town just before the transfer 'deadline' failed to save their place in Division One, although he scored six goals in only 11 matches. His final move in League circles was to Tranmere Rovers and he helped them to secure promotion from Division Four in season 1966-7. Hudson's career figures amply illustrate his talents as a goalscorer — 297 appearances (plus one as sub), 164 goals.

HUGHES, Leonard Chester **1926-27**
Half-back. 5ft 8in; 10st 12lb.
Born: Edmonton, London, 1899 (April quarter).
Debut v Hartlepools United (a) 18 September 1926.
Appearances: 38.
Career: Gnome Athletic; Leyton (London League, Premier Division); Burnley 8 January 1925; STANLEY 17 September 1926 (fee £250); Folkestone September 1927; Dartford; Margate July 1932.
Len Hughes assisted Leyton to win the championship of the London League in season 1923-4 and moved to Burnley late in the following term. He quickly won a first-team place at Turf Moor, appearing in 26 First Division matches and two FA Cup ties in 1925-6. Hughes cost Stanley a fair-sized fee and whilst he was a regular at left-half during 1926-7, he was operating in a poor side which finished next-to-bottom in the table.

HUNT, S(amuel) Walter **1938**
Centre-forward. 5ft 11½in; 11st 12lb.
Born: Doe Lea, Derbyshire, 9 January 1909. Died: Rochdale, 2 August 1963.
Debut v Halifax Town (a) 27 August 1938.
Appearances: 5; Goals: 1.
Career: Junior football; Lincoln City 10 May 1933; Mansfield Town 23 July 1934; Torquay United 19 June 1935; Rochdale 13 August 1936; Stockport County 24 December 1937 (fee £400); STANLEY 8 July 1938; Carlisle United 21 October 1938 to September 1939; Wartime guest player with Rochdale and Southport.
Another cricketer-footballer to assist Stanley, Wally Hunt was a member of Derbyshire's groundstaff at 17 years of age. He remained for four years, but when cricket and soccer interests clashed, he choose the latter. He arrived at Accrington with a fine reputation as a goalscorer and created an individual record in scoring seven goals for Stanley Reserves, in an 11-2 win at Lancaster Town. That apart, he did not 'come off' at Peel Park, scoring only once — and that from a penalty — for the first team. Ironically enough, on being transferred to Carlisle United, he was an immediate success. During the season when he scored exactly half of Carlisle's goals, he scored four against Lincoln City, four against Stanley and three against Rochdale. All three clubs for whom he had previously played. He ended the 1938-9 season as leading goalscorer in the Northern Section with 34 goals. After League football was suspended he served as a wartime reserve policeman and as a fireman. In the post-war years he was a well-known cricketer in the Central Lancashire League, as both an amateur and a professional. He also assisted Northumberland in the Minor Counties Championship.

HUNTER, Albert Edward **1934-35**
Full-back. 5ft 9in; 11st 8lb.
Born: Sheffield, 7 August 1902. Died: Sheffield, August 1982.
Debut v New Brighton (h) 25 August 1934.
Appearances: 38; Goals: 1.
Career: Norton Woodseats Amateurs; Sheffield United amateur 24 April, signing professional 2 May 1924; Brighton & Hove Albion 7 August 1925; Scarborough Town; Bradford 29 May 1930; Walsall 10 August 1931; Doncaster Rovers 15 July 1932; STANLEY 19 June 1934; Barrow 9 July 1935; Frickley Colliery season 1936-7.
A dour defender and a great favourite with the Accrington supporters, Albert Hunter was a strong tackler who cleared his lines heftily. Walsall gave him his Football League debut in 1931 which was rather late, considering that he was 29 years old and had begun with Sheffield United seven years earlier. Once established at League level, however, he gave excellent service, totalling 167 appearances in his final five seasons of senior football.

HUNTER, Edward **1954-59**
Wing-half. 5ft 8in; 11st 3lb.
Born: Tillicoultry, 7 March 1928.
Debut v Southport (h) 21 August 1954.
Appearances: 169; Goals: 4.
Career: Alva Albion Rangers; Falkirk season 1951-2; STANLEY 16 June 1954, released on a free transfer May 1959.

Representative honour: Third Division North v Third Division South at Stockport, season 1956-7.
One of Stanley's best signings, Eddie Hunter first came to manager Galbraith's notice when he played for Falkirk against Grimsby Town in a floodlit friendly match, when Stanley's manager was a player at Blundell Park. A thrustful player with a strong tackle, Hunter was also a clever ball-player with a highly developed positional sense. In his first three seasons at Peel Park he missed only a handful of matches, but then in season 1957-8 he was dogged by injury. In September 1958 he asked for a transfer but remained until the end of the season, when he announced his intention to retire. He took a newsagency business in Great Harwood and later worked as a progress clerk.

HURST, William Robert **1948-49**
Wing-forward. 5ft 7in; 10st 10lb.
Born: Brierfield, Lancashire, 4 March 1921.
Debut v Southport (a) 26 March 1949.
Appearances: 1.
Career: Burnley amateur 18 August 1937, signing professional 5 March 1938; Plymouth Argyle 7 June 1939; Nelson cs 1947; Bury 8 September 1947; Northwich Victoria cs 1948; STANLEY 29 October 1948 to May 1949.
Bill Hurst began as a colt with Burnley at 17 years of age and joined Plymouth just before the war. After only four League appearances he returned north and was playing for Nelson when Bury brought him back into League football. Stanley signed him after two earlier unsuccessful attempts. He was originally going to be part of the deal which took Walter Keeley to Bury, but at the last minute, Hurst declined to join Stanley. Again in the early part of season 1948-9 he refused a move to Peel Park. He finally signed for Stanley, for a small fee, in October 1948. In the event, he made only one first-team appearance, when he deputized for Walter Keeley, who was out of action with a fractured toe. Of Hurst's debut, the *Accrington Observer* commented: 'He did some neat things, but received no support from behind'.

HUTTON, Thomas Osborne **1944-47**
Full-back.
Born: Gateshead, 10 September 1922.
Debut v Hull City (h) 21 December 1946.
Appearances: 18.
Career: Red Rose FC; Newcastle United (wartime guest) season 1940-41; STANLEY amateur 13 November 1944, signing professional 25 May 1945; Carlisle United 5 August 1947; Rochdale 15 July 1949 to 2 January 1950; Nelson February 1950; Tranmere Rovers 15 August 1950; Chorley player-coach August 1951.
Tom Hutton first played for Stanley four days after returning from the Middle East, following his 'demob'. He had originally come to the match as a spectator, but when one of Stanley's players failed to turn up, he was pressed into action. In services football, Hutton played for Red Rose, an East Lancashire Army team based at the village of Whalley. Variously described as 'sound rather than spectacular' and 'hard working with particularly good distribution', he was also usefully versatile, appearing in all three half-back positions and at full-back. Outside of football, Tom Hutton was a joiner.

IVILL, Edward **1935-37**
Full-back. 5ft 9½in; 11st 10lb.
Born: Little Hulton, Lancashire, 7 December 1898.
Died: Blackburn, 24 November 1979.
Debut v Lincoln City (a) 31 August 1935.
Appearances: 16.
Career: Bolton Wanderers amateur; Atherton; Oldham Athletic 15 July 1924; Charlton Athletic 7 November 1932 (fee £1,700); Wolverhampton Wanderers 20 January 1933; STANLEY 26 July 1935, appointed reserve-team coach 27 August 1936; Clitheroe 31 August 1937.
Teddy Ivill, a former teammate of Stanley's manager Jack Hacking at Oldham Athletic, was approaching 37 years of age when he made his debut for Stanley. His experience was put to good use, however, when he was signed as coach to the second team in 1936. In earlier days he set up an outstanding record with Oldham Athletic, totalling 277 Football League appearances which included a run of five consecutive seasons (1927-32) when he did not miss a single League or Cup match. After the war in Europe had ended, Ivill was appointed to take charge of Stanley's Lancashire Combination side. His son, Jeffrey Ivill, also a full-back, played for the Reserves in season 1945-6.

JACK, Vincent **1959-60**
Centre-half or full-back. 6ft 4in; 13st.
Born: Rosemarkie, Ross and Cromarty, 6 August 1933.
Debut v Wrexham (h) 29 August 1959.
Appearances: 22.
Career: Inverness junior football; Bury 14 April 1954; Swindon Town 27 October 1956; STANLEY 9 July 1959; Gravesend & Northfleet October 1960.
Vince Jack was one of Harold Bodle's first signings when the new Stanley manager took over at Peel Park in June 1959. He obtained Jack's signature after a fee of £1,500, placed on him by Swindon Town, had been removed by the Football League. A formidable barrier to opposing forwards, at 6ft 4in and 13st, he had outstanding physical advantages for his position. At either centre-half or right-back, he could be relied upon for total commitment in an overworked defence, in the season which saw Stanley drop into Division Four.

JEAVONS, William Henry **1933-34**
Outside-right. 5ft 5½in; 10st 4lb.
Born: Woodhouse Mill, near Sheffield, 9 February 1912.
Debut v New Brighton (a) 4 November 1933 (scored two goals).
Appearances: 17; Goals: 7.
Career: Woodhouse Brunswick; Huddersfield Town (trial) 4 October 1930; Chesterfield amateur 28 August, signing professional 2 December 1931; Burnley 24 June 1932; STANLEY 24 June 1933; Oldham Athletic 24 February 1934; Southport 19 July 1934; Wrexham 30 July 1935; Shrewsbury Town 18 December 1935; Burton Town August 1936; Worcester City January 1938; Burnley (wartime guest).
Billy Jeavons did not break into Stanley's first team until early November 1933, but as he had scored in every reserve-team match up until then, his promotion was not unexpected. Stanley had not won for over a month when he made his debut, but he scored within 15 minutes of the kick-off, added another in the second half and Stanley won 3-0. Although of frail physique,

Jeavons' speed and footwork could take him through the most compact defences. His form made him a target for the scouts and it was Oldham Athletic who signed him, making him the third Stanley winger to join the Latics, Agar and Pears having earlier made the move from Accrington to Oldham.

JEPSON, John James **1925-27 & 1928-30**
Centre-forward. 5ft 10in; 11st 2lb.
Born: Heaton Norris, 1899 (July quarter).
Debut v Nelson (a) 10 October 1925.
Appearances: 117; Goals: 82.
Career: New Mills FC; Atherton 1921-2; New Mills FC 1922-24; Notts County 10 May 1924; STANLEY 26 August 1925; Carlisle United June 1927; STANLEY 16 June 1928; Wigan Borough 6 June 1930; Mansfield Town 30 July 1931; Altrincham February 1932; Nelson August 1933 to cs 1934.
John Jepson came into prominence by scoring 81 goals in two seasons for New Mills. Notts County signed him but did not give him a League outing and Stanley obtained him on a free transfer. He was an unlikely-looking footballer, tallish, stoop-shouldered and prematurely balding. His general play also was not for the purist, but he certainly knew how to put the ball into the net. In 1925-6 he scored six hat-tricks for Stanley in registering 30 League and six FA Cup goals. He was also leading scorer for the Reserves with 20 goals. As something of a marked man, he found less success in the following season and was allowed to move to Carlisle United. He was recalled by Stanley when Carlisle gained admission to the Football League in 1928. In the next two seasons he scored 41 goals in 61 appearances. He also scored five goals in a Lancashire Senior Cup tie against Wigan Borough in October 1929. In the following season he joined Wigan Borough and was their leading goalscorer with 28 in 35 appearances. He did not appear in the League with Mansfield Town in 1931-2, the Stags' first season as a League club. In 1933-4 Jepson rounded off his career by scoring 32 goals for Nelson.

JOHNSON, Joseph **1932-33**
Inside-forward. 5ft 7½in; 11st 4lb.
Born: Wednesbury, *c.*1907.
Debut v Halifax Town (h) 27 August 1932.
Appearances: 26; Goals: 7.
Career: Wigan Borough 24 May 1930; Halifax Town amateur 18 July, signing professional 22 October 1931; STANLEY 24 June 1932 to May 1933.
Joe Johnson's first season of League football was with Wigan Borough and he started well by scoring twice on his debut at Darlington. His return of nine goals in 30 matches assisted the Borough to finish tenth in the Northern Section, but it proved to be their last completed campaign, as they resigned from the Football League after fulfilling only 12 of their matches the following term. Johnson, in the meantime, had joined Halifax Town as an amateur and he was signed as a professional only four days prior to his old club's demise. With Stanley he missed only two matches up to mid-season, when an injury and subsequent loss of form saw him out of the side for all but six of the final 20 fixtures.

JOHNSON, John Charles **1938-39**
Half-back. 5ft 8½in; 11st 8lb.
Born: South Kirkby, 3 October 1905.
Debut v Halifax Town (a) 27 August 1938.
Appearances: 39.
Career: Denaby United; Sheffield Wednesday 30 April 1927; Bournemouth & Boscombe Athletic 1 June 1928; Rotherham United 7 November 1930; Barnsley 6 September 1933; Carlisle United 9 June 1934; STANLEY 9 June 1938 to September 1939.
A half-back capable of filling any position in the middle line, Jack Johnson was Stanley's most consistent defender in 1938-9, missing only three matches. One of the oldest players in the side, he joined Stanley after four seasons with Carlisle United, for whom he appeared in 139 League matches. Earlier, he had played in nine matches for Barnsley in season 1933-4, when they won the Third Division North championship. Johnson retired during World War Two, after a career which spanned 289 Football League appearances and ten goals. A brother, C.Johnson, was a Doncaster Rovers half-back and a cricketer on Yorkshire's groundstaff.

JOHNSON, Michael James **1951-52**
Inside-forward. 5ft 10in; 10st 12lb.
Born: Oxford, 24 February 1928.
Debut v Halifax Town (h) 25 September 1951.
Appearances: 3.
Career: Lytham junior football; Preston North End 19 September 1950; STANLEY 18 June 1951; Frickley Colliery July 1952.
Mike Johnson had made 15 Central League appearances for Preston North End Reserves in the 1950-51 season, when they finished fourth in the table and the first team won the Second Division championship. Five other League clubs were said to be interested in him when he sought a move, but manager Crook was successful in bringing him to Peel Park, in return for a small fee, in June 1951. Equally effective in either inside-forward berth, Johnson's debut was nevertheless made at outside-left, when he deputized for George Glaister in the 2-2 draw against Halifax Town. He was called upon for only a further two League appearances during the course of the season and was released on a free transfer in May 1952.

JOHNSON, Sydney **1931**
Centre-forward.
Debut v New Brighton (h) 10 January 1931.
Appearances: 7; Goals: 3.
Career: Barnoldswick Town; STANLEY 10 January 1931; Barnoldswick Town cs 1931; Rossendale United during season 1932-3.
Syd Johnson, a young centre-forward from Barnoldswick Town was a mid-season recruit. Although no fee was paid for him, Stanley played a game at Barnoldswick in late January 1931, with the Town club taking the proceeds. Johnson was said to have scored 35 goals for Barnoldswick in the season when Stanley signed him and he was quickly given a run in the first team. Of his debut performance, the *Sports Telegraph* reported: 'He showed promise in positional play and was quick to send a pass out to a well-placed wingman'. The young centre-forward scored three goals in seven appearances which seemed a reasonable return, but he was not retained in the close season and returned to Barnoldswick.

JONES, Eric **1959-60**
Inside or wing-forward. 5ft 10in; 11st 4lb.
Born: Ulverston, 23 June 1931.
Debut v Tranmere Rovers (a) 22 August 1959.
Appearances: 18.
Career: Blackburn Rovers amateur; Nottingham Forest amateur; Notts County amateur; Preston North End 4 January 1952; Nottingham Forest 5 September 1955; Doncaster Rovers 15 March 1958; STANLEY 14 July 1959; Southport 5 July 1960; Lancaster City August 1962 to September 1963.
Eric Jones was said to be the first player bought by Stanley (as opposed to the usual free-transfer signings) for two years, when Harold Bodle brought him from Doncaster Rovers to Peel Park in July 1959. In the relegation season which followed, Jones was not alone in failing to find his best form. it was not until mid-season that he was given an extended run at inside-left and his reintroduction coincided with the best spell of the campaign. Jones' final move in League circles proved his most productive, as he appeared in 45 League matches and scored 12 goals for Southport in 1960-61 and added a further 31 appearances and six goals in 1961-2. Off the field, Jones was employed in the motor trade.

JONES, James Alfred **1954-55**
Goalkeeper. 5ft 10in; 12st 6lb.
Born: Birkenhead, 3 August 1927.
Debut v Chesterfield (a) 20 February 1954.
Appearances: 46.
Career: Everton amateur 7 May, signing professional 1 December 1945; Ellesmere Port Town; Everton re-registered 2 August 1948; New Brighton 19 August 1950; Lincoln City 20 August 1951 (fee £408); STANLEY 19 February 1954 (fee £550); Rochdale 13 September 1955 (fee £750), retired June 1961.
Club honour: Lincoln City, Third Division North champions season 1951-2.
Jimmy Jones began in football as an inside-forward and only went into goal by accident. He did so well that he totalled 331 League appearances. His initial senior experience came with New Brighton, in what proved to be the Rakers' last season as a League club. He had been one of Walter Galbraith's earliest signings, following his appointment as player-manager to New Brighton. Some three and a half years later, Galbraith signed him again, this time on behalf of Stanley. Jones remained first-choice goalkeeper at Peel Park until February 1955. In a classic 'insult to injury' situation, he was taken unconscious to hospital after diving into a goalpost and then lost his first-team place to his deputy, Tommy McQueen. In September 1955 Jones requested a transfer and was quickly snapped up by Rochdale. He stayed for six seasons at Spotland, making 175 League appearances before announcing his retirement. He then became a licensee in Lincoln.

JONES, Thomas **1937-39**
Centre-half. 6ft; 12st 2lb.
Born: Little Hulton, Lancashire, 1916.
Debut v Chester (h) 7 May 1938.
Appearances: 10; Goals: 1.
Career: Little Hulton FC; STANLEY amateur 5 May, signing professional 25 August 1937; Oldham Athletic 14 January 1939; STANLEY and Rochdale (wartime guest).
Tall and fast moving with nice constructive ideas, Tom Jones made 35 Lancashire Combination appearances in 1937-8 when Stanley Reserves bid strongly for championship honours. In the following season, after nine first-team appearances, Oldham Athletic signed him. Whilst serving with the British liberation armies in North-West Europe in April 1945, he was seriously wounded and had to have both feet amputated. In September of the same year he was able to attend two games arranged for his benefit. Stanley played Rochdale at Peel Park and at Spotland, both games drawing good attendances. Elder brother William (*qv*) was also on Stanley's books in season 1931-2.

JONES, T(homas) Benjamin **1953-54**
Wing-forward. 5ft 9in; 11st 10lb.
Born: Frodsham, 23 March 1920. Died: December 1972.
Debut v Workington (h) 26 August 1953.
Appearances: 14.
Career: Ellesmere Port Town; Tranmere Rovers 3 September 1941; Chelsea 1 November 1947; STANLEY 9 July 1953; Dartford July 1954.
Benny Jones was one of several new signings made by Stanley's new player-manager, Walter Galbraith, in the summer of 1953. The former Chelsea winger was one of several widely-experienced recruits, in what was probably one of Stanley's oldest line-ups. Five players were aged 33 and over, whilst the only 'youngster' was Joe Devlin, who was 22 years old. Jones had starred with Tranmere Rovers in 1946-7, scoring 14 goals in 42 appearances and was signed by First Division Chelsea the following season. his best seasonal return with the Pensioners was in 1948-9, when he scored six goals in 28 appearances; thereafter he was mainly a reserve-team player at Stamford Bridge. A classy winger, accomplished on either flank, Jones' League career totalled 109 appearances and 30 goals, a fair return for a wingman.

JONES, William W. **1931-32**
Inside-forward. 5ft 9½in; 11st 3lb.

Born: Little Hulton, Lancashire, *c.*1910.
Debut v Wrexham (h) 25 December 1931 (scored one goal).
Appearances: 22; Goals: 3.
Career: Junior football; Aston Villa 27 January 1928; Scarborough Town; Manchester Central; Bacup Borough cs 1931; STANLEY 23 December 1931 to May 1932.
Bill Jones had scored 13 goals for Bacup Borough in the season that Stanley recruited him, just prior to Christmas 1931. Whilst he found goals more difficult to come by in League football, he held his place in Stanley's attack. Mainly from inside-left he showed marked ability in using the ball to advantage when organizing subtle attacks. Jones spent much of his career on the non-League circuit, after a very early association with Aston Villa. In October 1937 he was reported to be playing in Ireland. His younger brother, Thomas Jones (*qv*) was a Stanley defender just before the war.

KASHER, Joseph W.R. 1925-27
Centre-half. 5ft 11in; 11st 6lb.
Born: Willington, Co Durham, 14 January 1894.
Debut v Walsall (a) 29 August 1925.
Appearances: 47; Goals: 2.
Career: Hunwick Juniors; Willington; Crook Town; Sunderland 17 May 1919; Stoke 19 October 1922; Carlisle United cs 1924; STANLEY 6 June 1925 to May 1927.

Joe Kasher, a tall, seasoned centre-half with a guardsman's bearing, had four seasons of First Division experience with Sunderland and Stoke. In the summer of 1924 he could not agree terms with Stoke, who placed a heavy transfer fee on him. Kasher returned home to Willington, secured a job and played part-time for Carlisle United, at that time a North Eastern League club. Once back into full-time training with Stanley he proved a fine pivot, playing clever and polished football. Always cool and collected, his resourcefulness when in difficult situations revealed his skill and experience. In March 1927 he retired and became licensee of the Peel Park Hotel, Accrington.
Note: At the time of writing, Joe Kasher is due to celebrate his 97th birthday.

KAY, Fred 1921-23
Full-back. 5ft 9in; 12st 7lb.
Born: Hindley, 1901 (April quarter).
Debut v Rochdale (a) 27 August 1921.
Appearances: 30.

Career: Ramsbottom British Legion; STANLEY April 1921, retired due to injury during 1922-3 season.
During their initial season of Third Division North football, Stanley's right-back Freddie Kay was generally acknowledged to be one of the best backs in the Division. A strong defender, seen at his best during intense periods of pressure, his only fault was probably attributable to his youthful enthusiasm. As the *Accrington Observer* delicately put it: 'He was apt to forget that fair play is a jewel'. Sadly, in a game against Southport in March 1922, he received such a serious knee injury that his career was effectively ended. He had a run in the Reserves nine months later and managed one more outing with the first team in January 1923. It was, however, obvious that a career which had promised so much was over. Freddie Kay was only 22 years old at the time.

KAY, Thomas **1923-25**
Outside-left. 5ft 6½in; 10st 8lb.
Born: Ramsbottom, 1904.
Debut v Wigan Borough (h) 10 November 1923 (scored one goal).
Appearances: 33; Goals: 5.
Career: Holcombe Church FC; Ramsbottom British Legion; STANLEY amateur 12, signing professional 16 November 1923 to 10 August 1925; Southport (one month's trial) September 1925; Manchester City (trial) 31 August to 29 September 1926.
Tommy Kay scored on his Football League debut and earned good Press notices. 'Fast, clever and controlled the ball well' was one verdict. The only critical note was that 'he seemed to lack confidence in taking corner kicks'. Although not registered by Accrington's management until November 1923, he had assisted Stanley, as an amateur, in the previous season. He scored for Stanley Reserves in their 2-0 victory over Lytham in the Richardson Cup Final, played at Deepdale, Preston, on 5 May 1923. A bout of ill health ended his Stanley career after he had originally been retained for a third season. Tommy Kay played cricket for Haslingden in the Lancashire League and after World War Two became a newsagent in Accrington and later had a grocery business in Radcliffe.

KEARNEY, Sydney Francis **1938-39 & 1946-47**
Inside-forward, later half-back. 5ft 8½in; 11st.
Born: Liverpool, 28 March 1917. Died: Chelsea, 1982 (October quarter).
Debut v Darlington (a) 5 November 1938.
Appearances: 30; Goals: 7.
Career: Liverpool junior football; Leicester City amateur April 1935 signing professional 20 August 1936; Tranmere Rovers 12 May 1937; STANLEY 7 November 1938 (fee £125); Bristol City 4 January 1947; Street FC (Somerset) 11 August 1950.
In his first two seasons of League football, Syd Kearney was a championship winner with Tranmere Rovers in 1937-8 (eight appearances, two goals), but he ended 1938-9 with Stanley who finished 22nd in Division Three North. His career spanned World War Two, part of which saw him stationed in Nairobi. After making a few appearances towards the close of season 1945-6, he was Stanley's first goalscorer when normal League football resumed in August 1946. A positional switch from inside-forward to wing-half was an immediate success, so much so that Bristol City signed him and he spent the next three and a half years at Ashton Gate.

KEATING, Robert **1946-47**
Outside-right. 5ft 8in; 10st 10lb.
Born: Oldham, 24 June 1917. Died: Werneth, Oldham, June 1985.
Debut v Tranmere Rovers (h) 7 December 1946.
Appearances: 5.
Career: Oldham Athletic 23 August 1941; Hereford United June 1946; STANLEY 6 December 1946 to May 1947.
Robert Keating began in wartime football with his local club, Oldham Athletic. He appeared in five seasons of regional football and was leading goalscorer for the Latics' reserve team in 1945-6, this despite his having played as much in defence as in attack. He left Boundary Park to join Hereford United, just before League football recommenced. His new club was also reported to have found him a job, to go with his part-time professional engagement. He returned north to sign for Stanley in December of the same year and played on both wings in a five-match run. Unfortunately, his inclusion did little to strengthen the attack, which managed to score only four goals in six matches during the month. All the goals, incidentally, were recorded by another transient recruit, Bert Robinson (*qv*).

KEELEY, John James **1959**
Inside-forward. 5ft 8½in; 12st 7lb.
Born: Anfield, Liverpool, 18 October 1936.
Debut v Tranmere Rovers (a) 22 August 1959.
Appearances: 10; Goals: 1.
Career: Liverpool Schoolboys; Everton amateur 4 May 1953, signing professional 12 May 1954; STANLEY 18 July 1959; Southport (trial) 25 December 1959; Prescot Cables January 1960; New Brighton; Colwyn Bay to 1962; Dolgellau 1962-3.
International honours: England Schoolboys and England Youth.
Jackie Keeley was a member of the England Schoolboys side, captained by the late Duncan Edwards, who won the Victory Shield in 1951-2. He scored twice against both Scotland and Wales. In 1953-4 he represented England in the International Youth Tournament, played in West Germany. On his Football League debut for Everton, he scored at Bolton Wanderers. This was in season 1957-8 and he appeared in seven League and FA Cup matches and scored three goals. He cost Stanley a substantial fee in July 1959, but he failed to command a first-team place and was released in mid December 1959, not having been included in any of Stanley's sides for a month. Briefly on trial with Southport, Keeley had gravitated into non-League football before the end of the season. Altogether a most disappointing outcome to a career which had shown such early promise.

KEELEY, Walter **1944-47 & 1948-51**
Inside-forward. 5ft 9in; 10st 12lb.
Born: Manchester, 1 April 1921.
Debut v Bradford City (a) 31 August 1946.
Appearances: 149; Goals: 56.
Career: RAF Football; STANLEY amateur 18 September, signing professional 11 December 1944; Bury 25 October 1947 (fee about £3,500); Port Vale 10 January 1948; STANLEY 24 September 1948 (fee £1,500); Rochdale 20 October 1951 (fee £300); Fleetwood February 1952.
Walter Keeley was a match-winning opportunist who began with Stanley during wartime football, whilst he was serving in the RAF. He was leading goalscorer, by a large margin, when Stanley won the championship of the Third Division North (West Region) in season 1945-6. He was joint leading scorer, with Stan Mercer, in 1946-7 and had netted eight times in only 12 appearances when Bury paid a record fee to take him to Gigg Lane. He soon moved again, joining Port Vale in an exchange deal which involved another player, Alf Bellis. Just less than a year after leaving Stanley, Walter Keeley was welcomed back. Predictably, he led the side's goalscoring charts at the end of the season. Keeley was just as adept at saving goals as he was at scoring them. In season 1946-7 he was selected, in an emergency, as goalkeeper for the visit to Southport.

He was very much the hero of the occasion as Stanley won 1-0. Subsequently, he was the player turned to when Stanley goalkeepers were injured during matches. He was called upon four times and remained unbeaten throughout. He suffered a broken leg at Chester in March 1951, having just scored his 13th goal of the season. He was to play only twice more for Stanley before joining Rochdale. Later in the same season he joined Fleetwood and scored five goals in his debut match. A plumber by trade, Keeley's father helped form Manchester North End FC and played for them for 14 seasons after World War One. Known locally as 'tough ginger', Keeley senior certainly lived up to his reputation. He once turned out, in an emergency, for a junior works team when he was 60 years old.

KERR, Daniel **1935-36**
Centre-forward. 5ft 8½in; 11st 6lb.
Born: Hamilton, Scotland, *c.*1915.
Debut v Rochdale (h) 7 September 1935.
Appearances: 2.
Career: Carluke Rangers; Manchester United 30 November 1934 to 8 March 1935; STANLEY 23 July 1935 to May 1936; Birmingham (trial) 21 May to 28 August 1937.
'Danny' Kerr joined Manchester United as a 19-year-old, but his stay at Old Trafford was brief. He had, however, done enough to impress Stanley's new player-manager, Jack Hacking, when the two players were teammates in Manchester United's Central League side. Kerr had an early but undistinguished debut for Stanley and, apart from one other first-team outing, spent his season at Peel Park in the Reserves. An enigmatic character who at times exhibited all the attributes of a born footballer, Kerr lacked consistency and thrust to combine with his sinuous dribbling skills.

KEETLEY, Joseph Frederick **1923**
Inside-forward. 5ft 9½in; 10st 13lb.
Born: Derby, 28 June 1897. Died: Allerton, 30 March 1958.

Debut v Darlington (a) 25 August 1923.
Appearances: 13; Goals: 8.
Career: Victoria Ironworks (Derby); Bolton Wanderers 17 August 1920; STANLEY 12 June 1923; Liverpool 9 November 1923 (fee £1,200); Wolverhampton Wanderers 26 May 1925; Wrexham 24 November 1925; Doncaster Rovers 29 January 1926; Horwich RMI later in the same year.
'A player of the artistic type, clever in ball-control and artful in beating an opponent,' remarked the *Accrington Observer* in September 1923. Joe Keetley had arrived from Bolton Wanderers on a free transfer, but after scoring eight goals in 13 appearances for Stanley he brought a four-figure fee from Liverpool. A younger brother, Harry Keetley, was given a trial in Stanley's reserve team in November 1923. He was a good player, but considered too young for League football. He later played for Doncaster Rovers. Joe Keetley was the eldest of a remarkable footballing family which boasted a quintet of League footballers. There were actually 11 boys and one girl and on one occasion the Victoria Ironworks team included seven of the brothers. Frank, Harry, Tom, Joe and Jack forming the forward line.

KELLY, J(ohn) Norman **1933-34**
Inside-forward. 5ft 10½in; 11st 4lb.
Born: Liverpool, *c.*1909.
Debut v New Brighton (a) 4 November 1933.
Appearances: 14; Goals: 8.
Career: Seaforth Ribble Motors; Blackburn Rovers 29 March 1932; Southport (trial) 11 August 1933; STANLEY 9 September 1933 to 4 April 1934.
During season 1922-3, Norman Kelly suffered a broken shin-bone when playing for Blackburn Rovers' Midweek League side at Preston. Released in the close season, he joined Stanley after a brief trial with Southport. He proved to be a most popular player with the Peel Park crowd. Brilliant in headwork, he seemed able to get to the ball from apparently impossible positions and scored several picture goals in this manner. He was injured at Barnsley in February 1934 and the problem proved more serious than had first been thought. He seemed to have recovered and was back in the team three weeks later. He broke down, however, after scoring a typical goal and had to leave the field. He did not play again and in September 1934 he was reported to have taken up a position outside of the game.

KELLY, William Muir **1957-58**
Centre-half.
Born: Hill O'Beath, Cowdenbeath, 14 August 1922.
Debut v York City (h) 21 September 1957.
Appearances: 24.
Career: Airdrieonians; Blackburn Rovers 17 September 1951; Mossley July 1957; STANLEY 23 September 1957, retired July 1958.
Willie Kelly was signed by Stanley at a time when the side was crippled by injuries and he proved to be an excellent short-term signing. He had been Blackburn Rovers' regular centre-half until Matt Woods was signed from Everton in November 1956. Kelly had been playing for Mossley (managed by a former Blackburn Rovers teammate, Eddie Quigley) in the season that Stanley signed him. Kelly's senior career eventually fell victim to the reorganization of the Third Divisions in 1958-9. He decided to retire because he felt that

he would be unable to get time off his work to undertake all the extra travelling that the new Third Division would involve. Younger brother, Walter Kelly, scored over a century of League goals in a career which took in Bury, Doncaster Rovers, Stockport County and Chester.

KENDALL, James Briden **1952-53**
Inside-forward. 5ft 9in; 11st.
Born: Birtley, 4 October 1922.
Debut v Grimsby Town (h) 27 September 1952.
Appearances: 26; Goals: 8.
Career: Gateshead United; Barrow 8 May 1947; Gateshead 25 November 1948; Barrow 24 October 1951; STANLEY 26 September 1952; Nelson cs 1953.
When Jimmy Kendall re-signed for Barrow from Gateshead in October 1951, the Holker Street programme editor commented: 'Whilst Jimmy is no international, for 100 per cent hard graft it would be difficult to find a better man. He still knows the shortest way to goal and he can hit a ball.' When Stanley signed him, they hoped that he would keep up the scoring form that he had always shown at their expense. In games against the Reds he had registered three hat-tricks (one a four-goal feat) with Gateshead and Barrow. Kendall scored eight of Stanley's 39 goals in 1952-3 to round off his senior career which totalled 149 appearances and 51 goals.

KIRK, John McCrae **1952-54**
Inside-forward. 5ft 9½in; 12st.
Born: Winnipeg, Canada, 13 March 1930.
Debut v Port Vale (h) 14 March 1953.
Appearances: 14; Goals: 1.
Career: Montrose (Scotland); Portsmouth amateur, signing professional 22 January 1951; STANLEY 13 March 1952, transfer listed 8 September 1953, registration cancelled February 1954.
John Kirk signed for Stanley on his 23rd birthday, beating the transfer 'deadline' by three days. In a long spell with Portsmouth, two years were spent away from Fratton Park on National Service. He was described as 'a Scot' by the local Press when signed, but he was actually Canadian and had moved to Scotland with his family when a boy. His inclusion into Stanley's ranks failed to lift the team off the foot of the table, as they won only two matches in the final two months of the season. Under new player-manager Walter Galbraith, Kirk played only once in the first team in 1953-4. He scored Stanley's goal against Wrexham in September, but then played exclusively in the reserve team, making several appearances at centre-half.

KIRKPATRICK, John **1924-25**
Inside-forward. 5ft 8½in; 11st 8lb.
Born: Annan, Dumfriesshire.
Debut v Bradford (h) 8 September 1924.
Appearances: 4.
Career: Workington (North Eastern League); STANLEY 25 June 1924 to May 1925.
A stocky, dark haired forward with two seasons experience of North Eastern League football. John Kirkpatrick proved a useful reserve forward, but his senior outings were infrequent. His younger brother, James Kirkpatrick, found more success in a career which took in Queen of the South, Leeds United and Watford.

LANCASTER, Joseph Gerard **1950-51**
Goalkeeper.
Born: Stockport, 28 April 1926.
Debut v Gateshead (h) 5 May 1951.
Appearances: 1.
Career: Heaton Mersey Old Boys; Manchester United 4 February 1950; STANLEY 25 November 1950, released on a free transfer 16 June 1951.
One of four goalkeepers used by Manchester United in League matches in season 1949-50, Joe Lancaster made his debut at Old Trafford before a crowd of almost 47,000. He kept his charge intact in a 1-0 win against Chelsea. He also appeared in one other League game and two of the season's FA Cup ties. He left Old Trafford at about the time when United paid what was then a record fee for a goalkeeper, £11,000, to bring Reg Allen from Queen's Park Rangers. With Stanley, Lancaster was understudy to Doug Daniels and appeared in only one first-team match. This was on the final Saturday of the 1950-51 season and less than 3,000 spectators were present at Redheugh Park, Gateshead, to witness his final League appearance. It was quite a contrast to his senior debut with Manchester United, only some 16 months earlier.

LANGSTRETH, H(orace) Lawrence **1952-55**
Full-back or half-back. 5ft 9½in; 11st 10lb.
Born: Blackburn, 19 July 1931.
Debut v York City (h) 5 December 1953.
Appearances: 3.
Career: Blackburn junior football; STANLEY amateur during season 1952-3, signing professional 9 July 1953; Netherfield 17 June 1955 (fee £75); Torquay United 14 August 1956 to June 1957.

'Lol' Langstreth, a stalwart defender in Stanley's reserve team, combined his football career with his profession as a master joiner in Blackburn. His only calls for first-team duty came in season 1953-4 when he appeared in three League matches and one FA Cup tie. In September 1954 he requested cancellation of his contract due to heavy calls upon his time by his business interests. He was persuaded to change his mind and reappeared in the Reserves a month later. In June 1955 he joined Netherfield, along with another of Stanley's reserve-team players, Tommy McKeown (*qv*).

LANSDALE, Joseph **1930-31**
Goalkeeper. 5ft 11½in; 11st 4lb.
Born: Little Lever, 4 March 1894. Died: South Africa, *c.*1977.
Debut v Stockport County (a) 22 November 1930.
Appearances: 26.
Career: Little Lever Congregational; Norwich City July 1912; Bolton Wanderers (wartime guest); Millwall April 1920; STANLEY 7 November 1930; Folkestone Town 27 August 1931.

Representative honours: Southern League v Welsh League at Fratton Park, Portsmouth 4 October 1922. The South v England at Millwall 12 February 1923.
Joe Lansdale was recruited in November 1930 after Stanley's first 16 League matches had seen 49 goals conceded. An early match report suggested that the new goalkeeper was as cool as the weather and his skill and cool judgement certainly helped tighten Stanley's defensive lines. On Boxing Day 1930, he saved two penalties at Wigan Borough. In a match lacking in Christmas spirit, Stanley won 3-2 and Frank Barson, Wigan's centre-half, was sent off the field. In over ten years with Millwall, Lansdale served the Lions in four different Divisions (Southern, Third, Third South and Second), totalling 239 appearances.

LAPHAM, E(dgar) Harold **1936**
Centre-forward. 5ft 8½in; 11st 7lb.
Born: Liverpool, *c.*1905.
Debut v Stockport County (h) 15 February 1935 (scored one goal).
Appearances: 7; Goals: 2.
Career: Marine FC (Liverpool); Everton (trial); Blackburn Rovers amateur November 1934, signing professional 25 June 1935; STANLEY 13 February 1936; Wrexham 25 July 1936 to May 1939.
Harold Lapham was signed by Stanley on the same day that Mortimer and Harker were transferred to Portsmouth. A bustler with a strong shot in either foot, he had scored ten goals in 17 Central League appearances for Blackburn Rovers Reserves. After scoring twice in his first three appearances in Stanley's colours, Lapham's goalscoring touch deserted him as the team ended the season in poor form. Moving to Wrexham for season 1936-7, he proved a big success, being leading goalscorer in his first two seasons at the Racecourse. He netted 21 goals in 30 appearances in 1936-7 (which included four against Gateshead on 29 March 1937) and 16 goals in 32 appearances in 1937-8.

LATHAM, Albert **1928-30**
Half-back. 6ft; 11st 10lb.
Born: Hucknall, Notts, 1904 (October quarter).
Debut v Carlisle United (h) 25 August 1928.
Appearances: 52; Goals: 3.

Career: Newark Town; Wolverhampton Wanderers 24 June 1927; STANLEY 21 July 1928; Rochdale 4 August 1930; Hurst cs 1931; York City 30 October 1931; Barnoldswick Town cs 1932; Fleetwood June 1933; Clitheroe April 1935; Lancaster Town (trial) October 1938.

Albert Latham became a regular first-team player for Stanley after Chris Dodds had been transferred to Sheffield Wednesday in October 1928. A thoughtful, constructive half-back, he was particularly useful in the air, by reason of his height. Apart from his 52 appearances for Stanley, Latham saw little senior football. He did not appear in the League for either Wolves or York City and played only eight times for Rochdale. In October 1938 he was reported to be on trial with Lancaster Town and was unfortunate to be in the Dollies' team which lost 11-2 to Stanley Reserves at the Giant Axe, when Wally Hunt broke the individual goalscoring record for Stanley Reserves by scoring seven goals in the match.

LATHAM, George **1938-39**

Inside-forward. 5ft 6½in; 10st 6lb.
Born: Blackburn, *c.*1918.
Debut v Oldham Athletic (h) 27 September 1938.
Appearances: 2.
Career: Blackburn Grammar School; Blackburn Rovers amateur; Liverpool amateur season 1937-8; STANLEY 17 August 1938; Bangor City 11 February 1939.

Signed following an impressive display at inside-left for the 'Reds' in the pre-season trial in August 1938, George Latham had played in the previous season with Liverpool's 'A' and reserve teams. A dapper little player with a neat touch and plenty of tricks in approaching goal, his one drawback was his lightweight physique. Latham departed Peel Park to join Bangor City who finished as runners-up for the championship, in their first season in the Lancashire Combination.

LAW, George Bramley **1930-32**

Full-back. 5ft 8in; 11st 3lb.

Born: Ramsbottom, 1905 (October quarter).
Debut v York City (h) 27 September 1930.
Appearances: 4.
Career: Ramsbottom United; Oldham Athletic (trial) August 1928; Ramsbottom United; STANLEY amateur 21 August 1930, signing professional 9 May 1931, released on a free transfer April 1932.

Basically a reserve-team player, George Law was understudy to Jimmy Armstrong, Stanley's long-serving defender. Law's first chance came when injury broke Armstrong's remarkable run of 150 consecutive appearances. With the departure of Tom Whittaker in May 1931, Law was signed as a professional. He remained on the side-lines, however, as Norman Price, a new signing from Bristol Rovers, took over the vacant left-back position.

LEADBETTER, Albert **1946-47**

Outside-left.
Born: Newton-le-Willows, 17 August 1921.
Debut v Carlisle United (a) 1 January 1947.
Appearances: 4.
Career: Earlestown; STANLEY amateur 4 December 1946 to June 1947.

After Accrington's success in winning the Third Division North West championship in 1945-6, the following season proved an absolute disappointment. Thirty-three players were used in League matches during 1946-7, a season which saw Stanley finish only one place above the re-election applicants, Southport and Halifax Town. Albert Leadbetter was one of seven amateur players who made a fleeting appearance on the League scene during the campaign. Each of the four matches in which he played ended in defeat, with an adverse goal-difference of 4-16.

LEE, Patrick Francis **1927-30**

Half-back. 5ft 9in; 11st 4lb.
Born: Uddington, Lanarkshire, 20 Janaury 1903. Died: Stonehouse Hospital, Lanarkshire, 1 March 1981.
Appearances: 112; Goals: 4.
Career: Vale of Clyde; Hull City 3 June 1925; STANLEY 6 June 1927; Southport (trial) 8 September to 13 October 1930; Ballymena (Ireland) October 1930; Dundee 1933-4; Hamilton Academical; Babcock & Wilcox FC.

One of a pair of Hull City players signed by Stanley in the close season of 1927, Pat Lee blended well with his former teammate George McLoughlin at Peel Park. For two seasons the left-wing triangle of McLoughlin and Barclay, skilfully prompted by Lee from left-half, initiated most of Stanley's attacking moves. Lee's studied approach and skill on the ball made him a good example of the typical Scottish craftsman.

LEEDHAM, Frederick A. **1933-35**

Inside-forward. 5ft 8½in; 11st.
Born: Lye, Worcestershire, 21 February 1909.
Debut v Stockport County (a) 26 August 1933.
Appearances: 51; Goals: 9.
Career: Worcestershire Amateurs; Kidderminster Harriers; West Bromwich Albion amateur 9 April 1926, signing professional 22 February 1928 (fee £300) to 28 May 1929; Kidderminster Harriers; Bradford 13 August 1931 (fee £160); STANLEY 10 June 1933; Oldham Athletic 8 February 1935 (in exchange for F.Britton, plus a fee of £225); Cheltenham Town season 1937-8.

International honours: England Schoolboys in 1924.
A stylish and neat ball worker, Fred Leedham was signed from Bradford who had transfer-listed him at £250. When, on appeal, the Football League reduced his fee, Stanley signed him. He could have hardly had a worse start to his career with the Reds. An injury sustained at Stockport on the opening day of the season kept him out until New Year's Day 1934. He scored on his return and his clever manoeuvring was seen to excellent effect in an unbroken run of 50 appearances. This was brought to an end in February 1935, when Oldham Athletic signed him.

LENNOX, Wilson **1933-34**
Inside-forward. 5ft 9in; 12st 3lb.
Born: Holytown, Lanarkshire, 27 May 1901. Died: Plumstead, 4 February 1976.
Debut v Chesterfield (h) 2 Sepember 1933.
Appearances: 31; Goals: 9.
Career: Mid Annandale; Charlton Athletic 25 July 1927; Thames 3 June 1931; Newport County 16 August 1932; STANLEY 8 August 1933; Enschede (Holland) as coach May 1934.
Club honour: Charlton Athletic, Third Division South champions season 1928-9.
One of Stanley's most experienced players in 1933-4, Wilson Lennox possessed ball-control and dangerous shooting, a combination which had earlier netted him 41 goals in 71 appearances for Charlton Athletic, his first Football League club. At Exeter on 2 February 1929, he scored all of his team's goals in a 5-2 win, breaking the club's individual goalscoring record at that time. Lennox assisted Thames in their final season as a League club and then was transferred to Newport County, who had been newly elected. This after they had failed to gain re-election in the previous season. With Stanley, Wilson Lennox teamed up again with Tommy Wyper (*qv*), who was also a member of Charlton Athletic's Third Division South championship side in 1928-9.

LEWIN, Derek J. **1957-58**
Inside-forward.
Born: Manchester, 18 May 1930.
Debut v Oldham Athletic (h) 5 October 1957.
Appearances: 1.
Career: St Anne's Athletic; Oldham Athletic amateur 31 August 1953; Bishop Auckland; STANLEY amateur 5 October 1957 to 26 February 1958; Bishop Auckland.
International honours: England Amateur, 5 caps. Also represented Great Britain in the 1956 Melbourne Olympic Games.
Derek Lewin's amateur registration was made only just before the noon 'deadline', in time to allow him to play against Oldham Athletic three hours later. He was signed at a time when all four of Stanley's recognized inside-forwards were injured. Lewin was only available for this one game, as his club, Bishop Auckland, required him. Lewin scored for the Bishops in each of their three FA Amateur Cup Final appearances at Wembley in 1955, 1956 and 1957. In season 1953-4 he appeared in ten Second Division games for Oldham Athletic, when the Latics were in the midst of an injury crisis.

LIDDLE, George **1937-38**
Outside-left.
Debut v New Brighton (a) 30 October 1937.
Appearances: 4.
Career: Bradford City amateur 24 February, signing professional 6 March 1937; STANLEY 15 July 1937; Frickley Colliery August 1938.
George Liddle, a young winger from Bradford City, initially came to Peel Park on trial, but was signed up for the remainder of the season on 19 October 1937. Later in the same month he deputized at outside-left for George Mee, but then found few subsequent opportunities. In the Lancashire Combination side he enjoyed a successful season, scoring 12 goals in 29 appearances for Stanley Reserves, who finished fourth in the League table.

LIGHTBOWN, Trevor J. **1959-60**
Inside or wing-forward.
Born: Blackburn, 21 November 1939.
Debut v Bradford City (h) 6 February 1960.
Appearances: 8.
Career: Burnley amateur 21 May 1957; STANLEY amateur 19 August 1959; Bradford amateur August 1960 to June 1961.
Trevor Lightbown, a Nottingham University student, was first given a run in Stanley's first team at centre-forward, after Harvey McCreadie had been transferred to Luton Town. In three matches, all of which were lost, he could not be faulted for effort, but he lacked support. Later in the season, he appeared in five matches as right winger, in place of Harry Anders, but then left Stanley to join Bradford. He made only two League appearances in his spell at Park Avenue before losing his place when another ex-Stanley winger, Jimmy Anders, was signed from Buxton.

LINDSAY, James **1925**
Inside-forward. 5ft 6½in; 10st 12lb.

Born: Johnstone, Scotland, *c.*1891.
Debut v Walsall (a) 29 August 1925.
Appearances: 5.
Career: Strathclyde; Clyde; Glentoran; Burnley 30 July 1914; Llanelly cs 1923; Larne FC (Ireland); STANLEY 20 July 1925 to 2 October 1925.
Club honour: Glentoran, Irish Cup winners v Linfield in 1914.
Representative honour: Central League v Southern League at Molineux 25 March 1922 and v North Eastern League at St James' Park, Newcastle, 3 February 1923.
The youngest of four brothers who all figured in high-class football, James Lindsay was a Scotsman who came into prominence whilst playing in Irish football. Shortly after assisting Glentoran to win the Irish Cup in 1914, he was transferred to Burnley. He had scored 20 goals for Glentoran in season 1913-14, but his scoring rate was less impressive in League football. He was, however, a clever schemer and he formed an excellent wing partnership with Eddie Mosscrop at Turf Moor. Listed by Burnley in April 1923, Lindsay returned to Ireland. Briefly associated with Stanley in the early part of season 1925-6, he left Peel Park by mutual consent in order to devote more time to his Scottish business interests.

LOCKIE, Thomas **1934-35**
Centre-half. 6ft ½in; 12st 4lb.
Born: Duns, Scotland, 13 January 1906. Died: New Earswick, Yorkshire, July 1977.
Debut v New Brighton (a) 25 August 1934.
Appearances: 36.
Career: Duns FC; Glasgow Rangers cs 1927; Leith Athletic season 1931-2; Barnsley 4 August 1932; York City 16 May 1933; STANLEY 11 July 1934; Mansfield Town 15 May 1935; York City reserve-team trainer August 1936, becoming head trainer September 1937. Subsequently serving as manager from July 1960 to October 1967.
A graduate from the Border junior club Duns, Tommy Lockie was a gritty defender, a full 90 minutes trier who never admitted defeat. He was something of a roamer during his playing career, but in management he proved exactly the opposite. As York City's reserve trainer, senior trainer and manager in turn, he was associated with the club for over 31 years. Subsequently employed as a manager in the wages office of Rowntree Mackintosh of York.

LOGUE, Samuel Walker **1960**
Inside-forward. 5ft 10in; 11st 5lb.
Born: Glasgow, 9 April 1934.
Debut v Crystal Palace (a) 20 August 1960.
Appearances: 2.
Career: Renfrew Juniors; Clyde season 1959-60; STANLEY 27 June 1960 to 12 October 1960.
Sam Logue's introduction to English football was a traumatic experience. His debut was at Selhurst Park, where Stanley went down 9-2 in their first-ever fixture in Division Four. Logue lost his place, he was one of five team changes for the next match, as manager Harrower was forced into an early reappraisal. The reshuffled side showed a great improvement and Logue had only one more senior outing, in a 2-1 defeat at Workington. Three weeks later he departed Peel Park, the club cancelling his registration in October 1960.

LORD, W(illiam) Graham **1957-62**
Full-back. 5ft 10in; 11st 7lb.
Born: Rawtenstall, 9 July 1936.
Debut v Tranmere Rovers (h) 29 November 1958.
Appearances: 67.
Career: Rossendale United; STANLEY 10 July 1957 to March 1962.
In Graham Lord's first season at Peel Park, Stanley finished as runners-up for the Third Division North championship. It was the final season of regionalized Third Division football. Lord made his League debut in the new Third Division in the following season, taking over at left-back from Jimmy Harrower in mid-term. A cool and plucky defender who was quick to recover and worked with efficiency and enthusiasm, Lord's senior career met a tragic end. On Christmas Eve 1960 he was carried off Peel Park with his leg broken in two places. He was out of training for almost a year and did not appear in the first team in Stanley's final, unfinished, season 1961-2.

LOVETT, Eric **1949-51**
Centre-half. 5ft 10½in; 12st 3lb.
Born: Radcliffe, Lancashire, 20 August 1925.
Debut v Wrexham (h) 26 December 1949.
Appearances: 41; Goals: 1.
Career: Bury junior football; STANLEY 2 November 1949 to May 1951.
Eric Lovett was discovered playing in a Bury Sunday School League by Stanley's manager, Jimmy Porter. In early reserve-team games he was reported to be 'of the right build and speeding up nicely'. Immediately following the Christmas games in 1949, he stepped into the first team in place of Cyril Briggs. In his third match he faced the Scottish wartime international centre-forward Jock Dodds and completely subdued him as Stanley beat Lincoln City 2-0. An unobtrusive but efficient defender, Lovett did less well in the following season, losing his place after appearing in the first 18 matches of the season, the last five of which had yielded but a single point.

LOWERY, Bernard **1934-35**
Half-back. 5ft 11in; 11st 12lb.
Born: Kirkdale, Liverpool, 1907 (July quarter).
Debut v Tranmere Rovers (a) 3 November 1934.
Appearances: 7.
Career: Local junior football; Liverpool amateur 13 May, signing professional 16 October 1930; Rochdale 22 August 1932; Chester (trial) October 1932; Yeovil & Petters United 1933-4; Southport June 1934; STANLEY 1 November 1934; South Liverpool October 1935; Notts County 8 August 1936 to June 1937.
When Bernard Lowery deputized for Sam McCulloch in Stanley's first team shortly after arriving at Peel Park, he was making what was only his second League appearance, despite having been on the books of five League clubs. The tall Merseysider had made his earlier Football League debut with Rochdale, after a lengthy spell in reserve at Anfield. Lowery left Stanley to join the revived South Liverpool club, who became the best side in the Lancashire Combination before the outbreak of World War Two.

LUNN, Lawrence **1926**
Goalkeeper. 5ft 10in; 12st 4lb.

Born: Huddersfield, 1896 (July quarter).
Debut v Crewe Alexandra (h) 3 April 1926.
Appearances: 5.
Career: Royton Amateurs; Rochdale (trial); Oldham Athletic amateur 3 June 1921; Ashton National June 1922; Royton amateurs later in the same season; Crewe Alexandra 1 August 1923; Nelson 1 July 1924; Barrow 1 June 1925; Llandudno January 1926; STANLEY 26 February 1926; Crewe Alexandra 6 July 1926 to June 1927.
Anticipation and clean handling were characteristics of Lawrence Lunn's goalkeeping. As an amateur he represented the Lancashire and Cheshire League before spending a season with Oldham Athletic. Something of a wanderer, he had only a brief stay at Peel Park, Stanley being his third club in season 1925-6. Strangely enough, Lunn's best display in Stanley's goal was in a 5-2 defeat. The game was the final of the Lancashire Senior Cup against Bury. The Shakers were a top First Division side in those days and scored 85 goals in finishing fourth in the table in season 1925-6.

LYNN, Stan **1945-50**
Full-back. 5ft 10½in; 12st 2lb.
Born: Bolton, 18 June 1928.
Debut v Lincoln City (h) 31 May 1947.
Appearances: 35; Goals: 2.

Career: Whitecroft Road School; Whitworth's FC; STANLEY amateur 14 August 1945, signing professional 22 July 1947; Aston Villa 16 March 1950 (fee £4,500); Birmingham City 21 October 1961 (fee £15,000); Stourbridge August 1966 to cs 1968.
Club honours: Aston Villa, FA Cup winners 1957. Second Division champions season 1959-60; Football League Cup winners 1961 (playing in the first leg of the two-legged final). Birmingham City, Football League Cup winners 1963.
Stan Lynn began in junior football as a winger and had a trial for Bolton Schoolboys at outside-right. After leaving school he worked at a mineral water factory and played for an under-18 team, Whitworth's FC. When a defender failed to turn up, he was switched to right-back. Soon afterwards he was offered a trial by Stanley. An early Press comment proved prophetic: 'An amateur full-back, full of possibilities and a wonderful kicker of a long ball'. He made his Football League debut one month before his 19th birthday. It proved a match to remember, as Stanley beat Lincoln City 8-4. Wisely 'nursed' in the reserve side, Lynn finally won promotion early in season 1949-50. Once into the team, he missed only one match before Aston Villa signed him, after Newcastle United had shown interest three months earlier. Stan Lynn enjoyed a splendid career, totalling 446 League appearances and scoring 64 goals. In season 1957-8 he scored a hat-trick from right-back for Aston Villa against Sunderland in a First Division fixture. Two of his three goals came from the penalty-spot and he had few peers as a penalty-taker.

LYTHGOE, Arnold **1945-47**
Half-back.
Born: Bolton, 7 March 1922.
Debut v Bradford City (a) 31 August 1946.
Appearances: 10.
Career: Ashton National; Linfield (Ireland); STANLEY amateur 29 August, signing professional 5 September 1945 to 24 January 1947.
Arnold Lythgoe joined Stanley in season 1945-6 and appeared in eight Regional League matches and six FA Cup ties. He made a splendid start, scoring the winning goal in a 2-1 victory at Crewe Alexandra in December 1945. He was retained for the resumption of normal League football in season 1946-7 and actually played in the first nine matches. He lost his place following a 4-0 defeat at New Brighton which put Stanley on the bottom of the League table. After only one subsequent senior appearance his contract was cancelled in January 1947. A younger brother, Derrick Lythgoe, was an inside-forward with Blackpool, Norwich City and Bristol City in the 1950s and early 1960s.

McCANDLESS, John **1923**
Outside-left. 5ft 10½in; 11st 10lb.
Born: Coleraine, 29 February (year unknown).
Debut v New Brighton (a) 15 September 1923.
Appearances: 2.
Career: Linfield; Bradford 27 March 1912; STANLEY 15 September to 10 October 1923; Barn FC (Ireland) January 1924; Mid-Rhondda July 1924.
International honours: 5 Ireland caps, 1912-21.
Said to have been listed by Bradford due to unspecified 'differences' in the close season of 1923, Jack McCandless arrived at Peel Park on a month's trial and was immediately selected for first-team duty. Stanley won at New Brighton on his debut, graphically

described by the *Accrington Observer*: 'McCandless was almost a second linesman, tall and trim and likely-looking, gently ambling just inside the touch-line. A quiet debut, but he laid on the winner for Keetley.' In his next match, at home to the Wolves, McCandless was injured after 15 minutes. His trial period was not extended and he returned to Ireland. An Irish international before World War One, McCandless won all of his caps whilst with Bradford, for whom he made over 200 League and Cup appearances.

McCLUSKEY, Ronald **1960-61**
Goalkeeper.
Born: Johnstone, Renfrew, 3 November 1936.
Debut v Southport (a) 3 December 1960.
Appearances: 4.
Career: East Fife; STANLEY 11 November 1960 to June 1961.
As deputy to the consistent Willie McInnes in Stanley's last line of defence, Ron McCluskey was called upon only four times to guard the net as senior level. All of his League games came in December 1960 and he was kept busy in one draw and three defeats, in which ten goals were conceded.

McCRAE, Ian **1957-61**
Full-back or centre-half. 5ft 11in; 11st 6lb.
Born: West Ham, 1 October 1935.
Debut v Halifax Town (a) 21 November 1959.
Appearances: 14.
Career: Blackburn junior football; STANLEY amateur, signing professional 10 July 1957; Darwen 18 August 1961.
A well-built defender who had a long time to wait for a first-team chance at Peel Park, Ian McCrae graduated through Stanley's 'A' and Reserve teams, and his first League chance came in a team reshuffle, following an injury to Graham Lord. McCrae gained in confidence as the game progressed and his fast, keen-tackling style won praise from the local correspondent. Stanley won at The Shay 2-0, thus maintaining a remarkable run of success on visits to Halifax Town. It was the fourth time that Stanley had won without conceding a goal in the same number of visits. Oddly enough, when McCrae was reintroduced later in the season, it was in the wake of a 5-0 home defeat by the same opponents.

McCREADIE, W(illiam) Harvey **1958-60**
Centre-forward. 5ft 9½in; 11st 3lb.
Born: Glenluce, 1 October 1942.
Debut v Wrexham (h) 21 February 1959.
Appearances: 28; Goals: 10.
Career: Girvan Amateurs; Stranraer; STANLEY amateur 31 January 1958, signing professional 6 October 1959; Luton Town 29 January 1960 (fee £5,500); Wrexham 10 November 1960; Northwich Victoria; Mossley October 1961; Hibernian October 1962.
On 21 February 1959, Harvey McCreadie became the youngest-ever player to appear in a League match for Stanley, at 16 years and 143 days. Earlier appearances in Stanley Reserves had shown that he could use the ball intelligently both in the air and on the ground. In the season following his debut he attracted the attention of several higher grade clubs and it was Luton Town who won the race for his signature. By the time he had reached his 19th birthday in October 1960, McCreadie had appeared in all four Division of the League and was currently playing in the Cheshire League. The remarkable sequence took in Stanley (Division Three), Luton Town (Divisions One and Two), Wrexham (Division Four) and Northwich Victoria. Another year on, he had returned to Scotland to play for Hibernian.

McCREDIE, Norman James **1955-57**
Full-back. 5ft 9in; 11st 7lb.
Born: Glasgow, 17 May 1928.
Debut v Rochdale (a) 29 August 1955 (scored one goal).
Appearances: 51; Goals: 3.
Career: Yoker Athletic; Partick Thistle 1946-55; Third Lanark (loan) 1954-5; STANLEY 20 May 1955; Southport 10 August 1957; Barrow 19 August 1958; Bacup Borough player-coach 1959-63; Accrington FC 12 December 1964.

A fine display against Stanley for Third Lanark in a floodlit friendly match was noted at Peel Park and in the following season, Norrie McCreadie was signed by Walter Galbraith. Normally a full-back, he made his debut for Stanley at outside-left and scored three goals in 14 appearances before resuming in his normal position at left-back. This came when Jimmy Harrower took over at centre-half, after John Ryden had been transferred to Tottenham Hotspur. A strong and resourceful player, McCreadie began and ended at outside-left for Stanley. Outside of football, he was a pattern-maker with an Accrington engineering firm.

McCULLOCH, Samuel S. **1931-35**
Half-back. 5ft 9½in; 11st 6lb.
Born: Glasgow, 21 May 1906.
Debut v Southport (a) 12 September 1931.
Appearances: 188; Goals: 3.
Career: Petershill FC; Blackburn Rovers 28 September

1926; Thames Association September 1929; STANLEY 20 August 1931; Bury 29 May 1936; Leyland Motors October 1938.
After three years and only one League appearance, Sam McCulloch left Blackburn Rovers for Thames Association in September 1929. He wore the distinctive red and blue quarters when the London club gained admission to the Third Division South in 1930-31, but left after a season to join Stanley. It was not until December 1931 that he established himself as a regular first-team player, but once into the team, he missed only six League matches in the next four seasons. Very much a 'stay at home' defender, McCulloch patrolled the edge of his penalty area, resolutely guarding the main entrance to goal. A move to Bury in 1936 saw him unable to break into the Shakers' first team in a two-year stay at Gigg Lane.

McDONALD, Alexander C. 1935-36
Centre-forward.
Born: *c.*1917.
Debut v Chester (a) 11 September 1935.
Appearances: 2.
Career: Haslingden Grane FC; STANLEY amateur 4 September 1935; Bacup Borough cs 1936.
Alex McDonald, an 18-year-old amateur centre-forward was reported to have scored 75 goals for Haslingden Grane FC in season 1934-5. He was one of new player-manager Jack Hacking's early signings and he was almost immediatley elevated into League action. In his second match, at York City, Stanley won their first point of the season in a 1-1 draw. When he made his debut at Chester, the *Accrington Observer* commented: 'McDonald created a good impression on his Football League debut. Several times he narrowly missed scoring, and his passing to the wings was good to watch.'

McDOUGALL, John 1926
Half-back. 5ft 7½in; 11st 7lb.
Born: Hamilton, Scotland, 1902.
Debut v Rochdale (h) 28 August 1926.
Appearances: 1.
Career: Hamilton Intermediates; Motherwell cs 1922; STANLEY 9 August to 29 September 1926.
Four years experience with Motherwell apparently did little to prepare McDougall for life in the Northern Section. On his Football League debut he was described as 'slow and lacking vim'. The local correspondent also noted that 'the Scotsman was deficient in the virility needed to be a success in Third Division football'. Like many before, and since, he must have found the lower reaches of English League football very different from the Scottish game.

McDOWELL, John 1922
Full-back. 5ft 6in; 10st 4lb.
Born: Londonderry.
Debut v Halifax Town (h) 17 April 1922.
Appearances: 1.
Career: Londonderry Distillery; STANLEY (trial) amateur 17 April 1922.
An amateur trialist from the same Irish club which provided Stanley with Pat Nelis (*qv*). McDowell was one of three different left-backs tried by Stanley in the last four fixtures of season 1921-2. With scarcely the physique generally demanded of a full-back, the Press comments following his debut were not surprising. 'McDowell occasionally showed resource in tackling, but his clearances lacked length.'

McEWAN, Stephen 1951
Inside-forward. 5ft 11in; 11st.
Born: Bowhill, 28 March 1930.
Debut v Gateshead (h) 18 August 1951 (scored one goal).
Appearances: 2; Goals: 1.
Career: Scottish junior football; Liverpool 14 July 1950; STANLEY 4 August to 3 November 1951.
Steve McEwan was one of two young forwards who joined Stanley from Liverpool in the summer of 1951, Malcolm Glazzard (*qv*) being the other Anfield recruit. Tall and slim and with an eye for an opening, McEwan was Stanley's first goalscorer of the season, in the opening 2-1 defeat by Gateshead at Peel Park. Despite his scoring debut, he was one of three players who were dropped after this initial reverse. McEwan featured in only one more senior game before requesting his release, in order to return to Scotland for domestic reasons.

McINNES, Joseph Clarke 1956
Outside-left. 5ft 7in; 11st.
Born: Glasgow, 9 December 1932.
Debut v Bradford City (h) 3 March 1956.
Appearances: 14; Goals: 2.
Career: Partick Thistle; STANLEY 1 March 1956; Third Lanark 11 August 1956.
Joe McInnes played regularly for Partick Thistle before and during his National Service. He was usually at

outside-left, which is where he played for Stanley, but he had appeared in every forward position but centre with the Jags. In a brief stay at Peel Park he was preferred to Bert Scott in 14 of the last 15 games of the season. He returned to Scotland in the close season, and was obviously glad to be back, as he scored five goals on his debut for Third Lanark, who beat Stenhousemuir 8-2.

McINNES, William **1955-61**
Goalkeeper. 5ft 11in; 12st 2lb.
Born: Douglas, Lanarkshire, 20 May 1931.
Debut v Workington (a) 24 March 1956.
Appearances: 153.
Career: Kirkmuirhill; Stonehouse Violet; Falkirk; Alloa Athletic (loan); Lesmahagow September 1955; STANLEY 15 October 1955; Southport 8 July 1961 to May 1963 when he retired.
Willie McInnes was yet another Scot who was 'spotted' whilst opposing Stanley in a floodlit friendly match. He was on loan to Alloa Athletic when they visited Peel Park in season 1954-5. McInnes spent almost six years with Stanley, becoming first-team goalkeeper in succession to Tommy McQueen. Having won senior status he retained it, despite cartilage trouble in late season 1957-8, which necessitated an operation. His only season of relative senior inactivity came in 1959-60, when he appeared in only 17 matches. Significantly, this was the campaign when the goals-against column registered 123. McInnes ended his career with Southport, retiring after two seasons at Haigh Avenue. He later ran a fish and chip shop in Huncoat.

McINTOSH, George **1924-25**
Centre-half. 6ft; 12st 1lb.
Born: Govan, Glasgow, 1899.
Debut v Rotherham County (h) 30 August 1924.
Appearances: 17; Goals: 1.
Career: Renfrew Juniors; Edinburgh Hibernian; Solway Star (Dumfriesshire); Workington season 1922-3; Exeter City 3 August 1923; STANLEY 19 July 1924; Boston Town December 1925.
An injury sustained at Crewe on 22 November 1924 prematurely ended George McIntosh's run as Stanley's centre-half after 17 matches. The injury proved more serious than had first been thought, when a scheduled comeback in the Reserves had to be put back after he broke down in training in January 1925. His previous League experience was gained with Exeter City, where he made 16 appearances as understudy to Ellis Crompton, the veteran defender with 20 seasons' experience of professional football.

McINTYRE, James **1957**
Goalkeeper.
Born: Motherwell, 22 March 1933.
Debut v Hull City (a) 19 April 1957.
Appearances: 4.
Career: Motherwell; STANLEY 16 March to May 1957.
A reserve goalkeeper from Motherwell, Jim McIntyre was signed on a free transfer to provide cover for Stanley's last line of defence, just prior to the transfer 'deadline' in March 1957. In a brief stay, he played in the final four fixtures of the season, conceding ten goals in three defeats and one win. It was a disappointing end to a season in which Stanley finished third in the table, five points behind the champions, Derby County. Less than two months after signing, McIntyre was released on a free transfer.

McKEOWN, Thomas **1954-55**
Inside-forward. 5ft 8in; 11st 4lb.
Born: Cleland, 2 October 1930.
Debut v Southport (h) 21 August 1954 (scored one goal).
Appearances: 12; Goals: 2.
Career: Queen of the South; STANLEY 13 May 1954; Netherfield 17 June 1955 (fee £75); Nelson September 1956; Berwick Rangers December 1957.
Tom McKeown was the first player signed by Stanley for season 1954-5. Agile, speedy and with good ball-control, he scored on his debut at Peel Park but was not able to hold a regular place in the first team. He was, however, a more than useful deputy throughout the campaign, appearing on both wings and at inside-right. He left Stanley, in company with Lol Langstreth, to join Netherfield. He assisted his new club to finish fourth in the Lancashire Combination in 1955-6, and they also won the Combination Cup, for the first time in the club's history.

McLOUGHLIN, George **1927-29**
Inside-forward. 5ft 8½in; 11st 2lb.
Born: Glasgow, 24 March 1904.
Debut v Nelson (a) 27 August 1927 (scored two goals).
Appearances: 76; Goals: 21.
Career: Glasgow Celtic; Clydebank; Darlington 27 August 1925; Hull City 11 June 1926; STANLEY 18 May 1927; Nelson 26 June 1929 to May 1930.
George McLoughlin had an outstanding debut for Stanley. He was on the score-sheet within 20 minutes of the kick-off and added a second in the Reds' fine 4-1 victory at Nelson on the opening Saturday of season 1927-8. Described as a 'tricky and clever inside-forward', his trickiness was always purposeful, and for two seasons he formed a fine left-wing partnership with fellow-Scot, Jack Barclay. McLoughlin's first-class career ended after a season with Nelson, when he was one of eight players who were given free transfers by the Seedhill management in the close season of 1930.

McNICHOL, Robert Hugh **1956-59**
Full-back. 5ft 11in; 12st 4lb.
Born: Cumbernauld, Dumbarton, 13 February 1933.
Debut v York City (h) 18 August 1956.
Appearances: 134; Goals: 5.
Career: Vale of Leven; Stirling Albion; STANLEY 29 May 1956 (fee £750); Brighton & Hove Albion 12 June 1959 (fee £4,700); Gravesend & Northfleet July 1962; Carlisle United 18 October 1963 to June 1964; Stalybridge Celtic; Great Harwood.
Bob McNichol was a product of the famed Scottish nursery, Vale of Leven. He joined Stanley after having played in 32 'A' Division matches for Stirling Albion in 1955-6. He settled so well into English football that he made 134 consecutive appearances before an injury broke the sequence. Ironically perhaps, he was injured whilst playing in goal at Bournemouth on Easter Monday 1959. Three of Stanley's recognized goalkeepers were already on the injured list and McNichol joined them when he fractured a toe in his right foot. He insisted that he was fit to continue, but after two more games he was forced to break his sequence. After three

seasons with Brighton & Hove Albion (93 appearances), he dropped out of League football, but helped Gravesend and Northfleet to reach the fourth round of the FA Cup in 1962-3, where they only lost after taking Sunderland to a replay. Carlisle United, one of the teams 'giantkilled' by Gravesend, signed him in October 1963, but he played in only one League match for the Cumbrians. Bob McNichol was later a newsagent in Church and was subsequently employed in the family coach and haulage business.

McQUEEN, Thomas **1954-57**
Goalkeeper. 6ft 1in; 12st 7lb.
Born: West Calder, Mid-Lothian, 21 February 1929.
Debut v Barnsley (h) 27 September 1954.
Appearances: 80.
Career: Kilburnie (Western League); Hibernian 1952-3; Queen of the South; STANLEY 15 June 1954; East Fife 22 February 1957.

Tommy McQueen joined Hibernian during his National Service, in which he was a military policeman. When he joined Queen of the South he was mainly understudy to Henderson and with Stanley he began as reserve-team goalkeeper. He had played in only one first-team game in the 1954-5 season when Jimmy Jones was injured in March. McQueen took his opportunity so well that Jones was allowed to move to Rochdale. Tall and ideally proportioned for his position, McQueen was a daring and often brilliant goalkeeper. He was also reputed to be one of the longest-kicking custodians in English football. He left Stanley for domestic reasons in February 1957 and returned to Scotland to play for East Fife. His son, Gordon McQueen, also began as a goalkeeper in junior football but switched to centre defence. He won 30 Scottish caps, a League Championship medal and an FA Cup winners' medal in his career with Leeds United and Manchester United.

MAIDMENT, James Henry C. **1933-34**
Goalkeeper. 5ft 10½in; 11st 4lb.
Born: Sunderland, 28 September 1901. Died: Rushcliffe, Notts, 1977 (January quarter).
Debut v Stockport County (a) 26 August 1933.
Appearances: 37.
Career: Thompson's Workers (Wearside League); Southend United amateur 23 May, signing professional 4 September 1923; Newport County 12 August 1924; Lincoln City 28 May 1930; Notts County 5 May 1931; STANLEY 3 July 1933 to June 1934.
A nephew of William Charlton, the Tranmere Rovers forward and an elder brother of Thomas Maidment, Lincoln City's inside-right. Jim Maidment was rarely absent in a season at Peel Park. He could not, however, have been sorry to miss the Barnsley home match on 3 February 1934, which Stanley lost 9-0. In a lengthy career he totalled 354 Football League appearances, of which 219 were made for Newport County. Maidment earned a rare distinction, for a goalkeeper, in October 1927. He scored, from the penalty-spot, in two consecutive games for Newport. He might have had an even more impressive record when, on 2 February 1929, he took two penalty-kicks for Newport County against Torquay United. He was successful in conveting the first award, but missed from the second.

MAKIN, James **1921-23**
Inside-forward. 5ft 7½in; 11st 5lb.
Born: Bury, 1900 (April quarter).
Debut v Rochdale (a) 27 August 1921.
Appearances: 39; Goals: 16.
Career: Stockport County during World War One; Exeter City cs 1919; STANLEY 27 May 1921 to May 1923.
A good initiator, Jim Makin was a neat dribbler whose passes were usually well-timed. Often content to work openings and allow others to apply the finishing touch, he nevertheless maintained a highly respectable striking rate in his first season, when he scored 16 goals in 31 matches. Towards the close of this season he was injured in a friendly match against Southport and was in hospital when the retained list was announced. He was kept on, but in 1922-3 he only played eight games in the first team and was released on a free transfer in May 1923.

MALCOLM, John M. **1944-47**
Half-back. 5ft 8½in; 11st.
Born: Clackmannan, 20 May 1917.
Debut v Barrow (a) 5 September 1946.
Appearances: 25.
Career: STANLEY amateur 21 August, signing professional 16 October 1944; Tranmere Rovers 14 July 1947 to June 1948.
A Stanley stalwart in wartime football, John Malcolm was a regular performer in seasons 1944-5 and 1945-6. In all matches for Stanley, his appearance total was in excess of 100. At either wing-half or full-back he was a tenacious defender but his value was at times discounted by erratic distribution. He left Peel Park on a free transfer and spent his final season of first-class football with Tranmere Rovers, making 22 appearances in season 1947-8.

MARCROFT, Edward Hollows **1934-35**
Outside-left. 5ft 6½in; 10st 12lb.

Born: Rochdale, 1910 (April quarter).
Debut v New Brighton (h) 25 August 1934 (scored one goal).
Appearances: 24; Goals: 4.
Career: Bacup Borough; Great Harwood 19 July 1930; Middlesbrough 28 December 1931 (fee £200); Queen's Park Rangers 10 May 1932; Cardiff City 14 June 1933 (in exchange for G.Emmerson); STANLEY 4 July 1934; Bacup Borough September 1935; Rochdale 18 July 1936; Macclesfield cs 1937.
When Ted Marcroft signed for Great Harwood, he was said to have scored 66 goals, in a run of 63 matches, for his previous club, Bacup Borough. Despite scoring for Middlesbrough at Sheffield Wednesday on his Football League debut, this match proved to be his only outing in First Division football. Two seasons in the Third Division South preceded his move to Peel Park. He was one of six new men in Stanley's line-up in the opening fixture of 1934-5 season. Despite scoring from the outside-left position, visitors New Brighton took the points in a 3-1 win. During the course of the season, Marcroft appeared on both wings and at centre-forward, but in the latter position his lack of height was a handicap. In 1933 *The Topical Times* revealed that his hobbies included swimming, tennis and playing the piano.

MARSDEN, Frederick **1934-35**
Full-back. 5ft 10½in; 11st 4lb.
Born: Blackburn, 6 September 1911.
Debut v Walsall (a) 1 December 1934.
Appearances: 5.
Career: STANLEY amateur 21 August, signing professional 1 October 1934; Wolverhampton Wanderers 31 January 1935 (with J.C.Aspin, for a combined fee of £750); Bournemouth & Boscombe Athletic 9 May 1936; Weymouth cs 1949.
Fred Marsden had a torrid first outing in League football as Stanley lost 6-0 at Walsall on his debut. In five first-team appearances he failed to collect a winning bonus, but it did not dissuade Wolves from signing him, after he had spent only four months as a professional. After only one First Division outing at Molineux, Marsden blossomed out with Bournemouth who converted him to centre-half and made him captain. He scored in what would have been Bournemouth's record League victory, a 10-0 win against Northampton Town. Unfortunately, this 2 September 1939 fixture proved to be the last in season 1939-40 as war broke out and the season's records were expunged. He was able to resume his League career after the war and did not miss a match in seasons 1946-7 and 1947-8. In the latter campaign, Bournemouth finished runners-up to Queen's Park Rangers for the championship of the Third Division South.

MARSHALL, Alexander Stewart **1960-61**
Inside-forward.
Born: Alloa, 27 November 1935.
Debut v Chester (a) 21 January 1961 (scored one goal).
Appearances: 8; Goals: 2.
Career: Stirling Albion; STANLEY 22 October 1960 to May 1961.
First-rate ball-control was a feature of Alex Marshall's play, and his game improved steadily with the benefits of full-time training. After some time spent in acclimatizing himself in the second team, his debut

came when he was a surprise replacement for Mike Ferguson at Chester in January 1961. Marshall scored after 25 minutes to assist in a 3-2 win, which was only the third away victory of the season. Despite scoring again in his third appearance at Oldham Athletic, he failed to win a regular berth in the side and eventually became one of nine players who were released on free transfers in May 1961.

MARSHALL, John **1957-61**
Goalkeeper. 5ft 11½in; 11st 5lb.
Born: Rawtenstall, 1 November 1938.
Debut v Crewe Alexandra (a) 25 December 1957.
Appearances: 7.
Career: Local junior football; STANLEY amateur, signing professional 10 July 1957 to May 1961.
A well-built local teenager who received an early opportunity, following promising displays in Stanley's 'A' and Reserve teams. In a hectic introduction to League football, he played in three matches within the space of five days over Christmas 1957. Stanley lost 4-1 at Crewe, but then won 2-0 and 5-2 and the young goalkeeper won high praise for his displays. He had a further four League outings in the following term, when a spate of injuries saw seven goalkeepers fielded in League matches. He did not reappear in senior football after completing his National Service, in which he served in the Ninth Signals Regiment in Cyprus. During his Army service he toured North Africa with a Combined Services XI, whose fixtures included a match against the Lybian Army, which was won 6-2.

MARSHALL, Thomas Albert **1925-26**
Goalkeeper.
Born: Blowick, Southport, 2 June 1897. Died: Southport, 17 February 1964.
Debut v Tranmere Rovers (a) 26 December 1925.
Appearances: 3.
Career: Southport amateur April 1922, signing professional May 1923 to May 1925; Skelmersdale United; STANLEY 21 November 1925 to May 1926.
Tom Marshall, a reserve goalkeeper with Southport, was transferred to Stanley and in his first game was opposed to Southport Reserves. An injury to Tom Holden gave Marshall his first senior opportunity and he rose to the occasion. His fine display at Tranmere Rovers on Boxing Day 1925 earned Stanley an unexpected point in a 2-2 draw. Unfortunately, his season ended prematurely after he had caught a chill during a game at Grimsby Town in January 1926. His cold was followed by pleurisy which in turn developed into pneumonia. Tom Marshall's brother, James Marshall, was a full-back with Southport from 1921 to 1926.

MARTIN, Edward **1950**
Inside-forward.
Born: Baillieston, 31 March 1921.
Debut v Crewe Alexandra (h) 23 August 1950.
Appearances: 2.
Career: Alloa Athletic; STANLEY (one month's trial) 9 August 1950.
Eddie Martin made 18 appearances and scored six goals for Alloa Athletic, who finished bottom of the 'B' Division of the Scottish League in season 1949-50. He was offered a month's trial by Stanley but this was not extended, despite the fact that he appeared on the winning side in both of his League outings. He later emigrated to Canada.

MARTIN, Frederick John **1950-52**
Half-back. 5ft 9in; 11st 7lb.
Born: Nottingham, 14 April 1925.
Debut v Gateshead (a) 19 August 1950.
Appearances: 64.
Career: Ipswich Town 7 January 1949; Blackburn Rovers 24 December 1949; STANLEY 20 July 1950 to 2 May 1952.
Some idea of the versatility of Fred Martin was revealed when he played at left-half, inside-left and inside-right, all of this within the space of his first three games for Stanley. Stocky and with a seemingly inexhaustable amount of energy and speed, his hard work and foraging abilities were best suited to a wing-half role. It was, however, his extreme adaptability which made him such a valuable member of the first-team squad at Peel Park.

MARTIN, James Joseph **1936-37**
Inside or wing-forward. 5ft 11½in; 11st 10lb.
Born: Patricroft, Manchester, 28 November 1908. Died: 1980.
Debut v Lincoln City (h) 29 August 1936.
Appearances: 5.
Career: Bacup Borough; Hull City amateur 8 May 1935; STANLEY 16 June 1936; Macclesfield June 1937; Great Harwood cs 1938; Bristol City (trial) November 1938.
In the pre-season trials of 1936-7 at Peel Park, Martin was tried in the first team attack as substitute for George Mee. Long-legged and raw-boned and reminiscent in style of Joe Clare (*qv*), he gave a good showing. Unfortunately, as an understudy to Stanley's 36-year-old wizard of the wing, George Mee, Martin found few first-team opportunities.

MARTIN, John **1926-28**
Wing-forward. 5ft 7½in; 11st 4lb.
Born: Gateshead, 1904.
Debut v Rochdale (h) 28 August 1926.
Appearances: 44; Goals: 8.
Career: Hebburn Colliery; Darlington cs 1920; Leeds United 19 July 1924 (fee £250); STANLEY 28 June 1926; Connah's Quay and Shotton August 1928; Bury 10 May 1929; Reading 13 June 1930; Doncaster Rovers 19 August 1931 to May 1932.
Jack Martin's form improved dramatically after a shaky debut when he was criticized for parting with the ball too early and being too often out of position. At his best, Martin worked the ball well along the line, centered effectively and made good use of almost every opportunity. He was Stanley's most impressive forward in 1926-7 and did particularly well in the season's Cup run, scoring a goal in each of the first three rounds. In 1927-8 he was deposed by new signing Jack Barclay and left Stanley to join Connah's Quay & Shotton for season 1928-9. He assisted his new club to win the championship of the Welsh National League, Northern Section.

MARTIN, John Charles **1924-26**
Centre-half. 6ft; 12st 2lb.
Born: North Leeds, 25 July 1903. Died: Padiham, Lancashire, 31 December 1976.

Debut v Darlington (h) 1 January 1925.
Appearances: 28; Goals: 1.
Career: Padiham junior football; Burnley 'A' team 1923; STANLEY amateur 29 July, signing professional 15 November 1924; Blackpool 5 February 1926 (fee £350); Southport 15 June 1927; Macclesfield 7 September 1929; Southport May 1930; Nelson 7 November 1930; Wigan Borough 29 July 1931; Oldham Athletic 3 November 1931 (fee £50) to May 1932.
John Martin's senior career began with Stanley and he showed early promise as a 'stopper' centre-half, although his distribution was inclined to be erratic. He was described in the *Lancashire Daily Post Annual* for 1925 as 'a great forager and breaker-up. His height, 6ft, is an asset in his main position, centre half-back.' Without leaving Lancashire, he assisted seven different League clubs. Two of them, Nelson and Wigan Borough, lost their League status whilst he was on their books. His career was ended by a knee injury, sustained whilst he was with Oldham Athletic. He was later a coal merchant in Padiham and then a loomer in the weaving industry.

MARTINDALE, Leonard **1951-52**
Half-back. 5ft 8in; 12st.
Born: Bolton, 30 June 1920.
Debut v Stockport County (a) 29 December 1951.
Appearances: 16.
Career: Folds Road School (Bolton); Rossendale United (trial); Burnley amateur 19 February, signing professional 17 July 1937; STANLEY 29 December 1951 to 2 May 1952.
A product of Folds Road School Bolton, which produced many famous footballers, including Tommy Lawton, Len Martindale was a Ribble Motors apprentice when he joined Burnley's groundstaff. He made rapid progress and was selected to make his Football League debut when only 17 years old. *The Topical Times Sporting Annual* named him as one of the best discoveries of season 1937-8, but the war was to seriously disrupt his promising career. He rejoined Burnley on his return from service in India in 1947, but then only made spasmodic League appearances. When he joined Stanley in mid-season 1951-2, he was immediately appointed captain, but he joined a struggling side and his debut brought the season's worst defeat, 6-0 at Stockport County. In his 16 appearances, Martindale collected only three winning bonuses and the side narrowly avoided a re-election application. A keen golfer, in October 1949 he won the Professional Footballers' Golf Championship at Chilwell.

MARVIN, Walter **1946-48**
Centre-forward. 5ft 9in; 11st 12lb.
Born: Derby, 6 July 1920.
Debut v Bradford City (h) 28 December 1946.
Appearances: 9; Goals: 3.
Career: Newport County amateur; STANLEY amateur 27 December 1946, signing professional 7 October 1947; Nelson 28 January 1948; Clitheroe April 1950.
Walter Marvin scored in two of his first three matches for Stanley in January 1947, but when Stan Mercer was signed from Leicester City in the same month, Marvin stepped down. An amateur middleweight boxer, he was not easily shaken off the ball, but he was inclined to try to bore through entire defences on his own. In looks and style, he was reminiscent of an earlier Stanley centre-forward, Bob Mortimer (*qv*).

MASON, James **1955-57**
Outside-left. 5ft 9in; 11st 6lb.
Born: Glasgow, 17 April 1933.
Debut v Gateshead (h) 20 August 1955.
Appearances: 14; Goals: 1.
Career: Rutherglen Glencairn; Dundee 1953; STANLEY 29 June 1955; Chester 6 June 1957; Chelmsford City; Crystal Palace 18 May to 30 December 1960.
Signed on completion of his National Service and after two seasons in Dundee's reserve team, Jimmy Mason was at outside-left in Stanley's first three fixtures of season 1955-6. He then lost his place to Norrie McCredie. In an otherwise fairly settled formation, the outside-left position was subject to a variety of changes. In Mason's two seasons at Peel Park he was one of the fringe contenders for the senior berth, which was finally settled when Jimmy Anders was signed from Bradford. Mason moved to Chester who became founder members of Division Four in 1958-9, after they had finished in 21st place in the final season of the Third Division North. He made 64 appearances and scored seven goals for the Sealand Road club but did not appear at League level with Crystal Palace.

MAYCOCK, Ranson **1932-33**
Inside-forward. 5ft 8½in; 11st 7lb.
Born: Waterhouses, Co Durham, 1905 (April quarter).
Debut v Barrow (a) 17 September 1932.
Appearances: 18; Goals: 3.
Career: Tow Law Town; South Shields 17 March 1928; Guildford City cs 1931; STANLEY 24 June 1932 to May 1933.
Ranson Maycock was brought back into League football by Stanley after he had spent a season in the London Combination with Guildford City. He took some time to readjust to League fare and he did not feature regularly until the last three months of the season and his name did not figure on a rather abbreviated retained list. Maycock had first played with South Shields in Division Two. They were relegated shortly after his arrival, but he led their goalscoring lists in the next two seasons. In 1928-9 he scored four goals in a match against Rotherham United, who were beaten 10-1. His career spanned both South Shields and Gateshead, when the club's name was officially changed in July 1930. In the final game played at Horsley Hill, on 3 May 1930, he scored the last of South Shields' two goals in their farewell fixture, a 2-2 draw against Stanley. He then scored Gateshead's first goal on the new Redheugh Park Stadium on 30 August 1930, when they beat Doncaster Rovers 2-1. Something of a record, no doubt.

MEADOWS, J(ohn) Ronald **1952-53**
Goalkeeper. 6ft 1in; 12st 5lb.
Born: Lancaster, 4 December 1920.
Debut v Hartlepools United (a) 23 August 1952.
Appearances: 18.
Career: Glason Dock (Lancaster); Burnley amateur, signing professional 7 September 1946; Bournemouth and Boscombe Athletic 22 April 1950; STANLEY 8 July 1952; Lancaster Town cs 1953.
Ron Meadows first appeared in Burnley's pre-season trial, 'Whites' v 'Clarets', at Turf Moor in August 1946. The attendance, incidentally, was about 10,000! He soon established himself in Burnley's Central League team, who were one of the best sides in the competition in the immediate post-war years. They won the championship in season 1948-9, conceding only 32 goals in the 42-match programme. When he left Burnley in April 1950, Meadows had not appeared in a League match. Senior goalkeeper Jimmy Strong having appeared in every match for four seasons. With Bournemouth he made 16 League appearances and began with Stanley as first-choice goalkeeper. He lost his place, however, in mid October after the team had sustained their seventh consecutive League defeat.

MEE, George Wilfred **1935-38 & 1939**
Outside-left. 5ft 5in; 11st.
Born: Bulwell, Notts, 12 April 1900. Died: Poulton-le-Fylde, 9 July 1978.
Debut v Stockport County (a) 12 October 1935.
Appearances: 123; Goals: 10.
Career: Highbury Vale Athletic (Nottingham junior League); Notts County August 1919; Blackpool 28 July 1920; Derby County 27 February 1926 (with J.Gill for a combined fee of £3,500); Burnley 2 September 1932; Mansfield Town 7 July 1933; Great Harwood November 1934; STANLEY 10 October 1935; Rochdale 21 July 1938 as reserve-team trainer-coach; STANLEY 27 January 1939 (in exchange for J.W.H.Gastall) as player-coach to May 1939.
The recipient of a gold watch to mark 162 consecutive appearances for Blackpool, a run which he extended to 194 matches. George Mee added a further 148 appearances with Derby County. By the time he arrived at Peel Park at the age of 35 years, his career total was approaching the 400 mark. Mee was 'ressurrected' by manager Jack Hacking (a former Blackpool teammate) after he had drifted into non-League football after relatively undistinguished spells with Burnley and Mansfield Town. With Stanley he was

an unqualified success, an artful dodger at outside-left, his sustenance of skill and liveliness was almost Peter Pan-like. He continued to bamboozle opposing defences until World War Two brought an end to League football, by which time he was 39 years old. A fine tenor singer, George Mee 'plugged the pops' in Lawrence Wright song booths at Blackpool during summer seasons. Later mine-host of a Blackpool hotel and coach to Blackpool's 'A' team during World War Two. Younger brother Bertie Mee was on the books of Derby County and Mansfield Town, but was best remembered as Arsenal's manager from 1966 to 1976.

MELLOR, William **1950-54**
Full-back. 5ft 10in; 12st.
Born: Manchester, 29 June 1925.
Debut v Bradford City (h) 11 November 1950.
Appearances: 138; Goals: 2.
Career: Droylsden; STANLEY 10 June 1950 to May 1954.

One of Stanley's best recruits from Cheshire League football, Bill Mellor quickly settled into League action. He became a fixture at right-back and was a popular and reliable defender who met opponents squarely and cleared well with either foot. In October 1953 he completed 100 consecutive appearances for Stanley, for which the Supporters' Club presented him with a cigarette lighter. Almost immediately afterwards he lost his place, as did his full-back partner, player-manager Walter Galbraith. The 'Boss' stood down to accommodate Armour Ashe, whilst Ken Holliday took over at right-back. In February 1953, Mellor was transfer listed, at his own request, along with Billy Robinson (*qv*) an earlier full-back partner, who was to lose his life in tragic circumstances only three months later.

MERCER, Stanley **1944-45 & 1947-48**
Centre-forward. 5ft 8½in; 11st 7lb.
Born: Birkenhead, 11 September 1919.
Debut v York City (a) 11 January 1947.
Appearances: 68; Goals: 36.
Career: Blackpool July 1944; Manchester United and

STANLEY (wartime guest) season 1944-5; Leicester City season 1945-6; STANLEY 10 January 1947 (fee £750); Mansfield Town 8 October 1948, appointed trainer following a knee injury sustained in the same season. Appointed manager August 1953, resigned January 1956.
As a wartime guest player for Stanley, Mercer began by scoring a hat-trick against Bolton Wanderers at Burnden Park and went on to total 24 goals in as many appearances. During the war he played for the RAF team against Portugal in Lisbon. Stanley signed him from Leicester City in mid-season 1946-7 and he made an immediate impact, scoring 13 goals in only 19 matches. A fast and aggressive leader with an excellent shot, he maintained a high goal-scoring ratio throughout his career, which ended prematurely. Shortly after leaving Accrington for Mansfield Town, where he had scored ten goals in 15 League and Cup matches, injury forced his retirement as a player, but he was to remain at Field Mill for over seven years, as trainer and then manager.

METCALF, Arthur **1922-23**
Inside-forward. 5ft 8in; 11st 6lb.
Born: Seaham Harbour, Sunderland, 8 April 1889.
Died: February 1926.
Debut v Darlington (h) 26 August 1922.
Appearances: 32; Goals: 18.

Career: Herrington Swifts; North Shields Athletic; Newcastle United 5 April 1909 (fee £100); Liverpool 25 May 1912 (fee £150); Stockport County August 1918; Swindon Town 17 June 1920; STANLEY 21 June 1922; Aberdare Athletic 1 June 1923; Norwich City 2 July 1925.
Club honour: Liverpool FA Cup runners-up 1914.
Probably Stanley's best capture of season 1922-3, Arthur Metcalf was an experienced inside-forward of clever and thoughtful style. Captain and leading goalscorer during his term at Peel Park, he signed off by collecting the East Lancashire Charity Shield after Darwen had been beaten, over two legs, in the Final. In retrospect, he would have been well worth a place on the retained list, as he gave his next club, Aberdare Athletic, two years of sterling service. Metcalf's career totalled 235 appearances and 76 goals. He was only 36 years old when he died and an obituary in the *Accrington Observer* recalled: 'He was a likeable man who knew the whole alphabet of the game'. A brother, George Metcalf, was a Sunderland and Huddersfield Town player.

MILLAR, William **1956-57**

Wing-forward. 5ft 8½in; 11st 10lb.
Born: Irvine, Strathclyde, 24 July 1924.
Debut v York City (h) 18 August 1956 (scored one goal).
Appearances: 26; Goals: 11.
Career: Ayrshire Schoolboys; Annbank United; Partick Thistle 1943; Aberdeen 1946; Stirling Albion 1950; Swindon Town 19 August 1950; Gillingham 21 July 1953; STANLEY 24 July 1956; Kettering Town cs 1957; Macclesfield Town; STANLEY as scout from 1960 and then as reserve-team coach in 1961-2; Great Harwood trainer-coach; Horwich RMI manager 1971; Luton Town scout 1974.
When Willie Millar signed for Stanley he must have immediately felt 'at home', as he became the 18th Scot on the club's books. He was a seasoned campaigner and initially appeared to have solved a long standing outside-left problem, when he scored in each of his first two games. The fact that he failed to secure a regular berth was a good indication of the strength of the playing squad at that time. His return of 11 goals in 26 matches would have made him an automatic selection in many other periods of the club's history.

MOIR, James MM **1937-39**

Centre-forward. 5ft 8in; 11st 4lb.
Born: Newcastle upon Tyne, 23 March 1918.
Debut v Gateshead (h) 6 November 1937 (scored one goal).
Appearances: 20; Goals: 9.
Career: Newcastle West End; STANLEY 19 October 1937 to September 1939; Carlisle United August 1946 to May 1948.
Boundless energy, combined with a somewhat awkward style and a flair for doing the unexpected, made Jim Moir a difficult opponent. Signed shortly after Bob Mortimer had been transferred to Blackburn Rovers, the 19-year-old centre-forward had an early introduction into League action and scored twice in three matches in November 1937. The senior centre-forward position was eventually claimed by another youngster, Jim Blakeney (*qv*), as Moir's game continued to develop in the Lancashire Combination side. In season 1938-9 he scored five hat-tricks, four with the Reserves, which included a five and a four and one with the League side. He was the Reserves' leading scorer, by a wide margin, with 27 goals. A move to Carlisle United after the war saw him open the Cumbrians' goalscoring account in the first peacetime season. His opener, at Oldham, was the first of 18 League goals which he scored during the season. Moir was awarded the Military Medal in World War Two.

MONTGOMERY, Harold **1924**

Outside-right. 5ft 5in; 10st 3lb.
Born: Hadfield, 1900 (January quarter).
Debut v Barrow (h) 30 September 1924.
Appearances: 2.
Career: Hyde United; Crewe Alexandra 20 October 1922; STANLEY 30 September to 14 November 1924.
In a brief stay at Peel Park, Harry Montgomery, an extremely lightweight winger, had two League outings. He was preferred to Fred Bedford at outside-right in consecutive home matches against Barrow and Grimsby Town, both of which were lost. Montgomery had two seasons with Crewe Alexandra (51 League appearances) and was released at the close of the 1923-4 season when the Railwaymen had finished 20th in the Third Division North.

MOON, Albert **1928-31**

Outside-left. 5ft 7in; 11st 6lb.
Born: Preston, 1904 (January quarter).
Debut v Tranmere Rovers (a) 2 February 1929.
Appearances: 3.
Career: Chorley; STANLEY 22 June 1928; Burscough Rangers August 1931; Rossendale United; Fleetwood 1933-37.

A good reserve winger, but one whose League debut caused the local Press to observe: 'Moon never failed for lack of effort but discovered that there is a wide difference between (Lancashire) Combination football and the Third Division'. In October 1929 he had the misfortune to suffer a broken leg in a reserve match at Southport, but he made a complete recovery. He moved into non-League football in the summer of 1931 and obviously proved to be a handy man at this level. The *Lancashire Daily Post* revealed that in season 1935-6 he had appeared in every position on the field, including goalkeeper, for Fleetwood.

MORAN, Thomas **1953-54**
Half-back. 5ft 9in; 11st 9lb.
Born: Glasgow, 31 May 1924.
Debut v Stockport County (h) 22 August 1953.
Appearances: 7.
Career: Third Lanark; Alloa Athletic; Hastings United cs 1952; STANLEY 3 August 1953 to 29 April 1954.
Tommy Moran was a strongly-built half-back who had maintained a regular place in the Alloa Athletic team until he failed to agree terms for season 1952-3. Transfer-listed at £2,000, he moved into Southern League football with Hastings United, leaving them for domestic reasons to return to Scotland in March 1953. He was one of Walter Galbraith's early Scottish imports, but after early-season appearances at right-half he lost his place, the new player-manager eventually settling on a wing-half pairing of Harold Bodle and Charlie Sneddon.

MORGAN, Donald **1947-48**
Half-back or inside-forward. 5ft 8in; 11st 12lb.
Born: Huddersfield, 8 June 1925. Died: 1976.
Debut v Darlington (a) 8 June 1925.
Appearances: 8; Goals: 1.
Career: Huddersfield Town amateur; STANLEY amateur 4 March, signing professional 19 June 1947; Tranmere Rovers 31 May 1948; Halifax Town (trial) 6 October to 2 November 1948.
Don Morgan first played for Stanley as an amateur wing-half in 1946-7, playing in five of the last six League matches. He was signed as a professional in the close season and in 1947-8 played mainly as an inside-forward. He often received good notices for his work in the Combination side, where he carried out a 'shoot on sight' policy to excellent effect. He left Peel Park to join Tranmere Rovers on a free transfer in May 1948, but in October of the same year he was reported to have left them, finding the journey from his home in Huddersfield too much.

MORGAN, Ronald **1939-47**
Centre-forward.
Born: Twynrodyn, 6 September 1915.
Debut v Bradford City (a) 31 August 1946.
Appearances: 4.
Career: Wolverhampton Wanderers groundstaff at 17 years of age; Bournemouth & Boscombe Athletic June 1935; Doncaster Rovers 8 May 1937; STANLEY 22 June 1939; Worcester City 3 January 1947.
Ron Morgan joined Stanley just prior to the outbreak of World War Two and played in the three League matches completed before the outbreak of hostilities, scoring one goal. The League closed down and Stanley's 100 per cent record of three straight victories was unfortunately expunged. Prior to enlistment, Morgan played in 19 matches in the Regional League competition of 1939-40. He did not reappear until April 1946, when he played in the final two matches of the 1945-6 season. In preparation for the resumption of normal League football in 1946-7, Morgan trained in South Wales and also with the Wolves, one of his earlier clubs. As in season 1939-40, he led Stanley's attack in the first three matches of the season, but was then deposed by amateur centre-forward, Charlie Hudson (*qv*).

MORRIS, Alfred **1945-48**
Wing-half. 5ft 11in; 12st 4lb.
Born: Cadishead, Manchester.
Debut v Carlisle United (h) 24 September 1946.
Appearances: 15.
Career: Manchester junior football; STANLEY amateur 12 May, signing professional 18 October 1945 to May 1948.
Alf Morris was serving in the Army when he first turned out for Stanley and he had just returned with his unit from Ireland when he was signed on as a professional. A tall, bustling wing-half, Morris 'kicked strongly and tackled unerringly', according to one match report in 1946. Despite these attributes, he did not manage to establish a regular senior berth during his two and a half years at Peel Park.

MORRIS, Robert **1922-23**
Centre-forward. 5ft 7in; 11st 5lb.
Born: Coppull, near Chorley.
Debut v Darlington (h) 26 August 1922.
Appearances: 17; Goals: 4.
Career: Copland FC (Chorley); Preston North End January 1916; Blackburn Rovers September 1916; West Ham United July 1919; Fleetwood cs 1920; Barnsley 28 October 1920; STANLEY 24 May 1922; Lancaster Town October 1923; Blackburn Rovers reserve-team coach, Liverpool scout after World War Two.
Over-demonstrative celebrations were rare in the 1920s, but Bob Morris would probably have been forgiven for his handstand after he had scored the winning goal in a 4-3 victory against Bradford City in January 1923. Stanley had been three goals down at one point against the eventual runners-up in the Division. A well-known centre-forward in East Lancashire, Morris had missed almost all of season 1921-2 after a leg injury. After starting at centre-forward with Stanley he lost his place and was later used as an outside-left.

MORTIMER, Robert **1935-36 & 1936-37**
Centre-forward. 5ft 8½in; 11st 4lb.
Born: Bolton, 1908 (April quarter).
Appearances: 76; Goals: 56.
Career: Connah's Quay & Shotton; Barrow amateur 25 February, signing professional 18 July 1927; Bolton Wanderers 29 August 1928; Northampton Town 13 June 1931; Brentford 15 May 1933; Bournemouth & Boscombe Athletic 11 May 1934; STANLEY 11 June 1935; Portsmouth 13 February 1936 (with W.Harker for a combined fee of £1,450); STANLEY 19 September 1936; Blackburn Rovers 4 October 1937 (with W.G.Tyson for a combined fee of £1,200); York City 27 June 1938 (fee approx £300) to September 1939; Horwich RMI 3 September 1946.
A stocky, flame-haired centre-forward, Bob Mortimer's sharp shooting attracted much attention after he had scored 15 goals in ten consecutive games, which included his having found the net in eight consecutive matches. Portsmouth signed him, but he was back at Peel Park some seven months later, on a free transfer. He scored with his first shot on his return, at Gateshead and went on to set up what was at that time a new goalscoring record of 33 League and five FA Cup goals during the season. In Stanley's wonderful FA Cup adventure of that season, he scored twice at Ewood Park and twice in the replay when Stanley knocked

out Blackburn Rovers. The reward was a visit to Maine Road where 39,135 spectators (the largest ever 'gate' in a match involving Stanley) saw Manchester City progress by a 2-0 scoreline. After eight matches and four goals in season 1937-8, Blackburn Rovers took him from Peel Park for the last time. In his final season of League football he was York City's leading goal-scorer with 22 in 35 appearances. Fondly remembered as the man with the 'deadly ginger head', Bob Mortimer had career figures of exactly 200 League appearances and 105 goals. He later had a grocery and mixed business at Bolton.

MULKERRIN, James **1957-59**
Inside-forward. 5ft 8½in; 11st 6lb.
Born: Dumbarton, 25 December 1931.
Debut v Derby County (a) 16 March 1957.
Appearances: 70; Goals: 36.
Career: Hibernian; Cheltenham Town 23 October 1953; Hibernian; STANLEY 16 March 1957; Tranmere Rovers 21 August 1959 (fee £3,000); Northwich Victoria cs 1961.
International honour: Scotland 'B' v England 'B', 29 February 1956.
Jimmy Mulkerrin scored one of his team's two goals when he made his international debut for Scotland 'B'. The game against England 'B' at Dens Park, Dundee, ending in a 2-2 draw. He joined Stanley about a year later and was an immediate success, scoring seven goals in his first eight matches. Despite being side-lined for almost three months of the following term, due to a shoulder injury, he still managed to score 19 goals in 30 matches. When he left Stanley, the club were said to have recouped roughly that they paid for him. If this was the case, he would have been one of the club's most expensive signings. In two seasons with Tranmere, Mulkerrin scored eight goals in 38 games. He later worked in Accrington as a painter and decorator and kept in touch with the game by managing a local boys team.

MUSGRAVE, David **1953-54**
Outside-left.
Born: South Shields, 20 April 1928.
Debut v Grimsby Town (a) 9 September 1953.
Appearances: 30; Goals: 7.
Career: Johannesburg (South Africa); Manchester United 25 December 1947; Northwich Victoria; Fleetwood; New Brighton 23 August 1950; Preston North End (trial) 16 August 1951; Southport 12 October 1951 (fee £300); STANLEY 9 September 1953; Fleetwood cs 1954; Lancaster City October 1954 to May 1955; Oldham Athletic (one month's trial) August 1955; Crewe Alexandra (one month's trial) 29 September to 26 October 1955; Northwich Victoria 1955-6; Winsford United 1956-7.
Although only in his mid-20s when signed by Stanley, David Musgrave had packed in a great deal of football experience before he arrived at Peel Park. Born in South Shields, he emigrated with his parents to South Africa in 1933. In due course he took up football and his form was noted by Berry Nieuwenhuys, a South Africa-born former Liverpool winger. 'Nivvy' recommended Musgrave to a former Anfield colleague, Matt Busby, at that time Manchester United's manager. The outcome was that Musgrave returned to England and signed forms at Old Trafford on Christmas Day 1947. The son of a former League footballer, Musgrave was a fast and tricky winger who could deliver a well-judged centre with either foot. In an early reserve-team game for Stanley he scored an unusual hat-trick, all three goals coming from the penalty-spot. He also scored four goals in seven matches for the first team in September 1953 which earned him a contract for the season, after he had originally signed for a month's trial. All of Musgrave's career total of 117 appearances (16 goals) were made in the colours of New Brighton, Southport and Stanley, three clubs who all subsequently lost their League status.

MUTCH, Adam **1924-25**
Inside-forward. 5ft 9in; 11st.
Born: Aberdeen, 1903.
Debut v Rotherham County (h) 30 August 1924 (scored one goal).
Appearances: 40; Goals: 7.
Career: Aberdeen; STANLEY 23 July 1923; Lincoln City 11 May to 9 November 1925.
'A rare forager and a smart tactician', was one verdict on Adam Mutch, who marked his Stanley debut with a fine goal against Rotherham County. Adaptable to either inside berth, but usually at inside-right, he proved a consistent performer, missing only two matches during the season. His one failing seemed to be in finishing, as he often disappointed in front of goal.

MUTCH, William **1935-36**
Outside-left. 5ft 10½in; 10st 9lb.
Born: Aberdeen.
Debut v Lincoln City (a) 31 August 1935.
Appearances: 19; Goals: 2.
Career: Scottish junior football; Manchester United 30 October 1934; STANLEY 26 August 1935 to May 1936.
Bill Mutch began 1935-6 season on Stanley's left wing. It was Jack Hacking's first season as player-manager and the team made a dreadful start, losing the opening four fixtures with a goal difference of 2-17. The arrival of veteran winger George Mee in October 1935 relegated Mutch to Lancashire Combination football. Later on, he had two spells with Mee as his inside partner. Elder brother George Mutch was a Scottish international inside-forward whose clubs included Manchester United and Preston North End.

NEAL, Richard Marshall **1938-39**
Born: Rotherham, 14 January 1906. Died: Fence, 26 December 1986.
Debut v Halifax Town (a) 27 August 1938.
Appearances: 21; Goals: 7.
Career: Dinnington Main; Blackpool amateur 28 January, signing professional 6 February 1926; Derby County 16 May 1931; Southampton 19 February 1932; Bristol City 7 May 1937; STANLEY 9 June 1938 to March 1939.
A slender but strong winger with the ability to occupy either flank, Neal was a product of a colliery team on the outskirts of Sheffield. Introduced to League football by Blackpool, he was unfortunate to be injured in season 1929-30 and managed only 11 appearances in the Seasiders' Second Division championship side. After a brief spell with Derby County, he then spent a little over five seasons with Southampton, making over 200 Second Division appearances. A season with

Bristol City preceded his spell with Stanley. He was first-choice outside-left until the arrival of George Mee from Rochdale in late January 1939. Neal's brother-in-law, Fred Gibson, was a goalkeeper whose clubs included Hull City, Middlesbrough and Bradford City. His son, Richard M.Neal, was a wing-half with Wolverhampton Wanderers, Lincoln City, Birmingham City and Middlesbrough. He made over 350 Football League appearances and won four England Under-23 caps in the 1950s and 1960s.

NELIS, Patrick **1920-22**
Centre-forward. 5ft 7in; 10st 11lb.
Born: Londonderry, 27 October 1898. Died: Londonderry, 22 April 1970.
Debut v Durham City (h) 5 November 1921 (scored three goals).
Appearances: 11; Goals: 14.
Career: Londonderry Distillery; STANLEY December 1920; Nottingham Forest 16 March 1922 (fee £2,000); Wigan Borough 27 June 1925 to April 1926.
International honour: 1 cap for Ireland v England in 1922.

When Pat Nelis first joined Stanley he was a pale-faced and rather sickly-looking Irishman. As he improved physically, so his game improved and he developed with remarkable rapidity. First introduced to Stanley by fellow countryman Pat Quigley (*qv*), Nelis was initially dropped after playing in his first two League matches, the first of which he had celebrated by scoring a hat-trick. He had three months to wait for another chance and this came only because Tom Green was injured. Nevertheless, in a run of nine games he scored 11 goals, which included a further two hat-tricks. Not surprisingly he was snapped up by Nottingham Forest and he assisted them in their run-in to the Second Division championship by scoring six goals in 11 appearances. Nelis' transfer fee was said to be the highest ever received for a Third Division player, the previous highest being £1,600, paid by Huddersfield Town to Nelson for Walter Wadsworth. Only seven months after his transfer, Stanley directors forwarded a telegram of congratulations to Nelis, on his selection for Ireland in the first international match of season 1922-3.

NESS, Hugh Preston **1959-60**
Outside-left. 5ft 6½in; 10st.
Born: Dunfermline, 30 April 1940.
Debut v Wrexham (h) 29 August 1959.
Appearances: 14; Goals: 1.
Career: Raith Rovers; Cowdenbeath; STANLEY 29 July 1959; Halifax Town 1 July 1960 to 30 June 1961; Nelson 1961-2; Great Harwood 1962-66.
A 19-year-old winger who had created a good impression in the Scottish Second Division. Hugh Ness was fast and fluent but had a tendency to hold the ball too long. He played in Stanley's first team with any regularity only in the first half of season 1959-60, being largely in the shadow of a much more experienced winger, Jimmy Anders.

NEWTON, William Alfred A. **1921-22**
Full-back. 5ft 8in; 11st 10lb.
Born: Romiley, Cheshire, 1896 (January quarter).
Debut v Rochdale (a) 27 August 1921.
Appearances: 2.
Career: Droylsden; Manchester City 16 February 1916; Burnley season 1916-17 (wartime guest); Southend United July 1920; STANLEY 7 July 1921, released on a free transfer 9 January 1922.
Newton's transfer from Manchester City was rather unusual. He was one of four players from Maine Road who joined Southend United in the close season of 1920. Tom Mather, Southend's manager, had earlier been assistant secretary with Manchester City, which probably influenced the 'bulk buy'. Newton returned north to join Stanley after making 29 appearances in Southend's initial season of League football, in the Third Division. He played in Stanley's first two games in the newly-formed Third Division North, but was then deposed. He was reported to have left Peel Park in early December 1921.

NICHOLSON, G(eorge) Henry **1958-59**
Goalkeeper. 6ft 2in; 12st 9lb.
Born: Wetheral, Cumberland, 25 January 1932.
Debut v Newport County (a) 4 September 1958.
Appearances: 1.
Career: Carlisle United amateur; Grimsby Town 13 August 1952; Nottingham Forest 5 July 1955; STANLEY 14 March 1958; Leyton Orient 17 March 1959 (fee £500); Bristol City 6 July 1960 to May 1961.
Harry Nicholson was the last player to be signed by Walter Galbraith before the Stanley manager resigned in August 1958. In season 1956-7 Nicholson played in 34 matches for Nottingham Forest, who won promotion to the First Division as runners-up to Leicester City. With Stanley he had only one senior outing, as deputy to Willie McInnes and was

transferred to Leyton Orient a year after first joining the Peel Park staff. Apart from his spell with Nottingham Forest, he was generally cast in a reserve role. Of his total career aggregate of 95 League appearances, all but 23 were made with Forest.

NIGHTINGALE, Ronald **1957-61**
Half-back. 5ft 10in; 11st 2lb.
Born: Darwen, 27 January 1937.
Debut v Halifax Town (a) 27 December 1958.
Appearances: 14.
Career: STANLEY amateur, signing professional 10 July 1957. Reverted to amateur status 27 October 1958 (to avoid exceeding income limit for grant when he became a student at Manchester University); Tranmere Rovers (trial) 19 August to 18 September 1961; Chorley.
Ron Nightingale graduated through Stanley's 'A' and reserve teams to make his Football League debut as a 21-year-old. The Reds won 2-0 at Halifax Town after Nightingale, a last-minute selection, had been rushed to the team's coach on the pillion of a motor-cycle, driven by reserve-team trainer, Les Cocker. Nightingale had a useful faculty of being able to fill any defensive position, but his career was retarded by a chest complaint which caused him to spend three weeks in hospital and left him unfit for football for much of season 1960-61.

NISBITT, Gavin **1936-37**
Half-back. 5ft 8in; 11st 7lb.
Born: Hamilton, Scotland, 1905.
Debut v Lincoln City (h) 29 August 1936.
Appearances: 31.
Career: Coalburn Juniors; Blantyre Victoria; Preston North End 27 November 1926; Burnley 21 September 1935; STANLEY 17 June 1936; Stalybridge Celtic September 1937.
In his second season at Deepdale, former bricklayer Gavin Nisbitt won promotion to the first team after scoring seven goals in a Central League match. It was, however, as a wing-half that he made his mark. Considered too slow to be a successful forward, he found his true position as an attacking wing-half, where his judgement of passes and ball-control left little room for complaint. In his nine years at Deepdale, he assisted North End to promotion into the First Division in 1933-4, when they were runners-up to Grimsby Town for the Second Dvision championship. A move to Burnley saw him play only twice in the League side and he arrived at Peel Park on a free transfer. Generally first-choice at right-half for Stanley, a typical Press comment on his style was: 'Nisbitt was a trifle slow in going to the ball, but when in possession he was an excellent craftsman'.

NOCK, John Edwin **1934-35**
Inside-forward. 5ft 8½in; 10st 12lb.
Born: Rotherham, 13 January 1909.
Debut v Southport (a) 19 January 1935.
Appearances: 1.
Career: Brinsworth Council School; Rotherham YMCA; Dinnington Athletic; Silverwood Colliery (Sheffield Association League); Rotherham United 9 July 1931; Scarborough Town July 1933; Bacup Borough cs 1934; STANLEY 14 December 1934; Rossendale United February 1935.
A prolific scorer in non-League football, John Nock began by netting 43 in one season with Dinnington Athletic and followed up by scoring 76 in one season with Silverwood Colliery. It seemed surprising that Rotherham United did not retain his services after two seasons in which he had scored 15 goals in 25 League appearances. A term with Scarborough Town saw him register over 30 goals in the North-Eastern League and he joined Stanley after having spent half a season with Bacup Borough, in which he scored 16 goals in as many games. Apart from one Third Division game, a scoreless draw at Southport, Nock's activities were confined to the reserve side. When Frank Britton was signed in early February, Nock was released to Rossendale United.

NUTTALL, Henry **1921-22**
Half-back. 5ft 6in; 9st 9lb.
Born: Oswaldtwistle.
Debut v Barrow (a) 7 January 1922.
Appearances: 2.
Career: Local junior football; STANLEY 11 May 1921; Great Harwood cs 1922; Darwen September 1924; Great Harwood June 1925.
Signed after trials at the close of season 1920-21, Harry Nuttall spent the following term in Stanley's reserve team, making just two first team appearances, as deputy for Billy Crawshaw. Moving into non-League football, he spent two seasons with Great Harwood and then assisted Darwen to finish third in the Lancashire Combination in 1924-5. A return to Great Harwood for the following season proved far less rewarding, as they finished at the foot of the table, having conceded 142 goals in their 38 games.

OGDEN, Harold **1922-23**
Half-back.
Debut v Chesterfield (a) 11 November 1922.
Appearances: 1.
Career: Local junior football; STANLEY amateur 17 June 1922 to May 1923.
A last-minute selection for Stanley's visit to Saltergate in their second Northern Section campaign, Harry Ogden's display was said to be only moderate. The *Accrington Observer* revealed, however, that he had worn a brand-new pair of boots, which had blistered his feet to a shocking degree.
Note: Football boots in those days bore no relation whatsoever to today's soft leather, low-cut styles. Players were usually recommended to soak the boots, whilst being worn without stockings, alternately in hot and then cold water. Runs through ploughed fields were also advocated! Professional players in particular were loathe to discard a pair of boots until they literally fell apart. The last thing any player wanted was to have to break in a new pair.

O'GRADY, Harry **1937-38**
Inside-forward. 5ft 9in; 11st 6lb.
Born: Tunstall, Staffs, 16 March 1907.
Debut v Carlisle United (h) 28 August 1937 (scored one goal).
Appearances: 23; Goals: 2.
Career: Nantwich Victoria (trial); Witton Albion 1928; Port Vale 9 November 1929; Southampton 14 August 1931; Leeds United 24 August 1932; Burnley 18 May 1933; Bury 10 May 1934; Millwall 29 June 1935;

Carlisle United 28 August 1936; STANLEY 31 May 1937; Tunbridge Wells Rangers October 1938.
Harry O'Grady's debut for Stanley was made against his previous club, Carlisle United, at Peel Park. Whilst he had the satisfaction of scoring against his former colleagues, the Reds made their almost customary poor start to a season by losing 4-1. In what proved to be his final season of League football, he made a slow start and did not win a regular place in the side until mid-November. Once established, he proved a hard-working link man but he often disappointed in front of goal. One of the games 'happy wanderers', O'Grady wore the colours of eight different League clubs in as many seasons, playing in all four Divisions of the League.

OLDHAM, John **1945-53**
Centre-half. 5ft 8in; 11st 6lb.
Born: Oswaldtwistle, 30 January 1926.
Debut v Darlington (h) 7 April 1951.
Appearances: 10.
Career: Oswaldtwistle Immanuel; STANLEY amateur 28 November, professional 5 August 1950 to May 1953.
A mainstay of the reserve team, Jack Oldham made all but two of his ten senior appearances at the close of season 1950-51. He was selected in preference to Eric Lovett at centre-half, following a 7-0 defeat at Bradford City. His inclusion in the side coincided with something of a revival, built around a more compact defence. The side took eight points from their final eight fixtures. This was a great improvement on what had gone before, but was insufficient in the event to lift them out of 23rd position. Stanley's first post-war re-election was successful, but New Brighton, in 24th place, failed to retain their League status.

OXLEY, Richard Lambert **1921-22**
Outside-right. 5ft 7½in; 10st 10lb.
Born: Wallsend-on-Tyne, 1895 (January quarter).

Died: Wallsend-on-Tyne, 3 July 1953.
Debut v Rochdale (a) 27 August 1921.
Appearances: 33; Goals: 3.
Career: Wallsend; Newcastle United (trial); STANLEY 11 May 1921; Southport 27 May 1922; Queen's Park Rangers 25 August 1923; Northampton Town 8 December 1925 to May 1926.
Stanley invited Richard Oxley for a trial towards the end of season 1920-21 and, on the strength of this, he was signed on in May 1921. A star of the running track, Oxley was a well-known sprinter who had won the Powderhall Handicap. He proved to be a good provider from the wing in a season when Stanley scored in every match but one of their 38 League engagements, finishing fifth in the table in their initial Northern Section campaign. A brother, William Oxley, was an inside-forward who figured on the books of no fewer than nine League clubs in the inter-war period.

PAGE, George **1922-23**
Full-back. 5ft 9in; 11st 12lb.
Born: Darlington, 30 November 1898.
Debut v Darlington (h) 26 August 1922.
Appearances: 31; Goals: 1.

Career: Rise Carr FC; Doncaster Rovers (when a Midland League club); Barnsley 25 May 1921; STANLEY 24 May 1922; Ashington 4 July 1923; Lincoln City 10 July 1924; Crewe Alexandra 30 June 1926 to May 1927.
In amateur days George Page captained Rise Carr and was first signed as a professional by Doncaster Rovers, before they gained Football League entry. Well built

and speedy, Page had only one Football League outing to his credit when he arrived at Peel Park. He had the confidence of the Stanley directors, however, and proved to be a great success at left-back. He was also a more than useful emergency goalkeeper and during his Lincoln City spell earned the soubriquet 'Deadshot George', after he had scored from the penalty-spot in each of three consecutive matches in season 1925-6.

PARKER, Samuel **1948 & 1949-50**
Centre-forward, later full-back. 5ft 9in; 12st 8lb.
Born: Liverpool, 5 April 1924.
Debut v Oldham Athletic (h) 28 August 1948.
Appearances: 49; Goals: 12.
Career: Marine (Crosby); STANLEY 5 July 1948; Barnsley 29 December 1948 (in exchange for E.Williams); STANLEY 6 September 1949; Crewe Alexandra 14 November 1950 to 2 December 1951.
Sam Parker had scored 23 goals in half a season with Marine and these included two hat-tricks against Stanley Reserves. Not surprisingly, he was snapped up by Stanley and in the pre-season trials broke the net with a bullet-like penalty-kick. On his first-team debut he revealed another great asset in his ability to propel throw-ins prodigious distances. He had scored six goals in 13 appearances for Stanley when Barnsley signed him, after Oakwell scouts had seen him score a goal and provide the winner against Darlington. He was to return to Peel Park about nine months later, shortly after regular centre-forward Don Travis had fractured a cheek bone, thus becoming the seventh man on the injury list. When Travis recovered, Parker spent some time in the Reserves, where he was successfully converted to right-back. It was in this position that he resumed in the first team, after Stan Lynn had been transferred to Aston Villa. Parker left Stanley for the last time in November 1950, along with Don Travis, to join Crewe Alexandra. He made 43 appearances and scored five goals for the Railwaymen.

PARKIN, John Turnbull **1927-29**
Centre-forward. 5ft 8in; 11st 3lb.
Born: Byker-on-Tyne, 31 July 1900.
Debut v Nelson (a) 27 August 1927 (scored two goals).
Appearances: 63; Goals: 36.
Career: Langley Moor; Durham City amateur 16 March 1925, signing professional 29 August 1925; STANLEY 6 July 1927; Chesterfield 22 May 1929; Stalybridge Celtic August 1930.
Jack Parkin began in first-class football with Durham City in company with his brother Tom. City's forward line also featured George Camsell, who later found fame with Middlesbrough and won nine English caps. In 1927-8, Parkin had a very successful season as Stanley's centre-forward, scoring 28 goals in 38 games. A fine attack leader, he was well supported by Butler and McLoughlin, two clever inside-forwards. Retained for a second season, he did less well, eventually losing his centre-forward birth to Jepson and moving to inside-right.

PARRY, Frank Thomas **1927-29**
Outside-right. 5ft 7in; 11st 2lb.
Born: Aigburth, Liverpool, 14 June 1898. Died: Southport, 13 March 1973.
Debut v Nelson (a) 27 August 1927.
Appearances: 81; Goals: 10.
Career: Local junior football; Everton 11 November 1921; Grimsby Town 22 June 1926; STANLEY 22 July 1927; Nelson 6 November 1929 to May 1930.
Frank Parry's departure from Peel Park after two seasons evoked controversy amongst the club's supporters. Even the *Athletic News* commented on his release: 'Accrington have not retained Frank Parry, the dainty outside-right. He will be sadly missed by those who admire skill and polish.' Parry had arrived at Accrington with only 13 League outings to his name. At Goodison Park he was understudy to Sam Chedgzoy for the best part of five seasons. With Stanley he missed only three first-team games in two seasons. A skilful winger, Parry's only flaw was said to be a lack of confidence in his own ability as a goalscorer. His father was Maurice Pryce Parry, a prominent wing-half with Liverpool and Wales in the early 1900s. An uncle, Tom D.Parry, also played for Oswestry and Wales in the same period.

PARSONS, Jacob **1929-30**
Inside-forward. 5ft 10in; 12st 4lb.
Born: Barrow, 27 February 1903.
Debut v Tranmere Rovers (a) 25 January 1930.
Appearnces: 15; Goals: 12.
Career: Whitehaven Athletic; Southport 1 July 1927; Barrow 16 February 1928; STANLEY 31 May 1929; Exeter City 16 May 1930; Thames 5 June 1931; Mansfield Town 13 October to 6 December 1932.
A powerfully-built centre or inside-forward who opened his career by scoring 60 goals for Whitehaven Athletic in 1926-7, setting up a new individual goalscoring record for the competition. With Southport he scored in total 36 goals in little more than half a season, including six in a friendly match against Wigan Borough in January 1928. Despite this, he played in only four first-team games, in which he scored three goals. This was to prove a recurring pattern throughout his career, as his next move saw him score 15 goals, including two hat-tricks, for Barrow whilst being unable to retain a first-team place. Stanley did not give him a League outing for six months but on his second first-team appearance he netted four goals against Halifax Town at Peel Park. One week later he scored four again, at Rotherham United. With Exeter City, Parsons was reserve to Percy Varco and made only three League appearances. For the Grecians Reserves he scored 34 goals which included six in one match against Taunton Town. A burly, swarthy-looking player, Parsons lacked pace but was the possessor of a lethal shot, once reported as being of 'howitzer power'.

PATEMAN, George Edward **1936-37**
Inside or centre-forward. 5ft 11in; 11st 12lb.
Born: Chatham, 8 May 1910. Died: Rochester, 23 March 1973.
Debut v Lincoln City (h) 29 August 1936 (scored one goal).
Appearances: 21; Goals: 8.
Career: Canterbury Waverley; Gillingham 3 June 1929; Portsmouth 20 July 1931; Oldham Athletic 12 May 1933; Bradford City 7 June 1934; Clapton Orient 31 July 1935; Reading 18 October 1935 (fee £350); STANLEY 12 August 1936 (fee £100); Southport 19 February 1937 (in exchange for F.Curran); Barrow 29

June 1937 to May 1939; Short's works team player and manager to 1947.
A widely-travelled forward and former shipyard worker, George Pateman began at centre-forward with Stanley but was moved to inside-left when Bob Mortimer returned to Stanley from Portsmouth. Supple and tall, he fitted well in the inside berth, running intelligently into open positions in midfield and distributing judiciously. He departed Stanley in a transfer which brought Frank Curran to Peel Park and, by coincidence, made his Southport debut at Accrington, one day after his transfer. He had the satisfaction of scoring twice against his former teammates, but his efforts did not bring success as Stanley won a high-scoring encounter by 6-3.

PATERSON, William **1949**
Centre-forward. 5ft 11in; 12st 2lb.
Born: Morton, *c.*1928.
Debut v Lincoln City (a) 3 September 1949.
Appearances: 1.
Career: Morton; STANLEY 3 August to 13 October 1949.
Billy Paterson, a 21-year-old Lanark boy, spent an unrewarding few weeks at Peel Park. Ideally built at almost 6ft tall, he had shown promise as a junior with Morton. He failed to reproduce his earlier form, however, and his contract was cancelled after only one Football League outing.

PATTISON, Joseph **1932-35**
Goalkeeper. 5ft 10in; 10st 12lb.
Born: Haslingden, 1912 (July quarter).
Debut v New Brighton (a) 3 September 1932.
Appearances: 16.
Career: Burnley amateur; STANLEY amateur 24 May 1932, signing professional May 1934; returned to Burnley as an amateur in 1935 and in 1938 was in junior football with Haslingden St Mary's.
Joe Pattison, a young reserve goalkeeper, had the misfortune to make one of his infrequent appearances in Stanley's goal on 3 February 1934. The visitors to Peel Park were Barnsley and they won 9-0 to record the second highest away victory in the Football League. (The record was a 10-0 victory by Sheffield United against Burslem Port Vale at Burslem on 10 December 1892). Barnsley had earlier beaten Stanley at Oakwell by 6-0 and they ran up 118 goals in winning the championship of the Northern section.

PEACOCK, Frederick **1921-22**
Goalkeeper. 5ft 9½in; 11st.
Born: Altrincham, 1891 (April quarter).
Debut v Crewe Alexandra (h) 10 September 1921.
Appearances: 4.
Career: Winsford United; STANLEY 1 August 1921 to May 1922.
Stanley recruited an entire playing staff for their first season in the Third Division North without paying a penny in transfer fees. It was not, therefore, unexpected that some players would not come up to expectations. The goalkeeping position was subject to several changes during the course of the season after Tattersall had begun as first-choice with Peacock as reserve. By the close of the season, Sloane was first-choice with Floyd the emerging youngster. Fred Peacock had joined Stanley after a highly successful season with Winsford United, Cheshire League champions in 1920-21. In isolated League appearances he proved a competent last line of defence, but his value was discounted somewhat by his goal-kicking, which was criticized for lacking length.

PEARS, John **1929-30**
Outside-left. 5ft 8½in; 11st 10lb.
Born: Ormskirk, 23 February 1904.
Debut v Doncaster Rovers (a) 31 August 1929.
Appearances: 21; Goals: 8.
Career: Westhead St James; Skelmersdale United cs 1926; Burscough Rangers December 1926; Liverpool amateur 25 August 1927; Rotherham United 4 August 1928; STANLEY 25 May 1929; Oldham Athletic 12 July 1930; Preston North End 15 March 1934; Sheffield United 8 November 1934 (fee £1,000); Swansea Town 15 August 1935 (fee £350); Hull City 11 June 1937 (fee £100); Mossley September 1938.
'A fast-moving winger who carries out to the full the modern tendency to cut in and shoot' was a *Topical Times* appraisal of Jack Pears in 1930. Despite having played in only half of Stanley's matches in 1929-30, he had done enough to impress Second Division Oldham Athletic. At Boundary Park he took over from Bill Hasson in season 1931-2 and gave excellent service to the Latics, scoring 34 goals in 92 League appearances. A move to Deepdale, just prior to the transfer 'deadline' in 1934, saw him help his new club to promotion to the First Division, as runners-up to Grimsby Town.

PETERS, Thomas J. **1949**
Inside-forward. 5ft 7in; 11st 6lb.
Born: Droylsden, Lancashire, 22 December 1920.
Debut v Gateshead (h) 29 October 1949.
Appearances: 4; Goals: 2.
Career: Everton and Chesterfield (wartime guest player); Doncaster Rovers 16 May 1944; Bury 30 December 1946; Leeds United 19 August 1948; Mansfield Town 17 March 1949; Droylsden cs 1949; STANLEY (trial) 18 October to 14 December 1949; Brighton and Hove Albion (one month's trial) 17 January to 14 February 1950.
Tom Peters originally came to Peel Park on a month's trial. This was extended by a further month after he had scored twice in a 3-0 win over Darlington on 12 November 1949. However, he did not win a permanent engagement and his eventual replacement was another former Bury forward, Andy Dolan (*qv*). Tom Peters' career totalled only 20 League games, half of which were made in Bury's colours.

PICKERING, William Harold **1937-38**
Full-back. 5ft 11in; 12st 12lb.
Born: Birmingham.
Debut v Carlisle United (h) 28 August 1937.
Appearances: 29.
Career: Latch & Batchelors FC (Birmingham League); Sunderland amateur 26 July 1924; Merthyr Town 25 August 1925; Gillingham 26 August 1926; Huddersfield Town 7 November 1927 (fee £1,000); Reading 31 May 1929; Colwyn Bay United August 1930; Bristol Rovers 18 May 1931 (fee £300); STANLEY 16 June 1937; Oswestry Town player-manager cs 1938.
A tall, strongly-built full-back of sound experience, Bill Pickering was a cool and calculating defender who

relied more on judgment than vigour. His height and blond hair made him easily recognizable on the field, and he was usually to be found where the action was thickest. Experienced in all Divisions of the League and associated at League level with six clubs during his career, Pickering's final total fell only one short of 300 appearances. He was a fine servant to Bristol Rovers in a six-year association, which included a run of four seasons in which he missed only three League matches. Pickering, who was also a good table-tennis player, represented Accrington in inter-League matches whilst he was at Peel Park.

PICKUP, Thomas **1930-31**
Half-back. 5ft 9in; 11st 3lb.
Born: Blackburn, 1908 (April quarter).
Debut v Crewe Alexandra (h) 30 August 1930.
Appearances: 5.
Career: Local junior football; Blackburn Rovers 10 May 1929; STANLEY 19 May 1930; Mossley May 1931; Great Harwood; Fleetwood January 1933; Haslingden Grane FC season 1938-9.
Stanley took five points from their opening three fixtures of the 1930-31 season, at that time, their best-ever start to a Third Division campaign. The promising start had, however, seen seven goals conceded, and the original half-back line was quickly dismantled, Tom Pickup being one who lost his place. A wholehearted and versatile player, but one lacking in experience, Pickup made a useful auxillary, his final League outing being made on the right wing.

PIGG, William **1930-31**
Half-back. 5ft 7½in; 11st 6lb.

Born: High Spen, Co Durham.
Debut v Crewe Alexandra (h) 30 August 1930.
Appearances: 10.
Career: Ashington amateur 20 October, signing professional 1 November 1921; Queen's Park Rangers 4 August 1924; Carlisle United cs 1926; STANLEY 9 June 1930 to May 1931.
Bill Pigg's career commenced in his native north-east with Ashington, at that time a Third Division North side. In three seasons he made 94 appearances, which included 40 in 1923-4 when Ashington finished eighth in the table, their best position in League football. Queen's Park Rangers signed him after they had experienced their worst-ever League season in 1923-4, but he left after two unrewarding seasons, at the close of which the Rangers had to seek re-election for the second time in three seasons. A four-year stint with Carlisle United followed and in season 1928-9 the Cumbrians were elected to the Football League. With Stanley, he joined former teammate Alf Agar (*qv*), who had also assisted Carlisle United in their first season as a League club. Pigg began as first-choice left-half with Stanley but lost his place to George Whyte. His career totals were 193 appearances, nine goals.

PINKNEY, Ernest **1922-23**
Outside-right. 5ft 8in; 11st 7lb.
Born: Glasgow, 23 November (year unknown).
Debut v Darlington (h) 26 August 1922.
Appearances: 12; Goals: 3.
Career: West Hartlepool; Everton 1 February 1910; Barrow cs 1912; Gillingham July 1913; Liverpool October 1915; Tranmere Rovers season 1919-20; Halifax Town 22 July 1921; STANLEY 1 June 1922 to May 1923.
On the closing Saturday of season 1922-3, Ernest Pinkney scored Stanley's winner in their 1-0 victory against Lincoln City at Peel Park. It proved to be insufficient to win him a place on the retained list, in what had been an unfortunate season for the experienced winger. He was carried off the field in the game against Durham City at Peel Park on 30 September 1922. After a lay-off of two months he was back in action, but he broke down again and had to undergo a cartilage operation. When he scored on his final appearance on 5 May 1923, it was his first senior outing since Boxing Day of the previous year.

PIRIE, Frederick William **1954-60**
Full-back. 5ft 7½in; 11st.
Born: Coupar Angus, 19 January 1934.
Debut v Tranmere Rovers (a) 6 November 1954.
Appearances: 17.
Career: Coupar Angus; STANLEY 12 January 1954 (fee £100); Horwich RMI cs 1960; Bacup Borough season 1962-3.
In a stay of six years with Stanley, Fred Pirie was signed as a full-time professional in February 1957, on being demobilized from the Army after two years service with the RASC. Powerfully built and with good positional sense, he was also outstanding in headwork, being able to outjump many taller opponents. When he left Stanley, after being released in May 1960, he joined Horwich RMI, who were managed by ex-Stanley inside-forward Archie Wright (*qv*). Pirie's career was ended by a broken leg injury, sustained in his first season with Bacup Borough.

PLATT, John **1930-31**
Goalkeeper.
Debut v Chesterfield (h) 11 October 1930.
Appearances: 1.
Career: STANLEY amateur 11 October 1930 to May 1931.
Few details of John Platt's football career have been unearthed, but his solitary Football League outing had some amusing aspects. His selection came when regular goalkeeper Dick Thornton was suffering from influenza. As Thornton had been beaten eight times the previous week, the *Accrington Observer's* correspondent wondered whether the flu had been caused by the draughts created by the eight goals scored against him! Platt's debut was a poor game which Stanley lost 3-1 to surrender their unbeaten home record. One report of the match stated that when the referee stopped play and called upon a policeman to eject a spectator, it provided some little break from the monotony. At least Platt missed the reserve-team match at Seedhill on the same afternoon, which Nelson Reserves won 10-3.

POLLITT, John **1960**
Centre-forward. 6ft; 11st 7lb.
Born: Farnworth, Lancashire, 29 March 1937.
Debut v Norwich City (a) 5 March 1960.
Appearances: 3; Goals: 1.
Career: Junior football; Bolton Wanderers 3 January 1955; Bury 19 August 1958; STANLEY 4 March 1960; Rochdale 17 August 1960 to June 1961.
One of manager Harold Bodle's late-season signings in 1959-60, John Pollitt had a good record in Bury's reserve team. He had appeared in 60 matches and was their leading Central League goalscorer. Some six weeks after his arrival, manager Bodle's engagement was terminated and Pollitt followed shortly afterwards. He was transfer-listed and a fee was placed on him, but following an appeal to the Football League, he was granted a free transfer. Despite his association with four different League clubs in his native county, Pollitt appeared in only 13 League matches, scoring two goals.

POPPLEWELL, Stanley **1921-24 & 1927-28**
Centre-half. 5ft 10½in; 12st 3lb.
Born: Bolton, 2 September 1892.
Debut v Rochdale (a) 27 August 1921.
Appearances: 71; Goals: 4.
Career: Barrow; Exeter City August 1919; Blackpool 14 May 1920; STANLEY 29 June 1921; Darwen 16 August 1924; Clitheroe August 1925; Colne Town September 1926; STANLEY 10 September 1927 to May 1928.
'A steady and reliable defender who tackled with skill and opened out the game with passes to the wings,' was one Press verdict on Stanley Popplewell during Stanley's first campaign in the Third Division North. He was the team's most consistent defender, missing only two matches due to injury. In his second season he began in his usual role as pivot, later switching to right half-back. In 1923-4 he was reserve centre-half to Billy Rooks, but marked his final two Football League appearances by scoring in consecutive games

against Rotherham County and Hartlepools United, in May 1924. In his second spell at Peel Park, he was exclusively a reserve-team player.

POWELL, Edgar Frederick **1925-27**
Inside-forward. 5ft 7½in; 10st 9lb.

Born: Cardiff, 6 January 1899.
Debut v Walsall (a) 29 August 1925.
Appearances: 65; Goals: 17.
Career: Barry Schoolboys; Barry FC; Denaby United; Huddersfield Town 11 May 1923; Stoke 16 May 1924; STANLEY 19 June 1925; Merthyr Town 8 August 1927; Barrow 28 July 1928 to May 1929.
International honour: Wales Schoolboys.
A star in schools football, Edgar Powell represented his country at this level, playing against England Schoolboys in 1913. He came to Huddersfield Town's notice whilst playing for Denaby United, but his Football League debut came with Stoke in season 1924-5. Powell began as a winger with Stanley but was switched to inside-left to accommodate Tommy Wyper on the right wing. He had an unfortunate ending to an otherwise excellent first season (41 appearances and 11 goals) when he was seriously injured in the semi-final of the Lancashire Senior Cup against Manchester United at Bury. He did not feature as a regular first teamer in the early months of the following season, when he totalled 24 League appearances and scored six goals.

PRICE, Norman **1931-34**
Full-back. 5ft 10in; 12st 1lb.
Born: Dumfries, 1908.
Debut v Rochdale (a) 29 August 1931.
Appearances: 88; Goals: 8.
Career: Ayr United 1928; Bristol Rovers 25 July 1930; STANLEY 29 June 1931; Coleraine 4 July 1934; Stalybridge Celtic 27 August 1935; Oldham Athletic 19 May 1936; Gainsborough Trinity 25 June 1938.
Too literal an interpretation of Boxing Day in 1931 saw Norman Price sent off the field at Wrexham for fighting. The subsequent suspension prevented him from obtaining an ever-present record in his first season with Stanley. Midway through the following term he was injured and his deputy, Tommy Corcoran, did so well that Price could not regain his place. At either full-back flank, he was generally in the first team in his final season. After spending two years out of League football, Oldham Athletic brought him back and he gave the Latics two seasons of sterling service. A strong, powerful defender who cleared his lines in the approved manner, Price was also a reliable man from the penalty-spot.

PRIDAY, Robert Herbert **1952-53**
Outside-left. 5ft 7½in; 12st 2lb.
Born: Cape Town, South Africa, 29 March 1925.
Debut v Gateshead (h) 13 December 1952.
Appearances: 5.
Career: South African football; Liverpool 1 December 1945; Blackburn Rovers 17 March 1949 (fee £10,000); Clitheroe cs 1951; Northwich Victoria cs 1952; STANLEY 13 December 1952; Rochdale (trial) 17 August to 10 October 1953.
Bob Priday revealed clever touches on his debut for Stanley, but was unfortunate to be injured in his initial outing. He was kept out for four months, by which time the 1952-3 season was in its final weeks. Priday was one of a number of South African footballers to be introduced into League football by Liverpool. His signing took place on board a liner, arriving in Southampton from South Africa. Some four years later, when he was on his way to the transfer meeting which made him a Blackburn Rovers player, he was

involved in a car crash, but escaped with a severe shaking.

PYE, Fred **1948-49**
Inside-forward.
Born: Stockport, 11 March 1928.
Debut v Hartlepools United (a) 28 April 1948.
Appearances: 4.
Career: Stalybridge Celtic; STANLEY amateur 27 April, signing professional 23 September 1948; Winsford United cs 1949; Altrincham.
Light of hair and light of step, Freddie Pye was a stocky, diminutive, amateur winger who made his debut for Stanley whilst he was stationed at Nuneaton in the Royal Navy. Two years earlier he had played against Stanley when he guested for Rochdale in the benefit match for war casualty Tom Jones (*qv*). An incessant worker throughout 90 minutes, Pye's best game for Stanley was against Mansfield Town in September 1948. The Reserve team left wing of Pye and Joe Rodwell (*qv*) were promoted to the first team and they combined well to bring a welcome injection of youthful dash and enthusiasm to the attack. Pye later had much success in non-League management with Stalybridge Celtic and notably with Altrincham. He took over the Robins in June 1963 and later became chairman of their board of directors. He also became a very successful businessman in the field of scrap metal.

QUIGLEY, Patrick H. **1920-22 & 1923-24**
Inside-forward. 5ft 9½in; 12st 7lb.
Born: Londonderry, 1898.
Debut v Chesterfield (h) 24 September 1921.
Appearances: 39; Goals: 5.
Career: Londonderry Distillery; Glentoran; STAN-

LEY November 1920; Rossendale United August 1922; STANLEY 21 September 1923; Preston North End (trial); Rossendale United October 1924; Chorley August 1925; Darwen August 1928 to 1934.
'Paddy' Quigley first joined Stanley before they gained Football League entry in 1921 and at first travelled on the Irish night boat every Friday to play for Stanley. He eventually settled in Accrington and in the early 1930s worked as a clerk at Accrington Post Office. Said to have been an Irish junior international, he was a player of individualistic methods, clever beyond question, but difficult to knit into an attacking formation. He had two spells with Stanley, but won local fame, and a fine collection of medals, in Lancashire Combination football. These included a League and Cup double in season 1930-31, and a League championship and Cup runners-up medal in 1931-2, both with Darwen FC.

RALSTON, Peter **1957-59**
Centre-half. 6ft; 12st 8lb.
Born: Fauldhouse, West Lothian, 31 January 1929.
Debut v Hartlepools United (h) 24 August 1957.
Appearances: 6.
Career: Falkirk cs 1951; STANLEY 3 August 1957 (fee £1,750); Bangor City August 1959.
Stanley paid a substantial fee for Peter Ralston, an ideally-built pivot with six season's experience in Scottish League football. He had played only in the opening two fixtures of the 1957-8 season, both of which ended in defeat, before he lost his first-team place. When Willie Kelly was signed in September 1957, the former Blackburn Rovers star took over the number-five jersey. Ralston spent the remainder of the campaign in the Reserves, where his form improved as the season went on. He was retained for 1958-9, but again failed to win a first-team place, understudying Gordon Stones for the centre-half berth.

RANDLE, Herbert Clarence **1937-39**
Half-back or full-back. 5ft 7½in; 11st 2lb.
Born: Stonebroom, Derbyshire, 31 July 1906. Died: Chesterfield, 7 August 1976.
Debut v Carlisle United (h) 28 August 1937.
Appearances: 74; Goals: 1.
Career: Shirebrook; Birmingham 13 May 1930; Southend United 8 August 1932; Gillingham 31 July 1934; STANLEY 27 May 1937; Barrow 19 May 1939.
An end of season review in the *Accrington Observer* in May 1938 named Herbert Randle as the best of the season's newcomers, considering him to have been the most consistently effective player on the staff. He maintained his high standard in the following season, when his untiring efforts at either wing-half or full-back made him the team's outstanding defender. For his earlier clubs, Randle made 40 appearances for Southend United and 109 appearances (two goals) for Gillingham.

RATTRAY, Charles Robert **1938-39**
Outside-right. 5ft 7in; 11st.
Born: Fleetwood, 10 May 1911.
Debut v Halifax Town (a) 27 August 1938.
Appearances: 19; Goals: 1.
Career: Fleetwood Windsor Villa; Blackpool 5 November 1929; Watford 1 July 1934; Mansfield Town 22 June 1936; Port Vale 22 May 1937; STANLEY 13 June 1938 to May 1939.

Both with Mansfield Town and Port Vale, Charlie Rattray had played fine games against Stanley, who signed him in June 1938. He had extensive experience, despite being only 27 years old, as he had started with Blackpool when only a youngster. His initial League experience came in season 1929-30, when he scored two goals in nine games to help Blackpool clinch the Second Division championship. After a stay of four and a half seasons at Bloomfield Road, he then made four moves in a similar period. He was one of five outside-rights used by Stanley in 1938-9, when constant team changes failed to arrest an alarming run of defeats. The team finished at the foot of the table, separated from the team above them by 11 points.

RAWCLIFFE, Roland **1923-24**
Half-back.
Born: Accrington, 1900 (July quarter).
Debut v Crewe Alexandra (a) 8 December 1923.
Appearances: 1.
Career: Local junior football; STANLEY amateur 18 April 1923 to 5 September 1925; Burnley (trial) 7 October 1924 registering as an amateur 16 January 1925 to May 1925.
Roland Rawcliffe, a younger brother of George Rawcliffe, a Stanley half-back in pre-League days, was first given a trial in December 1922. He did not sign amateur forms until the following April. In his one Football League appearance he had the satisfaction of assisting Stanley to win 2-1 at Crewe, which was the team's first victory for over two months. In the same match, a much shuffled line-up included another Football League debutant, centre-forward Jack Sagar (*qv*).

REEDAY, Maurice J. **1936-37**
Full-back. 5ft 9½in; 11st 7lb.
Born: Darwen, 28 August 1909.
Debut v Lincoln City (h) 29 August 1936.
Appearances: 22.
Career: Darwen; Blackpool 9 May 1934; STANLEY 6 May 1936; Leicester City 11 March 1937 (fee £1,200); STANLEY, Blackburn Rovers and Burnley (wartime guest player). After 18 months out of football, appointed player-coach to Darwen FC October 1947.
One of a pair of full-backs signed by Blackpool from Darwen in the close season of 1934, Maurice Reeday did not appear in the first team during a stay of two seasons at Bloomfield Road. His early form with Stanley suggested that he would solve the club's left full-back problem and his displays in the season's FA Cup ties confirmed this early impression. Against such noted wingers as Bruton (Blackburn Rovers) and Toseland (Manchester City), his displays bore the stamp of class well above Third Division level. Leicester City's manager Frank Womack, a fine full-back himself in his playing days, took Reeday to Filbert Street, where he made 74 appearances before the outbreak of World War Two ended his League career.

REYNOLDS, Walter **1935-38**
Outside-right. 5ft 9in; 11st.
Born: Sheffield, 24 November 1906.
Debut v Lincoln City (a) 31 August 1935.
Appearances: 125; Goals: 28.
Career: Sheffield Wednesday amateur; Leeds United 11 November 1930; Clapton Orient 18 August 1931; Burnley 24 June 1932; Newport County 10 August 1933; STANLEY 13 June 1935; York City 24 June 1938; Rochdale 19 November 1938 to September 1939; Sheffield Wednesday (wartime guest).
Walter Reynolds' record with Stanley was quite outstanding. In three seasons he missed only one League or FA Cup game, clocking up 102 consecutive appearances between August 1935 and October 1937. He was also in the same position, outside-right, in every game but one, and in this match he scored the winning goal from outside-left. A crack half-mile runner, he had very few equals as a speed merchant. His consistently good form in every match made him an outstanding asset to the team and his speedy, direct approach was the perfect foil to George Mee's more subtle machinations on the opposite flank. During wartime football, Walter Reynolds assisted Sheffield Wednesday to the runners-up position for the League North championship in season 1942-3.

RHODES, Harold **1930-31**
Centre-half.
Debut v Doncaster Rovers (a) 8 November 1930.
Appearances: 1.
Career: STANLEY amateur 8 November 1930 to May 1931.
Harold Rhodes' first trial in Stanley's Reserve team was at Lancaster Town and he had a good match. 'Opened out the game well and showed a surprising turn of speed,' was the verdict by the local correspondent. One week later, he was literally 'thrown in at the deep end' when he was selected for the first team. It was a rather unfamiliar-looking Stanley team which journeyed to Doncaster Rovers and they got off to the worst possible start. Reserve full-back George Law put through his own goal and in the end Doncaster ran out easy winners by 6-1. In the *Accrington Observer*, Rhodes was praised for 'a commendable performance, considering his very limited experience'.

RHODES, Irvine **1936 and 1938**
Full-back. 5ft 11in; 12st.
Born: Rotherham, 1916 (July quarter).
Debut v York City (h) 29 January 1938.
Appearances: 5.
Career: Rotherham United amateur 16 October 1935; STANLEY amateur 21 February 1936; Great Harwood cs 1936; Preston North End 6 August 1937; STANLEY as a professional 28 January 1938 (fee £50); Boston United August 1938.
After an initial brief spell on amateur forms, Irvine Rhodes left Stanley to join Great Harwood. He returned, as a professional, some two years later but again his stay lasted only a matter of months. In five League matches he failed to bolster a shaky defence in a season which saw Stanley finish at the foot of the table.

RICHARDSON, John MM **1920-25**
Full-back. 5ft 7½in; 11st 3lb.
Born: Church, 1895 (April quarter). Died: Accrington, 8 November 1957.
Debut v Stockport County (a) 1 April 1922.
Appearances: 95.
Career: Great Harwood; STANLEY (trial) 1914; Moscow Mill United Methodists 1919; STANLEY February 1920; Great Harwood August to September 1925.
In the early 1920s the *Accrington Observer* described John Richardson thus: 'Speedy, a sure kick with either foot and a rare worker. A very reliable player.' He returned to Accrington after World War One, in which he had served in the Howitzer Brigade as a sergeant and was awarded the Military Medal in France. He played his first game in February 1920 against Fleetwood, this being prior to Stanley's election into the Football League. He became an established first-team player in 1923 and embarked upon a long run of consecutive appearances which was broken only by a family bereavement. He was awarded a benefit match in 1924, a reserve match against Southport in October

drawing a crowd of over 2,500, a better attendance than some of the season's League fixtures.

RIGBY, Ernest **1950-53**
Full-back. 5ft 10in; 12st.
Born: Kirkham, 8 April 1928
Debut v Chester (a) 16 March 1951.
Appearances: 10.
Career: Lancashire Amateurs; Blackpool amateur season 1949-50; STANLEY amateur September 1950, signing professional 21 February 1951 to 1 May 1953.
In season 1949-50, Ernie Rigby went to Holland with the Lancashire FA touring party and was a regular choice for Lancashire County Amateurs. He joined Stanley in the following season, initially as an amateur, and made his Football League debut shortly after winning a professional contract in February 1951. A sound reserve-team defender, Rigby also proved a capable deputy when called upon for infrequent first-team appearances. His longest spell of senior action came in September 1951, when he deputized at right-back for Bill Mellor in a six-match run.

RILEY, Harold **1930-31**
Inside-forward. 5ft 6½in; 10st 8lb.
Born: Hollinwood, near Oldham, 22 November 1909.
Died: Lincoln, 1982 (April quarter).
Debut v Crewe Alexandra (h) 30 August 1930.
Appearances: 32; Goals: 18.
Career: Altrincham; Hurst; Birmingham amateur 13 December 1928; Ashton National season 1929-30; STANLEY 14 June 1930; Lincoln City 19 June 1931 (with G.Whyte); Notts County 12 June 1933; Cardiff City 25 June 1934; Northampton Town 20 June 1936; Exeter City 19 September 1938 to September 1939; retired during World War Two period.
International honour: England Schoolboys.
Club honour: Lincoln City, Third Division North champions season 1931-2.
In season 1930-31 Stanley scored eight goals from the penalty-spot, seven of the penalties awarded were said to be the result of unlawfully terminated dribbles by Harold Riley. On his final appearance in Stanley's colours he scored a hat-trick against Lincoln City, who were beaten 5-3. It was the last Saturday of the season and Lincoln had journeyed to Peel Park in need of maximum points to secure the Third Division North championship. The Imps also needed Chesterfield to lose, but they won 8-1 against Gateshead and took the title by one point. Lincoln signed Riley in the close season (along with George Whyte). Having missed out so narrowly, Lincoln succeeded in winning the championship in the following season. It was another nail-biting finish, however, the Imps succeeding only on goal-average over runners-up Gateshead. Riley's contribution that season was 18 goals in 33 appearances.

RIMMER, Albert **1936-37**
Inside-forward. 5ft 9in; 11st 6lb.
Born: Scarisbrick, 27 February 1908. Died: Southport, 11 January 1980.
Debut v Lincoln City (h) 29 August 1936.
Appearances: 2.
Career: Crossens Juniors; Southport 7 September 1927; Lancaster Town August 1933; Clapton Orient 12 January 1935 (also assisting Ashford, Orient's nursery side, during the season); Fleetwood 17 August 1935; STANLEY 20 July 1936; Fleetwood September 1937; Hartwood Hosiery (Southport) 1938-9; High Park (Southport & District League) to 1945-6.
In an early appearance at Peel Park, Albert Rimmer was described as 'a useful bustler, but one whose passes to his partner were somewhat obviously advertised'. Stanley signed him from Fleetwood, but he was best remembered for his seven-year stint with Southport. A strong, versatile performer, he was said to have

occupied every outfield position for Southport, for whom he appeared in 27 League matches and over 200 reserve-team games. Rimmer spent his season at Peel Park in the Lancashire Combination side, making 35 appearances and scoring 20 goals which included four in one match against Great Harwood in February 1937.

RITCHIE, John **1949-50**
Half-back. 5ft 7in; 10st 9lb.
Born: Blairhill, Fifeshire, 31 March 1927.
Debut v Mansfield Town (a) 29 August 1949.
Appearances: 13.
Career: Crossgates Primrose; STANLEY 20 June 1949 to May 1950.
Jack Ritchie immediately impressed in reserve-team matches in August 1949. Following one early outing against Southport Reserves the *Accrington Observer* commented: 'Ritchie took the eye with constructive

work as neat as you are likely to see in a (Lancashire) Combination game'. He quickly won promotion in what was a sweeping reshuffle by manager Porter for the visit to Field Mill. Ritchie was one of six team changes, one positional, brought about by the side's customary bad start to the season. After playing in 13 League games and one FA Cup tie, Ritchie lost his place when Stanley's half-back line was reorganized to accommodate Eric Lovett at centre-half. Ritchie's final League match, a 6-0 defeat by Rotherham United on 24 December 1949, also marked the final appearance of Stanley's long-serving centre-half, Cyril Briggs.

RIVERS, Walter **1936-38**
Inside-forward or half-back. 5ft 11in; 12st.
Born: Throckley, Newcastle, 8 January 1909.
Debut v Stockport County (h) 10 October 1936.
Appearances: 56; Goals: 4.
Career: Walbottle FC; Throckley Welfare; Gillingham 13 September 1927; Crystal Palace 3 August 1929; Queen's Park Rangers 22 May 1933; Gateshead 6 August 1934; Aldershot 4 January 1936; Carlisle United 24 June 1936; STANLEY 10 October 1936 (in exchange for J.Singleton); Scarborough Town August 1938.
The exchange-transfer which brought Walter Rivers to Peel Park proved an inspired move. Stanley had won only one of their first eight League fixtures when he arrived, but in a most impressive debut he was the source of a revitalized attack. A tall, stalwart figure, he was not easily shaken off the ball and he opened up play with impressive distribution. At either inside-forward or wing-half he gave sterling service. His vision and astute passes down the middle did much to assist Bob Mortimer's goal-blitz in 1936-7. In a career spent in both Northern and Southern Sections of the Third Division, Rivers totalled 221 appearances and scored 21 goals.

ROBERTS, D(ouglas) Gordon **1951-52**
Wing-forward. 5ft 8½in; 10st 12lb.
Born: Foleshill, 30 May 1925.
Debut v Gateshead (h) 18 August 1951.
Appearances: 39; Goals: 11.
Career: Wolverhampton Wanderers 19 September 1942; Northampton Town (wartime guest) season 1944-5; Brighton & Hove Albion 17 March 1949; STANLEY 24 July 1951 to 2 May 1952; Rugby Town cs 1952.
Fleet-footed and with an aptitude for doing the unexpected, Gordon Roberts was a dangerous raider with plenty of confidence when approaching goal. On Christmas Day 1951 he scored a hat-trick at Darlington in a high-scoring encounter which Stanley won 5-4. It was the first League treble by a Stanley winger for almost 14 years, the feat having last been achieved by Walter Reynolds against Wrexham on 3 January 1938. When Roberts scored for Stanley against Oldham Athletic on 23 February 1952, he became the first Stanley winger for 15 years to record ten or more goals in a season. In 1960 he was living in Northampton and was working as a draughtsman.

ROBERTSON, Alfred Joseph **1936-39**
Goalkeeper. 6ft; 12st 4lb.
Born: Sunderland, 2 July 1908. Died: Clayton-le-Moor, May 1984.
Debut v Lincoln City (h) 29 August 1936.
Appearances: 81.
Career: Bank Head FC; Newcastle United (trial); Notts County 4 May 1928; Grantham Town; Bradford 6 May 1930; Clapton Orient 8 July 1933; Bristol Rovers 8 May 1935; STANLEY 26 June 1936 to May 1939.
On his day, Alf Robertson was one of the most brilliantly spectacular goalkeepers in the Northern Section. In Stanley's last line of defence he had ample opportunities to demonstrate his ability, which he did splendidly. One of his best games was in the FA Cup fourth-round tie against Manchester City at Maine Road in January 1937. He treated a crowd of over 39,000 to a display of immaculate handling, mobility and some sixth sense which enabled him to be in just the right spot at the right moment. One national match report observed: 'Robertson tipped Tilson's fierce drive over the crossbar as effortlessly as a man taps the ash off his cigarette'. He was not a goalkeeper who would leave anybody in doubt as to his intentions. On one occasion the *Accrington Observer* commented: 'Anyone within 150 yards range and with normal hearing could not fail to hear Robertson's instructions from the goalmouth'. In March 1945 he was reported to be living in Accrington and keeping goal with Dunkenhalgh FC, a local junior team. Before becoming a footballer, he had worked as a rivetter in the shipbuilding industry.

ROBERTSON, Leonard Verdun **1948**
Inside-forward. 5ft 10in; 11st 7lb.
Born: Middlesbrough, 1 March 1916.
Debut v Darlington (a) 21 August 1948.
Appearances: 3.
Career: Newcastle Schoolboys; Stockton FC; Hartlepools United and Grimsby Town during World War Two; Watford June 1946; Hull City 30 May 1947; Scunthorpe United March 1948; STANLEY 16 July 1948; released on a free transfer 24 December 1948, when he was reported to have joined a North-Eastern League club, near to his home.
Len Robertson joined Hull City at the end of May 1947, yet was still in time to play in two League matches. Due to adverse weather conditions the season ran on until early June. Hull City, incidentally, used 42 players in League fixtures that season, much the highest number of any League club. He joined Stanley from Scunthorpe United, having assisted the then Midland League club to the runners-up position in season 1947-8. He failed to impress at Peel Park, his three appearances coming within the space of the first six matches of the season. By mid-term, manager Hacking had recruited an entirely new forward line and Len Robertson was released on Christmas Eve.

ROBINSON, Alfred **1921-22**
Centre-half. 5ft 7½in; 10st 12lb.
Born: Belfast.
Debut v Durham City (a) 12 November 1921.
Appearances: 3.
Career: South Liverpool; STANLEY 11 May 1921 to May 1922.
In a trio of senior appearances, Alf Robinson deputized in all three half-back positions. He was primarily a centre-half, yet in this position his lack of inches and light build was a distinct disadvantage. Press comments on one of his League outings, at Halifax, illustrated the point: 'The Halifax backs kicked a fine length and

a tall centre-half would have been much more likely to intercept many of the returns. It was Robinson's misfortune to have made one of his infrequent appearances against such a virile team, for he was bustled until he must have been sore and weary.'

ROBINSON, Charles Alexander **1935-36**
Half-back. 5ft 11in; 11st 12lb.
Born: Pegswood, near Ashington, 1906 (April quarter).
Debut v Lincoln City (a) 31 August 1935.
Appearances: 24.
Career: Bedlington United; Blackpool 10 May 1928; Exeter City 29 May 1931; Gillingham 26 July 1933; STANLEY 11 June 1935; Rochdale 27 June 1936; Blyth Spartans August 1938.
Charlie Robinson graduated from a local church team in his native Pegswood to Bedlington United, the North-Eastern League Second Division club. He moved into League circles with Blackpool, where he spent three seasons, mainly as a wing-half in the Reserves. Two seasons with Exeter City saw him given few senior opportunities and his first experience of regular League football came with Gillingham. After joining Stanley, he did not establish himself until mid-season, but then went on to appear in every match but one before the end of the campaign. He was unfortunate during his Rochdale spell to suffer a broken leg, sustained in a collision with one of his own teammates. Off the field, he was a pianist of above average ability.

ROBINSON, Herbert **1946-48**
Centre-forward. 6ft; 12st 2lb.
Born: Barnoldswick, 1924.
Debut v Tranmere Rovers (h) 7 December 1946 (scored two goals).
Appearances: 5; Goals: 4.
Career: Middlesbrough amateur 1 May 1945; Barnoldswick Town; STANLEY 6 December 1946 to May 1948.
A well-built, fearless bustler, Robinson had scored 13 goals in the five games which preceded his move from Barnoldswick Town to Stanley. He was immediately thrust into the limelight, taking over as centre-forward in the League team and scoring both of Stanley's goals in a 2-1 win. In five consecutive appearances he scored a total of four goals, a return incidentally, which constituted the team's total of goals in the same period. Despite his commendable efforts, Robinson lost his place to another new signing, Walter Marvin (*qv*). The team's problems with the centre-forward role were finally resolved by the signing of Stan Mercer from Leicester City in January 1947.

ROBINSON, John James **1935-37**
Goalkeeper. 5ft 10in; 11st 7lb.
Born: Oswaldtwistle, 23 April 1918.
Debut v Southport (a) 2 May 1936.
Appearances: 16.
Career: Sacred Heart FC; STANLEY amateur 7 March, signing professional 17 May 1935; Manchester City 17 April 1937 (with W.Gregg for a combined fee of £1,350); STANLEY (wartime guest) season 1939-40; Bury 26 November 1946; Southend United 7 August 1947 to April 1948 when a shoulder injury ended his career.
Jack Robinson attracted Stanley's attention at an early age and was signed as a professional on passing the age limit of 17 years. He made his League debut as an 18-year-old, on the closing day of season 1935-6. In the following term he provided Alf Robertson with some stiff competition for the first-team jersey, appearing in 15 League matches. Despite inevitable errors of immaturity, his talents were easily discernable and he left Stanley, along with full-back Willis Gregg, to join Manchester City in April 1937. The two new recruits did much to stiffen City Reserves defence, thus ensuring that a second consecutive re-election application to the Central League was unnecessary.

ROBINSON, William **1950-53**
Utility. 5ft 7in; 11st.
Born: Manchester, 17 November 1925. Died: Salford, 16 May 1953.
Debut v Southport (a) 23 December 1950.
Appearances: 96; Goals: 2.
Career: Stockport County 4 August 1949; STANLEY 15 December 1950 to his death.
Billy Robinson was a fine clubman, with a fighting spirit out of all proportion to his size. An adaptable footballer with a wonderful faculty for filling all sorts of positions, he settled eventually at left-back and became one of the best in the Northern Section. It came as a great shock to all associated with Stanley when it was learned that their popular full-back had been murdered in Salford. He had been shot, along with a young women, Mrs Marie Waddington, by the husband of the woman, 31-year-old John Waddington of Deane Street, Salford.

RODWELL, Joseph **1948-49**
Wing-forward.
Born: Southport, 13 October 1928.
Debut v Mansfield Town (h) 11 September 1948.
Appearances: 2.
Career: Birkdale Athletic; STANLEY amateur 8 September 1948 to May 1949.
Joe Rodwell showed early promise in Lancashire Combination matches and was very quickly given a trial in the League side. Of his debut at Mansfield Town, the *Accrington Observer* commented: 'Although sometimes on the wrong side of his full-back, Rodwell continued to do his duty by slinging over centres, from one of which, in the last minute, Stanley might have snatched an undeserved victory'. The match ended in a draw of one goal each and the Stanley faithful had to wait until 16 October before they saw the Reds record their first victory of the season, after eight defeats and four draws.

ROGERS, Dennis **1959**
Goalkeeper. 6ft; 12st 4lb.
Born: Chorley, 28 March 1936.
Debut v Queen's Park Rangers (a) 21 March 1959.
Appearances: 3.
Career: Netherfield; STANLEY (loan) 20 to 28 March 1959.
On the eve of their match against QPR at Loftus Road, Stanley found themselves without a goalkeeper. Both McInnes and Marshall were unfit and Nicholson had been transferred to Leyton Orient four days earlier. In one of the most dramatic 'beat the deadline' transfers ever made by Stanley, Dennis Rogers came to Peel Park, courtesy of his club, Netherfield. He made a good debut and although he received a knee injury,

he also played against Norwich and Bournemouth whilst not fully recovered. In his last game, Stanley beat Bournemouth 3-2 to provide a high spot on which to end an eventful few days for the young goalkeeper.

ROOKS, William **1922-27**
Half-back. 5ft 7½in; 11st 6lb.
Born: Grangetown, near Sunderland, 13 December 1890.
Debut v Darlington (h) 26 August 1922.
Appearances: 132; Goals: 4.
Career: Willington FC; Sunderland Rovers; Blackpool 4 May 1913; STANLEY 29 July 1922; Hurst player-manager August 1927.
Representative honour: Central League v Lancashire Combination at Tranmere 25 April 1921.
Billy Rooks was a live-wire performer who obviously enjoyed his football and was prepared to play in any position. He began with Blackpool as an outside-left but eventually evolved as a utility defender, making over 100 appearances for the Seasiders. He was appointed captain by Stanley but a cartilage operation restricted him to only 13 matches in his first season.

In the following term he was the recognized centre-half and in 1924-5 he alternated between wing-half and full-back. It was a continuing pattern, for in the course of his five years association with Stanley he played in all outfield defensive positions and even had the odd game at centre-forward. In recognition of his services, Rooks was awarded a benefit and in May 1927 a Reds v Blues match was played at Peel Park. Both teams included guest players from Blackburn Rovers, Blackpool and Preston North End.

ROSE, James **1937-47**
Goalkeeper. 5ft 11in; 11st 4lb.
Born: Clayton-le-Moor, 4 March 1918.
Debut v Crewe Alexandra (h) 25 February 1939.
Appearances: 20.
Career: Clayton Villa; STANLEY amateur 30 October 1937, signing professional 21 February 1939 to May 1947.
Jim Rose had appeared in occasional matches for Stanley Reserves in season 1936-7. In this term his team, Clayton Villa, had won the championship of the Accrington & District Combination and also lifted the Walmsley Cup. After a lengthy spell on amateur forms, he was signed as a professional in February 1939 and made his Football League debut in the same month. The war years took away a large part of his career, after he had played in eight matches in the final peacetime season. It was not until 1945-6 that he reappeared and in 1946-7 he was one of five goalkeepers used in League matches. His career was ended prematurely by a torn thigh muscle injury. Outside of the game, Jim Rose had a successful career with Galbraiths Garage in Accrington, where he eventually became secretary-director.

ROSS, Alan **1959**
Goalkeeper. 6ft; 12st 2lb.
Born: Ellesmere Port, 7 February 1933.
Debut v Rochdale (h) 28 March 1959.
Appearances: 1.
Career: Bishop Auckland; Oldham Athletic amateur 4 September 1956; West Bromwich Albion amateur 7 February 1957; Formby; Southport amateur May 1957; Blackburn Rovers amateur 23 August 1957; Rochdale amateur 9 February 1959; Oldham Athletic amateur 27 February 1959; STANLEY amateur 28 March 1959; Wigan Rovers cs 1959.
Alan Ross was signed only half an hour before the kick-off of his debut game at Rochdale. Soon after the start, a pulled muscle made him the third Stanley goalkeeper to be injured within the space of 15 days. For the third game in this period, full-back Bob McNicholl went into goal for the last 30 minutes. He continued his remarkable run by extending his 'clean sheet' to 150 minutes as emergency 'keeper. A Liverpool civil servant, Ross made only three other Football League appearances, with Oldham Athletic, where he turned down the offer of a professional contract during season 1956-7.

ROTHWELL, George **1944-52**
Inside-forward or half-back. 5ft 6in; 10st 10lb.
Born: Bolton, 22 November 1923.
Debut v Stockport County (a) 14 September 1946.
Appearances: 202; Goals: 10.
Career: Bolton Schoolboys; Lancashire Schoolboys; Chorley; STANLEY 28 August 1944; Clitheroe February 1952.
In August 1945 Stanley did one of their best strokes of business when they signed on one of their outstanding wartime guest players, George Rothwell, from Chorley. He had originally come to play for Stanley because his club was not engaged in the Lancashire Combination at that time. An inside-forward of unusual craft and possessing remarkable ball-control, he soon blended well into Stanley's fast-moving forward line. A prodigious worker, Rothwell

was never slow to assist a harrased defence, often acting as a fourth half-back in moments of pressure. If he had one fault, it was that of excessive pattern-weaving, but he certainly coloured play with his footcraft, perkiness and his droll Bolton accent. One amusing snippet from an October 1946 match report stated: 'Rothwell returned to his habit of beating opponents and teammates with strict impartiality'. In 1948 he left his job as an iron-moulder in a Bolton factory to take up football as a full-time career. After retiring from the game he worked for a Bolton bookmaker. He later took up bowls, and won many prizes.

ROWBOTHAM, Harry **1933-34**
Inside-forward. 5ft 8in; 11st 2lb.
Born: Willington Quay, Northumberland, 1911 (April quarter).
Debut v Wrexham (h) 14 October 1933.
Appearances: 4.
Career: Cheddleton Mental Hospital; Port Vale April 1931; Hyde United; Southampton cs 1932; STANLEY 16 October 1933; Barrow cs 1934; Rochdale cs 1936; Tunbridge Wells Rangers cs 1937.
Said to have been a regular member of Southampton's London Combination side when signed, Harry Rowbotham's move to Peel Park came in the wake of early-season injuries to both first-team inside-forwards, Fitton and Leedham. After four matches Rowbotham lost his place to Norman Kelly and did not appear again in Stanley's first team. He did much better in two season's with Barrow, totalling 60 appearances and scoring 15 goals. These included a hat-trick against Rochdale on Boxing Day 1935. At the close of the same season he moved to Rochdale, ending his senior career with 19 appearances and one goal in season 1936-7.

RUDD, Edward **1951-52**
Half-back. 5ft 10in; 11st 6lb.
Born: Wigan, 7 January 1929.
Debut v Mansfield Town (a) 27 August 1951.
Appearances: 2.
Career: Lancashire Schoolboys; Bolton Wanderers 28 September 1950; STANLEY 3 August 1951 to 2 May 1952.
A Bury schoolteacher living at Wigan, Ted Rudd captained Lancashire Schoolboys and had made 25 consecutive appearances for Bolton Wanderers Reserves in season 1950-51. In Walter Crook's first full season in charge, he tried Rudd at left-half in two consecutive, early season matches, both of which resulted in 3-0 defeats. Thereafter, he was confined to reserve-team football, where he assisted Stanley's second string to finish in fourth place in the Lancashire Combination table.

RYAN, Kenneth **1959**
Goalkeeper.
Born: Accrington, 20 September 1936.
Debut v Southampton (a) 22 April 1959.
Appearances: 1.
Career: Accrington Collieries; STANLEY amateur 21 April 1959.
Ken Ryan was recruited from the Accrington & District Combination League to help out in the remarkable goalkeeping crisis of season 1958-9. In the final 12 matches of the season, Stanley used six different goalkeepers. Ryan showed few signs of nerves on his debut at The Dell, but he was unable to prevent Stanley going down by 3-1. The three goals he conceded were slightly better than par for the course, as 39 goals were scored against Stanley in the final 12 matches of the season.

RYDEN, John Johnston **1954-55**
Centre-half. 6ft ½in; 12st 1lb.
Born: Alexandra, Dumbartonshire, 7 April 1943.
Debut v Bradford City (h) 13 February 1954.
Appearances: 80; Goals: 1.
Career: Duntocher Hibernian 1949; Alloa Athletic 1950; STANLEY 12 February 1954 (fee £1,000); Tottenham Hotspur 2 November 1955 (fee £8,400); Watford 24 June 1961; Romford October 1962.
Representative honour: Third Division North v Third Division South at Peel Park in season 1955-6.
Stanley's manager, Walter Galbraith, was said to have first 'spotted' John Ryden when he was 17 years old and playing for Duntocher Hibs. He began in senior football as a wing-half and even had a spell at centre-forward, but an injury to Alloa's centre-half led to Ryden being tried in that position, which proved to be his best. Tall and slim and with a shock of wavy hair, he was a richly-talented defender, good in the air and a fearless tackler. He had played in 80

consecutive Football League matches for Stanley when Spurs took him to White Hart Lane. He scored on his first-team debut for Tottenham and was later appointed club captain (August 1957). In almost six years at White Hart Lane, his best season was in 1957-8, when he appeared in 35 matches in which he assisted his team to finish third in the First Division. John Ryden had two brothers who played in senior football, George with Dundee, and Hugh, who began with Leeds United in 1960 and made 367 Football League appearances and scored 78 goals.

RYMER, George H. **1947**
Goalkeeper. 5ft 8½in; 11st 8lb.
Born: Barnsley, 6 October 1923.
Debut v Doncaster Rovers (h) 1 February 1947.
Appearances: 8.
Career: Ardsley Victoria; Barnsley 29 December 1943; STANLEY 1 February 1947 to May 1947.
George Rymer arrived at Peel Park as Sam Hayes departed for Rossendale United in February 1947. On Barnsley's books for a little over three years, Rymer worked as a collier and it was a pit injury to his fingers which lost him his place in Barnsley's first team. In a brief stay with Stanley he began well, but was then beaten 12 times in his final three outings. His last game, on the final Saturday of season 1946-7, saw him beaten four times but in a most entertaining encounter Stanley won 8-4 against Lincoln City.

SAGAR, James **1923-24**
Centre-forward.
Born: Padiham, Lancashire, *c*.1901.
Debut v Crewe Alexandra (a) 8 December 1923.
Appearances: 10.
Career: Padiham junior football; STANLEY amateur 9 May, signing professional 7 December 1923; Barnoldswick Town August 1924.
Jim Sagar, a dashing and enthusiastic young centre-forward, netted on his first appearance for Stanley Reserves against Leyland in August 1923. He was awarded a professional contract in December 1923 and made his debut in the Football League. In a three-match run at centre-forward, he failed to solve a chronic goalscoring problem. He was later tried at outside-right but in a season marked by the lack of a settled team formation, Stanley managed to score only 48 goals in 42 League matches. It remained their worst return in pre-war football until 1937-8, when only 45 were scored.

SALT, Ernest **1923-25**
Goalkeeper. 5ft 10in; 12st 1lb.
Born: Walsall, 10 February 1897.
Debut v Darlington (a) 25 August 1923.
Appearances: 72.
Career: Talbot Stead FC (Birmingham Combination); Everton 1 November 1920; STANLEY 7 July 1923; Wigan Borough 25 May 1925 to May 1926.
For two seasons Stanley's recognized custodian, Ernie Salt's career began with Everton, but in two and a half years he played in only four League matches. He took over from Peter Floyd in Stanley's goal and looked rather small in comparison to the 6ft 1in Huncoat collier. Salt was, however, able to field high balls with the best and one early Press verdict was 'cool, confident and collected'. His final season in senior football was with Wigan Borough, for whom he played in 26 League matches in season 1925-6.

SCHOFIELD, John **1935-36**
Half-back. 5ft 8in; 11st 4lb.
Born: Waterfoot, Lancashire, 1913.
Debut v Barrow (h) 21 September 1935.
Appearances: 10.
Career: Bacup Borough; Burnley amateur 13 May, signing professional 28 August 1931; STANLEY 20 May 1935; Rossendale United 22 May 1937.
A Rossendale Valley native, Jack Schofield was discovered in West Lancashire League football and graduated to Turf Moor via Bacup Borough. In a lengthy spell with Burnley he was a reserve wing half, but had played in nine League matches for the Clarets. Without ever establishing himself in the League side at Peel Park, he was a fine clubman whose versatility was his strongest point. He had a 'field day' on 25 January 1936, when playing at centre-forward for Stanley Reserves against New Brighton Reserves at Peel Park. On a pitch covered with frozen snow he scored five times in a 7-0 win. In his second season, a dislocated knee kept him out of action for a long spell. A neat summing-up of Schofield's capabilities came in September 1936, when the *Accrington Observer* reported on reserve-team selections: 'Schofield, who sparkled at centre-forward last Saturday, moves to right full-back in place of Gregg. Schofield's technique is very elastic, he has now appeared in every position but goal for Stanley.'

SCHOFIELD, Robert **1932-33**
Inside-forward. 5ft 7½in; 11st 5lb.
Born: Rochdale.
Debut v Gateshead (h) 3 December 1932.
Appearances: 1.
Career: Local junior football; Rochdale amateur 12 August, signing professional 23 December 1926; Newton Heath cs 1928; Halifax Town 28 May 1929; Rochdale amateur 1930; Bacup Borough 1931-2; STANLEY 12 May 1932 to 23 August 1933.
Robert Schofield's first season in League football proved to be his best. As a local amateur he made a sensational start with Rochdale, scoring five goals in his first three appearances. He scored two goals on his debut against Chesterfield on 18 December 1926 and the 8-1 victory still stands as Rochdale's best-ever win in the Football League. During the season he made 14 appearances, assisting the Dale to the runners-up position in the Third Division North. Thereafter, his career proved to be something of an anticlimax, ending with a solitary outing for Stanley which ended in a 3-0 home defeat against Gateshead.

SCOTT, Robert **1954-59**
Inside or wing-forward. 5ft 9in; 10st 10lb.
Born: Bellshill, Glasgow, 20 May 1930.
Debut v Workington (h) 4 September 1954.
Appearances: 149; Goals: 32.
Career: Stonehouse Violet 1947; Burnbank Athletic 1948; Dunfermline Athletic 1951; Alloa Athletic season 1953-54; STANLEY 6 September 1954; Wrexham 14 July 1959; Oldham Athletic 3 October 1959; Nelson cs 1960; Bacup Borough.
A teammate of John Ryden (*qv*) at Alloa Athletic, Bert Scott had joined the Scottish 'B' Division side after being 'demobbed' from the Forces. He began at Peel Park as an outside-left, a problem position for many years and made 37 appearances and scored four

goals in his first season. Fast, strong and two-footed, he was an adaptable forward whose impressive approach work on either flank made many openings for his colleagues. In his final season with Stanley, when he was mainly used as an inside-forward, he scored 19 League and Cup goals in 37 appearances. He did particularly well in the season's FA Cup ties, scoring seven goals in five games, which included a 'hat-trick' against Workington in the first round. After retiring from football, Bert Scott ran a window-cleaning business.

SEED, Trevance F. **1950-51**
Centre-half or full-back.
Born: Preston, 3 September 1923.
Debut v Rotherham United (h) 1 January 1951.
Appearances: 1.
Career: Junior football; Preston North End 4 July 1946; Carlisle United 23 December 1946; STANLEY 6 September 1950 to May 1951.
Despite the famous footballing surname, 'Trevor' Seed was not related to the Charlton Athletic and Barnsley managers. A Prestonian who began with North End but whose Football League debut came with Carlisle United, in three and a half seasons at Brunton Park he made 81 appearances. Seed finally lost his place to Geoff Twentyman, who later played in 170 Football League matches for Liverpool. Signed by Stanley a few days after his 27th birthday, Seed waited three months for a League outing with the Reds. His debut came at Rotherham United on New Year's Day 1951. Stanley sustained their fifth consecutive defeat, to round off a depressing holiday programme.

SENIOR, Colin **1951-52**
Half-back. 6ft 1in; 13st 4lb.

Born: Thornhill, 3 June 1927.
Debut v Gateshead (h) 18 August 1951.
Appearances: 27; Goals: 1.
Career: Stocksbridge FC; Huddersfield Town amateur 7 June, signing professional 23 October 1945; STANLEY 13 June 1951; Corby Town cs 1952.
Colin Senior was first associated with Huddersfield Town as an 18-year-old, but he had some time to wait for a senior opportunity. This finally came in October 1950 in rather unusual circumstances. Senior was introduced in a wholesale reshuffle which saw seven team changes made for a visit to Sunderland. The previous three games had seen 18 goals conceded, so the goalless draw at Roker Park was doubly welcomed. Signed by Stanley's manager Walter Crook as his first move in team-building, one week after the Reds had been re-elected, after their 23rd place finish in 1950-51, Senior began well at Peel Park. Tall, fair-haired and with an impressive physique, his progress was halted by a broken arm, suffered in the first month of the season. His deputy, Dennis Winterbottom did so well that Senior remained on the side-lines, only regaining the position when Winterbottom was unavailable, due to illness.

SHAW, George Rickerby **1926**
Outside-left. 5ft 8½in; 11st 1lb.
Born: Withnall Mill, near Chorley, 7 April 1904.
Debut v Coventry City (a) 27 February 1926.
Appearances: 7; Goals: 1.
Career: Withnall St Joseph's; Horwich RMI; Brinscall FC; STANLEY amateur 30 January 1926; Preston North End 17 September 1926; Wigan Borough 3 September 1927; Southport 10 October 1927; Darwen June 1928 to 1939.
A Lancashire Junior Cup winner with Horwich RMI in season 1924-5, George Shaw made a promising debut for Stanley Reserves in a 5-1 win against Colne Town. Two months later he was selected for the first team, in their first-ever visit to Coventry City. The amateur winger won high praise for his dashing display and excellent use of the ball and he held his place in the team for a run of seven matches. Preston North End eventually offered him a professional contract and he later assisted Wigan Borough and Southport without making any great impact at League level. He did, however, enjoy a remarkable career with Darwen, who won the Lancashire Combination championship in consecutive seaons, 1930-31 and 1931-2. In January 1932, Darwen played at Arsenal in the third round of the FA Cup, they went under 11-1 but shared a 'gate' of over 37,000. Shaw was at outside-left at Highbury and when he last turned out in Darwen's colours (in an emergency) he was 43 years old.

SHAW, John **1922-23**
Centre-half.
Born: Oswaldtwistle.
Debut v Crewe Alexandra (a) 25 November 1922.
Appearances: 3.
Career: Oswaldtwistle St Mary's RC; STANLEY amateur 14 October 1922, signing professional 11 January 1923 to 10 August 1923.
After two League appearances as an amateur, Jack Shaw was awarded a professional contract. Contemporary reports spoke of his sound methods and good headwork, but his stamina was said to be suspect,

doubtless not helped by the customary heavy going at Peel Park. In three League outings he did not appear in a losing side and he was on the retained list published in May 1923, but was later removed and given a free transfer.

SHORROCK, Richard **1922-24**
Full-back. 5ft 8in; 10st 10lb.
Born: Blackburn, 1901 (April quarter).
Debut v Grimsby Town (h) 22 April 1922.
Appearances: 3.
Career: Brinscall FC; Darwen; STANLEY amateur 17 March 1922 to May 1924.
An injury to Jimmy Wilde gave an opportunity to Richard Shorrock who, after a shaky opening to his Football League debut, improved finely and made a distinctly creditable first appearance. Stanley won 1-0 and the *Sports Telegraph* commented: 'Shorrock is built on the right lines and clears strongly with either foot'. Unfortunately, after only one more first-team outing he was injured, just as the season closed. It was nearing the end of October in the following season before he made a reappearance in the Reserves. During this season, no fewer than six different players occupied the right-back position in the League side, but Shorrock played only once, in a 0-0 draw at Halifax Town.

SIMPSON, Harry **1949**
Outside-left.
Born: Ashton-under-Lyne, Lancashire, 2 August 1926.
Debut v Gateshead (h) 30 April 1949.
Appearances: 1.
Career: Oxford Amateurs (a Blackpool junior XI); Lytham FC; STANLEY amateur 29 April to June 1949.
Due to the timing of his arrival at Peel Park (after the transfer 'deadline'), Harry Simpson had to seek special permission from the Football League to make his debut against Gateshead. As neither team were involved in the re-election issue, permission was granted. In reserve-team football he had made an excellent start, scoring on his debut at Clitheroe and then scoring twice in his next match, a Combination Cup tie against Darwen. At the time of his League debut, he had scored six goals in seven Combination matches. Direct in method yet studied in distribution, his one drawback was a lack of speed. The *Accrington Observer's* comments on his debut illustrated the point: 'Several times Simpson beat his man neatly, but he needs to move more quickly to the ball'.

SIMPSON, Samuel **1937-38**
Full-back. 6ft 1in; 13st 4lb.
Born: Lanarkshire, 1915.
Debut v Hartlepools United (a) 1 September 1937.
Appearances: 26.
Career: Shettleston Rovers; Hull City 18 May 1936; STANLEY 10 June 1937; Barrow 10 June 1938 to September 1939.
Without senior experience when he arrived at Peel Park, Sam Simpson was quickly introduced into League action with Stanley. Adaptable to either flank but usually at left-back, his strong physique was coupled with excellent mobility and a powerful kick. He left Stanley after a year to join Barrow and in season 1938-9, he was one of only 22 Northern Section players who appeared in every match for their club.

SINGLETON, James **1936**
Inside-forward. 5ft 9in; 11st 6lb.
Born: Egremont, Cumberland.
Debut v Hartlepools United (a) 2 September 1936.
Appearances: 5.
Career: Cumberland Schoolboys; West Bromwich Albion amateur 22 March, signing professional 8 May 1934; STANLEY 14 July 1936; Carlisle United 16 October 1936 (in exchange for W.Rivers); Bournemouth & Boscombe Athletic 31 May to 8 October 1937.
As a junior Jim Singleton set up a new goalscoring record as centre-forward in a Cumberland district schoolboys competition. Without League experience when he joined Stanley, his sojourn at Peel Park covered five League matches and three Lancashire Combination games. He was praised for his handsome style and fine dribbling and passing skills but as a marksman he was disappointing.

SKILLEN, James **1924-25**
Inside-forward. 5ft 11in; 11st 3lb.
Born: Ballochmyle.
Debut v Rotherham County (h) 30 August 1924 (scored one goal).
Appearances: 25; Goals: 8.
Career: Auchinleck Talbot; Kilmarnock December 1922; STANLEY 7 July 1924; Barrow 20 July 1925; Morton February 1927; Royal Albert March 1927.
One pithy Press comment described Jim Skillen as 'a thrustful player, but one who is inclined to neglect his wing partner'. He scored on his debut in League football and was a regular in Stanley's attack until mid-season. At this point he seemed to lose form and was superceded by Jimmy Gee. In a second season in English football, with Barrow, he was their leading goalscorer by a wide margin. Skillen scored 14 goals in 28 appearances, whilst the second-highest scorer, Hatch, scored five.

SLATER, Frank **1926-28**
Wing-forward. 5ft 7in; 10st 7lb.

Born: Blackburn, 1907 (April quarter).
Debut v Halifax Town (a) 26 February 1927.
Appearances: 17; Goals: 1.
Career: Bolton Wanderers amateur; STANLEY 17 June 1926; Stalybridge Celtic May 1928; Manchester City amateur May 1930.
Frank Slater joined Stanley as a 19-year-old reserve winger. He was a talented all-round sportsman, as he was also a fast bowler with East Lancashire Cricket Club, the Blackburn based Lancashire League club. He headed their bowling averages in 1925, when only 18 years old. Slater's chance with Stanley came when Tommy Wyper, the regular first-team outside-right, was transferred to Hull City. He proved a good deputy, holding his place for the final 13 games of the season. He was retained for the following campaign, but one of the close-season signings, Frank Parry, the former Everton and Grimsby Town winger dominated the outside-right berth in season 1927-8.

SLATTERY, Joseph William **1950-51**
Centre-forward. 5ft 10in; 12st.
Born: Newcastle upon Tyne, 3 June 1926.
Debut v York City (a) 4 September 1950.
Appearances: 13; Goals: 2.
Career: Newcastle United amateur on leaving school and again in 1947 after wartime Naval Service; Hexham Hearts 1948; Bury (trial); STANLEY 9 June 1959; Nelson cs 1951; Morecambe 1956; Rossendale United.
Joe Slattery's 66 goals in 32 Northern Alliance matches in season 1949-50 was noted by several League clubs. He was offered a contract by Barnsley, but opted to move to Accrington as he had previously met Stanley's manager, Jimmy Porter. This was during his Bury trial, undertaken when Mr Porter was assistant manager at Gigg Lane. The departure of Don Travis to Crewe Alexandra in November 1950 saw Slattery given a run at centre-forward. In a poor side, he lacked support and was deposed in mid-January when Bill Watkinson, a £3,000 signing from Liverpool was introduced. Slattery won his place back in late season, actually scoring the last goal of the campaign in a 2-2 draw at Gateshead. Joe Slattery settled in Accrington and has recently retired from a managerial post with a chemical company in Church, near Accrington.

SLINGER, James William **1935**
Centre-forward. 5ft 9½in; 12st 2lb.
Born: Leeds, 1906 (July quarter).
Debut v Lincoln City (a) 31 August 1935.
Appearances: 2.
Career: Army football; Carlisle United 23 March 1932; STANLEY 21 June to 4 October 1935.
A prolific goalscorer with Carlisle United, Jim Slinger was their leading marksman in seasons 1932-3 and 1933-4. In the latter term he scored 31 goals in 38 matches, scoring almost half of his team's 66 goals for the season. His tally included one return of four goals in a match and two hat-tricks. The Third Division North provided a bonanza of goals during this season, as Slinger was one of 18 players who scored four goals in a match and four players netted fives. His overall record with Carlisle United was 53 goals in 80 Football League appearances but he failed to live up to his reputation at Peel Park, playing twice without scoring in a very brief stay.

SLOANE, J(ohn) Joseph **1921-23**
Goalkeeper. 6ft ½in; 11st 3lb.
Born: Preston.
Debut v Chesterfield (a) 1 October 1921.
Appearances: 33.
Career: Preston North End amateur 23 August 1920; Morecambe; STANLEY amateur 30 September, signing professional 15 October 1921; Morecambe cs 1923.
The signing of Joe Sloane, a Preston schoolteacher, alleviated early-season goalkeeping problems. In the previous term he had impressed Stanley officials by his displays for Morecambe, in opposition to the Reds. A neat and safe goalkeeper with good anticipation, he was first choice until Peter Floyd was tried, late

in season 1921-2. When the new season opened, Floyd continued in the first team and Sloane was restricted to only seven League appearances. He returned to Morecambe and assisted them to the Lancashire Combination Championship in 1924-5 and to the runners-up spot in the following season, when they additionally won the Lancashire Junior Cup.

SMELT, Tom **1922-24**
Centre-forward. 5ft 7in; 10st 5lb.
Born: Rotherham, 25 November 1900. Died: Rotherham, 1980 (January quarter).
Debut v Chesterfield (a) 11 November 1922.
Appearances: 40; Goals: 16.
Career: Mexborough Town; Chesterfield; Rotherham Town; Burnley amateur January 1921; Wombwell June 1921; STANLEY 4 October 1922; Exeter City 23 September 1924; Chesterfield 16 July 1925; Morecambe 1925-6; Manchester City 28 April 1927; Oldham Athletic 8 May 1928; Crewe Alexandra 3 June 1930; Scunthorpe United 27 August 1931; Rotherham United 9 September 1932 to June 1933.
'Is neat and clever in footwork, is an opportunist and

always a trier,' commented the *Lancashire Daily Post Annual* for 1923. In the previous season Tom Smelt had satisfactorily filled a position which had proved difficult in early season matches. He was, in fact, Stanley's seventh centre-forward within the space of 12 matches at the start of 1922-3. He ended the season with 13 goals in 25 appearances. Under new player-manager, Curtis Booth, Stanley opened 1923-4 with an entirely new forward line and Smelt found few opportunities. Younger brother of Len Smelt, the Burnley full-back, Tom was a good all-round cricketer and was professional for Crompton Cricket Club (Central Lancashire League) in 1930.

SMETHURST, Henry **1919-22**
Centre-half. 5ft 6in; 10st 4lb.
Born: Burnley, 1893 (January quarter).
Debut v Ashington (h) 27 December 1921.
Appearances: 8.
Career: Burnley junior football; STANLEY September 1919 to May 1922.
Six of Harry Smethurst's eight Football League appearances were made in April and May 1922. In this period, the team's form evaporated as they took only three points from their last seven fixtures. It was a disappointing end to their first season in the Third Division North, despite a final placing of fifth in the table. A pre-League signing, Smethurst was one of several lightweight defenders who found less success in League football than they had enjoyed in Lancashire Combination circles.

SMITH, Charles **1950-51**
Inside-forward.
Born: Oswaldtwistle, 27 June 1930.
Debut v Hartlepools United (a) 28 April 1951.
Appearances: 1.
Career: Oswaldtwistle Immanuel; STANLEY amateur June 1950 to May 1951.
Charlie Smith was pressed into first-team service when Stanley found themselves with eight men unfit out of their total professional staff of 20. He had to be given time off work to play at Hartlepools. The match was played on an iron-hard surface and in a high wind. In a scrappy encounter, Stanley lost by the only goal of the game. A point-saving chance fell to the young debutant late in the game, but having been put clear, his shot from the edge of the penalty area cleared the crossbar.

SMITH, Dennis **1947-54**
Half-back or forward. 6ft; 11st 12lb.
Born: Nelson, 22 August 1925.
Debut v Chester (h) 22 November 1947.
Appearances: 155; Goals: 15.
Career: Nelson Schoolboys; Sheffield Training College; Frickley Colliery; Hull City 19 July 1946; STANLEY 18 October 1947 to 29 April 1954.
Although a Lancashire lad, Dennis Smith's early football development took place in Yorkshire. A former 'Bevin Boy', he progressed as a forward with Frickley Colliery before Hull City enrolled him in 1946. After a season in which he appeared in three different forward positions and at centre-half, he was signed by Stanley. He remained on the Peel Park playing strength for seven years and gave sterling service. In his first season he scored eight goals in 24 appearances, mainly operating at inside-left. In subsequent seasons he revealed a wonderful faculty for filling all sorts of positions, appearing at senior level in every outfield position except left full-back in the course of his 155 appearances. A schoolteacher and Lancashire League cricketer with Nelson CC, Smith shared a benefit match with Dick Webster and Tommy Butler in March 1954. Despite incessant sweeping rain, a crowd of 7,000 attended the match in which Stanley beat an All Star Manager's XI by 3-2. The All Star XI included Carey (Blackburn Rovers), Hill (Burnley), Hardwick (Oldham Athletic), Powell (Bradford City), Welsh (Liverpool) and Russell (Bury).

SMITH, Norman Henry **1945-48**
Inside-forward. 6ft; 11st 4lb.
Born: Burton upon Trent, 27 January 1924.
Debut v Wrexham (h) 21 September 1946.
Appearances: 39; Goals: 6.
Career: Army football; STANLEY amateur 30 October 1945 signing professional 6 February 1946; Oldham Athletic 17 June 1948 (fee £400); Congleton Town 15 July 1949.
Norman Smith, an apprentice printer at Burton upon Trent, signed for Stanley from Services football. He was offered full-time terms but declined, preferring to play as a part-time professional. Tall, long-striding and a prodigious worker, Smith's game featured clever footwork and a willingness to assist in both defence and attack. Oldham Athletic paid a fee for him in June 1948, but he appeared only once at League level for the Latics, in a 6-0 defeat at Hull City. Smith's left-wing partner in this match was Ronnie Birkett (*qv*), also making his debut for Oldham.

SMITH, William Henry **1960-62**
Wing half-back. 5ft 11in; 11st 7lb.
Born: Plymouth, 7 September 1926.

Debut v Crystal Palace (a) 20 August 1960.
Appearances: 34; Goals: 3.
Career: Plymouth Argyle 21 August 1945; Reading 20 August 1947; Northampton Town 16 July 1948; Birmingham City 30 March 1950; Blackburn Rovers 1 December 1952; STANLEY player-coach 4 July 1960 to March 1962.
In February 1958 Bill Smith was reported to have filled every position on the field for Blackburn Rovers, an emergency having presented him with the chance to try his hand as goalkeeper in the Reserve team. He began his career as a centre-half with Plymouth Argyle and then was Reading's centre-forward for a spell. With Birmingham City, he scored in the FA Cup semi-final replay against Blackpool in season 1950-51, but the Blues were beaten 2-1. Signed along with George Hudson from Blackburn Rovers, the new arrivals linked up with another ex-Rovers player on the Peel Park staff, Jack Swindells. As captain and player-coach the veteran half-back lent valuable experience to Stanley's cause in the final seasons of League football at Peel Park.

SMYTH, H(erbert) Robert **1951**
Half-back. 5ft 10in; 12st.
Born: Manchester, 28 February 1921.
Debut v Barrow (h) 27 January 1951.
Appearances: 7.
Career: Navy football; Ipswich Town 22 December 1945; Halifax Town 2 August 1950; Rochdale 30 September 1950; STANLEY 26 January to 16 April 1951.
Bob Smyth's seven League appearances with Stanley constituted exactly half of his career aggregate, despite his association with four Football League clubs. One of manager Porter's last signings before his resignation in March 1951, Smyth also departed Peel Park about a month later on a free transfer. In an initial six-match run, which terminated on 3 March after a 9-1 defeat at Lincoln City, Smyth had revealed skill on the ball and good headwork, but he lacked speed when moving into the tackle and was slow in recovery.

SNARY, John Edward **1930-31**
Full-back. 5ft 8in; 11st 5lb.
Born: Washington, Co Durham, 1907 (April quarter).
Debut v Hartlepools United (a) 18 October 1930.
Appearances: 4.
Career: Washington Colliery; STANLEY amateur 9 June, signing professional 11 August 1930 to May 1931.
A reserve full-back whose unrewarding role was to understudy Stanley's long-running defensive duo of Armstrong and Whittaker. Jack Snary made only four League appearances and failed to collect a winning bonus. Stanley's defensive record for the season was 108 goals against, a total exceeded only by Nelson, who conceded 113 and lost their League status.

SNEDDON, Charles **1953-61**
Wing-half. 5ft 9in; 11st 7lb.
Born: Carriden, West Lothian, 10 June 1930.
Debut v Chesterfield (h) 3 October 1953.
Appearances: 213; Goals: 3.
Career: Carriden Hearts 1945-6; Forth Rangers (Grangemouth) 1946-7; Stenhousemuir cs 1947; STANLEY 5 October 1953 (fee £650) to June 1961; Padiham briefly in 1961-2 before retiring.
Representative honour: Third Division North v Third Division South at Coventry season 1956-57.
Charlie Sneddon was a professional with Stenhousemuir at 17 years of age. He was a regular first-team player, except for two years' National Service in the Army, spent in Greece and Cyprus, before signing for Stanley in October 1953. Often described as 'the football artist of the Peel Park staff', he was a skilled initiator, clever at tricking an opponent and able to see a a move beyond the next. Awarded a joint

testimonial match with Les Cocker in 1959, the game was attended by 3,285 spectators (which was more than the 'gate' at a League match at Peel Park two days earlier). Sixteen goals were scored, the All Stars XI beating a Stanley XI by 9-7. Don Revie, at that time a Leeds United player, scored four of the All Stars' goals. After leaving Stanley in 1961, Charlie Sneddon became an optical mechanic with an Accrington firm, a position which he still holds.

SOUTAR, Henry William **1929-30**
Goalkeeper. 5ft 10½in; 11st 12lb.
Born: Invergowrie, Dundee, 1905.
Debut v Doncaster Rovers (a) 31 August 1929.
Appearances: 7.
Career: Dundee; Rhyl Athletic; STANLEY 28 June 1929; Notts County 29 July 1930; Rotherham United 18 July 1931 to May 1932; Rhyl Athletic; Brechin City.
International honour: Scottish Juniors.
Club honour: Rhyl Athletic, Welsh Cup runners-up, season 1926-7.
Harry Soutar, a Scottish junior international recruited from Welsh football, made his Football League debut with Stanley. After appearing in the opening seven fixtures of 1929-30 he lost his place to Richard Thornton. Notts County signed him to understudy Jimmy Ferguson and Soutar made only seven first-team appearances, but he assisted in maintaining the

best defensive record in the four Divisions, as County won the Third Division South championship. In his final season of League footall, he made 25 appearances for Rotherham United in season 1931-2.

SOWDEN, Peter Tasker **1956-58**
Inside-forward. 5ft 5in; 10st 10lb.
Born: Bradford, 1 May 1929.
Debut v Tranmere Rovers (a) 4 September 1956 (scored one goal).
Appearnces: 54; Goals: 13.
Career: Yorkshire Schoolboys; Blackpool amateur, signing professional 14 June 1947; Bacup Borough; Hull City 23 September 1948; Elgin City cs 1950; Aldershot 27 October 1950; Hull City 10 August 1951; Gillingham August 1952; STANLEY 1 September 1956; Wrexham 9 June 1958 (fee approx £2,000); Chorley 16 July 1962; Great Harwood as player-manager; Rossendale United; Darwen as player-manager 1967; Horwich RMI manager; Blackpool as youth-team manager; Luton Town as assistant-manager; Cambridge United as assistant-manager, appointed general manager 1977 to 1978.
Stanley were said to have signed 'Paddy' Sowden after failing to secure Eddie Quigley from Blackburn Rovers. Sowden had refused to resign for Gillingham, for whom he made 131 appearances and scored 27 goals, as he wished to return north. Only 5ft 5in, but squarely-built, Sowden was a clever ball-player with a deceptive body swerve, which made him a difficult man to tackle. He followed Archie Wright as Stanley's inside-right and he enjoyed an excellent first season. In the following term, after playing in the first nine matches he was injured, joining three other inside-forwards on the side-lines. When he came back, after an absence of almost three months, he was unable to command a regular first-team place.

SPENCER, John Shepherd **1951-52**
Inside-forward. 5ft 11in; 11st 6lb.
Born: Bacup, 24 August 1920.
Debut v Gateshead (h) 18 August 1951.
Appearances: 29; Goals: 7.
Career: Burnley amateur, signing professional 23 June 1948; STANLEY 14 June 1951, retired May 1952.
'Jack' Spencer began with Burnley and made a scoring first-team debut against Rotherham United in the FA Cup on 29 January 1949. His best season at Turf Moor was 1949-50, when he made 29 League appearances and scored seven goals. He also scored two goals in three FA Cup ties and assisted his team to win the Lancashire Senior Cup against Liverpool in May 1950. A good attacking player, Spencer occupied both inside-forward berths for Stanley, yet played almost as a second centre-forward. After playing in most matches until mid-March, he then lost his place and in May announced his intention to retire from the game. As company secretary to a large firm in Padiham, he felt that he could not give the time required to football, because of his work.

STAFFORD, Harold **1925**
Outside-right. 5ft 9in; 11st 7lb.
Born: Clayton, Manchester.
Debut v Halifax Town (h) 3 October 1925.
Appearances: 1.
Career: Stalybridge Celtic cs 1921; Manchester United 16 May 1923; Crewe Alexandra 6 June 1924; STANLEY (trial) 25 September to 9 November 1925.
Harry Stafford assisted Stalybridge Celtic during their sojourn as a Football League club between 1921-23. He appeared in 53 matches, scoring two goals, and moved on when they resigned from the Third Division North. He signed for Manchester United after the Football League had initially refused to sanction the transfer, but he did not play in the League team during his season at Old Trafford. His one match trial at Peel Park was preceded by a season with Crewe Alexandra, for whom he made 22 appearances and scored one goal.

STEWART, George Thompson Scott **1954-58**
Centre-forward. 5ft 10in; 11st 9lb.
Born: Buckie, 17 February 1927.
Debut v Scunthorpe United (a) 2 October 1954.
Appearances: 182; Goals: 136
Career: Buckie Thistle 1944; Dundee 1946; St Mirren 1950; Worcester City cs 1954; STANLEY 1 October 1954 (fee £1,500); Coventry City 28 November 1958 (fee £3,750); Carlisle United 22 June 1960 (fee £2,000) to 30 June 1961.
Representative honour: Third Division North v Third Division South, 2 appearances in season 1954-5 and 1957-8.

Within two months of his arrival at Peel Park, George Stewart scored the first five of Stanley's six goals against Gateshead. His feat equalled Billy Harker's record, set up in 1935, also against Gateshead. In the following season, Stewart broke the club scoring record with 35 League goals, previously held by Bob Mortimer with 33 in 1936-7. His century of League goals was completed when he scored two against Rochdale at Peel Park on 2 September 1957, a game fittingly witnessed by 15,454 spectators, the best home 'gate' of the season. Stewart's century had been achieved in

123 matches and was reported to be the second-fastest in Football League history. A non-smoker and teetotaller, George Stewart was extremely fast, had a powerful shot and was one of the best headers of the ball in the game. In all matches for Stanley, he netted 152 goals in 208 appearances and was quite simply the club's most prolific goalscorer of all time. After leaving Stanley, he assisted Coventry City to gain promotion from the Fourth Division a runners-up to Port Vale in season 1958-9. A season with Carlisle United concluded his Football League career which spanned 229 matches and 160 goals. He returned to Scotland, settling in Buckie, where he worked as a ship's chandler.

STINSON, Hugh Michael John **1955-59**
Inside-forward. 5ft 7in; 10st 10lb.
Born: Waterfoot, Lancashire, 18 May 1937.
Debut v Brentford (a) 31 January 1958.
Appearances: 3.
Career: Whitewell Bottom FC (Rossendale); STANLEY amateur, signing professional 27 May 1955; Gillingham July 1959; Hastings United cs 1960; Bedford Town; Ramsgate Athletic; Folkestone; Dartford; Chatham Town; Sheppey United.
Hugh Stinson had a lengthy spell with Stanley, beginning as a 17-year-old amateur in the 'A' team in season 1954-5. He was then signed as a part-time professional before starting his National Service at 18 years of age. His first senior game was a third round FA Cup tie, against Darlington at Peel Park on 10 January 1958, and he had the satisfaction of scoring one of the team's goals in a 3-0 win. This victory put Stanley into the fourth round for the first time in 22 years and the opponents were First Division Portsmouth. Stinson played in the goalless draw at Peel Park and in the replay at Fratton Park which Portsmouth won 4-1. At the end of an eventful month, he made his Football League debut at Brentford. He left in the close season after the team had slumped to 19th position in a staggering decline, largely due to an injury crisis which saw five inexperienced deputy goalkeepers fielded. Moving south for a season with Gillingham, he was unable to establish himself, making only one first-team appearance. He then did the rounds in southern non-League football.

STODDART, William Michael C. **1933-34**
Centre-half. 5ft 8½in; 12st 6lb.
Born: Leadgate, 1907 (October quarter).
Debut v Stockport County (a) 26 August 1933.
Appearances: 31; Goals: 1.
Career: Medomsley Edge FC; West Stanley; Manchester City 17 March 1926; Coventry City 26 May 1927; Southampton 21 June 1928; Bristol Rovers 6 July 1931; STANLEY 14 July 1933 to May 1934.
In his final season of League football, Bill Stoddart's 31 appearances with Stanley constituted his highest seasonal return. Basically a reserve-team player with Manchester City, Coventry City and Southampton, he then made 38 League appearances in two seasons with Bristol Rovers, prior to joining Stanley. Usually at centre-half but occasionally at right-half, he was a regular in the first team until March 1934, when a loss of form let in Ray Crawshaw, the young reserve centre-half. Bill Stoddart was, despite his bulk, an exceptionally clean player. He could kick and throw-in, from tremendous distances. Some of his long throw-ins were said to be almost the equivalent of a free-kick.

STONES, Gordon **1954-61**
Defender. 6ft; 11st 7lb.
Born: Kearsley, 18 November 1934.
Debut v Chesterfield (a) 7 September 1955.
Appearances: 109; Goals: 1.
Career: Kearsley FC (Bolton & District League); Little Lever FC; Bury amateur 29 May 1953; STANLEY 3 September 1954 to May 1961.
Gordon Stones played for Little Lever in the Lancashire Amateur Cup Final at Peel Park in 1953 and a year later was signed by Stanley as a 19-year-old part-time professional. His first extended run in the first team came in 1956-7 when he deputised at centre-half for Jimmy Harrower. In the same season he scored two goals, from centre-half, against Morecambe in the first round of the FA Cup. In

1957-8 he deputized for the Cup-tied Willie Kelly and did so well that the ex-Blackburn Rovers pivot lost his place. Late call-up for RAF National Service — he had been previously exempt because of his employment as a miner — restricted his opportunities in his final two seasons.

STOREY, Sidney **1957-59**
Inside-forward. 5ft 7in; 10st 2lb.
Born: Darfield, South Yorkshire, 25 December 1919.
Debut v Scunthorpe United (h) 12 October 1957.
Appearances: 30; Goals: 2.
Career: Ardsley Welfare; Grimethorpe Athletic; Huddersfield Town amateur 19 November 1942; Wombwell Athletic; York City 3 May 1947 (fee £100); Barnsley 15 May 1956; STANLEY 11 October 1957; Bradford reserve-team player-coach July 1959; York City trainer-coach 1960-63.

Sid Storey was almost 38 years old when he was signed by Stanley as a stop-gap during the Reds' long run of injuries in early season 1957-8. The veteran inside-forward did so well that he held his place in the team for most of the season and played his final League game for Stanley at 39 years and four months of age. Throughout his football career, Storey worked as a miner at Wombwell and he is best remembered for his long association with York City, particularly as their arch-schemer in the City's famous run to the FA Cup semi-final in 1955. Storey joined Stanley from Barnsley where he had been signed with the intention of taking charge of the reserve team at Oakwell. In the event, an injury to a first-team player saw him step up into the seniors, where he played in 29 Second Division matches and scored four goals. His final career figures were 390 Football League appearances, 45 goals.

STOREY, Thomas **1938-39**
Inside or wing-forward. 5ft 8in; 11st.
Born: Foulridge, near Colne, Lancashire, 23 November 1914.
Debut v Oldham Athletic (h) 27 September 1938.
Appearances: 26; Goals: 3.
Career: Darwen; Nelson amateur; Burnley 10 October 1935; STANLEY 24 September 1938 to September 1939.
A prominent schoolboy footballer, Tom Storey's first professional engagement was with Burnley, where he appeared in 35 League matches, scoring seven goals, in a three-year stay. At the time of his move to Peel Park, it was stated that he had been loaned to Stanley, but this was obviously made permanent, as Stanley re-signed him in August 1939. A quick-thinking player who revealed clever touches, Storey was adept in all forward positions and actually played in every front line position but centre for Stanley.

SUMMERS, George Moffet **1930-31**
Outside-left.
Born: Durham, 1906 (October quarter).
Debut v Crewe Alexandra (h) 30 August 1930.
Appearances: 26; Goals: 2.
Career: Willington FC; Huddersfield Town 4 November 1929; STANLEY 5 August 1930; Barrow 11 July 1931 to May 1932.
George Summers' season came to a premature end on a 'skating rink' surface at Peel Park. He was injured in the January fixture against New Brighton. To that point, the former Huddersfield Town winger had formed a progressive left-wing partnership with Harry Broome, whose strategy and placing of passes brought out Summers' chief assets of pace and a seemingly inexhaustible supply of energy.

STURROCK, David **1960-61**
Wing-forward. 5ft 7½in; 10st 4lb.
Born: Dundee, 22 February 1938.
Debut v Workington (a) 17 September 1960.
Appearances: 17; Goals: 5.
Career: Dundee United; STANLEY 4 July 1960 to 20 October 1961.
David Sturrock had two season's experience with Dundee United and had made several first-team appearances. When signed by Stanley, he was doing his National Service in the RAF in Surrey, but was expected to be able to get leave for most weekend matches. He made his debut as stand-in for the injured Lawson Bennett at outside-right and made a good impression with his all-action style and never-say-die spirit. During his first season he appeared in every forward position but centre and would probably have added to his 19 appearances, had he not been restricted by his National Service commitments. Somewhat ironically, he was released by Stanley only a matter of weeks after he had completed his RAF service. He had played in nine matches and scored one goal in the ill-fated 1961-2 season.

SWINDELLS, Jack **1959-61**
Centre-forward. 5ft 9in; 11st 10lb.
Born: Manchester, 12 April 1937.
Debut v Tranmere Rovers (h) 19 December 1959.
Appearances: 65; Goals: 28.
Career: Manchester City amateur 18 May 1955; Blackburn Rovers amateur 29 June, signing professional 20 November 1957; STANLEY 18 December 1959 (fee £1,250); Barnsley 15 June 1961; Workington February 1962; Torquay United 11 July 1963; Newport County 7 July 1964 to 30 June 1965.
International Honour: England Youth.
In season 1954-5, Jack Swindells played for England Youth against Ireland at Watford and also in the International Youth Tournament held in Italy. A Manchester boy, he began on City's books, but made his League debut with Blackburn Rovers. He was signed by Stanley shortly after they had released two forwards, Jack Keeley (*qv*) and Keith Marsden, who was a reserve-team player. The 22-year-old centre-forward arrived with an impressive goalscoring record in Blackburn Rovers' Central League team, his total being 56 goals in two and a half seasons. In his first five games in Stanley's colours he scored six goals and was joint leading scorer for the season, despite having played in less than half of the season's fixtures. His efforts unfortunately failed to save Stanley from relegation to Division Four, where, in tandem with George Hudson, the pair scored between them 52 of Stanley's 74 goals during the 1960-61 season.

TATTERSALL, John **1919-22**
Goalkeeper. 5ft 7½in; 10st 8lb.
Born: Church, Lancashire.
Debut v Rochdale (a) 27 August 1921.
Appearances: 3.
Career: St Mary's RC (Oswaldtwistle); STANLEY August 1919 to May 1922; Barnoldswick Town 1924-5.
When Stanley played Southport at Peel Park on 24 March 1923, a collection taken for John Tattersall raised £18. Stanley's former goalkeper, badly hurt in the club's service, was awaiting another operation. A product of St Mary's RC, a prolific Stanley nursery, Tattersall joined the Reds for their first season after World War One. He was a confident goalkeeper with a businesslike style, but his career was badly blighted by injuries. Perhaps too brave for his own good, he ignored medical advice on one occasion and played with a splintered collarbone, only to be carried off the field having received another knock. He was badly hurt again in November 1921, suffering severe concussion and broken ribs in a match at Durham City. He missed the remainder of the season and was

out of football altogether for some considerable time, eventually making a comeback with Barnoldswick Town in 1924.

TAYLOR, John James **1952-53**
Full-back. 5ft 9½in; 11st.
Born: Manchester, 12 October 1928.
Debut v Carlisle United (a) 4 September 1952.
Appearances: 16.
Career: Manchester junior football; Blackpool 27 September 1949; STANLEY 11 July 1952 to May 1953; Stalybridge Celtic cs 1954.
Blackpool Reserves won the championship of the Central League in John Taylor's first season at Bloomfield Road, but in a three-year stay he did not have a senior outing. His position was undoubtably a handicap, as the outside-right position at Bloomfield Road was illustriously filled by Stanley Matthews. When the maestro was unavailable, Albert Hobson was the usual deputy. Having waited three years at Bloomfield Road, Taylor waited only three weeks at Peel Park before playing in his first Football League fixture. During the season, in which Stanley's return of 39 League goals was the worst in the four Divisions, Taylor was one of seven different players tried at outside-right.

THOMAS, Dennis **1950-51**
Outside-left. 5ft 7in; 11st 2lb.
Born: Hebburn-on-Tyne, 2 February 1926.
Debut v Gateshead (a) 19 August 1950.
Appearances: 34; Goals: 5.
Career: Wardley Welfare (North-Eastern Alliance); Bury 25 January 1949; STANLEY 11 July 1950 to May 1951.
Stanley's manager Jimmy Porter went back to his old club to recruit Dennis Thomas, a Central League player with Bury who had also played in three Second Division matches. At outside-left for Stanley he completed an all-English XI (a situation which changed radically a few years later, when Stanley fielded an all-Scottish XI under Walter Galbraith's managership). Thomas had a good season at Peel Park, but his goalscoring was disappointing after a bright start which saw him second only to Walter Keeley as the team's most penetrative marksman.

THOMPSON, James **1924-25**
Wing-forward. 5ft 7in; 10st 3lb.
Born: Chadderton, Lancashire, 24 January 1899.
Debut v Rotherham County (h) 30 August 1924.
Appearances: 42; Goals: 8.
Career: Bathgate FC; Oldham Athletic 7 January 1920; Manchester City 19 August 1920; Stalybridge Celtic 11 June 1921; Ashton National 16 September 1922; Port Vale 13 January 1923; Blackpool 5 June 1923; STANLEY 14 June 1924; Swindon Town 9 June 1925; Crewe Alexandra 16 July 1926; Hurst 10 August 1928.
Jimmy Thompson was the first Stanley player to complete an ever-present season in the Third Division North. Typically, after initially appearing on the retained list, he was later transfer-listed due to lack of funds to pay summer wages. Earlier in his career, Thompson played in Stalybridge Celtic's first-ever game in the Football League. He had a big hand in what proved to be a record-breaking occasion, as his hat-trick helped to set up a 6-0 win against Chesterfield. The result remains Stalybridge Celtic's record victory in a Football League match.

THOMPSON, Robert **1924-25**
Centre-forward. 6ft; 12st 4lb.
Born: Eldon, near Bishop Auckland.
Debut v Rotherham County (h) 30 August 1924.
Appearances: 33; Goals: 17.
Career: Durham City August 1919; Leeds United 20 July 1920; Ashington 25 May 1921; Luton Town 5 June 1922; Pontypridd cs 1923; STANLEY 30 June 1924; Bury 4 May 1925; Hartlepools United 21 October 1926; Goole Town January 1927.
Representative honour: Welsh League v Free State League at Dalymount Park, Dublin, 9 February 1924.
Robert Thompson's best performance at Peel Park came on Monday, 23 February 1925, when he scored a hat-trick in a 6-0 win against Durham City. It was the first time that Stanley had scored six goals in a Northern Section match. Unfortunately, due to adverse weather conditions, only 500 spectators attended, receipts being an all-time low of £22. Leading goalscorer, by a wide margin, in his season at Peel Park, Thompson had justified his reputation as a goalscorer, following his 51 goals for Pontypridd in season 1923-4.

THORNTON, Richard G. **1928-31**
Goalkeeper. 5ft 10in; 11st 4lb.
Born: Bearpark, Co Durham.
Debut v Barrow (a) 16 March 1929.
Appearances: 61.
Career: Esh Winning; Bearpark; Leeds United amateur 19 May, signing professional 5 September 1925; STANLEY 9 November 1928; York City 27 June 1931 to May 1932; Bridlington Town; Leyland Motors.
Richard Thornton was promoted from Stanley's Reserve team in March 1929, following the transfer of Alf Tootill to Wolverhampton Wanderers. 'Occasionally brilliant but sometimes erratic,' was one early verdict, but Thornton improved notably in technique. He guarded the breach with fine judgment in season 1929-30 in a long run of consecutive appearances. In 1930-31 he lot his place to new signing Joe Lansdale, after a shaky opening to the season had seen 34 goals conceded in the team's first seven away fixtures.

THORPE, Percy **1934-35**
Full-back. 5ft 8½in; 12st 8lb.
Born: Nottingham, 18 July 1899.
Debut v Mansfield Town (h) 19 September 1934.
Appearances: 2.
Career: Nottingham Schoolboys; Sutton Town; Blackpool 6 May 1924; Connah's Quay & Shotton August 1928; Reading 5 October 1928; Sheffield United 13 June 1930; West Ham United 10 June 1933; STANLEY 18 September 1934; Port Vale 2 November 1934.
Percy Thorpe began as a centre-half but was converted into a full-back during his stay with Blackpool. He was appointed captain at Bloomfield Road in 1926-7. A very capable, strong-tackling defender, Thorpe could occupy either flank and was said to be particularly in his element on a heavy ground. He made 114 appearances and scored six goals for Blackpool, adding a further 71 appearances in a little under two seasons with Reading. In three seasons with Sheffield

United he clocked up 103 First Division appearances, but a season with West Ham United was spent mainly in reserve (three appearances). After a fine career, spent in Divisions One and Two, his move to Stanley saw him make only two appearances. These came when both Hunter and Fieldsend, Stanley's regular backs, were on the injured list.

TIGHE, Terence William **1957-60**
Half-back. 5ft 8in; 11st 7lb.
Born: Edinburgh, 12 August 1934.
Debut v Rochdale (a) 28 August 1957.
Appearances: 117; Goals: 20.
Career: Newton Grange Star; Hibernian 1953-56; Dumfermline 1956-7; STANLEY 3 June 1957; Crewe Alexandra 16 December 1960; Southport 23 August 1963; Runcorn 1964-5; Great Harwood.
Terry Tighe joined Stanley as an inside-forward but blossomed out as a wing-half. He had been switched to the middle line after recovering from a fractured jaw, received whilst playing for the Reserves. Strong in the tackle and with good distribution, he was a valuable clubman who played under four different managers and one 'caretaker' boss in his three and a half seasons at Peel Park. After leaving Stanley he gave equally good service to Crewe Alexandra (86 appearances, five goals) and ended his first-class career with a season at Southport (36 appearances, three goals).

TINDALL, John Thomas **1924-25**
Full-back. 5ft 9in; 12st 2lb.
Born: Barnsley, 1891 (April quarter).
Debut v Ashington (a) 25 October 1924.
Appearances: 12.

Career: St Barnabas FC; Barnsley 10 May 1911; STANLEY 22 August 1924, appointed club trainer November 1924 to June 1925.
A solid, sturdy full-back with a powerful kick and in excess of 12st to throw usefully into the fray. Jack Tindall was an importation from Barnsley where he gained sound experience in a career which was interrupted by World War One. Rather unusually, he took on a dual role in November 1924, when he was appointed club trainer, whilst continuing as a player.

TODD, Ronald **1956-60**
Half-back. 5ft 9in; 11st.
Born: Bellshill, Lanarkshire, 4 October 1935.
Debut v Bradford City (a) 19 September 1959.
Appearances: 5.
Career: Lesmahagow; STANLEY 1 February 1956; Chelmsford City July 1960.
One of the first Scottish juniors brought to Peel Park by Walter Galbraith, Ron Todd had caught the eye of Stanley's manager when he was in Scotland watching another player. An engineering apprentice and part-time professional, Todd's period with Stanley was interrupted by RAF National Service. He was a long time in reserve, making his League debut some three and a half years after first signing. In his initial outing, Stanley won an exciting match against Bradford City by 5-4 to record the season's first away victory. His Stanley career ended painfully when he fractured an arm in a Reserves match at Doncaster, late in season 1959-60.

TOMLINSON, James **1925-29**
Half-back. 5ft 11in; 11st 7lb.
Born: Leyland, 1904 (July quarter).
Debut v Halifax Town (a) 13 February 1926.
Appearances: 20; Goals: 1.
Career: Preston junior football; STANLEY amateur 24 August 1925, signing professional 15 February 1926; Morecambe August 1929 to cs 1930.
Jim Tomlinson was one of several amateur players who applied for a place in the pre-season trial matches at Peel Park in August 1925. He was one of five who impressed enough to be signed up, initially on amateur forms. In the Reserves he developed into a very servicable half-back, being well-built, enthusiastic and speedy. He made his Football League debut in February 1926 and was signed as professional immediately afterwards. In a stay of four years, calls for first-team duty were infrequent, but he was a good reserve-team player and a valuable clubman. In civilian life he became chairman of Leyland District Council and was chairman of the National Savings Committee there in the early post-war years.

TOOTILL, Alfred **1927-29**
Goalkeeper. 5ft 10in; 11st.
Born: Ramsbottom, 12 November 1908. Died: 31 August 1975.
Debut v Durham City (h) 12 November 1927.
Appearances: 31.
Career: Ramsbottom United; STANLEY (trial) February 1926; Ramsbottom United; STANLEY amateur 5 November, signing professional 10 November 1927; Wolverhampton Wanderers 16 March 1929 (fee £450); Fulham 1 December 1932 (fee £1,000); Crystal Palace 26 November 1938, retired in 1945.

Club honour: Wolverhampton Wanderers, Division Two champions, season 1931-2.
Stanley had spotted Alf Tootill's promise very early, as he was invited for a trial in the Midweek XI when he was only 17 years old. He was a week short of his 19th birthday when he signed amateur forms and, in a matter of days, had been signed up as a professional. After spending a season in the Reserves, he took over the first-team jersey in place of Finnigan, in the early stages of season 1928-9. Possessing a fine eye and a safe pair of hands, his form was so impressive that Wolverhampton Wanderers signed him later in the same season. He was ever-present when the Wolves won the Second Division title in 1931-2 and later made over 200 appearances for Fulham. With Crystal Palace he appeared in only one League match, but was a regular performer throughout the wartime seasons. Alf Tootill was also a fine cricketer, assisting Ramsbottom in the Lancashire League between 1927-35. He had a career record of over 1,800 runs which included two centuries and he headed his club's batting and bowling averages in 1930, when he was also fifth in the League batting averages.

TRAVIS, Donald **1948-50**
Centre-forward. 6ft 3in; 12st 12lb.
Born: Moston, Manchester, 21 January 1924.
Debut v Doncaster Rovers (a) 25 December 1948.
Appearances: 71; Goals: 36.
Career: Manchester Schoolboys; Ferranti FC; Blackpool amateur 13 July 1939; Southend United and Plymouth Argyle (wartime guest); West Ham United 3 September 1945; Southend United 7 May 1948; STANLEY 23 December 1948; Crewe Alexandra 14 November 1950; Oldham Athletic 19 October 1951; Chester 15 February 1952; Oldham Athletic 17 August 1954 (fee £570); Yeovil Town 13 July 1957.
Standing at 6ft 3in and weighing close on 13st, Don Travis was ideally built for his centre-forward role. He was remarkably nimble for such a big man and his height enabled him to give most opposing centre-halves an uncomfortable time in the air. Strong shooting, mainly with his left foot, and good distribution and line-holding abilities combined to make him a very dangerous opponent. In a career spent mainly in the Northern Section, he was a consistent marksman, his best season coming in 1954-5 with Oldham Athletic when he scored 32 goals in 40 League appearances. Younger brother of Harry Travis (*qv*), Don also began as a butcher's boy and, as one correspondent noted, he put plenty of 'meat' into his shots.

TRAVIS, Henry **1933-34**
Inside-forward. 5ft 11in; 12st 3lb.
Born: Manchester, 26 December 1911.
Debut v Mansfield Town (a) 10 February 1934.
Appearances: 4; Goals: 1.
Career: Manchester Schoolboys; Manchester City 24 October 1931; Oldham Athletic 18 June 1932; STANLEY 8 July 1933; Leeds United 13 June 1924; Bradford City 11 June 1935; Derby County 20 February 1937 (fee £825); Tranmere Rovers 25 November 1938; Kidderminster Harriers July 1939.
Harry Travis, a rosy-cheeked former butcher's boy, made several moves before winning his spurs with Bradford City. He changed his League grade each time he changed his club and no fee was involved in any of his first four moves. He made his League debut with Stanley, where he was generally used as a wing-half in the Reserves. He was leading goalscorer for Bradford City in his first season at Valley Parade with 16 goals in 24 appearances, but subsequently did little at senior level. Travis' father was said to have been a junior with Manchester City at 17 years of age. Younger brother Don (*qv*) was a Stanley centre-forward in post-war football.

TREANOR, James Leslie **1935-36**
Half-back. 6ft ½in; 11st 7lb.
Born: Heap, near Bury, 11 October 1913. Died: Manchester, 1966 (April quarter).
Debut v Barrow (h) 21 September 1935.
Appearances: 40.
Career: Bury Grammar School; Winsford United; Bury 16 August 1933; STANLEY 20 September 1935; Hull City 26 September 1936 (fee £500) to May 1939; post-war with Chorley FC.
One of Stanley's finest left-halves in pre-war football, Jim Treanor missed only two games, due to injury, during his year at Peel Park. His arrival in September 1935 coincided with the team's first win of the season, and he contributed materially to the ensuing revival. Young and speedy, he covered a tremendous amount of ground and was a great asset in both defence and attack. One of the tallest wing-halves in the Northern Section, he also used his height to great advantage. Hull City signed him in September 1936, after he had played a particularly fine game against the Tigers, earlier in the same month. During his Stanley spell he was employed by a cotton firm in Manchester. During military service as a sergeant wireless operator in the Royal Armoured Corps, his Army representative honours included an appearance for the Northern Command against Combined Universities in March 1945.

TURNBULL, George Frederick **1951-52**
Goalkeeper. 5ft 11in; 12st 4lb.
Born: Gateshead, 4 February 1927.
Debut v Mansfield Town (h) 22 August 1951.
Appearances: 33.
Career: Alnwick Town; Grimsby Town 18 August 1950; STANLEY 20 August 1951; Gateshead 28 July 1952 to May 1953.
George Turnbull made his Football League debut with Grimsby Town in season 1950-51, when the Mariners were relegated from Division Two. One of four goalkeepers on the Blundell Park staff, he was restricted to only two first-team outings in which, incidentally, he conceded only one goal. He took over from Doug Daniels in Stanley's goal and was generally kept busy in a season when 92 goals were conceded, and a re-election application was only narrowly avoided. Moving to Gateshead, he played in only three League matches in 1952-3, being in the shadow of Bob Gray, one of the Northern Sections best goalkeepers.

TURNER, Philip S. **1955-56**
Inside-forward. 5ft 8in; 12st.
Born: Chester, 20 February 1927.
Debut v Barrow (a) 14 January 1956 (scored one goal).
Appearances: 14; Goals: 5.
Career: Local junior football; Chester amateur, signing

professional July 1946; Carlisle United 13 September 1948 (fee £300); Bradford 29 June 1951 (fee £3,000); Scunthorpe United 1 July 1954; STANLEY 28 October 1955; Chester 3 November 1956 to May 1957; Winsford United cs 1958; Barrow (one month's trial) 5 September to 2 October 1958; Rhyl player-manager (after a month's trial) December 1959; Prestatyn manager August 1962; Rhyl FC promotions manager 1979.
When signed by Stanley in October 1955, the local Press felt it necessary to point out that Phil Turner was not a Scotsman. He was being introduced into a team with only one other Englishman, Les Cocker. Despite scoring in each of his first three matches for Stanley, he failed to win a permanent berth in the side, a good indication of the strength of the squad at that time. Turner's best season was with Bradford in 1951-2 when he was leading scorer with 27 goals in League and Cup matches. A season earlier, he had been Carlisle United's top marksman with 13 goals in 31 matches. Turner's career figures were 194 appearances and 59 goals and considering his extraordinary catalogue of injuries (five fractures and twenty operations) he did well to total as many as he did. After retiring as a player, he was in business in Rhyl and Chester, running a sports shop and a café.

TYLER, William **1929-30**
Half-back. 5ft 7in; 11st 3lb.
Born: Manchester, 28 May 1900. Died: Withington, Manchester, 24 March 1974.
Debut v Nelson (h) 24 September 1929.
Appearances: 7.
Career: New Cross; Manchester United 10 May 1922; Southport 26 May 1925; Bradford City 8 September 1926; Bournemouth & Boscombe Athletic (trial) 22 August to 17 October 1927; Grimsby Town 31 October 1927; Hurst June 1928; STANLEY 25 June 1929; Ashton National 26 July 1930.
Despite appearing in a losing side only once in his seven appearances, Bill Tyler found few first-team opportunities with Stanley. He had been brought back into League football after a season with Hurst, in the Cheshire County League. A hard-working half-back who could always be relied upon to pull his weight, Tyler's most productive spell was with Southport, where his 30 appearances and three goals constituted the major part of his modest career aggregate of 50 appearances and three goals.

TYSON, William George **1936-37**
Inside-forward. 5ft 7in; 10st 12lb.
Born: Skerton, Lancaster, 1916 (January quarter).
Debut v Carlisle United (h) 19 December 1936.
Appearances: 31; Goals: 13.
Career: Lancaster Schoolboys; Skerton Athletic; Southport amateur 14 June 1933; Glentoran 1934; Lancaster Town October 1935; STANLEY 10 September 1936; Blackburn Rovers 4 October 1937 (with R.Mortimer for a combined fee of £1,200); Boston United August 1938; STANLEY 8 October 1938; Southport 13 June to September 1939; STANLEY (wartime guest) August 1944.
Seven goals in his first 13 Lancashire Combination games paved the way for Billy Tyson's Football League debut with Stanley in December 1936. One of several footballing brothers, he quickly became a great favourite at Peel Park. He combined bustle with intelligent distribution and great agility in the air, despite his lack of inches. He left Stanley in October 1937 to join Blackburn Rovers, but returned 12 months later. Unfortunately, in the month of his return, he was injured in the first minute of a game at Crewe and later had to undergo a cartilage operation. He returned to Stanley when wartime football resumed in season 1944-5. After the war Tyson worked at a Lancaster hospital, and in season 1948-9 was reported to be playing for the hospital team.

VALENTINE, Albert Finch **1937-38**
Centre-forward. 5ft 7in; 12st.
Born: Higher Ince, near Wigan, 3 June 1907.
Debut v Doncaster Rovers (h) 9 October 1937.
Appearances: 7; Goals: 1.
Career: Ashton St Thomas'; Southport amateur 9 November 1928, signing professional 9 January 1929; Cardiff City 20 July 1929; Wigan Borough 18 July 1931; Chester 2 November 1931; Crewe Alexandra 19 August 1932; Macclesfield season 1933-4; Halifax Town 7 July 1934 (fee £500); Stockport County 11 June 1937; STANLEY 6 October 1937 (fee £225); Oldham Athletic 13 August 1938, retired cs 1941.
Albert Valentine was signed by Stanley as a replacement for Bob Mortimer, who had been transferred to Blackburn Rovers a week earlier. He found Mortimer a hard act to follow and after seven matches and only one goal he was superseded by Jim Blakeney. In the Reserves, Valentine scored 19 goals in 16 Lancashire Combination appearances, plus three in the Combination Cup. He scored the only goal of the Combination Cup Final against Clitheroe on 4 May 1938, when Stanley's Reserves won the trophy for the first time in their history. The game at Peel Park was watched by a crowd of 6,100, a record attendance for a reserve-team match. Valentine travelled widely in his career, and his best days were spent with Halifax Town, who signed him after he had scored 84 goals for Macclesfield in season 1933-4. In three seasons at the Shay he scored 88 goals. His total of 34 in season 1934-5 remains the club record for goals by an individual player in one season.

VINER, Ronald Jesse **1930-33**
Centre-half. 6ft; 12st 7lb.
Born: Reading.
Debut v Southport (h) 10 September 1930.
Appearances: 96; Goals: 2.
Career: Reading amateur 10 October 1923; Kettering Town July 1924; Leicester City 23 December 1925 (fee £850); Guildford City July 1927; STANLEY 4 September 1930; Chester 13 February 1933 (fee £250); Barrow 12 June 1933; Nelson August 1934.
Ron Viner first came into prominence with Kettering Town and he cost Leicester City a substantial fee in December 1925. He did not progress beyond reserve-team standard at Filbert Street, and he was transfer listed at £750. On appeal his fee was reduced to £500, but Leicester City received nothing when he signed for a non-League club, Guildford City. When he joined Stanley, he quickly made his presence felt. He caused some anxiety, however, when he made an application to join the Reading police force after one season at Peel Park. Fortunately for Stanley, there were no vacancies in the Reading area and Viner remained in Accrington to record over a century of first-team

appearances in League and Cup. Chester signed him when an injury crisis left them short of defensive cover, but he played in only one League match before signing for Barrow. Some indication of the parlous financial position of the Barrow club was revealed on 13 April 1934, when the FA ordered them to pay the £50 balance due on Viner's fee within 14 days, or face suspension.

VIPHAM, Peter **1960-62**
Goalkeeper. 5ft 7in; 10st 7lb.
Born: Rawtenstall, 9 September 1942.
Debut v Mansfield Town (a) 22 March 1961.
Appearances: 6.
Career: Local junior football; STANLEY amateur 9 August 1960, signing professional 16 June 1961 to March 1962; Chorley; Rossendale United 1965-6.
Peter Vipham began with Stanley Reserves in the North Regional League whilst still a 17-year-old. His unexpected chance came due to an early-season injury to John Marshall. Vipham took his chance well, prompting the *Accrington Observer* to comment: 'There is not much of him, but he is all heart and skill and he puts himself in the line of fire with agility and sureness'. Later in the same season, he made his League debut at Mansfield Town and was applauded off the field for his part in earning Stanley a share of the points in a goalless draw.

WADDINGTON, John Mercer **1938-39**
Inside-forward.
Born: Clayton-le-Moors, 26 August 1914.
Debut v Lincoln City (a) 8 October 1938.
Appearances: 5; Goals: 1.

Career: Clayton Villa; Stanhill FC; STANLEY amateur 4 October 1938 to September 1939. During wartime football assisted Citheroe; Howard & Bullough FC; STANLEY and Rossendale United. Clitheroe season 1946-7.
Stanley only narrowly beat Blackburn Rovers in the race to sign John Waddington, an outstanding amateur forward with the Stanhill club in the Blackburn Combination. Strong and clever on the ball, he did so well in two Lancashire Combination matches that he was selected for his debut in Third Division football without further preliminaries. He scored at Crewe on his third appearance and, considering his lack of top-class experience, did well in a poor side. After appearing in five consecutive matches he was deposed, losing his place to the newly-signed former England international 'Pongo' Waring. During wartime football he had to pass up the opportunity of joining Rochdale, which would have presented travelling difficulties, and elected to join Clitheroe instead. John Waddington was later employed in the woodworking industry and today lives in retirement at Huncoat.

WALKER, Andrew McQueen **1922-23**
Centre-half. 5ft 10in; 12st 7lb.
Born: Dalkeith, *c.*1892.
Debut v Darlington (a) 2 September 1922.
Appearances: 13.
Career: Dundee; Chelsea 20 May 1913; Newport County 1920; STANLEY 21 June 1922 (fee £50) to May 1923. Later in the same year he emigrated to the USA.
Club honour: Chelsea FA Cup runners-up 1915.
Stanley were well covered in the half-back division for season 1922-3. Despite losing wing-half Billy Rooks with cartilage trouble in mid-season, Andy Walker was

left out of the side at the same time. He had started well at right-half, revealing high-class football in both defence and attack. He lost his place, however, after a 7-1 Christmas Day defeat by Grimsby Town. An FA Cup Finalist with Chelsea, Walker had captained Newport County before joining Stanley, making 75 appearances and scoring 14 goals for the Welsh side. He left Stanley to take up a coaching appointment in the USA.

WALMSLEY, John W. **1924-26**
Defender. 5ft 9½in; 12st 4lb.
Born: Accrington, 1903 (April quarter)
Debut v Halifax Town (a) 24 January 1925.
Appearances: 17.
Career: Accrington St Peter's; Bacup Borough; Nelson 15 August 1921; Barnoldswick Town 1923-4; STANLEY 21 August 1924 to May 1926.
Discovered in Accrington Sunday School football, John Walmsley arrived at Peel Park after a variety of experience which included a season with Nelson. Curly-haired and hefty, he was a useful utility defender, strong and challenging and a great stumbling block to opposing attackers. In the close season of 1925, Walmsley was one of only six players on Stanley's retained list.

WALTON, George **1929-33**
Inside-forward. 5ft 6½in; 10st 7lb.
Born: Burnley, 1911 (January quarter).
Debut v South Shields (h) 21 April 1930 (scored one goal).
Appearances: 79; Goals: 21.
Career: Burnley Works XI; STANLEY (trial) 27 April, amateur 28 November 1929, signing professional 18 May 1931; Bolton Wanderers 13 February 1933 (fee £300); Cardiff City 23 October 1936; Walsall 19 August 1939; STANLEY (wartime guest).
Stanley's best 'find' of season 1930-31, George Walton was given occasional trials in the first team but it was not until mid-term that he was given an extended run. Keen and enthusiastic, he was a hard-working inside man and he quickly acquired a few tricks as a very useful stock-in-trade. He eventually earned Stanley a useful fee when Bolton Wanderers signed him, but in three and a half years at Burnden Park he found only limited opportunities. In 1934-5 he played in ten Second Division matches and scored two goals to assist the Trotters to promotion to Division One as runners-up to Brentford. Additionally, they progressed to the FA Cup semi-final, losing only after a replay against West Bromwich Albion. Walton scored his team's goal in

the first match, a 1-1 draw at Elland Road, Leeds. A move to Cardiff City followed (54 appearances, nine goals) and then, just prior to the outbreak of World War Two, a move to Walsall. In the same season (1939-40), he was back at Peel Park as a wartime guest player. In October 1945 he was reported to have been demobbed from the Services, but he did not figure in post-war League football.

WALTON, Joseph W. **1961-62**
Full-back. 5ft 6½in; 10st 10lb.
Born: Manchester, 5 June 1925.
Debut v Aldershot (h) 18 February 1961.
Appearances: 18.
Career: Manchester United amateur 25 April 1940; Preston North End, 13 March 1948 (fee £10,000, then

a record for a full-back); STANLEY 18 February to March 1962.
International honour: England 'Victory' v Scotland (Bolton Disaster Fund Match) 24 August 1946.
Representative honour: Football League, 1 appearance v League of Ireland 14 April 1948.
Club honour: Preston North End, FA Cup runners-up, 1954.
Joe Walton was one of the best uncapped full-backs in the early post-war years, yet it did not prevent him from losing his place in the Manchester United side. Out for several weeks due to injury, he then found John Carey impossible to dislodge. Following his record-breaking transfer to Preston North End, he made 70 appearances in his first two seasons at Deepdale and then in the next three seasons made only slightly more than half that number. He eventually regained his place and in 1953 helped North End to finish runners-up for the League Championship. A year later, he was an FA Cup Finalist. After almost 13 years at Deepdale and over 400 League appearances, he joined Stanley and played in the last 18 matches of season 1960-61. He was 36 years old when 1962-3 season began and whilst he was not as nimble as in his heyday, his sound knowledge of the game and highly developed positional sense made him a match for most wingers in the Fourth Division.

WARD, Thomas Henry **1922-24**
Outside-right.
Born: Padiham, Lancashire, 1901 (April quarter).
Debut v Wigan Borough (h) 7 October 1922.
Appearances: 20.
Career: Padiham junior football; STANLEY 17 August 1922; Burnley (trial) September 1923; returned to STANLEY October 1923; Wigan Borough (trial) 23 September to 4 October 1924.
A slightly-built winger of incisive and speedy style, Tom Ward showed distinct promise of developing into a first-rate player. Misfortune in the shape of injuries to both senior wingers, Pinkney and Harrold, gave him an unexpected and early opportunity at League level. He made 18 first-team appearances in his first season, but then refused Stanley's terms for 1923-4. He was offered a trial by Burnley, and initially appeared in what was virtually the Clarets' first team in a Lancashire Senior Cup tie against Bolton Wanderers. Burnley won 2-0, but the local correspondent was not impressed, reporting that 'Ward did a few good things at outside-right, but he was not in his class'. He returned to Peel Park, presumably accepting the previously declined terms, but played in only two more League matches. He left Stanley in the summer of 1924, when newspaper speculation linked him with Lancaster Town. In the event, he joined Wigan Borough on trial, but he did not obtain a permanent engagement.

WARING, Thomas **1938-39**
Centre-forward. 6ft 1½in; 13st 4lb.
Born: High Tranmere, Birkenhead, 12 October 1906.
Died: Liverpool, 20 December 1980.
Debut v Hartlepools United (h) 12 November 1938.
Appearances: 22; Goals: 10.
Career: Birkenhead Schoolboys; Tranmere Celtic 1921; Tranmere Rovers amateur 16 February, signing professional 29 February 1926; Aston Villa 17 February 1928 (fee £4,750); Barnsley 2 December 1935; Wolverhampton Wanderers 23 July 1936; Tranmere Rovers 16 October 1936; STANLEY 10 November 1938 (with W.Hamilton for a combined fee of £660); Bath City July 1939; New Brighton (wartime guest); South Liverpool and Ellesmere Port Town during season 1945-6.
International honours: 5 England caps, 1931-2.
Club honour: Tranmere Rovers, Third Division North champions season 1937-8.
'Pongo' Waring, as he was popularly known, began in senior football with Tranmere Rovers. In early 1928 he scored six goals against Durham City in an 11-1 win, and Aston Villa won the race to obtain his signature. In nine seasons at Villa Park he scored 167 goals in 226 matches, but his efforts failed to bring the League Championship trophy to the Villa, although they were twice runners-up. In season 1930-31 he was the First Division's leading goalscorer with 49 goals, as Villa totalled a record-breaking 128 in 42 League matches. Moves in quick succession to Barnsley and Wolverhampton Wanderers preceded his return to Tranmere Rovers, where he helped his old club to win the championship of the Third Division North. Amazingly enough, it was the only medal that he ever won. Stanley proved to be his final fling in League circles. Always a controversial character, Waring was soon in trouble with Stanley's directorate, who fined him £10 and severely reprimanded him for his conduct on Boxing Day 1938. On the return journey from the Barnsley match, a bottle of whisky was taken from the trainer's baggage and dispatched, assisted by two other Stanley players. Aside from the disciplinary problems, Waring headed the season's goalscoring lists, despite having played in only 22 matches.

WATKINSON, John W. **1922**
Outside-left. 5ft 6½in; 10st 8lb.
Born: Bradford, 29 January 1901.
Debut v Stalybridge Celtic (h) 11 February 1922 (scored one goal).
Appearances: 8; Goals: 1.
Career: Bank Top White Star; Queensbury United; STANLEY amateur 7 January, signing professional 16 February 1922 to June 1922.
John Watkinson was one of seven different outside-lefts fielded by Stanley in their initial Northern Section campaign. A nippy, lightweight winger, he made a distinctly promising first appearance against Stalybridge Celtic in a 4-1 win. His performance drew praise from the *Accrington Observer* which reported: 'Watkinson showed no little versatility in eluding the opposition and his ball-control was very good. He also centred very accurately, and the splendid way he flashed the ball into the net showed that he can turn openings to account.'

WATKINSON, William W. **1951-54**
Centre-forward. 5ft 10in; 11st 3lb.
Born: Prescot, 16 March 1922.
Debut v Oldham Athletic (h) 20 January 1951 (scored one goal).
Appearances: 105; Goals: 45.
Career: Prescot Cables; Liverpool February 1946; STANLEY 20 January 1951 (fee approx £3,000); Halifax Town 20 September 1954 (fee £2,500); Prescot Cables July 1956.
Bill Watkinson's record with Stanley was quite

outstanding, as he managed to maintain a consistent striking rate, despite receiving scant support. He began with Liverpool, scoring on his debut at Villa Park, and in six matches at the end of season 1946-7 helped the Reds to win the League Championship, five wins and one draw clinching the title. He cost Stanley what was a record fee at that time and began by scoring three goals in his first four matches. In season 1951-2 he netted 22 League and one FA Cup goal and led the goalscoring charts by a wide margin. He was top marksman again in 1952-3, but in the close season it was revealed that he was suffering from a slipped disc and an operation in September 1953 kept him out of action for a lengthy spell. In September 1954 he was selected as a late replacement for the injured Ian Brydon in a home game against Oldham Athletic, and hit an 18-minute hat-trick. His senior career ended with Halifax Town, for whom he scored 24 goals in 60 appearances.

WATSON, J(ames) William **1923-25**
Half-back. 5ft 8½in; 11st 3lb.
Born: Darwen, 1896 (July quarter).
Debut v Darlington (a) 25 August 1923.
Appearances: 72; Goals: 3.
Career: Darwen Olympic; Blackburn Rovers 1 September 1920; STANLEY 30 May 1923; Clitheroe August 1925; Darwen cs 1926 to cs 1928.
William Watson played in 11 First Division matches for Blackburn Rovers in season 1920-21. He was at left-half in most matches, following his debut in March 1920. In an unfortunate start to the following term, he was injured in a pre-season practice match and was on the side-lines for two months, and then was unable to win back a first-team place. Joining Stanley, he gave good service for two seasons. Usually from right-half, he showed an immense capacity for work. His fearless tackling made him a commanding figure in the defence and, although his goals were infrequent, he twice celebrated New Year's Day, in 1923 and 1924, by scoring in Stanley victories. He left Peel Park in 1925 and joined several other ex-Reds in Clitheroe's initial season of Lancashire Combination football. He later captained Darwen for two seasons.

WATSON, Thomas Linton **1931-32**
Centre-forward. 5ft 8½in; 11st 6lb.
Born: Chester-le-Street, 1912 (October quarter).
Debut v Rochdale (a) 29 August 1931.
Appearances: 19; Goals: 9.
Career: Shiney Row Swifts; Grimsby Town 10 January 1931; STANLEY 24 June 1931; Rochdale 6 August 1932 to May 1933.
Tom Watson had only a sojourn in senior football, despite an impressive striking rate which saw him net 15 goals in 37 League appearances. He figured briefly with Grimsby Town Reserves before joining Stanley where he began in sparkling form, averaging a goal-a-game in his first five matches. His form deserted him in mid-season, however, and he lost his place in a reshuffle to accommodate the newly-signed Bill Jones (*qv*). Watson was one of six players granted a free transfer by Stanley in April 1932 and he joined Rochdale in the summer. On 3 September 1932 he netted four of Rochdale's goals in a 6-2 win against York City. It was Rochdale's first win since 7 November in the previous year and ended a barren spell of 28 League matches without a victory. It must have delighted the Willbutt's Lane faithful, but for Watson it proved an isolated success, as he was released at the end of the season, having appeared in only seven League matches.

WATSON, William **1925-26**
Half-back. 5ft 9½in; 11st 10lb.
Born: Kirkdale, 11 September 1890. Died: Southport, 1 September 1955.
Debut v Walsall (a) 29 August 1925.
Appearances: 6.
Career: All Saints Wennington Road School; Blowick Wesleyans; Southport Central amateur 1907, signing professional 1908; Burnley 26 March 1909; STANLEY player-coach to reserve team 28 May 1925; Blackburn Rovers coach from November 1926.
International honours: 3 England caps, and one Victory International appearance in 1919.
Representative honours: 5 appearances for the Football League.
Club honours: Burnley, FA Cup winners 1914, Football League champions 1921.
One-third of one of the most celebrated half-back lines in the game's history, Halley, Boyle and Watson, the trio who helped Burnley to win the FA Cup in 1914, and the League Championship in 1921. Bill Watson cost Burnley £250 in 1909, a great deal of money for an 18½-year-old in those days. It proved to be a wonderful investment, as he stayed for 16 years at Turf Moor. He appeared in every match when Burnley set up a new record of 30 undefeated League matches in 1920-21 and altogether appeared in 346 League matches, scored 18 goals, and was awarded three

benefits. Engaged as player-coach to Stanley's reserve team, he additionally appeared in six first-team games, ending his Football League career on a winning note at Peel Park on 3 April 1926, when Crewe Alexandra were beaten 2-0. The son of a high-diving champion, Watson was also a swimmer and a cricketer. A talented batsman, he had headed the Southport League averages and later served on the committee of the same competition. Engaged in the ironmongery trade and as a painter and decorator, he also served as a Liberal councillor in Southport.

WATSON, William Thomas **1933-34**
Outside-left. 5ft 8in; 11st 6lb.
Born: Morpeth, 16 March 1899. Died: Littleborough, Lancashire, 5 April 1969.
Debut v Stockport County (a) 26 August 1933.
Appearances: 25; Goals: 3.
Career: Blyth Spartans; Ashington 4 August 1923; Carlisle United 14 June 1928; Rochdale 6 August 1932; STANLEY 26 June 1933 to May 1934.
William Watson's senior career began with Ashington, the most northerly of the clubs in the Northern Section of the Third Division. He was a fixture in their team, averaging 40 appearances per season in a five-year stay. He then spent four seasons with Carlisle United, scoring 17 goals in 31 appearances in 1931-2. He was leading goalscorer in a season with Rochdale before joining Stanley. Although at the veteran stage, Watson had plenty of good football left, and it was mainly a lack of speed which prevented him from being a regular in the side. He completed his 400th Football League appearance with Stanley, all of his football being played in the Northern Section of the Third Division. His aggregate career figures were 406 appearances and 89 goals.

WEBSTER, Richard **1937-39 & 1945-51**
Half-back, later full-back. 5ft 9in; 11st 8lb.
Born: Accrington, 6 August 1919. Died: Accrington, 11 October 1979.
Debut v Tranmere Rovers (a) 22 January 1938.
Appearances: 227; Goals: 3.
Career: Accrington Schoolboys; Baxenden Rovers; Woodnook Amateurs; STANLEY amateur 6 May, signing professional 18 November 1937; Sheffield United 14 January 1939 (fee £1,000); STANLEY, Burnley; Rochdale and Blackburn Rovers (wartime guest) returned to STANLEY cs 1945 (fee £800), retired due to injury July 1951.
A prolific goalscorer at centre-forward for Accrington Schoolboys, Dick Webster joined Baxenden Rovers on leaving school. He then moved to Woodnook Amateurs before joining Stanley as a left-half. Despite being introduced at a time when the club's playing resources were at their lowest ebb, he nevertheless managed to shine in a very poor side and was quickly snapped up by Sheffield United. After returning to Peel Park as a guest player during wartime football, he was re-signed by Stanley, for a then record fee of £800. Appearing mainly at full-back, he clocked up 186 post-war appearances. Despite having played in 42 matches in 1950-51 season, he decided to retire, having been troubled by a persistent groin injury. He was at once elected vice-president of the Oswaldtwistle branch of Stanley's Supporters' Club. In March 1954, he shared a benefit match with Dennis Smith and Tommy Butler. Dick Webster ran a local plumbing business until 1974 and later was a technician with Hyndburn Council.

WHALLEY, Harold **1946-47**
Outside-left.
Born: Nelson, 4 April 1923.
Debut v Tranmere Rovers (h) 7 December 1946.
Appearances: 3.
Career: Barnoldswick Town; STANLEY amateur 6 December 1946 to May 1947.
Harold Whalley was one of three new players brought to Peel Park by manager Hacking in early December 1946. With a heavy Christmas programme looming and the team second from the bottom of the table, Whalley joined Bert Robinson and Robert Keating as newcomers into Stanley's first team. The trio made their debuts in the same match, but all three had been discarded before the month was out. Whalley provided the opening for Stanley's winner, two minutes from time, in the 2-1 victory against Tranmere Rovers. He did less well in his second appearance, however, missing two acceptable openings in the 3-1 defeat by Barrow at Peel Park.

WHITE, William **1953-54**
Goalkeeper. 6ft; 12st 3lb.
Born: Clackmannon, 25 September 1932.
Debut v Carlisle United (h) 28 September 1953.
Appearances: 18.
Career: Motherwell; STANLEY 3 August 1953; Mansfield Town 26 May 1954; Derby County 1 September 1955 (temporary transfer); Mansfield Town 28 September 1955 to May 1956; Bacup Borough cs 1956 to 1958.
A month after signing for Stanley, Willie White began working as a miner at Huncoat Pit, as part of his

National Service. He had been a colliery worker in Scotland before coming to Lancashire, so that training between shifts was not a new experience for him. An early Football League debut came when first-team goalkeeper Joe Henderson injured a hand in a match at Bradford City in late September 1953. In a run of six matches he conceded 14 goals and then lost his place. He regained it within a matter of weeks and during December and January gave some sound displays, but was deposed again when Jimmy Jones was signed from Lincoln City. White played little League football after leaving Stanley, appearing in three games for Mansfield Town and three whilst on a temporary transfer to Derby County. An injury sustained at work ended his career in non-League football in 1958.

WHITTAKER, Thomas **1925-31**
Full-back. 5ft 8½in; 11st 3lb.
Born: Boothstown, Lancashire.
Debut v Walsall (a) 29 August 1925.
Appearances: 221.
Career: Astley Bridge; Skelmersdale United; Darwen; STANLEY 30 May 1925; Stalybridge Celtic May 1931; Rossendale United June 1933.
When Stanley signed Tom Whittaker he was on Darwen's retained list. The move cost the Peel Park directorate a fine of £50, but they could never have regretted it. In six seasons as Stanley's left-back he had a run of 131 consecutive appearances, from 13 November 1926 until 24 September 1929. He also appeared in 99 consecutive matches with Jimmy Armstrong as his full-back partner. In over 200 outings, one of his very best displays was made in Stanley's epic third round FA Cup tie against Bolton Wanderers at Burnden Park. In a match which had several internationals on view, his display was not surpassed by any player on the field. A cool and resourceful defender with a strong tackle, after robbing an opponent he would invariably dribble the ball a few yards whilst scanning the position before deciding where best to place his clearance.

WHYTE, George **1929-31**
Wing-forward or half-back. 5ft 9in; 11st 3lb.
Born: Cowdenbeath, 24 March 1909.
Debut v Nelson (h) 24 September 1929 (scored one goal).
Appearances: 73; Goals: 15.
Career: Dunfermline Athletic amateur season 1927-8; Rhyl Athletic cs 1928; STANLEY 9 July 1929; Lincoln City 19 June 1931; Gainsborough Trinity cs 1939.
Club honour: Lincoln City, Third Division North champions season 1931-2.
Originally signed as an outside-left, George Whyte proved to be a much more effective wing-half. He was a fine striker of the ball, effective from the penalty-spot and on one occasion scoring from 60 yards against Doncaster Rovers. Within the space of one week in September 1930, he converted four penalty-kicks, two in a Lancashire Senior Cup tie against Nelson at Seedhill, and two against Barrow in a League match at Peel Park. He scored from the spot in his final game for Stanley, a 5-3 win against Lincoln City. One month later, he joined the Imps and was awarded a benefit during a seven-year stay. In four consecutive seasons from 1934-38 he did not miss a single League match. His total career figures truly reflected his consistency. In ten seasons of League fare, he appeared in 369 matches and scored 41 goals.

WILDE, James F. **1921-22 & 1923-24**
Full-back. 5ft 10½in; 11st 10lb.
Born: Tinsley, Sheffield.
Debut v Crewe Alexandra (h) 10 September 1921.
Appearances: 34.
Career: Rotherham Town; Burnley 9 June 1914; Reading May 1920; STANLEY 8 September 1921 to May 1922; re-signed 23 November 1923 to May 1924.
In Stanley's initial Third Division campaign, their regular full-back pairing of Kay and Wilde was the equal of any in the section. Unfortunately, before the

season was out, both were side-lined with serious injuries. Wilde met with knee ligament damage which kept him out of football for over a year, from the 1922 close season to November 1923. Jimmy Wilde was a reserve full-back with Burnley, his only League appearance coming in October 1914. He joined Reading in May 1920 and after one season was placed on the transfer list with a fee of £400 on him. After appeals, the fee was removed and Stanley signed him. One glimpse of his playing style was revealed in a February 1922 match report which noted that 'Wilde showed a rare turn of speed, cleared soundly and extricated the ball from some dangerous places'.

WILLIAMS, Emlyn **1948-49**
Full-back. 5ft 10in; 11st 8lb.
Born: Maesteg, Glamorgan, 15 January 1912.
Debut v Doncaster Rovers (h) 27 December 1948.
Appearances: 15.
Career: Buxton Town; Barnsley 6 October 1936; Preston North End 15 June 1939; Barnsley 21 April 1948; STANLEY as player-coach 24 December 1948 to May 1949.
Club honour: Barnsley, Third Division North champions, season 1938-9.
An experienced and great-hearted defender, Emlyn Williams began as a left-back with Barnsley but became a centre-half with Preston North End after the war. In season 1938-9 he played excellently in 41 matches for Barnsley, who won the Third Division North championship. They equalled the previous tally of 67 points and their goal-difference was 94-34. A brief return to Oakwell in April 1948 preceded his move to Stanley. It was felt that Williams would fill a much-needed want in the team, that of an experienced defender and leader on the field of play. Stanley had won only four out of 22 matches when he arrived and his influence was immediately apparent on his debut, a 2-0 win against third-placed Doncaster Rovers. The team were successful in pulling away from the foot of the table before the season's close, but an unexpected name on the open-to-transfer list was that of Emlyn Williams. His sojourn as player-coach having lasted a little over four months.

WILLIAMSON, William Gallacher ('Tim') **1931-32**
Inside-forward. 5ft 9in; 11st 6lb.
Born: Pollokshaws, Glasgow, 7 April 1900.
Debut v Rochdale (a) 29 August 1931.
Appearances: 27; Goals: 14.
Career: Glencraig Rovers; Lochgelly United; Broxburn United; Heart of Midlothian 13 May 1922; Portsmouth 3 October 1924; Clyde; Hamilton Academical 27 November 1925; Dunfermline Athletic 20 January 1927; Crystal Palace 25 May 1927; Dunfermline Athletic 18 November 1927; Ebbw Vale September 1928; Clyde later in season 1928-9; Shirebrook July 1929; Dundee United season 1930-31; STANLEY 16 July 1931; Southport 9 March 1932; Rochdale 13 October 1932 to 20 February 1933; Alloa Athletic 1934-5; Leith Athletic; Belfast Distillery; Montrose 1937-8.
Representative honour: Welsh League v Irish League 6 October 1928.
Tim Williamson, one of soccer's happy wanderers, joined Stanley from Dundee United, for whom his 25 goals in season 1930-31 materially assisted their promotion to Division One of the Scottish League. A virile attacker, clever and strong on the ball and with a great shot, he headed Stanley's goalscoring charts despite leaving in March 1932 to join Southport. His 15 goals included four in one match against Wrexham on Christmas Day, whilst earlier in the same month he had recorded a hat-trick against Rotherham United in a first-round FA Cup replay. Williamson had the unusual distinction of serving in the Army in both world wars. Successfully posing as an 18-year-old, although he was only 16, he enlisted in the Black Watch and saw action on the Somme. He served in the Medical Corps in World War Two and was severely wounded, spending three years in hospital with back and internal injuries. After a playing career which took in clubs in England, Scotland, Ireland and Wales, he returned to Scotland and held coaching appointments with Lochgelly Albert, Lochgelly Violet (where he coached Billy Liddell). Crossgates and Bowhill Rovers.

WILSON, George Wilfred **1935-37**
Full-back. 5ft 8in; 11st 10lb.
Born: Arlecdon, Cumberland, 1907 (January quarter).
Debut v Lincoln City (a) 31 August 1935.
Appearances: 73.
Career: Workington; Stockport County 14 June 1934; STANLEY 16 July 1935 to May 1937.
A collier who was a product of North-Eastern League football, George Wilson fully atoned for his lack of inches by clever anticipation coupled with bulldog tenacity. He had a fine season in 1935-6, missing only one match. Despite being slightly less consistent in

1936-7, he missed only ten matches, returning regularly to the side after Maurice Reeday's transfer to Leicester City. George Wilson returned to the mines after finishing with football.

WILSON, James Murray **1949-50**
Inside-forward.
Born: Saltcoates, Ayr, 19 March 1923.
Debut v York City (a) 1 October 1949.
Appearances: 4.
Career: Queen of the South; Dundalk (Ireland) 1948-9; STANLEY 26 July 1949 to May 1950.
Representative honour: League of Ireland v Scottish League 29 September 1948 at Ibrox Park, Glasgow.
Jim Wilson had an unfortunate start with Stanley, as he suffered a groin strain in his first reserve-team match and did not make his first-team debut until October 1949. Scottish-born but signed from Irish football, Wilson did extremely well with Dundalk in 1948-9, being the second-highest goalscorer. He was rewarded with a place in the League of Ireland team, whose visit to Ibrox Park attracted an attendance of 57,600 spectators. During manager Porter's first season in charge, Wilson was one of several inside-forwards tried and discarded up to the mid-season point. Afer this, a more settled formation emerged with Walter Keeley and Andy Dolan occupying the inside berths.

WILSON, John **1948-50**
Inside-forward. 5ft 8in; 11st 6lb.
Born: Airdrie, Lanarkshire, 29 October 1916.
Debut v Halifax Town (a) 2 October 1948.
Appearances: 28; Goals: 1.
Career: Glasgow Celtic; Chesterfield 18 May 1939; Ballantyne Juniors; Hamilton Academical and Cowdenbeath (wartime guest); Oldham Athletic 25 July 1947; STANLEY 2 October 1948 (fee £650) to 31 July 1950.
Schemer-in-chief of Stanley's attack, John Wilson's ball-control and adroit passing skills were capable of throwing the best defences into disarray. All too often, however, there was no one to take advantage of his prompting, as Stanley sadly lacked an opportunist. As a pre-war player, Wilson was approaching the veteran stage when he joined Stanley and his appearances were restricted by injuries, notably a groin strain which kept him out for some time towards the close of season 1948-9. During the war he helped Ballantyre Juniors to victory in the Hampden Park Cup.

WILSON, Joseph Henry **1946-51**
Full-back. 5ft 11in; 11st 12lb.
Born: Manchester, 17 May 1925.
Debut v Rochdale (h) 5 October 1946.
Appearances: 109; Goals: 4.
Career: Goslings FC: Manchester United 22 August 1941; STANLEY 1 October 1946 (after appearances as a wartime guest player during seasons 1944-5 and 1945-6); Buxton 1951-2.
A product of Goslings FC, a famous Manchester nursery, Joe Wilson began during the war with Manchester United, but found more outlet for his skill when he joined Stanley. He first appeared at Peel Park as a wartime guest player, and manager Hacking was successful in bringing Wilson to Stanley on a permanent basis in October 1946. Usually seen at left-back, he proved a strong stopper and a hard worker and in his final season proved exceptionally versatile in occupying the centre-half role and finally the centre-forward position. As attack leader he scored three goals in five matches, netting against Gateshead in his final appearance at Peel Park in a 2-2 draw, on the final Saturday of season 1950-51.

WILSON, Norman Henry **1926-27**
Half-back. 5ft 10in; 11st 8lb.
Born: Bishop Auckland, *c.*1900.
Debut v Crewe Alexandra (h) 25 September 1926.
Appearances: 32.
Career: Blyth Spartans; Dundee cs 1924; Bury 12 May 1925; STANLEY 21 September 1926 (fee £250); Aldershot Town player-coach June 1927.
Norman Wilson first came to the fore with Blyth Spartans in the 1922-3 season, when they were runners-up for the North-Eastern League championship, and also reached the first round of the FA Cup. One of only two Englishmen to be recruited by Dundee for season 1924-5, he played in six matches before joining Bury, at that time a leading First Division club, in May 1925. He had not appeared at senior level when Stanley recruited him, after they had taken only three points from the opening seven fixtures of the 1926-7 season. Wilson missed only three matches in the League and appeared in all the season's FA Cup ties, which saw Stanley reach the fourth round for the first time. Despite the Cup run, League form had been erratic and a dreadful record away from home (only one win) saw them re-election candidates for the first time. Wilson left Peel Park in the close season to join the fledgeling Aldershot Town club, for their first season in the Eastern Section of the Southern League.

WINSKILL, William **1928-29**
Inside-forward. 5ft 10in; 11st 7lb.
Born: Salford, 1906 (January quarter).
Debut v Carlisle United (h) 25 August 1928.
Appearances: 5.
Career: Adelphi FC; Manchester North End; Manchester City amateur 10 November 1924, signing professional 16 January 1925; Ashton National; Congleton Town 1927-8; STANLEY 8 May 1928 to May 1929.
Bill Winskill scored 40 goals for Congleton in season 1927-8, and it was hoped that he would supplement Jack Parkin as a scoring force in Stanley's attack. After appearing in the opening four fixtures, three of which were lost, he was deposed by John Chadwick. Winskill made only one more League appearance, at right-half against Ashington in March 1929. The *Accrington Observer* commented: 'Winskill made a good deputy, his one weakness being a lack of resource in tackling, but he made capital use of the ball when he secured it'. Winskill's father was a Rugby League player with the Broughton Rangers club.

WINTERBOTTOM, Dennis Trevor Wilson **1951-52**
Centre-half. 6ft 1in; 11st 8lb.
Born: Glossop, 23 October 1928.
Debut v Stockport County (h) 1 September 1951.
Appearances: 12.
Career: Stalybridge Celtic; STANLEY 18 June 1951 to May 1952.
A tall, willowy centre-half, whose outstanding aerial

ability and long, raking stride effectively tightened Stanley's defensive lines in the early months of 1951-2. Dennis Winterbottom's opportunity had arisen after the first-team pivot, Colin Senior, had broken an arm in the first month of the campaign. Ironically, he only lost his place through illness, playing his last senior match in December 1951. It was a sad loss to both club and player, as Winterbottom's League career did not extend beyond his dozen appearances with the Reds.

WOODHEAD, Dennis **1948-49**
Outside-left. 5ft 7in; 10st 5lb.
Born: Huddersfield, 2 September 1924.
Debut v Darlington (a) 21 August 1948.
Appearances: 6.
Career: Bradford City amateur, signing professional 10 January 1948; STANLEY 6 May 1948 to May 1949.
A free transfer signing from Bradford City, Dennis Woodhead made his Football League debut with Stanley. A short but strongly-built winger, Woodhead brought neatness and shooting power to the left wing in pre-season trials. He began 1948-9 season as first-team outside-left, but after five games in which only two points were gathered, he was deposed. Three weeks later, the return of an old Peel Park favourite, Reg Edwards, effectively tied up the outside-left position for the remainder of the season.

WOODS, William **1950-51**
Inside-forward. 5ft 8in; 10st 12lb.
Born: Farnworth, Lancashire, 12 March 1926.
Debut v Bradford City (h) 11 November 1950.
Appearances: 3.
Career: Moss Grove; Rochdale April 1945; Bradford 18 January 1947 (fee £4,500); Rochdale 13 January 1949 (fee £1,000); Barrow 4 November 1949 (fee £1,000); Crewe Alexandra 29 July 1950; STANLEY 11 November 1950 to 16 April 1951.
Originally recruited by Rochdale just prior to VE Day in 1945, Billy Woods outstanding form in the FA Cup in season 1946-7 induced Second Division Bradford to pay £4,500 for the flame-haired inside-forward. Two years and five senior appearances later, he left Park Avenue to return to Rochdale for a bargain fee of £1,000. Some ten months later he left Rochdale for the last time to join Barrow. Stanley obtained his services from Crewe Alexandra, where he had not appeared in the League side. The transfer involved both Don Travis and Sam Parker moving to Gresty Road and, as Woods played in only three League matches for Stanley in a five-month stay, it was the Railwaymen who appeared to come best out of the transaction.

WORTHINGTON, William **1928-29**
Inside-forward.
Debut v Ashington (a) 2 March 1929.
Appearances: 2.
Career: STANLEY amateur 16 December 1928; Stalybridge Celtic May 1929.
Bill Worthington worked hard and usefully on his Stanley debut at Ashington. The Reds were twice in arrears but fought back well to win a share of the points in a 2-2 draw. It was only the fourth point gained in away matches, but Worthington was back in the Combination side a week later, when George McLoughlin was recovered from injury. In a second senior outing, again brought about by injuries to first-team players, Stanley lost 4-1 at Wrexham in a match played over the Easter holiday period. Worthington was not retained in a virtual 'clean sweep' of reserve-team players, only R.Haworth, H.Haworth and A.Moon being offered terms. He moved to Stalybridge Celtic and made a good start, scoring twice on his debut against Chester Reserves in a 5-4 win.

WRIGHT, Archibald Watson **1954-57**
Inside-forward. 5ft 6in; 11st 3lb.
Born: Glasgow, 23 November 1924.
Debut v Southport (h) 21 August 1954.
Appearances: 80; Goals: 27.
Career: Rutherglen; Glencairn Juniors; Hamilton Academical 1946-7; Clyde 1947-8 (fee £6,000); Falkirk 1949-50; Blackburn Rovers 26 May 1951 (fee £10,000); Grimsby Town 27 July 1953; STANLEY 7 June 1954 (fee £1,000); Netherfield cs 1957; Horwich RMI manager 1960; Airdrieonians manager February 1963.
International honour: Scotland Schoolboys.
Club honour: Clyde, Scottish Cup runners-up 1949.

Archie Wright caught the eye of Blackburn Rovers when he played in a friendly match for Falkirk at Ewood Park. The former Ibrox Park ball-boy found only limited opportunities during his two seasons with the Rovers, despite his return of ten goals in 22 League outings. Wright joined Stanley from Grimsby Town, manager Galbraith's previous club, and he filled the role of main schemer in Stanley's attack for two seasons, eventually losing his place to Paddy Sowden. An astute and quick-thinking link man, Wright did much to help Stanley finish as runners-up in 1954-5 and to finish third a season later. During the war he served in Air-Sea Rescue launches and later in France, Belgium and Germany. He represented BOAR in Services football.

WRIGHT, James F. **1947-48**
Goalkeeper.
Born: Whitfield, Lancashire, 19 February 1924.
Debut v Darlington (a) 18 October 1947.
Appearances: 1.
Career: Bury Amateurs; STANLEY amateur September 1947 to May 1948.
Jim Wright was spotted by Stanley whilst playing in Bury junior football and within a few weeks he was given his Football League debut. First given a trial in the Lancashire Combination team in September 1947, Wright did so well that he took over from Reg Savage, the former Leeds United and Nottingham Forest veteran goalkeeper, as first choice for Stanley Reserves. When injury prevented Bill Harris from appearing at Darlington, Wright was selected for his League debut. Alas, he did not recover his composure after conceding an early goal and spent an altogether anxious 90 minutes which ended in a 3-1 defeat for his side.

WRIGHT, Norman **1931-33**
Outside-left. 5ft 8½in; 10st 10lb.
Born: Ushaw Moor, Co Durham, 27 December 1908.
Died: Newcastle upon Tyne, 30 January 1974.
Debut v Rochdale (a) 29 August 1931 (scored one goal).
Appearances: 78; Goals: 21.
Career: Esh Winning; Grimsby Town season 1928-9; Crewe Alexandra 14 June 1930; STANLEY 13 July 1931; Manchester City 20 May 1933; Watford 31 May 1935 to May 1936.

Stanley's only ever-present player in his first season, Norman Wright began in Northern League football, was a junior with Grimsby Town and joined Stanley after a season with Crewe Alexandra. A stylish, direct and thrustful winger, Wright scored on his debut for Stanley and repeated the feat with Manchester City. He was unable to secure a first-team place at Maine Road, however, due to the brilliance of Eric Brook.

WRIGHT, Tom Birtles **1947-48**
Half-back. 5ft 10½in; 10st 12lb.
Born: Glossop, 11 January 1917.
Debut v Mansfield Town (a) 15 November 1947.
Appearances: 20; Goals: 4.
Career: Droylsden; Manchester City 11 June 1937; Altrincham; Hull City 11 July 1947; STANLEY 9 October 1947; Stalybridge Celtic 6 November 1948.
Tom Wright became a professional with Manchester City in 1937, but he did not make his Football League debut until ten years later with Stanley. Like so many footballers of his generation, the war totally disrupted his career. He made a quiet start with Stanley, appearing once as a stand-in at left-half shortly after signing, and then playing in the Combination team until late February 1948. At this point, he was tried at outside-left in the League team and responded by scoring twice at Halifax Town and once at Gateshead in his first two appearances on the wing. After playing in only six League matches in the following term, he was allowed to move to Stalybridge Celtic, having requested a move to a club nearer his home.

WYPER, (H)enry Thomas Hartley **1925-27 & 1933-34**
Outside-right. 5ft 7in; 10st 7lb.
Born: Calton, Glasgow, 8 October 1900.
Debut v Hartlepools United (a) 16 September 1925.
Appearances: 90; Goals: 21.
Career: Glengarnock Vale; Southport amateur 30 December 1921, signing professional 19 January 1922; Motherwell cs 1922; Southport 22 November 1922; Wallasey United September 1923; Burscough Rangers 1924-5; STANLEY 27 August 1925; Hull City 4 February 1927 (fee 'over £500'); Arsenal (trial) August 1928; Charlton Athletic 7 September 1928; Queen's Park Rangers 13 June 1931; Chester 26 February 1932; Bristol Rovers 21 January 1933; STANLEY 19 May 1933; Crewe Alexandra 1 March 1935; Rossendale United 1935-6.
Club honour: Charlton Athletic, Third Division South champions, season 1928-9.
Tommy Wyper applied for a trial with Stanley after he had initially failed to secure a place in Southport's League side. He soon struck up a productive right-wing partnership with Jimmy Gee, becoming a firm favourite with Stanley's supporters. A lightweight winger with sleek black hair and twinkling feet, he scored ten goals in 36 appearances in his first season. He was transferred to Hull City in the following term, but five years (and five clubs) later, he returned to play for Stanley. He also took over the tenancy of the Peel Park Hotel, opposite the Stanley ground. He later had a boarding house in Bournemouth and by 1951 had emigrated to Australia.

YATES, Thomas **1935-39**
Half-back.
Born: Blackburn, 1915 (January quarter).
Debut v Darlington (h) 26 September 1935.
Appearances: 3.
Career: Blackburn junior football; STANLEY amateur 15 August 1935 to September 1939.
Representative honour: Lancashire Amateurs.

International trial honour: North v South (Amateur) at Ilford, October 1936.
An amateur in Stanley's reserve team for four seasons, Tom Yates' style was all-action, as instanced by one match report: 'Young Yates grew red in the face with zealous striving, but his work was not praiseworthy for its enthusiasm alone'. A grandson of Jimmy Forrest, the famous Blackburn Rover who won five FA Cup medals, Yates had an outstanding season in 1936-7. He made several appearances for Lancashire Amateurs, played in an Amateur international trial and also made his Football League debut.

YOUNG, John **1929-30**
Full-back. 5ft 10in; 12st 8lb.
Born: Whitburn, Co Durham.
Debut v Halifax Town (a) 28 September 1929.
Appearances: 4.
Career: Whitburn Villa; South Shields; Southend United 1919-20; West Ham United 29 April 1920 (fee £600); Queen's Park Rangers 10 May 1926; STANLEY 15 August 1929, retired 17 February 1930.
Club honour: West Ham United, FA Cup runners-up 1923.

Briefly associated with Stanley at the close of a distinguished career, Jack Young actually requested his release in February 1930 to enable him to take over a farm near Sunderland. He began his career as a winger and joined West Ham United in that capacity before being successfully converted into a defensive role. His 124 League and 14 FA Cup games for the Hammers included an appearance at left-back in the first Wembley Cup Final and 25 League appearances in the same season, when West Ham won promotion to the First Division as runners-up to Notts County. Two seasons as captain of Queen's Park Rangers followed, but his final spell in League football saw him unable to dislodge Tom Whittaker, Stanley's long-serving left-back.

YOUNG, Jerry L. **1936-39**
Outside-right.
Born: Farnworth, near Bolton, 1915 (April quarter).
Debut v Chester (h) 21 November 1936.
Appearances: 4.
Career: Morecambe; Horwich RMI; STANLEY amateur 19 October 1936 to May 1939. Post-war assisted Horwich RMI.
Jerry Young held a good post outside of football and played as an amateur by choice. At times he was unable to get time off work to enable him to travel to away matches, but in three seasons at Peel Park he played a major role in Stanley Reserves' attack. His senior appearances were very infrequent, for during most of his stay the senior wingers were Reynolds and Mee. Nevertheless, he had a splendid Football League debut, which included his having a hand in George Pateman's winning goal against Chester. At the time, Chester were runaway leaders of the Section, and they had previously taken 17 points from Stanley in ten League meeting. An all-round sportsman, Jerry Young spent his summers playing cricket with Farnworth CC in the Bolton League.

Accrington Stanley 4 Stalybridge Celtic 2

THE sight which greeted those wending their way to Accrington Stanley's new Peel Park home was a ground of meagre furnishings and a sloping pitch. The surroundings may have been spartan, but gate receipts of £107 for this opening home encounter in the Lancashire Combination brought a smile to the faces of the committee members.

Although concern had been expressed about the rough and uneven playing surface, this opening match was in every respect an auspicious occasion for Stanley. The game was full of incident, although the Accrington team always had the edge. The Reds' attack always looked lively, whilst the defence gave a solid display throughout.

In the first half, Stanley played up the slope with the wind in their favour. Both sides made light of the conditions — a poor playing surface and strong wind — and play moved from end to end. After 20 minutes, Stanley were awarded a penalty for a foul on Adams, but Hemsley wasted the opportunity by driving the ball against the crossbar. Stalybridge, too, spurned a chance of a lead when Tetlow allowed Briggs to foil him when only the Accrington custodian stood between him and the goal.

After 30 minutes, Peel Park witnessed its first goal. Woods managed to outwit two opponents and from an acute angle he crashed the ball into the net. The Stanley fans had hardly stopped celebrating when they saw Hemsley go close to adding a second and Petrie go near to equalizing.

Whilst the first half had been entertaining, the second period was to prove explosive. The veteran former Blackburn Rovers player, George Chapman, began a succession of sweeping passes which opened up the visiting defence. It was from one of these that Benson got possession on the left and drove in a magnificent shot. The visiting goalkeeper failed to hold the ball which was quickly bustled into the net. Within minutes the ever-dangerous Petrie had pulled a goal back for Stalybridge. Disaster struck Stanley some 20 minutes into the half. Briggs left his goal to make a dash for the ball but was beaten to it by Micheson. The visiting outside-left sent over a pin-point centre and Knox had the simplest of tasks to put the ball into the unguarded goal.

The Reds now renewed their efforts to christen Peel Park with a win. They were rewarded when Chapman drove a free-kick from eight yards outside the penalty area into the net. Almost immediately Briggs did his best to squander this precious lead by misfielding a long-range effort. Fortunately for the home crowd, Micheson inexplicably put the loose ball into the net with his hands and it was left to Charlie Hemsley to calm the home nerves by sealing victory with a fourth goal.

Accrington Stanley: Briggs; Finney, Alker, Walsh, Chapman, Burgin, Woods, Adams, Hemsley, Proctor, Benson.

Stalybridge Celtic: Wood; Caldwell, Greenhalgh, Jones, Kershaw, Parkes, Knox, Tetlow, Richards, Petrie, Micheson.
Referee: F. Robinson (Blackburn) *Attendance: 3,000*

Rochdale 6 Accrington Stanley 3

ACCRINGTON Stanley's first match in the newly-created Third Division North proved to be a game of two halves. In the opening 45 minutes, Stanley coasted along and ended a goal to the good. In the second half they were hit by a goal glut and ended their first 90 minutes of League action on the wrong end of 6-3 scoreline.

Having looked impressive in the pre-season practice games, Stanley quickly began to get in their stride and put former Blackburn Rovers goalkeeper James Crabtree under early pressure. However, there was a shock in store for the 3,000 Stanley fans at Spotland, when it was Rochdale who opened the scoring. The opening blow occured in the tenth minute when Aaron Crawshaw had the misfortune to divert a Hoade centre into his own goal.

Undismayed by this early set-back, Stanley continued to dominate. Crawshaw put his bad luck behind him and gave a masterly performance at right-half, whilst Makin was prominent in initiating many of the attacking moves. After intense pressure the home defence finally cracked after 23 minutes when Hosker forced a cross from the right past Crabtree and Nuttall for the equalizing goal. The Rochdale goalkeeper was now called upon to make a succession of saves, but was beaten again after 36 minutes by Hosker. Within a minute, Hartles drove the ball into the Rochdale net. Controversially the referee ruled the goal out, claiming that another Stanley player was in an offside position.

From the start of the second half it was clear that Rochdale were a team transformed. They started at a tremendous pace and the Stanley defence found it impossible to hold them. Although Crawshaw continued in the same magnificent vein as the first half, both Newton and Baines looked completely bewildered by the situation. For 24 minutes an increasingly jittery defence kept Rochdale at bay. Then, just when it appeared that Stanley might have weathered the storm, Newton got in a tangle and Dennison equalized. Two minutes later Dennison raced toward the Stanley goal with the defence nowhere in sight. Tattersall appeared totally mesmerized and kept to his line as Dennison coolly placed the ball out of his reach.

Before the visitors had a chance to reorganize Rochdale struck again, thanks to a confrontation between Newton and Carney. The Accrington full-back tackled Carney and the latter kicked out at Newton. Showing a total lack of restraint, Newton returned the compliment and was spotted by the referee. Carney had the last laugh as he made no mistake with his spot kick.

If three goals in eight minutes was not sufficient misery for Accrington's travelling fans, Owens proceeded to walk past Newton and flash the ball out of Tattersall's reach and into the net. As Stanley tried to steady a rapidly sinking ship they gifted Rochdale with a sixth goal. The ball was with Crawshaw on the left wing when, for some reason, the Stanley players all stopped. Possibly intrigued by this new tactic, Crawshaw left the ball and walked away. To everyone's amazement the referee waved play on and Owens simply took the ball on a few yards before blasting it past an incredulous Tattersall.

With seven minutes remaining Green grabbed a consolation goal for Stanley and brought the scoring to an end. Despite the result, disappointment was tempered by the fact that Stanley had given a fine exhibition of football before their abberation in the second half.

Rochdale: Crabtree; Nuttall, Shehan, Hill, Farrer, Yarwood, Hoade, Sandiford, Dennison, Owens, Carney.
Accrington Stanley: Tattersall; Newton, Baines, Crawshaw, Popplewell, Burkinshaw, Oxley, Makin, Green, Hosker, Hartles.
Referee: A.F.Kirby (Lostock Hall) *Attendance: 8,500*

Accrington Stanley in 1921-2. Back row (left to right): G.Brennand (director), S.Pilkington (secretary-manager), Popplewell, Kay, Sloane, Wilde, Crawshaw, Unknown, J.Brown, J.Holland. Front row: Oxley, Makin, Burkinshaw, Hosker, Nellis, F.Brennand (trainer).

Match to Remember 3 — 3 September 1921

Accrington Stanley 4 Rochdale 0

LEAGUE football returned to Accrington after an absence of 28 years, on the second Saturday of the 1921-2 campaign. A return encounter with Rochdale presented Stanley with an early opportunity to extract revenge for the previous week's 6-3 defeat at Spotland. The prospect of League soccer brought the fans out in force and a crowd of over 11,000 streamed into Peel Park for Stanley's inaugural home match in the Third Division North.

Attacking up the slope, Stanley looked rather unsettled early on and allowed Owens the opportunity to run clean though the defence. As Tattersall came out to meet him, Owens was presented with an open goal when the Accrington custodian slipped. Incredibly, and to the relief of all Accringtonians, Owens pushed the ball wide of the gaping goal. This early scare awakened the home forwards and James Crabtree, the former Blackburn Rovers goalkeeper, was called upon to make a fine save from Hosker.

After 15 minutes the home side got the sort of break which often win matches. Although Crabtree made a brilliant save from Green, he was powerless to prevent Makin driving the rebound into the net before a flat-footed defence could react. The goal was rough justice on Crabtree, who had enjoyed an inspired first 45 minutes.

Having dominated much of the first half, Stanley disappointed their supporters with an insipid opening period after the break. Fortunately, Rochdale showed no signs of the form which had brought them six goals the previous week and the match developed into a rather lacklustre affair.

A disappointing half was brought to life 15 minutes after the break when Hosker registered Stanley's second goal with a low shot. This awakened Stanley from their slumbers and they again began to bombard the Rochdale goalmouth. A rasping drive by Green struck the bar as Accrington totally overwhelmed their visitors.

With Rochdale back-pedalling, the result was a formality and after 75 minutes Green found himself with the easiest of openings as he practically walked the ball into the Rochdale net. Minutes from the end, a snap shot by Green gave Stanley their fourth goal and ended a memorable day for the home club.

Accrington Stanley: Tattersall; Kay, Newton, Crawshaw, Popplewell, Burkinshaw, Oxley, Makin, Green, Hosker, Hartles.
Rochdale: Crabtree; Nuttall, Mort, Hill, Barnes, Yarwood, Hoade, Sandiford, Dennison, Owens, Carney.
Referee: A.F.Kirby (Lostock Hall) *Attendance: 11,500*

Match to Remember 4 — 24 October 1925

Wrexham 5 Accrington Stanley 6

THE journey to Wales had rarely been a happy one for Accrington Stanley. Four previous visits to Wrexham in the Football League had seen Stanley return to Lancashire pointless. Thus it was not without a certain amount of trepidation that they ventured once more into foreign territory, particulary as they had failed to score in their last three games on Welsh soil.

Accrington hearts sank after only two minutes when Goode, Wrexham's veteran inside-right, drove the ball past Holden. Both Wyper and Gee spurned early chances to equalize in a game which was being dominated by Goode and Archie Longmuir. Fortunately for Stanley, Holden was in top form while at the other end Wyper tested Wilkinson on two occasions.

On 18 minutes, Stanley were on level terms when Gummery crossed from near the left touch-line and Wyper's deflected shot fell to Jepson who promptly drove it into the net. Three minutes later, Jepson almost gave Stanley the lead but his header flashed against the crossbar. Longmuir continued to cause the visitors problems and it was from his cross that Walmsley handled. Longmuir took the penalty-kick himself and placed the ball wide of Holden.

Within two minutes Stanley were again on level terms. Jepson dribbled down the field and passed to Wyper, who eluded two opponents before crossing for Jepson to head the ball into the net. The second goal encouraged Stanley to move forward with greater determination and they began to dominate the exchanges with Gummery and Wyper dictating play. However, despite having more possession, it required a 25 yard effort from Gee to give Stanley a deserved lead. Wrexham immediately caught Accrington off guard and Longmuir equalized from a corner. As half-time beckoned, Stanley once again edged in front when Wyper scored after a Jepson effort had been blocked.

It had been a sparkling 45 minutes of football, but fans had no time to get their breath back as the second half opened with a flurry of activity. Within minutes of the restart, Gummery placed a corner neatly for Jepson to cleverly deflect into goal. The home team stormed back in an effort to reduce the two-goal deficit. Goode blotted a fine performance by blasting over from only five yards out. However, Wrexham's efforts were finally rewarded with a goal by Holland and after 72 minutes Longmuir equalized for the home team.

The game continued to be an end-to-end affair as the crowd applauded both sides and, in particular, Holden, who was enjoying an inspired afternoon in the Stanley goal. After 80 minutes, Stanley grabbed what proved to be the winner when Gee finished another fine move with a low drive.

Ironically, many of Accrington Stanley's directors had missed what was truly a match to remember. On the way to Wrexham they had been dropped off at various venues to look at potential future signings. When they were picked up on the way back many no doubt found it hard to believe what they had missed!

Wrexham: Wilkinson; Bennett, Lumberg, D.Jones, Parker, Beevor, Longmuir, Goode, J.Jones, Holland, Nock.
Accrington Stanley: Holden; Walmsley, Whittaker, Field, Martin, Rooks, Wyper, Gee, Jepson, Powell, Gummery.
Referee: L.E.Vickery (Birmingham) *Attendance: 6,095*

Match to Remember 5 — 29 January 1927

Chelsea 7 Accrington Stanley 2

A TRIP to London was always a special occasion for Stanley and the third round FA Cup tie with Chelsea in 1927 was a truly glamour occasion with over 30,000 fans in Stamford Bridge. Stanley followers dreamed of glory, but Chelsea and Mr Pinckston turned the dream into a nightmare.

From the very start the afternoon became an anticlimax when Hayes and Whittaker got in a tangle and presented Thain with the simpliest of scoring chances. A goal to the good and playing fast and open football, Chelsea literally overran Stanley in the first ten minutes. After six minutes, a right-wing cross was driven into the net by Wilson before the Stanley defence had chance to clear the ball. Three minutes later, Stanley's cup of woe was complete when Crawford tapped the ball to Wilson, who hit a glorious drive past Hayes.

Three goals in the first ten minutes was enough to put a damper on even the most optimistic of the 300 Stanleyites at Stamford Bridge. Perhaps even more worrying than the score was the ineptitude with which Stanley played. Chelsea toyed almost contemptuously with their visitors and only overelaboration in front of goal spared Stanley from a more embarassing scoreline. In fact, Chelsea's generosity in front of goal enabled their visitors to claw their way back into the match. A brilliant save by Millington prevented Clarkson from pulling a goal back, but he was powerless to prevent Powell from scoring after his initial header had hit the post. Gee and Clarkson produced further efforts and suddenly the Stanley followers gained new heart.

Chelsea responded by pressuring the Stanley goal but found Hayes in superb form. On the one occasion he was beaten, Rooks was on hand to clear off the line. At the other end, Clarkson missed a golden opportunity to bring Stanley closer to Chelsea. After 39 minutes a seemingly lost cause was revived when Wyper met Martin's centre and coolly headed past Millington. Incredibly, a game which should have been a formality was in danger of slipping away as prospects of Stanley bringing Chelsea north for a replay began to grow.

The second half began with Chelsea attacking the Stanley goal in an all-out assault to settle the tie. After 64 minutes an increasingly desperate Chelsea got the break they wanted. The ball found its way to Turnbull, who was virtually standing on the Stanley goal-line. Seemingly legitimate appeals for offside were waved away and Chelsea had a two-goal lead once more.

It was a blow which visibly drew the strength from the Stanley team. Six minutes later, Thain looked yards offside when he received a ball which was quickly transferred to Turnbull who scored goal number-five. The Stanley defence again asked in vain for an offside decision when Turnbull added a sixth goal to complete his hat-trick.

Obviously disillusioned by the decisions which had gone against them Stanley were now totally outclassed in every aspect of the game. The will to win, or even survive, had evaporated and Chelsea were able to do as they wished. Thain registered a seventh goal and it was a major surprise that Stanley avoided conceding further goals.

Chelsea: Millington; Smith, Law, Priestley, Wilding, Ferguson, Crawford, Thain, Turnbull, A.Wilson, Pearson.
Accrington Stanley: Hayes; Bell, Whittaker, N.H.Wilson, Rooks, Hughes, Wyper, Gee, Clarkson, Powell, Martin.
Referee: E.Pinckston (Birmingham) *Attendance: 30,142*

Match to Remember 6 — 5 February 1927

Accrington Stanley 7 Hartlepools United 2

SEVEN days earlier, Accrington Stanley had visited Chelsea in the FA Cup and been humiliated by a 7-2 defeat. This, coupled with heavy morning rain, meant that only 3,000 supporters gathered on the sodden Peel Park terraces for the visit of Hartlepools. A further blow to the home side had been the loss of Wyper and the return of heavy rain and high winds gave few expectations of the sort of match which followed.

Accrington Stanley in 1926. Edgar Powell (extreme right, front row) gave Stanley the lead against Hartlepools for the first time in the 11-goal thriller.

Playing up the slope in the first half, Hartlepools had the advantage of the wind and rain at their backs. Incredibly, the visitors made little attempt to adapt their game to the conditions and persisted with a close-passing game which was obviously doomed to failure on the Peel Park bog. Perhaps United were persuaded to continued with these tactics following their early success. With only five minutes gone, Boland's shot from a wide position landed in the far corner of the net with Hayes stranded at the other post.

Although the first 15 minutes had seen Hartlepools United on top in terms of possession, they had actually created very few chances apart from their early goal. An outstanding figure in the Stanley defence was Jim Tomlinson, who had been drafted in from the Reserves and was revelling in his promotion.

Gradually Stanley established a foothold on the match and, despite the wind and rain, repeatedly attacked the United goal. Indeed, John Martin should have equalized but drove the ball tamely at Little from only a few yards out. However, a few minutes before the interval, Richard Clarkson finally did the trick when he was on hand to steer a loose ball into the net after Little had stopped a long-range effort from Jimmy Gee.

Both teams appeared in a new strip after the interval with United wearing yellow striped jerseys. Eight minutes into the second half, the visitors went into a surprise lead when Myers netted from Boland's cross. The crowd began to grow restless as thoughts drifted back to the nightmare of seven days earlier.

However, the Stanley players were in no mood for capitulation and they roared back at the visiting defence. Despite the atrocious conditions the home team moved the ball about with ease. Attack followed attack as Little nervously dealt with a succession of Stanley efforts. After 55 minutes, Gee received the ball from Johnny Jepson and hit a blistering shot past Little for the equalizing goal. Four minutes later, Stanley obtained the lead for the first time when Edgar Powell beat Little with an unexpected shot.

Showing superior stamina and speed, Stanley set about their visitors with renewed vigour. A terrific shot by Jepson was parried by Little, and Clarkson was on hand to tap in number-four. Jepson soon gained a just reward for his unstinting efforts when he hit a low shot from point-blank range past the bemused Little. The Stanley centre-forward had a hand in the sixth goal when he gave a neat pass to Clarkson, who in turn passed to Gee. The winger quickly returned the ball to Clarkson, who drove it into the net.

United were now playing with the same lacklustre organization which had been a feature of Stanley's second-half performance at Chelsea. Recognizing the signs of defeat, Stanley ploughed forward to make merry at the North-Easterners' expense. After 85 minutes, Clarkson delighted the crowd by scoring the seventh goal. The spectre of Stamford Bridge had been laid to rest far quicker than anyone could have expected.

Accrington Stanley: Hayes; Bell, Whittaker, Wilson, Tomlinson, Rooks, Gee, Clarkson, Jepson, Powell, Martin.
Hartlepools United: Little; Arch, Kell, Hall, Jobson, Richardson, McClenn, Waite, Wensley, Myers, Boland.
Referee: A.Shuker (Mansfield) *Attendance: 2,877*

Match to Remember 7 — 31 December 1927

Accrington Stanley 7 Nelson 1

ACCRINGTON Stanley concluded 1927 with a memorable victory over their near-neighbours and old rivals from Nelson. Unfortunately the winter weather and a home match at Burnley meant a suprisingly low crowd turned up to watch Stanley record their second League double over Nelson.

The ground, carpeted with snow, was frostbound and slippery, yet Stanley made light of the conditions and gave a fine exhibition of attacking football. They ought to have opened their account after only ten minutes, but Frank Parry missed an opportunity through choosing to dribble rather than shoot. However, after 17 minutes John Parkin opened the scoring when he went through a stationary defence that stood appealing for an offside decision which never came.

Nelson were stunned into retaliation but found Armstrong, Whittaker, Curran and Dodds an impregnable barrier. Their cause was not helped by a disallowed goal and this disappointment was compounded a few minutes later when Reuben Butler beat Sam Warhurst to another though ball and fired it into the net.

Totally subdued, Nelson found themselves further in arrears when Parkin scored his second goal. Surprised at the ease in which a three-goal lead had been accumulated, Stanley gave Ruffell too much space as the interval approached. The Nelson forward hit a fierce shot but to his dismay the ball hit the upright. Nelson then had their one stroke of luck when the ball rebounded to Ruffell and he made no mistake with his second effort.

The second half began with Accrington in total control as Parkin ran the Nelson defence ragged. Not surprisingly it was Parkin who claimed the fourth goal with the Nelson defenders again appealing vainly for offside. This was the signal for the visitors to capitulate completely and further goals from George McLoughlin, Andrew Curran and John Martin gave Stanley a convincing victory.

Accrington Stanley: Finnigan; Armstrong, Whittaker, Carrick, Curran, Dodds, Parry, Butler, Parkin, McLoughlin, Martin.
Nelson: Warhurst; McClure, Rigg, Halliwell, Wilson, Sharpe, Bottrill, Ruffell, McGuire, Radford, Bedford.
Referee: A.Haworth (Blackpool) *Attendance: 4,207*

Match to Remember 8 3 February 1934

Accrington Stanley 0 Barnsley 9

HIGH-FLYING Barnsley went to Peel Park looking to complete a double as they stepped up their quest for the Third Division North championship. Lying third in the table and nine points ahead of Stanley, the Yorkshiremen had crushed the Reds 6-0 when the teams had met at Oakwell earlier in the season. Since that reversal, Stanley had strengthened their team and though their form remained erratic, many thought that they were capable of stretching Barnsley at Peel Park.

The first half produced plenty of entertainment and, whilst the visitors had the edge, Stanley always looked capable of causing them problems. The Accrington team had experienced an early set-back with Blight took advantage of a left-wing move to put the visitors one up. Another move down the left enabled Smith to add a second goal after 25 minutes. The goal highlighted the problems the ageing Jimmy Armstrong was experiencing in holding Barnsley's quick forwards.

However, a succession of free-kicks allowed Stanley to exert pressure on the Barnsley defence and Dodds, Leedham and McCulloch all went close to getting on the score-sheet. Just before the interval the referee came to Stanley's aid when he ruled that Pattison had been fouled as Barnsley scored what they thought was their third goal.

As the fans enjoyed the entertainment on the pitch, the fog which had drifted around Peel Park all afternoon began to thicken. Doubts were expressed as to whether the game would finish and the referee asked the players to forego the usual interval. However, three Accrington men ran off the pitch and the resumpton of play was delayed for five minutes.

With the slope in their favour, Stanley ought to have turned the game around. Instead the home supporters were to endure an all too frequent nightmare. Scarcely a minute of the half had elapsed before Barnsley increased their lead. Smith and Spence worked the ball along the line before Smith outpaced Corcoran and crossed for Andrews to crash the ball into the net.

Stanley responded with a McCulloch shot from Clare's corner but Ellis proved equal to it. Another corner saw Lennox head over the bar and for a time Stanley swarmed around the Barnsley area, threatening to reduce the arrears. Unfortunately the threat was only short-lived and after 56 minutes, Corcoran, not for the first time, was found trailing in the wake of Spence, whose cross was converted by Blight. Within 60 seconds, Spence put the finishing touch to another Barnsley move to score the fifth goal.

Any pretence of resistance crumbled as Stanley were totally overwhelmed by the visiting forwards. Only Leedham was able to bring occasional relief with neat, if ultimately futile, runs into the opposition's half of the field. On 74 minutes, Blight completed a deserved hat-trick. Two minutes later, Spence collected his second goal of the match and further goals by Blight (79 minutes) and Ashton (80 minutes) completed the rout.

Accrington Stanley: Pattison; Armstrong, Corcoran, Dodds, Stoddart, McCulloch, Jeavons, Lennox, Kelly, Leedham, Clare.
Barnsley: Ellis; Cookson, Shotton, Harper, Henderson, Whitworth, Spence, Smith, Blight, Andrews, Ashton.
Referee: H.T. Wright (Macclesfield) *Attendance: 2,814*

Match to Remember 9 17 March 1934

Accrington Stanley 8 New Brighton 0

ACCRINGTON Stanley had gone seven League matches without a win before entertaining New Brighton on a wintery Saturday afternoon in March 1934. Included in that dismal sequence was a record 9-0 home defeat at the hands of Barnsley. Little wonder that less than 1,500 people defied the rain, hail and snow to make their way to Peel Park. However, those who braved the cheerless weather were rewarded with a match which would claim a place in the record books for all the right reasons.

Playing up the slope and with the wind at their backs, Stanley made an unusually auspicious start. Barely a minute had elapsed when Henry Wyper pounced on a centre from Watson and had the goal at his mercy. Instead of shooting, he chose to tap the ball to John Cheetham, whose rather tame effort was partially saved by Bradshaw. However, before the goalkeeper could recover, Cheetham dashed in to make no mistake with his second attempt. Within a minute, a red-faced Cheetham missed a glorious opening by shooting wide. If the supporters found such early goalmouth incidents hard to believe, they were positively dumbfounded when a mazy run by Watson ended in Lennox notching a second goal.

It was hard to believe that the now-rampant Stanley was the same team which had endured such a depressing run of results. In attack, Leedham and Lennox were showing the deft, incisive footwork of which both were capable but had so rarely displayed in recent weeks. After 17 minutes, Leedham latched on to a long ball down the middle and hit a glorious drive past the bemused Bradshaw.

So one-sided had the game become that Chris Dodds and Sam McCulloch were able to leave their defensive duties and add weight to the attack. Throughout the first 45 minutes only the brilliance of the overworked Bradshaw kept Accrington at bay, but even he was powerless to prevent Cheetham adding a fourth goal before the interval. In truth, the score ought to have been five as a venomous shot by

Fred Leedham hit the rear net support with such force that it rebounded into play and deceived the referee who waved play on.

The second-half was just as one-sided as the first and Stanley again scored in the opening minute. Cheetham dribbled towards goal and evaded Bradshaw as he rushed out to score his fourth goal of the match. After 62 minutes, Accrington went further ahead when Lennox scored. Although they had netted six, the Accrington forwards were guilty of some indifferent finishing as the home team totally dominated the play.

The New Brighton forwards had little opportunity to display their finishing powers. Even then, on a rare excursion into the Stanley area Davis fluffed the simpliest of chances.

Stanley continued to create and miss chances before Leedham added a seventh. A brilliant penalty save by Bradshaw from Price appeared to have deprived Stanley of reaching eight. However, after 85 minutes a second penalty gave Armstrong the opportunity to demonstrate how spot-kicks should be taken and he created a record club victory for Stanley — a record which was destined never to be broken.

Accrington Stanley: Maidment; Armstrong, Price, Dodds, Crawshaw, McCulloch, Wyper, Lennox, Cheetham, Leedham, Watson.
New Brighton: Bradshaw; Bower, Carr, Amery, Major, McPherson, Allen, Butter, Davis, Miller, Pegg.
Referee: H. Taylor (Wigan) *Attendance: 1,429*

Match to Remember 10 — 16 January 1937

Blackburn Rovers 2 Accrington Stanley 2

AFTER disposing of two non-League teams, Accrington Stanley were given a plum tie in the third round of the FA Cup when they were paired with neighbouring Blackburn Rovers.

Stanley approached the game with the confidence of three straight wins behind them, whilst the Rovers had lost five of their previous six matches. The clubs had last met in the competiton in 1909, when Blackburn handed out a 7-1 drubbing at Ewood Park. Whilst few of those who crowded on to the 11 special trains, or joined the exodus by road, felt that Stanley could topple Blackburn, none expected a repeat of the 1909 scoreline. Over 31,000 gathered at Ewood Park to witness this local derby, even though the home side were represented by a number of men more familiar with Central League football.

The opening period was fiercely contested with the referee having to work hard to control some fairly tough tackling from the visiting defenders. After 14 minutes there was a shock for home fans when George Mee got the better of two defenders and swung over the perfect cross for Bob Mortimer to gleefully head past Pratt.

Realizing that this was going to be no formality, the home team became a little more assertive and were unlucky not to equalize when John Robertson cleared a header from Vause on the line. The increased Blackburn pressure finally brought a goal after 24 minutes. An unfortunate slip by Willis Gregg allowed Rutherford a clear run at goal and, in attempting to clear Rutherford's low shot, Joe Craven merely kicked the ball into the roof of his own net.

Accrington Stanley, 1936-7. Back row (left to right): F.Brennand (trainer), Nesbitt, Craven, Gregg, Robertson, Reeday, Andrews, Mee. Front row: Reynolds, Rivers, Mortimer, Pateman, Tyson.

Understandably, the goal knocked some of the spirit out of the visitors and for a spell it looked like Blackburn would make their extra class count. With Arnold Whiteside prompting the home attack, Stanley found themselves in a grim struggle to stay on level terms.

However, the second half got off to a sensational start when Accrington managed to snatch the lead. Once again George Mee was the instigator as he dribbled towards the Rovers area before placing the perfect centre on to Mortimer's head. The leader of the Stanley attack gratefully accepted the invitation to power a header past the unsighted Pratt.

The goal gave Stanley new-found confidence as the Blackburn players became more and more unsettled by the keen tackling of their opponents. The game was developing into a classic derby battle, with very little real football played and passes going astray with almost unfailing regularity.

If George Mee was providing most of the football for Stanley on the wing, then so too was Jack Bruton for Blackburn. After 22 minutes of the second half, Bruton slipped past two men on the right before delivering an inch-perfect cross for Fraser to head past Robertson. As the game flowed from end to end, both Mee and Bruton saw much of the ball, and their respective teammates hoped that they would hold the key to a winning goal. However, neither man was able to deliver the *coup de grâce* and the game ended in a draw with Blackburn facing a daunting trip to Peel Park. It was one of the great results in Stanley's history, and yet one which would be bettered only four days later.

Blackburn Rovers: Pratt; Lanceley, Crook, Whiteside, Christie, Pryde, Bruton, Fraser, Vause, Sale, Rutherford.
Accrington Stanley: Robertson; Gregg, Reeday, Nesbitt, Craven, Andrews, Reynolds, Rivers, Mortimer, Tyson, Mee.
Referee: G.Hewitt (St Helens) *Attendance: 31,080*

Accrington Stanley 3 Blackburn Rovers 1
(after extra-time)

OVER 11,000 people squeezed into Peel Park to watch this FA Cup third round replay between local rivals. To add spice to the affair, a plum tie at Maine Road awaited the victors and many Stanleyites believed that the local side had the perfect opportunity to snatch a piece of Cup glory.

After an impressive performance the previous Saturday, the home side were happy to remain unchanged. However, the visitors were forced into making a number of changes and included Jack Lee, an Oxford Blue and Blackburn lad who had played in the Central League team.

The home team gave their visitors the benefit of the slope in the first half and the Rovers made full use of their hosts' generosity. After only four minutes play, a right-wing cross from Sale was swept in off the post by Calladine. Within minutes, Blackburn had almost increased their lead when Robertson was called upon to beat out a drive from Sale. The Accrington defence was rocked again when a Bruton cross was blasted fractionally too high by Calladine.

However, Stanley refused to be overawed by the impressive start by Blackburn and gradually pulled themselves back into the match. A mix-up between Pratt and Christie ought to have resulted in a goal, but Bob Mortimer's shot struck the inside of the post and rebounded across the goal where Tyson could do no better than head wide.

Encouraged by the signs of panic in the Blackburn defence, Stanley began to take complete control. Wave after wave of high crosses were launched into the Blackburn area. However, Frank Christie proved to be an outstanding figure in the Rovers' defence as he headed clear a succession of dangerous crosses. Stanley became more penetrative, particularly down the right wing where Walter Reynolds and Gavin Nisbet were giving Walter Crook an unusually torrid time.

After so much pressure it was not surprising that Stanley should snatch an equalizer. Responsibility for the goal rested on the shoulders of Pratt, who allowed a low centre to slip from his grasp when under no challenge. Needless to say, Bob Mortimer was on hand to bang the ball into the back of the net.

The second half saw Accrington continue to dominate the game, although in truth they appeared to lack the skill required to break down a resolute defence. The only response from the Rovers were a couple of drives from Sale. At the other end, Reynolds continued to torture Crook and, whilst the Mee-Mortimer combination was not as effective as in the previous encounter, it did produce a Mortimer header which flashed narrowly over the bar.

As the 90 minutes drew to a close, Blackburn began to show a little more enterprise and just on time Sale netted, only to find the referee had whistled for an infringement.

The period of extra-time proved to be a trial of strength in the clinging Peel Park mud. If Stanley were wanting in finesse, extra-time was to prove they lacked nothing in fitness. The Rovers' defence finally began to show signs of flagging and after 14 minutes a rare mistake by Christie gave Mortimer the opportunity to give the home team the lead.

Urged on by the crowd, Stanley coasted through the second-half of extra-time as the visitors looked more and more incapable of changing the result. With only five minutes remaining, Rivers scored a third for Stanley and gave them one of the greatest victories in their history.

Accrington Stanley: Robertson; Gregg, Reeday, Nisbet, Craven, Andrews, Reynolds, Rivers, Mortimer, Tyson, Mee.
Blackburn Rovers: Pratt; Lanceley, Crook, Whiteside, Christie, Pryde, Bruton, Lee, Sale, Calladine, Baxendale.
Referee: G.Hewitt (St Helens) *Attendance: 11,636*

Match to Remember 12 — 31 May 1947

Accrington Stanley 8 Lincoln City 4

THE first season of League football after World War Two was a particularly long one. Having kicked-off on 31 August 1946, Accrington Stanley finally brought the curtain down on the last day of May 1947. Most Stanley fans could be forgiven for turning their thoughts to Lancashire League Cricket rather than watching the last act in another disappointing season at Peel Park. Only 2,500 people watched what turned out to be a feast of goals, the like of which Peel Park had never seen before, or indeed would see again.

The final goal tally was all the more remarkable in that there was nothing in the early stages of the game to suggest that this would be anything other than a drab end-of-season affair. In fact, Stanley started on the all-too-familiar note of defensive blundering which allowed the visitors to notch a two-goal lead in 20 minutes. Indeed, but for the heroics of George Rymer, Lincoln could well have added to their tally.

The man who rallied the home troops was the ever-reliable Walter Keeley, who began to cause panic in the visitors' defence with his dribbling and shooting ability. It was Keeley who pulled a goal back for Accrington and then Norman Smith made matters even with an opportunist goal. Indeed, Smith might well have given Stanley an interval lead but was guilty of an appalling double miss.

After the restart, Stanley unexpectedly raced into a commanding lead. Once again it was Keeley who hustled the defence and created the opportunity for Reg Edwards to put Accrington in front. This was quickly followed by a glorious through-pass by Stan Mercer which found its way to Smith. The Stanley inside-forward evaded a tackle before scoring with a shot which Footitt could scarcely have seen. Before Lincoln had time to recover, an almost identical move saw Keeley streak through and smack the ball past the goalkeeper with equal venom.

Rocked by the sudden goal blitz which Stanley had launched, Footitt and his defenders strove manfully to keep their goal intact. However, not even their best efforts could prevent Mercer from darting through to the right of goal and coolly placing the ball into the far corner of the net.

Having stormed into a 6-2 lead, the Stanley team began to sit back and allowed their visitors more and more possession. If the home side felt they were in an impregnable position, the visiting forwards were obviously not reading the same script. The Lincoln number-nine, Tom Cheetham, completed his hat-trick with goals in the 66th and 67th minutes. Suddenly, Stanley's seemingly invincible lead looked distinctly shaky.

The fans, who had already witnessed ten goals, urged the home forwards to greater efforts and Mercer relieved the pressure with two late goals. The first was a pile driver from the edge of the area and the second was an example of his usual clinical finishing when he was put clean through a spread-eagled defence. The goals signalled the end of a goal glut which gave the fans more than enough memories to see them through the close season.

Accrington Stanley: Rymer; Lynn, Wilson, Hutton, Briggs, Webster, Rothwell, Smith, Mercer, Keeley, Edwards.
Lincoln City: Footitt; Watford, Bean, Grummitt, Johnson, Owen, Davies, Hutchinson, Cheetham, Parr, Marlow.
Referee: C. Womersley (Cheshire) *Attendance: 2,504*

Match to Remember 13 — 27 November 1954

Accrington Stanley 6 Gateshead 2

GATESHEAD arrived at Peel Park with a remarkable away record — the best in the Football League. However, what should have proved an extremely close contest ended as a stroll for Stanley and a personal triumph for George Stewart.

Considering the visitors away form, home supporters could have been forgiven a howl of anguish when George Stewart missed an absolute 'sitter' after only four minutes. Fortunately, four minutes later the number-nine made amends when he put Stanley ahead. The goal stemmed from a Joe Devlin cross which both Gray and Tom Callender rose to reach. However, before either man could make contact, Stewart made a perfectly-judged leap to get the ball into the net off the inside of the post.

After 23 minutes, Harold Bodle started another move which ended in Stewart notching his second goal with a rocket-like shot. Stanley were giving a sparkling display, despite the thick mud, and cleverly used the wing areas where Devlin and Scott tore into the visiting defence. After 42 minutes, a fine dribble and centre by Archie Wright was once again met by Stewart, who headed the ball past Gray.

Although 3-0 up at half-time, Gateshead gave Stanley a shock immediately after the interval. Straight from the kick-off, a swift move down the left saw Ingham slide the ball to Anderson, who drew the home defence to the near post and crossed a low centre for Smith to tap into the empty net. However, ten minutes into the half, Stanley had once again established a three-goal cushion. A glorious run on the left wing by Les Cocker ended in a cross to the far post. Once again, George Stewart was in the perfect position to hit the ball low and true past Gray.

After 76 minutes, Stanley and Stewart went nap when the centre-forward darted in to flick a short centre past the luckless Gray. The sixth goal was not credited to Stewart, but none the less he played a major role in the build-up. Archie Wright began the move and a lovely touch by Stewart gave Cocker the opportunity to dribble round Cairns and Gray and slam the ball into the back of the net.

Outplayed and overwhelmed, Gateshead were fortunate to escape a double-figure score and only the acrobatic Gray kept the score respectable. The visitors managed to get on the score sheet in the gathering gloom when Tom Callender scored with a left-foot shot from the acutest of angles. The ball flew past Jones in the fading light and his reaction suggested that he simply had not seen it.

Naturally, George Stewart stole the headlines by becoming the first Stanley player since 1935 to score five goals in a League match. However, it was a team effort which crushed the best away record in the League and was an indication of the good times which lay ahead for Walter Galbraith's new team.

Accrington Stanley: Jones; Pirie, Ashe, Hunter, Ryden, Bodle, Devlin, Cocker, Stewart, Wright, Scott.
Gateshead: Gray; Cairns, March, J.Callender, T.Callender, Brown, Ingham, Smith, Campbell, Anderson, Oliver.
Referee: A.Holland (Barnsley) *Attendance: 6,503*

Match to Remember 14 15 November 1954

Accrington Stanley 2 Blackburn Rovers 2

WHEN Accrington Stanley took the decision to install floodlights at Peel Park, there were many who doubted the wisdom of such action by a struggling Third Division North club. However, this was the night when the decision of the Accrington directors proved totally justified. A record attendance of 17,634 poured into Peel Park for a floodlight friendly against neighbouring Blackburn Rovers.

The treacherous conditions underfoot meant that the game was never going to be a classic, but with local pride at stake, it proved a grand battle for those assembled. The opening 45 minutes confirmed the improvement which had taken place at Peel Park since the arrival of Walter Galbraith. The home team found that they had little trouble in containing their more illustrious neighbours during the opening period, but they in turn were causing all sorts of problems to the visiting defence.

After only seven minutes play, George Stewart raced through and dribbled round Reg Elvy, only to find himself facing a difficult angle to score from. Instead of shooting, he steadied himself and swung over a lovely high centre which Scott raced forward to head into the back of the Blackburn net. Hardly had the cheers died down when Stanley found themselves two up. Once again, a through-pass again set Stewart on his way but this time as Elvy came out to meet him the Accrington number-nine blasted the ball into the back of the net.

Although Blackburn were struggling to get their game together, a snap-shot by Eddie Crossan brought a magnificent save from Alf Jones at the foot of the post. However, it was Elvy who was the busier of the two goalkeepers and only a breathtaking save prevented Stewart from scoring a third goal for Stanley.

Although only a friendly, Blackburn were obviously stung by finding themselves two goals behind at the break. The second half saw them in a more determined mood as they finally got to grips with the situation. After 55 minutes, Eddie Quigley pulled a goal back when he hooked a pass from Tommy Briggs into the net. The Rovers now piled on the pressure and seven minutes later they managed to equalize. This was a somewhat fortunate goal as a clearance by John Ryden rebounded into the open and fell at the feet of Briggs. With a clear run on goal, the Blackburn goal-machine made no mistake.

The match developed into a stirring struggle in the mud and with a hint of November fog in the air. Stanley fought back strongly and could even have won the match in the final minutes but Les Cocker drove over the bar from six yards.

In the end, the result was probably a fair one, but of greater importance was

Accrington Stanley, 1954-5. Back row (left to right): Walter Galbraith (manager), Ferguson, Holliday, Farrell, Henderson, McQueen, Hunter, Ryden, Eastham, Jones, Harry Hubbick (trainer), Ashe. Front row: Devlin, McKeown, Brydon, Wright, Scott.

the fact that the largest home crowd in Accrington Stanley's history had gathered to watch a match by floodlight. It was the perfect answer to those sceptics who had mocked Stanley's pioneering efforts.

Accrington Stanley: Jones; Pirie, Ashe, Hunter, Ryden, Holliday, Devlin, Cocker, Stewart, Wright, Scott.
Blackburn Rovers: Elvy; Suart, Eckersley, Clayton, Kelly, Bell, Mooney, Crossan, Briggs, Quigley, Langton.
Referee: J. Clough (Bolton) *Attendance: 17,634*

Match to Remember 15 — 16 March 1957

Derby County 2 Accrington Stanley 2

THIS match had all the hallmarks of a classic top-of-the-table confrontation. Derby County were riding high at the head of the Third Division North, whilst Stanley were hot on their heels having not conceded a goal in their previous four matches. In fact, only three points separated the teams and Accrington had the advantage of a game in hand. On the eve of the match, Walter Galbraith sprang a surprise when he signed Scottish 'B' international Jimmy Mulkerrin from Hibernian. After arriving in Accrington in the early hours of Saturday morning, Mulkerrin had less than five hours sleep before hitting the road to Derby with the rest of the team.

A crowd of over 24,000 were at the Baseball Ground to witness what promised to be a titanic struggle. There were early scares for the home fans as Stanley began promisingly and could easily have been two up in the first six minutes. However, not to be denied, Stanley finally went ahead after only 11 minutes play. Newcomer Mulkerrin slid a clever pass out to Jimmy Anders, who neatly beat Martin McDonnell before slipping the ball square for Wattie Dick to smash a glorious 25-yard effort into the net past Terry Webster. A moment later, the industrious Mulkerrin created a chance for Anders but the winger shot hastily wide.

Stanley were in complete control for the first 20 minutes before double-Irish international Reg Ryan finally managed to prompt some life into the home team. Gradually the game shifted more and more into the Accrington half of the field and after 34 minutes the scores were level. The Derby goal was set up by Dennis Woodhead, whose cross was driven home by Albert Mays. The goal gave the home side further encouragement and two minutes before half-time, Accrington suffered a shattering blow. Again Woodhead did the damage after McNichol had made a hash of an attempted clearance. Ryan dashed into the area and receiving the ball from Woodhead blasted the home side in front.

The second half became a test of Stanley's character and the men from Peel Park passed with flying colours. The half was only four minutes old when Scott fluffed a chance to put them on level terms. However, after 21 minutes, Accrington gained the second goal that their play so richly deserved when Bert Scott hit a cracking shot past Webster. Once again the architect was Jimmy Mulkerrin, who was enjoying an inspired debut.

The home side responded by mounting a frenzied attack on the Stanley goal and the game became an end-to-end affair. As the match drew to a close, Derby came closest to snatching a winning goal. A cross from Woodhead was met by

Accrington Stanley, 1956-7. Back row (left to right): McNicol, Ashe, McQueen, Stones, Hunter, Sneddon. Front row: Scott, Sowden, Stewart, Dick, Mason.

Ray Straw, who blasted the ball toward the Stanley goal from only six yards. It looked like the winner, but to the home fans dismay, the ball hit the inside of the post and ricocheted across the goal before McNichol cleared.

The game had lived up to all expectations and Stanley had thoroughly earned their point against the eventual Third Division North champions.

Derby County: Webster; McDonnell, Barrowcliffe, Mays, Young, Davies, Powell, Brown, Straw, Ryan, Woodhead.
Accrington Stanley: McInnes; McNichol, Ashe, Hunter, Harrower, Dick, Scott, Sowden, Stewart, Mulkerrin, J.Anders.
Referee: J.V.Sherlock (Sheffield) *Attendance: 24,272*

Match to Remember 16 8 April 1957

Accrington Stanley 4 Stockport County 0

THIS was a match which Accrington Stanley had to win to keep the pressure on Derby County in the promotion race. The importance of the match was not lost on the public of Accrington and over 11,000 fans flocked to Peel Park. The fans were not to be disappointed as Stanley stretched an unbeaten run to ten games and made it five wins in a row.

The game had a sensational start when the Reds took the lead after only 30 seconds. A clearance from Eddie Hunter found Jimmy Mulkerrin on the half-way line. Dribbling upfield, the inside-forward played a one-two with Stewart before crashing the ball into the net. After seven minutes there was cause for further celebrations when Stanley went into a two-goal lead. Paddy Sowden beat left-back Seemley beautifully and sent him slithering the wrong way. Sowden then flicked the ball into the open where Stewart pounced on it and ran through to hit a long shot into the net.

After Stewart missed a glorious chance of adding a third goal, Stockport gradually fought back. The architect of much of County's good work was Bill Holden, the former Burnley forward. However, Stanley delivered the third and crucial blow after 24 minutes. A brilliant piece of inter-passing along the left between Jimmy Anders and Stewart saw the left winger flash across a centre. The ball was met by Paddy Sowden, who, diving forward at full-length, steered the ball into the roof of the net with his head.

In the face of mounting pressure, Stanley answered in the best possible way after 41 minutes. A short corner gave Anders the chance to lash in a shot from 20 yards which Stewart flicked with his head and the ball flew past Barnard into the far corner of the net. Within minutes, Mulkerrin almost added a fifth when he drove over from a pass by Anders.

The second half brought wave after wave of Stanley attacks as the County side hung on grimly. In the 75th minute, Stanley looked like going nap when Seemley handled in the area as Sowden was sneaking past him. There was a hush as Bob McNichol took the penalty, but Barnard made a remarkable save and pushed the ball clear. The second period remained goalless as the County defence escaped time and again in the wake of countless Stanley attacking moves.

The match ended with Stanley claiming another two points, but unfortunately it was the prelude to yet another disappointing run-in. After this convincing victory, Stanley managed to win only one of their remaining five games and promotion once again slipped through their grasp.

Accrington Stanley: McInnes; McNichol, Ashe, Hunter, Harrower, Dick, Millar, Sowden, Stewart, Mulkerrin, Anders.
Stockport County: Barnard; Murray, Seemley, Porteous, Wilmot, Rowland, Wilson, Moir, Holden, Jackson, Daley.
Referee: A.E.Ellis (Halifax) *Attendance: 11,266*

Match to Remember 17 — 18 April 1959

Tranmere Rovers 9 Accrington Stanley 0

WHAT ought to have been a strictly end-of-season affair ended up in the record books as Stanley experienced a harrowing record away defeat. This was Accrington's darkest hour on away soil and equalled their humiliation at the hands of Barnsley at Peel Park in 1934.

Although George Eastham had been forced to reshuffle his defence through the loss of Bob McNichol, the manager's concern over the future of the club — which brought about his resignation two months later — was well expressed in this dire performance.

The proceedings opened ominously for the visitors when Tranmere roared through their defence twice in the opening two minutes. Accrington hearts missed a few

Accrington Stanley, 1957-8. Back row (left to right): Mulkerrin, Ashe, McInnes, Dick, Tighe. Second row: Les Cocker (assistant trainer), Sneddon, Stones, Scott, Ralston, Hunter, Harry Hubbick (trainer). Front row: Snowden, Anders, Harrower, Walter Galbraith (manager), Pirie, Stewart, McNicol.

beats when John Marshall — the fourth of five men employed between the posts during March and April — completely missed a cross from the veteran Bell.

An early goal was obviously on the cards and after only three minutes play, Marshall stood transfixed as Eglington's tame header hit the net. Valiant defending by Gordon Stones could not turn the tide and after 20 minutes, Marshall dropped a low, slow-moving cross at the feet of Rowley. The Tranmere number-nine's first effort was blocked by Harrower, but he made no mistake with the rebound. If the defence looked all at sea, the forwards strove manfully to get Stanley back in the match. Both Ken Garrity and Jimmy Mulkerrin showed plenty of ideas on their recall to the team and Jimmy Anders provided his usual sparkle on the left wing. As Accrington fought their way back into the match, Payne was called upon to make great saves from Garrity, Jimmy Anders and Terry Tighe before the first half drew to a close.

The performance of Stanley's front men meant hope remained alive at half-time, despite a two-goal deficit. However, hopes of a fight-back ended after 61 minutes when Rowley capitalized on a slip by Stones and put the home side three in front. With the third goal, all attempts at resistance ended and Rowley grabbed two more goals, after 67 and 69 minutes. Incredibly, Williams had managed to squeeze a goal in between Rowley's strikes. Three goals in as many minutes left the Stanley team utterly shell-shocked.

After only three minutes respite, Sneddon had the misfortune to beat his own goalkeeper and on 79 minutes, Stones did likewise. A late goal by Finney meant Stanley had equalled their heaviest-ever loss and created a new record defeat away from Peel Park.

Tranmere Rovers: Payne; Bell, Frith, Farrell, Millington, Charlton, Finney, K.Williams, Rowley, McDonnell, Eglington.
Accrington Stanley: Marshall; Lord, Harrower, Tighe, Stones, Sneddon, H.Anders, Gibson, Garrity, Mulkerrin, J.Anders.
Referee: E.Crawford (Doncaster) *Attendance: 8,394*

Match to Remember 18 — 7 January 1961

Preston North End 1 Accrington Stanley 1

THE history of Accrington Stanley is not littered with many moments of glory in the FA Cup. Indeed, until this game at Deepdale, their most famous hour in the competition had been way back in 1937, when they had eliminated neighbouring Blackburn Rovers. However, this thrilling Cup tie was to provide the followers of Accrington Stanley with one final fleeting glimpse of Cup glory. The task facing Stanley was a daunting one, for whilst Preston were struggling in the First Division, the visitors were languishing in the Fourth Division and quietly slipping into the oblivion which would envelop them a mere 14 months hence. Even the most ardent of Accrington supporters could not have had much faith in a Cup shock.

However, after 90 minutes of thrilling football, several thousand happy Stanley fans stood and cheered the team as they trooped off at the finish. They were joined by most of the Preston followers, who heaved a mighty sigh of relief that North End had survived to fight another day.

Yet Stanley had the kind of start which could easily have drained all self-confidence. After only a few minutes play, Tommy Thompson hit a powerful drive which rattled the crossbar before being cleared by a grateful Gordon Stones. Stanley suffered a major blow after only eight minutes, when George Forrester was carried off after a collision with Mayers. The diagnosis was a dislocated elbow, but Forrester, despite great pain, insisted on having the arm strapped up and returning to the field.

The game appeared to drift further away from Stanley after 21 minutes when the home side took the lead. A harmless-looking centre from Sneddon managed to find its way between Stones and Hamilton, although McInnes looked certain to collect the loose ball. Fatally, a moment's hesitation on the goalkeeper's part allowed Tommy Thompson to dart forward and head a simple goal.

North End could have been forgiven for expecting the Stanley team to lie down and die. But within a minute of the goal, Jack Swindells and Willie Devine carved a path through the right side of the home defence. When Devine sent over an inch-perfect cross, Willie Duff was on hand to lash home a low shot which just beat the outstretched fingers of the diving Else.

Clearly shaken by the goal, the home team became more and more unsettled. A scorching drive by Duff looked goal-bound until Cunningham somehow managed to deflect it over the bar. Ferguson then dashed through the static defence only to see the ball bobble as he was poised to shoot. Rarely can a game have changed so dramatically in such a short space of time.

The inspiration behind the Stanley rival was player-manager Jimmy Harrower. The quietly-spoken Scotsman continually yelled instructions and marshalled his defence in superb fashion. It was not simply a case of a physical assault on the craftsmen from the top flight by the lower basement journeymen. Accrington had come to play good football and, after an indifferent start, they played far better than their hosts.

During the second half, Harrower changed his tactics and decided to play a little more conservatively. Packing his defence, Harrower chose to try to win the game by hitting Preston on the break. Despite the home side being given more possession, it was the acrobatic Else who was under most pressure in the second period. Indeed, a save from Swindells' downward header showed just why Else was regarded as the finest uncapped 'keeper in the country. It was a save which gave North End the chance to fight again and when they did they proved victorious.

Preston North End: Else; Cunningham, O'Neill, Fullam, Singleton, Wylie, Alston, T.Thompson, P.Thompson, Sneddon, Mayers.
Accrington Stanley: McInnes; Forrester, Harrower, Smith, Stones, Hamilton, Devine, Swindells, Hudson, Ferguson, Duff.
Referee: P.G.Brandwood (Kidderminster) *Attendance: 20,268*

Match to Remember 19 24 February 1962

Accrington Stanley 0 Rochdale 2

WHEN the Stanley team took the field, few of those watching could have imagined the significance of the occasion. On 3 September 1921, Rochdale had visited Peel

Park for Accrington Stanley's first home match in the newly-created Third Division North. Now, a little over 40 years later, they visited Accrington for what was to prove to be Stanley's last home match as a League club.

Becalmed at the foot of the Fourth Division and immersed in a financial crisis, the Accrington club saw the public rally to the latest call for support and Stanley took to the field in front of their largest home attendance for some months.

There was an early scare for the home supporters when only a brilliant point-blank save by Alex Smith prevented Richardson giving the visitors the lead. Unfortunately, Rochdale were not to be denied. After only five minutes play, Wragg beat teenage debutant Alan Gregory and crossed for Louis Bimpson to head home. After the former Blackburn favourite had opened the scoring, Stanley were lucky not to fall further behind. Deputizing for the injured Joe Walton, Gregory had a torrid opening and was fortunate to escape having a penalty awarded against him for a desperate tackle on Wragg.

Fortunately, the young full-back settled down and, along with George Forrester and the ever reliable Alex Smith, the Stanley defence held firm. In truth, though, the match was completely dominated by the Rochdale attacking players. However, as half-time approached, Stanley spurned an excellent opportunity to draw level.

Rochdale goalkeeper Ted Burgin is well-beaten and right-back Stan Milburn and centre-half Ray Aspden look on helplessly. Yet this effort by Accrington Stanley's Mike Ferguson (centre) went wide in one of the few Reds' attacks which promised any reward.

Unfortunately, efforts by Pickup and Devlin were kicked off the line by veteran full-back Stan Milburn, then Paddy Mulvey saw an effort blocked by Aspden.

The only other opportunity which presented itself to the home team came midway through the second half. Watched by scouts from at least two clubs, the hard-working Mike Ferguson managed to break through the visiting defence. With only Burgin to beat, Ferguson managed to pull his effort wide of the goal. It was a bad miss and symptomatic of Stanley's poor finishing throughout the season.

For the rest of the match, Stanley struggled to make any impression. Those who thought that the visitors' veteran full-backs might prove an Achilles' heel were sorely disappointed. Both Milburn and Winton found that they could outpace the Stanley front men with almost contemptuous ease.

The match saw the return to Stanley colours of Joe Devlin, who had first played for the club in 1953. Sadly, despite great encouragement from the crowd, the winger's speed had deserted him and like the team as a whole, he had little left to offer. The final blow was surprisingly delayed until the last minute. Once again defensive frailties allowed Ronnie Cairns, another ex-Blackburn Rovers player, to hit a blistering shot past Smith from the edge of the area. A depressing day was mercifully brought to a close and the Accrington Stanley players left Peel Park after a Football League match for the last time .

Accrington Stanley: A.Smith; Forrester, Gregory, Hamilton, Wilson, Cuddihy, Devlin, Bades, Pickup, Ferguson, Mulvey.
Rochdale: Burgin; Milburn, Winton, Bodell, Aspden, Thompson, Wragg, Cairns, Bimpson, Richardson, Whittaker.
Referee: K.Howley (Middlesbrough) *Attendance: 2,727*

Match to Remember 20 — 2 March 1962

Crewe Alexandra 4 Accrington Stanley 0

AS the Accrington Stanley players took to the Gresty Road pitch, few Stanleyites could have realized that this would be the last time the Reds would be seen in the Football League. Despite the gathering financial storm clouds, many were optimistic that Stanley would achieve their first double of the season. The last victory they had enjoyed in the League had been at Peel Park way back in October, when Crewe were the visitors. And their performance at Doncaster a few days earlier suggested that Accrington might well shock a team in the top half of the table.

Conditions for Accrington Stanley's last excursion in the Fourth Division were hardly ideal as the entire match was played during a snowstorm. However, the match began brightly for Stanley and they almost took an early lead, thanks to a Peel Park old boy. In the poor conditions, Terry Tighe totally misjudged a back-pass and had to thank Eric Barnes for clearing off the line. Alas, it proved to be a rare sortie into the Crewe area, with frost-bite proving a greater danger to Crewe 'keeper Jim Ferguson, than the Stanley forwards.

At the other end of the field, the Crewe defence was once again working overtime.

Alex Smith again showed why he was rated as one of the best goalkeepers in the Fourth Division, as he kept the home forwards at bay. Ironically, Smith, who was called upon to make three brilliant saves in the first five minutes, almost missed the match. He had to dash by car to join the team at Knutsford after missing the coach. Fortunately for Stanley, he missed little that came into the area. Bill Smith, the veteran player-coach, made a valiant effort to coax some cohesion and method into a struggling team. Unfortunately, the forwards who had sparkled only a couple of days previously, appeared totally devoid of attacking ideas.

In the face of such relentless pressure it was creditable that Accrington reached the interval only one goal in arrears. Even then, there had been a hint of good fortune about Crewe's 24th-minute opener. As Wheatley went for a centre by Leigh, he appeared to slip as he tried to control the ball with his left foot and yet somehow contrived to recover and smash a right-foot shot past Smith.

The second half produced a steady procession of chances which somehow managed to evade the Crewe forwards. However, after 65 minutes a corner by Tighe was met by a perfect header from Frank Lord to put Crewe further ahead. The beleaguered defence made a brave effort to keep their goal intact for the rest of the half. After running themselves into the ground, they finally collapsed like a pack of cards. Two goals in the last five minutes from Wheatley and Lord, although not unexpected, simply served to underline Crewe's all-round superiority.

As in their very first League match, Accrington Stanley tasted defeat in their last. Unfortunately, unlike 1921, there was no chance to make amends the following week.

Crewe Alexandra: J.Ferguson; Maloney, Leigh, Keery, Barnes, Tighe, Haydock, Connolly, Lord, Wheatley, R.Smith.
Accrington Stanley: A.Smith; Forrester, Gregory, Pickup, Wilson, Hamilton, Devine, Bennett, W.Smith, M.Ferguson, Mulvey.
Referee: K.G.Aston (Ilford) *Attendance: 4,272*

Accrington Against Other League Clubs

Accrington played 16 clubs in the Football League between 1888-1893. Below is the Accrington's record against each club.

		HOME					AWAY				
	P	W	D	L	F	A	W	D	L	F	A
Aston Villa	10	2	2	1	10	9	1	0	4	12	26
Blackburn Rovers	10	1	2	2	4	9	0	4	1	12	13
Bolton Wanderers	10	2	1	2	8	9	2	0	3	11	20
Burnley	10	2	2	1	9	8	1	2	2	8	9
Darwen	2	0	1	0	1	1	0	0	1	2	5
Derby County	10	3	1	1	17	7	2	2	1	10	10
Everton	10	2	1	2	10	10	0	2	3	6	11
Newton Heath	2	0	1	0	2	2	0	1	0	3	3
Nottingham Forest	2	0	1	0	1	1	0	0	1	0	3
Notts County	10	3	0	2	11	14	0	1	4	4	22
Preston North End	10	0	2	3	5	10	0	2	3	3	10
Sheffield Wednesday	2	1	0	0	4	2	0	0	1	2	5
Stoke	8	4	0	0	12	3	1	1	2	8	14
Sunderland	6	1	0	2	7	12	0	1	2	5	10
West Bromwich Albion	10	4	1	0	12	7	0	1	4	5	18
Wolverhampton Wanderers	10	3	1	1	18	11	0	0	5	4	19

Accrington in the Football League

	P	W	D	L	F	A	Pts	Pos
1888-89	22	6	8	8	48	48	20	7
1889-90	22	9	6	7	53	56	24	6
1890-91	22	6	4	12	28	50	16	10
1891-92	26	8	4	14	40	78	20	11
DIVISION ONE								
1892-93	30	6	11	13	57	81	23	15

Summary of League Record

	P	W	D	L	F	A
Total	122	35	33	54	226	313

Accrington in the Lancashire League 1893-1895

	P	W	D	L	F	A	Pts	Pos
1893-94	22	11	4	7	51	39	26	4
1894-95	26	10	2	14	62	63	22	12

Summary of Lancashire League Record

	P	W	D	L	F	A
Total	48	21	6	21	113	102

Accrington in the Lancashire Combination 1895-1896

Accrington failed to complete their fixtures. Their record at the time of the last League match stood as follows:

	P	W	D	L	F	A	Pts	Pos
1895-96	5	1	1	3	12	18	3	13

1888-89

Manager: Committee

No	Month	Day	Venue	Opponent	Result	Score	Scorers	Attendance
1	Sep	8	(a)	Everton	L	1-2	Holden	12,000
2		15	(a)	Blackburn R	D	5-5	Kirkham 2, Holden, Chippendale, James Southworth (og)	5,000
3		22	(a)	Derby C	D	1-1	Brand	2,000
4		29	(a)	Stoke	W	4-2	Brand 2, Barbour, Holden	3,000
5	Oct	6	(h)	Wolves	D	4-4	Barbour 2, Holden, Brand	5,000
6		13	(h)	Derby C	W	6-2	Barbour, Brand 3, Kirkham 2	3,000
7		20	(h)	Preston NE	D	0-0		7,000
8		27	(a)	Aston Villa	L	3-4	Kirkham, Barbour, Brand	600
9	Nov	3	(a)	West Brom A	D	2-2	Barbour 2	3,000
10		10	(a)	Notts C	D	3-3	Barbour 2, Lofthouse	8,000
11		17	(a)	Preston NE	L	0-2		7,000
12		24	(h)	West Brom A	W	2-1	Kirkham, Barbour	3,000
13	Dec	1	(h)	Burnley	W	5-1	Barbour 2, Brand 2, Kirkham	5,000
14		8	(a)	Wolves	L	0-4		3,000
15		15	(h)	Aston Villa	D	1-1	Kirkham	5,000
16		22	(a)	Bolton W	L	1-4	Bullough (og)	5,000
17		29	(h)	Everton	W	3-1	Brand, Haworth, Lofthouse	2,000
18	Jan	12	(a)	Burnley	D	2-2	A.Wilkinson, Kirkham	6,000
19		19	(h)	Blackburn R	L	0-2		4,000
20		26	(h)	Notts C	L	1-2	Kirkham	'large'
21	Mar	23	(h)	Bolton W	L	2-3	Kirkham 2	4,000
22	Apr	20	(h)	Stoke	W	2-0	Gallocher, Barbour	2,000

FINAL LEAGUE POSITION: 7th in The Football League

Appearances
Goals

FA Cup

No	Month	Day	Venue	Opponent	Result	Score	Scorers	Attendance
1	Feb	2	(h)	Blackburn R	D	1-1	Wilkinson	3,000
R		9	(a)	Blackburn R	L	0-5		8,000

Appearances
Goals

Horne JK	Stevenson J	McLellan J	Haworth G	Wilkinson JT	Pemberton L	Lofthouse JM	Bonar J	Kirkham JB	Holden J	Chippendale P	Tattersall J	Barbour A	Brand R	Singleton SS	Woods J	Wilkinson A	Robertson J	Macbeth R	Parkinson H	Galbraith H	Gallocher P	
1	2	3	4	5	6	7	8	9	10	11												1
1	2	3	4	9	6	7	8	11	10	5												2
1	2	3	4			7	8		10	5	6	9	11									3
1	2	3	4		6	7	8		10	5		9	11									4
1	2	3	4			7	8		10	5	6	9	11									5
1	2	3	4		6	7	8	10		5		9	11									6
1	2	3	4	5	6	7	8	10				9	11									7
1	2		4		6	7	8	10			5	9	11	3								8
1	2		4		6	7	8	10			5	9	11	3								9
1	2		4		6	7	8	10			5	9	11		3							10
1	2	3	4		6	7	8	10			5	9	11									11
1	2	3	4		6	7	8	10			5	9	11									12
1	2	3		4	6			10			5	9	11			7	8					13
1	2	3	4		6	7		10			5	9	11				8					14
1	2	3	4			7		10			5	9	11		6		8					15
1	2	3	4		6	7	8	10			5	9	11									16
1	2	3	4		6	7	8	10			5	9	11									17
1	2	3	4		6	7	8	10	11		5					9						18
1	2	3	4		6	7	8	10			5	9						11				19
1	2	5	4			9	8	10			6	11		3		7						20
1	2	3	4			7		10			5	9	11						6	8		21
1	2	3	4			7		10			5	9		6		11					8	22
22	22	19	21	4	16	21	17	19	6	6	17	19	16	4	2	4	3	1	1	1	1	
			1			2		12	4	1		13	11			1					1	

2 own-goals

Horne JK	Stevenson J	McLellan J	Haworth G	Wilkinson JT	Pemberton L	Lofthouse JM	Bonar J	Kirkham JB	Holden J	Chippendale P	Tattersall J	Barbour A	Brand R	Singleton SS	Woods J	Wilkinson A	
1	2	5	4			9	8	10			6	11		3		7	1
1	2	5	4			11	8	10			6	9		3		7	R
2	2	2	2			2	2	2			2	2		2		2	
																1	

1889-90

Manager: Committee

1	Sep	14	(a)	Bolton W	W 4-2	A.Wilkinson 2, McLuggage, Kirkham	5,000
2		21	(a)	Burnley	D 2-2	McLuggage, Haworth	3,000
3		28	(h)	Blackburn R	D 2-2	Entwistle 2	6,000
4	Oct	5	(a)	Wolves	L 1-2	A.Wilkinson	3,000
5		12	(h)	Notts C	L 1-8	Kirkham	1,500
6		19	(h)	Burnley	D 2-2	Barbour 2	2,000
7		26	(a)	Everton	D 2-2	Entwistle, Barbour	8,000
8	Nov	9	(a)	Preston NE	L 1-3	Entwistle	8,000
9		16	(h)	Derby C	W 6-1	Gallocher 2, Bromage (og), A.Wilkinson 2, Kirkham	3,000
10		23	(a)	Blackburn R	L 2-3	A.Wilkinson, Kirkham	8,000
11		30	(h)	Aston Villa	W 4-2	Pendergast 2, Haworth, Entwistle	2,000
12	Dec	21	(a)	West Brom A	L 1-4	Entwistle	3,500
13		26	(a)	Aston Villa	W 2-1	Barbour, A.WIlkinson	2,000
14		28	(h)	Stoke	W 2-1	A.Wilkinson, Gallocher	1,500
15	Jan	1	(h)	Wolves	W 6-3	A.Wilkinson, Barbour, Pendergast 2, Scorer unknown 2	3,000
16		4	(h)	Bolton W	W 3-1	Pendergast, Barbour, Entwistle	
17	Feb	8	(h)	West Brom A	D 0-0		2,100
18		15	(a)	Derby C	W 3-2	Entwistle, Barbour, A.Wilkinson	1,500
19		22	(h)	Everton	W 5-3	Entwistle, A.Wilkinson, Barbour 2, Pendercast	6,000
20	Mar	1	(a)	Stoke	L 1-7	Opp own-goal	2,000
21		13	(a)	Notts C	L 1-3	Barbour	2,000
22		15	(h)	Preston NE	D 2-2	Kirkham, Barbour	6,000

FINAL LEAGUE POSITION: 6th in The Football League

Appearances
Goals

FA Cup

*1	Jan	25	(h)	West Brom A	W 3-0	Entwistle 2, Barbour	5,300
2	Feb	1	(a)	Sheffield W	L 1-2	A.Wilkinson	8,000

* Originally due to be played on 18 January 1890, but after a pitch inspection it was declared the match should not be a cup-tie and a replay was ordered. Details of the match played on 18 January 1890 can be found in *Accrington's Other Matches 1888-1893* section.

Appearances
Goals

Lindsay J	Stevenson J	McLellan J	Haworth G	Pemberton L	Tattersall J	Wilkinson A	Gallocher P	Barbour A	Kirkham JB	McLuggage J	Entwistle J	Pendergast T	Marsh G	Haworth P	Brand R	Wilkinson JT	Chippendale P	
1	2	3	4	5	6	7	8	9	10	11								1
1	2	3	4	5	6		8	9	10	11	7							2
1	2	3	4	5	6		8	9	10	11	7							3
1	2	3	4	5	6	7	8	9	10	11								4
1	2	3	4	5	6	7	8	9	10	11								5
1	2	3	4	5	6			9	8	11	7	10						6
1	2	3		6	4		9	5	8	11	7	10						7
1	2	3	4	5	6		9		8	11	7	10						8
1	2	3	4	5	6	11	9		8		7	10						9
1	2	3	4	5	6	11	9		8		7	10						10
1	2	3	4	5	6	11	9		8		7	10						11
1		3	4	5	6	11	9		8		7	10	2					12
1	2	3	4	5	6	11		9	8		7	10						13
1	2	3	4	5	6	7	9		11		8	10						14
1	2	3	4	5	6	7		9	11		8	10						15
1	2	3	4	5	6	7		9	11		8	10						16
	2	3		4	6	7	5	9	11		8	10		1				17
1	2	3		4	6	7	5	9	11		8	10						18
1	2	3		4	6	7	5	9	11		8	10						19
1	2	3		4	6	7	5	9	11		8	10						20
1	2	3			6	7	5	9	10		4	8			11			21
1	2	3	5			7	6	9	10		8				11	4		22
21	21	22	16	20	21	17	18	16	22	8	19	16	1	1	2	1		
			2			11	3	11	5	2	9	6						

2 scorers unknown, 2 own-goals

Lindsay J	Stevenson J	McLellan J	Haworth G	Pemberton L	Tattersall J	Wilkinson A	Gallocher P	Barbour A	Kirkham JB	McLuggage J	Entwistle J	Pendergast T	Marsh G	Haworth P	Brand R	Wilkinson JT	Chippendale P	
1	2	3		4	6	7	10	9			8					5	11	1
1	2	3	5	4	6	11	8	9	7		10							2
2	2	2	1	2	2	2	2	2	1		2					1	1	
						1		1			2							

1890-91

Manager: Committee

1	Sep	6	(h)	Burnley	D 1-1	Barbour	8,000
2		13	(a)	Blackburn R	D 0-0		10,000
3		20	(a)	Notts C	L 0-5		
4		27	(h)	Everton	L 1-2	Whitehead	5,000
5	Oct	4	(a)	Wolves	L 0-3		2,500
6		11	(h)	Preston NE	L 1-3	Pendergast	4,000
7		18	(a)	Sunderland	D 2-2	Barbour, Whitehead	4,000
8		25	(h)	Notts C	W 3-2	Barbour, Shelton (og), Sanders	
9	Nov	1	(a)	Preston NE	D 1-1	Thomson	6,000
10		8	(h)	Derby C	W 4-0	Gallocher, Pendergast, Barbour 2	2,000
11		15	(a)	Aston Villa	L 1-3	Pendergast	3,000
12		22	(h)	Sunderland	W 4-1	Whitehead, Barbour 2, Thomson	1,000
13		29	(a)	Burnley	L 0-2		6,000
14	Dec	6	(a)	Derby C	W 2-1	Whitehead, Gallocher	2,500
15		13	(a)	Bolton W	L 0-6		
16		26	(a)	Everton	L 2-3	Barbour, Whitehead	14,000
17	Jan	1	(h)	Wolves	L 1-2	Barbour	6,000
18		10	(h)	Bolton W	W 2-1	Whitehead, A.Wilkinson	
19	Mar	4	(h)	Blackburn R	L 0-4		'moderate'
20		7	(a)	West Brom A	L 1-5	Kirkham	800
21		21	(h)	Aston Villa	L 1-3	Kirkham	1,500
22	Apr	18	(h)	West Brom A	W 1-0	McPherson	3,300

FINAL LEAGUE POSITION: 10th in The Football League

Appearances
Goals

FA Cup

1	Jan	17	(h)	Bolton W	D 2-2	Whitehead, Kirkham	
R		24	(h)	Bolton W	W 5-1	Gallocher, Kirkham, Scorer unknown, Whitehead, Pendergast	
2		31	(h)	Wolves	L 2-3*	Pendergast, Kirkham	8,500

* After extra-time

Appearances
Goals

Hay T	McDermid R	McLellan J	Haworth G	Sanders M	Tattersall J	Gallocher P	Kirkham JB	Barbour A	Thomson S	Macbeth R	Stevenson J	Orr J	Nisbet J	Wilkinson JT	Wilkinson A	Whitehead J	Barlow JM	Holding J	Smith D	Pendergast T	Pemberton L	Horne W	Horne JK	Shuttleworth W	McPherson M	Sneddon J	
1	2	3	4	5	6	7	8	9	10	11																	1
1	2		4	5	6	7	8	9	10		3	11															2
1	3			6	4	7	8	9	10				2	5	11												3
1	2		5	4	6	7		11	10				3			8	9										4
1	2		5	4	6			11					3			7	9	8	10								5
1	2	3	5	4	6	7		9								8			11	10							6
1	2	3		4	6	7		9				11				8				10	5						7
1	2	3	5	11	6	7		9								8				10	4						8
1	2	3	5	4	6	7		11	10							8				9							9
1	2	3	5	4	6	9		7	8							10				11							10
1	2	3	5	4	6	7		10	11							8				9							11
1	2	3	5	4	6	7		9	10							11						8					12
1	2	3	5	4	6	7	8	9	10							11											13
	2	3		5	6	7	10	11								8				9	4		1				14
1	2	3		5	6	7		11	10							8				9	4						15
1	2	3	5	4	6	7		11			10					8				9							16
1	2	3		5	6	7	10	11								8				9	4						17
1	2				6	5	10	11					3		7	8				9				4			18
1	2		5			7	10			11	3					8				9	4			6			19
1	2		5			7	10			11	3					8				9	4			6			20
1	2		5			9	11						3			8	7			10	4			6			21
1	2	3			6	5	11									8				10	4				7	9	22
21	22	14	15	17	19	21	11	18	10	3	4	2	5	1	2	19	3	1	2	15	9	1	1	4	1	1	
				1		2	2	9	2						1	6				3					1		

1 own-goal

Hay T	McDermid R	McLellan J	Haworth G	Sanders M	Tattersall J	Gallocher P	Kirkham JB	Barbour A	Thomson S	Macbeth R	Stevenson J	Orr J	Nisbet J	Wilkinson JT	Wilkinson A	Whitehead J	Barlow JM	Holding J	Smith D	Pendergast T	Pemberton L	Horne W	Horne JK	Shuttleworth W	McPherson M	Sneddon J	
1	2	3	4		6	5	10	9							7	8				11							1
1	2	3	5		6	9	10								7	8				11				4			R
1	2	3	5		6	9	10								7	8				11				4			2
3	3	3	3		3	3	3	1							3	3				3				2			
						1	3									2				2							

1 scorer unknown

1891-92

Manager: Committee

1	Sep	5	(h)	Burnley	W 1-0	Kirkham	7,000
2		12	(a)	Derby C	L 1-3	Elliott	3,500
3		14	(a)	Wolves	L 0-5		3,500
4		19	(a)	Darwen	L 2-5	Whitehead, Faulds	4,000
5		26	(h)	Everton	D 1-1	Elliott	
6	Oct	3	(a)	Bolton W	W 4-3	Whitehead, Pendergast 2, Faulds	5,000
7		10	(h)	Darwen	D 1-1	Pendergast	3,000
8		24	(h)	Wolves	W 3-2	Thomson, Whitehead, Tattersall	3,000
9		31	(a)	Sunderland	L 1-4	Irvine	7,000
10	Nov	7	(h)	Bolton W	L 0-3		6,000
11		14	(a)	Burnley	L 1-2	Thomson	7,000
12		21	(h)	Notts C	W 2-0	Thomson, Whitehead	very small
13		28	(a)	Notts C	L 0-9		3,000
14	Dec	5	(a)	West Brom A	L 1-3	Kirkham	6,000
15		19	(a)	Stoke	L 1-3	Whitehead	3,000
16		26	(a)	Blackburn R	D 2-2	Elliott, Irvine	3,000
17	Jan	2	(h)	Preston NE	L 1-3	Kirkham	6,000
18		4	(h)	Aston Villa	W 3-2	Irvine 2, Elliott	3,500
19		9	(h)	Stoke	W 3-0	Tattersall, Kirkham, Irvine	1,500
20		23	(h)	West Brom A	W 4-2	Bowman, Thomson 2, Kirkham	4,200
21	Feb	27	(h)	Blackburn R	W 1-0	Irvine	3,000
22	Mar	5	(h)	Sunderland	L 3-5	Bowman, Irvine, Elliott	2,000
23		12	(a)	Aston Villa	L 2-12	Whitehead, Elliott	8,000
24		19	(a)	Everton	L 0-3		8,000
25	Apr	2	(h)	Derby C	D 1-1	Bowman	2,000
26		15	(a)	Preston NE	L 1-4	Elliott	6,000

FINAL LEAGUE POSITION: 11th in The Football League

Appearances

Goals

FA Cup

1	Jan	16	(a)	Crusaders	W 4-1	Haworth, Thomson, Kirkham, Whitehead	3,000
*2	Feb	6	(h)	Sunderland	L 1-3	Whitehead	8,000

* Originally due to be played on 30 January 1892, but after a pitch inspection it was decided the match should not be a cup-tie. A friendly match was played and details can be found in *Accrington's Other Matches 1888-1893* section.

Appearances

Goals

Hay T	McVickers J	McLellan J	Barr J	Haworth G	Tattersall J	Faulds W	Whitehead J	Irvine J	Elliott A	Kirkham JB	McKay W	Pendergast T	Thomson S	Stevenson J	Marsh G	Shuttleworth W	Barlow JM	Bowman WW	Clegg JR	Morgan E	
1	2	3	4	5	6	7	8	9	10	11											1
1	2	3	4	5	6	7	8	9	10		11										2
1	2	3	4	5	6	7	8	9	10		11										3
1	2	3	4	5	6	7	8	9	10		11										4
1	2	3	4	5	6	7	8		10	11		9									5
1	2	3	4	5	6	7	8		10	11		9									6
1	2	3	4	5	6	7	8		10	11		9									7
1	2	3	4	5	6	7	8		10	11			9								8
1	2	3	4		6		8	7	10	11			9	5							9
1	2	3	4	5	6		8		10	11		9	7								10
1	2	3	4	5	6	7	8		10	11			9								11
1		3		5	6	7	8		10	11			9		2	4					12
1		3		5	6		8		10	11			9		2	4	7				13
1		3	4	5	6		8		10	11			9	2			7				14
1	4	3		5	6		8	7	10	11			9	2							15
1	2	3		5	6		8	11	10	7			9	4							16
1	2	3		5	6		8	9	10	7			11	4							17
1	2	3		5	6		8	9	10	7			11	4							18
1	2	3		5	6		8	11		7		10	9	4							19
1	2	3		5	6		8	9		7			11	4				10			20
1	2	3		5				11	8	7			9	4		6		10			21
1		3		5	6			11	10	7			9	2		4		8			22
1	2	3		5	6		8	11	10	7			9	4							23
1		3			6		8	11	10	7			9	2		4			5		24
1		3			6		8		10	7			11	5		4		9		2	25
1		3			6		8	9	10	7			5			4		11		2	26
26	19	26	12	22	25	10	24	16	24	23	3	5	19	13	2	7	2	5	1	2	
					2	2	6	7	7	5		3	5					3			

Hay T	McVickers J	McLellan J	Barr J	Haworth G	Tattersall J	Faulds W	Whitehead J	Irvine J	Elliott A	Kirkham JB	McKay W	Pendergast T	Thomson S	Stevenson J	Marsh G	Shuttleworth W	Barlow JM	Bowman WW	Clegg JR	Morgan E	
1	2	3		5	6		8	9	10	7			11	4							1
1	2	3		5			8	9	10	7			11	4		6					2
2	2	2		2	1		2	2	2	2			2	2		1					
				1			2			1			1								

1892-93

Manager: Committee

1	Sep	3	(h)	Sunderland	L 0-6		
2		10	(a)	Sheffield W	L 2-5	Kirkham, H.Lea	15,000
3		17	(a)	Stoke	D 2-2	Whitehead, Kirkham	5,000
4		24	(h)	Sheffield W	W 4-2	H.Lea 2, Cookson 2	3,000
5	Oct	1	(a)	Blackburn R	D 3-3	H.Lea, Kirkham, T.Lea	
6		8	(h)	Bolton W	D 1-1	Kirkham	4,000
7		15	(a)	Sunderland	L 2-4	Whitehead, Cookson	
8		22	(a)	Everton	D 1-1	Whitehead	14,000
9		29	(a)	Burnley	W 3-1	Cookson, Kirkham, T.Lea	8,000
10	Nov	5	(h)	Preston NE	L 1-2	Ross (og)	8,000
11		12	(a)	West Brom A	L 0-4		4,000
12		19	(a)	Wolves	L 3-5	Kirkham 3	2,000
13		26	(h)	Newton Heath	D 2-2	Alexander, Whitehead	3,000
14	Dec	3	(a)	Derby C	D 3-3	Kirkham, Cookson, H.Lea	1,500
15		10	(h)	Notts C	W 4-2	H.Lea, Cookson 2, Whitehead	1,500
16		17	(h)	West Brom A	W 5-4	H.Lea, Cookson, T.Lea 2, Whitehead	3,000
17		26	(h)	Stoke	W 5-2	Almond, Cookson 3, T.Lea	5,000
18		31	(h)	Wolves	W 4-0	Whitehead 2, Cookson, H.Lea	2,500
19	Jan	2	(h)	Blackburn R	D 1-1	Cookson	8,000
20		7	(a)	Nottingham F	L 0-3		3,000
21		14	(h)	Burnley	L 0-4		6,000
22	Feb	11	(a)	Notts C	L 0-2		4,000
23		25	(h)	Everton	L 0-3		4,000
24	Mar	4	(a)	Bolton W	L 2-5	Bowie, Whitehead	
25		18	(h)	Nottingham F	D 1-1	Whitehead	1,500
26		25	(a)	Aston Villa	L 4-6	Higham 2, T.Lea, Cookson	5,000
27		31	(h)	Derby C	L 0-3		2,000
28	Apr	3	(a)	Preston NE	D 0-0		5,000
29		8	(a)	Newton Heath	D 3-3	H.Lea 2, Clements (og)	5,000
30		15	(h)	Aston Villa	D 1-1	Whitehead	2,000

FINAL LEAGUE POSITION: 15th in Division One

Appearances
Goals

FA Cup

1	Jan	21	(h)	Stoke	W 2-1	Cookson, H.Lea	
2	Feb	4	(h)	Preston NE	L 1-4	H.Lea	

Appearances
Goals

Test Match

	Apr	22	(n*)	Sheffield U	L 0-1		6,000

* Played at the Town Ground, Nottingham

Appearances
Goals

Hay T	Ditchfield JC	McLellan J	Stevenson J	Shuttleworth W	Tattersall J	Cookson H	Whitehead JW	Kirkham JB	Lea H	Lea T	Alexander D	Almond W	Hodge W	Bowie W	Horne JK	Matthew J	Higham W	Mason W	
1	2	3	4	5	6	7	8	9	10	11									1
1	2	3	4	5	6	9	8	11	10	7									2
1	2	3	4	5	6	9	8	11	10	7									3
1	2	3	4	5	6	9	8	11	10	7									4
1	2	3	4	5	6	9	8	11	10	7									5
1	2	3	4	5	6	9	8	11	10	7									6
1	2	3		4	6	11	8	10	5	7	9								7
1	2	3	11	4	6	10	8		5	7	9								8
1	2	3	4	5	6	10	8	11		7	9								9
1	2	3	4	5	6	10	8	11		7	9								10
1	2		3	4	6	9	8	11	10	7		5							11
1	2		3	4	6		8	11	10	7	9	5							12
1	2	3		4	6		8	11	10	7	9	5							13
1	2	3	4	6		10	8	11	9	7		5							14
1	2	3	4	6		10	8	11	9	7		5							15
1	2	3	4	6	5	10	8	11	9	7									16
1	2	3	4	6		10	8	11	9	7		5							17
1	2	3	4	6		9	8	11	10	7		5							18
1	2	3	4	6		9	8	11	10	7		5							19
1	2	3	4	6		9	8	11	10	7		5							20
1	2	3	4	5	6	9	8	11	10	7									21
1		2	7	6	3	9	8	11	10				4	5					22
1	3		4	6		11	8	10	9	7			2	5					23
	3			6	4	11	8	10	5	7			2	9	1				24
	3			4	6		8	11	10	7			2	9	1	5			25
	3					9	8	10	6	7			2	4	1	5	11		26
	3					9	8	10	6	7			2	4		5	11	1	27
	3			6		9	8	11	10	7			2	4		5		1	28
	3			6		9	8	11	10	7			2	4		5		1	29
	3			6		9	8	11	10	7			2	4		5		1	30
23	29	20	21	28	18	27	30	29	28	29	6	9	9	9	3	6	2	4	
						14	11	9	10	6	1	1		1			2		

2 own-goals

1	2	3	4	5	6	9	8	11	10	7		1
1	2	3	4	5	6	9	8	11	10	7		2
2	2	2	2	2	2	2	2	2	2	2		
						1			2			

	3		5	6		9	8	11	10	7			2	4				1
	1		1	1		1	1	1	1	1			1	1				1

Stanley Against Other League Clubs

ACCRINGTON Stanley met 60 clubs in the Football League between 1921-22 and 1960-61. Below is their record against each club. Some clubs modified their names (eg Hartlepools United became Hartlepool and then Hartlepool United). In all cases the current name used by each club covers all games under previous names. The records of matches against South Shields are included with Gateshead, whilst those against Rotherham County are included with Rotherham United. It should be noted that the results of matches played during the 1961-62 season and the three League games played at the start of the 1939-40 season are not included in these records.

		HOME					*AWAY*				
	P	W	D	L	F	A	W	D	L	F	A
AFC Bournemouth	4	2	0	0	5	3	0	0	2	3	8
Aldershot	2	1	0	0	1	0	0	0	1	1	3
Ashington	16	5	1	2	17	7	2	3	3	14	14
Barnsley	12	3	0	3	9	15	1	0	5	3	25
Barrow	62	20	4	7	64	33	7	6	18	35	62
Bradford	30	8	4	3	46	28	1	4	10	18	44
Bradford City	36	6	4	8	24	24	5	4	9	28	41
Brentford	4	0	1	1	4	5	0	0	2	1	5
Bury	6	1	0	2	4	5	1	1	1	3	4
Carlisle United	48	14	4	6	47	37	2	3	19	37	74
Chester City	42	11	3	7	42	28	2	4	15	16	52
Chesterfield	44	11	6	5	36	26	5	3	14	21	47
Colchester United	4	0	1	1	2	3	0	0	2	1	6
Coventry City	4	1	0	1	3	3	0	0	2	2	4
Crewe Alexandra	62	22	4	5	64	27	7	4	20	42	75
Crystal Palace	2	0	0	1	2	3	0	0	1	2	9
Darlington	58	24	4	1	59	15	4	5	20	29	74
Derby County	4	1	1	0	2	0	0	1	1	4	8
Doncaster Rovers	38	8	6	5	36	26	1	3	15	16	63
Durham City	14	7	0	0	27	7	0	0	7	4	21
Exeter City	2	0	0	1	0	1	1	0	0	4	2
Gateshead	46	10	5	8	46	37	1	7	15	14	59
Gillingham	2	1	0	0	3	0	0	0	1	1	2
Grimsby Town	22	6	0	5	17	14	0	0	11	6	36
Halifax Town	64	18	8	6	70	39	7	9	16	38	50
Hartlepool United	62	17	6	8	69	41	5	6	20	30	62
Hull City	24	1	3	8	10	20	1	2	9	13	31
Lincoln City	42	11	3	7	43	34	2	6	13	22	60
Mansfield Town	38	8	7	4	34	25	4	3	12	23	40
Millwall	2	0	1	0	3	3	0	1	0	2	2

		HOME					*AWAY*				
	P	W	D	L	F	A	W	D	L	F	A
Nelson	18	6	1	2	26	15	3	0	6	12	21
New Brighton	42	14	2	5	64	27	6	4	11	24	43
Newport County	4	0	2	0	2	2	1	0	1	4	3
Northampton Town	2	1	0	0	3	2	0	0	1	1	2
Norwich City	4	0	0	2	3	6	1	0	1	4	6
Notts County	2	1	0	0	3	0	0	1	0	1	1
Oldham Athletic	32	3	5	8	28	29	6	0	10	22	31
Peterborough United	2	1	0	0	3	2	0	0	1	0	3
Plymouth Argyle	2	0	1	0	1	1	1	0	0	4	2
Port Vale	12	1	2	3	8	12	1	1	4	5	13
Queen's Park Rangers	4	0	0	2	3	6	0	0	2	2	8
Reading	4	1	1	0	4	3	0	0	2	0	7
Rochdale	64	15	4	13	58	54	6	6	20	40	70
Rotherham United	42	10	3	8	44	35	4	4	13	27	54
Scunthorpe United	16	4	2	2	10	7	3	0	5	11	21
Shrewsbury Town	4	1	1	0	4	2	1	0	1	1	5
Southampton	4	0	2	0	2	2	0	0	2	2	8
Southend United	4	1	0	1	3	4	0	0	2	3	10
Southport	62	18	10	3	69	36	5	9	17	36	62
Stalybridge Celtic	4	2	0	0	5	1	0	0	2	1	4
Stockport County	54	15	4	8	54	43	3	8	16	24	58
Stoke City	2	0	0	1	0	1	0	0	1	0	1
Swindon Town	4	1	1	0	3	1	2	0	0	3	1
Tranmere Rovers	62	18	5	8	61	38	7	5	19	31	87
Walsall	22	5	3	3	23	22	1	3	7	13	36
Wigan Borough	20	7	2	1	26	9	2	0	8	8	25
Wolverh'ton Wanderers	2	1	0	0	1	0	0	0	1	1	5
Workington	16	5	1	2	17	7	3	1	4	7	12
Wrexham	66	18	6	9	59	40	5	5	23	34	75
York City	48	18	3	3	60	22	5	6	13	25	46

Accrington Stanley
in the Football League
1921 to 1962

	P	W	D	L	F	A	Pts	Pos
DIVISION THREE NORTH								
1921-22	38	19	3	16	73	57	41	5th
1922-23	38	17	7	14	59	65	41	8th
1923-24	42	16	8	18	48	61	40	13th
1924-25	42	15	8	19	60	72	38	17th
1925-26	42	17	3	22	81	105	37	18th
1926-27	42	10	7	25	62	98	27	21st
1927-28	42	18	8	16	76	67	44	9th
1928-29	42	13	8	21	68	82	34	18th
1929-30	42	14	9	19	84	81	37	16th
1930-31	42	15	9	18	84	108	39	13th
1931-32	40	15	6	19	75	80	36	14th
1932-33	42	15	10	17	78	76	40	13th
1933-34	42	13	7	22	65	101	33	20th
1934-35	42	12	10	20	63	89	34	18th
1935-36	42	17	8	17	63	72	42	9th
1936-37	42	16	9	17	76	69	41	13th
1937-38	42	11	7	24	45	75	29	22nd
1938-39	42	7	6	29	49	103	20	22nd
1946-47	42	14	4	24	56	92	32	20th
1947-48	42	20	6	16	62	59	46	6th
1948-49	42	12	10	20	55	64	34	20th
1949-50	42	16	7	19	57	62	39	13th
1950-51	46	11	10	25	42	101	32	23rd
1951-52	46	10	12	24	61	92	32	22nd
1952-53	46	8	11	27	39	89	27	24th
1953-54	46	16	10	20	66	74	42	15th
1954-55	46	25	11	10	96	67	61	2nd
1955-56	46	25	9	12	92	57	59	3rd
1956-57	46	25	8	13	95	64	58	3rd
1957-58	46	25	9	12	83	61	59	2nd
DIVISION THREE								
1958-59	46	15	12	19	71	87	42	19th
1959-60	46	11	5	30	57	123	27	24th
DIVISION FOUR								
1960-61	46	16	8	22	74	88	40	18th
1961-62	Failed to complete fixtures							

Note: The record of Accrington Stanley at the time of their resignation from the Football League stood as follows:

	P	W	D	L	F	A	Pts	Pos
DIVISION FOUR								
1961-62	33	5	8	20	19	60	18	24

These figures are not included in the summary below.

Summary of League Record

	P	W	D	L	F	A
Third Division North	1282	467	240	575	2013	2343
Third Division	92	26	17	49	128	210
Fourth Division	46	16	8	22	74	88
Total	1420	509	265	646	2215	2641

Accrington Stanley president Sir W.W.Cocker (second left) makes a presentation to secretary Jack Wrigglesworth. Manager Jack Hacking is pictured between them.

Peel Park pictured from the air before Stanley's demise as a League club.

1921-22

Secretary/Manager: Samuel T.Pilkington

1	Aug	27	(a)	Rochdale	L 3-6	Hosker 2, Green	8,500
2	Sep	3	(h)	Rochdale	W 4-0	Makin, Hosker, Green 2	11,500
3		10	(h)	Crewe A	W 2-0	Green 2	10,000
4		17	(a)	Crewe A	L 1-2	Green	8,000
5		24	(h)	Chesterfield	W 3-1	Makin, Green 2	8,000
6	Oct	1	(a)	Chesterfield	W 1-0	Makin	7,500
7		8	(h)	Nelson	W 4-1	Hosker, Makin, Green 2 (1 pen)	12,000
8		15	(a)	Nelson	W 1-0	Green	14,000
9		22	(h)	Wrexham	W 1-0	Makin	5,000
10		29	(a)	Wrexham	L 1-2	Hosker	7,000
11	Nov	5	(h)	Durham C	W 5-1	Makin 2, Nelis 3	8,000
12		12	(a)	Durham C	L 1-3	Patchett (og)	3,000
13		26	(h)	Barrow	W 3-0	Makin, Green, Oxley	
14	Dec	10	(a)	Halifax T	L 1-2	Green	4,000
15		17	(a)	Lincoln C	D 1-1	Green	4,000
16		24	(h)	Lincoln C	W 2-0	Hosker, Green	5,000
17		26	(a)	Southport	D 1-1	Green	11,250
18		27	(h)	Ashington	W 3-0	Hosker, Makin 2	6,250
19		31	(a)	Darlington	L 0-3		7,000
20	Jan	2	(a)	Ashington	L 1-2	Hosker	5,000
21		7	(a)	Barrow	L 1-3	Makin	
22		14	(h)	Darlington	W 1-0	Burkinshaw (pen)	5,470
23		21	(a)	Tranmere R	W 4-2	Makin 3, Oxley	4,500
24		28	(h)	Tranmere R	W 3-0	Nelis, Makin, Quigley	7,100
25	Feb	4	(a)	Stalybridge C	L 1-3	Hosker	
26		11	(h)	Stalybridge C	W 4-1	Makin, Nelis 2, Watkinson	6,180
27		18	(h)	Wigan B	W 4-0	Hosker, Nelis 3	5,120
28		25	(a)	Wigan B	W 1-0	Nelis	5,000
29	Mar	4	(a)	Hartlepools U	L 1-2	Nelis	7,500
30		11	(h)	Hartlepools U	W 4-1	Hosker, Nelis 3	7,000
31		18	(h)	Southport	L 1-2	Oxley	7,000
32	Apr	1	(a)	Stockport C	L 1-2	Green	10,000
33		8	(h)	Stockport C	L 1-3	Green	5,000
34		15	(a)	Grimsby T	L 1-2	Green	10,000
35		17	(h)	Halifax T	L 1-2	Hosker	6,000
36		22	(h)	Grimsby T	W 1-0	Brown	6,000
37		29	(h)	Walsall	D 3-3	Green 3	
38	May	6	(a)	Walsall	L 1-6	Green	4,000

FINAL LEAGUE POSITION: 5th in Division Three North

Appearances
Goals

FA Cup

4Q	Nov	19	(h)	Nelson	L 0-1		10,106

Appearances
Goals

Tattersall J	Newton WAA	Baines F	Crawshaw A	Popplewell S	Burkinshaw JDL	Oxley RL	Makin J	Green T	Hosker J	Hartles W	Kay F	Peacock F	Wilde J	Quigley PH	Cragg R	Sloane JJ	Bolton F	Nelis P	Robinson A	Smethurst H	Foster J	Nuttall H	Cooper F	Watkinson J	Richardson J	Floyd P	Brown RG	McDowell J	Shorrock R	Farrington R	Goldie J	
1	2	3	4	5	6	7	8	9	10	11																						
1	3		4	5	6	7	8	9	10	11	2																					2
			4	5	6	7	8	9	10	11	2	1	3																			3
			4	5	6	7	8	9	10	11	2	1	3																			4
			4	5	6	7	8	9			2	1	3	10	11																	5
			4	5	6	7	8	9	10	11	2		3			1																6
			4	5	6	7	8	9	10		2		3	11		1																7
			4	5	6	7	8	9	10	11	2		3			1																8
			4	5	6	7	8	9	10		2		3			1	11															9
			4	5	6	7	8	9	10	11	2		3			1																10
			4	5	6	7	8	11	10		2		3			1		9														11
1		2	4	5		7	8	11	10				3					9	6													12
			4	5	6	7	8	9	10		2		3	11		1																13
			4	3	6	7	8	9	10		2			11		1			5													14
			4	5	6	7	8	9	10		2		3	11		1																15
			4	5	6	7	8	9	10	11	2		3			1																16
			4	5	6	7	8	9	10	11	2		3			1																17
			4	3		7	8	9	10	11	2					1				5	6											18
				5		7	8	9	10	11	2		3			1				4	6											19
				5		7	8	11	9		2		3		10	1			4		6											20
				5			8	9	10		2	1	3	11							6	4	7									21
				5	6	7		9	10		2		3	11		1		8				4										22
				5	4	7	8		10	6	2		3	11		1		9														23
				5	4	7	8		10	6	2		3	11		1		9														24
			4	5		7	8		10	6	2		3	11		1		9														25
			4	5	6	7	8		10		2		3			1		9						11								26
			4	5	6	7	8		10		2		3			1		9						11								27
			4	5	6	7	8		10		2		3			1		9						11								28
			4	5	6	7	8		10		2		3			1		9						11								29
			4	5	6	7	8	11	10		2		3			1		9														30
			4	5	6	7	8	9	10		2		3			1								11								31
			4	3	6	7		9	10					11	8	1				5					2							32
			4	3	6	7		9	10					11	8	1				5					2							33
			4	3	6			9	10						8					5	11				2	1	7					34
			4	5	6	9		11	10						8										2	1	7	3				35
			4		6				9					10						5				11	2	1	7		3	8		36
			4		6			9	10											5				11	2	1	7		3		8	37
			4	3			8	9	10											5	6			11	2	1	7					38
3	2	2	32	36	31	33	31	30	37	14	29	4	27	13	6	26	1	11	3	8	6	2	1	8	7	5	5	1	2	1	1	
					1	3	16	23	12					1				14						1			1					

1 own-goal

			4	5	6		8	11	10		2	1	3	7				9														4Q
			1	1	1		1	1	1		1	1	1	1				1														

1922-23

Secretary/Manager: Samuel T.Pilkington

1	Aug	26	(h)	Darlington	W 2-1	Metcalf, Hosker	10,000
2	Sep	2	(a)	Darlington	L 0-4		7,000
3		9	(a)	Tranmere R	L 1-4	Challinor	
4		16	(h)	Tranmere R	W 4-1	Pinkney, Popplewell, Harrold, Metcalf	6,000
5		23	(a)	Durham C	L 1-4	Morris	3,000
6		30	(h)	Durham C	W 3-1	Metcalf, Rooks, Popplewell	6,000
7	Oct	7	(h)	Wigan B	D 0-0		7,000
8		14	(a)	Wigan B	L 0-2		13,000
9		21	(h)	Wrexham	W 1-0	Graham	5,000
10		28	(a)	Wrexham	L 0-2		5,500
11	Nov	4	(h)	Chesterfield	L 0-4		5,000
12		11	(a)	Chesterfield	L 1-3	Metcalf	6,000
13		25	(a)	Crewe A	D 1-1	Smelt	
14	Dec	9	(a)	Hartlepools U	D 0-0		3,000
15		23	(h)	Walsall	W 2-1	Hosker, Morris	4,000
16		25	(a)	Grimsby T	L 1-7	Page (pen)	
17		26	(h)	Ashington	W 4-1	Metcalf 2, Pinkney, Hosker	4,000
18		30	(h)	Halifax T	W 4-1	Smelt, Morris, Bradburn, Metcalf	5,000
19	Jan	1	(h)	Grimsby T	W 4-0	Metcalf 2, Smelt, Hosker	7,000
20		6	(a)	Halifax T	D 0-0		18,000
21		13	(h)	Crewe A	D 0-0		5,000
22		20	(h)	Bradford	W 4-3	Metcalf, Smelt, Hosker, Morris	7,500
23		27	(a)	Bradford	L 1-5	Metcalf	14,000
24	Feb	3	(h)	Rochdale	W 2-1	Metcalf, Hosker	6,000
25		10	(a)	Rochdale	D 1-1	Hosker	4,000
26		17	(h)	Barrow	L 3-4	Helliwell, Metcalf, Smelt (pen)	6,000
27		24	(a)	Barrow	L 2-5	Metcalf, Smelt	
28	Mar	3	(a)	Ashington	W 5-2	Hosker 3, Smelt 2	5,000
29		10	(h)	Harltepools U	W 2-1	Smelt, Hosker	5,000
30		17	(a)	Southport	W 2-1	Smelt 2	
31		24	(h)	Southport	W 3-1	Metcalf 3	6,000
32		31	(a)	Stalybridge C	L 0-1		2,000
33	Apr	2	(a)	Walsall	W 2-0	Smelt 2	
34		7	(h)	Stalybridge C	W 1-0	Metcalf	5,000
35		14	(a)	Nelson	L 1-2	Hosker	10,000
36		21	(h)	Nelson	L 0-1		11,000
37		28	(a)	Lincoln C	D 0-0		8,000
38	May	5	(h)	Lincoln C	W 1-0	Pinkney	5,000

FINAL LEAGUE POSITION: 8th in Third Division North

Appearances
Goals

FA Cup

5Q	Dec	2	(h)	Halifax T	D 1-1	Hosker	7,000
R		4	(a)	Halifax T	L 0-1		7,000

Appearances
Goals

Floyd P	Richardson J	Page G	Crawshaw A	Challinor S	Rooks W	Pinkney E	Metcalf A	Morris R	Hosker J	Harrold S	Walker A	Popplewell S	Makin J	Congdon J	Donnelly J	Childs W	Ward TH	Graham	Howell H	Cummings D	Sloane JJ	Ogden H	Smelt T	Shaw J	Bradburn R	Shorrock R	Kay F	Helliwell T	Barnes KS	Entwistle W	Allinson C	
1	2	3	4	5	6	7	8	9	10	11																						1
1	2	3			6	7	9		10	11	4	5	8																			2
1	2	3		4	6	7	8		10	11		5		9																		3
1	2	3		9	6	7	8		10	11	4	5																				4
1	2	3			6	7	8	9	10	11	4	5																				5
1		3			6	7	8	9	10	11	4	5			2																	6
1		3			6		8		10		4	5	9	11		2	7															7
1		3	6		9				10		4	5	8	11		2	7															8
1		3			6		8		10		4	5				2	7	11	9													9
1		3		6				11			4	5	8			2	7		9	10												10
1		3	4	6					11		9	5	8			2	7		10													11
		3			6		10					5	8	11		2	7				1	4	9									12
		3	6			7		11	10		4					2	8				1		9	5								13
		3	6		5	7	8	11	10		4					2					1		9									14
		3	6		5	7		11	10		4		8			2					1		9									15
		3	6		5	7			10		4			11		2	8				1		9									16
1	2	3	6			7	8	11	10			4											9	5								17
1		3	6				8	11	10			4			5	2							9		7							18
1	2	3	6	5			8	11	10			4											9		7							19
1		3	6	5			8	11	10			4	9												7	2						20
1		3	6				8	11	10			4											9	5	7		2					21
1		3	6	5			8	11	10			4			2								9		7							22
1		3	6	5			8	11	10			4			2								9		7							23
		3	6	5			8		10			4			2						1		9		7			11				24
		3	6	5			8		10			4			2						1		9		7			11				25
		3	6	5			8		10			4				2							9		7			11	1			26
		3	6	5			8		10			4			2		7						9					11	1			27
1		3	6	5			8	11	10			4			2		7						9									28
1		3	6	5			8	11	10			4			2		7						9									29
1	2		6	5			8		10			4			3		7						9					11				30
1	2			5			8	11	10			4			3		7						9							6		31
1	2		4	5			8		10						3		11						9		7					6		32
1	2	5	4				8		10						3		7						9		11					6		33
1	2		4	5			8		10						3		7						9		11					6		34
1			4	5			8		10			2			3								9		7			11		6		35
1		3		5			8		10			4			2		7						9					11		6		36
1	2		4	5			8		10						3		7						9					11		6		37
1	2		4	5		7	8		10						3													11		6	9	38
29	14	31	27	23	13	12	32	17	36	6	13	28	8	5	18	12	18	1	3	1	7	1	25	3	13	1	1	9	2	8	1	
		1		1	1	3	18	4	12	1		2						1					13		1			1				

Floyd P	Richardson J	Page G	Crawshaw A	Challinor S	Rooks W	Pinkney E	Metcalf A	Morris R	Hosker J	Harrold S	Walker A	Popplewell S	Makin J	Congdon J	Donnelly J	Childs W	Ward TH	Graham	Howell H	Cummings D	Sloane JJ	Ogden H	Smelt T	Shaw J	Bradburn R	Shorrock R	Kay F	Helliwell T	Barnes KS	Entwistle W	Allinson C	
		3	6		5	7		11	10		4					2	8				1		9									5Q
		3	6		5	7		11	10		4					2	8				1		9									R
		2	2		2	2		2	2		2					2	2				2		2									
									1																							

1923-24

Player/Manager: Curtis Booth

1	Aug	25	(a)	Darlington	L 1-2	Keetley	
2	Sep	1	(h)	Darlington	W 2-0	Hosker, Cooke	8,500
3		3	(a)	Barrow	D 0-0		4,000
4		8	(h)	New Brighton	D 0-0		6,000
5		15	(a)	New Brighton	W 2-1	Keetley 2	7,000
6		22	(h)	Wolves	W 1-0	Keetley	9,000
7		25	(h)	Barrow	W 3-1	Cooke, Keetley 2	
8		29	(a)	Wolves	L 1-5	Keetley	14,486
9	Oct	6	(h)	Walsall	L 0-3		6,000
10		13	(a)	Walsall	L 0-2		6,000
11		20	(a)	Ashington	D 1-1	Keetley	4,000
12		17	(h)	Ashington	L 0-1		5,000
13	Nov	3	(a)	Wigan B	L 0-2		
14		10	(h)	Wigan B	D 2-2	Kay, Cooke	5,000
15		24	(a)	Durham C	L 0-3		
16	Dec	8	(a)	Crewe A	W 2-1	Rooks (pen), Quigley	
17		22	(a)	Hartlepools U	L 0-3		3,000
18		25	(a)	Southport	L 0-1		
19		26	(h)	Southport	W 2-0	Entwistle, Smelt	6,000
20		29	(a)	Halifax T	L 0-3		
21	Jan	1	(h)	Grimsby T	W 2-0	Rooks, Watson	6,000
22		5	(h)	Halifax T	L 1-2	Cooke	
23		19	(a)	Lincoln C	W 2-0	Smelt, Quigley	
24		26	(h)	Lincoln C	W 3-1	Heap 2, Watson	4,500
25	Feb	2	(a)	Tranmere R	L 0-2		6,000
26		9	(h)	Tranmere R	W 3-1	Quigley, Kay, Rooks	
27		11	(h)	Crewe A	D 1-1	Heys	1,200
28		16	(a)	Bradford	D 1-1	Cooke	7,000
29		23	(h)	Bradford	D 2-2	Heys, Black	6,000
30	Mar	1	(a)	Chesterfield	L 0-3		4,000
31		8	(h)	Chesterfield	W 2-0	Hosker, Black	
32		15	(h)	Rotherham C	W 3-2	Kay, Popplewell (pen), Hosker	
33		17	(h)	Hartlepools U	W 2-0	Kay, Popplewell	1,500
34		22	(a)	Rotherham C	L 0-2		8,000
35		29	(h)	Wrexham	W 1-0	Black	4,000
36	Apr	5	(a)	Wrexham	L 0-1		
37		12	(a)	Doncaster R	W 2-1	Smelt, Entwistle	5,000
38		18	(a)	Grimsby T	L 0-2		
39		19	(h)	Doncaster R	D 0-0		
40		26	(h)	Rochdale	L 0-1		7,000
41		30	(h)	Durham C	W 5-4	Black 2, Hosker 2, Quigley	2,000
42	May	3	(a)	Rochdale	L 1-4	Brown	5,000

FINAL LEAGUE POSITION: 13th in Division Three North

Appearances
Goals

FA Cup

5Q	Dec	1	(h)	Rochdale	W 1-0	Kay	7,000
6Q		15	(h)	Wrexham	W 1-0	Hosker	6,000
1	Jan	12	(h)	Charlton A	D 0-0		11,310
R		17	(a)	Charlton A	L 0-1		6,344

Appearances
Goals

Salt E	Richardson J	Donnelly J	Watson W	Rooks W	Duffus RMD	Brown T	Booth C	Cooke FR	Keetley JJ	Helliwell T	Hosker J	McCandless J	Quigley PH	Smelt T	Ward TH	Entwistle W	Kay T	Rawcliffe R	Sagar J	Popplewell S	Halshaw JT	Heap D	Heys R	Black JR	Wilde J	Crabtree JJ	Bradburn R	Haigh C	Childs W	
1	2	3	4	5	6	7	8	9	10	11																				1
1	2	3	4	5	6	7		9	10	11	8																			2
1	2	3	4	5	6	7		9	10	11	8																			3
1	2	3	4	5	6	7		9	10	11	8																			4
1	2	3	4	5	6	7		9	10		8	11																		5
1	2	3	4	5	6	7		9	10		8	11																		6
1	2	3	4	5	6	7		9	10		8		11																	7
1	2	3	4	5	6	7		9	10		8		11																	8
1	2	3	4	5	6			8	10		7		11	9																9
1	2	3	4	5	6				10	11	8		9		7															10
1	2	3	4	5	6	7			10	11	8		9																	11
1	2	3	4	5	6	7			10	11	8		9																	12
1	2	3		5	6	7		9	10		8		11			4														13
1	2	3		5	6	7		9					10	8		4	11													14
1	2	3	4	5	6	7		9					10	8			11													15
1	2	3		5	6	7					10		8				11	4	9											16
1	2	3	4	5	6			8			10				7		11		9											17
1	2	3	4								10		8	7		6	11		9	5										18
1	2	3	4					7			10		8	9		6	11			5										19
1	2	3	4		6			7			10		8	9			11			5										20
1	2	3	4	5	6			7		11	10		8	9																21
1	2	3	4	5	6			9		11			10			7					8									22
1	2	3	4	5	6			9					7	8			11					10								23
1	2	3	4	5	6			9					7	8			11					10								24
1	2	3	4	5	6			9					7	8			11					10								25
1	2	3	4	6	5								7				11					10	8	9						26
1	2	3	4		6								7				11			5		10	8	9						27
1	2		4		5			7					11			6						10	8	9	3					28
1	2		4		5			7								6	11					10	8	9	3					29
	2		4	5							10					6	11		7				8	9	3	1				30
	2	3	4	5							10		7			6	11						8	9		1				31
	2	3	4								10					6	11		7	5			8	9		1				32
	2	3	4								10						11		7	5			8	9	6	1				33
	2		4					7			10					6	11			5			8	9	3	1				34
	2		4	5				7			10					6							8	9	3	1	11			35
1	2		4	5							10			8		6	11		7					9	3					36
1	2	3		6							10			9		4	11						8	7				5		37
1	2	3	4								10			9		6	11		7				8					5		38
1	2	3	4			7					10		8	9		6	11											5		39
1		3	4	5							10		11	9		6							8	7					2	40
1	2	3	4	6	5						10		11						7				8	9						41
1	2	3	4	5	6	7		8			10		11						9											42
36	41	36	38	31	29	16	1	25	13	9	31	2	26	15	2	17	22	1	10	7	1	7	14	14	7	6	1	3	1	
			2	3		1		5	8		5		4	3		2	4			2		2	2	5						

Salt E	Richardson J	Donnelly J	Watson W	Rooks W	Duffus RMD	Brown T	Booth C	Cooke FR	Keetley JJ	Helliwell T	Hosker J	McCandless J	Quigley PH	Smelt T	Ward TH	Entwistle W	Kay T	Rawcliffe R	Sagar J	Popplewell S	Halshaw JT	Heap D	Heys R	Black JR	Wilde J	Crabtree JJ	Bradburn R	Haigh C	Childs W	
1	2	3	4	5	6	7		9			10		8				11													5Q
1	2	3	4	5	6						10		8		7		11		9											6Q
1	2	3	4	5	6			10					7	8			11		9											1
1	2	3	4	5	6			10		7			8	9			11													R
4	4	4	4	4	4	1		3		1	2		4	2	1		4		2											
											1						1													

1924-25

Secretary/Manager: Samuel T.Pilkington until 14 November 1924 then Ernest Blackburn

1	Aug	30	(h)	Rotherham C	W 2-0	Skillen, Mutch	7,496
2	Sep	1	(a)	Bradford	L 0-3		7,000
3		6	(a)	Chesterfield	L 0-1		10,000
4		8	(h)	Bradford	D 2-2	J.Thompson, Gee	6,000
5		13	(h)	Nelson	W 2-0	Skillen, Mutch	7,000
6		17	(h)	Wigan B	W 3-1	J.Thompson (pen), R.Thompson, Skillen	5,000
7		20	(h)	Halifax T	W 2-0	Mutch, Bedford	8,000
8		24	(a)	Wrexham	L 0-1		6,000
9		27	(a)	New Brighton	L 0-4		
10		30	(h)	Barrow	L 1-2	R.Thompson	
11	Oct	4	(h)	Grimsby T	L 0-3		
12		11	(a)	Hartlepools U	L 0-3		4,000
13		18	(h)	Rochdale	D 2-2	Skillen 2	7,000
14		25	(a)	Ashington	W 2-1	Skillen, R.Thompson	
15	Nov	1	(h)	Southport	W 5-1	Mutch, McIntosh, J.Thompson, Skillen, Bedford	4,000
16		8	(a)	Doncaster R	L 1-4	Skillen	
17		22	(a)	Crewe A	L 2-4	R.Thompson 2	
18	Dec	6	(a)	Walsall	D 1-1	R.Thompson	
19		20	(a)	Lincoln C	L 0-3		
20		26	(a)	Barrow	L 1-3	J.Thompson	5,000
21		27	(a)	Rotherham C	D 1-1	J.Thompson	3,000
22	Jan	1	(h)	Darlington	W 2-0	Watson, R.Thompson (pen)	4,000
23		3	(h)	Chesterfield	D 2-2	Heys, Bedford (pen)	5,000
24		17	(a)	Nelson	L 1-4	R.Thompson	8,000
25		24	(a)	Halifax T	D 2-2	Heap 2	5,000
26	Feb	7	(a)	Grimsby T	L 0-4		
27		14	(h)	Hartlepools U	W 4-1	R.Thompson 2 (1 pen), Mutch, J.Thompson	3,000
28		21	(a)	Rochdale	W 1-0	R.Thompson	6,000
29		23	(h)	Durham C	W 6-0	Gee 2, R.Thompson 3, Kay	600
30		28	(h)	Ashington	D 2-2	Hall, R.Thompson	4,000
31	Mar	7	(a)	Southport	L 1-3	Gee	
32		14	(h)	Doncaster R	W 3-2	Mutch, R.Thompson, Gee	
33		21	(h)	Durham C	L 0-2		
34		28	(h)	Crewe A	W 1-0	R.Thompson	
35	Apr	4	(a)	Wigan B	W 2-1	Bedford, Gee	3,000
36		10	(a)	Darlington	L 1-2	Mutch	
37		11	(h)	Walsall	D 1-1	Smith (og)	4,000
38		18	(a)	Tranmere R	L 1-2	J.Thompson	3,000
39		22	(h)	Tranmere R	W 2-1	Bedford, Martin	
40		25	(h)	Lincoln C	L 0-2		
41		27	(h)	New Brighton	L 0-1		1,000
42	May	8	(h)	Wrexham	W 1-0	J.Thompson	

FINAL LEAGUE POSITION: 17th in Division Three North

Appearances
Goals

FA Cup

5Q	Nov	29	(a)	New Brighton	D 0-0		
R	Dec	1	(h)	New Brighton	W 3-2	R.Thompson 2, Hall	
6Q		13	(h)	Chesterfield	W 1-0	J.Thompson	5,313
1	Jan	10	(h)	Portsmouth	L 2-5	R.Thompson 2 (1 pen)	10,852

Appearances
Goals

Salt E	Richardson J	Crawley F	Watson W	McIntosh G	Rooks W	Bedford F	Mutch A	Thompson R	Skillen J	Thompson J	Gee J	Kirkpatrick J	Entwistle W	Montgomery H	Crabtree JJ	Childs W	Tindall TJ	Haigh C	Hall J	Martin JC	Heys R	Blackadder W	Heap D	Kay T	Walmsley JW	Blake J	
1	2	3	4	5	6	7	8	9	10	11																	1
1	2	3	4	5	6	7	8	9	10	11																	2
1	2	3	4	5	6		8	9	10	11	7																3
1	2	3	4	5	6		8		9	11	7	10															4
1	2	3	4	5	6	7	8		9	11		10															5
1	2	3	4	5	6	7	8	9	10	11																	6
1	2	3	4	5	6	7	8	9	10	11																	7
1	2	3	4	5	6	7	8	9	10	11																	8
1	2	3	4	5	6	7	8	9	10	11																	9
1		2	4	5	3		8	9	10	11			6	7													10
1	2		4	5	3		8	9		11		10	6	7													11
	3		4	5	6	7	8		9	11		10			1	2											12
1	2	3	4	5	6	7	8	9	10	11																	13
1	2			5	6	7	8	9	10	11							3	4									14
1	2		4	5	6	7	8	9	10	11							3										15
1	2		4	5	6	7	8	9	10	11							3										16
1	2		4	5	6	7	8	9	10	11							3										17
1	2		4				8	9	10	11			6				3	5	7								18
1	2		4		6		8	9	10	11							3	5	7								19
1	2		4		6		8	9	10	11							3	5	7								20
1	2		4		6		8	9	10	11							3	5	7								21
1	2		4		6	7	8	9	10	11							3			5							22
1	2		4			7	8		10	11			6				3			5	9						23
1	2				6		8	9		7							3	5				4	10	11			24
1			4		6		8	9		7						2		5					10	11	3		25
1	3				6		8	9		7						2		5				4	10	11			26
1			4		3		10	9		7	8					2				5		6		11			27
			4		3		10	9		7	8					2				5		6		11		1	28
			4		3		10	9		7	8					2				5		6		11		1	29
			6		3			9		7	8					2			10	5		4		11		1	30
1			4		3		10		9	7	8					2				5		6		11			31
	2		4		3	7	10	9		11	8							5				6				1	32
	3		6		5	11	8	9		7	10											4			2	1	33
1	2		4		6	7	10	9		11	8									5					3		34
1	3				2	7	10	9		11	8									5		6			4		35
1	2				3	7	10	9		11	8									5		6			4		36
1	2				3	7	10	9		11	8									5		6			4		37
1	2		6		3		10	9		11	8									5		7			4		38
1	2				3	9	10			7	8									5		6		11	4		39
1	2				3	9	10			7	8									5		6		11	4		40
1			4		2	7	10		9	11	8						3			5		6					41
1			4		3	7			9	10	8					2				5		6		11			42
36	33	11	34	17	40	25	40	33	25	42	18	4	4	2	1	9	12	9	5	16	1	17	3	11	9	5	
			1	1		5	7	17	8	8	6								1	1	1		2	1			

1 own-goal

Salt E	Richardson J	Crawley F	Watson W	McIntosh G	Rooks W	Bedford F	Mutch A	Thompson R	Skillen J	Thompson J	Gee J	Kirkpatrick J	Entwistle W	Montgomery H	Crabtree JJ	Childs W	Tindall TJ	Haigh C	Hall J	Martin JC	Heys R	Blackadder W	Heap D	Kay T	Walmsley JW	Blake J	
1	2		4		6		8	9	10	11							3	5	7								5Q
1	2		4		6		8	9	10	11							3	5	7								R
1	2		4		6		8	9		11		10					3	5	7								6Q
1	2		4		6	7	8	9	10	11							3			5							1
4	4		4		4	1	4	4	3	4		1					4	3	3	1							
								4		1									1								

1925-26

Secretary/Manager: Ernest Blackburn

1	Aug	29	(a)	Walsall	D 3-3	Crockford 2, Gummery	4,777
2	Sep	2	(h)	Hartlepools U	L 1-2	Cowell (og)	5,177
3		5	(h)	Chesterfield	W 2-0	Crockford, Greenhalgh	5,322
4		9	(a)	Durham C	L 1-5	Greenhalgh	2,291
5		12	(a)	Bradford	L 0-3		12,388
6		16	(a)	Hartlepools U	L 1-5	Gummery	3,698
7		19	(h)	Grimsby T	W 1-0	Greenhalgh	2,981
8		26	(a)	Rotherham U	L 1-3	Crockford	6,405
9		29	(h)	Durham C	W 3-1	Gee, Crockford, Powell	5,608
10	Oct	3	(h)	Halifax T	L 0-1		4,798
11		10	(a)	Nelson	L 0-1		9,119
12		17	(h)	Coventry C	W 3-1	Jepson 3	3,948
13		24	(a)	Wrexham	W 6-5	Jepson 3, Gee 2, Wyper	6,095
14		31	(h)	Ashington	W 2-1	Jepson 2	4,823
15	Nov	7	(a)	Barrow	W 2-1	Wyper, Gummery	1,969
16		14	(h)	Lincoln C	W 3-1	Gee, Powell, Jepson	5,649
17		21	(a)	Crewe A	L 0-3		4,149
18	Dec	5	(a)	Wigan B	L 0-5		4,421
19		19	(a)	Southport	W 3-1	Powell 2, Gee	3,924
20		25	(h)	Tranmere R	W 4-3	Jepson 3, Gee	5,413
21		26	(a)	Tranmere R	D 2-2	Wyper, Powell	6,635
22	Jan	2	(h)	Walsall	W 5-2	Gee 3, Jepson 2	4,237
23		16	(a)	Chesterfield	L 2-7	Gee, Wyper	3,160
24		20	(h)	New Brighton	L 0-2		2,352
25		23	(h)	Bradford	L 1-4	Jepson	5,575
26		30	(a)	Grimsby T	L 2-5	Powell, Wyper	8,573
27	Feb	6	(h)	Rotherham U	L 2-3	Wyper 2	3,947
28		13	(a)	Halifax T	D 1-1	Powell	5,110
29		20	(h)	Nelson	W 3-2	Powell, Jepson 2	7,153
30		27	(a)	Coventry C	L 1-2	Wyper	9,388
31	Mar	6	(h)	Wrexham	W 4-2	Jepson 3, Gee (pen)	4,355
32		13	(a)	Ashington	L 1-3	Shaw	4,353
33		20	(h)	Barrow	W 2-0	Jepson 2	3,721
34		27	(a)	Lincoln C	L 1-3	Wyper	3,107
35	Apr	2	(h)	Rochdale	L 1-3	Gee (pen)	5,264
36		3	(h)	Crewe A	W 2-0	Jepson, Powell	3,423
37		5	(a)	Rochdale	L 2-3	Gee 2	7,890
38		10	(a)	New Brighton	L 1-4	Wyper	4,136
39		14	(h)	Doncaster R	L 2-3	Jepson, Powell	1,701
40		17	(h)	Wigan B	W 4-0	Jepson 3, Barrington (og)	2,028
41		24	(a)	Doncaster R	L 2-6	Jepson 2	4,215
42	May	1	(h)	Southport	W 4-3	Gee, Powell, Kasher, Jepson	1,745

FINAL LEAGUE POSITION: 18th in Division Three North

Appearances
Goals

FA Cup

1	Nov	28	(h)	Wrexham	W 4-0	Jepson 3, Rooks	7,368
2	Dec	12	(h)	Blyth S	W 5-0	Gummery, Jepson 3, Powell	9,030
3	Jan	9	(a)	Bolton W	L 0-1		32,875

Appearances
Goals

Holden T	Bell A	Whittaker T	Field R	Kasher JWR	Watson W	Powell EJ	Greenhalgh JS	Crockford H	Lindsay J	Gummery W	Haworth J	Wyper HT	Rooks W	Walmsley JW	Gee J	Stafford H	Martin JC	Jepson JJ	Marshall TA	Tomlinson J	Shaw G	Lunn L	Gregory E	Armitt T	Hall R	
1	2	3	4	5	6	7	8	9	10	11																1
1	2	3	4	5	6	7	8	9	10	11																2
1	2	3	4	5	6	7	8	9	10	11																3
1	2	3	4	5	6	7	8	9	10	11																4
1	2	3	4	5	6	7	8	9	10	11																5
	2	3	4	5		11	10	8		9	1	7	6													6
1		3	4	5		10	8	9		11		7	6	2												7
1		3	4	5		10		9		11		7	6	2	8											8
1		3	4	5		10		9		11		7	6	2	8											9
1		3	4	5		10		9		11			6	2	8	7										10
1		3	4					10		11		7	6	2	8		5	9								11
1		3	4			10				11		7	6	2	8		5	9								12
1		3	4			10				11		7	6	2	8		5	9								13
1		3	4			10				11		7	6	2	8		5	9								14
1	2	3	4			10				11		7	6		8		5	9								15
1	2	3	4			10				11		7	6		8		5	9								16
1	2	3	4			10				11		7	6		8		5	9								17
1	2	3	4			10	9			11		7	6		8		5									18
1	2	3	4			10				11		7	6		8		5	9								19
1	2	3	4	5		10				11		7	6		8			9								20
	2	3	4	5		10				11		7	6		8			9	1							21
	2	3	4	5		10				11		7	6		8			9	1							22
1	2	3	4	5		10				11		7	6		8			9								23
1	2	3	4			10	8			11		7	6				5	9								24
1	2	3	4			10				11		7	6		8		5	9								25
	2	3	4			10	11					7	6		8		5	9	1							26
1	2	3	4	5		10	11					7	6		8			9								27
1	2	3	6	5		10	11					7			8			9		4						28
1	2	3	6	5		10	11					7			8			9		4						29
1	2	3	6	5		10						7	9		8					4	11					30
1	2	3	6	5		10						7			8			9		4	11					31
1	2	3	6	5		10						7			8			9		4	11					32
1	2	3	4	5		10						7	6		8			9			11					33
1	2	3	6	5		10						7			8			9		4	11					34
1	2		6	5		10						7	3		8			9		4	11					35
			4	5	6	10						7	2		8			9			11	1	3			36
	2		4	5		10				11		7	6		8			9				1	3			37
	2		4	5		10				11		7	6		8			9				1	3			38
	2		4	5		10				11		7	6		8			9				1	3			39
1	2		4	6		10				11		7			8			9					3	5		40
1	2		4	6		10				11		7			8			9					3		5	41
	2	3	4	6		10				11		7			8			9				1			5	42
33	33	35	42	30	6	41	13	11	5	31	1	36	29	8	34	1	12	30	3	7	7	5	6	1	2	
				1		11	3	5		3		10			15			30			1					

2 own-goals

Holden T	Bell A	Whittaker T	Field R	Kasher JWR	Watson W	Powell EJ	Greenhalgh JS	Crockford H	Lindsay J	Gummery W	Haworth J	Wyper HT	Rooks W	Walmsley JW	Gee J	Stafford H	Martin JC	Jepson JJ	Marshall TA	Tomlinson J	Shaw G	Lunn L	Gregory E	Armitt T	Hall R	
1	2	3	4			10				11		7	6		8		5	9								1
1	2	3	4			10				11		7	6		8		5	9								2
1	2	3	4	5		10				11		7	6		8			9								3
3	3	3	3	1		3				3		3	3		3		2	3								
						1				1			1					6								

1926-27

Secretary/Manager: Ernest Blackburn

1	Aug	28	(h)	Rochdale	L 0-1		7,335
2		30	(a)	Chesterfield	D 1-1	Jepson	5,304
3	Sep	4	(a)	Southport	L 1-2	Gee	5,599
4		11	(h)	Stockport C	L 2-4	Gee, Field	4,574
5		13	(a)	Lincoln C	L 0-4		3,340
6		18	(a)	Hartlepools U	L 1-3	Wyper	3,285
7		20	(h)	Durham C	W 3-0	Clarkson 2, Gee	3,009
8		25	(h)	Crewe A	W 3-1	Wyper, Gee, Jepson	3,868
9		28	(h)	Lincoln C	D 1-1	Jepson	5,292
10	Oct	2	(a)	Barrow	D 1-1	Jepson	5,854
11		9	(h)	Halifax T	W 4-2	Jepson 2, Benyon, Chadwick	3,914
12		16	(a)	Walsall	L 1-5	Wyper	6,085
13		23	(h)	Nelson	L 0-5		6,804
14		30	(a)	Ashington	L 1-2	Gee	2,048
15	Nov	6	(h)	New Brighton	L 2-3	Clarkson, Kasher	3,301
16		13	(a)	Wrexham	L 0-5		3,099
17		20	(h)	Wigan B	W 3-1	Gee 2, Powell	2,867
18	Dec	4	(h)	Stoke C	L 0-1		5,803
19		18	(h)	Bradford	L 2-3	Martin, Clarkson	4,407
20		25	(h)	Tranmere R	L 2-3	Clarkson 2	4,468
21		27	(a)	Durham	L 0-2		1,843
22	Jan	1	(h)	Chesterfield	W 2-1	Gee (pen), Wyper	5,114
23		15	(a)	Rochdale	L 1-2	Gee	2,992
24		22	(h)	Southport	D 2-2	Tomlinson, Gee	3,920
25		24	(a)	Rotherham U	D 1-1	Clarkson	1,631
26	Feb	5	(h)	Hartlepools U	W 7-2	Clarkson 4, Gee, Powell, Jepson	2,877
27		8	(a)	Stockport C	D 3-3	Powell, Jepson, Clarkson	3,689
28		12	(a)	Crewe A	L 0-4		3,915
29		19	(h)	Barrow	L 0-1		3,287
30		26	(a)	Halifax T	L 3-4	Martin, Gee, Dodds	7,547
31	Mar	5	(h)	Walsall	L 3-5	Dodds, Gee 2	1,816
32		12	(a)	Nelson	L 0-7		7,046
33		19	(h)	Ashington	W 3-0	Powell 2, Jepson	3,450
34		26	(a)	New Brighton	W 1-0	Martin	1,760
35	Apr	2	(h)	Wrexham	D 1-1	Jepson	3,351
36		9	(a)	Wigan B	L 0-3		1,911
37		16	(h)	Doncaster R	W 2-0	Clarkson, Martin	3,644
38		18	(a)	Tranmere R	L 1-2	Martin	4,651
39		23	(a)	Stoke C	L 0-1		8,502
40		25	(a)	Doncaster R	L 0-2		
41		30	(h)	Rotherham U	W 3-1	Chadwick, Powell, Jepson	2,991
42	May	7	(a)	Bradford	L 1-6	Slater	4,470

FINAL LEAGUE POSITION: 21st in Division Three North

Appearances

Goals

FA Cup

1	Nov	27	(h)	Rochdale	W 4-3	Gee (pen), Clarkson 2, Martin	6,500
2	Dec	11	(a)	Chilton Colliery	W 3-0	Gee, Clarkson, Martin	
3	Jan	8	(a)	Exeter C	W 2-0	Clarkson, Martin	13,647
4		29	(a)	Chelsea	L 2-7	Powell, Wyper	30,142

Appearances

Goals

Hayes W	Bell A	Davis SS	Kasher JWR	Hall R	McDougall J	Wyper HT	Gee J	Jepson JJ	Chadwick J	Martin J	Field R	Rooks W	Gregory E	Powell EJ	Clarkson R	Whittaker T	Hughes LC	Wilson NH	Benyon J	Dodds C	Tomlinson J	Holden T	Slater F	Haworth H	Curran A	
1	2	3	4	5	6	7	8	9	10	11																1
1	2	3	6	5		7	8	9	10	11	4															2
1	2		6	5		7	8	9	10	11	4	3														3
1	2		5			7	8	9		11	4	6	3	10												4
1	2		5			7	8	9		11	4		3	10	6											5
1				5		7	8	10		11	4	3			9	2	6									6
1	2		5			7	8	10		11	4	3			9		6									7
1	2		5			7	8	10		11		3			9		6	4								8
1	2		5			7	8	10		11		3			9		6	4								9
1	2		5			7		9		11		3		10	8		6	4								10
1	2		5			7		9	10			3			8		6	4	11							11
1	2		5			7		9	10			3			8		6	4	11							12
1			5			7	8	9	10			3				2	6	4	11							13
1	2		5			7	8	9	10	11	4	3					6									14
1	2		5			7	8		9	10		3					6	4	11							15
1	2					7	8	9		11	4			10		3	5	6								16
1	2					7	8			11	4			10	9	3	6	5								17
1	2					7	8			11	5			10	9	3	6	4								18
1	2					7	10	9		11		5			8	3	6	4								19
1	2					7	10	9		11		5			8	3	6	4								20
1	2		5			7		10		11		6			9	3		4		8						21
1	2		5			7	8			11				10	9	3	6	4								22
1	2					7	8			11		5		10	9	3	6	4								23
1	2					7	8			11				10	9	3	6	4			5					24
1	2					7	8			11				10	9	3	6	4			5					25
1	2						7	9		11		6		10	8	3		4			5					26
1	2						7	9		11				10	8	3	6	4			5					27
1	2						7	9		11				10	8	3	6	4			5					28
	2						7	9		11				10	8	3	6	4			5	1				29
1	2		6				8			11				9		3		4		10	5		7			30
1	2						8								9	3	11	4		10	5		7	6		31
1	2						8			11		4			9	3				10	5		7	6		32
1							8	9		11		2		10		3	6	4					7		5	33
1							8	9		11			2	10		3	6	4					7		5	34
1							8	9		11			2	10		3	6	4					7		5	35
1	2						8	9		11				10		3	6	4					7		5	36
1	2								8	11				10	9	3	6	4					7		5	37
1	2								8	11				10	9	3	6				4		7		5	38
1	2						8			11				10	9	3	6	4					7		5	39
1	2						8			11				10	9	3	6	4					7		5	40
1	2								8	11				10	9	3	6	4					7		5	41
1	2								10	11					8	3	6	4		9			7		5	42
41	37	2	17	4	1	25	34	26	12	38	10	19	4	24	29	29	33	32	4	5	10	1	13	2	10	
			1			4	14	11	2	5	1			6	13				1	2	1		1			

Hayes W	Bell A	Davis SS	Kasher JWR	Hall R	McDougall J	Wyper HT	Gee J	Jepson JJ	Chadwick J	Martin J	Field R	Rooks W	Gregory E	Powell EJ	Clarkson R	Whittaker T	Hughes LC	Wilson NH	Benyon J	Dodds C	Tomlinson J	Holden T	Slater F	Haworth H	Curran A	
1	2		5			7	8			11				10	9	3	6	4								1
1	2					7	10	9		11		5			8	3	6	4								2
1	2					7	8			11		5		10	9	3	6	4								3
1	2					7	8			11		5		10	9	3	6	4								4
4	4		1			4	4	1		4		3		3	4	4	4	4								
						1	2			3				1	4											

1927-28

Secretary/Manager: Ernest Blackburn

1	Aug	27	(a)	Nelson	W 4-1	McLoughlin 2, Parkin 2	8,007
2	Sep	3	(h)	Wigan B	L 2-4	Butler, Parkin	8,330
3		10	(a)	Doncaster R	D 0-0		6,143
4		17	(h)	Darlington	D 0-0		7,392
5		24	(a)	Ashington	D 1-1	Clarkson	2,853
6		27	(h)	Hartlepools U	D 2-2	Armstrong (pen), McLoughlin	6,353
7	Oct	1	(h)	Crewe A	W 5-0	Parkin 2, McLoughlin, Butler, Armstrong (pen)	3,675
8		8	(a)	Halifax T	L 1-3	Butler	7,173
9		15	(h)	Bradford C	D 1-1	Parry	7,428
10		22	(a)	Southport	L 0-5		2,655
11		29	(h)	Rotherham U	W 3-1	Carrick, Parkin, Clarkson	4,930
12	Nov	12	(h)	Durham C	W 2-0	Parkin 2	4,459
13		19	(a)	Wrexham	W 1-0	Clarkson	2,070
14	Dec	3	(a)	Bradford	D 3-3	McLoughlin, Clarkson, Parkin	10,337
15		10	(h)	Chesterfield	D 0-0		3,771
16		17	(a)	Stockport C	D 3-3	Parkin 2, Parry	7,020
17		24	(h)	Barrow	W 5-1	Parkin, Barclay (pen), Armstrong, Parry, McLoughlin	3,127
18		26	(h)	New Brighton	W 2-1	Laycock (og), Martin	5,644
19		27	(a)	New Brighton	L 1-3	McLoughlin	5,384
20		31	(h)	Nelson	W 7-1	Parkin 3, Butler, McLoughlin, Curran, Martin	4,207
21	Jan	2	(h)	Lincoln C	W 1-0	Martin	5,682
22		7	(a)	Wigan B	L 0-2		2,756
23		14	(a)	Chesterfield	L 1-3	Parkin	3,358
24		21	(h)	Doncaster R	L 1-3	Parkin	4,931
25		28	(a)	Darlington	L 0-3		3,132
26	Feb	4	(h)	Ashington	W 3-1	Butler, Ridley (og), Parkin	2,526
27		11	(a)	Crewe A	W 3-2	Parkin, Barclay (pen), McLoughlin	2,576
28		15	(h)	Tranmere R	L 2-3	Barclay (pen), Butler	2,017
29		18	(h)	Halifax T	W 3-2	Dodds, Butler, Parkin	3,241
30		25	(a)	Bradford C	L 0-2		10,930
31	Mar	3	(h)	Southport	W 4-1	Butler 2, Parkin 2 (1 pen)	4,573
32		10	(a)	Rotherham U	L 1-2	Curran	3,763
33		17	(h)	Rochdale	W 1-0	Barclay (pen)	3,885
34		24	(a)	Durham C	L 1-2	Parkin	1,343
35		31	(h)	Wrexham	W 2-0	McLoughlin, Parkin	3,188
36	Apr	6	(a)	Lincoln C	L 1-3	Barclay	8,810
37		7	(a)	Tranmere R	L 2-3	Parkin 2	6,169
38		9	(a)	Hartlepools U	W 2-0	Parry, Parkin	2,245
39		14	(h)	Bradford	W 2-1	Parry, Lee	4,948
40		28	(h)	Stockport C	W 1-0	Chadwick	5,225
41	May	1	(a)	Rochdale	L 2-3	Barclay (pen), Barber (og)	1,443
42		8	(a)	Barrow	L 0-1		6,561

FINAL LEAGUE POSITION: 9th in Division Three North — Appearances

Goals

FA Cup

1	Nov	26	(h)	Lincoln C	L 2-5	Clarkson, Parkin	10,000

Appearances

Goals

Finnigan RJ	Brooke P	Whittaker T	Carrick J	Curran A	Lee P	Parry FT	Butler R	Parkin JT	McLoughlin G	Barclay JB	Armstrong J	Clarkson R	Martin J	Chadwick J	Tootill A	Dodds C	Slater F	Hall R	
1	2	3	4	5	6	7	8	9	10	11									1
1	2	3	4	5	6	7	8	9	10	11									2
1		3	4	5	6	7	8	9	10	11	2								3
1		3	4	5	6	7	8	9	10	11	2								4
1		3	4	5	6	7	8		10	11	2	9							5
1		3	4	5	6	7			8	11	2	9	10						6
1		3	4	5	6	7	8	9	10	11	2								7
1		3	4	5	6	7	8	9	10	11	2								8
1		3	4	5	6	7	8	9	10	11	2								9
1		3	4	5	6	7	8	9		11	2			10					10
1		3	4	5	6	7		8	10	11	2	9							11
		3	4	5	6	7		9	10	11	2	8			1				12
		3	4	5	6	7		9	10	11	2	8			1				13
1		3	4	5	6	7		9	10	11	2	8							14
1		3	4	5	6	7		9	10	11	2	8							15
1		3	4	5		7	8	9	10	11	2					6			16
1		3	4	5		7	8	9	10	11	2					6			17
1		3	4	5		7	8	9	10		2		11			6			18
1		3	4	5		7	8	9	10		2		11			6			19
1		3	4	5		7	8	9	10		2		11			6			20
1		3	4	5		7	9		10		2		11	8		6			21
1		3	4	5		7	9		10	11	2			8		6			22
1		3	4	5		7	8	9	10	11	2					6			23
1		3	4	5		7		9	10	11	2	8				6			24
1		3		5	6			8	10	11	2	9				4	7		25
1		3		5	6		8	9	10	11	2					4	7		26
1		3		5	6	7	8	9	10	11	2					4			27
1		3		5	6	7	8	9	10	11	2					4			28
1		3	5		6	7	8	9	10	11	2					4			29
1		3	5		6	7	8	9	10	11	2					4			30
1		3		5	6	7	8	9	10		2		11			4			31
1		3		5	6	7	8	9	10	11	2					4			32
1		3		5	6	8		9	10	11	2					4	7		33
1		3	5		6	8		9	10	11	2					4	7		34
1		3		5	6	7	8	9	10	11	2					4			35
1		3			6	7	8	9	10	11	2					4		5	36
1		3		5	6	7	8	9	10	11	2					4			37
1		3		5	6	7	8	9	10	11	2					4			38
1		3		5	6	7		9	10	11	2			8		4			39
1		3		5	6	7		9	10	11	2			8		4			40
1		3		5	6	7		9	10	11	2			8		4			41
1		3		5	6	7		9	10	11	2			8		4			42
40	2	42	27	38	33	40	28	38	41	37	40	9	6	7	2	27	4	1	
			1	2	1	5	9	27	10	6	3	4	3	1		1			

3 own-goals

		3	4	5	6	7		9	10	11	2	8			1				1
		1	1	1	1	1		1	1	1	1	1			1				
								1				1							

1928-29

Secretary/Manager: Ernest Blackburn

1	Aug	25	(h)	Carlisle U	L 2-3	Barclay (pen), Lee	6,714
2	Sep	1	(a)	Rotherham U	L 1-2	Parry	5,652
3		8	(h)	Wigan B	W 2-0	Parkin, Barclay	5,133
4		15	(a)	Crewe A	L 0-4		3,443
5		22	(h)	Tranmere R	W 2-0	Parry, McLoughlin	4,409
6		25	(h)	Hartlepools U	D 2-2	Chadwick 2	4,488
7		29	(a)	Stockport C	L 1-6	Barclay (pen)	10,250
8	Oct	6	(h)	Halifax T	D 1-1	Chadwick	4,480
9		13	(a)	Lincoln C	L 1-3	Parkin	6,431
10		20	(h)	Ashington	L 0-1		3,411
11		27	(a)	Doncaster R	L 1-4	Parkin	3,808
12	Nov	3	(h)	Barrow	W 1-0	McLoughlin	3,196
13		10	(a)	Chesterfield	L 1-4	Barclay	2,897
14		17	(h)	Wrexham	W 4-3	Parkin, Taylor (og), Jepson 2	4,631
15	Dec	1	(h)	Rochdale	D 2-2	Armstrong (pen), McLoughlin	4,711
16		15	(h)	Darlington	W 4-0	Jepson 2, Parry, McLoughlin	4,007
17		22	(a)	Nelson	W 2-0	Curran, Jepson	4,791
18		25	(h)	Bradford C	L 0-1		7,357
19		26	(a)	Bradford C	L 1-4	Parkin	23,671
20		29	(a)	Carlisle U	L 3-4	Parkin, Jepson 2	6,662
21	Jan	1	(h)	South Shields	W 2-0	Parkin, Jepson	7,039
22		5	(h)	Rotherham U	L 1-3	Parkin	3,319
23		19	(a)	Wigan B	L 2-5	McLoughlin, Curran	5,245
24		26	(h)	Crewe A	W 2-0	Chadwick, Jepson	2,892
25	Feb	2	(a)	Tranmere R	D 1-1	Chadwick	2,876
26		6	(a)	New Brighton	L 1-2	Jepson	1,535
27		9	(h)	Stockport C	W 2-0	McLoughlin, Parry	5,851
28		16	(a)	Halifax T	L 2-4	Chadwick, Jepson	3,768
29		23	(h)	Lincoln C	L 0-1		3,377
30	Mar	2	(a)	Ashington	D 2-2	Chadwick, Jepson	1,124
31		9	(h)	Doncaster R	W 6-0	McLoughlin 3, Chadwick, Jepson, Barclay	4,177
32		16	(a)	Barrow	L 1-2	McLoughlin	5,439
33		23	(h)	Chesterfield	D 0-0		3,507
34		29	(a)	South Shields	L 0-3		5,940
35		30	(a)	Wrexham	L 1-4	McLoughlin	5,629
36	Apr	1	(a)	Hartlepools U	W 3-1	Parkin, Jepson 2	2,331
37		6	(h)	New Brighton	W 3-1	Jepson 2, McDonald (og)	3,645
38		9	(a)	Southport	L 1-3	Jepson	2,175
39		13	(a)	Rochdale	L 1-2	Jepson	2,894
40		20	(h)	Southport	W 2-0	Martin (og), Parry	3,343
41		27	(a)	Darlington	D 0-0		2,020
42	May	4	(h)	Nelson	D 4-4	Chadwick, Jepson 2, Latham	2,671

FINAL LEAGUE POSITION: 18th in Division Three North

Appearances
Goals

FA Cup

1	Nov	24	(h)	South Shields	W 2-1	Parkin, Parry	5,354
2	Dec	8	(h)	Spennymoor U	W 7-0	Jepson 3, Parry 2, McLoughlin 2	7,230
3	Jan	12	(h)	Bournemouth	D 1-1	Jepson	8,027
R		16	(a)	Bournemouth	L 0-2		10,486

Appearances
Goals

Finnigan RJ	Armstrong J	Whittaker T	Dodds C	Latham A	Lee P	Parry FT	Winskill W	Parkin JT	McLoughlin G	Barclay JB	Curran A	Tootill A	Chadwick J	Tomlinson J	Jepson JJ	Haworth J	Haworth H	Moon A	Arnold HS	Worthington W	Thornton R	
1	2	3	4	5	6	7	8	9	10	11												1
1	2	3	4		6	7	8	9	10	11	5											2
	2	3	4		6	7	8	9	10	11	5	1										3
	2	3	4		6	7	8	9	10	11	5	1										4
	2	3	4		6	7		9	10	11	5	1	8									5
	2	3	4		6	7		9	10	11	5	1	8									6
	2	3			6	7		9		11	5	1	8	4	10							7
	2	3	4	10	6	7		9		11	5	1	8									8
	2	3	4	10	6	7		9	8	11	5	1										9
	2	3	4	10	6	7		9	8	11	5	1										10
	2	3			6	7		9	10	11	5	1	8	4								11
	2	3		4	6	7		9	10	11	5	1	8									12
	2	3		6	4	7		8	10	11	5	1			9							13
	2	3		4	6	7		8	10	11	5	1			9							14
	2	3		4	6	7		8	10			1		5	9	11						15
	2	3		4	6	7		8	10	11	5	1			9							16
	2	3		4	6	7		8	10	11	5	1			9							17
	2	3		4	6	7		8	10	11	5	1			9							18
	2	3		4	6	7		9	10	11	5	1	8									19
	2	3		4	6	7		8	10	11	5	1			9							20
	2	3		4	6	7		8	10	11	5	1			9							21
	2	3		4	6	7		8	10	11	5	1			9							22
	2	3		4	6	7			10	11	5	1	8		9							23
	2	3		4	6	7			10	11	5	1	8		9							24
	2	3		4		7			10		5	1	8		9		6	11				25
	2	3		4	6	7			10		5	1	8		9				11			26
	2	3		4	6	7			10	11	5	1	8		9							27
	2	3		4	6	7			10	11	5	1	8		9							28
	2	3		4	6	7			10	11	5	1	8		9							29
	2	3			6	7	4			11	5	1	8		9					10		30
	2	3		4	6	7			10	11	5	1	8		9							31
	2	3		4	6	7			10	11	5		8		9						1	32
	2	3		4	6	7			10	11	5		8		9						1	33
	2	3		4	6	7			10	11	5		8		9						1	34
	2	3		4	6				8	11	5		7		9					10	1	35
	2	3		4	6	7		8		11	5		10		9						1	36
	2	3		4	6	7		8		11	5		10		9						1	37
	2	3		4	6	7		8		11	5		10		9						1	38
	2	3		4	6	7		8		11	5		10		9						1	39
	2	3		4	6	7			10	11	5				9			8			1	40
	2	3		4	6	7			10	11	5		8		9						1	41
	2	3		4	6	7			10	11	5		8		9						1	42
2	42	42	9	34	41	41	5	26	35	39	40	29	26	3	30	1	1	2	1	2	11	
	1			1	1	5		9	11	5	2		9		21							

3 own-goals

	2	3		4	6	7		8	10	11	5	1			9							1
	2	3		4	6	7		8	10	11	5	1			9							2
	2	3		4	6	7		8	10	11	5	1			9							3
	2	3		4	6	7		8	10	11	5	1			9							R
	4	4		4	4	4		4	4	4	4	4			4							
						3		1	2						4							

1929-30

Secretary/Manager: Ernest Blackburn

1	Aug	31	(a)	Doncaster R	L	1-3	Hawes	4,794
2	Sep	2	(a)	Hartlepools U	D	2-2	Jepson, Curran	4,953
3		7	(h)	Chesterfield	W	3-0	Jepson 2, Pears	6,335
4		9	(h)	Hartlepools U	W	3-0	Jepson 3	4,966
5		14	(a)	Lincoln C	D	3-3	Hawes, Hamilton, Pears	6,040
6		21	(h)	Tranmere R	D	3-3	Hawes, Jepson 2	5,108
7		24	(h)	Nelson	W	3-0	Ferguson, Whyte, Lee	7,108
8		28	(a)	Halifax T	D	1-1	Armstrong (pen)	4,763
9	Oct	5	(h)	Rotherham U	W	2-0	Jepson, Hamilton	5,183
10		12	(a)	Rochdale	L	0-4		5,362
11		19	(h)	Wigan B	W	3-1	Hawes, Jepson 2	5,007
12		26	(a)	Wrexham	W	1-0	Hamilton	4,299
13	Nov	2	(h)	Barrow	W	3-1	Lee, Jepson, Whyte	4,457
14		9	(a)	Port Vale	L	2-5	Jepson 2	11,294
15		16	(h)	New Brighton	W	5-0	Latham, Whyte, Jepson, Hamilton, Hawes	4,121
16		23	(a)	Stockport C	L	0-1		8,720
17	Dec	7	(a)	Crewe A	L	1-2	Jepson	3,909
18		21	(a)	Nelson	L	1-2	Jepson	3,806
19		25	(a)	Darlington	W	4-2	Hamilton 3, Hawes	3,739
20		26	(h)	Darlington	W	3-1	Ferguson 2, Latham	5,114
21	Jan	1	(h)	Carlisle U	W	7-2	Jepson 2, Whyte, Hamilton 2, Hawes, Ferguson	4,138
22		4	(a)	Chesterfield	L	2-4	Ferguson 2	4,831
23		18	(h)	Lincoln C	L	0-3		4,513
24		25	(a)	Tranmere R	D	2-2	Hamilton, Pears	4,219
25	Feb	1	(h)	Halifax T	W	7-1	Parsons 4, Pears, Hamilton 2	3,467
26		8	(a)	Rotherham U	W	4-2	Parsons 4	4,096
27		15	(h)	Rochdale	W	6-2	Hawes, Ferguson 2, Pears 2, Parsons	4,361
28		22	(a)	Wigan B	L	1-2	Parsons	4,197
29		24	(h)	Doncaster R	D	3-3	Pears, Hawes, Whyte	2,143
30	Mar	1	(h)	Wrexham	L	1-3	Pears	4,353
31		5	(h)	York C	D	1-1	Hamilton	2,017
32		8	(a)	Barrow	L	1-3	Hamilton	2,438
33		15	(h)	Port Vale	L	0-2		4,431
34		22	(a)	New Brighton	L	0-5		4,129
35		29	(h)	Stockport C	L	0-1		4,552
36	Apr	5	(a)	York C	L	0-2		4,529
37		12	(h)	Crewe A	L	0-3		2,777
38		18	(a)	Carlisle U	L	1-2	Parsons	5,682
39		19	(a)	Southport	L	0-2		2,788
40		21	(h)	South Shields	L	1-2	Walton	2,789
41		26	(h)	Southport	D	1-1	Parsons	1,818
42	May	3	(a)	South Shields	D	2-2	Littlewood (og), Jepson	1,752

FINAL LEAGUE POSITION: 16th in Division Three North

Appearances
Goals

FA Cup

1	Nov	30	(h)	Rochdale	W	3-1	Jepson 2, Armstrong (pen)	5,456
2	Dec	14	(a)	Bristol R	L	1-4	Ferguson	7,844

Appearances
Goals

Soutar HW	Armstrong J	Whittaker T	Latham A	Curran A	Lee P	Hamilton W	Ferguson D	Jepson JJ	Hawes AR	Pears J	Tyler W	Whyte G	Thornton R	Young J	Haworth J	Parsons J	Carrick J	Haworth H	Haworth Ralph	Chadwick J	Walton G	
1	2	3	4	5	6	7	8	9	10	11												1
1	2	3	4	5	6	7	8	9	10	11												2
1	2	3	4	5	6	7	8	9	10	11												3
1	2	3	4	5	6	7	8	9	10	11												4
1	2	3	4	5	6	7	8	9	10	11												5
1	2	3	4	5	6	7	8	9	10	11												6
1	2	3		5	6	7	8	9	10		4	11										7
	2			5	6	7	8	9	10		4	11	1	3								8
	2			5	6	7	8	9	10		4	11	1	3								9
	2		4	5	6	7	8	9	10			11	1	3								10
	2			5	6	7	8	9	10		4	11	1	3								11
	2	3		5	6	7	8	9	10			4	1		11							12
	2	3		5	6	7	8	9	10		4	11	1									13
	2	3		5	6	7	8	9	10		4	11	1									14
	2	3	4	5	6	7	8	9	10			11	1									15
	2	3	4	5	6	7	8	9	10			11	1									16
	2	3	4	5	6	7	8	9	10			11	1									17
	2	3	4	5	6	7	8	9	10			11	1									18
	2	3	4	5	6	7	8	9	10			11	1									19
	2	3	4	5	6	7	8	9	10			11	1									20
	2	3		5	6	7	8	9	10	11		4	1									21
	2	3	4	5	6	7	8	9	10			11	1									22
	2	3	4	5	6	7	8	9	10			11	1									23
	2	3		5	6	7	8		10	11		4	1			9						24
	2	3		5	6	7	8		10	11		4	1			9						25
	2	3		5	6	7	8		10	11		4	1			9						26
	2	3		5	6	7	8		10	11			1			9	4					27
	2	3		5	6	7	8		10	11		4	1			9						28
	2	3		5	6	7	8		10	11		4	1			9						29
	2	3		5		7	8		10	11		4	1			9		6				30
	2	3		5	6	7	8	9		11	4	10	1									31
	2			5	6	7	8	9	10	11		4	1						3			32
	2	3	4	5	6	7		9	8	11		10	1									33
	2	3	4		6		9		8			10	1		11				5	7		34
	2	3			6	7	8		10	11		4	1			9	5					35
	2	3		5	6	7	8		10	11		4	1			9						36
	2	3		5	6	7	8		10	11		4	1			9						37
	2	3			6	7	4	9		11		10	1			8	5					38
	2				3	7	4	9	10			6	1		11	8	5					39
	2			3		7	4	10				6	1		11	9	5				8	40
	2	3	4	5		7	8	11	10			6	1			9						41
	2	3		5		7	8	11	10			6	1			9	4					42
7	42	35	18	38	38	41	41	31	39	21	7	35	35	4	4	15	6	1	2	1	1	
	1		2	1	2	14	8	20	9	8		5				12					1	

1 own-goal

Soutar HW	Armstrong J	Whittaker T	Latham A	Curran A	Lee P	Hamilton W	Ferguson D	Jepson JJ	Hawes AR	Pears J	Tyler W	Whyte G	Thornton R	Young J	Haworth J	Parsons J	Carrick J	Haworth H	Haworth Ralph	Chadwick J	Walton G	
	2	3	4	5	6	7	8	9	10			11	1									1
	2	3	4	5	6	7	8	9	10			11	1									2
	2	2	2	2	2	2	2	2	2			2	2									
	1						1	2														

1930-31

Secretary/Manager: Ernest Blackburn

1	Aug	30	(h)	Crewe A	W	3-1	Abel 2, Agar	5,011
2	Sep	1	(a)	Barrow	D	0-0		4,970
3		6	(a)	Wrexham	L	1-6	Riley	7,050
4		10	(h)	Southport	W	2-0	Abel, Whyte (pen)	3,833
5		13	(h)	Tranmere R	W	5-2	Riley 2, Whyte (pen), Abel, Broome	4,706
6		16	(a)	Southport	D	3-3	Whyte (pen), Abel 2	2,325
7		20	(a)	Carlisle U	L	3-7	Summers 2, Riley	6,704
8		27	(h)	York C	W	4-2	Abel, Agar, Riley 2	4,295
9		30	(h)	Barrow	W	3-1	Whyte 2 (2 pens), Abel	4,427
10	Oct	4	(a)	Rotherham U	L	1-8	Riley	7,070
11		11	(h)	Chesterfield	L	1-3	Whyte (pen)	4,168
12		18	(h)	Hartlepools U	L	0-2		3,344
13		25	(a)	Nelson	L	2-4	Abel, Agar	2,756
14	Nov	1	(h)	Hull C	L	1-3	Walton	2,758
15		8	(a)	Doncaster R	L	1-6	Abel	3,331
16		15	(h)	Gateshead	W	2-1	Riley, Broome	2,811
17		22	(a)	Stockport C	L	1-4	Broome	4,691
18	Dec	6	(a)	Halifax T	D	1-1	Walton	4,330
19		15	(h)	Darlington	W	2-1	Broome, Abel	1,175
20		20	(a)	Lincoln C	L	2-5	Whyte, Abel	5,731
21		25	(h)	Wigan B	W	3-0	Riley 2, Agar	4,155
22		26	(a)	Wigan B	L	2-3	Abel 2	5,597
23		27	(a)	Crewe A	L	1-2	Whyte	4,082
24	Jan	1	(h)	Rochdale	L	2-3	Broome, Abel	3,724
25		3	(h)	Wrexham	L	1-3	Agar	2,871
26		10	(h)	New Brighton	W	3-0	Walton, Whyte (pen), Agar	1,843
27		17	(a)	Tranmere R	L	0-8		4,473
28		24	(h)	Carlisle U	W	3-0	Agar, Walton, Abel	1,680
29	Feb	7	(h)	Rotherham U	W	3-2	Abel, Agar, Viner	2,396
30		14	(a)	Chesterfield	L	3-7	Agar 2, Abel	4,514
31		21	(a)	Hartlepools U	D	3-3	Johnson 2, Walton	2,370
32		28	(h)	Nelson	W	3-1	Johnson, Walton, J.Haworth	2,216
33	Mar	7	(a)	Hull C	D	1-1	Agar	2,834
34		14	(h)	Doncaster R	W	2-0	J.Haworth 2	2,571
35		21	(a)	Gateshead	L	0-4		5,034
36		28	(h)	Stockport C	D	2-2	Riley 2	2,555
37	Apr	3	(a)	Rochdale	W	6-1	Broome 4, Agar, Riley	3,024
38		4	(a)	New Brighton	D	0-0		2,323
39		6	(a)	York C	L	1-3	J.Haworth	4,933
40		11	(h)	Halifax T	D	1-1	Riley	2,658
41		18	(a)	Darlington	D	1-1	Riley	1,108
42		25	(h)	Lincoln C	W	5-3	Riley 3, Agar, Whyte (pen)	3,844

FINAL LEAGUE POSITION: 13th in Division Three North

Appearances

Goals

FA Cup

1	Nov	29	(h)	Lancaster T	W	3-1	Agar 2, Abel	4,110
2	Dec	13	(h)	Torquay U	L	0-1		6,009

Appearances

Goals

Thornton R	Armstrong J	Whittaker T	Pickup T	Curran A	Pigg W	Agar A	Riley H	Abel S	Broome WH	Summers GM	Ferguson D	Whyte G	Viner RV	Law GB	Walton G	Haworth R	Haworth J	Platt J	Snary JE	Fletcher J	Rhodes H	Moon A	Lansdale J	Johnson S	Finn J	
1	2	3	4	5	6	7	8	9	10	11																1
1	2	3	4		6	7	8	9	10	11	5															2
1	2	3	4		6	7	8	9		11	5	10														3
1	2	3				7	8	9	10	11	4	6	5													4
1	2	3				7	8	9	10	11	4	6	5													5
1	2	3				7	8	9	10	11	4	6	5													6
1		3	4			7	8	9	10	11	2	6	5													7
1		3		5		7	8	9	10	11	4	6		2												8
1		3		5			8	9	10	11	4	6		2	7											9
1		3		5			8	9	10	11	4	6				2	7									10
	2	3		5	6		8	9	7	11	4	10						1								11
1		3	7				8	9	10	11	4	6	5						2							12
1		3				7	8	9	10	11	4	6	5						2							13
1		3						9	10	11	4	6	5		8				2	7						14
1		3				7		9		11	4	6		2	8						5	10				15
1	2	3			6	7	8		10	9	4	11	5													16
	2	3			6		8	9	10	11	4	7	5										1			17
		3		2	6	7		9	10	11	4		5		8								1			18
	2	3			6		8	9	10	11	4	7	5										1			19
	2	3				7	8	9	10	11	4	6	5										1			20
	2	3				7	8	9	10	11	4	6	5										1			21
	2	3				7	8	9		11	4	6	5		10								1			22
	2	3		4		7	8	9		11	10	6	5										1			23
	2	3				7	8	9	10	11	4	6	5										1			24
	2	3				7	9		10	11	4	6	5		8								1			25
	2	3		4		7				11	8	6	5		10								1	9		26
	2	3		4		7					8	6	5		10		11						1	9		27
	2	3				7	8	9			4	6	5		10		11						1			28
	2	3				7	8	9			4	6	5		10		11						1			29
	2	3				7	8	9			4	6	5		10		11						1			30
	2					7			10		4	6	5		8		11						1	9	3	31
	2					7			10		4	6	5		8		11						1	9	3	32
	2	3				7			10		4		5		8		11						1	9	6	33
	2					7			10		4	6	5		8		11						1	9	3	34
	2			5		7			10		4	6			8		11						1	9	3	35
		3				7	10		9		4	6	5		8		11		2				1			36
	2	3				7	10		9		4	6	5		8		11						1			37
	2	3				7	10		9		4	6	5		8		11						1			38
	2	3				7	10		9		4	6	5		8		11						1			39
	2	3				7	8		9		4	6	5		10		11						1			40
	2	3			6	7	8		9		4	11	5		10								1			41
	2	3			6	7	8		9		4	11	5		10								1			42
15	32	38	5	10	10	35	32	26	33	26	41	38	33	3	23	1	15	1	4	1	1	1	26	7	5	
						13	18	18	9	2		10	1		6		4							3		

Thornton R	Armstrong J	Whittaker T	Pickup T	Curran A	Pigg W	Agar A	Riley H	Abel S	Broome WH	Summers GM	Ferguson D	Whyte G	Viner RV	Law GB	Walton G	Haworth R	Haworth J	Platt J	Snary JE	Fletcher J	Rhodes H	Moon A	Lansdale J	Johnson S	Finn J	
		3		2	6	7		9	10	11	4	8	5										1			1
	2	3			6	7	8	9	10	11	4		5										1			2
	1	2		1	2	2	1	2	2	2	2	1	2										2			
						2		1																		

1931-32

Secretary/Manager: Ernest Blackburn until 16 January then Amos Wade from 23 January 1932.

1	Aug	29	(a)	Rochdale	D 2-2	Wright, Viner	6,974
2	Sep	2	(h)	Carlisle U	W 5-3	Watson 2, Williamson (pen), Wright, Ferguson	3,288
3		5	(h)	Doncaster R	W 3-2	Watson, Birch, Williamson (pen)	4,854
4		7	(a)	Crewe A	L 1-3	Watson	5,578
5		12	(a)	Southport	L 2-4	Watson, Williamson (pen)	6,161
6		19	(h)	York C	W 2-1	High, Walton	4,468
7		26	(a)	Tranmere R	L 1-8	Wright	6,116
8		29	(h)	Crewe A	W 2-0	Walton, Watson	4,002
9	Oct	3	(h)	Rotherham U	W 5-2	Agar, Ferguson, Williamson 3 (1 pen)	3,983
10		10	(a)	Stockport C	L 0-3		5,254
11		17	(a)	Chester	L 0-1		7,094
12		24	(h)	Hartlepools U	W 5-0	Agar, Wright, Watson 2, Walton	2,978
13	Nov	7	(h)	Darlington	W 4-0	Walton 2, Wright, Agar	3,434
14		14	(a)	Halifax T	L 0-1		5,015
15		21	(h)	Walsall	W 1-0	Watson	3,539
16	Dec	5	(h)	New Brighton	W 4-1	Agar 3, Garbutt	3,124
17		19	(h)	Hull C	D 1-1	Agar	3,671
18		25	(h)	Wrexham	W 5-0	Williamson 4, Jones	4,307
19		26	(a)	Wrexham	L 1-2	Williamson	8,084
20	Jan	1	(h)	Lincoln C	D 2-2	Agar, Williamson	6,511
21		2	(h)	Rochdale	W 3-0	Williamson, Agar, Jones	1,824
22		9	(a)	Gateshead	L 0-4		6,480
23		16	(a)	Doncaster R	L 1-3	Spargo (og)	4,164
24		30	(a)	York C	L 0-1		3,860
25	Feb	6	(h)	Tranmere R	D 2-2	Williamson, Wright	3,497
26		10	(h)	Southport	D 1-1	Walton	1,816
27		13	(a)	Rotherham U	W 3-2	Garbutt, Price (pen), Wright	2,672
28		18	(a)	Barrow	L 0-3		3,113
29		20	(h)	Stockport C	W 2-0	Price (pen), Wright	3,159
30		27	(h)	Chester	L 2-3	Ferguson 2	3,981
31	Mar	5	(a)	Hartlepools U	L 0-1		3,051
32		19	(a)	Darlington	L 1-4	Agar	2,165
33		25	(a)	Lincoln C	L 1-5	Agar	11,796
34		26	(h)	Halifax T	W 4-0	Agar 2, Garbutt 2	2,591
35	Apr	2	(a)	Walsall	D 5-5	Jones, Cooper (og), Garbutt 2, Walton	2,726
36		9	(h)	Gateshead	L 1-2	Price (pen)	3,786
37		16	(a)	New Brighton	L 1-2	Garbutt	2,334
38		23	(h)	Barrow	W 2-0	Agar, Wright	1,610
39		30	(a)	Hull C	L 0-3		3,535
40	May	7	(a)	Carlisle U	L 0-3		2,540

FINAL LEAGUE POSITION: 14th in Division Three North

Appearances
Goals

FA Cup

1	Nov	28	(a)	Rotherham U	D 0-0		6,118
R	Dec	2	(h)	Rotherham U	W 5-0	Williamson 3, Watson, Agar	2,964
2		12	(a)	Halifax T	L 0-3		

Appearances
Goals

Bell JC	Armstrong J	Price NN	Ferguson D	Viner RV	High S	Agar A	Walton G	Watson TL	Williamson TW	Wright N	Birch W	McCulloch SS	Law GB	Garbutt HP	Jones WW	Foster R	Heap C	Benson J	Henderson W	
1	2	3	4	5	6	7	8	9	10	11										1
1	2	3	4	5	6	7	8	9	10	11										2
1	2	3	4	5	6		8	9	10	11	7									3
1	2	3	4	5	6		8	9	10	11	7									4
1	2	3	8	5	6	7		9	10	11		4								5
1	2	3	4	5	6	7	10	9	8	11										6
1	2	3	8	5	6	7	10	9		11		4								7
1	2	3	4	5	6	7	10	9	8	11										8
1	2	3	4	5	6	7	10	9	8	11										9
1	2	3	4	5	6	7	10	9	8	11										10
1		3	4	5	6	7	10	9	8	11			2							11
1	2	3	4	5	6	7	8	9	10	11										12
1	2	3	4	5	6	7	8	9	10	11										13
1	2	3	4	5	6	7	8		10	11				9						14
1	2	3	4	5		7	8	9	10	11		6								15
1	2	3	4	5	6	7	8		10	11				9						16
1	2	3	4	5	6	7	8	9	10	11										17
1	2	3	4	5		7	8		9	11		6			10					18
1	2	3	4	5		7	8		9	11		6			10					19
1	2	3	4	5		7	8		9	11		6			10					20
1	2	3	4	5		7	8		9	11		6			10					21
1	2	3	4	5		7	8		9	11		6			10					22
	2		4	5		7	8		9	11		6			10	1	3			23
	2	3	4	5		7	8		9	11		6			10	1				24
	2	3	4	5		7	8		9	11		6			10	1				25
1	2	3	8	5	4	7	10			11		6			9					26
1		3	4	5		7	8			11		6		9	10		2			27
1		3	4	5		7	8			11		6		9	10		2			28
1		3	4	5		7	8		10	11		6			9		2			29
1	2	3	8	5	4	7			10	11		6			9					30
1	2	3	4		6	7		9	8	11		5			10					31
	2	3			6	7	4	9		11		5		8	10	1				32
	2	3		5	6	7		9		11		4		8	10	1				33
	2	3		5	6	7	8			11		4		9	10	1				34
	2	3		5	6	7	8			11		4		9	10	1				35
	2	3		5	6	7	8			11		4		9	10	1				36
	2	3		5	6	7	8			11		4		9	10	1				37
	2	3		5	6	7	8			11		4		9	10	1				38
	2	3		5	6	7	10	8		11		4		9		1				39
	2	3		5	6	7	10			11		4			9			1	8	40
28	36	39	31	38	28	38	36	19	27	40	2	26	1	12	22	11	4	1	1	
		3	4	1	1	14	7	9	14	9	1			7	3					

2 own-goals

1	2	3	4	5	6	7	8	9	10	11	1
1	2	3	4	5	6	7	8	9	10	11	R
1	2	3	4	5	6	7	8	9	10	11	2
3	3	3	3	3	3	3	3	3	3	3	
						1		1	3		

1932-33

Secretary/Manager: Amos Wade

1	Aug	27	(h)	Halifax T	W 4-1	Eddleston, Wright 2, Fitton	5,082
2		29	(h)	Rotherham U	W 5-1	Price, Wright, Johnson, Fitton 2	3,402
3	Sep	3	(a)	New Brighton	D 2-2	Johnson, Fitton	3,803
4		5	(a)	Rotherham U	W 3-2	Fitton, Johnson, Eddleston	3,064
5		10	(h)	Chester	L 1-4	Price (pen)	5,569
6		17	(a)	Barrow	L 0-5		5,068
7		24	(h)	Carlisle U	W 3-1	Eddleston, Fitton 2	3,518
8		27	(h)	Southport	D 1-1	Johnson	4,828
9	Oct	1	(a)	York C	D 0-0		4,553
10		8	(h)	Crewe A	W 2-0	Walton 2	2,244
11		15	(a)	Rochdale	L 0-2		7,041
12		22	(h)	Hartlepools U	W 7-1	Johnson 2, McCulloch, Eddleston, Fitton 2, Wright	2,927
13		29	(a)	Barnsley	L 0-4		4,023
14	Nov	5	(h)	Hull C	L 1-2	Eddleston	4,478
15		12	(a)	Doncaster R	D 2-2	Hunter (og), Wright	3,780
16		19	(h)	Darlington	W 2-0	Maycock, Walton	3,137
17	Dec	3	(h)	Gateshead	L 0-3		2,847
18		12	(a)	Walsall	L 0-1		1,414
19		17	(h)	Wrexham	W 5-3	Fitton 2, Johnson, Eddleston 2	1,858
20		24	(a)	Tranmere R	L 0-4		3,193
21		26	(a)	Southport	W 3-2	Fitton, Wright, Little (og)	5,933
22		31	(a)	Halifax T	D 0-0		5,585
23	Jan	2	(h)	Mansfield T	W 6-0	Fitton 3, Walton, Eddleston 2	2,477
24		7	(h)	New Brighton	W 5-4	Fitton, Wright, Walton, McCulloch, Eddleston	2,958
25		14	(a)	Stockport C	L 0-2		4,488
26		21	(a)	Chester	L 2-4	Fitton, Wright	4,980
27		28	(h)	Barrow	D 0-0		1,829
28	Feb	4	(a)	Carlisle U	D 2-2	Fitton, McCulloch	1,927
29		11	(h)	York C	W 5-0	Eddleston, Fitton 2, Walton 2	2,199
30		18	(a)	Crewe A	L 1-3	Dewsnap	2,943
31	Mar	4	(a)	Hartlepools U	L 1-3	Eddleston	3,410
32		11	(h)	Barnsley	W 2-0	Fitton, Armstrong (pen)	3,122
33		18	(a)	Hull C	L 2-4	Fitton, Dewsnap	9,708
34		25	(h)	Doncaster R	D 1-1	Maycock	2,544
35	Apr	1	(a)	Darlington	D 2-2	Fitton, Dewsnap	1,923
36		8	(h)	Stockport C	D 1-1	Wright	2,404
37		15	(a)	Gateshead	L 0-1		1,929
38		17	(a)	Mansfield T	W 3-1	Fitton, Maycock, Wright	3,869
39		22	(h)	Walsall	L 1-3	Wright	2,073
40		29	(a)	Wrexham	L 0-1		4,048
41	May	3	(h)	Rochdale	L 0-3		1,013
42		6	(h)	Tranmere R	W 3-0	Wright, Hobson, Bentley	1,079

FINAL LEAGUE POSITION: 13th in Division Three North

Appearances
Goals

FA Cup

1	Nov	26	(h)	Hereford U	W 2-1	Maycock, Price (pen)	4,365
2	Dec	10	(h)	Aldershot	L 1-2	Johnson	4,851

Appearances
Goals

Allen T	Armstrong J	Price NN	McCulloch SS	Viner RV	Dodds C	Hackett CE	Fitton F	Eddleston J	Johnson J	Wright N	Pattison J	Walton G	Maycock R	Haworth, Robert	Farrell F	Bentley W	Schofield R	Corcoran T	Dewsnap GH	Hobson E	
1	2	3	4	5	6	7	8	9	10	11											1
1	2	3	4	5	6	7	9	8	10	11											2
	2	3	4	5	6	7	9	8	10	11	1										3
	2	3	4	5	6	7	9	8	11		1	10									4
	2	3	4	5	6	7	9	8	10	11	1										5
	2	3	4	5	6	7	9		10	11	1		8								6
1	2	3	6	5	4		9	7	10	11		8									7
1	2	3	6	5	4		9	7	10	11		8									8
1	2	3	6	5	4		9	7	10	11		8									9
1		3	6	5	4		9	7	11			10	8	2							10
1	2	3	6	5	4		9	7	10	11		8									11
1	2	3	6	5	4		9	7	10	11		8									12
1	2	3	6		4		9	7	10	11		8			5						13
1	2	3	6		4		9	7	10	11		8			5						14
1		3	6	5	4		10	7		11		8	9	2							15
1	2	3	6	5	4		9	7	11			10	8								16
1	2	3	6	5			9	7				10	8			4	11				17
1	2		5		4	7	8	9	10	11						6		3			18
1	2	3	6	5	4		9	8	10	11									7		19
1	2		6	5	4		9	8	10	11								3	7		20
1	2		6	5	4		9	8	10	11								3	7		21
1	2		6	5	4		9	8	10	11								3	7		22
1	2		6	5	4		9	8		11		10						3	7		23
1	2		6	5			9	8		11		10				4		3	7		24
1	2		6	5	4		9	8		11		10						3	7		25
1	2		6	5	4		9	8		11		10	7					3			26
1	2		6	5	4		9	8	7	11		10						3			27
1	2		6	5	4		9	8	7	11		10						3			28
1	2		5		4		9	8		11		10				6		3	7		29
1	2		5		4		9		10	11			8			6		3	7		30
1	2		6		5		9	10		11			8			4		3	7		31
1	2		5		4		9	10		11			8			6		3	7		32
1	2		5		4		9	10		11			8			6		3	7		33
1	2		5		4		9	10		11			8			6		3	7		34
1	2		5		4		9	10		11			8			6		3	7		35
1	2		5		4		9	10		11			8			6		3	7		36
	2		5		4		9	10		11	1		8			6		3	7		37
	2		5		4		9	10		11	1		8			6		3	7		38
	2		5		4		9	10		11	1		8			6		3	7		39
1	2		5		4		9	7	10	11			8			6		3			40
1	2		5		4		9	7	10	11			8			6		3			41
1	2		5				8	7	10	11				4		6		3		9	42
35	40	18	42	25	39	7	42	40	26	38	7	19	18	3	2	17	1	24	18	1	
	1	2	3				24	12	7	12		7	3			1			3	1	

2 own-goals

Allen T	Armstrong J	Price NN	McCulloch SS	Viner RV	Dodds C	Hackett CE	Fitton F	Eddleston J	Johnson J	Wright N	Pattison J	Walton G	Maycock R	Haworth, Robert	Farrell F	Bentley W	Schofield R	Corcoran T	Dewsnap GH	Hobson E	
1	2	3	6	5	4			7	10	11		8	9								1
1	2	3	5		4				10	11		8	9	6					7		2
2	2	2	2	1	2			1	2	2		2	2	1					1		
		1							1				1								

1933-34

Secretary/Manager: Amos Wade

1	Aug	26	(a)	Stockport C	L 0-3		7,301
2		29	(a)	Southport	D 1-1	Wyper	4,416
3	Sep	2	(h)	Chesterfield	W 1-0	Cheetham	4,867
4		9	(a)	Rochdale	W 1-0	Watson	7,437
5		11	(h)	Gateshead	W 5-2	Cheetham, Dulson, Lennox, Dodds, Price (Pen)	4,457
6		16	(h)	Tranmere R	D 2-2	Cheetham, Wyper	6,146
7		23	(a)	Barnsley	L 0-6		9,671
8		26	(h)	Southport	W 3-2	Cheetham 2, Lennox	4,381
9		30	(h)	Mansfield T	D 1-1	Wyper	4,271
10	Oct	7	(a)	Hartlepools U	L 0-3		4,605
11		14	(h)	Wrexham	D 1-1	Price (pen)	3,827
12		21	(a)	Halifax T	L 1-2	Watson	7,334
13		28	(h)	Crewe A	L 0-2		2,705
14	Nov	4	(a)	New Brighton	W 3-0	Jeavons 2, Wyper	3,535
15		11	(h)	Rotherham U	D 2-2	Kelly, Cheetham	3,020
16		18	(a)	Walsall	L 0-5		5,769
17	Dec	2	(a)	Chester	L 0-7		4,795
18		16	(a)	Barrow	W 6-2	Lennox, Kelly 2, Dodds, Jeavons, Cheetham	2,874
19		23	(h)	Carlisle U	W 2-1	Kelly, Jeavons	2,967
20		26	(a)	Gateshead	L 0-2		4,348
21		30	(h)	Stockport C	L 0-3		2,665
22	Jan	1	(h)	Darlington	W 2-0	Cheetham, Leedham	2,577
23		3	(h)	Doncaster R	W 4-1	Kelly 2, Stoddart (pen), Lennox	2,077
24		6	(a)	Chesterfield	L 0-1		8,213
25		20	(h)	Rochdale	L 1-3	Kelly	2,851
26		24	(h)	York C	W 4-1	Leedham 2, Jeavons 2 (1 pen)	1,306
27	Feb	1	(a)	Tranmere R	L 0-2		1,788
28		3	(h)	Barnsley	L 0-9		2,814
29		10	(a)	Mansfield T	L 0-5		4,441
30		17	(h)	Hartlepools U	D 2-2	Travis, Jeavons	1,977
31		24	(a)	Wrexham	L 2-3	Kelly, Price (pen)	5,273
32	Mar	3	(h)	Halifax T	D 1-1	Leedham	1,934
33		10	(a)	Crewe A	L 2-4	Lennox, Wyper	2,826
34		17	(h)	New Brighton	W 8-0	Cheetham 4, Lennox 2, Leedham, Armstrong (pen)	1,429
35		24	(a)	Rotherham U	L 1-3	Lennox	2,866
36		31	(h)	Walsall	W 1-0	Clare	2,716
37	Apr	2	(a)	Darlington	L 1-3	Wyper	4,457
38		7	(a)	York C	L 2-3	Lennox, Cheetham	3,928
39		14	(h)	Chester	W 4-1	Cheetham 2, Watson, Dodds	2,096
40		21	(a)	Doncaster R	L 1-5	Wyper	5,005
41		28	(h)	Barrow	L 0-4		1,676
42	May	5	(a)	Carlisle U	L 0-3		2,716
FINAL LEAGUE POSITION: 20th in Division Three North							Appearances
							Goals

FA Cup

1	Nov	25	(a)	Scunthorpe U	D 1-1	Kelly	6,499
R		29	(h)	Scunthorpe U	W 3-0	Lennox, Cheetham 2	3,350
2	Dec	9	(h)	Bristol R	W 1-0	Cheetham	5,991
3	Jan	13	(a)	Millwall	L 0-3		20,980
							Appearances
							Goals

Maidment JHC	Armstrong J	Corcoran T	Dodds C	Stoddart W	McCulloch SS	Wyper HT	Fitton F	Cheetham J	Leedham F	Watson WT	Dulson J	Price NN	Lennox W	Crawshaw R	Rowbotham H	Kelly JN	Jeavons WH	Clare J	Bentley W	Pattison J	Travis H	Match
1	2	3	4	5	6	7	8	9	10	11												1
1	2	3	4	5	6	7	8	9		11	10											2
1		3	4	5	6	7		9		11	10	2	8									3
1		3	4	5	6	7		9		11	10	2	8									4
1		3	4	5	6	7		9		11	10	2	8									5
1		3	4	5	6	7		9		11	10	2	8									6
1		3	4	5	6	7		9		11	10	2	8									7
1		3	4	5	6	7		9		11	10	2	8									8
1		3	4	5	6	7		9		11	10	2	8									9
1		3		5	6	7		9		11	10	2	8	4								10
1		3	4	5	6	7		9		11	8	2			10							11
1	2			4	6	7	10	9		11		3		5	8							12
1	2			4	6	7		9		11		3	10	5	8							13
1	2			4	6	7		9				3		5	8	10	11					14
1	2			4	6	7		9		10		3		5		8	11					15
1	2			4	6	8		9		11		3		5		10	7					16
1	2		4	5	6	7					10	3	8			9	11					17
1	2		4	5	6			9				3	8			10	7	11				18
1	2		4	5	6			9				3	8			10	7	11				19
1	2	3		5	6			9					8			10	7	11	4			20
1	2			5	6			9				3	8			10	7	11	4			21
1	2	3		5	6			9	10				8				7	11	4			22
1	2	3		5	6				10				8	4		9	7	11				23
1		3		5	6			11	10			2	8			9	7		4			24
1	2			5	6			9	10			3				8	7	11	4			25
1		3	6	5					10			2	8	4		9	7	11				26
		3	4		6			9	10			2	8	5			7	11		1		27
	2	3	4	5	6				10				8			9	7	11		1		28
1		3	4		6				10			2	8	5			7	11			9	29
1		3	4		6			8	10	11		2		5			7				9	30
1	2		4		6	7		9	10	11		3		5		8						31
	2		4		6	7		9	10	11		3		5						1	8	32
	2		4		6	7		9	10	11		3	8	5						1		33
1	2		4		6	7		9	10	11		3	8	5								34
1	2		4		6	7		9	10	11		3	8	5								35
1	2	3	4		6	7		9	10				8	5				11				36
1	2	3	4		6	7		9	10				8	5				11				37
1	2	3	4		6	7		9	10				8	5				11				38
1	2	3	4	5	6	7		9	10	11			8									39
1	2	3	4	5	6	7		9	10	11			8									40
1	2		4	5	6	7		9	10	11		3	8									41
	2			5	6	7		9	10	11		3	8							1	4	42
37	28	25	29	31	41	29	3	37	22	25	11	31	31	19	4	14	17	14	5	5	4	
	1		3	1		7		15	5	3	1	3	9			8	7	1			1	

Maidment JHC	Armstrong J	Corcoran T	Dodds C	Stoddart W	McCulloch SS	Wyper HT	Fitton F	Cheetham J	Leedham F	Watson WT	Dulson J	Price NN	Lennox W	Crawshaw R	Rowbotham H	Kelly JN	Jeavons WH	Clare J	Bentley W	Pattison J	Travis H	Round
1	2		4	5	6	7		9				3	8			10	11					1
1	2		4	5	6	7		9				3	8			10	11					R
1	2		4	5	6	7		9		11		3	8			10						2
1	2	4		5	6			11	10			3	8			9	7					3
4	4	1	3	4	4	3		4	1	1		4	4			4	3					
								3					1			1						

1934-35

Secretary/Manager: Amos Wade

1	Aug	25	(h)	New Brighton	L 1-3	Marcroft	4,249
2		30	(a)	Carlisle U	L 0-2		6,203
3	Sep	1	(a)	Chester	L 0-4		8,932
4		8	(h)	Southport	D 1-1	Corcoran (pen)	2,776
5		15	(a)	Doncaster R	L 1-2	Marcroft	5,687
6		19	(h)	Mansfield T	W 2-0	Harker 2	1,604
7		22	(h)	Hartlepools U	L 0-4		1,993
8		25	(h)	Carlisle U	W 1-0	Marcroft	3,039
9		29	(a)	Crewe A	L 2-4	Harker, Leedham	2,420
10	Oct	6	(h)	Stockport C	W 3-1	Brown, Harker, Leedham	2,792
11		13	(a)	Gateshead	D 1-1	Brown	5,173
12		20	(a)	Rochdale	D 2-2	Brown, Harker	5,263
13		27	(h)	Lincoln C	W 3-0	Harker, Brown, Cull	2,609
14	Nov	3	(a)	Tranmere R	L 1-2	Brown	5,892
15		10	(h)	Wrexham	D 2-2	Jones (og), Cull	4,153
16		17	(a)	Halifax T	L 1-2	Leedham	10,899
17	Dec	1	(a)	Walsall	L 0-6		5,976
18		8	(h)	Chesterfield	W 1-0	Leedham	2,607
19		15	(a)	Mansfield T	L 1-2	Cull	4,327
20		22	(h)	Barrow	W 5-2	Cull, Dodds (pen), Deacon 2, Brown	2,446
21		25	(a)	York C	L 2-5	Harker, Dodds	3,867
22		26	(h)	York C	W 5-2	Hunter, Deacon, Brown 2, Harker	3,877
23		29	(a)	New Brighton	L 1-2	Harker	2,815
24	Jan	1	(a)	Darlington	L 0-5		3,827
25		5	(h)	Chester	D 1-1	Deacon	3,733
26		12	(h)	Rotherham U	L 2-3	Deacon 2	2,518
27		19	(a)	Southport	D 0-0		2,211
28		26	(h)	Doncaster R	L 1-5	Cull	1,777
29	Feb	2	(a)	Hartlepools U	L 2-4	Brown 2	2,259
30		9	(h)	Crewe A	W 3-0	Deacon 2, Britton	2,424
31		20	(a)	Stockport C	L 1-5	Deacon	1,714
32		23	(h)	Gateshead	W 4-2	Deacon, Britton 3	2,220
33	Mar	2	(h)	Rochdale	L 2-5	Britton 2 (1 pen)	2,019
34		9	(a)	Lincoln C	L 0-1		2,448
35		16	(h)	Tranmere R	W 1-0	Dodds (pen)	3,519
36		23	(a)	Wrexham	D 2-2	Harker, Cull	1,972
37		30	(h)	Halifax T	D 1-1	Britton	3,155
38	Apr	6	(a)	Rotherham U	L 0-2		5,126
39		13	(h)	Walsall	D 3-3	Britton, Brown, Deacon	2,541
40		20	(a)	Chesterfield	D 0-0		1,938
41		22	(h)	Darlington	W 2-1	Britton, Marcroft	2,432
42	May	4	(a)	Barrow	W 2-0	Duckworth, Brown	2,225

FINAL LEAGUE POSITION: 18th in Division Three North

Appearances
Goals

FA Cup

1	Nov	24	(a)	Mansfield T	L 1-6	Brown	7,750

Appearances
Goals

Pattison J	Hunter AE	Fieldsend GH	Dodds C	Lockie T	McCulloch SS	Cull JE	Harker W	Cheetham J	Leedham F	Marcroft EH	Gill JA	Corcoran T	Clare J	Thorpe P	Brown FW	Lowery B	Marsden F	Deacon H	Aspin J	Nock JE	Britton F	Duckworth A	
1	2	3	4	5	6	7	8	9	10	11													1
	2	3	4	5	6	7	8		10	11	1	9											2
		3	4	5	6	7	8		10	9	1	2	11										3
		3	4	5	6	7	8	9	10	11	1	2											4
	2		4	5	6	7	8		10	9	1	3	11										5
			4	5	6	7	9		10	11	1	3		2	8								6
			4	5	6	7	9		10	11	1	3		2	8								7
	2		4	5	6	7	9		10	11	1	3			8								8
	2		4	5	6	7	9		10		1	3	11		8								9
	2		4	5	6	7	8		10		1	3	11		9								10
	2		4	5	6	7	8		10		1	3	11		9								11
	2		4	5	6	7	8		10		1	3	11		9								12
	2		4	5	6	7	8		10		1	3	11		9								13
	2		4	5		7	8		10		1	3	11		9	6							14
	2		4	5	6	7	8		10		1	3	11		9								15
	2		4	5	6	7	8		10		1	3	11		9								16
	3		4	5	6	7	8		10		1		11		9		2						17
	2	3	4	5	6	7			10	11	1				9			8					18
	2	3	4	5	6	11	9		10		1				7			8					19
	2	3	4	5	6	11	9		10		1				7			8					20
	2	3	4	5	6	11	9		10		1				7			8					21
	2	3	4	5	6	11	9		10		1				7			8					22
	2	3	4	5	6	11	9		10		1				7			8					23
	2	3	4	5	6		9		10		1				11			8	7				24
	3		4	5	6		9		10	11	1				7		2	8					25
	3		4	5	6	7	9		10		1				11		2	8					26
	3		4	5		7			10		1				11	6	2	8		9			27
	3		4	5	6	7	9		10		1				11		2	8					28
	2	3	4	5		7			10	11	1				9	6		8					29
	2	3	4	5		7				11	1				8	6		10			9		30
1	2	3	4	5		7				11					8	6		10			9		31
1	2	3		5	4	7				11					8	6		10			9		32
1	2	3	5		4	7				11					8	6		10			9		33
	2	3	4	5	6	11	9			7	1				8			10					34
	2	3	4	5	6	11				7	1				8			10			9		35
	2	3	4		5	11	6			7	1				8			10			9		36
	2	3	6		5	7	4			11	1				8			10			9		37
	2	3	4	5	6		7			11	1				8			10			9		38
	2	3	4	5	6		8			11	1				7			10			9		39
	2	3	4		5	7	6			11	1				8			10			9		40
	2	3	4		5	7	6			11	1				8			10			9		41
	2	3	4		5	7	6			11	1				8			10				9	42
4	38	25	41	36	37	38	34	2	29	24	38	15	11	2	37	7	5	25	1	1	11	1	
	1		3			6	10		4	4		1			12			11			9	1	

1 own-goal

Pattison J	Hunter AE	Fieldsend GH	Dodds C	Lockie T	McCulloch SS	Cull JE	Harker W	Cheetham J	Leedham F	Marcroft EH	Gill JA	Corcoran T	Clare J	Thorpe P	Brown FW	
	2		4	5	6	7	8		10		1	3	11		9	1
	1		1	1	1	1	1		1		1	1	1		1	
															1	

1935-36

Player/Manager: John Hacking

1	Aug	31	(a)	Lincoln C	L 0-6		7,190
2	Sep	2	(h)	Chester	L 0-3		4,227
3		7	(h)	Rochdale	L 2-4	Mortimer, Brown	4,212
4		11	(a)	Chester	L 0-4		6,521
5		14	(a)	York C	D 1-1	Mortimer	3,430
6		21	(h)	Barrow	W 2-0	Mutch, Mortimer	3,197
7		24	(h)	Southport	W 1-0	Brown	2,600
8		28	(a)	New Brighton	W 3-2	Brown 2, Reynolds	3,409
9	Oct	5	(h)	Chesterfield	L 0-1		4,709
10		12	(a)	Stockport C	W 2-1	Brown 2	8,066
11		19	(h)	Hartlepools U	W 3-2	Brown 2, Reynolds	2,677
12		26	(a)	Carlisle U	L 1-3	Harker	6,083
13	Nov	2	(h)	Walsall	W 3-1	Reynolds, Brown, Mortimer	3,514
14		9	(a)	Tranmere R	L 0-6		6,993
15		16	(h)	Gateshead	W 6-1	Harker 5, Brown	3,537
16		23	(a)	Darlington	L 1-2	Brown	3,403
17	Dec	7	(a)	Oldham A	L 0-3		5,017
18		14	(h)	Wrexham	L 0-1		2,569
19		21	(a)	Rotherham U	W 3-1	Mortimer 3	4,035
20		25	(a)	Crewe A	L 0-4		4,469
21		26	(h)	Crewe A	W 2-1	Mortimer 2	2,760
22		28	(h)	Lincoln C	D 2-2	Reynolds, Mortimer	3,673
23	Jan	4	(a)	Rochdale	D 2-2	Harker, Mortimer	4,822
24		11	(h)	Halifax T	W 2-0	Mutch, Mortimer	2,306
25		18	(h)	York C	W 7-2	Mortimer 2, Harker 3, Reynolds, Brown	2,345
26		25	(a)	Barrow	W 1-0	Mortimer	3,316
27	Feb	1	(h)	New Brighton	W 5-2	Harker 3, Mortimer 2 (1 pen)	3,645
28		8	(a)	Chesterfield	W 3-0	Mortimer 2, Reynolds	8,119
29		15	(h)	Stockport C	D 1-1	Lapham	4,928
30		22	(a)	Hartlepools U	L 1-2	Green	4,056
31		29	(h)	Tranmere R	W 3-1	Mee, Fairhurst (og), Lapham	3,754
32	Mar	7	(a)	Walsall	L 0-2		3,889
33		14	(h)	Carlisle U	D 0-0		3,560
34		21	(a)	Gateshead	D 0-0		3,496
35		28	(h)	Darlington	W 1-0	Green	3,551
36	Apr	4	(a)	Halifax T	L 0-1		4,229
37		10	(a)	Mansfield T	L 1-3	Reynolds	6,165
38		11	(h)	Oldham A	W 1-0	Mee	3,689
39		13	(h)	Mansfield T	D 1-1	Reynolds	2,771
40		18	(a)	Wrexham	L 0-3		1,506
41		22	(h)	Rotherham U	D 1-1	Reynolds	2,154
42	May	2	(a)	Southport	L 1-2	Brown	1,748
	FINAL LEAGUE POSITION: 9th in Division Three North						Appearances
							Goals

FA Cup

1	Nov	30	(a)	Darlington	L 2-4	Reynolds, Brown	5,586
							Appearances
							Goals

Hacking J	Ivill E	Wilson GW	Dodds C	Robinson C	McCulloch SS	Reynolds W	Harker W	Slinger JW	Brown FW	Mutch W	Fieldsend GH	Mortimer R	Kerr D	McDonald AC	Schofield J	Treanor JL	Mee GW	Aspin J	Gill JA	Green JH	Lapham H	Ash JW	Robinson JJ	
1	2	3	4	5	6	7	8	9	10	11														1
1		2	4	5	6	7	10	9		11	3	8												2
1	2		4		5	7	6		8	11	3	9	10											3
1		2	6		5	7	4		8	11	3	10		9										4
1		2	6		5	7	4		8	11	3	10		9										5
1		2			5	7	8		9	11	3	10			4	6								6
1		2			5	7	8		9	11	3	10			4	6								7
1		2			5	7	8		9	11	3	10			4	6								8
1		2			5	7	8		9	11	3	10			4	6								9
1		2			5	7	8		9		3	10			4	6	11							10
1		2			5	7	10		9		3				4	6	11	8						11
1		2			5	7	8		9		3	10			4	6	11							12
1		2			5	7	8		9		3	10			4	6	11							13
1		2			5	7	8		9		3				4	6	11	10						14
1		2			5	7	8		9		3	10			4	6	11							15
1		2		4	5	7	8		9		3	10				6	11							16
1		2	4		5	7	8		9		3	10				6	11							17
		2	4		5	7	8		9		3	10				6	11		1					18
		2		6	5	7	4		8	11	3	9					10		1					19
		2		6	5	7	4		8	11	3	9					10		1					20
		2			5	7	4		8	11	3	9				6	10		1					21
		2			5	7	4		8	11	3	9				6	10		1					22
		2		4	5	7	8				3	9				6	11		1	10				23
		2		4	5	7	8			11	3	9				6	10		1					24
		2		4	5	7	10		8		3	9				6	11		1					25
		2		4	5	7	10		8		3	9				6	11		1					26
		2		4	5	7	10		8		3	9				6	11		1					27
		2		4	5	7	10		8		3	9				6	11		1					28
		2		4	5	7			8		3					6	11		1	10	9			29
	3	2		4	5	7			8							6	11		1	10	9			30
	3	2		4	5	7			8							6	11		1	10	9			31
	3	2		4	5	7			8							6	11		1	10	9			32
	3	2		4	5	7			8				9			6	11		1	10				33
	3	2		4	5	7			8	9						6	11		1	10				34
	3	2		4	5	7			8	9						6	11		1	10				35
	3	2		4	5	7			8							6	11		1	10	9			36
		2		4	5	7			10		3					6	11		1	8		9		37
		2		4	5	7			9	11	3					6	10		1	8				38
		2		4	5	7			9	11	3					6	10		1	8				39
		2		4	5	7			9	11	3					6	10		1	8				40
	3	2		4	5	7			8							6	11		1	10	9			41
	3	2			5	7			8							6	11			10	9	4	1	42
17	11	41	7	24	42	42	28	2	39	19	32	25	2	2	10	35	33	2	24	15	7	2	1	
						9	13		13	2		19					2			2	2			

1 own-goal

Hacking J	Ivill E	Wilson GW	Dodds C	Robinson C	McCulloch SS	Reynolds W	Harker W	Slinger JW	Brown FW	Mutch W	Fieldsend GH	Mortimer R	Kerr D	McDonald AC	Schofield J	Treanor JL	Mee GW	Aspin J	Gill JA	Green JH	Lapham H	Ash JW	Robinson JJ	
1		2			5	7	8		9		3	10			4	6	11							1
1		1			1	1	1		1		1	1			1	1	1							
						1			1															

1936-37

Manager: John Hacking

1	Aug	29	(h)	Lincoln C	L 1-2	Pateman	5,300
2	Sep	2	(a)	Hartlepools U	L 0-1		7,342
3		5	(a)	New Brighton	D 1-1	Pateman	4,711
4		12	(h)	Hull C	L 0-1		3,136
5		19	(a)	Gateshead	D 1-1	Mortimer	3,760
6		26	(h)	Darlington	W 1-0	Pateman	3,907
7		29	(h)	Hartlepools U	L 1-2	Mortimer	3,919
8	Oct	3	(a)	Wrexham	L 0-1		5,364
9		10	(h)	Stockport C	W 2-1	Pateman, Mortimer	4,066
10		17	(a)	Southport	L 1-3	Mortimer	5,479
11		24	(h)	Tranmere R	W 4-0	Pateman, Rivers, Mortimer 2	3,370
12		31	(a)	Halifax T	L 0-3		7,242
13	Nov	7	(h)	Mansfield T	L 0-3		3,334
14		14	(a)	Crewe A	D 2-2	Mortimer 2 (1 pen)	3,629
15		21	(h)	Chester	W 2-1	Mortimer, Pateman	4,727
16	Dec	5	(h)	Barrow	W 5-0	Mee, Pateman, Mortimer, Wood (og), Rivers	2,331
17		19	(h)	Carlisle U	W 2-1	Mortimer, Mee	3,285
18		25	(h)	Port Vale	L 2-3	Reynolds, Tyson	5,997
19		26	(a)	Lincoln C	D 3-3	Reynolds, Mortimer, Tyson	9,305
20		28	(a)	Port Vale	D 1-1	Mortimer	8,030
21	Jan	1	(h)	Rotherham U	W 3-0	Rivers, Mortimer 2	4,924
22		2	(h)	New Brighton	W 5-0	Reynolds, Mortimer 3 (1 pen), Tyson	2,897
23		9	(a)	Hull C	W 3-0	Mee, Reynolds, Pateman	6,165
24		23	(h)	Gateshead	W 2-1	Reynolds, Tyson	3,145
25	Feb	3	(a)	Darlington	L 1-4	Tyson	1,447
26		6	(h)	Wrexham	D 2-2	Tyson 2	3,514
27		13	(a)	Stockport C	L 2-3	Mortimer, Tyson	13,515
28		20	(h)	Southport	W 6-3	Reynolds 2, Mortimer 4	2,548
29	Mar	6	(h)	Halifax T	W 3-2	Curran 2, Mortimer	3,338
30		13	(a)	Mansfield T	L 1-2	Mortimer	3,385
31		20	(h)	Crewe A	W 4-1	Mortimer 2, Andrews, Tyson	3,487
32		26	(h)	Oldham A	D 1-1	Mortimer	4,760
33		27	(a)	Chester	D 1-1	Curran	6,197
34		29	(a)	Oldham A	L 1-3	Tyson	9,638
35	Apr	3	(h)	Rochdale	W 3-1	Mortimer 2, Mee	4,096
36		10	(a)	Barrow	L 0-1		4,193
37		14	(a)	York C	L 2-4	Reynolds, Rivers	3,065
38		17	(h)	York C	W 2-1	Hann, Mortimer	2,318
39		19	(a)	Tranmere R	W 2-1	Mortimer, Reynolds	1,162
40		24	(a)	Carlisle U	L 0-2		5,470
41		27	(a)	Rochdale	L 1-4	Reynolds	2,820
42	May	1	(a)	Rotherham U	D 2-2	Mortimer, Reynolds	3,152

FINAL LEAGUE POSITION: 13th in Division Three North

Appearances
Goals

FA Cup

1	Nov	28	(h)	Wellington T	W 3-1	Mortimer, Mee, Reynolds	5,254
2	Dec	12	(h)	Tunbridge Wells R	W 1-0	Mee	4,109
3	Jan	16	(a)	Blackburn R	D 2-2	Mortimer 2	31,080
R		20	(h)	Blackburn R	W 3-1*	Mortimer 2, Rivers	11,636
4		30	(a)	Manchester C	L 0-2		39,135

*After extra-time

Appearances
Goals

Robertson A	Wilson GW	Reeday M	Nesbitt G	Craven J	Treanor JL	Reynolds W	Rimmer A	Pateman GE	Martin JJ	Mee GW	Singleton J	Andrews H	Gregg W	Mortimer R	Robinson JJ	Yates T	Rivers W	Young JL	Tyson WG	Curran F	Hann L	Ivill E	
1	2	3	4	5	6	7	8	9	10	11													1
1	2	3	4	5	6	7		9		11	8	10											2
1	2	3	4	5	6	7		9		11	8	10											3
1	2		4	5	6	7		9		11	8	10	3										4
1	2		4	5	6	7				11	8	10	3	9									5
	2		4	5		7	8	10		11			3	9	1	6							6
	2		4	5		7		8		11		10	3	9	1	6							7
	2		4	5		7		10		11	8		3	9	1	6							8
	2	3	4	5		7		10		11			6	9	1		8						9
	2	3	4	5		7		10		11			6	9	1		8						10
	2	3	4	5		7		10		11			6	9	1		8						11
	2	3	4	5		7		10		11			6	9	1		8						12
	2	3	4	5		7		10		11			6	9	1		8						13
	2	3	4	5		7		10	11				6	9	1		8						14
	2	3		5		7		10				4	6	9	1		8	11					15
	2	3		5		7		10		11		6	4	9	1		8						16
	2		4	5		7				11		6	3	9	1		8		10				17
	2		4	5		7		8		11		6	3	9	1				10				18
1		3	4	5		7				11		6	2	9			8		10				19
1		3	4	5		7				11		6	2	9			8		10				20
1		3	4	5		7				11		6	2	9			8		10				21
1		3	4	5		7				11		6	2	9			8		10				22
1		3	4	5		7		9		11		6	2				8		10				23
1		3	4	5		7		8	11				2	9			6		10				24
		3	4	5		7		8		11			2	9	1		6		10				25
1		3		5		7		8		11		6	2	9			4		10				26
1	2	3		5		7		8		11		6		9			4		10				27
1		3		5		7				11		6	2	9			4		10	8			28
1		3		5		7				11		6	2	9			4		10	8			29
1	2			5		7				11		6	3	9			4		10	8			30
1	2			5		7				11		6	3	9			4		10	8			31
1	2			5		7				11		6	3	9			4		10	8			32
1	2		4	5		7				11		6	3	9			10			8			33
1	2		4	5		7				11		6	3	9			8		10				34
	2			5		7				11		6	3	9	1		4		10	8			35
1	2			5		7				11		6	3	9			4		10	8			36
1	2		4	5		7				11		6	3	9			8				10		37
1	2		4	5		7				11		6		9			8				10	3	38
1	2		4	5		11						6		9			8			7	10	3	39
1	2		4	5		7				11		6		9			8				10	3	40
1	2		4	5		7			11			6		9			8		10			3	41
1	2		4	5		7			11			6		9			8		10			3	42
27	32	22	31	42	5	42	2	21	5	36	5	31	33	37	15	3	33	1	21	9	4	5	
						11		8		4		1		33			4		10	3	1		

1 own-goal

	2	3		5		7		10		11		4	6	9	1		8						1
	2	3		5		7		10		11		6	4	9	1		8						2
1		3	4	5		7				11		6	2	9			8		10				3
1		3	4	5		7				11		6	2	9			8		10				R
1		3	4	5		7		8		11			2	9			6		10				4
3	2	5	3	5		5		3		5		4	5	5	2		5		3				
						1				2				5			1						

1937-38

Manager: John Hacking

1	Aug	28	(h)	Carlisle U	L 1-4	O'Grady	7,970
2	Sep	1	(a)	Hartlepools U	L 0-2		7,751
3		4	(a)	Halifax T	W 2-1	Mortimer, Curran	7,065
4		6	(h)	Hartlepools U	W 2-1	Curran, Mortimer	4,812
5		11	(h)	Tranmere R	L 0-1		5,891
6		18	(a)	York C	D 1-1	Mortimer	7,033
7		25	(h)	Bradford C	W 3-1	Mortimer, Tyson 2	5,278
8		28	(h)	Chester	D 0-0		6,442
9	Oct	2	(a)	Southport	L 1-2	Andrews (pen)	4,915
10		9	(h)	Doncaster R	L 0-1		6,542
11		16	(a)	Lincoln C	L 0-2		8,198
12		23	(h)	Hull C	L 0-2		3,198
13		30	(a)	New Brighton	L 1-2	Valentine	3,179
14	Nov	6	(h)	Gateshead	L 1-5	Moir	4,647
15		13	(a)	Oldham A	L 0-1		7,456
16		20	(h)	Darlington	W 2-1	Moir, Reynolds	3,949
17	Dec	4	(h)	Crewe A	W 3-2	Mee, Randle, Reynolds	2,313
18		25	(a)	Rochdale	W 1-0	Curran	9,146
19		27	(h)	Rochdale	L 0-1		4,700
20	Jan	1	(a)	Carlisle U	L 1-3	Curran	9,492
21		3	(h)	Wrexham	W 4-0	Reynolds 3, Blakeney	4,330
22		8	(a)	Port Vale	L 1-4	Blakeney	5,443
23		15	(h)	Halifax T	L 3-4	Blakeney 2, Reynolds	2,081
24		22	(a)	Tranmere R	L 0-5		6,310
25		29	(h)	York C	L 1-2	Curran	3,067
26	Feb	5	(a)	Bradford C	D 2-2	Blakeney, Curran	5,520
27		12	(h)	Southport	W 3-0	Blakeney, Curran 2 (1 pen)	3,556
28		19	(a)	Doncaster R	L 1-5	Blakeney	9,834
29		26	(h)	Lincoln C	L 0-3		3,985
30	Mar	5	(a)	Hull C	D 0-0		10,343
31		12	(h)	New Brighton	W 3-1	O'Grady, Blakeney, Curran	3,710
32		19	(a)	Gateshead	L 0-1		7,788
33		26	(h)	Oldham A	L 1-2	Curran	5,077
34	Apr	2	(a)	Darlington	L 0-3		3,403
35		9	(h)	Port Vale	W 2-1	Blakeney 2	2,990
36		15	(h)	Rotherham U	D 0-0		3,831
37		16	(a)	Crewe A	L 1-3	Reynolds	4,388
38		18	(a)	Rotherham U	D 1-1	Blakeney	7,187
39		23	(h)	Barrow	W 2-0	Mee (pen), Curran	2,861
40		25	(a)	Barrow	D 0-0		2,226
41		30	(a)	Wrexham	L 0-2		1,412
42	May	7	(a)	Chester	L 1-3	Reynolds	1,940

FINAL LEAGUE POSITION: 22nd in Division Three North

Appearances

Goals

FA Cup

1	Nov	27	(h)	Lancaster C	D 1-1	Moir	5,122
R	Dec	1	(a)	Lancaster C	D 1-1	Curran	3,575
2R		6	(n*)	Lancaster C	W 4-0	Curran 2, O'Grady, Andrews	2,963
2		11	(h)	Crystal P	L 0-1		5,400

*Played at Deepdale, Preston.

Appearances

Goals

Robertson A	Pickering WH	Hall J	Randle HC	Craven J	Andrews H	Reynolds W	Rivers W	Mortimer R	O'Grady H	Mee GW	Simpson S	Tyson WG	Curran F	Hann L	Valentine AF	Bowles JC	Young JL	Liddle G	Moir J	Ash JW	Cuthbert W	Blakeney J	Webster R	Rhodes I	Jones T	
1	2	3	4	5	6	7	8	9	10	11																1
1	2		4	5	6	7		9	8	11	3	10														2
1	2		4	5	6	7		9		11	3	10	8													3
1	2		4	5	6	7		9		11	3		8	10												4
1	2		4	5	6	7		9		11	3		8	10												5
1	2		4	5	6	7	8	9		11	3	10														6
1	2		4	5	6	7	8	9		11	3	10														7
1	2		4	5	6	7	8	9		11	3	10														8
1	2		4	5	6	7	8		9	11	3			10												9
1	2		4	5	6	7	8			11	3			10	9											10
	2		4	5	6	7	8			11	3			10	9	1										11
1	2		4	5	6	7	8			11	3			10	9											12
1	2			5	6		4				3		8	10	9		7	11								13
1	2		4	5	8	7	6				3			10				11	9							14
	2		4		6	7	8		10	11	3					1			9	5						15
	2		4		6	7	8		10	11	3					1			9	5						16
	2		4		6	7			10	11	3		8		9	1				5						17
	2		4		6	7			10	11			8		9	1				5	3					18
	2		4		6	7			10	11			8		9	1				5	3					19
	2		4		8	7	6		10	11			9			1				5	3					20
	2		4		8	7	6		10	11						1				5	3	9				21
	2		4		8	7	6		10	11						1				5	3	9				22
	2		4		8	7	6		10	11						1				5	3	9				23
	2		8		6	7	4				3					1		11		5		9	10			24
			4			7	10				2		8			1		11		5		9	6	3		25
1			4			7	10			11	2		8							5		9	6	3		26
1			4			7	10			11	2		8							5		9	6	3		27
1			4			7	10			11	2		8							5		9	6	3		28
1			4			7	10			11	2		8							5		9	6	3		29
1	2	3	4			7			10	11			8							5		9	6			30
1	2	3	4			7			10	11			8							5		9	6			31
1	2	3	4			7			10	11			8							5		9	6			32
1	2	3	4		6	7			10	11			8							5		9				33
1	2	3	4		6	7			10	11			8							5		9				34
1		3	2		4	7				11			8	10						5		9	6			35
1		3	2		4	7			8	11			9	10						5			6			36
1		3	2		4	7			8	11			9	10						5			6			37
1		3	2		4	7			10	11			8							5		9	6			38
1			2		4	7			10	11	3		8							5		9	6			39
1			2		4	7			10	11	3		8							5		9	6			40
1			2		4	7			10	11	3		8							5		9	6			41
1		3		4	8	7	10				2						11					9	6		5	42
30	29	11	40	15	34	41	23	8	23	37	26	5	25	11	7	12	2	4	3	27	6	20	17	5	1	
			1		1	8		4	2	2		2	11		1				2			11				

Robertson A	Pickering WH	Hall J	Randle HC	Craven J	Andrews H	Reynolds W	Rivers W	Mortimer R	O'Grady H	Mee GW	Simpson S	Tyson WG	Curran F	Hann L	Valentine AF	Bowles JC	Young JL	Liddle G	Moir J	Ash JW	Cuthbert W	Blakeney J	Webster R	Rhodes I	Jones T	
	2		4		6	7	8		10	11	3					1			9	5						1
	2		4		6	7			10	11	3		8			1			9	5						R
	2		4		6	7			10	11	3		8			1			9	5						2R
	2		4		6	7			10	11	3		8			1			9	5						2
	4		4		4	4	1		4	4	4		3			4			4	4						
					1				1				3						1							

1938-39

Manager: John Hacking

1	Aug	27	(a)	Halifax T	L 0-2		7,153
2		29	(a)	Stockport C	L 0-3		9,772
3	Sep	3	(h)	New Brighton	L 1-2	Clarke	4,348
4		5	(a)	Oldham A	L 0-2		8,493
5		10	(a)	Barrow	W 3-2	Neal 2, Alexander	8,702
6		17	(h)	Chester	L 2-3	Gastall, Neal	4,728
7		24	(a)	Bradford C	L 1-2	Chapman	6,200
8		27	(h)	Oldham A	L 1-3	Hunt (pen)	4,551
9	Oct	1	(h)	Hull C	D 1-1	Moir	3,799
10		8	(a)	Lincoln C	L 0-3		4,422
11		15	(h)	Southport C	L 1-4	Rattray	4,194
12		22	(a)	Crewe A	L 1-2	Waddington	5,755
13		29	(h)	Carlisle U	D 1-1	Neal	3,765
14	Nov	5	(a)	Darlington	L 0-3		3,637
15		12	(h)	Hartlepools U	D 0-0		5,063
16		19	(a)	Gateshead	L 1-4	Gastall	3,947
17	Dec	3	(a)	York C	D 2-2	Neal, Alexander	4,561
18		10	(h)	Rochdale	L 0-5		3,836
19		17	(a)	Rotherham U	L 1-2	Jones	2,654
20		24	(h)	Halifax T	L 1-2	Tyson	2,663
21		26	(a)	Barnsley	L 1-4	Hall (pen)	19,062
22		27	(h)	Barnsley	L 0-2		5,094
23		31	(a)	New Brighton	L 1-4	Neal	4,779
24	Jan	7	(h)	Wrexham	W 3-1	Waring, Dooley, Neal	2,630
25		14	(h)	Barrow	L 0-2		3,224
26		28	(h)	Bradford C	L 2-3	Waring, Hall (pen)	3,700
27	Feb	4	(a)	Hull C	L 1-6	Storey	5,502
28		11	(h)	Lincoln C	L 3-4	Moir 3	2,825
29		15	(a)	Chester	L 0-1		1,728
30		18	(a)	Southport	L 0-1		4,296
31		25	(h)	Crewe A	W 2-1	Keanery, Waring	2,542
32	Mar	4	(a)	Carlisle U	L 4-6	Mee, Waring 3	3,859
33		11	(h)	Darlington	W 3-0	Waring 2, Hall	2,270
34		18	(a)	Hartlepools U	L 1-2	Dooley	2,463
35		25	(h)	Gateshead	D 1-1	Moir	2,810
36	Apr	1	(a)	Wrexham	L 0-2		1,660
37		7	(a)	Doncaster R	L 1-7	Waring	12,257
38		8	(h)	York C	W 3-1	Kearney, Kelly (og), Moir	2,545
39		10	(h)	Doncaster R	D 0-0		2,819
40		15	(a)	Rochdale	L 1-4	Waring	3,981
41		22	(h)	Rotherham U	W 2-1	Storey, Moir	2,059
42		29	(h)	Stockport C	W 3-2	Storey, Harker (og), Mee	2,338

FINAL LEAGUE POSITION: 22nd in Division Three North

Appearances
Goals

FA Cup

1	Nov	26	(a)	Hartlepools U	L 1-2	Alexander	7,068

Appearances
Goals

Robertson A	Randle HC	Done R	Johnson JC	Howshall JH	Webster R	Rattray CR	Alexander S	Hunt SW	Clarke WV	Neal RM	Hall J	Jones T	Hann L	Gastall JWH	Chapman E	Storey T	Laytham G	Moir J	Green J	Waddington JM	Tyson WG	Dooley TE	Daniels J	Kearney SF	Hamilton H	Waring T	Calvert J	Young JL	Mee GW	Coupe J	Rose J	
1	2	3	4	5	6	7	8	9	10	11																						1
1	2	3	4	5	6	7	8	9	10	11																						2
1	2		4	5	6	7	8	9	10	11	3																					3
1	2		4	6	10		7			11	3	5	8	9																		4
1	2		4	6	10		7			11	3	5	8	9																		5
1	2		4	6	10		7			11	3	5	8	9																		6
1	4	3	2	5	6		8			11			10	9	7																	7
1	4	3	2	5	6		7	9		11						8	10															8
1	4	3			6					11	2	5			7	8	10	9														9
1	4	2			6	7		9		11		5							3	8	10											10
1					6	7				11	2	5		9					3	8	10	4										11
			5		6	7					2			9		11			3	8	10	4	1									12
			5		6	7				10	2					11		9	3	8		4	1									13
			5		6	7					2			9		11			3	8		4	1	10								14
			5		6					11						7		9	3			4	1	10	2	8						15
			5		6	7	10			11				9					3			4	1		2	8						16
1			5		6	7	8			11	3	9										10			2		4					17
1			5		6	7	8			11	3											10			2	9	4					18
1	4		5		6	7						9				11			3			10			2	8						19
1	4		5		6		7				2	9				11			3		10					8						20
1	4		5		6		7			11	3							9			10				2	8						21
1	2		5		6	7	8			11	3					10		9				4										22
1	2		5		6	7	8			11	3					10						4				9						23
1	2		5		6		9			11	3				7	10						4				8						24
1	2		5				8			11	3		6		7	10						4				9						25
1	2		5				4				3					8						6		10		9		7	11			26
1	2		4				8				3					7		9				6		10					11	5		27
	2		5				8				3		6			7		9				4	1	10					11			28
	2		5				8				3		6			7		9				4	1	10					11			29
1	2		5				8				3		6			7		9				4		10					11			30
	4		5								3		6			7		9						10	2	8			11		1	31
	4		5								3		6			7						8		10	2	9			11		1	32
	4		5			8					2		6			7			3				1	10		9			11			33
	4		5								2		6			7			3			8		10		9			11		1	34
	4		5								2					7		9	3			6		10		8			11		1	35
	4		5								2					7		9	3			6		10		8			11		1	36
	3		5			8					2					7						6		10		9	4		11		1	37
1	3		5			7					2							9				6		10		8	4		11			38
	3		5			7					2							9				6		10		8	4		11		1	39
	3		5			7					2							9				6		10		8	4		11		1	40
	3		5										6			7		9				10	1		2	8	4		11			41
	3		5										10			7		9				6	1		2	8	4		11			42
24	34	6	39	8	24	19	22	5	3	21	32	9	14	8	4	26	2	17	13	5	5	28	10	17	10	22	8	1	17	1	8	
						1	2	1	1	7	3	1		2	1	3		7		1	1	2		2		10			2			

2 own-goals

Robertson A	Randle HC	Done R	Johnson JC	Howshall JH	Webster R	Rattray CR	Alexander S	Hunt SW	Clarke WV	Neal RM	Hall J	Jones T	Hann L	Gastall JWH	Chapman E	Storey T	Laytham G	Moir J	Green J	Waddington JM	Tyson WG	Dooley TE	Daniels J	Kearney SF	Hamilton H	Waring T	Calvert J	Young JL	Mee GW	Coupe J	Rose J	
1	4		5		6	7	8			11	3			9								10			2							1
1	1		1		1	1	1			1	1			1								1			1							
							1																									

1939-40

Manager: John Hacking

1	Aug	26	(a)	Bradford C	W 2-0	Robbins, Conroy	7,224
2		28	(a)	Barrow	W 2-1	Morgan, Conroy	5,867
3	Sep	2	(h)	Oldham A	W 2-0	Robbins, Swinden (pen)	5,427

Above games played in Third Division North before the Football League closed down upon the outbreak of World War Two

Appearances
Goals

4	Oct	21	(a)	Carlisle U	D 0-0		4,500
5		28	(h)	Oldham A	L 1-2	Swinden	1,500
6	Nov	4	(a)	Oldham A	L 1-3	Morgan	4,000
7		11	(a)	Rochdale	L 1-5	Sams	3,500
8		18	(h)	Blackburn R	D 2-2	Swinden, Conroy	3,500
9		25	(h)	Blackpool	L 2-3	Kearney, Morgan	1,500
10	Dec	2	(h)	Barrow	D 2-2	Morgan, Sutherland	1,000
11		9	(a)	Southport	L 2-3	Dooley, Kearney	500
12		23	(h)	Bury	L 3-5	Johnson, Dooley, Swinden (pen)	1,700
13		26	(a)	Barrow	D 3-3	Johnson, A.Ainsworth, Sams	4,604
14	Jan	6	(h)	Bolton W	D 1-1	McShane	3,000
15		20	(a)	Preston NE	L 1-3	Conroy	2,000
16	Mar	9	(h)	Rochdale	W 4-1	Higham 2, Swinden (pen), Harker	300
17		16	(a)	Blackburn R	W 2-0	Higham 2	1,329
18		23	(a)	Blackpool	L 1-8	Morgan	7,000
19	Apr	6	(h)	Southport	D 1-1	Dooley	5,000
20		27	(a)	Carlisle U	L 1-6	Moir	
21	May	4	(a)	Bury	L 0-7		
22		18	(a)	Bolton W	L 1-4	Jones	500
23		22	(h)	Preston NE	L 1-10	Dyson	750
24		29	(h)	Burnley	L 1-2	Webster	
25	Jun	1	(a)	Burnley	L 0-7		

FINAL LEAGUE POSITION: 12th in Regional League North West Division

Appearances
Goals

League War Cup

P	Apr	13	(a)	Rochdale	L 0-3		1,000

Appearances
Goals

Owen CL	Ash JW	Swinden SA	Dooley TE	Johnson JC	Smith WS	Conroy RM	Robbins P	Morgan R	Kearney SF	Mauchline R	Hall G	Sams A	Robinson JJ	Reeday M	Webster R	Gale A	Ainsworth A	Sutherland HR	Jones T	Walton G	McShane H	Higham N	Harker W	Bargh GW	Barker W	Moir J	Hargreaves T	Ainsworth F	Wightman JR	Dyson J	Jackson H	Ward F	Mortimer R	Seddon H	Aspin A	Parr JE	Pollard	Dodds	
1	2	3	4	5	6	7	8	9	10	11																													1
1	2	3	4	5		7	8	9	10	11	6																												2
1	2	3	4	5		7	8	9	10	11		6																											3
3	3	3	3	3	1	3	3	3	3	3	1	1																											
		1				2	2	1																															
	2		4	5		7		9	10	11		8	1	3	6																								4
	2	11	4	5		7		9	10			8	1	3	6																								5
		3	4	5				9	10	11		8	1	2	6	7																							6
1	4	3	8	5				9	10	11		7		2	6																								7
1		3	4	5		7		9	10	11		8		2	6																								8
1		3	4	5		7		9	10			11		2	6		8																						9
1	2	3	4	5				9	10			11			6		8	7																					10
1	5	3	10	4				9	8			11		2	6			7																					11
1	5	3	6	8		7		9	10			11		2					4																				12
1	5	3	6	7				9	10			11		2			8		4																				13
1		3	4	7				9						2	6		8		5	10	11																		14
1	5	3	4			7		9				10		2	6					8	11																		15
1	5	3	4	7				9						2	6					10		8	11																16
1	5	3	6	4		7		9						2						10	11	8																	17
1	5	3	4			7		9						2	6					10	11	8																	18
1	5	3	7	4				9						2	6						11			8	10														19
	2			4									1	3	6				5	8	11					7	9	10											20
				2									1	3	6				5	8							9	10	4	7	11								21
	5			2									1	3	6				9									10		8		4	7	11					22
	5			2									1	3	6				7									10		8		4	9	11					23
	2			4										3	9				5									10		8		7		11	1	6			24
	2			9										3					5									10		8		4		7	1	6	11		25
13	17	15	16	20		8		16	10	4		11	7	21	18	1	4	2	9	7	6	3	1	1	1	1	2	6	1	5	1	4	2	4	2	2	1		
		4	3	2		2		4	2			2			1		1	1	1		1	4	1			1				1									
1	5	3	7	4										2	6					10						9		8										11	P
1	1	1	1	1										1	1					1						1		1										1	

1940-41

Secretary/Manager: Jack Wigglesworth

1	Oct	5	(h)	Blackburn R 'A'	W	3-1	Nuttall, F.Ainsworth, Parr
2		12	(a)	Blakey Moor OB	W	4-3	F.Ainsworth 2, Lingard 2
3		26	(h)	Darwen Cor	W	7-1	Wolstenholme, Nuttall 5, Ash
4	Nov	2	(a)	Blackburn Tech	W	7-0	F.Ainsworth, Nuttall, Moulding Ash 2, Wolstenholme 2
5		16	(h)	Mill Hill St Peters	D	2-2	Wolstenholme, Lingard
6		30	(a)	Feniscowles	D	2-2	Haworth, Fish
7	Dec	7	(h)	Feniscowles	W	3-1	Cobb, Lingard, Haworth
8		14	(h)	Rishton	D	1-1	Haworth
9	Jan	4	(a)	Rishton	L	2-4	Fish, Ash
10		11	(h)	Blakey Moor OB	W	5-0	Newsham, Aspden 2, Baldwin, Waddington
11		18	(h)	Clitheroe	L	3-6	F.Ainsworth, Baldwin, Wolstenholme
12		25	(a)	Mill Hill St Peter's	L	1-2	Haworth
13	Feb	1	(a)	Wellington Am	W	3-2	Newsham, Haworth, F.Ainsworth
14	Mar	8	(a)	Old Blackburnians	W	11-0	L.H.Haworth (og), L.Pilkington 3, J.Haworth 2, F.Ainsworth 2, Kenyon, McKay, Taylor
15		15	(h)	Spring Hill Am	L	3-5	Kenyon, L.Pilkington, Wood
16		22	(h)	Old Blackburnians	W	12-1	Wood 2, Parr (pen), Dodgson 6, L.Pilkington, F.Ainsworth, Haworth
17		29	(a)	Darwen Cor	W	5-1	Dodgson 3, McLachlan, Webb
18	Apr	5	(h)	Novas	W	8-1	Wood 2, Dodgson 5, Haworth
19		19	(a)	Spring Hill Am	W	5-4	Wood 2, F.Ainsworth, Dodgson, McCarthy
20	May	15	(h)	Blackburn Tech	W	6-1	Haworth 3, Taylor, Newsham, Chadwick
21		17	(a)	Clitheroe	L	3-4	Rushton, F.Ainsworth 2
22		21	(a)	Blackburn R 'A'	W	7-2	Brindle 2, Rushton, Haworth 2, F.Ainsworth, Newsham

FINAL LEAGUE POSITION: 4th in Blackburn Combination — Appearances

Goals

Birtwistle Cup

1	Feb	8	(a)	Novas*	W	5-0	L.Pilkington 3, F.Ainsworth, Taylor
		15	(h)	Novas	W	4-0	Gill 3, L.Pilkington
2	Mar	1	(a)	Clitheroe	W	4-1	Kenyon, Dooley, Gill, F.Ainsworth
SF	Apr	26	(n†)	Feniscowles	W	2-0	L.Pilkington, Dodgson
F	May	7	(n‡)	Rishton	W	3-2	Dodgson, Jones (pen), Haworth

*Match abandoned at half-time due to a waterlogged pitch. — Appearances

†Played at Mill Hill St Peter's, Blackburn. ‡Played at Ewood Park, Blackburn. — Goals

1	2	3	4	5	6	7	8	9	10	11	
Aspin A	Maddox	Ramsbottom	Moulding	Waddington J	Parr JE	Lingard	Jones	Nuttall	Ainsworth F	Holden J	1
Aspin A	Maddox	Moulding	Gill	Ash J	Parr JE	Ellison	Lingard	Nuttall	Ainsworth F	Haworth J	2
Aspin A	Maddox	Waddington J	Moulding	Ash J	Ward RA	Lingard	Wolstenholme	Nuttall	Ainsworth F	Haworth J	3
Aspin A	Maddox	Waddington J	Moulding	Ash J	Webster R	Lingard	Wolstenholme	Nuttall	Ainsworth F	Haworth J	4
Aspin A	Maddox	Waddington J	Moulding	Gill	Webster R	Lingard	Wolstenholme	Nuttall	Ainsworth F	Haworth J	5
Aspin A	Maddox	Waddington J	Silcock	Jones	Parr JE	Lingard	Fish	Nuttall	Ainsworth F	Haworth J	6
Aspin A	Maddox	Waddington J	Ward RA	Worswick	Ainsworth F	Nuttall	Fish	Cobb	Lingard	Haworth J	7
Aspin A	Maddox	Taylor W	Parr JE	Worswick	Ainsworth F	Lingard	Fish	Cobb	Waddington J	Haworth J	8
Aspin A	Taylor W	Waddington J	Worswick	Ash J	Parr JE	Butterworth F	Fish	Baldwin	Ainsworth F	Haworth J	9
Aspin A	Taylor W	Maddox	Ward RA	Worswick	Parr JE	Newsham	Ainsworth F	Baldwin	Waddington J	Aspden	10
Aspin A	Taylor W	Waddington J	Ward RA	Worswick	Parr JE	Newsham	Wolstenholme	Baldwin	Ainsworth F	Haworth J	11
Aspin A	Cook C	Ward RA	McKay GA	Hughes	Parr JE	Newsham	Wolstenholme	Nuttall	Ainsworth F	Haworth J	12
Hunt	Cook C	Taylor W	AinsworthFA	Gill	Parr JE	Pilkington ST	McKay GA	Newsham	Wolstenholme	Haworth J	13
Aspin A	Taylor W	Lyons A	Ward RA	Robinson S	Parr JE	McKay GA	Pilkington L	Kenyon J	Ainsworth F	Haworth J	14
Hurst	Lyons A	Sharples	Lomax J	Lang	Parr JE	Wood H	Pilkington L	Dooley T	Ainsworth F	Kenyon J	15
Watts	Lyons A	Sharples	Lomax J	Ward RA	Parr JE	Wood H	Pilkington L	Dodgson KS	Ainsworth F	Haworth J	16
Watts	Singleton	Lyons A	Ward RA	Waddington J	Parr JE	Aspin A	Ainsworth F	Dodgson KS	McLachlan	Webb	17
Nuttall	Ainsworth T	Waddington J	Boyd	Wharton	Hepple	Parr JE	Wood H	Dodgson KS	Ainsworth F	Haworth J	18
Watts	Lyons A	Taylor W	Eaton J	Waddington J	Parr JE	Wood H	Aisnworth F	Dodgson KS	McCarthy	Brawn	19
Aspin A	Smith	Hope	Chadwick	Jones	Parr JE	Newsham	Taylor W	Brindle	Ainsworth F	Haworth J	20
Holt	Taylor W	Waddington J	Nuttall	Pugh	Parr JE	Newsham	Rushton	Brindle	Ainsworth F	Kenyon J	21
Watts	Taylor W	Waddington J	Ward RA	Parr JE	Bass	Newsham	Rushton	Brindle	Ainsworth F	Haworth J	22

Aspin A	Taylor W	Sillence	Lomax J	Hughes	Parr JE	Newsham	Pilkington L	Gill	Ainsworth F	Haworth J	1
Aspin A	Taylor W	Greenwood	Ward RA	Hughes	Parr JE	Newsham	Pilkington L	Gill	Ainsworth F	Haworth J	
Aspin A	Taylor W	English	Ward RA	Dooley T	Parr JE	Gill	Pilkington L	Kenyon J	Ainsworth F	Haworth J	2
Watts	Lyons A	Taylaor W	Ward RA	Waddington J	Parr JE	Newsham	Pilkington L	Dodgson KS	Ainsworth F	Haworth J	SF
Watts	Taylor W	Waddington J	Ward RA	Jones	Parr JE	Newsham	Pilkington L	Dodgson KS	Ainsworth F	Haworth J	F

Blackburn Combination Appearances
Ainsworth F. 22, Ainsworth T. 1, Ash J. 4, Aspden 1, Aspin A. 15, Baldwin 3, Bass 1, Boyd 1, Brawn 1, Brindle 3, Butterworth F. 1, Chadwick 1, Cobb 2, Cook C. 2, Dodgson K.S. 4, Dooley T. 1, Eaton J. 1, Ellison 1, Fish 4, Gill 3, Haworth J. 16, Hepple 1, Holden J. 1, Holt 1, Hope 1, Hughes 1, Hunt 1, Hurst 1, Jones 3, Kenyon J. 3, Lang 1, Lingard 8, Lomax J. 2, Lyons A. 5, McCarthy 1, McKay G.A. 3, McLachlan 1, Maddox 9, Moulding 5, Newsham 7, Nuttall 10, Parr J.E. 18, Pilkington L. 3, Pilkington S.T. 1, Pugh 1, Ramsbottom 1, Robinson S. 1, Rushton 2, Sharples 2, Silcock 1, Singleton 1, Smith 1, Taylor W. 10, Waddington J. 15, Ward R.A. 9, Watts 4, Webb 1, Webster R. 2, Wharton 1, Wolstenholme 6, Wood H. 4, Worswick 5.

Birtwistle Cup Appearances
Ainsworth F. 5, Aspin A. 3, Dodgson K.S. 2, Dooley T. 2, English 1, Gill 3, Greenwood 1, Haworth J. 5, Hughes 2, Kenyon J. 1, Jones 1, Lomax J. 1, Lyons A. 1, Newsham 4, Parr J.E. 5, Pilkington L. 5, Sillence 1, Taylor W. 4, Waddington J. 2, Ward R.A. 4, Watts 2.

Blackburn Combination Goalscorers
Dodgson K.S. 15, Haworth J. 14, Ainsworth 13, Nuttall 7, Wood H. 7, Pilkington L. 5, Wolstenholme 5, Ash J. 4, Lingard 4, Newsham 4, Aspden 2, Baldwin 2, Brindle 2, Fish 2, Kenyon 2, Rushton 2, Taylor W. 2, Parr J.E. 2, Chadwick 1, Cobb 1, McCarthy 1, McKay G.A. 1, McLachlan 1, Moulding 1, Waddington J. 1, Webb 1, Haworth L.H. (own goal) 1.

Birtwistle Cup Goalscorers
Pilkington L. 5, Gill 4, Ainsworth F. 2, Dodgson K.S. 2, Dooley T. 1, Haworth J. 1, Kenyon J. 1, Jones 1, Taylor W. 1.

1941-42

Secretary/Manager: Jack Wigglesworth

1	Aug	30	(a)	Bacup Borough	L	3-7	Clarkson 2, Carey
2	Sep	6	(h)	Bacup Borough	W	4-2	Rushton 2, Brindle, Ireland (og)
3		13	(h)	Chorley	L	3-5	Clarkson 2, Dodgson
4		20	(a)	Chorley	L	3-6	Brindle 2, Wood
5		27	(h)	Preston NE Res	W	4-2	Dooley 2, J.Hargreaves, Wood
6	Oct	4	(a)	Preston NE Res	L	0-4	
7		18	(h)	Blackpool Services	L	2-5	Wood, J.Hargreaves (pen)
8		25	(h)	Rossendale U	L	2-6	Wood, Baldwin
9	Nov	1	(a)	Rossendale U	L	2-3	Haworth, J.Hargreaves
10		8	(h)	Morecambe Services	L	0-2	
11		15	(a)	Morecambe Services	L	1-2	Wood
12		22	(h)	Leyland Motors	W	6-1	Wood 2, Preedy 2, Haworth, McLean
13		29	(a)	Leyland Motors	W	6-4	Jackson, Preedy 4 (1 pen), Baldwin
14	Dec	6	(a)	Blackburn R Res	W	4-1	Wood 2, T.Jones (pen), Jackson
15		13	(h)	Blackburn R Res	W	6-2	Hayes, Haworth, Duckhouse, J.Hargreaves 3
16		20	(a)	Burnley Res	D	3-3	J.Hargreaves 2, T.Jones (pen)
17		25	(h)	Burnley Res	W	7-3	T.Jones (pen), Wood 2, Dodgson, J.Hargreaves 2, Preedy
18	Jan	1	(a)	Blackpool Services	L	1-2	T.Jones (pen)

FINAL LEAGUE POSITION: 7th in Lancashire Combination — Appearances

Goals

Lancashire Combination Cup

19	Dec	27	(h)	Bacup Borough	L	3-6	Haworth, Preedy (pen), Wood
20	Mar	14	(a)	Burnley Res	W	3-2	Wood, Haworth 2
21		21	(h)	Burnley Res	W	9-2	Thornton 3, J.Hargreaves 5, Sullivan
22		28	(a)	Chorley	L	1-4	J.Hargreaves
23	Apr	4	(a)	Bacup Borough	L	2-5	J.Hargreaves, Thornton
24		11	(h)	Morecambe Services	W	1-0	Haworth
25		18	(a)	Morecambe Services	L	0-2	
26	May	16	(h)	Chorley	L	1-3	Livesey

FINAL LEAGUE POSITION: 6th in Lancashire Combination Cup Competition — Appearances

Accrington Stanley did not qualify for the knock-out stage. — Goals

Lancashire Junior Cup

1	Jan	3	(h)	Rossendale U	L	2-4	Pilkington, D.Wood
		10	(a)	Rossendale U	L	2-7	Haworth, Preedy

Appearances

Goals

1	2	3	4	5	6	7	8	9	10	11	
Watts	Singleton	Waddington J	Baldwin	Jones T	Parr JE	Butterworth F	Burrows	Carey	Brindle	Clarkson	1
Watts	Ward	Waddington J	Baldwin	Jones T	Parr JE	Wood H	Rushton	Dodgson KS	Brindle	Clarkson	2
Aspin A	Ward	Waddington J	Baldwin	Hargreaves H	Parr JE	Wood H	Rushton	Dodgson KS	Brindle	Clarkson	3
Adams	Hargreaves H	Waddington J	Baldwin	Parr JE	Ainsworth F	Wood H	Rushton	Preedy	Brindle	Clarkson	4
Adams	Richardson	Waddington J	Baldwin	Jones T	Parr JE	Wood H	Dooley T	Hargreaves J	Brindle	Ormisher	5
Adams	Richardson	Waddington J	Baldwin	Jones T	Parr JE	Wood H	Hargreaves J	Ball	Brindle	Clarkson	6
Adams	Mangham	Waddington J	Baldwin	Parr JE	Clarkson	Wood H	Hargreaves J	Pearson	Brindle	Haworth J	7
Adams	Singleton	Schofield	Baldwin	Waddington J	Parr JE	Wood H	Hargreaves J	Green	Brindle	Clarkson	8
Watts	Singleton	Hargreaves H	Baldwin	Waddington J	Parr JE	Wood H	Chrispin	Hargreaves J	Ainsworth F	Haworth J	9
Watts	Singleton	Hargreaves H	Baldwin	Johnson	Parr JE	Wood H	Waddington J	Pearson	Butterworth A	Haworth J	10
Holt	Singleton	Hargreaves H	Baldwin	Waddington J	Parr JE	Wood H	Hargreaves J	Preedy	Ainsworth F	Haworth J	11
Holt	Hargreaves H	Waddington J	Pugh	Jones T	Parr JE	Wood H	McLean	Preedy	Hargreaves J	Haworth J	12
Holt	Hargreaves H	Hope	Baldwin	Jones T	Parr JE	Wood H	McLean	Preedy	Jackson	Haworth J	13
Holt	Hargreaves H	Waddington J	Baldwin	Jones T	Parr JE	Wood H	Hargreaves J	Preedy	Jackson	Haworth J	14
Parkinson	Hargreaves H	Waddington J	Baldwin	Jones T	Parr JE	Wood H	Hargreaves J	Duckhouse	Hayes	Haworth J	15
Watts	Hargreaves H	Waddington J	Baldwin	Jones T	Parr JE	Wood H	Richardson	Hargreaves J	Hayes	Haworth J	16
Watts	Smith TE	Hargreaves H	Baldwin	Jones T	Waddington J	Wood H	Dodgson KS	Preedy	Hargreaves J	Haworth J	17
Watts	Hargreaves H	Waddington J	Baldwin	Jones T	Parr JE	Simmister	Herbert	Jones B	Wood D	Haworth J	18

Gorton	Hargreaves H	Waddington J	Baldwin	Jones T	Parr JE	Wood H	Preedy	Dodgson	Butterworth A	Haworth J	19
Watts	Hargreaves H	Thornton	Baldwin	Jones T	Parr JE	Wood H	Wolstenholme	Hargreaves J	Cox	Haworth J	20
Watts	Hargreaves H	Mangham	Baldwin	Jones T	Parr JE	Wood H	Sullivan	Hargreaves J	Thornton	Haworth J	21
Watts	Hargreaves H	Mangham	Baldwin	Jones T	Parr JE	Myles	Wolstenholme	Hargreaves J	Thornton	Haworth J	22
Watts	Hargreaves H	Waddington J	Baldwin	Jones T	Parr JE	Simmister	Sullivan	Hargreaves J	Thornton	Haworth J	23
Pilkington L	Hargreaves H	Mangham	Baldwin	Jones T	Parr JE	Herbert	Thornton	Hargreaves J	Haworth J	Hill	24
Watts	Hargreaves H	Mangham	Baldwin	Jones T	Parr JE	Wolstenholme	Beardwood	Livesey	Thornton	Ormisher	25
Watts	Hargreaves H	Mangham	Baldwin	White	Webster R	Holt	Pearson	Livesey	Seed	Butterworth F	26

Watts	Smith TE	Mangham	Baldwin	Jones T	Parr JE	Wood H	Pilkington L	Herbert	Wood D	Haworth J	1
Watts	Ward RA	Hargreaves H	Baldwin	Waddington J	Parr JE	Wood H	McLean	Preedy	Hargreaves J	Haworth J	

Lancashire Combination Appearances
Adams 5, Ainsworth F. 3, Aspin A. 1, Baldwin 17, Ball 1, Brindle 8, Burrows 1, Butterworth A. 1, Butterworth F. 1, Carey 1, Chrispin 1, Clarkson 7, Dodgson K.S. 3, Dooley T. 1, Duckhouse 1, Green 1, Hargreaves H. 12, Hargreaves J. 11, Haworth J. 11, Hayes 2, Herbert 1, Holt 4, Hope 1, Jackson 2, Johnson 1, Jones B. 1, Jones T. 11, McLean 2 Mangham 1, Ormisher 1, Parkinson 1, Parr J.E. 17, Pearson 2, Preedy 6, Pugh 1, Richardson 3, Rushton 3, Schofield 1, Simmister 1, Singleton 5, Smith T.E. 1, Waddington J. 17, Ward R.A. 2, Watts 7, Wood D. 1, Wood H. 16

Lancashire Combination Cup Appearances
Baldwin 8, Beardwood 1, Butterworth A. 1, Butterworth F. 1, Cox 1, Dodgson K.S. 1, Gorton 1, Hargreaves H. 8, Hargreaves J. 5, Haworth J. 6, Herbert 1, Hill 1, Holt 1, Jones T. 7, Livesey 2, Mangham 5, Myles 1, Ormisher 1, Parr J.E. 7, Pearson 1, Pilkington L. 1, Preedy 1, Seed 1, Simmister 1, Sullivan 2, Thornton 6, Waddington J. 2, Watts 6, Webster R. 1, White 1, Wolstenholme 3, Wood H. 3

Lancashire Junior Cup Appearances
Baldwin 2, Hargreaves H. 1, Hargreaves J. 1, Haworth J. 2, Herbert 1, Jones T. 1, McLean 1, Mangham 1, Parr J.E. 2, Pilkington L. 1, Preedy 1, Smith T.E. 1, Waddington J. 1, Ward R.A. 1, Watts 2, Wood D. 1, Wood H. 2.

Lancashire Combination Goalscorers
Wood H. 11, Hargreaves J. 10, Preedy 7, Clarkson 4, Jones T. 4, Brindle 3, Haworth J. 3, Baldwin 2, Dodgson K.S. 2, Dooley T. 2, Jackson 2, Rushton 2, Carey 1, Duckhouse 1, Hayes 1, McLean 1, Ireland (own goal) 1.

Lancashire Combination Cup Goalscorers
Hargreaves J 7, Haworth J. 4, Thornton 4, Wood H. 2, Livesey 1, Preedy 1, Sullivan 1

Lancashire Junior Cup Goalscorers
Haworth J. 1, Pilkington L. 1, Preedy 1, Wood D. 1

1944-45

Manager: John Hacking

1	Aug	26	(h)	Oldham A	W 5-1	Tuson, Curran 2, Rothwell 2	3,600
2	Sep	2	(a)	Oldham A	L 1-2	Maudsley	3,000
3		9	(a)	Bradford C	L 0-4		3,000
4		16	(h)	Bradford C	L 2-3	Conroy (pen), Malcolm	3,500
5		23	(h)	Blackpool	L 3-4	Kearney, Curran 2	5,500
6		30	(a)	Blackpool	L 0-6		8,000
7	Oct	7	(a)	Blackburn R	W 2-1	Seddon, Curran	4,648
8		14	(h)	Blackburn R	L 1-4	Maudsley	5,772
9		21	(h)	Rochdale	L 1-2	Clark	3,400
10		28	(a)	Rochdale	L 0-3		2,200
11	Nov	4	(a)	Bolton W	D 3-3	Mercer 3	4,301
12		11	(h)	Bolton W	L 2-3	Waddington, Clark	3,588
13		18	(a)	Burnley	D 0-0		4,700
14		25	(h)	Burnley	L 0-5		4,560
15	Dec	2	(h)	Preston NE	L 0-3		2,360
16		9	(a)	Preston NE	W 3-1	Mercer 3	4,000
17		16	(a)	Southport	W 2-0	Conroy, Eastwood	2,500
18		23	(h)	Southport	W 4-1	Mercer 2, Conroy, Clark	4,260

FINAL LEAGUE POSITION: 45th in Football League (Northern Section) — First Championship

19	Dec	25	(h)	Rochdale	L 0-1		5,800
20		30	(a)	Rochdale	D 1-1	Conroy	2,000
21	Jan	6	(a)	Preston NE	W 2-1	Mercer 2	4,000
22		13	(h)	Preston NE	W 2-1	Conroy (pen), Mercer	3,882
23		20	(h)	Burnley	L 0-4		4,000
24		27	(a)	Burnley	L 0-3		3,200
25	Feb	3	(a)	Blackpool	W 3-0	Mercer 3	8,000
26		10	(h)	Blackpool	W 4-2	Keeley 3, Mercer	6,091
27		17	(h)	Blackburn R	W 3-2	Clark, Mercer, Keeley	7,000
28		24	(a)	Blackburn R	L 0-3		7,500
29	Mar	3	(h)	Blackpool	W 4-1	Cook, Conroy 2, Mercer	4,729
30		10	(a)	Blackpool	W 2-1	Mercer 2	8,000
31		17	(a)	Southport	D 2-2	Conroy, Rothwell	15,000
32		24	(a)	Bolton W	D 0-0		14,215
33		31	(h)	Bolton W	L 0-4		11,721
34	Apr	2	(a)	Blackburn R	D 4-4	Conroy, Mercer 2, Capstick	4,000
35		7	(a)	Burnley	L 0-1		5,211
36		14	(h)	Burnley	W 4-0	Keeley, Cockburn, Mercer 2	3,000
37		21	(h)	Bury	L 0-1		3,000
38		28	(a)	Bury	D 2-2	Whittle, Conroy	1,000
39	May	5	(h)	Everton	D 1-1	Rudd	2,348
40		12	(a)	Everton	W 2-0	Keeley, Conroy	9,806
41		19	(a)	Blackburn R	L 0-2		6,726
42		26	(h)	Blackburn R	L 3-4	Conroy, Malcolm, Rothwell	800

FINAL LEAGUE POSITION: 25th in Football League (Northern Section) Second Championship

Matches 19-28 were also in the Football League War Cup Qualifying Competition. Matches 32 and 33 were also in the Football League War Cup Knock-out Competition. Matches 29, 30, 35, 36 39-42 were also in the Lancashire Cup, the matches against Blackburn Rovers being the Final.

1	2	3	4	5	6	7	8	9	10	11	
Walmsley J	Male CG	Reeday M	Johnson J	Ash J	Malcolm JM	Clark H	Rothwell G	Curran F	Tyson W	Maudsley RC	1
Walmsley J	Male CG	Reeday M	Johnson J	Ash J	Malcolm JM	Clark H	Rothwell G	Curran F	Tyson W	Maudsley RC	2
Walmsley J	Ash J	Reeday M	Johnson J	Holt G	Malcolm JM	Conroy M	Clark H	Curran F	Maudsley RC	Rotherham E	3
Walmsley J	Ash J	Reeday M	Molloy P	Johnson J	Malcolm JM	Conroy M	Fogg J	Waddington J	Tyson W	Clark H	4
Walmsley J	Ash J	Reeday M	Molloy P	Johnson J	Malcolm JM	Clark H	Rothwell G	Curran F	Kearney SF	Maudsley RC	5
Walmsley J	Ash J	Rotherham E	Molloy P	Johnson J	Malcolm JM	Tyson W	Rothwell G	Curran F	Kearney SF	Maudsley RC	6
Walmsley J	Ash J	Rotherham E	Waddington J	Johnson J	Malcolm JM	Seddon H	Rothwell G	Curran F	Tyson W	Jessop W	7
Walmsley J	Ash J	Rotherham E	Molloy P	Porter W	Johnson J	Conroy M	Rothwell G	Curran F	Malcolm JM	Maudsley RC	8
Walmsley J	Roach JE	Topping H	Waddington J	Ash J	Molloy P	Conroy M	Rothwell G	Curran F	Tyson W	Clark H	9
Walmsley J	Roach JE	Reeday M	Johnson J	Ash J	Molloy P	Clark H	Waddington J	Curran F	Malcolm JM	Conroy M	10
Walmsley J	Roach JE	Holt G	Johnson J	Ash J	Molloy P	Clark H	Waddington J	Mercer S	Rothwell G	Conroy M	11
Walmsley J	Roach JE	Reeday M	Johnson J	Ash J	Molloy P	Conroy M	Waddington J	Mercer S	Jones W	Clark H	12
Walmsley J	Reeday M	Wilson J	Johnson J	Ash J	Molloy P	Conroy M	Waddington J	Mercer S	Johnson J	Clark H	13
Walmsley J	Reeday M	Wilson J	Johnson J	Ash J	Molloy P	Conroy M	Waddington J	Mercer S	Malcolm JM	Clark H	14
Wilson R	Clark G	Reeday M	Molloy P	Briggs JC	Malcolm JM	Conroy M	Rothwell G	Waddington J	Keeley W	Clark H	15
Walmsley J	Reeday M	Wilson J	Molloy P	Briggs JC	Malcolm JM	Conroy M	Rothwell G	Mercer S	Keeley W	Clark H	16
Walmsley J	Reeday M	Wilson J	Molloy P	Briggs JC	Malcolm JM	Conroy M	Rothwell G	Mercer S	Eastwood R	Clark H	17
Walmsley J	Reeday M	Wilson J	Molloy P	Johnson J	Malcolm JM	Conroy M	Rothwell G	Mercer S	Eastwood R	Clark H	18
Walmsley J	Reeday M	Wilson J	Molloy P	Johnson J	Malcolm JM	Waddington J	Rothwell G	Mercer S	Ainsworth F	Clark H	19
Walmsley J	Reeday M	Wilson J	Molloy P	Hutton T	Malcolm JM	Conroy M	Rothwell G	Mercer S	Briggs F	Clark H	20
Walmsley J	Reeday M	Wilson J	Molloy P	Briggs JC	Malcolm JM	Conroy M	Rothwell G	Mercer S	Briggs F	Clark H	21
Walmsley J	Reeday M	Wilson J	Molloy P	Briggs JC	Malcolm JM	Conroy M	Rothwell G	Mercer S	Keeley W	Clark H	22
Walmsley J	Reeday M	Wilson J	Molloy P	Briggs JC	Malcolm JM	Conroy M	Rothwell G	Mercer S	Keeley W	Clark H	23
Holdcroft GH	Reeday M	Wilson J	Eastwood R	Briggs JC	Malcolm JM	Conroy M	Rothwell G	Mercer S	Waddington J	Simpson J	24
Holdcroft GH	Reeday M	Wilson J	Cockburn H	Molloy P	Malcolm JM	Conroy M	Rothwell G	Mercer S	Keeley W	Clark H	25
Holdcroft GH	Reeday M	Wilson J	Molloy P	Briggs JC	Malcolm JM	Conroy M	Rothwell G	Mercer S	Keeley W	Clark H	26
Holdcroft GH	Reeday M	Wilson J	Molloy P	Briggs JC	Malcolm JM	Conroy M	Rothwell G	Mercer S	Keeley W	Clark H	27
Holdcroft GH	Eastwood R	Reeday M	Hutton T	Briggs JC	Malcolm JM	Rothwell G	Keeley L	Baldwin H	Keeley W	Conroy M	28
Holdcroft GH	Eastwood R	Reeday M	Cockburn H	Briggs JC	Malcolm JM	Conroy M	Rothwell G	Mercer S	Keeley W	Cook L	29
Holdcroft GH	Reeday M	Wilson J	Cockburn H	Briggs JC	Malcolm JM	Clark H	Rothwell G	Mercer S	Eastwood R	Conroy M	30
Holdcroft GH	Reeday M	Wilson J	Cockburn H	Briggs JC	Malcolm JM	Conroy M	Rothwell G	Mycock A	Eastwood R	Duckworth J	31
Holdcroft GH	Reeday M	Wilson J	Burrows A	Eastwood R	Malcolm JM	Conroy M	Rothwell G	Reid JM	Keeley W	Shaw K	32
Holdcroft GH	Reeday M	Wilson J	Burrows A	Briggs JC	Malcolm JM	Conroy M	Rothwell G	Mutch G	Keeley W	Clark H	33
Holdcroft GH	Ash J	Rotherham E	Hutton T	Eastwood R	Malcolm JM	Conroy M	Rothwell G	Mercer S	Capstick A	Duckworth J	34
Holdcroft GH	Roach JE	Snowden R	Cockburn H	Briggs JC	Malcolm JM	Conroy M	Rothwell G	Mercer S	Keeley W	Clark H	35
Holdcroft GH	Eastwood R	Wilson J	Hutton T	Briggs JC	Malcolm JM	Conroy M	Rothwell G	Mercer S	Cockburn H	Keeley W	36
Holdcroft GH	Eastwood R	Wilson J	Molloy P	Gibson F	Malcolm JM	Conroy M	Rothwell G	Keeley W	Cockburn H	Winterburn E	37
Holdcroft GH	Eastwood R	Wilson J	Molloy P	Briggs JC	Cockburn H	Conroy M	Rothwell G	Whittle A	Keeley W	Rotherham E	38
Holdcroft GH	Eastwood R	Wilson J	Cockburn H	Briggs JC	Malcolm JM	Conroy M	Rothwell G	Livingstone A	Keeley W	Rudd J	39
Holdcroft GH	Eastwood R	Wilson J	Cockburn H	Briggs JC	Malcolm JM	Conroy M	Rothwell G	Livingstone A	Keeley W	Rudd J	40
Holdcroft GH	Eastwood R	Clark G	Cockburn H	Briggs JC	Malcolm JM	Conroy M	Rothwell G	Ardron W	Keeley W	Rudd J	41
Holdcroft GH	Eastwood R	Wilson J	Molloy P	Briggs JC	Malcolm JM	Conroy M	Rothwell G	Ardron W	Keeley W	Cockburn H	42

Appearances
Ainsworth F. 1, Ardron W. 2, Ash J. 15, Baldwin H. 1, Briggs F. 2, Briggs J.C. 21, Burrows A. 2, Capstick 1, Clark G. 2, Clark H. 26, Cockburn H. 12, Conroy R.M. 36, Cook L. 1, Curran F. 9, Duckworth J. 2, Eastwood R. 16, Fogg J. 1, Gibson F. 1, Holdcroft G.H. 19, Holt G. 2, Hutton T. 4, Jessop W. 1, Johnson J. 15, Johnson J. 1, Jones W. 1, Kearney S.F. 2, Keeley L. 1, Keeley W. 19, Livingstone A. 2, Malcolm J.M. 37, Male C.G. 2, Maudsley R.C. 6, Mercer S. 21, Molloy P. 25, Mutch G. 1, Mycock A. 1, Porter W. 1, Reeday M. 28, Reid J.M. 1, Roach J.E. 5, Rotherham E. 6, Rothwell G. 36, Rudd J. 3, Shaw K, 1, Seddon H. 1, Simpson J. 1, Snowden R. 1, Topping H. 1, Syson W. 6, Waddington J. 11, Walmsley J. 22, Whittle A. 1, Wilson J. 24, Wilson R. 1, Winterburn E. 1.

Goalscorers
Mercer S. 23, Conroy R.M. 12, Keeley W. 6, Curran F. 5, H.Clark 4, G.Rothwell 4, Malcolm J.M. 2, Maudsley R.C. 2, Capstick A. 1, Cockburn H. 1, Cook L. 1, Eastwood, R. 1, Kearney S.F. 1, Rudd J. 1, Seddon H. 1, Tyson W. 1, Waddington J. 1, Whittle A. 1.

1945-46

Manager: John Hacking

1	Aug	25	(a)	Tranmere R	W 3-1	Rothwell, Thomas, Keeley	4,315
2	Sep	1	(h)	Tranmere R	L 2-3	Keeley 2	4,500
3		8	(h)	Wrexham	W 2-1	Keeley 2	4,235
4		15	(a)	Wrexham	L 0-1		4,918
5		22	(a)	Oldham A	W 3-0	Keeley, Rothwell 2	3,788
6		29	(h)	Oldham A	D 1-1	Keeley (pen)	5,000
7	Oct	6	(h)	Stockport C	W 3-0	Conroy 2, Davison (og)	4,773
8		13	(a)	Stockport C	D 0-0		4,647
9		20	(a)	Southport	D 0-0		2,754
10		27	(h)	Southport	W 1-0	Mauchline	4,200
11	Nov	3	(h)	Chester	W 5-2	Hudson 2, Keeley 3	5,023
12		10	(a)	Chester	D 3-3	Keeley 2, Rotherham	4,342
13	Dec	1	(h)	Barrow	W 4-1	Keeley, Rothwell 2, Hudson	3,654
14		22	(a)	Crewe A	W 2-1	Rothwell, Lythgoe	2,199
15		25	(a)	Rochdale	L 0-2		7,614
16		26	(h)	Rochdale	W 4-2	Mauchline, Keeley 2 (1 pen), Mercer	8,043
17		29	(a)	Barrow	W 4-0	Hudson, Rothwell 2, Mauchline	5,984
18	Jan	1	(h)	Crewe A	L 0-1		4,905

FINAL LEAGUE POSITION: 1st in Third Division North West (First Championship) — Appearances

Goals

19	Jan	12	(a)	Barrow	W 5-0	Rothwell, Morris 2, Rotherham, Keeley	2,033
20		26	(h)	Tranmere R	W 1-0	Rothwell	2,616
21	Feb	2	(h)	Oldham A	D 3-3	Hudson, Rothwell 2	2,913
22		9	(a)	Oldham A	L 1-2	Conroy	7,287
23		16	(a)	Southport	L 0-3		3,481
24		23	(h)	Southport	W 4-0	Keeley, Cain 3	2,790
25	Mar	2	(a)	Chester	L 1-4	Cain	3,583
26		6	(a)	Tranmere R	W 2-1	Kearney, Hudson	2,470
27		9	(h)	Chester	W 2-1	Cain 2	4,389
28		16	(h)	Barrow	W 5-3	Keeley, Hudson 2, Conroy 2 (1 pen)	2,852

FINAL LEAGUE POSITION: 3rd in Third Division North West (Cup Qualifying Competition) — Appearances

Goals

29	Mar	23	(h)	York C	W 1-0	Cain	4,508
30		30	(a)	York C	L 1-3	Clark	6,433
31	Apr	6	(h)	Darlington	D 2-2	Cain, Kearney	3,167
32		13	(a)	Darlington	L 3-4	Clark, Kearney, Moir	4,254
33		19	(h)	Bradford C	W 3-1	Kearney 2, Keeley	3,233
34		22	(a)	Bradford C	L 0-2		3,931
35		27	(h)	Lincoln C	W 2-1	Morgan, Kearney	1,772
36	May	4	(a)	Lincoln C	L 1-5	Keeley	6,000

FINAL LEAGUE POSITION: 14th in Third Division North West (Second Championship) — Appearances

Matches 29 and 30 were also the first round matches of the Competition Proper of the Third Division North Cup — Goals

FA Cup

1	Nov	17	(a)	Chorley	L 1-2	Keeley	4,019
		24	(h)	Chorley	W 2-0	Rothwell, Hudson	6,223
2	Dec	8	(a)	Oldham A	L 1-2	Hudson	6,729
		15	(h)	Oldham A	W 3-1	Hudson, Shipman (og), Rothwell	6,308
3	Jan	5	(h)	Manchester U	D 2-2	Conroy, Keeley	9,968
		9	(a)	Manchester U	L 1-5	Keeley	15,339

Appearances

Goals

Hacking J	Eastwood R	Webster R	Malcolm JM	Briggs JC	Hutton T	Conroy RM	Rothwell G	Thomas DSL	Keeley W	Clark H	Wilson JH	Rotherham E	Morris E	Ash JW	Hudson CA	Mauchline R	Lythgoe A	Wood C	Cornwell E	Mercer S	Molloy P	Seatree F	Dooley TE	Kearney SF	Cain D	Rose J	Haworth WE	Smith H	Moir J	Morgan R	
1	2	3	4	5	6	7	8	9	10	11																					1
1	2	3	4	5	6	7	8	9	10	11																					2
1	2	3	4	5	6	7	8	9	10	11																					3
1	2		4	5	6	7	8	9	10	11	3																				4
1	2	3	4	5	6	7	8	9	10	11																					5
1		6	4	5	2		8	9	10	7	3	11																			6
1	2	3	6	5	4	7	8		10	11			9																		7
1	2	3	6	5	4	7	8		10	11			9																		8
1	2	3	6	5	4	7	8		10	11			9																		9
1		3	6	5	4	7	8		10					2	9	11															10
1		3	6	5	4	7	8		10			11		2	9																11
1	5	3	6		4	7	8		10			11		2	9																12
1		3	4	5		7	8		10			11			9			6	2												13
1		3	6	5			8		10	7					9	11	4		2												14
1		3	6	5			8		10	7						11	4		2	9											15
1		3	6	5			8		10	7						11	4		2	9											16
1		3	6	5		4	8		10	7						11			2	9											17
1		3	6			4	8		10	7		11							2		5	9									18
18	9	17	18	16	12	14	18	6	18	14	2	5	3	3	5	5	3	1	6	3	1	1									
						2	8	1	15			1			4	3	1			1											

1 own-goal

Hacking J	Eastwood R	Webster R	Malcolm JM	Briggs JC	Hutton T	Conroy RM	Rothwell G	Thomas DSL	Keeley W	Clark H	Wilson JH	Rotherham E	Morris E	Ash JW	Hudson CA	Mauchline R	Lythgoe A	Wood C	Cornwell E	Mercer S	Molloy P	Seatree F	Dooley TE	Kearney SF	Cain D	Rose J	Haworth WE	Smith H	Moir J	Morgan R	
1		3	6	5		4	8		10	7		11	9						2												19
1		3	6	5		4	8		10	7		11	9						2												20
1		3	6	5		4	8		10	7					9				2				11								21
1		3	6	5		4	8		10	7					9				2				11								22
1		3	6	5		4	8		9	7					11				2					10							23
1		3	6	5		4	8		10	7					11				2						9						24
1		3		5		4	8		10	7					11		6		2						9						25
1		3	6	5		4			10	7					11				2					8	9						26
		3	6	5		4	8		10	7					11				2						9	1					27
		3	6	5		4	8		10	7					11				2						9	1					28
8		10	9	10		10	9		10	10		2	2		8		1		10				2	2	5	2					
						3	4		3			1	2		4									1	6						

Hacking J	Eastwood R	Webster R	Malcolm JM	Briggs JC	Hutton T	Conroy RM	Rothwell G	Thomas DSL	Keeley W	Clark H	Wilson JH	Rotherham E	Morris E	Ash JW	Hudson CA	Mauchline R	Lythgoe A	Wood C	Cornwell E	Mercer S	Molloy P	Seatree F	Dooley TE	Kearney SF	Cain D	Rose J	Haworth WE	Smith H	Moir J	Morgan R	
1		3	6	5		4	8		10	7					11				2						9						29
1		6	3	5			8		10	7									2				4	11	9						30
1		6	3	5		4	8		10										2					11	9		7				31
1		3	6	5		4	8			11									2					10				7	9		32
1		3	6	5			8		10	7							4		2					11					9		33
1		3	6	5			8		10	7							4		2					11					9		34
1		3		5		4	8		10								6		2					11					7	9	35
1		3	6	5		7	8		10								4		2					11						9	36
8		8	7	8		5	8		7	5					1		4		8				1	7	3		1	1	4	2	
									2	2														5	2				1	1	

Hacking J	Eastwood R	Webster R	Malcolm JM	Briggs JC	Hutton T	Conroy RM	Rothwell G	Thomas DSL	Keeley W	Clark H	Wilson JH	Rotherham E	Morris E	Ash JW	Hudson CA	Mauchline R	Lythgoe A	Wood C	Cornwell E	Mercer S	Molloy P	Seatree F	Dooley TE	Kearney SF	Cain D	Rose J	Haworth WE	Smith H	Moir J	Morgan R	
1			6	5	3	7	8		10			11		2	9		4														1
1			3	5	2	7	8		10	11					9		4	6													
1		3	6	5	2	7	8		10						9	11	4														2
1		3	6	5	2		8		10	7					9	11	4														
1		3	6	5		9	8		10	7						11	4		2												3
1		3	6	5		9	8		10	7						11	4		2												
6		4	6	6	4	5	6		6	4		1		1	4	4	6	1	2												
						1	2		3						3																

1 own-goal

1946-47

Secretary-Manager: John Hacking

1	Aug	31	(a)	Bradford C	L 1-3	Kearney	10,395
2	Sep	5	(a)	Barrow	W 3-1	Keeley, Edwards, Bond	6,562
3		7	(h)	Oldham A	L 2-3	Kearney 2	6,129
4		14	(a)	Stockport C	L 0-2		8,298
5		21	(h)	Wrexham	L 0-1		3,917
6		24	(h)	Carlisle U	W 4-3	Smith, Hudson, Keeley, Edwards	5,556
7		28	(a)	Doncaster R	L 0-5		12,873
8	Oct	5	(h)	Rochdale	L 2-3	Keeley (pen), Hudson	4,865
9		12	(a)	New Brighton	L 0-4		6,450
10		19	(a)	Hartlepools U	W 2-0	Hudson, Keeley	8,945
11		26	(h)	Crewe A	L 2-3	Keeley 2	3,951
12	Nov	2	(a)	Lincoln C	D 1-1	Kearney (pen)	8,253
13		9	(h)	Southport	W 1-0	Kearney	3,803
14		16	(a)	Rotherham U	L 1-4	Smith	12,032
15		23	(h)	Chester	L 1-4	Conroy	3,583
16	Dec	7	(h)	Tranmere R	W 2-1	Robinson 2	2,740
17		14	(h)	Barrow	L 1-3	Robinson	2,613
18		21	(h)	Hull C	D 0-0		2,672
19		25	(a)	Gateshead	L 1-2	Robinson	3,540
20		26	(h)	Gateshead	L 0-3		5,099
21		28	(h)	Bradford C	D 0-0		3,733
22	Jan	1	(a)	Carlisle U	L 2-4	Keeley, Marvin	11,522
23		4	(a)	Oldham A	W 2-1	Marvin, Keeley	14,735
24		11	(a)	York C	W 1-0	Bond	2,273
25		18	(h)	Stockport C	W 2-1	Keeley, Mercer	5,330
26		25	(a)	Wrexham	L 0-4		6,267
27	Feb	1	(h)	Doncaster R	L 0-1		4,114
28		22	(h)	Hartlepools U	W 2-1	Bond 2	3,560
29	Mar	15	(a)	Southport	W 1-0	Mercer	4,158
30		22	(h)	Rotherham U	L 2-3	Keeley 2	4,840
31		29	(a)	Chester	L 1-3	Mercer	3,287
32	Apr	4	(h)	Halifax T	D 1-1	Mercer	4,716
33		7	(a)	Halifax T	L 1-2	Edward	2,747
34		12	(a)	Tranmere R	W 1-0	Edwards	8,005
35		19	(h)	Darlington	W 3-0	Mercer 3	4,067
36		26	(a)	Hull C	L 0-3		13,023
37	May	3	(a)	Darlington	L 0-5		3,377
38		10	(h)	New Brighton	W 3-1	Mercer 2, Wilson	2,406
39		14	(h)	York C	L 1-2	Edwards	3,252
40		17	(a)	Crewe A	L 0–5		4,562
41		24	(a)	Rochdale	L 1-5	Mercer	6,758
42		31	(h)	Lincoln C	W 8-4	Keeley 2, Smith 2, Edwards, Mercer 3	2,504

FINAL LEAGUE POSITION: 20th in Division Three North

Appearances

Goals

FA Cup

1	Nov	30	(a)	Doncaster R	D 2-2	Conroy, Keeley	15,223
R	Dec	4	(h)	Doncaster R	L 0-5		6,163

Appearances

Goals

Hacking J	Eastwood R	Webster R	Conroy RM	Briggs JC	Lythgoe A	Bond A	Kearney SF	Morgan R	Keeley W	Edwards RC	Malcolm JM	Cornwell E	Rothwell G	Hudson CA	Smith NH	Morris A	Wilson JH	Hayes S	Haworth H	Rose J	Keating R	Robinson H	Whalley H	Hutton T	Marvin W	Leadbetter	Mercer S	Rymer GH	Bretherton T	Hallard W	Morgan D	Lynn S	
1	2	3	4	5	6	7	8	9	10	11																							1
1	2	3		5	6	7	8	9	10	11	4																						2
1	2	3		5	6	7	8	9	10	11	4																						3
1		3		5	6	7	9		10	11	4	2	8																				4
1		3		5	4	7			11		6	2	8	9	10																		5
1		3		5	6				10	11	2		7	9	8	4																	6
1		3		5	6				10	11		2	7	9	8	4																	7
1		6		5	4				10	11		2	7	9	8		3																8
		6		5	4	7		9	11		2		8		10		3	1															9
		6		5		7	4		11		2			9	10		3	1	8														10
		3	4	5		7	6		11		2			9	10			1	8														11
		3	2	5		7	6		10	11			8	4	9			1															12
		3	2			7	6		10	11			8	4	9		5	1															13
		3	2	5		7	6		10	11			8	4	9			1															14
		2	9	5		7	6		10	11				4	8		3	1															15
			4	5			6		10		3	2	8							1	7	9	11										16
		2	7	5	6		4		10				8				3			1	11	9											17
		2		5			6		10				8				3			1	7	9	11	4									18
		3	2	5					10		6		8							1	7	9	11	4									19
		3	2	5		7			10		6			8						1	11	9		4									20
		2	4	5		7			10	11	6		8				3	1							9								21
		2	4	5		7			10		3		8					1						6	9	11							22
		2	4	5		7			8	11	6		10				3	1							9								23
		2	4	5		7			10	11	6		8				3	1									9						24
		2	4	5		7			10	11	6		8				3	1									9						25
		2	4	5		7			10	11	6		8				3	1									9						26
		3	4	5		7			10	11	6													2			9	1	8				27
		3	4	5		7			10	11	6													2			9	1	8				28
			2	5		7			1	11	4					10	3										9		8	6			29
		3	4	5		7			10	11														2			9	1	8	6			30
		2	8	5		7				11			10				3			1				4			9			6			31
			4	5		7				11	6		10				3			1				2	8		9						32
			4	5		7			10	11	6		8				3			1				2			9						33
				5		7				11	6		8		10	4	3							2			9	1					34
				5		7				11	6		8		10	4	3							2			9	1					35
				5		7				11	6		8		10	4	3							2			9	1					36
		6		5					8	11			7		10		3							2			9	1			4		37
		2							6	11			8		10		3			1				5	7		9				4		38
		2							6	11			8		10		3			1				5		7	9				4		39
		2		5					10						8		3			1				6	9	11	7				4		40
		2		5									8		10	4	3			1					7	11	9				6		41
		6		5					10	11			7		8		3							4			9	1				2	42
8	3	35	23	39	10	29	13	4	36	30	25	5	30	11	20	7	25	13	2	12	5	5	3	18	7	4	19	8	4	3	5	1	
			1			4	5		13	6				3	4		1					4			2		13						

Hacking J	Eastwood R	Webster R	Conroy RM	Briggs JC	Lythgoe A	Bond A	Kearney SF	Morgan R	Keeley W	Edwards RC	Malcolm JM	Cornwell E	Rothwell G	Hudson CA	Smith NH	Morris A	Wilson JH	Hayes S	Haworth H	Rose J	Keating R	Robinson H	Whalley H	Hutton T	Marvin W	Leadbetter	Mercer S	Rymer GH	Bretherton T	Hallard W	Morgan D	Lynn S	
		2	9	5		7	6		10	11			8	4			3	1															1
		3	9	5		7	6		10	11	4	2	8					1															R
		2	2	2		2	2		2	2	1	1	2	1			1	2															
			1						1																								

1947-48

Secretary/Manager: John Hacking

1	Aug	23	(h)	Hartlepools U	W 4-2	Rothwell, Webster, Mercer, N.H.Smith	6,104
2		30	(a)	Hull C	L 2-4	T.Butler, Hassall (og)	23,356
3	Sep	3	(a)	New Brighton	W 1-0	Keeley	4,458
4		6	(h)	Stockport C	W 5-2	Gleave (og), Keeley 2, N.H.Smith, Rothwell	7,055
5		9	(a)	Rochdale	W 3-1	Mercer 2, Rothwell	8,551
6		13	(a)	Bradford C	W 2-1	Keeley, Mercer	12,229
7		20	(h)	Barrow	L 0-1		8,688
8		22	(a)	Rotherham U	L 0-1		10,630
9		27	(a)	Wrexham	D 1-1	Mercer	12,045
10		30	(h)	New Brighton	W 5-3	Rothwell, Mercer 2, Keeley 2	8,385
11	Oct	4	(h)	Halifax T	W 2-0	Keeley 2	6,969
12		11	(h)	Gateshead	W 1-0	Marvin	7,265
13		18	(a)	Darlington	L 1-3	Mercer	6,638
14		25	(h)	Tranmere R	W 1-0	Edwards	6,945
15	Nov	1	(a)	Oldham A	L 0-1		15,118
16		8	(h)	York C	W 1-0	Rothwell	6,305
17		15	(a)	Mansfield T	L 0-1		12,527
18		22	(h)	Chester	W 1-0	Webster	3,660
19	Dec	6	(h)	Carlisle U	L 1-2	Morgan	4,867
20		13	(a)	Carlisle U	W 3-2	T.Butler, Briggs, D.Smith	11,514
21		25	(a)	Lincoln C	W 3-2	D.Smith, Mercer 2 (1 pen)	14,352
22		27	(h)	Lincoln C	W 2-1	Mercer (pen), T.Butler	9,293
23	Jan	1	(h)	Rochdale	L 1-2	Mercer	5,785
24		3	(h)	Hull C	L 2-4	D.Smith 2	7,363
25		17	(a)	Stockport C	D 1-1	Mercer	8,932
26		31	(h)	Bradford C	W 2-0	D.Smith, Mercer	5,771
27	Feb	7	(a)	Barrow	L 0-3		4,721
28		14	(h)	Wrexham	L 0-2		5,371
29		21	(a)	Halifax T	D 3-3	T.Wright 2, D.Smith	4,055
30		28	(a)	Gateshead	L 2-4	D.Smith, T.Wright	7,262
31	Mar	6	(h)	Darlington	W 3-0	Dyson, Mercer, T.Butler	4,612
32		13	(a)	Tranmere R	W 1-0	Mercer	6,945
33		20	(h)	Oldham A	L 2-3	Mercer, T.Wright	5,213
34		26	(a)	Southport	D 1-1	T.Butler	11,401
35		27	(a)	York C	W 2-1	Mercer, D.Smith	10,156
36		29	(h)	Southport	D 0-0		5,227
37	Apr	3	(h)	Mansfield T	W 1-0	Mercer	4,622
38		7	(a)	Crewe A	D 0-0		5,110
39		10	(a)	Chester	L 0-1		5,811
40		17	(h)	Crewe A	W 2-1	Webster, Rothwell	4,795
41		28	(a)	Hartlepools U	L 0-4		6,126
42	May	1	(h)	Rotherham U	L 0-1		6,545

FINAL LEAGUE POSITION: 6th in Division Three North

Appearances
Goals

FA Cup

1	Nov	29	(a)	Stockport C	L 1-3	T.Butler	15,016

Appearances
Goals

Harris W	Butler MP	Wilson JH	Conroy RM	Briggs JC	Webster R	Butler T	Rothwell G	Mercer S	Smith NH	Edwards RC	Keeley W	Morris A	Lynn S	Marvin W	Wright JF	Egerton F	Wright TB	Smith D	Morgan D	Harrison HKG	Coates F	Dyson G	Pye F	
1	2	3	4	5	6	7	8	9	10	11														1
1	2	3	4	5	6	7	8	9	10		11													2
1	2	3		5	6	7	8	9	10		11	4												3
1	2	3		5	6	7	8	9	10		11	4												4
1	2	3		5	6	7	8	9	10		11	4												5
1	2	3		5	6	7	8	9	10		11	4												6
1	2	3		5	6	7	8	9	10		11	4												7
1	2	3	4	5	6	7	8	9	10		11													8
1	2	3		5	6	7	8	9	10		11	4												9
1	2	3		5	6	7	8	9	10		11	4												10
1		3	2	5	6	7	8	9	10		11	4												11
1	3		4	5	6	7	8		10		11		2	9										12
	3		4	5	6	7	8	9	10		11		2		1									13
1	3		4	5	6	7	8	9	10	11			2											14
1	3		4	5	6	7	8	9	10	11			2											15
1	3		4	5	6	7	8	9	10	11			2											16
1			4	5	3	7	8		10	11				9		2	6							17
1	3		7	5	6	11	4	9	8							2		10						18
1	3			5	6	7	4	9		11						2		10	8					19
1	3		2	5	6	7	4	9		11								10	8					20
1	3		2	5	6	8	4	9		11								10		7				21
1			2	5	6	8	4	9		11						3		10		7				22
1			2	5	6	8	4	9		11						3		10		7				23
1			2	5	6	7	4	9	10							3		11	8					24
1	3		2	5	6	11	4	9										10			7	8		25
1	3		2	5	6	11	4	9										10			7	8		26
1	3		2	5	6	10	4	9										11			7	8		27
1	3		2	5	6	10	4	9										11			7	8		28
1	3		2	5	6	7	4	9									11	10				8		29
1	3		2	5	6	7	4	9									11	10				8		30
1	3		2	5	6	7	4	9									11	10				8		31
1	3		2	5	6	7	4	9									11	10				8		32
1	3		2	5	6	7	4	9									11	10				8		33
1	3		2	5	6	7	4	9									11	10				8		34
1		3	2	5	6	7	4	9									11	10				8		35
1	6	3	2	5		7	4	9									11	10				8		36
1		3	2	5	6	7	4	9									11	10				8		37
1	3		2	5	6	7	4	9									11	10				8		38
1	3		2	5	6	7	4	9									11	10				8		39
1		3	2	5	6	7	4	9									11	10				8		40
1		3	2	5	6	7	4	9									11					8	10	41
1		3	2	5	6	7	4	9		11								10				8		42
41	32	17	34	42	41	42	42	40	19	11	12	8	5	2	1	6	14	24	3	3	4	18	1	
				1	3	5	6	19	2	1	8			1			4	8	1			1		

2 own-goals

1	3		7	5	6	11	4	9	8							2		10						1
1	1		1	1	1	1	1	1	1							1		1						
						1																		

1948-49

Secretary/Manager: John Hacking

1	Aug	21	(a)	Darlington	L 0-3		9,624
2		25	(h)	Rotherham U	L 2-3	Mercer 2	7,681
3		28	(h)	Oldham A	D 1-1	Mercer	8,595
4		30	(a)	Rotherham U	L 0-1		15,249
5	Sep	4	(a)	Tranmere R	D 2-2	Smith, Parker	10,016
6		9	(a)	Hull C	L 1-3	Mercer	33,512
7		11	(h)	Mansfield T	D 1-1	Parker	6,160
8		18	(a)	Barrow	D 0-0		8,578
9		25	(h)	Wrexham	L 0-1		6,757
10		28	(h)	Hull C	L 1-2	Keeley	13,162
11	Oct	2	(a)	Halifax T	L 0-1		10,976
12		9	(a)	Rochdale	L 1-4	Parker	11,151
13		16	(h)	New Brighton	W 5-1	Parker 2, Keeley, Butler 2	5,800
14		23	(a)	Chester	L 0-3		7,558
15		30	(h)	Southport	W 3-1	Cutting, Wilson, Butler	6,591
16	Nov	6	(a)	Crewe A	L 0-2		7,565
17		13	(h)	York C	W 2-1	Keeley (pen), Butler	3,617
18		20	(a)	Stockport C	L 1-2	Edwards	9,836
19	Dec	4	(a)	Gateshead	D 1-1	Edwards	3,564
20		11	(h)	Hartlepools U	L 1-2	Edwards	3,408
21		18	(h)	Darlington	W 3-2	Keeley 2, Parker	3,744
22		25	(a)	Doncaster R	D 0-0		12,220
23		27	(h)	Doncaster R	W 2-0	Goodfellow (og), Travis	9,105
24	Jan	1	(a)	Oldham A	L 3-4	Keeley 2, Butler	13,205
25		8	(a)	Hartlepools U	L 0-1		5,724
26		15	(h)	Tranmere R	L 0-2		3,139
27		22	(a)	Mansfield T	L 0-2		11,735
28		29	(h)	Carlisle U	W 2-1	Keeley, Travis	7,844
29	Feb	5	(h)	Barrow	D 1-1	Travis	5,560
30		19	(a)	Wrexham	L 0-1		7,380
31		26	(h)	Halifax T	W 1-0	Keeley	3,951
32	Mar	12	(a)	New Brighton	W 3-1	Travis 2, Cutting	5,296
33		19	(h)	Chester	W 3-1	Travis, Butler, Cutting	4,767
34		26	(a)	Southport	L 0-3		5,005
35	Apr	2	(h)	Crewe A	W 2-0	Cutting, Travis	4,286
36		9	(a)	York C	D 1-1	Rothwell	8,409
37		16	(h)	Stockport C	W 2-1	Travis, Cutting	6,094
38		18	(h)	Bradford C	W 6-0	Travis 2, Keeley 2, Butler 2	6,750
39		19	(a)	Bradford C	D 2-2	Keeley 2	9,519
40		23	(a)	Carlisle U	L 1-4	Travis	6,613
41		27	(h)	Rochdale	D 0-0		5,446
42		30	(h)	Gateshead	L 1-2	Rothwell	3,564

FINAL LEAGUE POSITION: 20th in Division Three North

Appearances

Goals

FA Cup

1	Nov	27	(a)	Hull C	L 1-3	Webster	21,926

Appearances

Goals

Harris W	Conroy RM	Wilson Joseph H	Rothwell G	Briggs JC	Webster R	Smith D	Cutting JA	Mercer S	Robertson LV	Woodhead D	Wright TB	Butler T	Dyson G	Parker S	Burrows A	Pye F	Rodwell J	Egerton F	Keeley W	Edwards RC	Wilson John	Travis D	Williams E	Capstick AL	Hurst WR	Simpson H	
1	2	3	4	5	6	7	8	9	10	11																	1
1	2	3	4	5			8	9	10	11	6	7															2
1	2	3	4	5				9		11	6	7	8	10													3
1	2	3	8	5				9		11	6	7		10	4												4
1	2		4	5	3	10		7		11		8		9	6												5
1	2		4	5	3			7	10		11	8		9	6												6
1	2		4	5	3			7			6	8		9		10	11										7
1	2			5	3		8				11	7	4	9		10		6									8
1	2		4	5	3							7		9		8		6	10	11							9
1	2	3	4	5	6		8	9				7							10	11							10
1	2	3	4	5	6			9									7		10	11	8						11
1	2	3	4	5	6							7		9					10	11	8						12
1	2		4	5	3	6						7		9					10	11	8						13
1	2		4	5	3	6						7		9					10	11	8						14
1	2	3	4	5		6	9					7							10	11	8						15
1	2	3	4	5		6	9					7							10	11	8						16
1	2	5	4		3	6	9					7							10	11	8						17
1	2	5	4		3	6	9					7							10	11	8						18
1	2	3	4	5			8					7		9	6					11	10						19
1	2	3	4	5	6		8					7		9						11	10						20
1	2	3	4	5		6						7		9					10	11	8						21
1	2	3	4	5		6						7							10	11	8	9					22
1	6	3	4	5								7							10	11	8	9	2				23
1	6	3	4	5								7							10	11	8	9	2				24
1	2	3	4			6						7							10	11	8	9	5				25
1		3	4		2	6				7									10	11	8	9	5				26
1		3	8	5	2	6													10	11	7	9	4				27
1		3	4		2	6						7			10				11		8	9	5				28
1		3	4		2	6						7			8				11		10	9	5				29
1		3	4	8	2	6	10					7								11		9	5				30
1		3	4	5	2		10					7							11		8	9		6			31
1		3	4	5	2		10					7			6				11		8	9					32
1		3	4	5	2		10					7			6				11		8	9					33
1	8	3	4	5	2		10					7			6							9			11		34
1		3	4	5	2	6	8					7							10	11		9					35
1	4		6	5	2		8					7							10	11		9	3				36
1	4		6	5	2		8					7							10	11		9	3				37
1	4		6	5	2		8					7							10	11		9	3				38
1			4	5	2	6	8					7							10	11		9	3				39
1			4	5	2	6	8					7							11		10	9	3				40
1		3	4		2	6	8					7							11		10	9	5				41
1	2		4		3	6	8					7							10			9	5			11	42
42	30	29	41	34	31	21	23	9	3	6	6	38	2	13	9	3	2	2	30	25	24	21	15	1	1	1	
			2			1	5	4				8		6					13	3	1	11					

1 own-goal

Harris W	Conroy RM	Wilson Joseph H	Rothwell G	Briggs JC	Webster R	Smith D	Cutting JA	Mercer S	Robertson LV	Woodhead D	Wright TB	Butler T	Dyson G	Parker S	Burrows A	Pye F	Rodwell J	Egerton F	Keeley W	Edwards RC	Wilson John	Travis D	Williams E	Capstick AL	Hurst WR	Simpson H	
1	2	3	4	5	9	6						7							10	11	8						1
1	1	1	1	1	1	1						1							1	1	1						
					1																						

1949-50

Manager: James Porter

1	Aug	20	(a)	Carlisle U	L 1-2	Travis (pen)	8,388
2		24	(h)	Mansfield T	D 2-2	Travis, Hogan	8,712
3		27	(h)	Rotherham U	L 1-4	Blunt	8,302
4		29	(a)	Mansfield T	L 0-2		15,454
5	Sep	3	(a)	Lincoln C	L 0-1		13,817
6		6	(a)	Oldham A	W 1-0	Parker	1,760
7		10	(h)	Barrow	W 1-0	Keeley	6,584
8		17	(a)	Crewe A	L 1-2	Parker	10,354
9		24	(h)	Tranmere R	W 2-0	Parker, Keeley	6,221
10		27	(h)	Oldham A	L 3-4	Keeley, Parker 2	10,176
11	Oct	1	(a)	York C	L 1-2	Lynn (pen)	7,274
12		8	(a)	Southport	L 0-1		7,827
13		15	(h)	Stockport C	W 4-2	Keeley, Hogan, Parker, Travis	7,395
14		22	(a)	Doncaster R	L 1-4	Rothwell	14,109
15		29	(h)	Gateshead	L 0-1		5,636
16	Nov	5	(a)	Hartlepools U	D 0-0		6,689
17		12	(h)	Darlington	W 3-0	Travis, Peters 2	2,985
18		19	(a)	New Brighton	L 0-3		4,661
19	Dec	3	(a)	Rochdale	L 0-2		5,349
20		17	(h)	Carlisle U	D 1-1	Butler	2,802
21		24	(a)	Rotherham U	L 0-6		9,448
22		26	(h)	Wrexham	W 2-0	Travis, Keeley	4,493
23		27	(a)	Wrexham	D 1-1	Dolan	9,350
24		31	(h)	Lincoln C	W 2-0	Travis 2	5,691
25	Jan	14	(a)	Barrow	L 1-2	Travis	5,003
26		21	(h)	Crewe A	D 1-1	Travis	5,005
27		28	(h)	Halifax T	W 1-0	Travis	4,244
28	Feb	4	(a)	Tranmere R	W 1-0	Birkett	8,480
29		11	(h)	Bradford C	W 3-2	Dolan, Lynn (pen), Butler	4,410
30		18	(h)	York C	D 0-0		6,059
31		25	(h)	New Brighton	W 3-0	Keeley, Butler, Smith	3,969
32	Mar	4	(a)	Halifax T	W 4-1	Travis 2, Hogan, Dolan	5,726
33		11	(h)	Doncaster R	D 2-2	Keeley, Travis	8,963
34		18	(a)	Gateshead	L 0-5		6,851
35		25	(h)	Hartlepools U	L 1-2	Keeley	4,771
36	Apr	1	(a)	Darlington	W 2-0	Hogan, Travis	4,985
37		7	(a)	Chester	L 0-1		13,747
38		8	(h)	Southport	W 4-0	Keeley (pen), Dolan, Travis, Butler	5,388
39		10	(h)	Chester	W 4-0	Travis 2, Birkett, Greenwood (og)	4,611
40		15	(a)	Stockport C	L 0-1		7,304
41		22	(h)	Rochdale	W 1-0	Travis	7,302
42		29	(a)	Bradford C	L 2-5	Travis 2	7,251

FINAL LEAGUE POSITION: 13th in Division Three North

Appearances
Goals

FA Cup

1	Nov	26	(h)	Hartlepools U	L 0-1		6,300

Appearances
Goals

Harris W	Webster R	Wilson Joseph H	Rothwell G	Briggs JC	Smith D	Coll LS	Blunt E	Travis D	Wilson John	Hogan C	Birkett R	Lynn S	Brown E	Ritchie J	Butler T	Keeley W	Paterson W	Parker S	Wilson James	Peters TJ	Daniels D	Lovett E	Dolan A	
1	2	3	4	5	6	7	8	9	10	11														1
1	2	3	4	5	6	7	8	9	10	11														2
1	2	3	4	5	6		8	9	10	11	7													3
1			6	5				9		11	7	2	3	4	8	10								4
1	3		6	5						11	7	2		4	8	10	9							5
1	3		6	5	11					7		2		4	8	10		9						6
1	3		6	5	11					7		2		4	8	10		9						7
1	3		6	5	11					7		2		4	8	10		9						8
1	3		6	5	11					7		2		4	8	10		9						9
1	3		6	5						7	11	2		4	8	10		9						10
1	3		6	5						7		2		4	8	11		9	10					11
1	3	5	6				10	11		7		2		4				9	8					12
1	3		6	5				10		7		2		4		11		9	8					13
1	2	3	6	5				10		7				4		11		9	8					14
1	3		6	5			4	10		7		2				11		9		8				15
	3		8	5	6		4	9		7	11	2								10	1			16
	3		8	5	6		4	9		7		2						11		10	1			17
	3		8	5	6		4	9		7		2						11		10	1			18
		3	4	5	6		10	9		7		2			8	11					1			19
		3	10	5	6			9		7		2		4	8	11					1			20
		3	8	5	6			9		7		2		4	10	11					1			21
	3		4		6			9			11	2			7	10					1	5	8	22
	3		4		6			9		11		2			7	10					1	5	8	23
1	3		4		6			9			11	2			7	10						5	8	24
	3		4		6			9			11	2			7	10					1	5	8	25
	3		4		6			9			11	2			7	10					1	5	8	26
	3		4		6			9		11		2			7	10					1	5	8	27
	3		4		6			9			11	2			7	10					1	5	8	28
	3		4		6			9			11	2			7	10					1	5	8	29
	3		4		6			9				2	11		7	10					1	5	8	30
		3	4		6			9		11		2			7	10					1	5	8	31
	3		4		6			9		11		2			7	10					1	5	8	32
	3		4		6			9		11		2			7	10					1	5	8	33
	2	3	4		6					11					7	10		9			1	5	8	34
	2	3	4		6			9		11					7	10					1	5	8	35
	3		4		6			9		7	11				8	10		2			1	5		36
	3		4		6			9		7	11				8	10		2			1	5		37
	3		4		6			9		11					7	10		2			1	5	8	38
	3		4		6			9		11	7					10		2			1	5	8	39
	3		4		6			9		11					7	10		2			1	5	8	40
	3		4		6			9		11					7	10		2			1	5	8	41
	3		4		6			9		11					7	10		2			1	5	8	42
16	37	11	42	20	34	2	9	34	3	35	14	29	2	13	31	35	1	20	4	4	26	21	19	
			1		1		1	20		4	2	2			4	9		6		2			4	

1 own-goal

		3	8	5	6			9		7		2		4				11		10	1			1
		1	1	1	1			1		1		1		1				1		1	1			

1950-51

Manager: James Porter: resigned 5 March, 1951. The directors then selected team in consultation with Walter Crook.

1	Aug	19	(a)	Gateshead	L 0-7		9,623
2		23	(h)	Crewe A	W 1-0	Thomas	2,930
3		26	(h)	Southport	W 3-1	Keeley, Thomas, Travis	7,265
4		30	(a)	Crewe A	L 0-3		7,708
5	Sep	2	(a)	Tranmere R	D 1-1	Keeley	9,936
6		4	(a)	York C	L 0-3		7,417
7		9	(h)	Bradford	D 3-3	Thomas, Keeley 2	6,503
8		16	(a)	Oldham A	L 1-2	Thomas	11,645
9		23	(h)	Wrexham	W 1-0	Lovett	4,789
10		26	(h)	York C	W 2-0	Rothwell, Butler	7,237
11		30	(a)	Scunthorpe U	L 0-3		7,861
12	Oct	7	(a)	Shrewsbury T	W 1-0	Travis	8,226
13		14	(h)	Lincoln C	W 3-1	Travis 2, Keeley	5,785
14		21	(a)	Rochdale	L 1-3	Keeley	8,027
15		28	(h)	Chester	L 1-2	Lee (og)	5,744
16	Nov	4	(a)	New Brighton	D 1-1	Travis	3,455
17		11	(h)	Bradford C	L 0-2		4,662
18		18	(a)	Darlington	L 0-3		5,582
19	Dec	2	(a)	Halifax T	D 2-2	Slattery, Keeley	4,883
20		9	(h)	Stockport C	L 2-3	Keeley (pen), Thomas	3,415
21		23	(a)	Southport	L 0-3		3,227
22		25	(a)	Carlisle U	L 1-3	Keeley	13,943
23		26	(h)	Carlisle U	L 0-4		4,947
24	Jan	1	(h)	Rotherham U	L 0-2		5,004
25		13	(a)	Bradford	L 0-3		8,883
26		20	(h)	Oldham A	L 1-2	Watkinson	5,192
27		27	(h)	Barrow	W 1-0	Watkinson	4,370
28	Feb	3	(a)	Wrexham	D 1-1	Keeley	7,593
29		10	(a)	Rotherham U	L 2-6	Robinson, Watkinson	14,504
30		17	(h)	Scunthorpe U	D 0-0		3,433
31		24	(h)	Shrewsbury T	W 2-0	Keeley, Watkinson	3,417
32	Mar	3	(a)	Lincoln C	L 1-9	Mellor	10,745
33		10	(h)	Rochdale	L 1-2	Keeley	4,281
34		17	(a)	Chester	D 2-2	Watkinson, Keeley	3,400
35		23	(a)	Mansfield T	L 0-5		4,504
36		24	(h)	New Brighton	D 1-1	D.Smith	3,495
37		26	(h)	Mansfield T	L 0-2		3,602
38		31	(a)	Bradford C	L 0-7		9,025
39	Apr	7	(h)	Darlington	W 1-0	D.Smith	3,245
40		14	(a)	Stockport C	D 0-0		5,264
41		16	(a)	Barrow	L 0-4		4,130
42		21	(h)	Halifax T	W 1-0	Wilson	4,550
43		25	(h)	Hartlepools U	W 2-0	Wilson, Robinson	4,091
44		28	(a)	Hartlepools U	L 0-1		3,568
45	May	2	(h)	Tranmere R	L 0-2		4,194
46		5	(h)	Gateshead	D 2-2	Wilson, Slattery	2,782

FINAL LEAGUE POSITION: 23rd in Division Three North

Appearances

Goals

FA Cup

1	Nov	25	(a)	Wrexham	L 0-1		10,370

Appearances

Goals

Daniels D	Parker S	Webster R	Rothwell G	Lovett E	Martin FJ	Hogan C	Butler T	Travis D	Keeley W	Thomas D	Martin E	Smith D	Slattery JW	Wilson JH	Coll LS	Mellor W	Woods W	Robinson W	Seed T	Watkinson WW	Smythe H	Rigby E	Oldham J	Smith C	Lancaster JG	
1	2	3	4	5	6	7	8	9	10	11																1
1	2	3	4	5	10		7	9	6	11	8															2
1	2	3	4	5			7	9	10	11	8	6														3
1	2	3	4	5	8	7		9	10	11		6														4
1	2	3	4	5	8	7		9	10	11		6														5
1	2	3	4	5			7	9	10	11		6	8													6
1	2	3	4	5		7	8	9	10	11		6														7
1	2	3	4	5		7	8	9	10	11		6														8
1	2	3	4	5	8		7	9	10	11				6												9
1	2	3	4	5	8		7	9	10	11				6												10
1	2	3	4	5	8	11	7	9	10					6												11
1	2	3	4	5			8	9	10	11				6	7											12
1	2	3	4	5	6		8	9	10	11					7											13
1	2	3	4	5	6		7	9	10	11					8											14
1	2	3	4	5	6			9	10	11		7			8											15
1	2	3	4	5	6		7	9	10	11					8											16
1		3	4	5	6				10	11			9		7	2	8									17
1		3	4	5	6				10	11			9		7	2	8									18
1		3			4		8		10	11		6	9	5	7	2										19
1		3			6		8		10	11		4	9	5	7	2										20
1		3	7		4		8		10			6	9	5		2		11								21
1		3	4		6		8		9	11				5	7	2		10								22
1		3	4		6	7	8		9			11		5		2		10								23
1			4				7		10	11		6	9	5		2		8	3							24
1		3	4				7		10	11		6	9	5		2		8								25
1		3	4			7			10	11		6		5		2		8		9						26
1		3			11	7	8		10					5		2		4		9	6					27
1		3			11	7	8		10					5		2		4		9	6					28
1		3			11	7	8		10					5		2		4		9	6					29
1		3	8		10	7			11					5		2		4		9	6					30
1		3	8		10		7		11					5		2		4		9	6					31
1		3	8		11		7		9			10		5		2		4			6					32
1		3	4	5	6		7		9	11		10				2		8								33
1			4		6		7		10	11				5		2		8		9		3				34
1			4		6		7			11		10	9	5		2		8				3				35
1		3	4		6		7					10		5		2		11		9	8					36
1		3	4		6		8					10	9	5	7	2		11								37
1		3	4	5	6	7	8					9				2	10	11								38
1		3	4		6	7	8			11		9				2		10					5			39
1		3	4		6	7	8			11		10				2				9			5			40
1		3	4		6	7	8			11						2		10		9			5			41
1		3	4		6	7	8			11				9		2		10					5			42
1		3	4		6	7	8			11				9		2		10					5			43
1			4		6	7				11			8	9		2						3	5	10		44
1		3	4		6	7	8			11			10	9		2							5			45
		3	4		6	7	8			11			10	9		2							5		1	46
45	16	42	41	20	38	21	38	16	34	34	2	22	13	27	11	30	3	22	1	10	7	3	8	1	1	
			1	1			1	5	13	5		2	2	3		1		2		5						

1 own-goal

Daniels D	Parker S	Webster R	Rothwell G	Lovett E	Martin FJ	Hogan C	Butler T	Travis D	Keeley W	Thomas D	Martin E	Smith D	Slattery JW	Wilson JH	Coll LS	Mellor W	Woods W	Robinson W	Seed T	Watkinson WW	Smythe H	Rigby E	Oldham J	Smith C	Lancaster JG	
1		3	4		6				10	11			9	5		2	7		8							1
1		1	1		1				1	1			1	1		1	1		1							

1951-52

Manager: Walter Crook

1	Aug	18	(h)	Gateshead	L 1-2	McEwan	9,189
2		22	(h)	Mansfield T	W 1-0	Watkinson	8,614
3		25	(a)	Carlisle U	L 1-4	Watkinson	12,015
4		27	(a)	Mansfield T	L 0-3		10,520
5	Sep	1	(h)	Stockport C	L 0-3		7,642
6		3	(a)	Halifax T	W 4-0	Watkinson 2, Spencer, Roberts	7,163
7		8	(a)	Workington	W 2-0	McAlone (og), Roberts	9,152
8		15	(h)	Barrow	D 1-1	Roberts	7,415
9		22	(a)	Grimsby T	L 1-2	Butler	13,095
10		25	(h)	Halifax T	D 2-2	Watkinson, Roberts	5,977
11		29	(h)	Wrexham	W 4-2	Spencer, Donnelly, Watkinson 2	7,667
12	Oct	6	(h)	Oldham A	L 1-2	Spencer	13,268
13		13	(a)	Hartlepools U	L 2-4	Roberts, Butler	8,617
14		20	(h)	Bradford C	L 0-1		6,643
15		27	(a)	York C	L 1-6	Smith	7,538
16	Nov	3	(h)	Chester	W 4-2	Watkinson 3, Roberts	5,712
17		10	(a)	Lincoln C	D 2-2	Forrest 2	11,822
18		17	(h)	Scunthorpe U	D 2-2	Watkinson, Spencer	6,381
19	Dec	1	(h)	Southport	D 0-0		5,812
20		8	(a)	Crewe A	D 3-3	Watkinson, Darcy 2	3,825
21		22	(h)	Carlisle U	L 0-2		3,873
22		25	(a)	Darlington	W 5-4	Roberts 3, Watkinson, Spencer	4,835
23		26	(h)	Darlington	L 1-3	Watkinson	7,623
24		29	(a)	Stockport C	L 0-6		11,278
25	Jan	5	(h)	Workington	D 0-0		5,223
26		15	(a)	Rochdale	L 1-3	Watkinson	1,792
27		19	(a)	Barrow	L 1-3	Darcy	7,051
28		26	(h)	Grimsby T	L 0-3		4,210
29	Feb	9	(a)	Wrexham	L 0-1		7,156
30		16	(a)	Oldham A	L 1-3	Roberts	11,661
31		23	(a)	Bradford	D 1-1	Butler	10,897
32	Mar	1	(h)	Hartlepools U	D 0-0		4,755
33		8	(a)	Bradford C	W 3-1	Roberts, Butler, Spencer	11,382
34		15	(h)	York C	W 2-1	Watkinson, Aveyard	6,439
35		22	(a)	Chester	L 1-3	Senior	4,533
36		26	(a)	Gateshead	L 0-1		622
37		29	(h)	Lincoln C	L 1-3	Glaister	3,358
38	Apr	2	(h)	Rochdale	D 0-0		4,081
39		5	(a)	Scunthorpe U	L 1-3	Spencer	4,801
40		11	(h)	Chesterfield	W 2-0	Aveyard, Watkinson	5,639
41		12	(h)	Tranmere R	D 1-1	Watkinson (pen)	6,247
42		14	(a)	Chesterfield	L 0-2		8,236
43		19	(a)	Southport	D 0-0		3,853
44		22	(a)	Tranmere R	L 1-3	Watkinson (pen)	4,964
45		26	(h)	Crewe A	L 2-3	Darcy, Watkinson	5,333
46		30	(h)	Bradford	W 5-1	Watkinson 2, Darcy 2, Hindle (og)	5,598

FINAL LEAGUE POSITION: 22nd in Division Three North

Appearances
Goals

FA Cup

1	Nov	24	(h)	Chester	L 1-3	Watkinson	8,212

Appearances
Goals

Daniels D	Mellor W	Cox S	Rothwell G	Senior S	Martin FJ	Roberts DG	McEwan S	Watkinson WW	Spencer JS	Robinson W	Turnbull GF	Butler T	Keeley W	Rudd E	Glazzard M	Rigby E	Winterbottom DTW	Glaister G	Donnelly J	Johnson M	Smith D	Forrest J	Darcy AJ	Martindale L	Aveyard W	Oldham J	
1	2	3	4	5	6	7	8	9	10	11																	1
	2	3	4	5	6	7		9	10		1	8	11														2
	2	3	4	5	6	7		9	10		1	8	11														3
	2	3	4	5		7		9		10	1	8		6	11												4
		3	4			7		9	10		1	8		6		2	5	11									5
		3			4	7	10	9	8	6	1					2	5	11									6
		3			4	7		9	8	6	1	10				2	5	11									7
		3			4	7		9	10	6	1	8				2	5	11									8
		3			4	7		9	8	6	1	10				2	5	11									9
		3			4	7		9		6	1	10				2	5		8	11							10
		3			4	11		9	10	6	1	7					5		8		2						11
	2	3			4	7		9	8	6	1	10					5	11									12
1	2	3			4	7			8	6		10					5	11			9						13
1	2	3		4	10	11			8	6		7					5				9						14
1	2		8	4	10	11				6		7				3	5				9						15
	2	3		5	4	7		9	8	6	1							11				10					16
	2	3		5	4	7		9	8	6	1							11				10					17
	2	3		5	4	7		9	8	6	1							11				10					18
	2	3		5		7		9		6	1									10	4	8	11				19
	2	3		5	10	7		9		6	1	8									4		11				20
	2	3				7		9	8	6	1	10					5				4		11				21
1	2	3			4	7		9	8	6		10									5		11				22
1	2	3			4	7		9	8	6		10									5		11				23
	2	3		5		7		9		6	1	8						11				10		4			24
	2	3		5		7		9	8	6	1	10											11	4			25
	2	3		5	11	7		9	8	6	1	10												4			26
	2	3		5	6	7			9		1	8								10			11	4			27
	2	3		5		8		9	10		1	7						11			6			4			28
	2			5		8		9	10	3	1	7						11			6			4			29
	2			5		8		9	10	3	1	7						11			6			4			30
	2	5		4		11		7	9	3	1	8									6			10			31
	2	5		4		11		9	8	3	1	7									6			10			32
	2	5		4		11		9	8	3	1	7									6			10			33
	2	5		4		11		9		3	1	7									6			10	8		34
	2	5		4		11		9	10	3	1	7									6				8		35
	2	5		4				9		3	1	7						10					11	6	8		36
	2	5				7		8		3	1							10	4		6		11		9		37
	2	5				11		8		3	1	7						10	4		6				9		38
	2	5			11			9	8	3	1	7						10			6			4			39
1	2	5		4				9		3		7						11			6			10	8		40
1	2	5		4				9		3		7						11			6			10	8		41
1	2	5		4	8			9		3		7						11			6			10			42
1	2	5			4	7		9		3		10						11			6				8		43
1	2	5			4			9		3		7						10			6		11		8		44
1	2	5			4	7		9		3		10									6		11		8		45
1	2	5						9		3		7						10			6		11		8	4	46
13	39	43	6	27	26	39	2	42	29	41	33	39	2	2	1	7	12	24	4	3	27	5	12	16	11	1	
				1		11	1	22	7			4						1	1		1	2	6		2		

2 own-goals

	2	3		5		7		9	8	6	1							11			4	10					1
	1	1		1		1		1	1	1	1							1			1	1					
								1																			

1952-53

Secretary/Manager: Walter Crook until 26 February 1953

1	Aug	23	(a)	Hartlepools U	L 1-4	Goodfellow	10,765
2		27	(h)	Carlisle U	W 1-0	Watkinson	7,117
3		30	(h)	Workington	L 0-1		7,600
4	Sep	4	(a)	Carlisle U	D 4-4	Watkinson 2, Butler, Smith	10,897
5		6	(a)	Chesterfield	L 0-3		10,088
6		10	(h)	Halifax T	D 1-1	Goodfellow	6,867
7		13	(h)	Tranmere R	L 0-2		6,642
8		15	(a)	Halifax T	L 0-3		8,883
9		20	(a)	York C	L 0-2		8,232
10		24	(a)	Bradford C	L 2-3	Aveyard 2	5,122
11		27	(h)	Grimsby T	L 1-2	Collins	5,774
12	Oct	4	(a)	Barrow	L 0-2		4,291
13		11	(a)	Southport	L 0-1		6,263
14		18	(h)	Crewe A	D 1-1	Watkinson	6,349
15		25	(a)	Port Vale	W 1-0	Watkinson	12,202
16	Nov	1	(h)	Chester	D 1-1	Collins	5,903
17		8	(a)	Scunthorpe U	L 2-5	Watkinson 2	7,334
18		15	(h)	Stockport C	L 1-4	Watkinson	4,974
19		29	(h)	Rochdale	W 2-1	Kendal, Bushel	4,060
20	Dec	13	(h)	Gateshead	D 1-1	Butler	4,278
21		20	(h)	Hartlepools U	D 1-1	Kendal	3,195
22		26	(a)	Wrexham	L 1-3	Kendal	14,880
23		27	(h)	Wrexham	L 1-2	Kendal	8,351
24	Jan	1	(h)	Bradford	W 3-2	Mellor (pen), Butler 2	5,638
25		3	(a)	Workington	L 0-3		7,233
26		17	(h)	Chesterfield	D 1-1	Kendal	4,977
27		24	(a)	Tranmere R	L 0-2		5,162
28		31	(h)	Mansfield T	D 2-2	Cooper, Grummett	3,274
29	Feb	7	(h)	York C	W 1-0	Darcy	4,336
30		14	(a)	Grimsby T	L 0-3		11,118
31		21	(h)	Barrow	W 1-0	Kendal	4,350
32		28	(h)	Southport	L 1-2	Kendal	7,422
33	Mar	7	(a)	Crewe A	L 2-3	Smith, Darcy	5,094
34		14	(h)	Port Vale	D 1-1	Watkinson	5,499
35		21	(a)	Chester	L 0-2		3,818
36		25	(a)	Darlington	L 0-1		3,361
37		28	(h)	Scunthorpe U	W 2-1	Darcy, Kendal	2,903
38	Apr	3	(a)	Oldham A	L 0-3		21,698
39		4	(a)	Stockport C	L 1-3	Watkinson	7,068
40		6	(h)	Oldham A	L 0-2		10,465
41		11	(h)	Bradford C	D 1-1	Watkinson	4,496
42		13	(a)	Mansfield T	D 0-0		5,465
43		18	(a)	Rochdale	L 0-1		4,706
44		22	(a)	Bradford	L 0-4		6,067
45		25	(h)	Darlington	W 1-0	Goodfellow	3,152
46		29	(a)	Gateshead	L 0-5		1,599

FINAL LEAGUE POSITION: 24th in Division Three North

Appearances
Goals

FA Cup

1	Nov	22	(a)	Horden Colliery	W 2-1	Watkinson 2	5,748
2	Dec	6	(h)	Mansfield T	L 0-2		8,606

Appearances
Goals

Meadows JR	Mellor W	Robinson W	Goodfellow S	Holliday KJ	Smith D	Collins A	Hazzleton J	Watkinson WW	Aveyard W	Darcy AJ	Butler T	Grummett J	Taylor JJ	Brocklehurst JF	Kendall JB	Daniels D	Green D	Oldham J	Cooper J	Bushel A	Priday RH	Kirk JM	No.
1	2	3	4	5	6	7	8	9	10	11													1
1	2	3	4	5	6	7	8	9		11	10												2
1	2	3	4	5	6	7	8	9		11	10												3
1	2	3	4	5	10			9		11	8	6	7										4
1	2	3	4	5	10			9		11	8	6	7										5
1	2	3	4	5	10			9		11	8	6	7										6
1	2	3	4	5	10			9		11	8	6	7										7
1	2	3	4	5	10		9				11	6	7	8									8
1	2	3	4	5	10			9		11	8	6	7										9
1	2	3	4	5		11		9	10		7	6		8									10
1	2	3		5		11		10	9			6	7	4	8								11
1	2	3	6	5		11		10	9				7	4	8								12
1	2	3		5				10	9	11		6	7	4	8								13
	2	3		5				10	9	11		6	7	4	8	1							14
	2	3		5	10	11		9				6	7	4	8	1							15
	2			5	10	11		9				6	7	4	8	1	3						16
	2			5	10			9		11		6	7	4	8	1	3						17
	2			3				9	8	11		6		4	10	1		5	7				18
	2	3	4	5				9		11	8	6			10	1				7			19
	2	3	4	5		7		9			8	6			10	1					11		20
	2	3	4	5		7		9			10	6			8	1				11			21
	2	3	5					9			10	6	7	4	8	1				11			22
	2	3	5			7		9			10	6		4	8	1				11			23
	2	3	5			7		8			10	6		4	9	1				11			24
	2	3	5			7		8			10	6		4	9	1				11			25
	2	3	6	5		7		8	11		10			4	9	1							26
	2	3	5			7		8	11		10	6		4	9	1							27
	2	3		5				8		11	7	6		4	10	1			9				28
	2	3		5	10					11	7	6		4	8	1			9				29
	2	3		5				9	10		7	6		4	11	1			8				30
	2		5	3		7		8	11		10	6		4	9	1							31
	2		5	3		7		9	11		10	6		4	8	1							32
	2	3	6	5	8			9		11		10		4		1			7				33
	2	3		5	10			9		11		6		4		1			7			8	34
	2	3		5	10			9		11	7	6		4		1						8	35
	2	3		5				9		11	7	6		4	10	1						8	36
	2			5				9		11	7	6		4	10	1	3					8	37
	2			5				9		11	7	6		4	10	1	3					8	38
1	2			5				10			7	6		4			3		9	11		8	39
1	5		10	2	6			9				11		4			3			7		8	40
1	5			2	6			9		7	10			4			3				11	8	41
1	2		10	5	4			9		7		6					3				11	8	42
1	2		10	5	9					11		6	7	4			3					8	43
	2			5					7	11	10	6		4	9	1	3					8	44
	2	11	10	5						7		6		4		1	3				9	8	45
	2	11	10	5								6	7	4		1	3				9	8	46
18	46	33	28	41	20	17	4	40	13	26	30	40	16	34	26	28	12	1	7	8	5	13	
	1		3		2	2		11	2	3	4	1			8				1	1			

Meadows JR	Mellor W	Robinson W	Goodfellow S	Holliday KJ	Smith D	Collins A	Hazzleton J	Watkinson WW	Aveyard W	Darcy AJ	Butler T	Grummett J	Taylor JJ	Brocklehurst JF	Kendall JB	Daniels D	Green D	Oldham J	Cooper J	Bushel A	Priday RH	Kirk JM	No.
	2	3	4	5				9		11	7	6			10	1			8				1
	2	3	4	5				9		11	8	6			10	1				7			2
	2	2	2	2				2		2	2	2			2	2			1	1			
								2															

1953-54

Player/Manager: Walter Galbraith

1	Aug	22	(h)	Stockport C	W 2-1	Bodle, Brown	9,133
2		26	(h)	Workington	W 4-2	Bodle 2 (2 pens), Brown, Cocker	9,596
3		29	(a)	Rochdale	L 0-1		8,375
4		31	(a)	Workington	L 1-3	Devlin	3,417
5	Sep	5	(h)	Wrexham	L 1-2	Kirk	8,298
6		9	(a)	Grimsby T	L 0-2		11,357
7		12	(a)	Mansfield T	D 1-1	Musgrave	7,627
8		16	(h)	Grimsby T	W 3-1	Cocker 2, Holliday	7,591
9		19	(h)	Barrow	W 3-2	Eastham, Devlin, Holliday	8,137
10		22	(a)	Carlisle U	L 1-2	Musgrave	6,153
11		26	(a)	Bradford C	L 0-1		13,224
12		28	(h)	Carlisle U	D 2-2	Musgrave 2	8,758
13	Oct	3	(h)	Chesterfield	D 2-2	Musgrave, Cocker	8,297
14		10	(h)	Hartlepools U	W 2-0	Cocker, Bodle (pen)	7,729
15		17	(a)	Darlington	L 1-4	Eastham	5,936
16		24	(h)	Barnsley	W 3-0	Holliday, Cocker 2	8,891
17		31	(a)	Bradford	L 4-6	Holliday 2, Cocker 2	11,108
18	Nov	7	(h)	Port Vale	D 2-2	Brydon, Cocker	7,895
19		14	(a)	Crewe A	W 3-0	Brydon 3	6,772
20		28	(a)	Southport	L 3-5	Devlin, Brydon 2	6,897
21	Dec	5	(h)	York C	W 2-0	Brydon 2	7,557
22		19	(a)	Stockport C	D 1-1	Bodle (pen)	9,273
23		25	(a)	Halifax T	L 0-2		5,517
24		26	(h)	Halifax T	W 3-0	Watkinson, Currie 2	8,717
25	Jan	1	(h)	Scunthorpe U	L 0-1		8,729
26		9	(a)	Gateshead	L 0-4		2,514
27		16	(a)	Wrexham	L 2-4	Cocker 2	5,374
28		23	(h)	Mansfield T	W 5-1	Cocker 3, Musgrave (pen), Bodle	5,617
29		30	(h)	Gateshead	D 2-2	Cocker, Musgrave	5,113
30	Feb	13	(h)	Bradford C	L 0-1		1,844
31		20	(a)	Chesterfield	D 0-0		7,013
32		27	(a)	Hartlepools U	W 1-0	Watkinson	7,518
33	Mar	6	(h)	Darlington	D 0-0		6,266
34		13	(a)	Barnsley	L 0-5		8,131
35		18	(a)	Scunthorpe U	W 2-1	Eastham, Watkinson	5,191
36		20	(h)	Bradford	D 0-0		6,814
37		30	(a)	Port Vale	L 0-1		9,367
38	Apr	3	(h)	Crewe A	W 2-1	Brydon 2	5,979
39		7	(h)	Rochdale	W 1-0	Brydon	5,124
40		10	(a)	Chester	L 0-3		7,013
41		16	(a)	Tranmere R	L 0-1		7,751
42		17	(h)	Southport	D 1-1	Brydon	6,234
43		19	(h)	Tranmere R	L 0-1		5,634
44		20	(a)	Barrow	L 3-4	Cocker 2, Brydon	3,680
45		24	(a)	York C	W 2-1	Brydon, Cocker	4,252
46		28	(h)	Chester	W 1-0	Brydon	4,687

FINAL LEAGUE POSITION: 15th in Division Three North

Appearances

Goals

FA Cup

1	Nov	21	(a)	Blyth Spartans	W 1-0	Cocker	8,011
2	Dec	12	(h)	Tranmere R	D 2-2	Eastham, Musgrave (pen)	14,390
R		16	(a)	Tranmere R	L 1-5	Brydon	7,789

Appearances

Goals

Henderson J	Mellor W	Galbraith WM	Moran T	Cadden J	Smith D	Cocker L	Bodle H	Brown W	Eastham H	Devlin J	Holliday KJ	Jones TB	Kirk JM	Musgrave D	White W	Sneddon C	Ashe AD	Brydon IF	Currie J	Longstreth HL	Watkinson WW	Ryden JJ	Jones AJ	
1	2	3	4	5	6	7	8	9	10	11														1
1	2	3		5		8	6	9	10	11	4	7												2
1	2	3	4	5		8	6	9	10	11		7												3
1	2	3	8	5			6	9	10	11	4	7												4
1	2		4	5		7	6	9	10	11	3		8											5
1	2	3		5		7	4	9	10	8	6			11										6
1	2	3		5		9	6		10	8	4	7		11										7
1	2	3		5		9	4		10	7	6	8		11										8
1	2	3		5		9	4		10	7	6	8		11										9
1	2	3		5		9	4		10	7	6	8		11										10
1	2	3		5		9	4		10	7	6	8		11										11
	2	3		5		9	4		10	7	6	8		11	1									12
	2	3		5		9	8		10	7	4			11	1	6								13
	2	3		5		9	8		10	11	4	7			1	6								14
	2	3		5		9	8		10	7	4			11	1	6								15
	2			5		8	4		10	7	9			11	1	6	3							16
	2			5		8	4		10	7	9			11	1	6	3							17
1	2					8	4		10	7	5			11		6	3	9						18
1		3				8	4		10	7	5			11		6	2	9						19
1		3				8	4			7	5			11		6	2	9	10					20
	2						6			10	5	7		11	1		3	9	8	4				21
		3			6		4		10	7	5			11	1		2	9	8					22
		3			6	8	4		10	7	5			11	1		2	9						23
	2	3			6	7	4		10	11	5				1				8		9			24
		3				7	4		10	11	5				1	6	2		8		9			25
		3			6	7	4		10	11	5				1		2		8		9			26
	2				4	7	5		10	11	9				1	6	3		8					27
	2					9	4		10	7	5			11	1	6	3		8					28
	2					9	4		10	7	5			11	1	6	3		8					29
						9	4		10	7	2			11	1	6	3		8			5		30
						9	4		10	7	2			11		6	3		8			5	1	31
						8	4		10	7	2			11		6	3				9	5	1	32
						8	4		10	7	2			11		6	3				9	5	1	33
						9	4		10	7	2			11		6	3		8			5	1	34
						8	4		10	7	2	11				6	3				9	5	1	35
						8	4		10	7	2	11				6	3				9	5	1	36
						9	4		10	7	2	11				6	3		8			5	1	37
						8	4		10	7	2			11		6	3	9				5	1	38
						8	4		10	7	2			11		6	3	9				5	1	39
					6	8	4		10	7	2			11			3	9				5	1	40
			6			8	4		10	7	2			11			3	9				5	1	41
			4			8	6		10	7	2			11			3	9				5	1	42
						8	4		10	7	2			11	1	6	3	9				5		43
			4			8	6			11	2				1			9	10	3	7	5		44
						8	4			11	2					6	3	9	10		7	5	1	45
						8	4		10	11						6	3	9		2	7	5	1	46
14	23	21	7	17	7	43	46	6	42	46	43	14	1	30	18	25	29	15	15	3	10	17	14	
						19	6	2	3	3	5		1	7				15	2		3			

Henderson J	Mellor W	Galbraith WM	Moran T	Cadden J	Smith D	Cocker L	Bodle H	Brown W	Eastham H	Devlin J	Holliday KJ	Jones TB	Kirk JM	Musgrave D	White W	Sneddon C	Ashe AD	Brydon IF	Currie J	Longstreth HL	Watkinson WW	Ryden JJ	Jones AJ	
1		3				8	4		10	7	5			11		6	2	9						1
1	2						6		10	8	5	7		11			3	9		4				2
1	2			5			6		10	7	4			11			3	8			9			R
3	2	1		1		1	3		3	3	3	1		3		1	3	3		1	1			
						1			1					1				1						

1954-55

Manager: Walter Galbraith

1	Aug	21	(h)	Southport	D 1-1	McKeown	11,293
2		24	(a)	Carlisle U	L 0-1		9,004
3		28	(a)	Barrow	W 2-1	Wright, Devlin	8,269
4	Sep	1	(h)	Carlisle U	W 3-2	Brydon 2, Cocker	9,818
5		4	(h)	Workington	W 2-0	Cocker, Brydon	9,430
6		8	(h)	Oldham A	W 4-0	Watkinson 3, Devlin	11,202
7		11	(a)	Mansfield T	D 2-2	Scott, Ryden	9,766
8		13	(a)	Oldham A	W 1-0	Watkinson	7,694
9		18	(h)	Crewe A	W 1-0	Cocker	9,812
10		22	(a)	Barnsley	W 2-1	Devlin, Wright	14,095
11		25	(h)	Wrexham	W 2-0	Cocker, Brydon	8,486
12		27	(h)	Barnsley	L 2-3	Wright, Devlin	12,735
13	Oct	2	(a)	Scunthorpe U	L 0-4		11,370
14		9	(a)	Chester	D 1-1	Wright	8,670
15		16	(h)	Grimsby T	W 3-0	Stewart, Devlin, Wright	8,416
16		23	(a)	Bradford	L 2-3	Cocker 2	13,731
17		30	(h)	Rochdale	W 5-4	Cocker 2, Stewart 3	12,626
18	Nov	6	(a)	Tranmere R	L 1-3	Devlin	5,652
19		13	(h)	Stockport C	L 0-1		7,023
20		27	(h)	Gateshead	W 6-2	Stewart 5, Cocker	6,503
21	Dec	4	(a)	Darlington	D 3-3	Wright, Devlin, Stewart	8,580
22		18	(a)	Southport	D 1-1	Bodle	4,216
23		25	(a)	Halifax T	D 1-1	Stewart	13,392
24		27	(h)	Halifax T	W 3-1	Cocker 2, Bodle	12,390
25	Jan	1	(h)	Barrow	W 6-3	Cocker 3, Stewart 3	9,812
26		3	(h)	Chesterfield	W 4-1	Cocker 3, Wright (pen)	10,752
27		15	(a)	Workington	W 1-0	Cocker	6,708
28		22	(h)	Mansfield T	W 3-2	Stewart, Bodle 2	8,527
29		29	(h)	Bradford C	W 1-0	Stewart	9,564
30	Feb	5	(a)	Crewe A	W 3-0	Wright, Scott, Cocker	5,353
31		12	(a)	Wrexham	L 1-3	Stewart	6,893
32		19	(h)	Scunthorpe U	W 2-1	McKeown, Wright	10,926
33		26	(h)	Chester	W 3-0	Bodle 2, Stewart	7,999
34	Mar	5	(a)	Grimsby T	L 1-2	Stewart	6,672
35		12	(h)	Bradford	W 4-3	Bodle, Wright 2, Stewart	8,430
36		19	(a)	Rochdale	D 0-0		11,654
37		26	(h)	Tranmere R	W 3-1	Scott, Stewart, Devlin	5,644
38	Apr	2	(a)	Stockport C	D 0-0		13,144
39		8	(a)	York C	D 1-1	Stewart	19,843
40		9	(h)	Hartlepools U	L 2-5	Cocker, Stewart	11,267
41		11	(h)	York C	D 2-2	Stewart, Currie	15,425
42		16	(a)	Gateshead	D 1-1	Stewart	3,132
43		23	(h)	Darlington	W 3-0	Wright, Stewart, Devlin	6,532
44		25	(a)	Hartlepools U	W 3-1	Stewart 2, Cocker	9,371
45		30	(a)	Chesterfield	L 1-6	Wright	8,813
46	May	4	(a)	Bradford C	W 3-0	Scott, Wright 2	4,435

FINAL LEAGUE POSITION: 2nd in Division Three North

Appearances
Goals

FA Cup

1	Nov	20	(h)	Cresswell Colliery	W 7-1	Devlin 2, Scott 2, Wright, Brydon, Cocker	11,070
2	Dec	11	(a)	Millwall	L 2-3	Scott, Bodle	17,086

Appearances
Goals

Jones AJ	Ferguson C	Ashe AD	Hunter E	Ryden JJ	Bodle H	Cocker L	McKeown T	Brydon IF	Wright AW	Devlin J	Holliday KJ	Sneddon C	Farrell J	Scott R	Watkinson WW	Dale FW	McQueen T	Stewart GTS	Pirie FW	Harrower JS	Heggie WC	Currie J	
1	2	3	4	5	6	7	8	9	10	11													1
1		3		5	4	7	8	9	10	11	2	6											2
1		3	4	5	6	8		9	10	7	2		11										3
1		3	4	5	6	8		9	10	7	2		11										4
1		3	4	5	6	8		9	10	7	2			11									5
1		3	4	5	6	8			10	7	2			11	9								6
1		3	4	5	6	8			10	7	2			11	9								7
1		3	4	5	6	8			10	7	2			11	9								8
1		3	4	5	6	8		9	10	7	2					11							9
1		3	4	5	6	8	11	9	10	7	2												10
1		3	4	5	6	8	7	9	10	11	2												11
		3		5	4	8	7	9	10	11	2	6					1						12
1		3	4	5	6	8			10	7	2			11				9					13
1		2	4	5	3	8			10	7		6		11				9					14
1		2	4	5	3	8			10	7		6		11				9					15
1		2	4	5	3	8		9	10	7		6		11									16
1		2	4	5	3	8			10	7		6		11				9					17
1		3	6	5		4	8		10	7				11				9	2				18
1		3	4	5		8			10	7		6		11				9	2				19
1		3	4	5	6	8			10	7				11				9	2				20
1		3	4	5	6	8			10	7				11				9	2				21
1		2	4	5	6	8			10	7				11				9		3			22
1		2	4	5	6	8			10	7				11				9		3			23
1		2	4	5	6	8			10	7				11				9		3			24
1		2	4	5	6	8			10	7				11				9		3			25
		2	4	5	6	8			10	7				11			1	9		3			26
1		3	4	5	6	8			10	7				11				9		2			27
1		2	4	5	6	8			10	7				11				9		3			28
1		2	4	5	6	8			10	7				11				9		3			29
1		2	4	5	6	8			10	7				11				9		3			30
1			4	5	6	8	7		10					11				9		3	2		31
1		2	4	5	6	8	7		10					11				9		3			32
		2	4	5	6	8	7		10					11			1	9		3			33
1		2	4	5	6	8	7		10					11				9		3			34
1		2	4	5	10		7		8			6		11				9		3			35
		2	4	5	10	11	7		8			6					1	9		3			36
		2	4	5	6	8			10	7				11			1	9		3			37
		2	4	5	6	8			10	7				11			1	9		3			38
		2	4	5	6	8			10	7				11			1	9		3			39
		2	4	5	6	8			10	7				11			1	9		3			40
		2	4	5					8	7		6		11			1	9		3		10	41
		2	4	5	10				8	7		6		11			1	9		3			42
		2	4	5	10				8	7		6		11			1	9		3			43
		2	4	5		8		7	10			6		11			1	9		3			44
		2	4	5		8		7	10			6		11			1	9		3			45
		2	4	5	10				8	11		6		7			1	9		3			46
32	1	45	44	46	41	41	12	12	46	38	12	15	2	37	3	1	14	33	4	25	1	1	
				1	7	21	2	4	15	9				4	4			28				1	

Jones AJ	Ferguson C	Ashe AD	Hunter E	Ryden JJ	Bodle H	Cocker L	McKeown T	Brydon IF	Wright AW	Devlin J	Holliday KJ	Sneddon C	Farrell J	Scott R	Watkinson WW	Dale FW	McQueen T	Stewart GTS	Pirie FW	Harrower JS	Heggie WC	Currie J	
1		3	4	5		8		9	10	7	6			11					2				1
1		3	4	5	6	9			10	7				11					2			8	2
2		2	2	2	1	2		1	2	2	1			2					2			1	
					1	1		1	1	2				3									

1955-56

Manager: Walter Galbraith

1	Aug	20	(h)	Gateshead	D	2-2	Dick, Hunter	10,795
2		24	(h)	Rochdale	W	3-0	Cocker, Scott, Dick	12,016
3		27	(a)	Darlington	L	0-2		7,104
4		29	(a)	Rochdale	D	1-1	McCredie	8,086
5	Sep	3	(h)	Stockport C	W	3-1	Wright, Stewart 2	8,834
6		7	(a)	Chesterfield	W	1-0	Scott	10,883
7		10	(h)	Barrow	W	2-0	Wright, Stewart	9,418
8		14	(h)	Chesterfield	W	5-1	Stewart 2, McCredie, Dick, Devlin	9,858
9		17	(a)	Chester	D	1-1	Stewart	10,994
10		20	(a)	Tranmere R	L	1-4	Stewart	6,499
11		24	(h)	Carlisle U	W	1-0	Kenny (og)	9,805
12		26	(h)	Bradford	W	7-0	Wright 3, Stewart, McCredie, Dick 2	9,553
13	Oct	1	(a)	Grimsby T	L	0-3		19,069
14		8	(a)	Wrexham	W	4-1	Stewart 3, Cocker	9,971
15		15	(h)	Hartlepools U	W	1-0	Wright	8,824
16		22	(a)	Bradford C	L	1-2	Stewart	14,720
17		29	(h)	Scunthorpe U	W	2-0	Stewart 2	7,443
18	Nov	5	(a)	Oldham A	W	3-1	Dick, Scott, Hunter	10,643
19		12	(h)	Workington	W	5-1	Wright 2, Stewart 3	8,577
20		26	(h)	Derby C	W	2-0	McDonnell (og), Stewart	10,282
21	Dec	3	(a)	Crewe A	W	3-0	Dick 2, Stewart	5,200
22		17	(a)	Gateshead	L	0-4		3,179
23		24	(h)	Darlington	W	2-1	Cocker, Scott	7,982
24		26	(a)	Southport	D	1-1	Stewart	10,753
25		31	(a)	Stockport C	W	2-1	Stewart, Cocker	12,206
26	Jan	14	(a)	Barrow	L	1-3	Turner	5,368
27		21	(h)	Chester	W	4-0	Turner, Devlin, Stewart 2	6,862
28		28	(h)	Halifax T	D	2-2	Dick, Turner	9,383
29	Feb	4	(a)	Carlisle U	W	4-0	Stewart, Dick 2, Turner	5,725
30		11	(h)	Grimsby T	L	0-1		13,305
31		18	(h)	Wrexham	W	3-1	Dick, Wright, Stewart	7,840
32	Mar	3	(h)	Bradford C	W	2-0	Dick, Stewart	9,165
33		10	(a)	Scunthorpe U	W	3-2	Stewart 3	10,049
34		17	(h)	York C	L	1-3	Stewart	9,905
35		24	(a)	Workington	D	0-0		6,453
36		30	(a)	Mansfield T	L	2-3	Sneddon, Stewart	17,331
37		31	(h)	Oldham A	D	2-2	Dick, McInnes	8,237
38	Apr	2	(h)	Mansfield T	W	3-1	Dick (pen), Stewart 2	8,179
39		7	(a)	Derby C	L	2-6	Dick, Devlin	22,993
40		14	(h)	Crewe A	W	5-1	Stewart 2, Dick, Wright, Devlin	5,755
41		16	(a)	York C	W	1-0	Wright	8,016
42		21	(a)	Halifax T	L	0-2		4,691
43		23	(a)	Bradford	L	0-1		4,606
44		28	(h)	Tranmere R	D	0-0		5,957
45		30	(h)	Southport	W	4-2	Devlin, Wright, McInnes, Dick	7,785
46	May	3	(a)	Hartlepools U	D	0-0		7,331

FINAL LEAGUE POSITION: 3rd in Division Three North

Appearances
Goals

FA Cup

1	Nov	19	(h)	Wrexham	W	3-1	Stewart 2, Wright	11,500
2	Dec	10	(a)	Darlington	W	1-0	Dick	12,646
3	Jan	7	(a)	Liverpool	L	0-2		48,385

Appearances
Goals

McQueen T	Ashe AD	Harrower JS	Hunter E	Ryden JJ	Bodle H	Scott R	Wright AW	Stewart GTS	Dick PW	Mason J	Cocker L	Sneddon C	McCredie NJ	Stones G	Devlin J	Turner PS	McInnes JC	McInnes W	
1	2	3	4	5	6	7	8	9	10	11									1
1	2	3	4	5	6	7		9	10	11	8								2
1	2	3	4	5	6	7		9	10	11	8								3
1	2	3	4	5		7	8	9	10			6	11						4
1	2	3	4	5		7	8	9	10			6	11						5
1	2	3	4	5		7		9			8	6	11	10					6
1	2	3	4	5		7	10	9			8	6	11						7
1	2	3	4	5	6		8	9	10				11		7				8
1	2	3	4	5			8	9	10			6	11		7				9
1	2	3	4	5	6		8	9	10				11		7				10
1	2	3	4	5				9	10		8	6	11		7				11
1	2	3	4	5			8	9	10			6	11		7				12
1	2	3	4	5			8	9	10			6	11		7				13
1	2	3		5		7	8	9	10		4	6	11						14
1	2	3		5		7	8	9	10		4	6	11						15
1	2	3		5		7	8	9	10		4	6	11						16
1	2	3	4	5		7	8	9	10			6	11						17
1	2	5	4			11	8	9	10		7	6	3						18
1	2	5	4			11	8	9	10		7	6	3						19
1	2	5	4			11	8	9	10		7	6	3						20
1	2	5	4			11	8	9	10		7	6	3						21
1	2	5	4			11	8	9	10		6		3		7				22
1	2	5	4			11	10	9			8	6	3		7				23
1	2	5	4			11		9	10		8	6	3		7				24
1	2	5	4			11	8	9	10		7	6	3						25
1	2	5	4			11		9	10		7	6	3			8			26
1	2	5	4			11		9	10			6	3		7	8			27
1	2	5	4			11		9	10			6	3		7	8			28
1	2	5	4			11		9	10			6	3		7	8			29
1	2	5	4			11	8	9	10			6	3		7				30
1	2	5	4				8	9	10	11		6	3		7				31
1	2	5	4				8	9	10			6	3		7		11		32
1	2	5	4					9	10			6	3		7	8	11		33
1	2	5	4					9	10			6	3		7	8	11		34
	2	5	4					9	10			6	3		7	8	11	1	35
	2	5	4					9	10		7	6	3			8	11	1	36
		5	4					9	10		8	6	3	2	7		11	1	37
	2	5	4			7	8	9	10			6	3				11	1	38
	2	5	4				8	9	10			6	3		7		11	1	39
	2	5	4				8	9	10			6	3		7		11	1	40
	2	5	4				10	9				6	3		7	8	11	1	41
	2	5	4				10	9				6	3		7	8	11	1	42
	2	5			4	11	10	9			8	6	3		7			1	43
	2	5	4					9	10			6		3	7	8	11	1	44
	2	5	4				8	9	10			6	3		7		11	1	45
1		5	4				8	9	10			6	3	2	7		11		46
35	44	46	42	17	6	26	31	46	40	4	20	40	42	4	27	11	14	11	
			2			4	12	35	18		4	1	3		5	4	2		

2 own-goals

McQueen T	Ashe AD	Harrower JS	Hunter E	Ryden JJ	Bodle H	Scott R	Wright AW	Stewart GTS	Dick PW	Mason J	Cocker L	Sneddon C	McCredie NJ	Stones G	Devlin J	Turner PS	McInnes JC	McInnes W	
1	2	5	4			11	8	9	10		7	6	3						1
1	2	5	4			11	8	9	10		7	6	3						2
1	2	5	4			11	8	9	10		7	6	3						3
3	3	3	3			3	3	3	3		3	3	3						
							1	2	1										

1956-57

Manager: Walter Galbraith

1	Aug	18	(h)	York C	W	3-0	Millar, Stewart, Devlin	11,026
2		20	(a)	Barrow	L	1-3	Millar	8,706
3		25	(a)	Oldham A	W	4-2	Stewart, Cocker 2, Scott	11,883
4		29	(h)	Barrow	W	4-1	Cocker, Stewart 2, Dick	9,711
5	Sep	1	(h)	Mansfield T	D	3-3	Millar 2, Stewart	9,817
6		4	(a)	Tranmere R	W	2-1	Sowden, Stewart	8,430
7		8	(a)	Southport	W	5-3	Sowden, Dick, Stewart 3	7,376
8		12	(h)	Tranmere R	W	1-0	Stewart	7,460
9		15	(h)	Chesterfield	D	1-1	Galley (og)	8,977
10		19	(a)	Bradford C	W	2-1	McNicol (pen), Stewart	15,239
11		22	(a)	Chester	W	2-0	Stewart, Millar	8,850
12		24	(h)	Bradford C	L	0-2		10,079
13		29	(h)	Hartlepools U	W	2-1	Dick, Stewart	10,969
14	Oct	6	(h)	Darlington	W	4-2	Dick 2, Stewart, Turner	8,255
15		13	(a)	Bradford	L	0-2		12,415
16		20	(h)	Halifax T	W	4-0	Millar, Sowden, Stewart, Scott	8,079
17		27	(a)	Wrexham	L	2-5	Dick, Sowden	12,007
18	Nov	3	(h)	Derby C	D	0-0		9,946
19		10	(a)	Crewe A	W	4-3	Stewart 2, Scott, Dick	5,375
20		24	(a)	Rochdale	W	2-0	Sowden, Dick	11,071
21	Dec	1	(h)	Gateshead	W	2-0	Stewart 2	7,677
22		15	(a)	York C	L	1-3	Stewart	8,161
23		22	(h)	Oldham A	D	2-2	Stewart, Hunter	4,860
24		25	(a)	Stockport C	L	1-2	Dick	8,902
25		29	(a)	Mansfield T	W	3-1	Dick 3	9,654
26	Jan	1	(h)	Scunthorpe U	L	0-1		8,880
27		12	(h)	Southport	W	4-2	Sowden, Millar 3	6,743
28		19	(a)	Chesterfield	L	0-1		11,288
29		26	(h)	Carlisle U	L	1-2	Stewart	6,915
30	Feb	2	(h)	Chester	W	4-0	Millar, Sowden, Stewart, Scott	6,661
31		9	(a)	Hartlepools U	L	1-2	Stewart	12,518
32		16	(a)	Darlington	D	0-0		6,764
33	Mar	2	(a)	Halifax T	W	1-0	Stewart	8,149
34		9	(h)	Wrexham	W	1-0	Cocker	6,596
35		16	(a)	Derby C	D	2-2	Dick, Scott	24,272
36		19	(a)	Carlisle U	D	2-2	Stewart, Mulkerrin	7,734
37		23	(h)	Crewe A	W	5-0	Stewart 3, Mulkerrin, Sowden	8,596
38		25	(h)	Bradford	W	5-0	Mulkerrin 2, Anders 2, Stewart	8,553
39		30	(a)	Scunthorpe U	W	3-2	Sowden, Mulkerrin, Hunter	6,602
40	Apr	6	(h)	Rochdale	W	2-1	Storey (og), Millar	9,527
41		8	(h)	Stockport C	W	4-0	Mulkerrin, Stewart 2, Sowden	11,266
42		13	(a)	Gateshead	D	1-1	Mulkerrin	3,225
43		19	(a)	Hull C	L	1-2	Scott	18,304
44		20	(h)	Workington	W	2-1	Stewart, Mason	8,940
45		22	(h)	Hull C	L	0-3		11,400
46		27	(a)	Workington	L	1-4	Mulkerrin	6,790

FINAL LEAGUE POSITION: 3rd in Division Three North

Appearances

Goals

FA Cup

1	Nov	17	(h)	Morecambe	W	4-1	Scott, Stones 2, Dick	8,989
2	Dec	8	(h)	Oldham A	W	2-1	Stewart 2	13,286
3	Jan	5	(a)	Bournemouth	L	0-2		17,212

Appearances

Goals

McQueen T	McNicol RH	McCreadie NJ	Hunter E	Harrower JS	Sneddon C	Devlin J	Wright AW	Stewart GTS	Dick PW	Millar W	Scott R	Cocker L	Stones G	Bodle H	Sowden PT	Ashe AD	Mason J	Turner PS	Anders J	McInnes W	Mulkerrin J	McIntyre J	
1	2	3	4	5	6	7	8	9	10	11													1
1	2	3	4	5	6	7	8	9	10	11													2
1	2	3	4	5	6			9	10	11	7	8											3
1	5	3	4		6			9	10	11	7	8	2										4
1	5	3	4					9	10	11	7	8	2	6									5
1	2	3	4		6			9	10	11	7		5		8								6
1	2		4		6			9	10		7		5		8	3	11						7
1	2		4		6			9	10		7		5		8	3	11						8
1	2		4		6			9	10	11	7		5		8	3							9
1	2		4		6	11		9	10		7		5		8	3							10
1	2		4		6			9	10	11	7		5		8	3							11
1	2		4		6			9	10	11	7	8	5			3							12
1	2	11	4		6			9	10		7		5			3		8					13
1	2	11		4	6			9	10		7		5			3		8					14
1	2	11	4		6			9	10		7		5			3		8					15
1	2		4	6				9	10	11	7		5		8	3							16
1	2		4	6				9	10	11	7		5		8	3							17
1	2		4	3	6			9	10	11	7		5		8								18
1	2		4	3	6			9	10	11	7		5		8								19
1	2		4	5	6			9	10		7	11			8	3							20
1	2		4	5	6			9	10		7	11			8	3							21
1	2		4	5	6			9	10		7	11			8	3							22
1	2		4	5				9	10		7	11	6		8	3							23
1	2		4	5					10	11	7	8			9	3	6						24
1	2		4	5			10		9		7	11			8	3	6						25
1	2		4	5	6				9		7	10			8	3	11						26
1	2		4		6				10	11	7	9	5		8	3							27
1	2		4					9	10	11	7		5		8	3	6						28
1	2		4					9	10		7		5		8	3	6		11				29
1	2		4	5				9		10	7				8	3	6		11				30
1	2		4	5	6			9		10	7				8	3			11				31
	2		4	5	6				10		7	9			8	3			11	1			32
	2		4	5				9	6		7	10			8	3			11	1			33
	2		4	5				9	6		7	10			8	3			11	1			34
	2		4	5				9	6		7				8	3			11	1	10		35
	2		4	5				9	6			7			8	3			11	1	10		36
	2		4	5				9	6	7					8	3			11	1	10		37
	2		4	5				9	6	7					8	3			11	1	10		38
	2		4	5				9	6			7			8	3			11	1	10		39
	2		4	5				9	6	7					8	3			11	1	10		40
	2		4	5				9	6	7					8	3			11	1	10		41
	2		4	5				9	6	7					8	3			11	1	10		42
	2		4	5				9	6	11	7				8	3					10	1	43
	2		4	5				9	6	7					8	3	11				10	1	44
	2		4	5				9	6	7					8	3			11		10	1	45
	2		4	5	6				10						8	3	11		7		9	1	46
31	46	9	45	32	24	3	3	40	44	26	34	17	20	1	37	38	10	3	16	11	12	4	
	1		2			1		33	13	11	6	4			10		1	1	2		8		

2 own-goals

McQueen T	McNicol RH	McCreadie NJ	Hunter E	Harrower JS	Sneddon C	Devlin J	Wright AW	Stewart GTS	Dick PW	Millar W	Scott R	Cocker L	Stones G	Bodle H	Sowden PT	Ashe AD	Mason J	
1	2		4	3	6			9	10		7		5		8		11	1
1	2		4	5	6			9	10		7	11			8	3		2
1	2		4	5	6		10		9		7	11			8	3		3
3	3		3	3	3		1	2	3		3	2	1		3	2	1	
								2	1		1		2					

1957-58

Manager: Walter Galbraith

1	Aug	24	(h)	Hartlepools U	L 1-2	Stewart	9,678
2		28	(a)	Rochdale	L 0-3		12,030
3		31	(a)	Bradford	W 3-1	Dick, Stewart 2	12,820
4	Sep	2	(h)	Rochdale	W 3-2	Stewart 2, Sowden	15,454
5		7	(h)	Carlisle U	W 3-2	Dick, Sowden 2	7,674
6		11	(a)	Chesterfield	L 0-1		10,091
7		14	(a)	Southport	D 3-3	J.Anders, H.Anders, Stewart	5,473
8		16	(h)	Chesterfield	L 0-4		4,441
9		21	(h)	York C	W 3-0	Scott, Stewart 2	6,082
10		28	(a)	Barrow	L 1-3	H.Anders	4,435
11		30	(h)	Chester	L 1-2	Scott	7,404
12	Oct	5	(h)	Oldham A	D 1-1	J.Anders	5,987
13		12	(h)	Scunthorpe U	W 2-1	Stewart 2	7,388
14		19	(a)	Stockport C	D 0-0		9,439
15		26	(h)	Hull C	W 3-0	McNicol, H.Anders, Mulkerrin	7,107
16	Nov	2	(a)	Bradford C	D 1-1	H.Anders	14,046
17		9	(h)	Workington	W 3-0	Storey, Mulkerrin, H.Anders	7,086
18		23	(h)	Gateshead	W 3-0	Mulkerrin 2, Stewart	6,895
19		30	(a)	Darlington	W 2-0	H.Anders, Stewart	5,636
20	Dec	14	(h)	Wrexham	W 2-1	Stewart, H.Anders	6,079
21		21	(a)	Hartlepools U	D 1-1	Stewart	7,179
22		25	(a)	Crewe A	L 1-4	Mulkerrin	4,519
23		26	(h)	Crewe A	W 2-0	Stewart, Byrom	7,633
24		28	(h)	Bradford	W 5-2	Scott 2, Rushby (og), Stewart, H.Anders	7,212
25	Jan	1	(a)	Bury	D 1-1	Stewart	18,067
26		11	(a)	Carlisle U	L 1-6	Stewart (pen)	6,854
27		18	(h)	Southport	D 2-2	Stewart, Mulkerrin	4,633
28		25	(a)	Mansfield T	W 2-0	Stewart, Watson (og)	7,154
29	Feb	1	(a)	York C	W 3-0	Storey, Stewart, Mulkerrin	7,900
30		15	(a)	Oldham A	W 3-0	Mulkerrin 2, H.Anders	5,850
31		22	(a)	Gateshead	W 3-1	Stewart 2, Mulkerrin	5,035
32	Mar	1	(h)	Stockport C	W 3-2	Mulkerrin, J.Anders, Stewart	8,185
33		5	(h)	Bury	W 3-0	Mulkerrin, Sneddon, Stewart	6,048
34		15	(h)	Bradford C	D 2-2	Dick, Mulkerrin	8,309
35		22	(a)	Scunthorpe U	L 0-1		11,304
36		25	(a)	Hull C	L 0-1		9,382
37		29	(h)	Mansfield T	W 4-1	Stewart, J.Anders, Mulkerrin, Stones	5,290
38	Apr	4	(h)	Tranmere R	W 2-1	Mulkerrin, Harrower	7,215
39		5	(a)	Halifax T	W 2-0	Mulkerrin, Dick	7,160
40		7	(a)	Tranmere R	W 1-0	Millington (og)	15,005
41		12	(h)	Darlington	D 0-0		6,448
42		14	(h)	Halifax T	W 2-1	Lonsdale (og), Stewart (pen)	4,458
43		19	(a)	Workington	W 1-0	Scott	4,706
44		24	(h)	Barrow	W 3-2	Mulkerrin 2, Scott	8,593
45		26	(a)	Wrexham	L 0-1		9,766
46		30	(a)	Chester	L 1-5	Mulkerrin	3,373
	FINAL LEAGUE POSITION: 2nd in Division Three North						Appearances
							Goals

FA Cup

1	Nov	16	(a)	Wrexham	W 1-0	Stewart (pen)	11,271
2	Dec	7	(a)	Carlisle U	D 1-1	Mulkerrin	13,171
R		11	(h)	Carlisle U	W 3-2	J.Anders 3	11,413
3	Jan	4	(h)	Bristol C	D 2-2	Stewart, Byrom	11,976
R		7	(a)	Bristol C	L 1-3	Sowden	32,196
							Appearances
							Goals

McInnes W	McNicol RH	Harrower JS	Hunter E	Ralston P	Dick PW	Scott R	Sowden PT	Stewart GTS	Mulkerrin J	Anders J	Anders H	Tighe TW	Ashe AD	Sneddon C	Kelly WM	Stones G	Cocker L	Lewin DJ	Storey S	Marshall J	Byrom R	
1	2	3	4	5	6	7	8	9	10	11												1
1	2	3	4	5	6		8	9		11	7	10										2
1	2	5	4		10		8	9		11	7		3	6								3
1	2	5	4		10		8	9		11	7		3	6								4
1	2	5	4		10		8	9		11	7		3	6								5
1	2	5	4		10	11	8	9			7		3	6								6
1	2	5	4		10		8	9		11	7		3	6								7
1	2	5	4		10		8	9		11	7		3	6								8
1	2	3	4			10	8	9		11	7			6	5							9
1	2	3	4			10		9		11	7			6	5	8						10
1	2	3	4			10		9		11	7			6	5		8					11
1	2	3	4			10		9		11	7			6	5			8				12
1	2	3	4			8		9		11	7			6	5				10			13
1	2	3	4					9	8	11	7			6	5				10			14
1	2	3	4					9	8	11	7			6	5				10			15
1	2	3	4					9	8	11	7			6	5				10			16
1	2	3	4					9	8	11	7			6	5				10			17
1	2	3	4					9	8	11	7			6	5				10			18
1	2	3	4					9	8	11	7			6	5				10			19
1	2	3					4	9	8	11	7			6	5				10			20
1	2	3					4	9	8	11	7			6		5			10			21
	2	3						9	8	11	7	4		6	5				10	1		22
	2	3				8		9			7	4		6	5				10	1	11	23
	2	3				8		9			7	4		6	5				10	1	11	24
1	2	3				11		9	8		7	4		6	5				10			25
1	2	3	4			7	8	9				6			5				10		11	26
1	2	3				7	8	9	10	11		4		6		5						27
1	2	3						9	8	11	7	4		6		5			10			28
1	2	3						9	8	11	7	4		6		5			10			29
1	2	3						9	8	11	7	4		6		5			10			30
1	2	3						9	8	11	7	4		6		5			10			31
1	2	3						9	8	11	7	4		6		5			10			32
1	2	3			10			9	8	11	7	4		6		5						33
1	2	3			10			9	8	11	7	4		6		5						34
1	2	3			10			9	8	11	7	4		6		5						35
1	2	3	4		6	7		9	8							5			10		11	36
1	2	3			6			9	8	11	7	4				5			10			37
1	2	3			10			9	8	11	7	4		6		5						38
1	2	3	4		10	7	8		9	11				6	5							39
1	2	3	4		10	7	8		9	11				6	5							40
1	2	3	4					9	8	11	7			6	5				10			41
1	2	3	4			7	10	9			11	8		6	5							42
1	2	3			10	7		9	8		11	4		6	5							43
1	2	3			10	11		9	8		7	4		6	5							44
1	2	3	4			11		9	8		7			6	5				10			45
1	2	3	4			7	10	9	8	11				6		5						46
43	46	46	27	2	18	20	17	44	30	36	39	20	6	41	24	15	1	1	23	3	4	
	1	1			4	6	3	27	19	4	9			1		1			2		1	

4 own-goals

McInnes W	McNicol RH	Harrower JS	Hunter E	Ralston P	Dick PW	Scott R	Sowden PT	Stewart GTS	Mulkerrin J	Anders J	Anders H	Tighe TW	Ashe AD	Sneddon C	Kelly WM	Stones G	Cocker L	Lewin DJ	Storey S	Marshall J	Byrom R	
1	2	3	4					9	8	11	7			6		5			10			1
1	2	3	4				9		8	11	7			6		5			10			2
1	2	3					4	9	8	11	7			6		5			10			R
1	2	3					4	9	8		7	6				5			10		11	3
1	2	3	4				8	9			7	6				5			10		11	R
5	5	5	3				4	4	4	3	5	2		3		5			5		2	
							1	2	1	3											1	

1958-59

Caretaker-manager: Harry Hubbick until 23 October 1958 then George Eastham, manager.

1	Aug	23	(a)	Notts C	D	1-1	Mulkerrin	14,872
2		27	(h)	Newport C	D	2-2	Stewart (pen), Mulkerrin	9,202
3		30	(h)	Mansfield T	W	2-0	Dick, J.Anders	6,096
4	Sep	4	(a)	Newport C	L	1-2	Stewart	8,893
5		6	(a)	Swindon T	W	2-1	J.Anders 2	13,880
6		8	(a)	Colchester U	L	0-1		7,380
7		12	(h)	Brentford	D	1-1	Stewart	9,918
8		17	(h)	Colchester U	D	1-1	H.Anders	8,108
9		20	(a)	Hull C	L	2-4	Scott, Stewart	11,858
10		22	(a)	Chesterfield	W	1-0	Stewart	8,979
11		27	(h)	Bradford C	L	1-3	Tighe	6,893
12		29	(h)	Chesterfield	W	3-1	Scott 2, Stewart	5,381
13	Oct	4	(a)	Wrexham	D	2-2	Stewart 2	11,785
14		8	(h)	Southampton	D	0-0		7,773
15		11	(a)	Norwich C	W	4-2	Scott, Tighe, Stewart 2	18,560
16		17	(h)	Southend U	W	3-0	J.Anders, Stewart, Tighe	8,133
17		25	(a)	Bury	L	1-3	Stewart (pen)	12,635
18	Nov	1	(h)	Queen's Park R	L	2-4	Stewart, J.Anders	6,498
19		8	(a)	Rochdale	L	0-1		6,288
20		22	(a)	Stockport C	D	0-0		10,219
21		29	(h)	Tranmere R	W	3-1	Dick, Mulkerrin, Scott	5,180
22	Dec	13	(h)	Reading	W	4-3	Tighe 2 (1 pen), Scott, J.Anders	5,246
23		20	(h)	Notts C	W	3-0	Mulkerrin, Tighe, Scott	5,299
24		26	(h)	Halifax T	W	4-2	J.Anders 2, Scott, Mulkerrin	9,838
25		27	(a)	Halifax T	W	2-0	Mulkerrin 2	7,285
26	Jan	1	(a)	Mansfield T	L	2-3	J.Anders 2	6,815
27		31	(a)	Brentford	L	1-2	Scott	11,260
28	Feb	7	(h)	Hull C	L	0-1		6,610
29		14	(a)	Bradford C	D	0-0		13,004
30		18	(h)	Swindon T	D	0-0		5,564
31		21	(h)	Wrexham	D	1-1	J.Anders	3,641
32	Mar	4	(a)	Plymouth A	W	4-2	Scott, McNicol, Garrity, Mulkerrin	12,033
33		7	(a)	Southend U	L	2-4	Garrity, McNicol	9,343
34		11	(h)	Doncaster R	W	2-0	J.Anders 2	3,892
35		14	(h)	Bury	L	0-2		6,778
36		21	(a)	Queen's Park R	L	1-3	Rutter (og)	8,005
37		23	(h)	Norwich C	L	0-2		7,848
38		26	(h)	Bournemouth	W	3-2	J.Anders, Gibson, McNicol	4,174
39		28	(h)	Rochdale	W	4-2	Gibson, Scott, J.Anders, Tighe	4,412
40		30	(a)	Bournemouth	L	2-5	Mulkerrin, Scott	8,465
41	Apr	4	(a)	Doncaster R	L	0-3		5,290
42		11	(h)	Stockport C	D	2-2	Gibson, J.Anders	4,538
43		18	(a)	Tranmere R	L	0-9		8,394
44		22	(a)	Southampton	L	1-3	Tighe	6,808
45		25	(h)	Plymouth A	D	1-1	Tighe	3,109
46		29	(a)	Reading	L	0-5		6,588

FINAL LEAGUE POSITION: 19th in Division Three

Appearances
Goals

FA Cup

1	Nov	15	(h)	Workington	W	5-1	Scott 3, H.Anders, Stewart	6,425
2	Dec	6	(h)	Buxton	W	6-1	Scott 2, J.Anders 3, Tighe	8,958
3	Jan	10	(h)	Darlington	W	3-0	J.Anders, Stinson, Scott	9,172
4		24	(h)	Portsmouth	D	0-0		12,395
R		28	(a)	Portsmouth	L	1-4	Scott	22,607

Appearances
Goals

McInnes W	McNichol RH	Harrower JS	Hunter E	Stones G	Sneddon C	Anders H	Mulkerrin J	Stewart GTS	Dick PW	Byrom R	Anders J	Nicholson GH	Tighe TW	Storey S	Scott R	Ralston P	Garrity K	Lord WG	Hamilton AM	Blackwood JDS	Nightingale R	Stinson HMJ	McCreadie WH	Marshall J	Rogers D	Gibson I	Ross A	Pirie FW	Bennett LH	Ryan K	
1	2	3	4	5	6	7	8	9	10	11																					1
1	2	3	4	5	6	7	8	9	10		11																				2
1	2	3	4	5	6	7	8	9	10		11																				3
	2	3	4	5	6	7	8	9	10		11	1																			4
1	2	3		5	6	7	8	9	10		11		4																		5
1	2	3		5	6	7		9	8		11		4	10																	6
1	2	3		5	6	7	8	9	10	11			4																		7
1	2	3		5	6	7	8	9	10	11			4																		8
1	2	3		5	6	7		9	10	11			4		8																9
1	2	3		5	6	7		9	4				8	10	11																10
1	2	3		5	6	7		9	4				8	10	11																11
1	2	3		5	6	7		9	10		11		4		8																12
1	2	3		5	6	7		9	10		11		4		8																13
1	2	3		5	6	7		9	10		11		4		8																14
1	2	3			6	7		9	10		11		4		8	5															15
1	2	3			6	7		9	10		11		4		8	5															16
1	2			3		7		9	6		11		4	10	8	5															17
1	2	3	6	5		7	8	9	10		11		4																		18
1	2	3		5	6	7			10	11			4		8		9														19
1	2	3		5	6	7		9	10		11		4		8																20
1	2			5	6	7	9		10		11		4		8			3													21
1	2			5		7	9		10		11		4		8			3	6												22
1	2		6	5		7	9		10		11		4		8			3													23
1	2			5		7	9				11		4		8			3	6	10											24
1	2			5		7	9				11		10		8			3	6		4										25
1	2		6	5		7	9				11		10		8			3			4										26
1	2			5		7	9				11		4		8		10	3				6									27
1	2			5	6	7	9				11		4		8			3				10									28
1	2			5	6	7	9				11		4		8			3		10											29
1	2	5			6	7	9				11		4		8		10	3													30
1	2		4	5	6	7	9				11		8					3					10								31
1	2			5	6	7	9				11		4		8		10	3													32
1	2			5	6	7	9				11		4		8		10	3													33
1	2	5			6	7	9				11		4		8		10	3													34
	2			5		7	9				11		4		8		10	3			6			1							35
	2			5	6	7	9				11		4		8		10	3							1						36
	2	11		5	6	7					10		4		9			3							1	8					37
	2	11		5	6	7					10		4		9			3							1	8					38
	2	5				7	10				11		4		9			3	6							8	1				39
	1	3		5		7	8				10		4		9				6							11		2			40
	2	3		5	6	7	10				11		4		9									1		8					41
	2	5			6	7					10		4		9			3						1		11			8		42
		3		5	6	7	10				11		4				9	2						1		8					43
		3	4								11		8	10		5	9		6							7		2		1	44
1		3	4			7					11		8	10			9		6		5							2			45
1		3	4								11		8	10			9				5	6				7		2			46
35	42	31	11	37	32	44	28	19	23	5	39	1	42	7	32	4	12	21	7	2	5	3	1	4	3	9	1	4	1	1	
	3					1	9	13	2		16		9		12		2									3					

1 own-goal

McInnes W	McNichol RH	Harrower JS	Hunter E	Stones G	Sneddon C	Anders H	Mulkerrin J	Stewart GTS	Dick PW	Byrom R	Anders J	Nicholson GH	Tighe TW	Storey S	Scott R	Ralston P	Garrity K	Lord WG	Hamilton AM	Blackwood JDS	Nightingale R	Stinson HMJ	McCreadie WH	Marshall J	Rogers D	Gibson I	Ross A	Pirie FW	Bennett LH	Ryan K	
1	2	3		5	6	7		9	10		11		4		8																1
1	2			5	6	7	9		10		11		4		8			3													2
1	2			5		7	9				11		4		8			3	6			10									3
1	2			5		7	9				11		4		8			3	6			10									4
1	2			6		7	9				11		4		8	5		3				10									R
5	5	1		5	2	5	4	1	2		5		5		5	1		4	2			3									
						1		1			4		1		7							1									

1959-60

Manager: Harold Bodle until 21 April 1960 then James S.Harrower, player-manager.

1	Aug	22	(a)	Tranmere R	L 1-5	H.Anders	12,537
2		24	(h)	Shrewsbury T	D 2-2	McCreadie 2	7,321
3		29	(h)	Wrexham	D 2-2	McCreadie, Tighe (pen)	6,253
4		31	(a)	Shrewsbury T	L 0-5		9,670
5	Sep	5	(a)	Grimsby T	L 0-4		14,448
6		7	(h)	Bournemouth	W 2-1	H.Anders, Tighe	5,877
7		12	(h)	Queen's Park R	L 1-2	Tighe	5,336
8		16	(a)	Bournemouth	L 1-3	McCreadie	10,385
9		19	(a)	Bradford C	W 5-4	McCreadie 2, Tighe 2, Keeley	9,744
10		23	(a)	Reading	L 0-2		13,267
11		26	(h)	Coventry C	L 0-2		5,663
12		28	(h)	Reading	D 0-0		4,189
13	Oct	3	(a)	York C	L 0-3		7,997
14		7	(a)	Swindon T	W 1-0	McCreadie	7,882
15		10	(a)	Port Vale	L 0-2		10,712
16		12	(h)	Swindon T	W 3-1	J.Anders 2, McCreadie	3,895
17		17	(h)	Norwich C	L 3-4	Blackwood, J.Anders, Harrower	4,780
18		24	(a)	Brentford	L 0-3		12,660
19		31	(h)	Southampton	D 2-2	Ness, Tighe (pen)	3,351
20	Nov	7	(a)	Southend U	L 1-6	J.Anders	9,397
21		21	(a)	Halifax T	W 2-0	J.Anders, Tighe	5,901
22		28	(h)	Bury	L 1-3	Tighe	8,473
23	Dec	5	(h)	Chesterfield	L 1-3	Garrity	2,418
24		12	(h)	Colchester U	L 1-2	Bennett	2,116
25		19	(h)	Tranmere R	L 1-3	H.Anders	2,343
26		26	(a)	Chesterfield	W 3-0	McCreadie, Swindells (pen), H.Anders	5,961
27	Jan	2	(a)	Wrexham	W 3-2	Swindells, McCreadie, H.Anders	7,048
28		9	(h)	Barnsley	W 2-1	Swindells 2	4,920
29		16	(h)	Grimsby T	L 2-4	Swindells 2	4,243
30		23	(a)	Queen's Park R	L 1-5	H.Anders	4,721
31	Feb	6	(h)	Bradford C	L 0-4		5,804
32		13	(a)	Coventry C	L 1-2	Swindells	10,708
33		27	(h)	Port Vale	L 1-3	J.Anders	3,109
34	Mar	5	(a)	Norwich C	L 0-4		21,127
35		11	(h)	Brentford	L 3-4	H.Anders, Swindells (pen), Sneddon	3,464
36		19	(a)	Bury	W 1-0	Swindells	8,197
37		21	(h)	Mansfield T	L 0-1		5,283
38		26	(h)	Southend U	L 0-4		2,018
39		30	(h)	York C	W 4-0	H.Anders, J.Anders, Garrity 2	925
40	Apr	2	(a)	Mansfield T	L 1-4	Pollitt	5,283
41		9	(h)	Halifax T	L 0-5		2,650
42		15	(a)	Newport C	W 3-1	Swindells, Tighe 2	3,314
43		16	(a)	Southampton	L 1-5	Swindells (pen)	20,356
44		18	(h)	Newport C	D 0-0		2,202
45		23	(a)	Barnsley	L 0-5		4,129
46		30	(a)	Colchester U	L 1-5	Tighe	5,215

FINAL LEAGUE POSITION: 24th in Division Three

Appearances
Goals

FA Cup

1	Nov	14	(h)	Mansfield T	L 1-2	Tighe	4,363

Appearances
Goals

McInnes W	Pirie FW	Harrower JS	Tighe TW	Stones G	Sneddon C	Anders H	Jones E	McCreadie WH	Keeley JJ	Anders J	Jack V	Lord WG	Bennett LH	Gray E	Ness HP	Brown WI	Garrity K	Hamilton AM	Blackwood JSD	Todd R	Nightingale R	McCrae I	Swindells J	Lightbown TJ	Pollitt J	Forrester GH	
1	2	3	4	5	6	7	8	9	10	11																	1
1	2	3	4	5	6	7	8	9	10	11																	2
1		5	4		6		10	9			2	3	7	8	11												3
		2	4		6		10	9			5	3	7	8	11	1											4
1			8	5	6	7		9		11		3		10			2	4									5
1			8	5	6	7		9		11	2			10			3	4									6
1		3	8	5	6	7		9		11	2							4	8								7
		3	8	5	6		7	9	10	11	2					1		4									8
		3	8	5			7	9	10	11	2					1				4	6						9
		3	8	5			7	9	10	11	2					1				4	6						10
		3	8	5			7	9	10	11						1	2			4	6						11
		3	4				7	9	8	11				10		1	2	6			5						12
		3	4			7		9		11	5		8	10		1	2				6						13
		3	8		6	7		9	10		5				11	1	2				4						14
		3	4		6	7		9	10		5		8		11	1	2										15
		3	4		6	7		9		10	5		8		11	1	2										16
		3	8		6	7				10	5				11	1	2		9		4						17
		3	4		6	7		9	8	10	5				11	1					2						18
1			4	5	6	7		9		10		3	8		11		2										19
1			4	5	6	7		9		10		3	8		11		2										20
		5	8		6			9		11	2		7			1	10	4				3					21
		5	8		6			9		11		2	7			1	10	4				3					22
	2	5	9		6	7				10					11	1	8	4				3					23
		5	8	2				9		10		3	7		11	1		6		4							24
		5			6	7					2	3	8		11	1		10		4			9				25
		5	4			7	10	9		11	2	3				1		6					8				26
		5	4			7	10	9		11	2	3				1		6					8				27
		5	4			7	10	9		11	2	3				1		6					8				28
		5	4			7	10	9		11	2	3				1		6					8				29
1		5	4			7	10	9		11	2	3						6					8				30
	2	5	4			7	10			11		3				1		6					8	9			31
	2	5	4			7	10			11		3				1		6					8	9			32
	2		4			7	10			11		3				1		6				5	8	9			33
			4		6	7	11				2	3				1		10				5	8		9		34
			4	2	10	7				11	5	3				1	9	6					8				35
		5	4		10	7				11		3				1	9	6					8			2	36
		5	4		10	7				11		3				1	9	6					8			2	37
		5	4		10	7						3			11	1		6					8		9	2	38
1		5	4		10	7				11		3					9	6					8			2	39
1		5	4			7				11		3					9	6					8		10	2	40
1	2	5	4		10	7				11		3					9	6					8				41
1		5	8		6					11							10	4				3	9	7		2	42
1		5	8		6					11							10	4				3	9	7		2	43
1		5	8		6					11							10	4				3	9	7		2	44
1	2		8		6					11		3					10	4				5	9	7			45
1	2		8		6							3			11		10	4				5	9	7			46
17	9	37	45	13	31	31	18	27	10	38	22	26	11	6	14	29	25	31	2	5	8	10	22	8	3	8	
		1	11		1	8		10	1	7			1		1		3		1				11		1		

McInnes W	Pirie FW	Harrower JS	Tighe TW	Stones G	Sneddon C	Anders H	Jones E	McCreadie WH	Keeley JJ	Anders J	Jack V	Lord WG	Bennett LH	Gray E	Ness HP	Brown WI	Garrity K	Hamilton AM	Blackwood JSD	Todd R	Nightingale R	McCrae I	Swindells J	Lightbown TJ	Pollitt J	Forrester GH	
		3	8		6			9		11	5	2	7			1	10				4						1
		1	1		1			1		1	1	1	1			1	1				1						
			1																								

1960-61

Player-manager: James S.Harrower

1	Aug	20	(a)	Crystal P	L 2-9	Hudson, Swindells	15,653
2		22	(a)	Millwall	D 2-2	Hudson 2	13,082
3		29	(h)	Millwall	D 3-3	Swindells 3	4,318
4	Sep	3	(a)	Crewe A	W 1-0	Hudson	7,085
5		7	(a)	Gillingham	L 1-2	Bennett	6,209
6		10	(h)	Chester	W 2-0	Hudson, Swindells (pen)	3,597
7		12	(h)	Gillingham	W 3-0	Hudson 3	4,941
8		17	(a)	Workington	L 1-2	Hudson	3,299
9		19	(a)	Barrow	D 1-1	Hudson	4,110
10		24	(h)	Oldham A	W 5-1	Hudson 3, Swindells, Smith	4,661
11		26	(h)	Barrow	D 0-0		4,661
12	Oct	1	(a)	Aldershot	L 1-3	Hudson	5,791
13		3	(h)	Northampton T	W 3-2	Hudson, Swindells (pen), Smith	4,603
14		8	(a)	Hartlepools U	L 1-4	Swindells	2,525
15		14	(h)	Wrexham	L 0-3		3,500
16		22	(a)	Carlisle U	L 1-3	Swindells	3,849
17		29	(h)	Rochdale	W 2-0	Hudson, Devine	4,243
18	Nov	12	(h)	Stockport C	W 4-1	Swindells, Hudson, Duff, Ferguson	3,774
19		19	(a)	Exeter C	W 4-2	Hudson 2, Swindells 2	4,993
20	Dec	3	(a)	Southport	L 0-3		4,313
21		10	(h)	Darlington	D 2-2	Devine 2 (1 pen)	3,564
22		17	(h)	Crystal P	L 2-3	Hudson 2	3,385
23		24	(h)	Bradford	L 1-2	Duff	5,040
24		31	(a)	York C	L 0-1		4,725
25	Jan	14	(h)	Crewe A	L 1-3	Hudson	2,763
26		21	(a)	Chester	W 3-2	Marshall, Swindells, Duff	3,878
27	Feb	4	(h)	Workington	L 1-2	Swindells	1,758
28		11	(a)	Oldham A	L 2-5	Marshall, Swindells	13,307
29		18	(h)	Aldershot	W 1-0	Hudson	2,514
30		25	(h)	Hartlepools U	W 3-0	Hudson, Swindells, Sturrock	2,059
31	Mar	4	(a)	Wrexham	L 0-3		4,375
32		11	(h)	Carlisle U	W 1-0	Hudson	2,771
33		18	(a)	Rochdale	L 2-3	Swindells, Smith	4,067
34		22	(a)	Mansfield T	D 0-0		2,414
35		25	(h)	Mansfield T	L 1-4	Sturrock	3,095
36		31	(a)	Doncaster R	L 0-1		5,901
37	Apr	1	(a)	Stockport C	W 3-0	Hudson, Sturrock 2	4,190
38		3	(h)	Doncaster R	D 2-2	Sturrock, Swallow (og)	3,631
39		8	(h)	Exeter C	L 0-1		2,702
40		11	(h)	Peterborough U	W 3-2	Hudson 3	5,736
41		15	(a)	Peterborough U	L 0-3		13,436
42		19	(h)	York C	W 2-0	Hudson 2	1,801
43		22	(h)	Southport	W 2-1	Devine 2 (1 pen)	2,762
44		25	(a)	Northampton T	L 1-2	Hudson	8,167
45		29	(a)	Darlington	L 2-3	Hudson, Devine	3,338
46	May	1	(a)	Bradford	D 2-2	Hudson 2	8,589
				FINAL LEAGUE POSITION: 18th in Division Four			Appearances
							Goals

FA Cup

1	Nov	5	(h)	Barrow	W 2-1	Swindells 2	4,202
2		30	(h)	Mansfield T	W 3-0	Swindells, Hudson, Duff	4,227
3	Jan	7	(a)	Preston NE	D 1-1	Duff	20,268
R		9	(h)	Preston NE	L 0-4		14,596
							Appearances
							Goals

League Cup

1	Oct	12	(a)	Everton	L 1-3	Sturrock	18,246
							Appearances
							Goals

McInnes W	Forrester GH	Smith WH	Tighe TW	Harrower JS	Sneddon C	Bennett LH	Swindells J	Hudson GA	Logue SW	Devine W	Stones G	Hamilton AM	Lord WG	Egan J	Ferguson MK	Sturrock D	Nightingale R	Entwistle R	Bailey M	Cuddiney R	Duff W	McCluskey R	McCrae I	Marshall AS	Walton J	Vipham P	
1	2	3	4	5	6	7	8	9	10	11																	1
1	2	4	10	3		7	8	9		11	5	6															2
1	2	4	10	3		7	8	9		11	5	6															3
1	2	4	10			7	8	9		11	5	6	3														4
1	2	4	10			7	8	9		11	5	6	3														5
1	2	4	10				8	9		11	5	6	3	7													6
1	2	4	10				8	9		11	5	6	3		7												7
1	2	4					8	9	10	11	5	6	3			7											8
1	2	4	10				8	9		11	5	6	3			7											9
1	2	4			10		8	9		11	5	6	3			7											10
1	2	4			10		8	9		11	5	6	3			7											11
1	2	10					8	9		7	5	6	3				4	11									12
1	2	4					8	9		11	5	6	3		10			7									13
1	2	4	10				8	9		11	5	6	3						7								14
1	2		10		4		8	9		11	5	6	3						7								15
1	2				4	7	8	9		11	5	6	3		10												16
1	2			5			8	9		7		4	3		10					6	11						17
1	2			5			8	9		7		4	3		10					6	11						18
1	2			5			8	9		7		4	3		10					6	11						19
	2			5			8	9		7		4	3		10					6	11	1					20
	2			5			8	9		7		4	3		10					6	11	1					21
	2	4		5			8	9		7		6	3		10						11	1					22
	2	4		5			8	9		7		6	3		10						11	1					23
1	2	4		3			8	9		7	5	6			10						11						24
1	2						8	9		7	5	4			10					6	11		3				25
1	2	4					9			7	5	6				8					11		3	10			26
1	2	4					9			7	5	6			8						11		3	10			27
1	2	4		5		7	8	9		11		6											3	10			28
1	2	4		5			8	9		7		6				11								10	3		29
1	2	4		5		7	8	9		11		6				10									3		30
1	2	4		5		7	8	9		11						10				6					3		31
1	2	4		5		7		9		11		6			8	10									3		32
1	2	4		5			8	9		7		6				10					11				3		33
	2	4		5			8	9		7		6			10						11				3	1	34
	2			5			8	9		7		4			6	10					11				3	1	35
	2			5			11	9		7		4				8				6				10	3	1	36
	2			5			11	9		7		4				8				6				10	3	1	37
	2			5			11	9		7		4				8				6				10	3	1	38
	2	4		5			11	9		7		6				8								10	3	1	39
1	2	4		5		7		9		11		6			8	10									3		40
1	2	4		5		7		9		11		6			8	10									3		41
1	2	4		5		7	10	9		11		6			8										3		42
1	2	4		5		7	10	9		11		6			8										3		43
1	2	4		5		7	10	9		11		6			8										3		44
1	2	4				7	10	9		11	5	6			8										3		45
1	2	4		5		7	10	9		11		6			8										3		46
36	46	34	10	29	5	17	43	44	2	46	20	44	20	1	23	17	1	2	2	10	14	4	4	8	18	6	
		3				1	17	35		6					1	5					3			2			

1 own-goal

1	2			5			8	9		7		4	3		10					6	11	1
1	2			5			8	9		7		4	3		10					6	11	2
1	2	4		3			8	9		7	5	6			10						11	3
1	2	4		3			8	9		7	5	6			10						11	R
4	4	2		4			4	4		4	2	4	2		4					2	4	
							3	1													2	

1	2	4	10				8	9		11	5	6	3			7	1
1	1	1	1				1	1		1	1	1	1			1	
																1	

1961-62

Manager: James S. Harrower, resigned 14 December 1961 then W.H.Smith and H.Hubbick, joint caretaker-managers.

1	Aug	19	(a)	Tranmere R	L 0-2		10,711
2		21	(h)	Darlington	W 3-1	Hudson 2, Greener (og)	3,846
3		26	(h)	Chester	L 0-1		4,106
4		28	(a)	Darlington	D 1-1	Sturrock	8,583
5	Sep	2	(a)	Colchester U	L 2-3	Hudson, Devine (pen)	5,129
6		4	(h)	Mansfield T	D 0-0		4,161
7		9	(h)	Carlisle U	W 1-0	Hudson	2,905
8		16	(a)	Bradford C	W 1-0	Hamilton	5,716
9		18	(a)	Barrow	L 1-3	Robinson (og)	3,895
10		23	(h)	Aldershot	L 0-2		2,472
11		25	(h)	Barrow	D 2-2	Devine, Sturrock	2,901
12		29	(a)	Stockport C	L 0-2		6,711
13	Oct	2	(h)	Oldham A	W 1-0	Milner	4,396
14		7	(a)	Rochdale	L 0-1		5,364
15		11	(a)	Oldham A	L 0-5		11,275
16		14	(h)	Crewe A	W 1-0	Milner	2,713
17		21	(a)	Exeter C	L 0-3		4,948
18		28	(h)	Wrexham	L 0-2		2,881
19	Nov	11	(h)	Workington	L 0-4		2,394
20		18	(a)	York C	L 0-1		5,192
21	Dec	2	(a)	Gillingham	L 1-5	Mulvey	5,987
22		9	(h)	Millwall	L 0-2		1,709
23		16	(h)	Tranmere R	D 1-1	Milner	1,936
24		23	(a)	Chester	D 0-0		2,153
25	Jan	13	(h)	Colchester U	L 0-4		1,430
26		20	(a)	Carlisle U	L 0-2		4,500
27		27	(h)	Chesterfield	D 0-0		1,810
28	Feb	3	(h)	Bradford C	L 0-2		1,554
29		9	(a)	Aldershot	D 2-2	Milner 2	6,988
30		16	(h)	Stockport C	L 1-2	Pickup	1,760
31		24	(h)	Rochdale	L 0-2		2,727
32		27	(a)	Doncaster R	D 1-1	Ferguson	1,981
33	Mar	2	(a)	Crewe A	L 0-4		4,272
							Appearances
							Goals

FA Cup

1	Nov	4	(a)	Stockport C	W 1-0	Pickup	4,797
2		25	(a)	Hartlepools U	L 1-2	Irving	5,230
							Appearances
							Goals

League Cup

1	Sep	13	(a)	Lincoln C	L 0-1		2,681
							Appearances
							Goals

Smith A	Forrester GH	Walton J	Wilson RSW	Richardson G	Hamilton AM	Devine W	Ferguson MK	Hudson GA	Smith WH	Sturrock D	Bennett LH	Mulvey P	Milner JE	Cuddihey R	Irving P	Pickup M	Smith JB	Gordon RJW	Hooley JW	Bonson R	Wareing J	Christie L	Bades B	Gregory A	Devlin J	
1	2	3	4	5	6	7	8	9	10	11																1
1	2	3	4	5	6	7	8	9			10	11														2
1	2	3	4	5	6	7	8	9			10	11														3
1	2	3	4	5	6	11	10	9	8	7																4
1	2	3	4	5	6	11	10	9	8	7																5
1	2	3	4	5	6	7	8	9				11	10													6
1	2	3	4	5	6	7	10	9				11	8													7
1	2	3	4	5	6	7		9		10		11	8													8
1	2	3	4	5	6	7	10			9		11	8													9
1	2	3	5		6		10	9	4		11		8	7												10
1	2	3	5		4	11		9		10	7		8	6												11
1	2	3	5		4	11		9		10	7		8	6												12
1	2	3	5		4	11			9	10	7		8	6												13
1	2	3	5		4	11			9	10			8	6	7											14
1	2	3	5		4	7	10		9			11	8	6												15
1	2	3	5		4		10		9		7		8	6		11										16
1	2	3	5		4		10		9		7		8	6		11										17
1	2	3	5		6	11	10		4		7		8				9									18
1	2	3	5				10						8	6		9	11	4	7							19
1	2	3	5		6		10						8		11	7	9	4								20
1	2		5		6				9		8	11	10		7	3		4								21
1	2	3	5		6	7	10		9				8			11		4								22
1	2	3	5		6		10		4			11	8							7	9					23
1	2	3	5		6	7	10		4			11	8								9					24
1	2	3	5		6	7	10		4			11	8								9					25
1	2	3	5		6		10		8		7	11	9			4										26
1	2	3	5		6		10		8		7	11				4						9				27
1	2	3	5		6		10		8		7	11				4					9					28
1	2	3	5		8		10				7	11	9	6		4										29
1	2	3	5		4		10				7	11		6		9							8			30
1	2		5		4		10					11		6		9							8	3	7	31
1	2		5		6	7	10		9		8	11				4								3		32
1	2		5		6	7	10		9		8	11				4								3		33
33	33	29	33	9	32	20	27	11	20	9	17	19	22	12	3	14	3	4	1	1	4	1	2	3	1	
					1	2	1	4		2		1	5			1										

2 own-goals

Smith A	Forrester GH	Walton J	Wilson RSW	Richardson G	Hamilton AM	Devine W	Ferguson MK	Hudson GA	Smith WH	Sturrock D	Bennett LH	Mulvey P	Milner JE	Cuddihey R	Irving P	Pickup M	Smith JB	Gordon RJW	Hooley JW	
1	2	3	5			11	10						8	6		9		4	7	1
1	2	3	5		6		8				10	11			7	9		4		2
2	2	2	2		1	1	2				1	1	1	1	1	2		2	1	
															1	1				

Smith A	Forrester GH	Walton J	Wilson RSW	Richardson G	Hamilton AM	Devine W	Ferguson MK	Hudson GA	Smith WH	Sturrock D	Bennett LH	Mulvey P	
1	2	3	4	5	6	7	10	9	8			11	1
1	1	1	1	1	1	1	1	1	1			1	

Third Division North v Third Division South

This was a series of six representative matches played between selected sides from each Third Division Section. The matches were played between 1955 and 1958.

Peel Park hosted the fixture played on 13 October 1955:

Third Division North 3 Third Division South 3
Connor 2, Ryan (pen) Morgan 2, Mills

North: R.Minshull (Southport); J.Fleming (Workington), V.Kenny (Carlisle United), D.Stokoe (Workington), J.Ryden (Accrington Stanley), R.Ryan (Derby County), R.Webb (Bradford City), I.Broadis (Carlisle United), J.Connor (Stockport County), G.Smith, D.Woodhead (both Chesterfield).
South: R.Matthews (Coventry City); A.Jardine (Millwall), S.Charlton (Leyton Orient), N.Simpson (Coventry City), D.Rees (Ipswich Town), R.Ashman (Norwich City), R.Mills (Northampton Town), D.Mills (Torquay United), M.Cook (Watford), S.Morgan (Leyton Orient), J.Wheeler (Reading).
Attendance: 10,521

The following Accrington Stanley players represented the Third Division North side during this series:
James S.Harrower 16 March 1955 at Elm Park, Reading (South 2 v North 0).
John Ryden 13 October 1955 at Peel Park, Accrington (North 3 v South 3).
Charles Sneddon 8 October 1956 at Highfield Road, Coventry (South 2 v North 1).
Edward Hunter 2 April 1957 at Edgeley Park, Stockport (North 2 v South 1).
George Stewart 16 March 1955 at Elm Park, Reading (South 2 v North 0).
30 October 1957 at Selhurst Park, London (South 2 v North 2).

The inter-divisional games were played alternately in the north and south. This is the Third Division North side that met the Third Division South at Coventry in 1956. Back row (left to right): Ryan (Derby County, reserve), Currie (Bradford City), Moore (Hartlepools United), Newlands (Workington), Brownsword (Scunthorpe United), Mays (Derby County), Sneddon (Accrington Stanley), Powell (Chesterfield, reserve). Front row: Billy Newton (Stockport County, trainer), Burrell (Chesterfield), Hewitt (Wrexham), Johnson (Hartlepools United), Smith (Chesterfield), Simm (Bradford City), Harry Storer (Derby County, manager).

Representative XI's at Peel Park 1921-1962

A number of benefit matches were played at Peel Park for Accrington Stanley players which involved representative XI's rather than an official Accrington Stanley teams.

2 May 1923
Sidney Harrold Benefit
Reds 2 Whites 0
Reds: Bowen (Halifax Town); Fare (Wigan Borough), Rigg (Nelson), Emerson (Burnley), Leaver (Blackpool), Page (Accrington Stanley), Douglas (Oldham Athletic), Kelly (Burnley), Dixon (Halifax Town), Quigley (Rossendale United), Stevenson (Wigan Borough).
Goalscorers: Stevenson, Dixon
Whites: Bennett (Nottingham Forest); Bulling (Nottingham Forest), Barrett (Nottingham Forest), Newton (Leicester City), Parker (Nottingham Forest), Thompson (Leicester City), Adcock (Leicester City), Nelis (Nottingham Forest), Cox (Nottingham Forest), King (Leicester City), Tomkins (Leicester City).
Attendance: 3,000

4 May 1927
William Rooks Benefit
Reds 4 Blues 5
Reds: Crawford (Blackburn Rovers); Rooks (Accrington Stanley), Thorpe (Blackpool), Watson (Blackpool), Campbell (Blackburn Rovers), Benton (Blackpool), Gee (Accrington Stanley), Devlin (Preston North End), Cowan (Barnoldswick Town), Quigley (Chorley), Cooper (Blackburn Rovers).
Goalscorers: Cowan 2, Quigley, Cheetham (og)
Blues: Hayes (Accrington Stanley); Cheetham (Bradford City), Whittaker (Accrington Stanley), Hughes (Accrington Stanley), Parkes (Rochdale), Christie (Rochdale), Wyper (Hull City), Bertram (Rochdale), Whitehurst (Rochdale), Martin (Accrington Stanley), Wright (Bradford City).
Goalscorers: Whitehurst 3, Bertram, Wyper

27 April 1959
Leslie Cocker/Charlie Sneddon Benefit
Accrington Stanley XI 7 All Stars XI 9
Accrington Stanley XI: Moffat (Ards); Pirie, Harrower, Tighe, Ralston (all Accrington Stanley), Shannon (Burnley), Gibson (Accrington Stanley), Booth (Bradford), Shackleton (Leeds United), Cheesebrough (Burnley), Newlands (Burnley).
Goalscorers: Shackleton, Booth 3, Shannon, Gibson 2
All Stars XI: McInnes (Accrington Stanley); Cummings (Burnley), Walton (Preston North End), Cush (Leeds United), Ryden (Tottenham Hotspur), Adamson (Burnley), Humphries (Leeds United), Eastham (Newcastle United), Revie (Leeds United), Thompson (Preston North End), Cocker (Accrington Stanley).
Goalscorers: Revie 4, Thompson 2, Cocker 3
Attendance: 3,285

Accrington FA Cup Record
1881 to 1888 & 1893 to 1896

The following section details all matches played by Accrington in the FA Cup prior to joining the Football League and after leaving the League. All FA Cup matches played during their period in the Football League will be found under the season-by-season statistics.

1881-82
Round 1
Oct 29 v Queen's Park (h) walk-over
Round 2
Nov 26 v Darwen (a) 3-1
Yates
R.Horne; W.J.Whittaker, Hindle, Talbot, Hartley, James Yates, J.Lonsdale, Eastham, J.Hargreaves, Hacking, French.
Att: 3,000

1882-83
Round 1
Nov 4 v Blackburn Olympic (a) 3-6
Brown, Bamber, Yates
Chew; W.J.Whittaker, Hindle, R.Bryce, J.Hargreaves, J.Wilkinson, Brown, Eastham, Bamber, James Yates, McGill.
Att: 2,000

1883-84
Round 1
Nov 10 v Blackpool (h) 4-0
Hacking, Bryce 2, Hargreaves
Chew; W.J.Whittaker, Hindle, G.Haworth, R.Bryce, Chippendale, J.Wilkinson, J.Hargreaves, Eastham, Hacking, Deakin.
Round 2
Nov 26 v Park Road (Blackburn) (a) 3-2
Harper (og), Hargreaves, MacBeth
R.Horne; Hindle, James Yates, Wade, R.Bryce, G.Haworth, W.J.Whittaker, Friel, Macbeth, J.Hargreaves, Hacking.
Att: 1,000
Note: Accrington were disqualified from the competition.

1884-85
Round 1
Oct 11 v Southport (h) 3-0
Scorers unknown
J.K.Horne; James Yates, Hindle, W.J.Whittaker, Chippendale, Jefferson, R.Horne, Bamber, J.Whittaker, Jack Yates, Hacking.
Att: moderate
Note: Accrington were disqualified from the competition.

1885-86
Round 1
Oct 17 v Witton (h) 5-4
F.Wood 2, Deakin, Hargreaves, Wade
J.K.Horne; A.Hargreaves, Robinson, F.Whittaker, Hindle, H.Wood, Deakin, Wade, Brown, Duckworth, F.Wood.
Round 2
Nov 21 v Darwen Old Wanderers (a) 1-2
Whittaker
Cowell; Robinson, A.Hargreaves, G.Haworth, F.Whittaker, Chippendale, Mackereth, Duckworth, Brown, Wade, Deakin.
Att: 1,000

1886-87
Round 1
Oct 30 v Renton (a) 0-1
J.K.Horne; J.Stevenson, Singleton, G.Haworth, Malpass, Chippendale, Mackereth, J.Whittaker, Conway, Macbeth, Jack Yates.

1887-88
Round 1
Oct 15 v Rossendale (h) 11-0
Lofthouse 3, Bonar, Yates, Conway 2, Fecitt 4
J.K.Horne; J.Stevenson, McLellan, J.Wilkinson, R.Bryce, Chippendale, Lofthouse, Bonar, Conway, Fecitt, Jack Yates.
Att: 2,000
Round 2
Nov 5 v Burnley (h) 3-2
Conway, Bonar, Lofthouse
J.K.Horne; J.Stevenson, McLellan, G.Haworth, J.Wilkinson, Chippendale, Lofthouse, Bonar, Conway, Fecitt, Jack Yates.
Att: 7,000
Round 3
Nov 26 v Blackburn Rovers (h) 1-3
Yates

J.K.Horne; J.Stevenson, McLellan, G.Haworth, J.Wilkinson, Chippendale, Lofthouse, Bonar, Conway, Fecitt, Jack Yates.
Att: 6,000

1893-94
Round 1
Jan 27 v Sunderland (a) 0-3
G.Haworth; Hodge, Ditchfield, Shuttleworth, Matthew, Frame, Gray, Laurie, Brown, Gillespie, Chadwick.

1894-95
Round 1
Oct 13 v Bacup (h) 0-4
Barnes; Broadley, Ditchfield, Parkinson, Shuttleworth, Frame, Gray, Laurie, Lambie, Carnie, Greenwood.
Att: 2,500

1895-96
Round 1
Oct 5 v West Manchester (a) 1-5
Cunliffe
Redfearn; Nuttall, Grimshaw, Livesey, Smith, Duffield, Dawson, Wilmington, Richards, Cunliffe, Rawcliffe.

Accrington Stanley FA Cup Record 1896-1921

The following section details matches played by Accrington Stanley in the FA Cup prior to joining the Football League in 1921.

1896-97
Qualifying Competition
Round 1
Oct 10 v Carlisle City walk-over
Round 2
Oct 31 v Chorley (a) 0-5
Cavanagh; Wood, Whitehead, Kay, Hardman, Duffield, Greenwood, Skinner, Oldham, Jane, Dawson.

1897-98
Qualifying Competition
Round 1
Sep 18 v Carlisle City (a) 4-0
Smith, Ross (og), Oldham, Nuttall
Shaw; Wood, Hartley, Nuttall, Hardman, Duffield, Swift, Smith, Oldham, Bowker, Tierney.
Round 2
Sep 25 v Horwich (a) 1-3
Hardman
Smith; Wood, Hartley, Duffield, Nuttall, Hardman, Bowker, Smith, Oldham, Pendergast, Robinson.
Att: 300

1898-99
Qualifying Competition
Round 1
Oct 1 v Oswaldtwistle Rovers (a) 4-2
Whittaker, Swift, J.Hartley, Brown
Walker; Morgan, Smith, C.Hartley, Hardman, Duffield, Swift, Whittaker, Brown, Pendergast, J.Hartley.
Round 2
Oct 15 v Frizington White Star (h) 8-0
J.Hartley 4, C.Hartley, Swift, Whittaker, Brown
Walker; Morgan, Smith, C.Hartley, Brown, Duffield, Swift, Whittaker, Richardson, Pendergast, J.Hartley.

Round 3
Oct 29 v South Shore (a) 1-5
Swift
Walker; Morgan, Smith, C.Hartley, Hardman, Duffield, Swift, Dawson, Brown, Pendergast, J.Hartley.
Att: 600

1899-1900
Preliminary Round
Sep 16 v Blackburn Park Road (a) 0-3
Walker; Whittaker, Hardman, Pendergast, Heyes, Ashworth, Golding, Howarth, Shutt, Slater, Turner.

1900-01
Accrington Stanley did not enter the competition.

1901-02
Qualifying Competition
Round 1
Oct 5 v Nelson (h) 2-1
Gardner, Watkins
Edmundson; Finney, Kenyon, Golding, J.Bradshaw, D.Ashworth, Knowles, Watkins, L.Ashworth, Oldham, Gardner.
Round 2
Oct 19 v Oswaldtwistle Rovers (h) 1-1
Oldham
Walker; Finney, J.Heywood, Golding, J.Bradshaw, D.Ashworth, Knowles, Watkins, Oldham, W.Heywood, Wilmington.
Att: 5,000
Replay
Oct 23 v Oswaldtwistle Rovers (a) 2-0
Leeming, Heywood
Walker; Finney, Hardman, Golding, J.Bradshaw, D.Ashworth, Knowles, Leeming, Oldham, W.Heywood, Gardner.
Att: 3,500
Round 3
Nov 2 v Darwen (a) 1-2
Bradshaw
Edmundson; Finney, Hardman, Golding, J.Bradshaw, D.Ashworth, Knowles, Watkins, Oldham, Leeming, W.Heywood.
Att: 8,000

1902-03
Qualifying Competition
Round 1
Oct 4 v Bacup (h) 5-0
Morgan, Brunton, Watkins 3
Walker; Finney, Boulton, Golding, J.Bradshaw, D.Ashworth, Morgan, Watkins, Brunton, Hargreaves, W.Bradshaw.
Round 2
Oct 18 v Rossendale United (h) 1-0
Brunton
Walker; Finney, Hardman, Golding, J.Bradshaw, W.Bradshaw, Morgan, Brunton, Watkins, Hargreaves, Gardner.
Round 3
Nov 7 v Manchester United (a) 0-7
Walker; Finney, Boulton, Riley, J.Bradshaw, W.Bradshaw, Morgan, Watkins, Brunton, Hargreaves, Gardner.
Att: 6,000

1903-04
Qualifying Competition
Round 1
Oct 3 v Padiham (a) 0-0
Coupe; Finney, Chorlton, Holden, J.Bradshaw, Harrison, Chamberlain, Morgan, Brunton, Hargreaves, Becton.
Replay
Oct 7 v Padiham (h) 4-0
Brunton 2, Morgan, Hargreaves
Coupe; Finney, Chorlton, Holden, J.Bradshaw, Harrison, Chamberlain, Morgan, Brunton, Hargreaves, Becton.
Att: 3,000
Round 2
Oct 17 v Nelson (h) 2-1
Hesham, Morgan
McGregor; Chorlton, Walmsley, Holden, Finney, Harrison, Morgan, Hesham, Brunton, Hargreaves, Becton.
Att: 5,000

1904-05
Qualifying Competition
Round 3
Oct 29 v Blackpool (h) 1-4
Heaton
McGregor; Wragg, Hampson, Becton, J.Bradshaw, Coates, Anderton, Street, Heaton, Russell, Hinks.

1905-06
Preliminary Round
Sep 23 v Nelson (h) 7-0
Dempsey 6, Smith
Turner; Stevenson, Shaw, Rigby, J.Bradshaw, Brindle, Smith, Dempsey, Brunton, Stott, Pope.
Round 1
Oct 7 v Burnley Belvedere (h) 5-0
Brunton 2, Morris, Rigby, Dempsey
Turner; Stevenson, Shaw, Rigby, J.Bradshaw, Barlow, Smith, Dempsey, Brunton, Morris, Stott.
Round 2
Oct 28 v Padiham (a) 4-1
Morris, Barlow, Dempsey, Smith
Turner; Hampson, Shaw, Rigby, Barlow, Brindle, Smith, Dempsey, Brunton, Morris, Stott.
Intermediate Round
Dec 9 v Burton United (a) 0-3
Turner; Barlow, Stevenson, Rigby, J.Bradshaw, Brindle, Smith, Dempsey, Brunton, Morris, Stott.

1906-07
Qualifying Round
Round 5
Dec 8 v West Norwood (a) 9-1
Garside 2, Randall 5, Brindle, McGuigan
Turner; Carter, Shaw, Chadwick, J.Bradshaw, Brindle, Pilkington, Wilson, Randall, McGuigan, Garside.
Competition Proper
Round 1
Jan 12 v Crewe Alexandra (a) 1-1
Randall
Turner; Hampson, Shaw, Chadwick, J.Bradshaw, Brindle, Wilson, Sheridan, Randall, McGuigan, Garside.
Att: 5,156
Replay
Jan 16 v Crewe Alexandra (h) 1-0
Sheridan
Turner; Hampson, Shaw, Chadwick, J.Bradshaw, Brindle, Wilson, Sheridan, Randall, McGuigan, Garside.
Round 2
Feb 2 v Bradford City (a) 0-1
Turner; Hampson, Shaw, Chadwick, J.Bradshaw, Brindle, Wilson, Sheridan,

Randall, McGuigan, Garside.
Att: 16,000

1907-08
Preliminary Round
Sep 21 v Chorley (a) 1-2
Ashton
Swann; Nain, Hampson, Rigby, J.Bradshaw, Carter, Collier, Dempsey, Greaves, Ashton, Garside.

1908-09
Preliminary Round
Aug 19 v Rochdale (a) 5-3
Garside, Bradley 2, Baldwin 2
Lowe; Carter, Hampson, Rigby, J.Bradshaw, Brindle, Whittaker, Whiteside, Baldwin, Bradley, Garside.
Qualifying Competition
Round 1
Oct 3 v Rossendale United (h) 2-0
Whittaker 2
Lowe: Hampson, Carter, Rigby, J.Bradshaw, Brindle, Whittaker, Dempsey, Baldwin, Bradley, Garside.
Round 2
Oct 17 v Darwen (h) 3-1
Garside, Bradley, Whittaker
Lowe; Hampson, Carter, Rigby, J.Bradshaw, Brindle, Whittaker, Dempsey, Baldwin, Bradley, Garside.
Round 3
Nov 7 v Colne (h) 1-1
Bradley
Lowe; Nairn, Carter, Rigby, J.Bradshaw, Brindle, Whittaker, Knowles, Baldwin, Bradley, Garside.
Replay
Nov 10 v Colne (a) 2-2
Dempsey, Baldwin
Lowe; Nairn, Carter, Rigby, J.Bradshaw, Brindle, Whittaker, Dempsey, Baldwin, Wells, Garside.
Note: Extra-time was begun, during which Colne took a 3-2 lead. However, after the first 15 minutes of extra-time the referee abandoned the match due to poor light.
Second Replay
Nov 16 v Colne (Turf Moor, Burnley) 1-0
Bradley
Lowe; Nairn, Carter, Rigby, J.Bradshaw, Brindle, Sinfield, Dempsey, Baldwin, Bradley, Garside.

Round 4
Nov 21 v Northern Nomads (h) 0-2
Lowe; Nairn, Carter, Rigby, J.Bradshaw, Brindle, Swift, Dempsey, Baldwin, Bradley, Garside.

1909-10
Qualifying Competition
Round 4
Nov 20 v Haslingden (a) 4-3
Rigby, Carter (pen), Bradley 2
Barber; Nairn, Carter, Swift, J.Bradshaw, Brindle, Laycock, Rigby, Ingham, Bradley, Sanderson.
Round 5
Dec 4 v Brentford (h) 1-0
Rigby
Barber; Nairn, Carter, Swift, J.Bradshaw, Brindle, Laycock, Rigby, Warburton, Bradley, Sanderson.
Att: 4,400
Competition Proper
Round 1
Jan 15 v Blackburn Rovers (a) 1-7
Bradley
Weaver; Nairn, Carter, Swift, J.Bradshaw, Brindle, Laycock, Rigby, Heywood, Bradley, Sanderson.

1910-11
Qualifying Competition
Round 4
Nov 19 v Haslingden (a) 1-0
Jones
Rollinson; Stevenson, Carter, Rigby, J.Bradshaw, Brindle, Valentine, Twigg, Woods, Ingham, Jones.
Round 5
Dec 3 v Torquay Town (h) 4-0
Grieve 2, Riley, Jones
Rollinson; Stevenson, Carter, Rigby, J.Bradshaw, Brindle, Valentine, Riley, Grieve, Woods, Jones.
Competition Proper
Round 1
Jan 14 v Wolverhampton Wanderers (a) 0-2
Rollinson; Stevenson, Carter, Rigby, J.Bradshaw, Brindle, Valentine, Grieve, Owen, Wood, Jones.
Att: 13,500

1911-12
Qualifying Competition
Round 4
Nov 18 v Carlisle United (h) 3-0
Grieve, Noble, Gettins
Rollinson; Stevenson, Carter, Martin, Hargreaves, Robinson, Noble, Jones, Gettins, Grieve, Winterhalder.
Round 5
Dec 2 v Walsall (a) 1-2
Gettins
Robinson; Stevenson, Carter, Martin, Hargreaves, Robinson, Noble, Jones, Gettins, Grieve, Winterhalder.

1912-13
Qualifying Competition
Round 4
Nov 30 v Rochdale (a) 1-6
Baldwin
Langtree; Jackson, Carter, Woods, Dewhurst, Maguire, Noble, Baldwin, Goodison, Jones, Lowe.

1913-14
Qualifying Competition
Round 4
Nov 29 v Stalybridge Celtic (a) 0-2
Wright; Nuttall, Smith, Yates, Mockett, Maguire, Noble, Cunliffe, Goodison, Brogden, Winterburn.

1914-15
Qualifying Competition
Preliminary Round
Sep 26 v Adlington (h) 1-1
Goodison
Duckworth; Kelly, Nuttall, Robertson, Naughton, Maguire, Rothwell, Brogden, Goodison, Rawlinson, Winterburn.
Replay
Sep 29 v Adlington (h) 2-3
Brogden 2
Smith; Kelly, Nuttall, Robertson, Naughton, Maguire, Ormerod, Levus, Goodison, Brogden, Winterburn.

Note: Accrington guaranteed a sum for the gate in advance and Adlington agreed to play the replay at Accrington.

1919-20
Qualifying Competition
Round 1
Sep 27 v Nelson (a) 1-2
Smethurst
Tattersall; Finney, Goodman, Walsh, Chapman, Burgin, Woods, Smethurst, Hemsley, Proctor, Benson.

1920-21
Qualifying Competition
Round 1
Sep 25 v Fleetwood (a) 0-8
Tattersall; Wilson, Kirkbright, Howarth, Glenndenning, Richardson, J.Yates, Jones, Proctor, Stevenson, H.Yates.
Att: 4,000

ACCRINGTON MATCHES 1878-1888

This section chronicles matches played by the old Accrington club before joining the Football League. Matches in the FA Cup will be found in a separate section. Details of scorers, teams and attendances are recorded if known. However, it should be noted that the spasmodic coverage of Accrington's early years in the local Press means that it is impossible to give a detailed account of all matches.

1878-79

Friendlies

Sep 28 v Church Rovers (h) 1-1

Lightfoot

Eaton; J.Clayton, W.J.Whittaker, Talbot, R.Clayton, Hartley, J.Lonsdale, Peat, Lightfoot, R.Horne, James Yates.

(Note: Records show that Accrington claimed to have won the game by one goal and one disputed goal to one goal)

Oct 5 v Clitheroe (a) 2-0

Scorers unknown

Eaton; W.J.Whittaker, R.Horne, Higham, Talbot, J.Lonsdale, J.S.Clayton, Hartley, Lightfoot, J.Clayton, James Yates.

Oct 12 v St Mark's Witton (a) 1-2

Oct 19 v Great Harwood (h) 1-0

Lonsdale

Oct 26 v Haslingden Rangers (h) 3-0

Nov 2 v Cob Wall (h) 2-0

Nov 4 v Blackburn Rovers (a) 0-3

Eaton; W.J.Whittaker, Moore, Higham, Talbot, R.Horne, Peat, Lightfoot, Hartley, J.Lonsdale, Hacking.

Att: 5,000

Nov 9 v Haslingden Grane (h) 1-0

Nov 13 v Church (h) 3-3

Scorers unknown 2, Lonsdale

R.Horne; W.J.Whittaker, Raynes, Heald, Talbot, James Yates, J.Lonsdale, Lightfoot, Hartley, Hacking, Peat.

Att: 3,000

(Note: This match was played under Wells Lights)

Nov 16 v Church Rovers (a) 0-0

Eaton; J.Clayton, Smith, Talbot, Raynes, J.Lonsdale, Hartley, Gray, Peat, James Yates, Lightfoot.

(Note: The club's official scorecard shows a 1-0 victory, but newspapers reported a 0-0 draw)

Nov 23 v Enfield (h) 4-1
Scorers unknown
Eaton; W.J.Whittaker, Higham, Talbot, Stocks, James Yates, J.Lonsdale, R.Horne, Hartley, Kay, Lightfoot.
Att: 600
Nov 30 v Darwen (h) 2-5
Dec 7 v Church (h) 2-0
Scorers unknown
Eaton; W.J.Whittaker, Smith, Talbot, Higham, J.Lonsdale, Hartley, Stocks, F.Lonsdale, James Yates, R.Horne.
Dec 14 v Blackburn Rovers (a) 1-4
Jan 1 v Church (a) 2-1
Scorers unknown
Bradley; J.Clayton, W.J.Whittaker, Lightfoot, A.N.Other, J.Lonsdale, J.T.Clayton, R.Horne, Talbot, Higham, James Yates.
Att: 1,000
Jan 25 v Haslingden Grane (a) 0-0
Eaton, W.J.Whittaker, Hindle, Stocks, Raynes, F.Lonsdale, J.Lonsdale, Lightfoot, R.Horne, James Yates.
(Note: Accrington fielded only ten players)
Feb 1 v Enfield (a) 0-2
Bradbury; W.J.Whittaker, Hindle, Raynes, Talbot, James Yates, R.Horne, Lightfoot, Higham, J.Lonsdale, Heald.
Feb 8 v Darwen (a) 0-6
Feb 15 v Haslingden Rangers (a) 1-0
Scorer unknown
Eaton; Stocks, Hall, R.Horne, Talbot, J.Lonsdale, Hartley, W.J.Whittaker, Lightfoot, Higham, James Yates.
Feb 22 v Blackburn Rovers (h) 1-3
Scorer unknown
Team included Heald, James Yates, Hacking, W.J.Whittaker
Mar 1 v Witton St Mark's (h) 1-0
Mar 15 v Great Harwood (a) 5-2
Scorers unknown
Eaton; Hindle, Jones, Talbot, Stocks, J.Lonsdale, Hartley, Lightfoot, W.J.Whittaker, James Yates, R.Horne.
Mar 22 v Cob Wall (a) 3-0
Scorers unknown
Eaton; Hindle, Stocks, Talbot, Head, J.Lonsdale, Hartley, Lightfoot, W.J.Whittaker, James Yates, R.Horne.
Mar 29 v Blackburn Rovers (h) 1-4
Scorer unknown
Team included Talbot, Hacking, Stocks, James Yates.
Apr 5 v District of Accrington (venue unknown) 6-0

Apr 19 v A 'Scratch Team' (h) 5-2
Scorers unknown
Team included R.Horne, James Yates
Att: 600

1879-80
Lancashire Cup
Round 1
Oct 18 v Halliwell (h) 4-1
Scorers unknown
Eaton; Hindle, W.J.Whittaker, Talbot, Stocks, J.Lonsdale, Hartley, Raynes, Boothman, James Yates, R.Horne.
Att: 1,800
Round 2
Nov 22 v St Mark's Witton (h) 3-0
Horne, Stock, Yates
Eaton; Hindle, Smith, Talbot, Stocks, James Yates, R.Horne, Raynes, Boothman, Hartley, J.Lonsdale.
Att: 400
Round 3
Jan 1 v Lower Darwen (h) 3-1
Raynes, Smith, Horne
Eaton; Hindle, W.J.Whittaker, Talbot, Stocks, Hartley, J.Lonsdale, Raynes, Smith, James Yates, R.Horne.
Att: 1,800
(Note: Some sources state that Accrington were awarded a disputed goal after the match to make the score 4-1)
Round 4
Feb 7 v Lower Chapel (h) 4-3
Hartley, Raynes 3
Eaton; W.J.Whittaker, Hindle, Talbot, Stocks, Hartley, Lonsdale, Raynes, Smith, Yates, R.Honre.
Att: 1,500
Semi-final
Mar 6 v Blackburn Rovers (a) 1-3
Lonsdale
Eaton; W.J.Whittaker, Hindle, Talbot, Stocks, Hartley, F.Lonsdale, Raynes, Eastham, Yates, R.Horne.
Att: 4,500
Friendlies
Sep 27 v Padiham (h) 6-0
Raynes 3, Lonsdale 2, Yates
Eaton; Jones, Eastham, Talbot, Plummer, Parkinson, Peat, Raynes, J.Lonsdale, Aspden, A.N.Other. *Att: 400*

Oct 4 v Blackburn Rovers (h) 2-3
O'Dell, Horne
Eaton; W.J.Whittaker, Hindle, Talbot, Hacking, Hartley, Lonsdale, O'Dell, Smith, R.Horne, James Yates.
Oct 11 v Eagley (a) 2-3
Smith, Yates
Eaton; Hindle, W.J.Whittaker, Talbot, Stocks, Hartley, J.Lonsdale, Boothman, Smith, James Yates, R.Horne.
Att: 400
Oct 25 v Astley Bridge (h) 5-1
Scorers unknown
Eaton; W.J.Whittaker, Hindle, Talbot, Stocks, Boothman, R.Horne, Raynes, Smith, Hartley, J.Lonsdale.
Nov 1 v Manchester Wanderers (h) 2-0
Smith, Lonsdale
Bradley; W.J.Whittaker, Hindle, Talbot, Weir, J.Lonsdale, Hartley, Sheffield, Smith, Hacking, R.Horne.
Nov 8 v Bolton Wanderers (a) 0-1
Eaton; Waddington, Plummer, Talbot, Stocks, Hartley, J.Lonsdale, Smith, Substitute, R.Horne, Newsham.
(Note: Newspaper sources only name ten players and state that a 'substitute centre' played. Newsham has also been reported as Newsome in some sources)

Nov 15 v Blackburn Olympic (h) 1-2
Yates
Bradley; Hindle, Jones, Stocks, Talbot, Hacking, J.Lonsdale, Peat, R.Horne, Waddington, James Yates.
Att: 'large'
Nov 29 v Enfield (a) 3-2
Horne, Raynes, Lonsdale
Eaton, Hindle, W.J.Whittaker, Talbot, Roberts, A.N.Other, J.Lonsdale, Raynes, James Yates, Hartley, R.Horne.
Dec 20 v St Mark's Witton (a) 2-2
Smith, Yates
Eaton; Hindle, W.J.Whittaker, Talbot, Stocks, Hartley, J.Lonsdale, Boothman, Smith, James Yates, R.Horne.
Att: 400
Dec 27 v Great Harwood (h) 2-1
Jan 1 v Manchester Wanderers (h) 1-1
Eastham
Eaton; Hindle, Eastham, Talbot, Stocks, James Yates, R.Horne, Raynes, Smith, J.Lonsdale, Hartley.
(Note: This was Accrington's second match in a day, playing the match immediately after the Lancashire Cup-tie against Lower Darwen).

Jan 3 v Turton (a) 2-1
Scorers unknown
Bradley; Hindle, R.Horne, Talbot, Newsham, J.Lonsdale, Hartley, Eastham, Smith, Hacking, James Yates.
Att: 400
Jan 10 v Blackburn Rovers (h) 1-1
Peat
Bradley; Eaton, Jones, Waddington, Newsham, J.Lonsdale, Brown, Peat, Lightfoot, Parkinson, Eastham.
Jan 17 v Astley Bridge (a) 1-1
Scorer unknown
Bradley; Hindle, Jones, Talbot, Waddington, Eastham, F.Lonsdale, Raynor, Smith, James Yates, W.J.Whittaker.
Feb 21 v Bolton Wanderers (h) 1-2
Smith
Eaton; W.J.Whittaker, Hindle, Smith, Stocks, Suddall, Hartley, Talbot, R.Horne, James Yates, Hacking.
Mar 13 v Enfield (h) 3-4
Eastham, Scorers unknown 2
Bradley; W.J.Whittaker, Hindle, Talbot, Stock, Hartley, J.Lonsdale, Eastham, R.Horne, James Yates, Hacking.
Apr 10 v Church (a) 5-3
Eastham 2, French, Scorers unknown 2
Team included Hartley, W.J.Whittaker, J.Lonsdale, Hacking, James Yates, Eastham, Waddington, R.Horne.
Att: 1,600
Apr 24 v Manchester Wanderers (h) 5-5
Att: 300

1880-81
Lancashire Cup
Round 1
Oct 23 v Astley Bridge (h) 3-1
Lonsdale, French 2
Moore; Hindle, W.J.Whittaker, Stocks, Talbot, J.Lonsdale, Hacking, French, Eastham, James Yates, R.Horne.
Att: 1,500
Round 2
Dec 11 v Padiham (h) 4-1
French, Hartley, Hacking, Eastham
Secker; Hindle, W.J.Whittaker, Talbot, Latham, J.Lonsdale, Hartley, Eastham, French, Hacking, R.Horne.
Round 3
Dec 18 v Witton (a) 6-2

Yates 2, Scorer unknown, Lonsdale, Hartley 2
Secker; Hindle, Waddington, Latham, Talbot, Hartley, J.Lonsdale, French, Eastham, R.Horne, James Yates.
Att: 'large'
Round 4
Feb 26 v Enfield (h) 3-0
Hartley, Yates, Eastham
R.Howorth; W.J.Whittaker, Hindle, Latham, Waddington, Talbot, J.Lonsdale, Hartley, Eastham, R.Horne, James Yates.
Semi-final
Bye
Final
Apr 23 v Park Road (Blackburn) (played at Darwen) 6-4
Eastham 2, Yates, Horne 2, Lonsdale
R.Howarth; Hindle, W.J.Whittaker, Latham, Talbot, Hartley, J.Lonsdale, French, Eastham, R.Horne, James Yates.

Friendlies
Oct 2 v Blackburn Rovers (a) 2-3
Hacking, Horrocks
Moore; W.J.Whittaker, Waddington, Talbot, Horrocks, J.Lonsdale, Hacking, French, Eastham, James Yates, R.Horne.
Att: 'large'
Oct 9 v Manchester Wanderers (a) 1-0
Talbot
Moore; Hindle, W.J.Whittaker, Talbot, Parker, J.Lonsdale, Clegg, Eastham, French, James Yates, R.Horne.
Oct 16 v Bolton Wanderers (h) 12-1
Eastham, French, Scorer unknown, Yates 3, Lonsdale 2, Talbot, Horne, Hacking 2
Moore; W.J.Whittaker, Hindle, Talbot, Stocks, J.Lonsdale, Hacking, Eastham, French, James Yates, R.Horne.
Oct 30 v Turton (h) 4-1
Eastham, Scorer unknown, Hacking, Yates
Moore; W.J.Whittaker, Hindle, Talbot, Parker, French, Hacking, Eastham, Cooper, James Yates, R.Horne.
Att: 1,000
Nov 6 v Enfield (h) 1-0
Horne
Moore; W.J.Whittaker, Hindle, Talbot, Parker, Hartley, Hacking, French, Eastham, James Yates, R.Horne.
Att: 1,500
Nov 13 v Eagley (h) 2-0
Scorer unknown, Talbot

Secker; Hindle, W.J.Whittaker, Latham, Williams, Hartley, Talbot, Eastham, Peat, James Yates, R.Horne.
Att: 'moderate'
Nov 20 v Church (h) 3-2
Scorers unknown
Moore; W.J.Whittaker, Hindle, Williams, Latham, Talbot, Hartley, Eastham, French, James Yates, R.Horne.
Att: 1,500
Dec 4 v Darwen (a) 1-4
Broughton (og)
Moore; W.J.Whittaker, Hindle, Latham, Talbot, Hartley, Hacking, Eastham, French, R.Horne, James Yates.
Att: 'large'
Jan 1 v Church (h) 8-2
West (og), Horne, Lonsdale 5, Hartley
Secker; W.J.Whittaker, Hindle, Talbot, Latham, Hartley, J.Lonsdale, French, Eastham, James Yates, R.Horne.
Jan 8 v Blackburn Olympic (h) 5-1
Horne, Yates 2, Eastham, French
Secker; W.J.Whittaker, Hindle, Talbot, Latham, R.Horne, James Yates, French, Eastham, J.Lonsdale, Hacking.
Jan 15 v Preston North End(a) 6-0
Lonsdale, Yates, Scorers unknown 4
Parker; W.J.Whittaker, Hindle, Latham, R.Howarth, J.Wilkinson, J.Lonsdale, French, Peat, R.Horne, James Yates.
(Note: Match abandoned after 23 minutes due to fog)
Jan 22 v Blackburn Olympic (a) 0-3
R.Howarth; W.J.Whittaker, Hindle, Talbot, Latham, Hartley, J.Lonsdale, Eastham, Peat, French, R.Horne.
Jan 29 v Bolton Wanderers (a) 8-1
Lonsdale, Yates 5, Eastham 2
R.Howarth; W.J.Whittaker, Hindle, Talbot, Waddington, Latham, J.Lonsdale, Eastham, French, R.Horne, James Yates.
Feb 5 v Turton (a) 0-2
Secker; Hindle, R.Howarth, Waddington, Latham, Talbot, Hartley, Eastham, W.J.Whittaker, James Yates, French.
Feb 19 v Enfield (a) 6-1
Hacking, Eastham 3, Horne, Haydock (og)
R.Howarth; W.J.Whittaker, Hindle, Talbot, Latham, Hartley, Hacking, French, Eastham, R.Horne, James Yates.
Mar 5 v Blackburn Rovers (a) 1-4
French
R.Howarth; W.J.Whittaker, Hindle, Latham, Talbot, J.Lonsdale, Hartley, French, Eastham, R.Horne, James Yates.

Mar 12 v Darwen (h) 2-4
Broughton (og), Pilkington
R.Howarth; W.J.Whittaker, Hindle, Latham, Talbot, J.Lonsdale, French, Eastham, Pilkington, James Yates, R.Horne.
Att: 2,500
Mar 19 v Eagley (a) 3-1
Eastham 2, Yates
Gastall; W.J.Whittaker, Hindle, Waddington, Talbot, Pilkington, Hartley, Parker, Eastham, R.Horne, James Yates.
Mar 26 v Church (a) 4-1
Talbot, Hartley, Scorer unknown, Yates
R.Howarth; W.J.Whittaker, Hindle, Talbot, Latham, J.Lonsdale, Hartley, French, Eastham, R.Horne, James Yates.
Apr 9 v Great Lever (a) 4-2
Yates 2, Lonsdale, Horne
R.Howarth; W.J.Whittaker, Hindle, Latham, Talbot, Hartley, J.Lonsdale, Eastham, Parker, James Yates, R.Horne.
Apr 15 v Great Lever (played at Whalley) 4-4
French, Yates 2, Lonsdale
R.Howarth; W.J.Whittaker, Hindle, Latham, Gibson, French, J.Wilkinson, Eastham, Parker, James Yates, R.Horne.
Apr 18 v Darwen (a) 3-1
French, Eastham, Parker
R.Howarth; W.J.Whittaker, Hindle, Latham, Gibson, Eastham, J.Wilkinson, French, Parker, R.Horne, James Yates.
Att: 1,000
May 7 v Witton (a) 5-3

1881-82
Lancashire Cup
Round 1
Oct 8 v Blackpool (h) 9-1
Eastham, Horne 2, Yates, Hargreaves, Lonsdale 2, Hacking 2
Moore; Hindle, W.J.Whittaker, Talbot, Latham, James Yates, J.Lonsdale, Eastham, J.Hargreaves, R.Horne, Hacking.
Round 2
Dec 10 v Rishton (h) 9-0
Hacking 4, Eastham, Hargreaves, Yates 2, French
R.Horne; W.J.Whittaker, Hindle, Gregson, J.Hargreaves, James Yates, Eastham, F.Hargreaves, J.Lonsdale, Hacking, French.
Round 3
Dec 24 v Halliwell (a) 5-0
French, Yates, Eastham, Hacking, Hargreaves
R.Horne; W.J.Whittaker, Hindle, Hartley, Gregson, James Yates, J.Lonsdale, Eastham, J.Hargreaves, French, Hacking.

Round 4
Feb 11 v Bolton Wanderers (h) 7-3
Cox 2, Lonsdale, Hargreaves, Hacking 2, Eastham
Gastall; W.J.Whittaker, Hindle, R.Bryce, Latham, Cox, J.Lonsdale, Eastham, J.Hargreaves, Hacking, James Yates.
Att: 4,000
Semi-final
Mar 11 v Witton (played at Darwen) 2-1
Eastham, Yates
Chew; W.J.Whittaker, Hindle, Latham, R.Bryce, J.Lonsdale, James Yates, Eastham, Hacking, J.Hargreaves, Hartley.
Att: 2,500
(Note: Lancashire FA ordered a replay after Witton protested over eligibility of Chew)
Semi-final Replay
Mar 27 v Witton (played at Darwen) 4-2
Wilkinson, Lonsdale, Yates, Eastham
Duff; Hindle, W.J.Whittaker, Talbot, R.Bryce, J.Hargreaves, Eastham, J.Lonsdale, James Yates, Hacking, J.Wilkinson.
Att: 2,500
Final
Apr 15 v Blackburn Rovers (played at Turf Moor, Burnley) 1-3
Hacking
Chew; W.J.Whittaker, Hindle, Talbot, R.Bryce, J.Hargreaves, Eastham, James Yates, Hacking, J.Lonsdale, J.Wilkinson.
Att: 5,000

Friendlies
Sep 17 v Accrington Wanderers (a) 4-3
Pilkington, Scorers unknown 3
Team included Gastall, W.J.Whittaker, Latham, J.Hargreaves, James Yates, Pilkington, French, Parker, Hacking.
Sep 24 v Blackburn Rovers (a) 2-3
Woolfall (og), Lonsdale
R.Howarth; Hindle, W.J.Whittaker, Talbot, Latham, James Yates, J.Lonsdale, Eastham, J.Hargreaves, Hacking, R.Horne.
Att: 3,000
Oct 1 v Padiham (h) 2-2
Eastham, Yates
R.Howarth; Hindle, W.J.Whittaker, Talbot, J.Hargreaves, James Yates, J.Lonsdale, Eastham, French, Hacking, R.Horne.
Att: 2,000

Oct 15 v Staveley (a) 0-1
R.Horne; W.J.Whittaker, Hindle, Hartley, Latham, James Yates, J.Lonsdale, Eastham, J.Hargreaves, Hacking, French.
Oct 22 v Enfield (a) 5-1
French 2, Eastham, Lonsdale, Scorer unknown
R.Horne; Hindle, W.J.Whittaker, Hartley, Talbot, Hacking, J.Lonsdale, James Yates, Eastham, French, J.Hargreaves.
Oct 29 v Burnley & District (a) 9-2
(Note: Accrington only fielded 10 men)
Nov 5 v Darwen (h) 7-5
Yates 2, Lonsdale, Hacking 3, French
R.Horne; W.J.Whittaker, Hindle, Latham, Talbot, Hacking, French, Eastham, J.Hargreaves, James Yates, J.Lonsdale.
Att: 'good'
Nov 12 v Edinburgh Hibernians (a) 2-6
Eastham 2
R.Horne; W.J.Whittaker, Hindle, Latham, Talbot, James Yates, J.Lonsdale, Eastham, J.Hargreaves, French, Hacking.
Att: 4,000
Nov 14 v Edinburgh University (a) 1-2
Eastham
R.Horne; W.J.Whittaker, Hindle, Latham, Talbot, James Yates, J.Lonsdale, Eastham, J.Hargreaves, French, Hacking.
Nov 19 v Blackpool (h) 4-0
Smith, Yates, Scorers unknown 2
R.Horne; Stansfield, Duff, J.Lonsdale, Waddington, Smith, Gregson, French, Pilkington, James Yates, J.Wilkinson.
Dec 3 v Nottingham Forest (a) 3-3
Duckworth, Yates, Hacking
R.Horne; W.J.Whittaker, Hindle, Talbot, Chippendale, J.Hargreaves, Duckworth, J.Lonsdale, James Yates, Hacking, French.
Dec 17 v Padiham (a) 7-2
Yates, Eastham 3, Hacking 2, Wilkinson
R.Horne; Hindle, W.J.Whittaker, Gregson, Duff, J.Hargreaves, Eastham, J.Wilkinson, Hacking, French, James Yates.
Dec 19 v Blackburn Olympic (a) 0-4
R.Horne; Hindle, Stansfield, Gregson, Calvert, J.Wilkinson, Eastham, James Yates, J.Hargreaves, Hacking, French.
Att: 'good'
Dec 26 v Enfield (h) 3-4
Dec 31 v Blackburn Olympic (a) 5-2
Jan 2 v Partick Thistle (h) 2-2
Scorers unknown
R.Horne; Hindle, W.J.Whittaker, Latham, Talbot, J.Hargreaves, James

Yates, Eastham, J.Lonsdale, Cox, A.N.Other.
Jan 7 v Sheffield Wednesday (h) 4-1
Eastham 2, Swallow (og), Cox
R.Horne; W.J.Whittaker, Hindle, Waddington, Latham, Cox, J.Lonsdale, Eastham, J.Hargreaves, Talbot, James Yates.
Jan 14 v Staveley (h) 7-2
Hargreaves 2, Hacking, Yates, Cox, Scorers unknown 2
Waddington; W.J.Whittaker, Hindle, R.Bryce, Latham, Cox, J.Lonsdale, Eastham, J.Hargreaves, James Yates, Hacking.
Jan 21 v Great Lever (a) 7-2
Hargreaves 3, Eastham 3, Scorer unknown
Gastall; W.J.Whittaker, Hindle, Talbot, R.Bryce, Latham, James Yates, J.Hargreaves, Eastham, J.Lonsdale, Cox.
Jan 28 v Witton (h) 3-1
Scorers unknown
Bradley; W.J.Whittaker, Hindle, Talbot, Latham, James Yates, J.Hargreaves, Eastham, J.Lonsdale, Cox, Hacking.
Feb 4 v Clitheroe (h) 10-0
Yates 2, Lonsdale 2, Aldersley (og), Scorers unknown 5
Gastall; W.J.Whittaker, Hindle, Talbot, R.Bryce, Cox, J.Lonsdale, Eastham, J.Hargreaves, Hacking, James Yates.
Feb 18 v Park Road (Blackburn) (h) 0-1
Chew; W.J.Whittaker, Hindle, Latham, R.Bryce, Cox, Hartley, Greaves, French, Smith, James Yates.
Feb 25 v Darwen (a) 2-2
Eastham 2
Chew; Hindle, W.J.Whittaker, R.Bryce, Latham, Talbot, J.Lonsdale, James Yates, J.Wilkinson, J.Hargreaves, Eastham.
Mar 4 v Accrington Wanderers (h) 5-3
Scorers unknown
Chew; W.J.Whittaker, Duff, R.Bryce, Latham, J.Lonsdale, Hartley, J.Hargreaves, James Yates, Hacking, J.Wilkinson.
Mar 18 v Aston Unity (h) 7-1
Yates 4, Scorers unknown 2, Opp own-goal
Chew; Hindle, Royston, R.Bryce, Talbot, J.Hargreaves, J.Lonsdale, J.Wilkinson, Eastham, James Yates, Hacking.
Mar 25 v Bolton Wanderers (a) 3-2
Hacking, Yates 2
Chew; W.J.Whittaker, Hindle, Talbot, R.Bryce, J.Hargreaves, J.Lonsdale, J.Wilkinson, Eastham, James Yates, Hacking.
Apr 1 v Blackburn Rovers (a) 0-3
Chew; W.J.Whittaker, Hindle, Talbot, R.Bryce, J.Hargreaves, J.Lonsdale, James Yates, Eastham, Hacking, J.Wilkinson.
Att: 7,600

Apr 8 v Nottingham Forest (h) 3-5
Hacking, Whittaker, Yates
Chew; Hindle, W.J.Whittaker, A.Lonsdale, J.Hargreaves, Chippendale, J.Wilkinson, J.Lonsdale, Eastham, Hacking, James Yates.
Att: 1,500
Apr 10 v Blackpool (a) 2-2
Scorers unknown
Gastall; Duff, Hindle, Waddington, J.Hargreaves, J.Wilkinson, J.Lonsdale, F.Haworth, Clegg, Hacking, James Yates.
(Note: Accrington also lost to Darwen 3-1 but date and venue are unknown)

1882-83
Lancashire Cup
Round 1
Oct 7 v Great Harwood (h) 7-0
Scorer unknown, Horne, Hargreaves 2, Bryce 3
Chew; Hindle, W.J.Whittaker, R.Bryce, G.Haworth, J.Wilkinson, Bamber, Brown, James Yates, R.Horne.
Att: 1,000
Round 2
Dec 9 v Park Road (Blackburn) (a) 2-3
Hargreaves 2
Chew; W.J.Whittaker, Hindle, G.Haworth, R.Bryce, Bamber, Hacking, J.Hargreaves, Brown, J.Wilkinson, Royston.

East Lancashire Cup
Semi-final
Apr 21 v Blackburn Olympic (a) 1-2
Beresford
Chew; W.J.Whittaker, R.Bryce, G.Haworth, Chippendale, Ewbank, Clegg, Friel, Beresford, J.Hargreaves, Gregson.

Friendlies
Sep 23 v Haslingden (a) 2-1
Brown, Yates
Chew; W.J.Whittaker, Duff, G.Haworth, Price, J.Wilkinson, Hartley, J.Hargreaves, Brown, James Yates, Royston.
Sep 30 v Northwich Victoria (a) 2-3
Bryce, Eastham
Chew; R.Horne, Lonsdale, R.Bryce, G.Haworth, Wilkinson, Hartley, Eastham, J.Hargreaves, James Yates, Bamber

Oct 14 v Padiham (h) 6-0
McGill, Yates 2, Brown, Hartley, Hargreaves
Chew; Hindle, Harwood, R.Bryce, Chippendale, Brown, Hartley, Eastham, McGill, James Yates, J.Hargreaves.
Att: 1,500
Oct 21 v Bolton Wanderers (h) 3-3
Yates 2, Hargreaves
Chew; W.J.Whittaker, Hindle, Chippendale, R.Bryce, G.Haworth, Eastham, J.Wilkinson, McGill, James Yates, J.Hargreaves.
Att: 5,000
Oct 28 v Blackburn Rovers (a) 0-1
Chew; Hindle, W.J.Whittaker, G.Haworth, Chippendale, R.Bryce, J.Wilkinson, Eastham, McGill, James Yates, J.Hargreaves.
Att: 4,000
Nov 11 v Halliwell (h) 8-0
McGill 3, Wilkinson 2, Gregson 2, Bryce
Chew; Hindle, W.J.Whittaker, G.Haworth, Chippendale, R.Bryce, J.Wilkinson, McGill, Eastham, J.Hargreaves, Gregson.
Nov 18 v Great Lever (a) 1-4
McGill
Chew; W.J.Whittaker, Hindle, G.Haworth, Chippendale, Ewbank, Eastham, R.Bryce, McGill, James Yates, J.Hargreaves.
Nov 25 v Darwen (a) 1-4
Wilkinson
Chew; Beverley, Hindle, G.Haworth, Chippendale, R.Bryce, Eastham, McGill, J.Hargreaves, James Yates, J.Wilkinson.
Att: 3,000
Dec 2 v Blackpool (a) 9-1
Whittaker, Bryce, Ewbank 3, Yates, Chippendale, Wilkinson, McGill
Barnes; W.J.Whittaker, R.Bryce, Chippendale, G.Haworth, Ewbank, J.Wilkinson, McGill, James Yates, Royston, Hanson.
Dec 16 v Enfield (h) 8-1
McGill 3, Hacking 2, Haworth, Bryce, Wilkinson
Chew; W.J.Whittaker, Hindle, G.Haworth, Chippendale, R.Bryce, Hacking, McGill, J.Hargreaves, J.Wilkinson, Ewbank.
Att: 1,000
(Note: Enfield only fielded ten men)
Dec 23 v Bootle (h) 12-0
Eastham 5, Hargreaves, McGill 3, Royston, Ewbank, Haworth
Chew; Hindle, R.Bryce, G.Haworth, Chippendale, J.Wilkinson, Ewbank, McGill, Eastham, J.Hargreaves, Royston.
Dec 26 v Small Heath Alliance (a) 3-0
McGill, Hargreaves 2
Chew; W.J.Whittaker, Hindle, G.Haworth, Chippendale, R.Bryce, Royston,

J.Wilkinson, Eastham, McGill, J.Hargreaves.
Att: 1,500
Dec 27 v Aston Unity (a) 5-2
Eastham, Scorers unknown 4
Chew; W.J.Whittaker, Hindle, G.Haworth, Chippendale, R.Bryce, Wilson, J.Wilkinson, Ewbank, McGill, J.Hargreaves.
Dec 30 v Glasgow Rangers (h) 3-2
McGill 2, Eastham
Chew; W.J.Whittaker, Hindle, G.Haworth, Chippendale, R.Bryce, J.Hargreaves, Eastham, McGill, J.Wilkinson, Ewbank.
Jan 1 v Aston Unity (h) 9-2
Bryce 2, Gregson 3, Hargreaves, Scorer unknown, Eastham, Chippendale
Parkinson; W.J.Whittaker, Hindle, G.Haworth, Chippendale, R.Bryce, J.Wilkinson, Gregson, J.Hargreaves, McGill, Eastham.
Jan 2 v Vale of Leven (h) 0-4
Chew; Hindle, Duff, G.Haworth, P.Chippendale, J.Wilkinson, Eastham, McGill, J.Hargreaves, Gregson, and a substitute.
Att: 2,000
(Note: Match abandoned 16 minutes into the second half due to a gale)
Jan 6 v Padiham (a) 3-5
Eastham 2, Royston
Chew; W.J.Whittaker, Hindle, G.Haworth, Duff, Ewbank, J.Wilkinson, McGill, Eastham, J.Hargreaves, Royston.
Jan 27 v Bolton Wanderers (a) 8-4
Hargreaves, Eastham 2, Beresford 2, Clegg 2, Wilkinson
Chew; W.J.Whittaker, Hindle, G.Haworth, Chippendale, J.Wilkinson, Beresford, Eastham, Clegg, J.Hargreaves, Hartley.
Feb 3 v Park Road (Blackburn) (h) 9-1
Parkinson, Scorers unknown 6, Clegg 2
Chew; W.J.Whittaker, Hindle, G.Haworth, Chadwick, Parkinson, Clegg, J.Hargreaves, Eastham, Beresford, J.Wilkinson.
Feb 10 v Bolton Wanderers (h) 4-2
Friel 3, Wilkinson
Chew; W.J.Whittaker, Hindle, G.Haworth, Chippendale, J.Wilkinson, Matthews (Blackburn Olympic), Friel, Clegg, Jack Yates (Blackburn Olympic), J.Hargreaves.
Att: 2,000
Feb 17 v Enfield (a) 4-2
Duckworth, Haworth, Opp own-goal, Hargreaves
Secker; W.J.Whittaker, Hindle, G.Haworth, Parkinson, S.Duckworth, James Yates, Eastham, Clegg, Friel, J.Hargreaves.
Feb 24 v Great Lever (h) 4-1
Eastham 3, Friel
Chew; W.J.Whittaker, Hindle, G.Haworth, Chippendale, James Yates,

Clegg, Friel, Eastham, J.Hargreaves, Hacking.
Att: 1,000
Mar 3 v Halliwell (a) 1-0
Friel
Chew; Hindle, G.Haworth, Chippendale, R.Bryce, James Yates, Eastham, Friel, J.Hargreaves, Clegg.
(Note: Accrington only fielded 10 men)
Mar 10 v Darwen (h) 0-4
Chew; Hindle, W.J.Whittaker, Chippendale, G.Haworth, Ewbank, Clegg, Eastham, Friel, J.Hargreaves, R.Bryce.
Mar 17 v Padiham (h) 3-0
Maudsley, Deakin, Clegg
Chew; W.J.Whittaker, R.Bryce, G.Haworth, Chippendale, J.Wilkinson, Clegg, J.Hargreaves, Deakin, Maudsley, Hacking.
Mar 23 v Corinthians (h) 4-3
Beresford, Wilkinson, Hargreaves 2
Chew; W.J.Whittaker, R.Bryce, G.Haworth, Chippendale, J.Wilkinson, Clegg, Friel, Beresford, J.Hargreaves, H.Gregson.
Att: 3,000
Mar 24 v Walsall Town (h) 3-3
Hargreaves, Yates 2
R.Howarth; W.J.Whittaker, R.Bryce, G.Haworth, Chippendale, J.Wilkinson, Clegg, Friel, James Yates, J.Hargreaves, Deakin.
Mar 26 v Walsall Swifts (h) 3-1
Scorer unknown, Hargreaves, Opp own-goal
Chew; Hindle, Heaton, G.Haworth, Chippendale, J.E.Clegg, J.Wilkinson, Friel, S.Duckworth, James Yates, J.Hargreaves.
Mar 31 v Preston North End (h) 5-3
Scorers unknown
Chew; Hindle, R.Bryce, G.Haworth, Chippendale, Clegg, J.Wilkinson, Maudsley, J.Hargreaves, James Yates, Deakin.
Att: 1,500
Apr 14 v Small Heath Alliance (h) 4-1
Friel, Beresford 2, Hacking
Chew: W.J.Whittaker, R.Bryce, G.Haworth, Chippendale, Hacking, Clegg, Beresford, Friel, J.Hargreaves, Gregson.
Apr 23 v Blackburn Rovers (h) 0-3
R.Howarth; R.Bryce, W.J.Whittaker, Chippendale, G.Haworth, J.Hargreaves, Gregson, Friel, Ewbank, Clegg, Beresford.
Att: 1,000
Apr 28 v Rossendale (a) 4-1
Scorers unknown 3, Friel
Team included Eaton, Chippendale, Beresford, Friel, Bamber, Deakin, Hartley, Gregson.

May 5 v Clitheroe (a) 1-3
Scorer unknown
Eaton; R.Bryce, W.J.Whittaker, Chippendale, G.Haworth, Clegg, Hartley, Beresford, Gregson, J.Hargreaves.

1883-84
Lancashire Cup
Round 1
Sep 29 v Burnley Ramblers (h) 10-1
Hacking 3, Wilkinson 4, Deakin, Haworth 2
Team included Hacking, Hindle, Clegg, J.Hargreaves, G.Haworth, Deakin, J.Wilkinson.
Round 2
Dec 15 v Park Road (Blackburn) (h) 3-0
Hargreaves, Eastham, Deakin
Chew; Hindle, W.J.Whittaker, G.Haworth, Chippendale, J.Hargreaves, Clegg, Eastham, R.Bryce, Deakin, Hacking.
Att: 1,000
Round 3
Dec 31 v South Shore (h) 3-0
Deakin, Hacking, Bryce
R.Horne; Hindle, Waddington, G.Haworth, Parkinson, Heaton, Hacking, R.Bryce, Eastham, J.Hargreaves, Deakin.
Round 4
Feb 2 v Church (h) 2-3
Hacking, Hargreaves
R.Horne; J.W.Whittaker, R.Bryce, G.Haworth, Chippendale, Hacking, Heaton, Eastham, Ward, J.Hargreaves, Deakin.
Att: 5,000
(Note: Church were later ejected from the competition)
Round 5
Feb 26 v Blackburn Rovers (a) 0-0
R.Horne; Hindle, R.Bryce, Chippendale, J.Hargreaves, Parkinson, Hacking, Heaton, Eastham, Deakin, Wade.
Att: 3,000
Replay
Mar 8 v Blackburn Rovers (h) 3-6
Deakin 2, Scorer unknown
R.Horne; W.J.Whittaker, R.Bryce, J.Hargreaves, Parkinson, Hindle, Hacking, Heaton, Eastham, Wade, Deakin.
Att: 2,000

East Lancashire Charity Cup
Semi-final
Apr 26 v Blackburn Rovers (a) 1-1
Friel
R.Horne; McConnell (Padiham), W.J.Whittaker, G.Haworth, Chippendale, Crawford (Church), Heaton, Friel (Burnley), Marshall (Burnley), T.Bryce (Burnley), Gallagher (Padiham).
Att: 3,000
Semi-final
May 10 v Blackburn Rovers (played at Padiham) 2-1
Friel, Gallagher
R.Horne; W.J.Whittaker, McConnell (Padiham), G.Haworth, Chippendale, Crawford (Church), R.Bryce, Marshall (Burnley), Friel (Burnley), T.Bryce (Burnley), Gallagher (Padiham).
Att: 3,000
Final
May 17 v Darwen (played at Leamington Road, Blackburn) 2-2
Gallagher 2
R.Horne; W.J.Whittaker, McConnell (Padiham), G.Haworth, Chippendale, Crawford (Church), R.Bryce, Marshall (Burnley), Friel (Burnley), T.Bryce (Burnley), Gallagher (Padiham).
Att: 3,500
Replay
May 19 v Darwen (played at Leamington Road, Blackburn) 0-1
R.Horne; W.J.Whittaker, McConnell (Padiham), G.Haworth, Chippendale, Crawford (Church), R.Bryce, Marshall (Burnley), Friel (Burnley), T.Bryce (Burnley), Gallagher (Padiham).
Att: 2,000

Friendlies
Sep 8 v Blackburn Rovers (h) 2-5
Yates, Clegg
Chew; R.Horne, R.Bryce, G.Haworth, Chippendale, J.Wilkinson, Macrae, Clegg, James Yates, J.Hargreves, Friel.
Att: 2,000
Sep 15 v Rossendale (a) 5-1
Beresford 2, Wilkinson 2, Opp own-goal
Sep 22 v Preston North End (a) 4-4
Friel, Hacking, Hargreaves, Yates
Chew; Hindle, R.Bryce, Chippendale, Clegg, James Yates, J.Wilkinson, Friel, Eastham, J.Hargreaves, Hacking.
Att: 3,000
Oct 6 v Great Lever (h) 2-3
Friel, Wilkinson

Chew; W.J.Whittaker, Hindle, R.Bryce, Chippendale, J.Wilkinson, G.Haworth, Eastham, Friel, Hacking, J.Hargreaves.
Att: 'fair'
Oct 13 v Darwen (h) 1-0
Bryce
Chew; W.J.Whittaker, Hindle, R.Bryce, Chippendale, J.Wilkinson, G.Haworth, Hacking, J.Hargreaves, Friel, Eastham.
Oct 20 v Blackburn Olympic (h) 1-3
Hargreaves
Chew; Whittaker, Hindle, G.Haworth, Chippendale, R.Bryce, J.Wilkinson, Eastham, Friel, J.Hargreaves, Deakin.
Oct 27 v Bolton Wanderers (a) 1-5
Hargreaves
Chew; W.J.Whittaker, Hindle, G.Haworth, R.Bryce, Chippendale, J.Wilkinson, Eastham, Macbeth, J.Hargreaves, Bishop.
Att: 6,000
Nov 3 v Abercorn (a) 2-3
Bishop 2
Chew; W.J.Whittaker, Hindle, G.Haworth, R.Bryce, Chippendale, J.Wilkinson, J.Hargreaves, Eastham, Macbeth, Bishop.
Nov 5 v Edinburgh University (a) 3-7
Eastham, Hargreaves, Bryce
Chew; W.J.Whittaker, Hindle, G.Haworth, R.Bryce, Chippendale, J.Wilkinson, J.Hargreaves, Eastham, Macbeth, Bishop.
Nov 17 v Small Heath Alliance (h) 2-1
Eastham, Scorer unknown
R.Horne; W.J.Whittaker, Hindle, Wade, Chippendale, J.Wilkinson, J.Hargreaves, Eastham, R.Bryce, Macbeth, Bishop.
Att: 2,000
Nov 24 v Blackburn Rovers (h) 1-3
Bryce
Chew; W.J.Whittaker, Hindle, Chippendale, R.Bryce, G.Haworth, Eastham, Macbeth, Bishop, J.Wilkinson, J.Hargreaves.
Att: 'good'
Dec 22 v Padiham (a) 0-1
Team included Hindle, G.Haworth, Chippendale, Bishop
Att: 3,000
Dec 25 v Darwen Old Wanderers (h) 4-2
Hargreaves 2, Macbeth, Bond
Bootham; Hindle, James Yates, Chippendale, G.Haworth, Bond, Heaton, Bishop, Macbeth, R.Bryce, J.Hargreaves.
Att: 2,000
Dec 29 v St Bernard's (h) 4-2
Heaton, Eastwood, Bishop, Scorer unknown

Chew; Hindle, Parkinson, R.Bryce, G.Haworth, Heaton, Hacking, J.Hargreaves, Eastham, Bishop, Macbeth.
Jan 1 v Pollickshields Athletic (h) 1-2
Heaton
Chew; R.Bryce, Hindle, Parkinson, Chippendale, G.Haworth, Heaton, Hacking, J.Hargreaves, Deakin, Bishop.
Att: 2,000
Jan 2 v Dumbarton (h) 0-4
Team included Beverley & Avery of Blackburn Rovers and Gibson, Costley, Yates of Blackburn Olympic.
Jan 5 v Abercorn (a) 6-0
Hacking, Scorer unknown, Heaton 2, Bishop 2
Chew; W.J.Whittaker, Hindle, G.Haworth, Chippendale, Hacking, Heaton, Eastham, J.Hargreaves, Bishop, Macbeth.
Jan 12 v Preston North End (h) 1-7
Eastham
Chew; W.J.Whittaker, Hindle, G.Haworth, R.Bryce, Chippendale, Hacking, J.Hargreaves, Eastham, Bishop, Macbeth.
Att: 3,000
Jan 19 v Darwen (a) 2-2
Eastham, Bishop
R.Horne; W.J.Whittaker, R.Bryce, G.Haworth, Chippendale, Heaton, James Yates, Eastham, J.Hargreaves, Bishop, Macbeth.
Att: 1,000
Jan 26 v Padiham (h) 0-0
R.Horne; R.Bryce, W.J.Whittaker, Chippendale, Wade, Hacking, Heaton, Eastham, J.Hargreaves, Bishop, Macbeth.
Att: 'large'
(Note: Match abandoned after 10 minutes due to gales)
Feb 9 v Bolton Wanderers (h) 1-0
Hargreaves
R.Horne; W.J.Whittaker, Robinson (Preston North End), Chippendale, R.Bryce, Heaton, Hacking, Eastham, J.Hargreaves, Macbeth, Bishop.
Att: 'moderate'
Feb 16 v Blackburn Rovers (a) 0-2
R.Horne; W.J.Whittaker, Hindle, R.Bryce, Chippendale, Hacking, Heaton, J.Hargreaves, Eastham, Bishop, Macbeth.
Att: 1,500
Feb 23 v Great Lever (a) 2-2
Hacking, Scorer unknown
R.Horne; Hindle, W.J.Whittaker, Chippendale, R.Bryce, Hacking, Heaton, Eastham, Wade, Bishop, Macbeth.
Mar 1 v Church (a) 1-6
Scorer unknown

R.Horne; Hindle, W.J.Whittaker, Chippendale, R.Bryce, Heaton, Hacking, Eastham, Higgins, Bishop, Macbeth.
Att: 2,500
Mar 15 v Halliwell (h) 4-3
Scorer unknown, Eastham, Deakin, Heaton
R.Horne; R.Bryce, J.Wood, Parkinson, Chippendale, Hacking, Heaton, Macbeth, Deakin, Eastham, Bishop.
Mar 22 v Bolton Wanderers (a) 0-7
Richard; W.J.Whittaker, Robinson (Preston North End), Parkinson, James Yates, Wade, Deakin, Heaton, Bishop, Eastham, Smalley (Preston North End)
Att: 3,000
Mar 29 v Blackburn Olympic (a) 1-5
Bishop
Chew; Robinson (Preston North End), Smith, Chippendale, W.J.Whittaker, Marshall, Heaton, Bishop, Wade, Macbeth, Deakin.
Apr 5 v Enfield (a) 0-0
R.Horne; Beverley (Blackburn Rovers), W.J.Whittaker, G.Haworth, Chippendale, Bishop, Heaton, Eastham, Sowerbutts (Blackburn Rovers), Macbeth, Deakin.
Att: 'moderate'
Apr 11 v Church (h) 4-1
Scorers unknown 2, Macbeth 2
R.Horne, Ward (Blackburn Olympic), W.J.Whittaker, G.Haworth, Chippendale, Heaton, Smalley (Preston North End), Holden (Edinburgh University), Hunter (Blackburn Olympic), Macbeth, Jack Yates (Blackburn Olympic).
Att: 4,000
May 8 v Baxenden (played at Peel Park) 0-0
R.Horne; Baldwin, W.J.Whittaker, G.Haworth, H.Wood, T.Bryce, Heaton, R.Bryce, J.Hargreaves, Marshall, Crawford.

1884-85
Lancashire Cup
Round 1
Nov 1 v Blackburn Olympic
The match was not played as Accrington scratched from the competition because of the row over professionalism.

East Lancashire Cup
Semi-final
Apr 25 v Blackburn Rovers (a) 1-0
Bonar
Cowell; J.Stevenson, McLellan, G.Haworth, R.Bryce, Chippendale, Bonar,

Gregson, Conway, Douglas, Macbeth.
Att: 4,000
Final
May 2 v Blackburn Olympic (at Leamington Round, Blackburn) 4-0
Ward (og), Scorer unknown, Conway 2
Cowell; J.Stevenson, McLellan, G.Haworth, R.Bryce, Chippendale, Gregson, Bonar, Conway, Douglas, Macbeth.
Att: 6,000
Friendlies
Sep 27 v Eagley (h) 4-0
Scorers unknown 3, Jefferson
Horne; J.Stevenson, James Yates, G.Haworth, Chippendale, Jefferson, Bonar, Jack Yates, Macbeth, Conway, Harrison.
Oct 4 v Church (h) 3-2
Scorers unknown
J.K.Horne; J.Stevenson, Hindle, Chippendale, Astley, Bonar, Jefferson, Conway, Heaton, Jack Yates, Macbeth.
Att: 4,000
Oct 18 v Bolton Wanderers (h) 4-3
Macbeth, Conway, Yates 2
Horne; Wells, J.Stevenson, G.Haworth, Chippendale, Astley, Jefferson, Bonar, Conway, Macbeth, Jack Yates.
Att: 4,000
Oct 22 v Baxenden (played at Peel Park) 5-1
Scorers unknown
Barnes; Stevenson, Wells, G.Haworth, Astley, Hindle, Jefferson, Bonar, Conway, Jack Yates, Macbeth.
Oct 25 v Preston North End (h) 3-2
Yates, Macbeth, Jefferson
J.K.Horne; J.Stevenson, Wells, Chippendale, Astley, G.Haworth, Jack Yates, Macbeth, Conway, Bonar, Jefferson.
Att: 5,000
Nov 1 v Preston Zingari (h) 3-0
Conway, Macbeth, Haworth
Horne; J.Stevenson, Wells, G.Haworth, Chippendale, Astley, Jefferson, Bonar, Macbeth, Ross, Conway.
Nov 8 v Park Road (Blackburn) (h) 5-1
Jefferson, Conway 2, Heaton, Scorer unknown
Horne; J.Stevenson, Wells, Chippendale, Hindle, Astley, Conway, Macbeth, Heaton, Jefferson, Bonar.
Nov 15 v Blackburn Rovers (a) 0-1
R.Horne; J.Stevenson, Wells, Robinson, G.Haworth, Hindle, Jefferson, Bonar, Conway, Macbeth, McNee.
Att: 3,000

Nov 22 v Padiham (h) 1-0
Bonar
Horne; J.Stevenson, Wells, G.Haworth, Hindle, Robinson, McNee, Bonar, Jefferson, Southworth, Conway.
Att: 2,000
Nov 29 v Church (a) 2-1
Yates 2
Horne; J.Stevenson, Wells, Hindle, G.Haworth, Robinson, Jefferson, Bonar, Conway, Hothersall, Jack Yates.
Dec 6 v Darwen (a) 3-2
Yates 3
Horne; J.Stevenson, Robinson, G.Haworth, Hindle, Chippendale, Jefferson, Bonar, Conway, Macbeth, Jack Yates.
Dec 13 v Halliwell (a) 2-0
Chippendale, Douglas
Hamer (Astley Bridge); J.Stevenson, Robinson, James Yates, Conway, Chippendale, Jefferson, Bonar, Douglas, Macbeth, Jack Yates.
Att: 1,000
Dec 15 v Great Lever (a) 0-0
Cowell; Stevenson, Robinson, G.Haworth, Forrest, James Yates, Macbeth, Jefferson, Bonar, Conway, Douglas.
Dec 20 v Burnley (h) 0-1
Horne; J.Stevenson, Robinson, G.Haworth, Hindle, Chippendale, Jefferson, Bonar, Conway, Macbeth, Douglas.
Att: 3,000
Dec 25 v Druids (h) 2-0
Macbeth 2
Horne; J.Stevenson, Robinson, G.Haworth, Hindle, H.Wood, Jefferson, Bonar, Conway, Douglas, Macbeth.
Att: 3,000
Dec 27 v Blackburn Rovers (h) 2-0
Douglas, Conway
Horne; J.Stevenson, McLellan, G.Haworth, Hindle, Robinson, Jefferson, Bonar, Conway, Douglas, Macbeth.
Att: 4,000
Dec 29 v Stoke (a) 2-0
Forrest, Bonar
Arthur; J.Stevenson, McLellan, W.Wood, Robinson, Forrest, Jefferson, Bonar, Conway, Macbeth, Douglas.
Jan 3 v St Mirren (h) 7-0
Bonar 2, Douglas 2, Macbeth, Conway, Jefferson
Horne; J.Stevenson, McLellan, G.Haworth, Hindle, Robinson, Jefferson, Bonar, Conway, Macbeth, Douglas.
Att: 2,000

Jan 10 v Padiham (a) 2-3
Scorers unknown
Horne; J.Stevenson, McLellan, G.Haworth, Hindle, Robinson, Jefferson, Bonar, Conway, Macbeth, Douglas.
Att: 2,000
Jan 17 v Burnley (a) 4-2
Conway 2, Macbeth, Bonar
Bateson (Bolton W), J.Stevenson, McLellan, Hindle, R.Bryce, Russell (Preston NE), Jefferson, Bonar, Macbeth, Douglas, Conway.
Att: 3,500
Jan 24 v Darwen (h) 3-1
Bonar 2, Scorer unknown
Bateson (Bolton W); J.Stevenson, McLellan, G.Haworth, Robinson, R.Bryce, Macbeth, Douglas, Conway, Bonar, Duckworth.
Att: 2,000
Jan 31 v Derby Midland (h) 4-2
Conway, Bonar 2, Scorer unknown
James Yates; J.Stevenson, McLellan, Hindle, G.Haworth, R.Bryce, Bonar, Chippendale, Conway, Macbeth, Douglas.
Feb 7 v Edinburgh University (h) 2-0
Conway, Macbeth
James Yates; J.Stevenson, McLellan, Hindle, Salthouse, Chippendale, Mackereth, Bonar, Conway, Macbeth, Douglas.
Att: 3,000
Feb 14 v Bolton Wanderers (a) 3-1
Bonar, Macbeth 2
Cowell; J.Stevenson, McLellan, G.Haworth, R.Bryce, Chippendale, Mackereth, Bonar, Conway, Macbeth, Douglas.
Att: 5,000
Feb 21 v Aston Villa (h) 4-3
Conway, Douglas 2, Mackereth
Cowell; J.Stevenson, McLellan, G.Haworth, R.Bryce, Chippendale, Mackereth, Bonar, Conway, Macbeth, Douglas.
Att: 1,500
Feb 28 v Great Lever (h) 3-0
Douglas 2, Macbeth
Cowell; J.Stevenson, McLellan, G.Haworth, R.Bryce, Chippendale, Mackereth, Bonar, Conway, Macbeth, Douglas.
Att: 4,000
Mar 7 v Preston North End (a) 1-4
Macbeth
Cowell; J.Stevenson, McLellan, G.Haworth, Robinson, Chippendale, Douglas, Macbeth, Bonar, Mackereth, Conway.
Att: 10,000

Mar 14 v Burnley (h) 4-1
Macbeth, Mackereth, Douglas, Friel (og)
Cowell; J.Stevenson, McLellan, G.Haworth, Robinson, R.Bryce, Douglas, Macbeth, Conway, Mackereth, Douglas.
Att: 4,000
Mar 21 v Bolton Wanderers (a) 2-2
Conway, Chippendale
Cowell; J.Stevenson, McLellan, G.Haworth, R.Bryce, Chippendale, Mackereth, Bonar, Conway, Douglas, Macbeth.
Att: 4,000
Mar 28 v Padiham (a) 2-0
Conway, Mackereth
Cowell; J.Stevenson, McLellan, G.Haworth, Robinson, R.Bryce, Mackereth, Bonar, Conway, Macbeth, Douglas.
Att: 3,000
Apr 4 v Wolverhampton Wanderers (a) 7-1
Bonar, Macbeth 2, Conway, Scorers unknown 3
Cowell; J.Stevenson, McLellan, Chippendale, R.Bryce, Robinson, Douglas, Macbeth, Bonar, Mackereth, Conway.
Att: 'moderate'
Apr 6 v Aston Villa (a) 2-2
Conway, Scorer unknown
Cowell; J.Stevenson, McLellan, G.Haworth, R.Bryce, Chippendale, Douglas, Macbeth, Mackereth, Bonar, Conway.
Att: 4,000
Apr 11 v Park Road (Blackburn) (a) 3-3
Douglas, Bryce, Conway
Cowell; J.Stevenson, McLellan, G.Haworth, R.Bryce, Robinson, Douglas, Macbeth, Conway, Bonar, Gregson.
Att: 500
Apr 18 v Great Lever (a) 1-1
Douglas
Cowell; J.Stevenson, McLellan, G.Haworth, Chippendale, R.Bryce, Gregson, Bonar, Macbeth, Douglas, Conway.
Att: 3,000

1885-86
Lancashire Cup
Round 1
Sep 12 v Clitheroe (a) 2-1
Chippendale 2
Cowell; Robinson, A.Hargreaves, Chippendale, G.Haworth, Wood, Brown, Wade, Deakin, Duckworth, Mackereth.

Round 2
Oct 31 v Cherry Tree (a) 0-2
Note: Accrington fielded a Reserve XI

East Lancashire Charity Cup
Semi-final
May 8 v Darwen (h) 5-0
Mackereth 2, Bonar, Gregson, Conway
Horne; J.Stevenson, McLellan, G.Haworth, R.Bryce, Chippendale, Mackereth, Bonar, Conway, Macbeth, Gregson.
Final
May 22 v Blackburn Rovers (a) 1-2
Scorer unknown
Cowell; J.Stevenson, McLellan, R.Bryce, G.Haworth, Chippendale, Mackereth, Bonar, Conway, Macbeth, Gregson.
Att: 5,000
Friendlies
Jul 25 v Blackburn Olympic (a) 0-0
Cowell; J.Stevenson, McLellan, Chippendale, R.Bryce, Robinson, Mackereth, Bonar, Douglas, Macbeth, Conway.
Att: 800
Sep 5 v Darwen Old Wanderers (h) 9-1
Douglas 3, Macbeth 3, Conway, Bryce, Mackereth
Cowell; J.Stevenson, McLellan, Robinson, R.Bryce, Wood, Conway, Macbeth, Douglas, Bonar, Mackereth.
Att: 1,800
Sep 19 v Everton (a) 3-2
Macbeth 2, Mackereth
Cowell; J.Stevenson, McLellan, G.Haworth, R.Bryce, Chippendale, Mackereth, Bonar, Conway, Macbeth, Douglas.
Att: 2,000
Sep 26 v Oldham (a) 16-0
Mackereth, Macbeth 5, Conway 4, Douglas, Haworth, Bryce, Chippendale, McLellan, Scorer unknown
Cowell; J.Stevenson, McLellan, G.Haworth, R.Bryce, Chippendale, Macbeth, Douglas, Conway, Bonar, Mackereth.
Oct 3 v Derby Midland (a) 1-0
Conway
Cowell; J.Stevenson, McLellan, G.Haworth, R.Bryce, Robinson, Bonar, Mackereth, Conway, Douglas, Macbeth.
Att: 'large'
Oct 5 v Stoke (a) 4-0
Mackereth 2, Bonar 2
Cowell; J.Stevenson, McLellan, G.Haworth, R.Bryce, Robinson, Bonar,

Mackereth, Conway, Douglas, Macbeth.

Oct 10 v Blackburn Rovers (h) 2-1

Douglas, Bonar

Cowell; J.Stevenson, McLellan, Chippendale, R.Bryce, G.Haworth, Mackereth, Bonar, Conway, Macbeth, Douglas.

Att: 4,000

Oct 17 v Blackburn Olympic (a) 4-3

Conway, Macbeth 2, Douglas

Cowell; J.Stevenson, McLellan, R.Bryce, G.Haworth, Chippendale, Mackereth, Bonar, Douglas, Macbeth, Conway.

Att: 3,000

Oct 24 v Bolton Wanderers (a) 0-2

Cowell; J.Stevenson, Robinson, R.Bryce, G.Haworth, Chippendale, Mackereth, Bonar, Douglas, Macbeth, Conway.

Oct 31 v Bolton Wanderers (h) 2-5

Bryce, Hutchinson (og)

Team included Cowell, J.Stevenson, R.Bryce, G.Haworth, Mackereth, Macbeth.

Att: 'large'

Nov 7 v Burnley (a) 1-4

Sugg (og)

J.K.Horne; J.Stevenson, McLellan, G.Haworth, R.Bryce, Chippendale, Macbeth, Deakin, Conway, Bonar, Mackereth.

Att: 5,000

Nov 14 v Church (h) 6-0

Mackereth, Bonar, Conway 2, Scorers unknown 2

Nov 21 v Wigan (a) 7-0

Conway, Bonar, Scorers unknown 5

Nov 28 v Burnley (h) 2-0

Bonar, Mackereth

Cowell; J.Stevenson, McLellan, G.Haworth, R.Bryce, Chippendale, Mackereth, Bonar, Conway, Macbeth, Douglas.

Att: 1,000

Dec 5 v Padiham (h) 3-1

Bonar 2, Scorer unknown

Team included McLellan, R.Bryce, Bonar, Conway, Douglas, Mackereth, Macbeth.

Att: 'moderate'

Dec 12 v Great Lever (h) 4-0

Bryce, Macbeth, Mackereth, Conway

Cowell; J.Stevenson, McLellan, G.Haworth, R.Bryce, Chippendale, Mackereth, Bonar, Conway, Macbeth, Douglas.

Dec 19 v Darwen (h) 7-0

F.Wood 4, Douglas 2, Bonar

Cowell; J.Stevenson, McLellan, Hindle, R.Bryce, H.Wood, F.Wood, Bonar, Conway, Douglas, Macbeth.

Dec 26 v Notts Wanderers (h) 8-0

Bonar, Bryce, Mackereth 2, Douglas 3, Macbeth

Cowell; J.Stevenson, McLellan, G.Haworth, R.Bryce, Chippendale, Mackereth, Bonar, Conway, Macbeth, Douglas.

Att: 2,000

Jan 1 v Walsall Town (h) 5-2

Scorers unknown

Cowell; W.Stevenson, McLellan, G.Haworth, R.Bryce, Chippendale, Duckworth, F.Wood, Conway, Macbeth, Douglas.

Jan 2 v Darwen (a) 2-5

Scorers unknown

Cowell; Robinson, McLellan, G.Haworth, Bryce, Chippendale, Mackereth, Duckworth, Macbeth, Douglas, Conway.

Jan 9 v Bolton Wanderers (h) 5-0

Macbeth 4, Conway

Cowell; J.Stevenson, McLellan, G.Haworth, Robinson, Chippendale, F.Wood, Bonar, Conway, Macbeth, Douglas.

Att: 300

Jan 16 v Aston Villa (a) 0-2

Cowell; J.Stevenson, McLellan, G.Haworth, H.Wood, Chippendale, F.Wood, Bonar, Douglas, Macbeth, Conway.

Att: 3,000

Jan 23 v Great Lever (h) 6-0

Conway 2, Mackereth 3, Bonar

Cowell: W.Stevenson, McLellan, G.Haworth, R.Bryce, Chippendale, Mackereth, Bonar, Conway, Macbeth, Douglas.

Jan 30 v Church (h) 4-1

Conway 2, Bonar, Bury

Cowell; J.Stevenson, McLellan, R.Bryce, Bury, Chippendale, Mackereth, Bonar, Conway, Douglas, Macbeth.

Feb 6 v Derby Midland (h) 1-0

Macbeth

Cowell; J.Stevenson, McLellan, R.Bryce, Bury, Hindle, Mackereth, Bonar, Conway, Douglas, Macbeth.

Feb 13 v Padiham (h) 1-1

Mackereth

Cowell; J.Stevenson, McLellan, R.Bryce, Bury, Chippendale, Mackereth, Bonar, Conway, Macbeth, Douglas.

Feb 20 v Great Lever (h) 1-6

Deakin

Cowell; R.Bryce, McLellan, Chippendale, Bury, Mackereth, Deakin, Bonar, Macbeth, Conway. (Note: Accrington only fielded ten men)

Feb 27 v Notts County (a) 2-3
Mackereth 2
McConnell; W.Stevenson, McLellan, H.Wood, R.Bryce, Hindle, Mackereth, Bonar, Conway, Deakin, Macbeth.
Att: 'good'
Mar 6 v Burnley (h) 2-1
Mackereth, Sugg (og)
Allanson; J.Stevenson, McLellan, H.Wood, R.Bryce, Chippendale, Mackereth, Bonar, Conway, Macbeth, Deakin.
Att: 2,000
Mar 13 v Notts County (h) 2-1
Macbeth, Bonar
J.T.Duckworth; J.Stevenson, McLellan, H.Wood, R.Bryce, Chippendale, Mackereth, Bonar, Conway, Macbeth, Deakin.
Att: 3,000
Mar 20 v Stoke (h) 3-2
Macbeth, Yates, Conway
Cowell; J.Stevenson, Robinson, H.Wood, R.Bryce, Chippendale, Mackereth, Bonar, Conway, Macbeth, Jack Yates.
Att: 3,000
Mar 27 v Church (a) 1-3
Chippendale
Cowell; J.Stevenson, A.Hargreaves, Conway, R.Bryce, Chippendale, Mackereth, Bonar, Douglas, Macbeth, Jack Yates.
Apr 5 v Burnley (a) 1-3
Scorer unknown
McConnell; McLellan, Robinson, H.Wood, R.Bryce, Chippendale, Mackereth, Bonar, Conway, Macbeth, Jack Yates.
Att: 2,000
Apr 10 v Halliwell (a) 3-4
Conway, Yates, Scorer unknown
Hindley: J.Stevenson, McLellan, Hindle, R.Bryce, Chippendale, Mackereth, Bonar, Conway, Macbeth, Jack Yates.
Att: 'small'

Apr 12 v Bolton Wanderers (a) 0-4
R.Horne; J.Stevenson, McLellan, G.Haworth, R.Bryce, Robinson, Parkinson, Bonar, Conway, Macbeth, Jack Yates.
Att: 1,500

Apr 17 v Aston Villa (h) 2-1
Yates, Haworth
R.Horne; J.Stevenson, McLellan, Haworth, Malpass, Chippendale, Mackereth, Bonar, Conway, Macbeth, Jack Yates.
Att: 'large'

Apr 23 v Vale of Leven (h) 3-1
Yates 2, Mackereth
R.Horne; J.Stevenson, McLellan, G.Haworth, R.Bryce, Hindle, Mackereth, Bonar, Conway, Macbeth, Jack Yates.
Apr 24 v Oswestry (h) 6-1
Yates 3, Bryce, Macbeth, Chippendale
R.Horne; J.Stevenson, McLellan, G.Haworth, R.Bryce, Chippendale, Mackereth, Bonar, Conway, Macbeth, Jack Yates.
Apr 26 v Preston North End (a) 3-2
Macbeth, Rose (og), Mackereth
J.K.Horne; J.Stevenson, McLellan, G.Haworth, R.Bryce, Chippendale, Mackereth, Bonar, Conway, Macbeth, Jack Yates.
Att: 10,000
May 1 v Blackburn Olympic (h) 3-1
Scorers unknown 2, Macbeth
May 15 v Bolton Wanderers (a) 0-3
Att: 800

1886-87
Lancashire Senior Cup
Round 1
Oct 9 v Darwen (h) 2-1
Conway, Yates
R.Horne; Singleton, A.Hargreaves, G.Haworth, J.Wilkinson, Chippendale, Mackereth, Bonar, Conway, Macbeth, Jack Yates.
Round 2
Nov 6 v Higher Walton (a) 6-1
Yates 3, Conway, Haworth, Mackereth
Greenwood; J.Stevenson, Singleton, G.Haworth, J.Wilkinson, Taylor, Bonar, Jack Yates, Mackereth, Macbeth, Conway.
Att: 1,000
Round 3
Note: Accrington were drawn to play Witton but scratched from the competition.

East Lancashire Cup
Semi-final
May 14 v Blackburn Olympic (a) 3-0
Yates, Mackereth, Scorer unknown
J.K.Horne; J.Stevenson, McLellan, G.Haworth, H.Wood, Chippendale, Mackereth, Bonar, Conway, Macbeth, Yates.
Att: 'large'

Final

May 21 v Blackburn Rovers (h) 1-0

Bonar

Horne; J.Stevenson, McLellan, Haworth, Parkinson, Chippendale, Mackereth, Bonar, Conway, Macbeth, Jack Yates.

Att: 5,000

Friendlies

Sep 4 v Dumbarton (a) 3-1

Bryce, Yates, Bonar

Arthur (Blackburn Rovers); J.Stevenson, McLellan, G.Haworth, R.Bryce, MacLean (Vale of Leven), Mackereth, Conway, Bonar, Macbeth, Jack Yates.

Sep 6 v Edinburgh St Bernards (a) 3-3

McLennan, Conway, Macbeth

Arthur (Blackburn Rovers); McLellan, Forbes (Vale of Leven), G.Haworth, R.Bryce, McLennan (Hibernian), Mackereth, Bonar, Conway, Macbeth, Jack Yates.

Att: 'several thousand'

Sep 11 v Church (a) 1-2

Scorer unknown

Marshall (Staveley); J.Stevenson, McLellan, G.Haworth, R.Bryce, Chippendale, Mackereth, Bonar, Conway, Jack Yates, Macbeth.

Att: 3,000

Sep 25 v Blackburn Rovers (a) 2-0

Mackereth, Macbeth

R.Horne; J.Stevenson, McLellan, G.Haworth, R.Bryce, Chippendale, Mackereth, Bonar, Conway, Macbeth, Jack Yates.

Att: 1,000

Oct 2 v Bolton Wanderers (h) 1-2

Scorer unknown

R.Horne; J.Stevenson, McLellan, G.Haworth, Bryce, Chippendale, Macbeth, Bonar, Conway, Macbeth, Jack Yates.

Att: 3,000

Oct 16 v Church (a) 1-0

Bonar

Greenwood; J.Stevenson, McLellan, G.Haworth, R.Bryce, Chippendale, Mackereth, Bonar, Conway, Whittaker, Jack Yates.

Oct 23 v Nottingham Forest (a) 4-1

Mackereth, Conway 2, Yates

J.K.Horne; J.Stevenson, McLellan, G.Haworth, R.Bryce, McIntyre, Mackereth, Bonar, Conway, Macbeth, Jack Yates.

Att: 2,000

Nov 13 v Burnley (h) 1-3
Bonar
Horne; J.Stevenson, McLellan, G.Haworth, R.Bryce, Chippendale, Mackereth, Bonar, Conway, Macbeth, Jack Yates.
Att: 1,700
Nov 15 v Burslem Port Vale (a) 2-3
Att: 8,000
Nov 20 v Halliwell (h) 1-4
Mackereth
J.K.Horne; J.Stevenson, W.Stevenson, G.Haworth, Chippendale, Bryce, Mackereth, Deakin, Conway, Macbeth, Jack Yates.
Nov 27 v Notts County (h) 8-0
Conway 3, Yates 2, Mackereth 3
Team included McLellan, J.Wilkinson, W.Stevenson, Chippendale, Mackereth, Conway, Macbeth, Jack Yates.
Dec 4 v Padiham (h) 7-1
Conway 3, Yates, Bryce, Macbeth, Scorer unknown
Horne; McLellan, J.Stevenson, G.Haworth, R.Bryce, Chippendale, Bonar, Mackereth, Conway, Macbeth, Jack Yates.
Dec 11 v Burnley (a) 0-2
Horne; J.Stevenson, McLellan, Chippendale, G.Haworth, R.Bryce, Mackereth, Bonar, Conway, Jack Yates, Macbeth.
Att: 'large'
Dec 18 v Stoke (h) 7-0
Conway 3, Mackereth, Scorers unknown 3
Horne; J.Stevenson, McLellan, R.Bryce, J.Wilkinson, Chippendale, Mackereth, Bonar, Conway, Macbeth, Jack Yates.
Dec 25 v Church (h) 1-1
Conway
J.K.Horne; J.Stevenson, McLellan, G.Haworth, R.Bryce, Chippendale, Mackereth, Bonar, Conway, Macbeth, Jack Yates.
Att: 6,000
Dec 27 v Blackburn Rovers (a) 0-1
Horne; J.Stevenson, McLellan, G.Haworth, J.Wilkinson, Chippendale, Mackereth, Bonar, Conway, Macbeth, Jack Yates.
Att: 3,000
Jan 1 v Nottingham Forest (h) 4-2
Bonar, Macbeth, Scorers unknown 2
Horne; J.Stevenson, McLellan, G.Haworth, J.Wilkinson, Chippendale, Mackereth, Bonar, Conway, Macbeth, Jack Yates.
Att: 2,000
Jan 3 v Burnley (a) 1-0
Macbeth
Horne; J.Stevenson, McLellan, G.Haworth, Chippendale, J.Wilkinson, Jack

Yates, Macbeth, Conway, Bonar, Shuttleworth.
Att: 1,500
Jan 8 v Church (a) 6-3
Mackereth 2, Conway, Wilkinson, Scorer unknown, Macbeth
J.K.Horne; J.Stevenson, McLellan, G.Haworth, J.Wilkinson, Chippendale, Mackereth, Bonar, Conway, Macbeth, Jack Yates.
Att: 3,000
Jan 15 v Burnley (h) 0-0
Horne; J.Stevenson, McLellan, J.Wilkinson, G.Haworth, R.Bryce, Mackereth, Bonar, Conway, Macbeth, Jack Yates.
Att: 4,000
Jan 22 v Bury (a) 4-1
Yates, Bryce 2, Scorer unknown
Jan 24 v Aston Villa (a) 2-2
Scorers unknown
Horne; J.Stevenson, McLellan, G.Haworth, R.Bryce, Chippendale, Macbeth, Jack Yates, Conway, Mackereth, Bonar.
Att: 2,000
Jan 29 v Blackburn Rovers (h) 1-2
Conway
Horne; W.Stevenson, McLellan, G.Haworth, R.Bryce, Chippendale, Mackereth, Bonar, Conway, Macbeth, Jack Yates.
Feb 5 v Padiham (a) 2-1
Conway, Macbeth
Greenwood; W.Stevenson, McLellan, J.Wilkinson, R.Bryce, Chippendale, Mackereth, Bonar, Conway, Macbeth, Jack Yates.
Feb 12 v Notts Jardines (h) 4-0
Mackereth 2, Yates 2
Horne; McLellan, J.Stevenson, G.Haworth, R.Bryce, Chippendale, Mackereth, Bonar, Conway, Macbeth, Jack Yates.
Feb 19 v Halliwell (a) 2-0
Macbeth, Mackereth
Horne; McLellan, J.Stevenson, G.Haworth, R.Bryce, Chippendale, Mackereth, Bonar, Conway, Macbeth, Jack Yates.
Att: 3,000
Feb 26 v Bolton Wanderers (a) 2-2
Yates, Bryce
Horne; McLellan, J.Stevenson, J.Wilkinson, R.Bryce, Chippendale, Mackereth, Bonar, Jack Yates, Deakin, Conway.
Att: 3,000
Mar 5 v Darwen (h) 6-1
Bonar, Macbeth 3, Opp own-goal, Conway
Horne; McLellan, J.Stevenson, G.Haworth, R.Bryce, Chippendale, Mackereth, Bonar, Macbeth, Jack Yates, Conway.

Mar 12 v Darwen (a) 1-3
Yates
Horne: J.Stevenson, McLellan, G.Haworth, J.Wilkinson, Chippendale, Mackereth, Bonar, R.Bryce, Macbeth, Jack Yates.
Mar 19 v Burnley (a) 2-3
Yates, Haworth
Horne; J.Stevenson, McLellan, Chippendale, R.Bryce, J.Wilkinson, Mackereth, Bonar, Conway, Macbeth, Jack Yates.
Att: 2,000
Mar 26 v Blackburn Rovers (a) 2-2
Scorers unknown
Horne; J.Stevenson, McLellan, G.Haworth, J.Wilkinson, Chippendale, Mackereth, Bonar, Conway, Macbeth, Jack Yates.
Att: 1,000
Apr 2 v Church (h) 5-1
Conway, Scorers unknown 2, Macbeth 2
Horne; J.Stevenson, McLellan, Chippendale, R.Bryce, J.Wilkinson, Mackereth, Bonar, Jack Yates, Macbeth, Conway.
Att: 3,000
Apr 8 v Dumbarton (h) 5-1
Apr 9 v Halliwell (h) 3-4
Conway, Mackereth 2
Horne; Leach(Haslingden Church Institute), McLellan, G.Haworth, R.Bryce, Chippendale, Mackereth, Bonar, Conway, Macbeth, Blades(Church).
Apr 11 v Newton Heath (a) 3-0
Conway 2, Macbeth
Horne; McLellan, J.Stevenson, R.Bryce, J.Wilkinson, G.Haworth, Mackereth, Deakin, Shuttleworth, Bonar, Conway.
Att: 7,000
Apr 16 v Accrington District (h) 2-0
Scorers unknown
Horne; McLellan, J.Stevenson, Taylor, J.Wilkinson, Hargreaves, Mackereth, Deakin, Shuttleworth, Bonar, Conway.
Att: 300
Apr 23 v Blackburn Rovers (h) 1-0
Yates
Horne; J.Stevenson, McLellan, G.Haworth, Parkinson, Chippendale, Mackereth, Bonar, Conway, J.Wilkinson, Jack Yates.
Att: 'moderate'
Apr 30 v Sunderland (a) 3-1
Scorers unknown
Horne; McLellan, J.Stevenson, G.Haworth, Webster, Chippendale, Hargreaves, Bonar, Conway, Parkinson, Jack Yates.

1887-88
Lancashire Cup
Round 1
Oct 1 v Lower Darwen (h) 20-1
Conway 5, Yates 4, Bonar 4, Chippendale 2, Fecitt 2, Bryce, Scorer unknown, Lofthouse.
Greenwood; J.Stevenson, McLellan, J.Wilkinson, R.Bryce, Chippendale, Lofthouse, Bonar, Conway, Fecitt, Jack Yates.
Att: 3,000
Round 2
Nov 19 v Higher Walton (a) 4-0
Bonar 2, Conway, Yates
J.K.Horne; J.Stevenson, McLellan, G.Haworth, J.Wilkinson, Chippendale, Lofthouse, Bonar, Conway, Fecitt, Jack Yates.
Att: 4,000
Round 3
Jan 21 v Darwen (a) 4-0
Conway 2, Yates, Pemberton
J.K.Horne; J.Stevenson, McLellan, G.Haworth, Pemberton, Chippendale, Lofthouse, Bonar, Fecitt, Conway, Jack Yates.
Semi-final
Feb 25 v Witton (a) 1-1
Conway
J.K.Horne; J.Stevenson, McLellan, G.Haworth, Pemberton, Chippendale, Lofthouse, Bonar, Jack Yates, Conway, Fecitt.
Att: 2,000
Replay
Mar 24 v Witton (h) 2-1
Bonar, Lofthouse
J.K.Horne; J.Stevenson, McLellan, G.Haworth, Chippendale, Pemberton, Lofthouse, Bonar, Fecitt, Conway, Jack Yates.
Final
Apr 21 v Preston North End (at Leamington Road, Blackburn)
Note: Preston scratched from the competition. See narrative history for details.

East Lancashire Charity Cup
Semi-final
May 26 v Darwen (a) 0-0
J.K.Horne; Wood, McLellan, G.Haworth, Pemberton, Chippendale, Lofthouse, Bonar, Fecitt, J.Wilkinson, Jack Yates.
Replay
Jun 2 v Darwen (h) 5-1
Bonar 2, Holden, Lofthouse, Yates

J.K.Horne; J.Stevenson, McLellan, G.Haworth, Chippendale, Pemberton, Lofthouse, Bonar, Fecitt, Jack Yates, Holden.
Att: 1,500
Final
Jun 9 v Blackburn Rovers (a) 3-3
Chippendale, Fecitt 2
J.K.Horne; Warburton, McLellan, G.Haworth, Chippendale, J.Wilkinson, Lofthouse, Bonar, Fecitt, Jack Yates, Holden.
Att: 3,000

Friendlies
Sep 2 v Newton Heath (a) 1-2
Lofthouse
Woolfall; J.Stevenson, McLellan, G.Haworth, R.Bryce, Chippendale, Lofthouse, Bonar, Conway, Fecitt, Jack Yates.
Att: 4,000
Sep 10 v Hurst (a) 7-0
Bryce, Fecitt, Scorer unknown, Chippendale 2, Conway, Lofthouse.
Woolfall; J.Stevenson, McLellan, G.Haworth, R.Bryce, Chippendale, Lofthouse, Bonar, Conway, Fecitt, Jack Yates.
Sep 17 v Helliwell (a) 2-2
Fecitt, Conway
Woolfall; J.Stevenson, McLellan, G.Haworth, R.Bryce, Chippendale, Lofthouse, Bonar, Conway, Fecitt, Jack Yates.
Att: 2,000
Sep 19 v Stoke (a) 3-5
Scorer unknown, Lofthouse, Bonar
Woolfall; J.Stevenson, McLellan, G.Haworth, R.Bryce, J.Wilkinson, Lofthouse, Bonar, Conway, Fecitt, Jack Yates.
Att: 3,000
Sep 24 v Bootle (a) 1-1
Conway
Greenwood; McLellan, J.Stevenson, G.Haworth, R.Bryce, Chippendale, Lofthouse, Bonar, Conway, Fecitt, Jack Yates.
Att: 4,000
Oct 8 v Bolton Wanderers (a) 1-1
Yates
J.K.Horne; J.Stevenson, McLellan, J.Wilkinson, R.Bryce, Chippendale, Lofthouse, Rowan, Conway, Fecitt, Jack Yates.
Att: 'few'
Oct 22 v Newton Heath (h) 2-1
Fecitt, Bryce
J.K.Horne; Singleton, R.Bryce, J.Stevenson, Gregory, J.Wilkinson, Shuttleworth, Bonar, Conway, Jack Yates, Fecitt.
Att: 2,000

Oct 29 v Church (h) 4-1
Fecitt 2, Conway, Lofthouse
J.K.Horne; J.Stevenson, McLellan, G.Haworth, R.Bryce, Chippendale, Lofthouse, Bonar, Conway, Fecitt, Jack Yates.
Nov 12 v Burnley (a) 2-0
Conway, Lawton
J.K.Horne; J.Stevenson, McLellan, G.Haworth, J.Wilkinson, Chippendale, Lawton, Bonar, Conway, Fecitt, Jack Yates.
Dec 3 v Blackburn Olympic (h) 6-1
Bonar 2, Conway, Scorer unknown 3
J.K.Horne; J.Stevenson, McLellan, G.Haworth, R.Bryce, Chippendale, Lofthouse, Bonar, Conway, Laycock, Jack Yates.
Dec 10 v Nottingham Forest (a) 0-2
J.K.Horne; J.Stevenson, McLellan, G.Haworth, Gregory, R.Bryce, Lofthouse, Laycock, Conway, Fecitt, Jack Yates
Att: 1,000
Dec 17 v Davenham (h) 7-0
Bonar 3, Fecitt, R.Bryce, Lofthouse 2
J.K.Horne; J.Stevenson, McLellan, Pemberton, R.Bryce, Chippendale, Lofthouse, Bonar, Conway, Fecitt, Jack Yates
Dec 24 v Burnley (h) 0-1
J.K.Horne; J.Stevenson, McLellan, G.Haworth, J.Wilkinson, Chippendale, Lofthouse, Bonar, Conway, Fecitt, Jack Yates.
Dec 26 v Witton (h) 3-3
Yates, Lofthouse 2
J.K.Horne; J.Stevenson, McLellan, G.Haworth, R.Bryce, Chippendale, Lofthouse, Bonar, Conway, Fecitt, Jack Yates.
Att: 'fair'
Dec 31 v Glasgow Northern (h) 4-1
Conway 2, Haworth, Fecitt
J.K.Horne; J.Stevenson, McLellan, G.Haworth, R.Bryce, Chippendale, Lofthouse, Bonar, Conway, Fecitt, Jack Yates.
Jan 2 v Thornliebank (h) 10-0
Conway 4, Yates 2, Bonar 2, Shuttleworth 2
J.K.Horne; J.Stevenson, McLellan, G.Haworth, Shuttleworth, Chippendale, Lofthouse, Bonar, Fecitt, Conway, Jack Yates.
Jan 7 v Wolverhampton Wanderers (h) 4-1
Fecitt, Lofthouse, Yates, Haworth
J.K.Horne; J.Stevenson, McLellan, G.Haworth, J.Wilkinson, Chippendale, Lofthouse, Bonar, Fecitt, Conway, Jack Yates.
Jan 14 v Bolton Wanderers (h) 3-1
Yates, Bonar, Shuttleworth
J.K.Horne; J.Stevenson, McLellan, G.Haworth, J.Wilkinson, Pemberton, Lofthouse, Bonar, Shuttleworth, Fecitt, Jack Yates.

Jan 16 v Burnley (a) 0-1
J.K.Horne; Gregory, McLellan, G.Haworth, J.Wilkinson, Pemberton, Lofthouse, Bonar, J.Stevenson, Jack Yates, Fecitt.
Jan 28 v Halliwell (h) 2-1
Yates, Scorer unknown
J.K.Horne; J.Stevenson, R.Bryce, G.Haworth, Pemberton, Chippendale, Lofthouse, Bonar, Fecitt, Conway, Jack Yates.
Feb 4 v Burnley (a) 3-0
Conway, Scorer unknown, Yates
Strachan; J.Stevenson, McLellan, G.Haworth, Pemberton, Chippendale, J.Wilkinson, Bonar, Shuttleworth, Conway, Jack Yates.
Att: 2,500
Feb 11 v Witton (a) 3-1
Yates 3
J.K.Horne; J.Stevenson, McLellan, G.Haworth, Pemberton, Chippendale, Lofthouse, Bonar, Fecitt, Jack Yates, Conway.
Att: 3,000
Feb 18 v Darwen (h) 4-0
Conway, Fecitt, Bonar, Chippendale
J.K.Horne; J.Stevenson, McLellan, G.Haworth, Pemberton, Chippendale, Lofthouse, Bonar, Fecitt, Jack Yates, Conway.
Mar 3 v Church (a) 10-2
Lofthouse 4, Yates, Conway 2, Fecitt 2, Chippendale
J.K.Horne; J.Stevenson, McLellan, G.Haworth, Chippendale, Pemberton, Lofthouse, Bonar, Fecitt, Conway, Jack Yates.
Mar 10 v Blackburn Rovers (h) 7-3
Bonar 2, Scorer unknown, Conway, Lofthouse, Fecitt 2
J.K.Horne; J.Stevenson, McLellan, G.Haworth, Chippendale, Pemberton, Lofthouse, Jack Yates, Conway, Bonar, Fecitt.
Att: 4,000

Mar 17 v Burnley Union Star (a) 4-2
Scorers unknown 3, Conway
J.K.Horne; J.Stevenson, McLellan, R.Bryce, Chippendale, Pemberton, Lofthouse, Shuttleworth, Fecitt, Conway, Bonar.

Mar 20 v Bottle (a) 1-1
Yates
J.K.Horne; McLellan, J.Stevenson, Pemberton, W.Stevenson, G.Haworth, Jack Yates, Conway, Fecitt, Bonar, Lofthouse.
Att: 3,000

Mar 30 v Vale of Leven (h) 3-3
Scorers unknown
J.K.Horne; Gregory, McLellan, G.Haworth, Pemberton, Chippendale, Lofthouse, Conway, A.Wilkinson, Bonar, Jack Yates.

Mar 31 v Preston North End (a) 0-2
J.K.Horne; J.Stevenson, McLellan, G.Haworth, Chippendale, Pemberton, Lofthouse, Bonar, Fecitt, Conway, Jack Yates.
Apr 2 v Newton Heath (a) 1-0
Scorer unknown
J.K.Horne; J.Stevenson, McLellan, G.Haworth, J.Wilkinson, Pemberton, Lofthouse, Bonar, A.Wilkinson, Conway, Jack Yates.
Att: 6,500
Apr 7 v Preston North End (h) 1-2
Scorer unknown
J.K.Horne; J.Stevenson, McLellan, G.Haworth, Chippendale, Pemberton, Lofthouse, Bonar, Jack Yates, Conway, Macbeth.
Att: 8,000
Apr 14 v Blackburn Rovers (a) 2-1
Fecitt, McColl
J.K.Horne; J.Stevenson, McLellan, G.Haworth, J.Wilkinson, Chippendale, Lofthouse, Bonar, Fecitt, Conway, McColl.
Att: 5,000
Apr 21 v Witton (at Leamington Road, Blackburn) 0-4
J.K.Horne; J.Stevenson, McLellan, G.Haworth, Chippendale, Pemberton, Lofthouse, Bonar, Fecitt, Jack Yates, Conway.
Att: 2,000
Apr 28 v Bolton Wanderers (a) 1-1
Lofthouse
J.K.Horne; J.Stevenson, McLellan, Chippendale, Pemberton, G.Haworth, Lofthouse, Bonar, Fecitt, Jack Yates, Conway.
May 5 v Halliwell (a) 3-0
Lofthoue, Yates, Holden
J.K.Horne; J.Stevenson, McLellan, G.Haworth, Chippendale, Pemberton, Kirkham, Lofthouse, Fecitt, Jack Yates, Holden.
Att: 2,000
May 9 v Blackburn Rovers (h) 3-4
Scorers unknown
J.K.Horne; Shorrock, Berry, Pemberton, J.Wilkinson, G.Haworth, Kirkham, Bonar, Cunliffe, Jack Yates, Grimshaw.
Att: 'Several thousand'
May 12 v Everton (a) 2-0
Holden, Fecitt
J.K.Horne; J.Stevenson, McLellan, G.Haworth, Chippendale, Pemberton, Lofthouse, Bonar, Fecitt, Holden, Jack Yates.
Att: 9,000

Notes on the Horne Brothers

Accrington were represented by two goalkeeping brothers, Richard and John

Kay Horne, during the 1880s. Although Richard Horne began his career as an outfield player, he eventually became the first-choice goalkeeper. By 1884, younger brother John was also making appearances in goal for the first team. Unfortunately newspaper reports do not always distinguish between the two. Although it is possible to make an educated guess for many of the matches, as to the identity of the brother; in the interests of accuracy, initials have only been used when a definite identification has been made.

Although John Kay Horne began his playing career with Accrington, he turned out for Windsor, Grimsby Town and Bury before returning to play with Accrington. He then joined Burslem Port Vale for the start of the 1886-7 season, but was quickly seen again playing for Accrington. He returned to Accrington on a permanent basis in October 1887 and was immediately installed as first-choice goalkeeper. John Kay Horne had later spells with Blackburn Rovers and Darwen.

Curiously, a third brother, William Horne, made one League appearance for Accrington during the 1890-91 season; but as an outfield player. In June 1891 he joined Blackburn Rovers and made 7 League appearances during the 1891-2 season as a goalkeeper!

Accrington Football Club

Other Matches 1888-1893

THIS section chronicles the results of minor cup matches and friendlies played by Accrington FC during the period of their Football League membership.

1888-89
Lancashire Senior Cup
1st Round
Bye
2nd Round
Nov 10 v Hurst (a) 4-0
3rd Round
Jan 5 v Halliwell (a) 1-1
3rd Round Replay
Feb 28 v Halliwell (a) 1-0
Semi-final
Mar 16 v Haydock (at Bootle) 1-1
Semi-final Replay
Apr 6 v Haydock (at Darwen) 6-1
Final
Apr 27 v Higher Walton
(at Leamington Road, Blackburn) 1-1
Final Replay
May 4 v Higher Walton
(at Deepdale, Preston) 1-0

East Lancashire Charity Cup
Semi-final
Jun 8 v Witton (a) 3-1
Final
Jun 15 v Blackburn Rovers (a) 1-3

Friendlies
Dec 25 v Wrexham (h) 2-0
Dec 31 v Kilmarnock (h) 3-2
Jan 1 v Partick Thistle (h) 10-0
Feb 16 v Darwen (a) 2-3
Mar 2 v Bootle (h) 4-0
Mar 30 v Bury (a) 5-0
Apr 1 v Bootle (a) 2-1
Apr 19 v Wolverhampton Wanderers (h) 2-1
Apr 22 v Blackburn Rovers (a) 5-4
Apr 23 v Derby County (a) 1-3
May 11 v Heywood Central (a) 3-3
May 15 v Ramsbottom (a) 6-4
May 18 v Sunderland (a) 0-4
May 25 v Everton (a) 0-1

1889-90
Lancashire Senior Cup
1st Round
Nov 2 v Bolton Wanderers (a) 2-4

Friendlies
Aug 31 v Oswaldtwistle Rovers (h) 5-0
Sep 2 v Irwell Springs (a) 7-1
Sep 7 v Southport Central (a) 4-0
Nov 4 v Burslem Port Vale (a) 9-0
Dec 14 v Preston North End (h) 0-0
Dec 25 v Halliwell (h) 5-3
Jan 11 v Heywood Central (a) 6-1
Mar 8 v Halliwell (a) 3-5
Mar 22 v Burnley (h) 2-4
Apr 4 v Blackburn Rovers (a) 2-5
Apr 5 v Burnley (a) 2-3
Apr 12 v Sunderland (a) 3-2
Apr 19 v Witton (h) 6-2
Apr 26 v Grimsby Town (a) 1-4
May 3 v Middlesbrough Ironopolis (a) 2-8
May 17 v Preston North End (a) 2-6

1890-91
Lancashire Cup
1st Round
Feb 10 v Rossendale (h) 7-0
2nd Round
Feb 21 v Darwen (a) 1-2

East Lancashire Charity Cup
Semi-final
May 9 v Blackburn Rovers (a) 1-5

Friendlies
Sep 18 v Bootle (a) 3-1
Sep 25 v Sheffield Wednesday (a) 1-0
Oct 16 v Stockton (a) 4-1
Nov 17 v Walsall Town Swifts (a) 2-2
Dec 25 v Chirk (h) 4-3
Dec 27 v Blackburn Rovers (h) 1-2
Jan 3 v Moss End Swifts (h) 4-0
Feb 7 v Blackburn Rovers (a) 1-4
Feb 14 v Everton (a) 1-2
Feb 28 v Darwen (h) 3-1
Mar 14 v Middlesbrough (a) 0-2
Mar 27 v Blackburn Rovers (h) 6-3
Mar 28 v Burnley (a) 1-4
Mar 30 v Newton Heath (a) 5-2
Apr 4 v Rotherham Town (a) 4-2
Apr 11 v Bury (a) 0-2
Apr 16 v Everton (a) 2-5
Apr 25 v Sheffield Wednesday (a) 2-6
Apr 30 v Burnley (a) 1-4

1891-92
Lancashire Cup
1st Round
Feb 10 v Ardwick (h) 6-0
2nd Round
Feb 20 v Bury (a) 0-4

Friendlies
Sep 1 v Burnley (a) 2-1
Sep 21 v Darwen (a) 5-2
Oct 5 v Chirk (a) 3-2
Oct 14 v Bolton Wanderers (h) 1-1
Oct 17 v Newcastle West End (a) 1-4
Dec 25 v Battlefield (h) 5-1
Jan 1 v Burnley (h) 3-1
Jan 20 v Blackpool (a) 5-4
Feb 13 v Linfield Athletic (a) 0-4
Feb 15 v United Ulster (a) 4-2
Mar 21 v Sheffield Wednesday (a) 0-6
Mar 26 v Preston North End (h) 3-1
Mar 30 v Ardwick (a) 3-3
Apr 9 v Sheffield United (a) 1-3
Apr 16 v Newton Heath (a) 2-0
Apr 18 v Blackburn Rovers (a) 3-1
Apr 23 v Sheffield Wednesday (h) 1-0
Apr 30 v Blackpool (a) 1-6

1892-93
Lancashire Cup
1st Round
Feb 18 v Bolton Wanderers (a) 0-4

East Lancashire Charity Cup
Semi-final
Mar 11 v Darwen (a) 1-2
Semi-final
Apr 19 v Darwen (h) 4-1

Friendlies
Sep 1 v Blackpool (a) 2-4
Sep 12 v Bootle (a) 1-3
Sep 24 v Bury (a) 1-4
Jan 28 v 1st Royal Scots (h) 3-0
Mar 27 v Bootle (h) 2-4
Apr 1 v Royal Arsenal (a) 1-3

Accrington Football Club

Results 1893-1896

THIS section chronicles matches played by the Accrington club after leaving the Football League in 1893 until their final match in 1896.

1893-94

Lancashire League

Sep 2 v Blackpool (h) 1-3
Sep 9 v Fleetwood Rangers (a) 1-2
Sep 16 v Bury (h) 0-0
Sep 23 v Fairfield (h) 3-0
Sep 30 v West Manchester (a) 2-2
Oct 14 v Rossendale (h) 1-0
Oct 28 v South Shore (h) 4-1
Nov 18 v Blackpool (a) 0-2
Dec 2 v Rossendale (a) 2-2
Dec 9 v West Manchester (h) 5-1
Dec 16 v Heywood Central (h) 4-3
Dec 23 v Heywood Central (a) 2-2
Jan 2 v Bacup (a) 3-0
Jan 6 v Bacup (h) 3-0
Feb 3 v Southport Central (a) 1-2
Feb 10 v South Shore (a) 1-5
Feb 21 v Nelson (h) 6-2
Feb 24 v Bury (a) 1-3
Mar 3 v Nelson (a) 2-6
Mar 7 v Fleetwood Rangers (h) 5-0
Mar 10 v Fairfield (a) 2-0
Mar 19 v Southport Central (h) 2-1

County Palantine League

Feb 6 v Newton Heath (a) 3-1
Feb 28 v Bury (h) 0-0
Mar 23 v Everton (a) 1-4
Apr 11 v Newton Heath (h) 1-2
Apr 14 v Bury (a) 0-4
Apr 21 v Everton (h) 0-2

Lancashire Senior Cup

1st Round

Jan 20 v Bury (a) 0-6

2nd Round

Feb 17 v Rossendale (h) 5-0

Semi-final

Mar 17 v Bolton Wanderers (a) 0-1

East Lancashire Charity Cup

Semi-final

Apr 20 v Blackburn Rovers (h) 1-1
Apr 27 v Blackburn Rovers (a) 0-4

Friendlies

Sep 1 v Southport Central (a) 1-5
Oct 7 v Millwall Athletic (h) 2-1
Oct 21 v Chatham (a) 2-2
Oct 23 v Sheerness (a) 2-3
Nov 4 v Crouch End (a) 0-0
Nov 6 v Chesham (a) 3-2
Nov 11 v Swindon Town (a) 0-1
Nov 25 v Burton Swifts (h) 2-0
Dec 25 v Liverpool (h) 1-0
Dec 26 v Burton Swifts (a) 3-2
Dec 30 v Nelson (h) 1-1
Jan 1 v Burnley (h) 3-2
Jan 13 v Woolwich Arsenal (a) 0-2
Mar 24 v Burnley (a) 1-3
Mar 26 v Liverpool (a) 0-6
Mar 31 v Accrington District (h) 2-2
Apr 7 v Bell's Temperance (a) 6-4
Apr 14 v Bury (a) 0-4
Apr 21 v Everton (h) 0-2

1894-95

Lancashire League

Sep 1 v Fairfield (a) 1-4
Sep 8 v Clitheroe (h) 2-1
Sep 15 v Blackpool (a) 1-5
Sep 22 v Clitheroe (a) 1-3
Sep 29 v Bacup (h) 3-3
Oct 6 v Blackpool (h) 1-0
Oct 20 v Stockport County (h) 5-0
Oct 27 v Rossendale (a) 2-3
Nov 10 v Stockport County (a) 4-2
Nov 17 v Fleetwood Rangers (h) 1-2
Nov 24 v Nelson (h) 2-3
Dec 1 v Rossendale (h) 3-0
Dec 8 v Chorley (h) 1-4
Dec 15 v Heywood Central (h) 13-0
Jan 5 v South Shore (h) 4-0
Jan 26 v Nelson (a) 1-0
Feb 16 v Heywood Central (a) 6-3
Feb 26 v Bacup (a) 1-2
Mar 2 v West Manchester (h) 2-2
Mar 20 v Fairfield (h) 1-2
Mar 23 v Southport Central (a) 0-4
Mar 30 v West Manchester (a) 1-3
Apr 6 v Fleetwood Rangers (a) 1-3
Apr 10 v South Shore (a) 1-7
Apr 13 v Chorley (a) 1-6
Apr 17 v Southport Central (h) 2-1

Lancashire Senior Cup
1st Round
Jan 19 v Southport Central (a) 3-1
2nd Round
Feb 9 v Fairfield (a) 1-0
Semi-final
Mar 9 v Preston North End
(at Ewood Park, Blackburn) 1-6

Friendlies
Nov 3 v Rotherham Town (h) 5-2
Dec 25 v Welsh Druids (h) 1-0
Dec 26 v Royal Ordnance (a) 2-0
Dec 27 v Kettering Town (a) 2-4
Dec 31 v Vale of Clyde (h) 4-0
Jan 1 v Glasgow Perthshire (h) 2-0
Jan 12 v Everton Reserves (a) 0-5
Feb 2 v Northwich Victoria (h) 4-0
Mar 16 v Sheffield United (a) 1-2
Feb 23 v Rotherham Town (a) 1-5
Feb 23 v Oswaldtwistle Rovers (h) 0-1
(Note: Accrington used a number of Accrington Stanley players in their team.)
Apr 15 v Macclesfield Town (a) 1-2

1895-96
Lancashire Combination
Sep 7 v Oswaldtwistle Rovers (h) 2-2
Sep 14 v Rawtenstall (h) 2-0
Sep 21 v Turton (h) 2-4
Sep 28 v Little Lever (h) 4-5
Oct 12 v Oswaldtwistle Rovers (a) 2-7

Lancashire Senior Cup
1st Round
Jan 18 v Darwen (a) 0-12

Friendlies
Sep 1 v Burnley Reserves (a) 1-2
Sep 4 v Blackburn Rovers Reserves (a) 0-3

ACCRINGTON LEAGUE & CUP CAREER RECORDS

A total of sixty-one players represented Accrington in the Football League. The second column denotes the first and last seasons in which the player appeared in the Football League. For players who appeared prior to 1888-89 and after 1892-93 the dates refer to when they appeared in their first and last FA Cup match.

		League		FA Cup		Test Match		Total	
Player	**Seasons played**	**Apps**	**Gls**	**Apps**	**Gls**	**Apps**	**Gls**	**Apps**	**Gls**
Alexander D.	1892-93	6	1	0	0	0	0	6	1
Almond W.	1892-93	9	1	0	0	0	0	9	1
Barbour A.	1888-89 to 1890-91	53	33	5	1	0	0	58	34
Barlow J.M.	1890-91 to 1891-92	5	0	0	0	0	0	5	0
Barr J.	1891-92	12	0	0	0	0	0	12	0
Bonar J.	1887-88 to 1888-89	17	0	5	2	0	0	22	2
Bowie W.	1892-93	9	1	0	0	1	0	10	1
Bowman W.W.	1891-92	5	3	0	0	0	0	5	3
Brand R.	1888-89 to 1889-90	18	11	0	0	0	0	18	11
Chippendale P.	1883-84 to 1888-89	6	1	7	0	0	0	13	1
Clegg J.R.	1891-92	1	0	0	0	0	0	1	0
Cookson H.	1892-93	27	14	2	1	1	0	30	15
Ditchfield J.C.	1892-93 to 1894-95	29	0	3	0	1	0	33	0
Elliott A.	1891-92	24	7	2	0	0	0	26	7
Entwistle J.	1889-90	19	9	2	2	0	0	21	11
Faulds W.	1891-92	10	2	0	0	0	0	10	2
Galbraith H.	1888-89	1	0	0	0	0	0	1	0
Gallocher P.	1888-89 to 1890-91	40	6	5	1	0	0	45	7
Haworth G.	1882-83 to 1891-92 & 1893-94	74	3	15	1	0	0	89	4
Haworth P.	1889-90	1	0	0	0	0	0	1	0
Hay T.	1890-91 to 1892-93	70	0	7	0	0	0	77	0
Higham W.	1892-93	2	2	0	0	0	0	2	2
Hodge W.	1892-93 to 1893-94	9	0	1	0	1	0	11	0
Holden J.*	1888-89 to 1890-91	7	4	0	0	0	0	7	4
Horne J.K.†	1884-85 to 1892-93	26	0	8	0	0	0	34	0
Horne W.	1890-91	1	0	0	0	0	0	1	0
Irvine J.	1891-92	16	7	2	0	0	0	18	7
Kirkham J.B.	1888-89 to 1892-93	104	33	10	4	1	0	115	37
Lea H.	1892-93	28	10	2	2	1	0	31	12
Lea T.	1892-93	29	6	2	0	1	0	32	6
Lindsay J.	1889-90	21	0	2	0	0	0	23	0
Lofthouse J.M.	1887-88 to 1888-89	21	2	5	4	0	0	26	6
Macbeth R.	1883-84 to 1886-87 & 1888-89 & 1890-91	4	0	2	1	0	0	6	1
McDermid R.	1890-91	22	0	3	0	0	0	25	0
McKay W.	1891-92	3	0	0	0	0	0	3	0

Player	Seasons played	League Apps	League Gls	FA Cup Apps	FA Cup Gls	Test Match Apps	Test Match Gls	Total Apps	Total Gls
McLellan J.	1887-88 to 1892-93	101	0	14	0	0	0	115	0
McLuggage J.	1889-90	8	2	0	0	0	0	8	2
McPherson M.	1890-91	1	1	0	0	0	0	1	1
McVickers J.	1891-92	19	0	2	0	0	0	21	0
Marsh G.	1889-90 to 1891-92	3	0	0	0	0	0	3	0
Mason W.	1892-93	4	0	0	0	1	0	5	0
Matthew J.	1892-93 to 1893-94	6	0	0	0	0	0	6	0
Morgan E.	1891-92	2	0	0	0	0	0	2	0
Nesbit J.	1890-91	5	0	0	0	0	0	5	0
Orr J.	1890-91	2	0	0	0	0	0	2	0
Parkinson H.	1888-89	1	0	0	0	0	0	1	0
Pemberton L.	1888-89 to 1890-91	45	0	2	0	0	0	47	0
Pendergast T.	1889-90 to 1891-92	36	12	3	2	0	0	39	14
Robertson J.	1888-89	3	0	0	0	0	0	3	0
Sanders M.	1890-91	17	1	0	0	0	0	17	1
Shuttleworth W.	1890-91 to 1894-95	39	0	7	0	1	0	47	0
Singleton S.S.	1888-89	4	0	2	0	0	0	6	0
Smith D.	1890-91	2	0	0	0	0	0	2	0
Sneddon J.	1890-91	1	0	0	0	0	0	1	0
Stevenson J.	1886-87 to 1892-93	81	0	12	0	1	0	94	0
Tattersall J.	1888-89 to 1892-93	100	2	10	0	0	0	110	2
Thomson S.	1890-91 to 1891-92	29	7	2	1	0	0	31	8
Whitehead J.W.	1890-91 to 1892-93	73	23	7	4	1	0	81	27
Wilkinson A.	1888-89 to 1890-91	23	13	7	2	0	0	30	15
Wilkinson J.	1882-83 to 1890-91	6	0	6	0	0	0	12	0
Woods J.	1888-89	2	0	0	0	0	0	2	0

* A number of sources have listed a player called Holding making one appearance during the 1890-91 season. Other sources have listed this players as J.Holden which is the position shown in the above list.

† J.K.Horne had several spells with clubs other than Accrington during the years mentioned above.

Note: Although the spellings of the above surnames are believed to be accurate, two players have caused some confusion. In a number of newspapers, John McLellan has on occasions been spelt as McLennan. Similarly, Robert Macbeth has been spelt as MacBeth, McBeth and even MacBeith on occasions. In both cases the spelling found to prevalent in the majority of sources has been used.

Note: Three FA Cup goals remain unidentified from 1884-85
One FA Cup goal remains unidentified from 1890-91
Two League goals remain unidentified from 1889-90

Accrington Stanley's Other Matches

This section deals with all other first team matches played by Accrington Stanley between 1921 and 1962. The spasmodic coverage of East Lancashire Charity Cup matches is due to the fact that Accrington fielded their reserve team in a number of these games, hence their exclusion from this section.

1921-22
Lancashire Senior Cup
First Round
Sep 5 v Barrow (a) 0-1
Peacock; Kay, Newton, Crawshaw, Popplewell, Burkinshaw, Oxley, Makin, Green, Hosker, Hartles.
Att: 5,500

East Lancashire Charity Cup
Sep 26 v Darwen (h) 1-2
Green
Tattersall; Kay, Wilde, Crawshaw, Popplewell, Burkinshaw, Oxley, Makin, Green, Quigley, Newton.
Att: 5,000
Apr 25 v Darwen (a) 0-3
Floyd; Richardson, Shorrock, Crawshaw, Smethurst, Foster, Cragg, Farrington, Hosker, Quigley, Watkinson.
Att: 4,000

Friendlies
Dec 3 v Doncaster Rovers (a) 3-0
Green 2, Hosker
Sloane; Kay, Wilde, Foster, Popplewell, Burkinshaw, Oxley, Nelis, Green, Hosker, Quigley.
Att: 4,000
Mar 25 v Southport (a) 0-1
Sloane; Kay, Shorrock, Crawshaw, Smethurst, Foster, Oxley, Makin, Green, Hosker, Cooper.

1922-23
Lancashire Senior Cup
First Round
Aug 30 v Rochdale (h) 1-2
Morris

Floyd; Richardson, Page, Crawshaw, Challinor, Rooks, Pinkney, Makin, Morris, Hosker, Harrold.
Att: 7,000

East Lancashire Charity Cup
Nov 18 v Darwen (h) 2-4
Metcalf, Smelt
Sloane; Childs, Page, Ogden, Popplewell, Smith, Ward, Makin, Smelt, Metcalf, Congdon.
Att: 6,000
May 1 v Darwen (a) 5-1
Helliwell, Metcalf 2, Hosker, Brindle (og)
Floyd; Richardson, Donnelly, Crawshaw, Challinor, Rooks, Ward, Metcalf, Allinson, Hosker, Helliwell.

1923-24
Lancashire Senior Cup
First Round
Sep 18 v Nelson (a) 3-2
Keetley (pen), Cooke, Hosker
Salt; Richardson, Donnelly, Watson, Rooks, Duffus, Brown, Hosker, Cooke, Keetley, Childs.
Second Round
Oct 1 v Manchester City (a) 1-2
Keetley
Salt; Richardson, Donnelly, Watson, Rooks, Duffus, Brown, Hosker, Cooke, Keetley, McCandless.

East Lancashire Charity Cup
Apr 15 v Darwen (a) 0-0
Salt; Richardson, Donnelly, Watson, Duffus, Rooks, Quigley, Heys, Sagar, Hosker, Kay.
Apr 28 v Darwen (h) 5-2
Hosker, Black 2, Rooks (pen), Quigley
Salt; Richardson, Donnelly, Watson, Duffus, Rooks, Sagar, Heap, Black, Hosker, Quigley.
Att: 2,000

1924-25
Lancashire Senior Cup
First Round
Sep 29 v New Brighton (h) 1-0
Watson
Salt; Crawley, Glennie, Watson, McIntosh, Entwistle, Bedford, Mutch,

R.Thompson, Kirkpatrick, J.Thompson.
Att: 4,000
Second Round
Oct 28 v Oldham Athletic (h) 0-2
Salt; Richardson, Crawley, Haigh, McIntosh, Rooks, Bedford, Mutch, R.Thompson, Skillen, J.Thompson.
Att: 2,500

East Lancashire Charity Cup
Apr 16 v Darwen (h) 0-1
Salt; Richardson, Rooks, Walmsley, Martin, Blackadder, Bedford, Gee, Skillen, Hall, Kirkpatrick.
Apr 28 v Darwen (a) 2-1 (after extra-time)
Salt; Childs, Rooks, Watson, Martin, Peplowe, Bedford, Gee, Skillen, Kirkpatrick, Heap.
Att: 3,000

1925-26
Lancashire Senior Cup
First Round
Oct 14 v Wigan Borough (h) 3-1
Gee (pen), Powell, Jepson
Blake; Gray, Whittaker, Field, Martin, Rooks, Wyper, Gee, Jepson, Powell, Gummery.
Att: 1,200
Second Round
Nov 11 v Stockport County (h) 1-1
Jepson
Holden; Bell, Whittaker, Field, Martin, Rooks, Wyper, Gee, Jepson, Powell, Gummery.
Att: 1,600
Second Round Replay
Nov 16 v Stockport County (a) 1-0
Jepson
Holden; Bell, Whittaker, Field, Martin, Rooks, Wyper, Gee, Jepson, Powell, Gummery.
Third Round
Dec 16 v Preston North End (h) 2-1
Gee 2
Holden; Bell, Whittaker, Field, Martin, Rooks, Wyper, Gee, Jepson, Powell, Gummery.
Att: 2,000

Semi-final
May 3 v Manchester City (played at Bury) 2-1
Gee (pen), Jepson
Lunn; Bell, Whittaker, Field, Hall, Kasher, Wyper, Gee, Jepson, Powell, Gummery.
Final
May 8 v Bolton Wanderers (a) 2-5
Greenhalgh, Gee
Lunn; Bell, Whittaker, Field, Hall, Kasher, Wyper, Gee, Jepson, Greenhalgh, Gummery.

East Lancashire Charity Cup
Apr 21 v Darwen (h) 9-2
Gummery, Gee, Wyper 2, Powell 2, Jepson 3
Holden; Bell, Gregory, Field, Hall, Kasher, Wyper, Gee, Jepson, Powell, Gummery.
Apr 27 v Darwen (a) 1-2
Jepson
Holden; Bell, Gregory, Field, Hall, Kasher, Wyper, Gee, Jepson, Powell, Gummery.

1926-27
Lancashire Senior Cup
Second Round
Sep 8 v Nelson (a) 2-2
Gee 2
Hayes; Bell, Rooks, Field, Armitt, Kahser, Wyper, Gee, Jepson, Powell, Martin.
Second Round Replay
Oct 11 v Nelson (h) 5-3
Clarkson 2, Jepson 2, Chadwick
Hayes; Bell, Whittaker, Field, Kasher, Rooks, Wyper, Clarkson, Jepson, Chadwick, Martin.
Third Round
Oct 25 v Manchester City (h) 3-5
Gee, Jepson, Martin
Hayes; Bell, Rooks, Field, Kasher, Hughes, Wyper, Gee, Jepson, Chadwick, Martin.
Att: 2,000

East Lancashire Charity Cup
Apr 4 v Darwen (h) 5-0
Powell 3, Jepson 2
Hayes; Gregory, Whittaker, Wilson, Bell, Hughes, Slater, Gee, Jepson, Powell, Martin.

Apr 26 v Darwen (a) 0-4
Hayes; Gregory, Whittaker, Rooks, Bell, Hughes, Slater, Clarkson, Jepson, Dodds, Martin.

1927-28
Lancashire Senior Cup
First Round
Sep 12 v Wigan Borough (h) 2-0
Butler, Parkin
Finnigan, Armstrong, Whittaker, Carrick, Curran, Lee, Parry, Butler, Parkin, McLoughlin, Barclay.
Att: 3,000
Second Round
Sep 20 v Oldham Athletic (h) 1-2
Butler
Finnigan; Armstrong, Whittaker, Carrick, Curran, Lee, Parry, Butler, Parkin, McLoughlin, Barclay.
Att: 1,500

Abandoned League Match
Nov 11 v Rochdale (a) 1-1
Barclay
Tootill; Armstrong, Whittaker, Carrick, Curran, Lee, Parry, Clarkson, Parkin, McLoughlin, Barclay.
Att: 3,079
(Abandoned after 76 minutes due to a waterlogged pitch and bad light)

1928-29
Lancashire Senior Cup
First Round
Sep 13 v Blackburn Rovers (a) 1-3
Parkin
Tootill; Armstrong, Whittaker, Latham, Curran, Lee, Parry, Parkin, Jepson, McLoughlin, Barclay.
Att: 6,000

1929-30
Lancashire Senior Cup
First Round
Sep 16 v Barrow (a) 4-2
Hawes, Jepson 3
Soutar; Armstrong, Whittaker, Latham, Curran, Lee, Hamilton, Ferguson, Jepson, Hawes, Pears.
Att: 3,861

Second Round
Oct 7 v Wigan Borough (h) 6-1
Jepson 5, Hawes
Thornton; Armstrong, Young, Latham, Curran, Lee, Hamilton, Ferguson, Jepson, Hawes, Whyte.
Att: 5,000
Third Round
Oct 28 v Burnley (h) 2-2
Hawes, Ferguson
Thornton; Armstrong, Whittaker, Whyte, Curran, Lee, Hamilton, Ferguson, Jepson, Hawes, J.Haworth.
Att: 3,000
Third Round Replay
Nov 11 v Burnley (a) 2-3
Jepson 2
Thornton; Armstrong, Whittaker, Whyte, Curran, Lee, Hamilton, Ferguson, Jepson, Hawes, J.Haworth.
Att: 2,000

Friendlies
Jan 11 v Nelson (a) 1-2
Curran
Thornton; Armstrong, Whittaker, Latham, Curran, H.Haworth, Hamilton, Ferguson, Jepson, Whyte, J.Haworth.
Att: 300

Thomas Whittaker Benefit Match
May 30 v Blackpool (h) 3-2
Jepson, Ferguson, Parsons
Thornton; Armstrong, Whittaker, Latham, Curran, Whyte, Hamilton, Ferguson, Parsons, Hawes, Jepson.
Att: 1,000

Abandoned League Match
Dec 28 v Doncaster Rovers (h) 1-1
Curran
Thornton; Armstrong, Whittaker, Latham, Curran, Lee, Hamilton, Ferguson, Jepson, Hawes, Whyte.
Att: 3,205
(Abandoned after 40 minutes due to a waterlogged pitch and bad light)

1930-31
Lancashire Senior Cup
First Round
Sep 23 v Nelson (a) 4-1

Abel, Agar, Whyte 2 (2 pens)
Thornton; Law, Whittaker, Ferguson, Curran, Whyte, Agar, Riley, Abel, Broome, Summers.
Att: 1,500
Second Round
Oct 15 v Burnley (h) 1-2
Riley
Thornton; Snary, Whittaker, Ferguson, Viner, Whyte, Pickup, Riley, Abel, Broome, Summers
Att: 1,000

East Lancashire Charity Cup
First Round
Oct 27 v Blackburn Rovers (h) 1-2
Summers
Thornton; Snary, Whittaker, Ferguson, Rhodes, Whyte, Pickup, Buchanan, Abel, Broome, Summers.
Att: 1,200

Friendlies
Jan 31 v Barnoldswick Town (a) 2-1
Haworth, Johnson
Lansdale; Armstrong, Whittaker, Ferguson, Viner, Whyte, Agar, Riley, Johnson, Walton, J.Haworth.
Att: 200

1931-32
Lancashire Senior Cup
First Round
Sep 22 v Rochdale (a) 1-0
Watson
Bell; Armstrong, Price, Ferguson, Viner, High, Agar, Williamson, Watson, Walton, Wright.
Second Round
Oct 7 v Bolton Wanderers (h) 0-0
Bell; Armstrong, Price, Ferguson, Viner, High, Agar, Garbutt, Watson, Walton, Wright
Second Round Replay
Oct 19 v Bolton Wanderers (h) 1-4
Wright
Bell; Armstrong, Price, Ferguson, Viner, High, Agar, Williamson, Watson, Walton, Wright.
Att: 2,000

1932-33
Lancashire Senior Cup
Qualifying Round
Sep 19 v Rochdale (a) 2-2
Fitton 2
Pattison; Armstrong, Price, McCulloch, Viner, Dodds, Eddleston, Maycock, Fitton, Walton, Johnson.
Qualifying Round Replay
Oct 5 v Rochdale (h) 4-2
Walton, Price 2 (2 pens), Johnson
Allen; Corcoran, Price, Dodds, Viner, McCulloch, Eddleston, Walton, Fitton, Johnson, Wright.
Att: 1,300
First Round
Oct 12 v Liverpool (a) 1-5
Viner
Allen; R.Haworth, Price, Dodds, Viner, McCulloch, Eddleston, Maycock, Fitton, Walton, Johnson.
Att: 2,000

East Lancashire Charity Cup
First Round
Oct 17 v Blackburn Rovers (h) 1-2
Eddleston
Allen; Armstrong, Price, Dodds, Viner, McCulloch, Hackett, Eddleston, Fitton, Schofield, Johnson.
Att: 1,200

1933-34
Northern Section Cup
First Round
Jan 29 v Halifax Town (h) 2-2
Cheetham, Lennox
Pattison; Armstrong, Price, Dodds, Stoddart, McCulloch, Jeavons, Lennox, Cheetham, Leedham, Clare.
Att: 882
First Round Replay
Feb 5 v Halifax Town (a) 3-0
Travis 2, Wyper
Maidment; Price, Corcoran, Dodds, Crawshaw, McCulloch, Wyper, Lennox, Travis, Leedham, Watson.
Second Round
Feb 19 v Stockport County (a) 0-1
Maidment; Price, Armstrong, Dodds, Stoddart, McCulloch, Jeavons, Aspin, Cheetham, Leedham, Clare.

Lancashire Senior Cup
First Round
Sep 20 v Preston North End (h) 2-1
Price, Wyper
Maidment; Price, Corcoran, Dodds, Stoddart, McCulloch, Wyper, Lennox, Cheetham, Dulson, Watson.
Att: 2,000
Second Round
Oct 4 v Bolton Wanderers (a) 2-5
Cheetham, Price (pen)
Maidment; Price, Corcoran, Crawshaw, Stoddart, McCulloch, Wyper, Lennox, Cheetham, Dulson, Watson.

1934-35
Northern Section Cup
First Round
Feb 27 v Stockport County (h) 1-2
Harker
Pattison; Hunter, Fieldsend, McCulloch, Lockie, Lowery, Cull, Harker, Britton, Brown, Miller.
Att: 500

Lancashire Senior Cup
First Round
Sep 12 v Wigan Athletic (h) 1-3
Harker
Gill; Hunter, Fieldsend, Buchanan, McCulloch, Dodds, Cull, Harker, Marcroft, Leedham, Clare.

1935-36
Northern Section Cup
First Round
Jan 1 v Barrow (a) 3-4
Mortimer, Green 2
Hacking; Wilson, Fieldsend, Harker, McCulloch, Robinson, Reynolds, Brown, Mortimer, Green, Mee.
Att: 3,000

Lancashire Senior Cup
First Round
Sep 5 v Preston North End (a) 1-4
Mortimer
J.Robinson; Sant, Fieldsend, Harker, C.Robinson, Schofield, Brown, Aspin, Mortimer, Kerr, Amos.

1936-37
Northern Section Cup
First Round
Sep 16 v Carlisle United (h) 3-3
Andrews, Singleton, Nesbit
Robertson; Wilson, Gregg, Nesbit, Craven, Treanor, Reynolds, Singleton, Schofield, Andrews, Mee.
First Round Replay
Oct 8 v Carlisle United (a) 0-3
Robertson; Wilson, Reeday, Nesbit, Craven, Gregg, Reynolds, Andrews, Mortimer, Pateman, Martin.

Lancashire Senior Cup
First Round
Sep 23 v Rochdale (h) 2-3
Mortimer, Rimmer
Robertson; Wilson, Gregg, Nesbitt, Craven, Treanor, Reynolds, Rimmer, Mortimer, Andrews, Mee.

1937-38
Northern Section Cup
First Round
Sep 20 v Barrow (a) 3-4
Mortimer 3
Robertson; Pickering, Simpson, Randle, Craven, Andrews, Reynolds, O'Grady, Mortimer, Tyson, Mee.

Lancashire Senior Cup
First Round
Apr 6 v Barrow (h) 4-2
Blakeney 2, Reynolds, Hann
Robertson; Randle, Rhodes, Andrews, Ash, Webster, Reynolds, Curran, Blakeney, Hann, Mee.
Att: 700
Second Round
May 2 v Manchester United (a) 0-1
Robertson; Randle, Hall, Andrews, Jones, Webster, Reynolds, O'Grady, Blakeney, Curran, Mee.
Att: 2,200

1938-39
Northern Section Cup
First Round
Jan 1 v Rochdale (h) 2-1

Waring, Alexander
Robertson; Randle, Hall, Dooley, Johnson, Webster, Rattray, Alexander, Waring, Storey, Neal.
Att: 1,663

Second Round

Mar 3 v Barrow (h) 4-3
Waring, Kearney 2, Mee
Rose; Hall, Green, Randle, Johnson, Hann, Storey, Rattray, Waring, Kearney, Mee.
Att: 250

Semi-final

Apr 19 v New Brighton (a) 0-0
Daniels; Hamilton, Randle, Calvert, Johnson, Dooley, Storey, Waring, Moir, Kearney, Mee.

Semi-final Replay

Apr 26 v New Brighton (h) 2-0
Waring, Storey
Daniels; Hamilton, Randle, Calvert, Johnson, Dooley, Storey, Waring, Moir, Hann, Mee.
Att: 1,400

Final

May 1 v Bradford City (a) 0-3
Daniels; Hamilton, Randle, Calvert, Johnson, Dooley, Storey, Waring, Moir, Hann, Mee.
Att: 3,500

Lancashire Senior Cup

First Round

Sep 19 v New Brighton (h) 3-3
Alexander, Hunt 2
Daniels; Randle, Done, Johnson, Jones, Howshall, Gastall, Alexander, Hunt, Webster, Hann.

First Round Replay

Oct 5 v New Brighton (a) 0-1
Robertson; Johnson, Done, Randle, Jones, Webster, Rattray, Alexander, Hunt, Storey, Neal.

Friendlies

Football League Jubilee Match

Aug 20 v Southport (a) 2-3
Alexander, Clark
Robertson; Randle, Done, Johnson, Howshall, Webster, Rattray, Alexander, Hunt, Clark, Neal.
Att: 3,000

1939-40
Friendlies
Football League Jubilee Match
Aug 19 v Southport (h) 6-1
Conroy, Mauchline 2, Kearney 2, Morgan
Owen; Ash, Swinden, Dooley, Johnson, Smith, Conroy, Robbins, Morgan, Kearney, Mauchline.
Att: 2,000
Sep 16 v Burnley (a) 1-2
Swinden (pen)
Rose; Ash, Swinden, Dooley, Johnson, Yates, Conroy, Morgan, Moir, Kearney, Gale.
Att: 3,000
Sep 23 v Rochdale (h) 6-4
Conroy, Kearney, Mauchline 3, Swinden (pen)
Rose; Reeday, Swinden, Dooley, Johnson, Webster, Conroy, Sams, Morgan, Kearney, Mauchline.
Att: 3,000
Sep 30 v Southport (h) 1-3
Mauchline
Rose; Hall, Swinden, Dooley, Johnson, Webster, Gale, Sams, Morgan, Kearney, Mauchline.
Att: 1,500
Oct 7 v Rochdale (a) 1-1
Morgan
Robinson; Reeday, Swinden, Dooley, Johnson, Webster, Conroy, Sams, Morgan, Kearney, Mauchline.
Oct 14 v Bradford City (h) 3-2
Mauchline, Kearney, Swinden
Robinson; Reeday, Swinden, Dooley, Johnson, Webster, Conroy, Sams, Morgan, Kearney, Mauchline.
Att: 1,000
Dec 25 v Preston North End (h) 2-3
Conroy, Kearney
Owen; Reeday, Swinden, Johnson, Ash, Dooley, Conroy, Kearney, Morgan, Sams, Haworth.
Att: 3,000
Dec 30 v New Brighton (h) 4-2
Conroy 2, Ainsworth, Morgan
Owen; Reeday, Swinden, Dooley, Ash, Johnson, Conroy, A.Ainsworth, Morgan, Walton, Sams. *Att: 1,000*
Jan 1 v New Brighton (a) 0-6
Owen; Reeday, Swinden, Johnson, Ash, Dooley, A.Ainsworth, Walton, Morgan, Kearney, Sams.

Jan 13 v Barnsley (h) 2-1
Ainsworth, Walton
Owen; Reeday, Swinden, Johnson, Ash, Dooley, Conroy, A.Ainsworth, Morgan, Walton, Sams.
Att: 700
Feb 24 v Bradford (h) 3-3
Jackson 3
Owen; Reeday, Swinden, Johnson, Ash, Webster, Morgan, A.Ainsworth, Jackson, Walton, McShane.
Mar 22 v Halifax Town (h) 5-2
Kearney 3, Morgan 2
Owen; Reeday, Swinden, Dooley, Johnson, Webster, McShane, Kearney, Morgan, Walton, Robbins.
Mar 30 v Halifax Town (a) 1-3
Higham
Robinson; Ash, Swinden, Dooley, Johnson, Webster, Conroy, Higham, Morgan, Earl.

1940-41
Oct 19 v Bristol Aviation Works (Dunkenhalgh) (h) 10-1
Wolstenholme, Webster 4, Ainsworth, Nuttall 2, Haworth 2
Aspin; Maddox, Waddington, Moulding, Gill, Webster, Lingard, Wolstenholme, Nuttall, F.Ainsworth, Haworth.
Apr 12 v Farnworth Town (h) 3-1
McKay 2, Dodgson
Watts; Lyons, Taylor, Robinson, Waddington, F.Ainsworth, Wood, McKay, Dodgson, Haworth, Hindle.
May 3 v Services XI (h) 2-1
Pilkington, Brindle
Nuttall; Taylor, Waddington, F.Ainsworth, Jones, Parr, Brindle, Pilkington, Newsham, McCarthy, Brawn.
May 26 v Blackburn Combination XI (h) result unknown
Watts; Smith, Waddington, Ward, Parr, Ellson, Newsham, Rushton, F.Ainsworth, Haworth.
(Note: The Blackburn Combination XI was a privately selected team and not an official representative team of the Combination).

1944-45
May 21 v English League XI (h) 1-2
Ivill
Hacking; Eastwood, Crook, Morris, Ash, Malcolm, Gardner, Brindle, Ivill, Capstick, Cook.

1945-46
Tom Jones Benefit Match
Sep 11 v Rochdale (a) 1-2

Clark
Hacking; Webster, Dickinson, Maddox, Ash, Wood, Clark, Reid, Hargreaves, Capstick, Smith.

Tom Jones Benefit Match

Sep 19 v Rochdale (h) 1-0

Wright
Hacking; Taylor, Hutton, Farrow(Blackpool), Woodruffe, Malcolm, Clark, Patterson(Celtic), Wright, Smith, Cook.
Att: 1,500

Sep 26 v Services XI (h) 0-0

Hunt; Hacking, Waite, Wood, Ash, Nuttall, Taylor, D.Smith, Lynch, G.Smith, Ivill.

1946-47

Lancashire Senior Cup

First Round (1st leg)

Oct 9 v Burnley (h) 0-0

Hayes; Malcolm, Webster, Lythgoe, Briggs, Kearney, Bond, Rothwell, Morgan, Keeley, Edwards.

First Round (2nd leg)

Oct 21 v Burnley (a) 0-3

Hayes; Malcolm, Webster, Conroy, Briggs, Kearney, Bond, Haworth, Hudson, N.H.Smith, Keeley.
Att: 4,700

Abandoned League Match

Apr 5 v York City (h) 1-0

Rothwell
Rose; Hutton, Wilson, Conroy, Briggs, Malcolm, Bond, Marvin, Mercer, Rothwell, Edwards.
Att: 1,955
(Abandoned after 45 minutes due to a waterlogged pitch)

1947-48

Lancashire Senior Cup

First Round

Oct 7 v Bury (a) 2-3

Smith, Marvin
Harris; Lynn, Wilson, Conroy, Egerton, Webster, T.Butler, Rothwell, Marvin, N.H.Smith, Keeley.
Att: 2,100

1948-49
Lancashire Senior Cup
First Round
Oct 27 v Bolton Wanderers (a) 1-3
Keeley
Harris; Conroy, Webster, Rothwell, Briggs, Robertson, Butler, John Wilson, Parker, Keeley, Edwards.

1949-50
Lancashire Senior Cup
First Round
Oct 5 v Bolton Wanderers (a) 1-4
Travis
Harris; Lynn, Webster, Ritchie, Joe Wilson, Rothwell, Butler, Jim Wilson, Parker, Blunt, Travis.
Att: 3,493

Friendly
Jan 7 v Bradford City (a) 2-7
Keeley, Dolan
Harris; Lynn, Webster, Rothwell, Briggs, Smith, Butler, Dolan, Travis, Keeley, Birkett.
Att: 3,051

1950-51
Lancashire Senior Cup
First Round
Oct 11 v Rochdale (h) 2-1
Thomas, Travis
Daniels; Parker, Webster, Rothwell, Lovett, Joe Wilson, Hogan, Coll, Travis, Keeley, Thomas.
Second Round
Jan 17 v Manchester United (h) 1-2
Slattery
Daniels; Mellor, Webster, Rothwell, Jim Wilson, Robinson, Hogan, Butler, Slattery, Keeley, Thomas.
Att: 1,500

Friendlies
Festival of Britain Matches
May 9 v Bohemians (h) 0-1
Lancaster; Holliday(Blackburn Rovers), Webster, Rothwell, Brierley(Mansfield Town), Bell(Blackburn Rovers), Henderson(Burnley), Beech(Mansfield Town), Martin, McLaren (Barrow), Hannah(Barrow).

May 16 v Cork Athletic (h) 1-1
Rigby
Lancaster; Mellor, Rigby, Rothwell, Oldham, Martin, Newman, Butler, Graham(Blackburn Rovers), Wharton(Blackburn Rovers), Fenton(Blackburn Rovers).

1951-52
Lancashire Senior Cup
First Round
Oct 9 v Southport (a) 1-3
Roberts (pen)
Daniels; Mellor, Rigby, Senior, Oldham, Rothwell, Roberts, Butler, McEwan, Keeley, Glaister
Att: 2,000

1952-53
Lancashire Senior Cup
First Round
Sep 30 v Blackburn Rovers (h) 2-1
Kendal, Collins
Meadows; Mellor, Robinson, Brocklehurst, Holliday, Grummett, Taylor, Kendal, Aveyard, Watkinson, Collins.
Att: 5,300
Second Round
Mar 4 v Chester (a) 1-3
Watkinson
Meadows; Mellor, Robinson, Brocklehurst, Holliday, Grummett, Collins, Farnworth, Watkinson, Aveyard, Darcy.

Abandoned League Match
Jan 14 v Mansfield Town (a) 1-1
Kendal
Daniels; Mellor, Robinson, Brocklehurst, Goodfellow, Grummett, Collins, Watkinson, Kendal, Butler, Aveyard.
Att: 3,335
(Abandoned after 64 minutes due to fog)

1953-54
Lancashire Senior Cup
First Round
Oct 21 v Oldham Athletic (h) 3-0
Holliday 2, Ashe (pen)
White; Mellor, Ashe, Moran, Cadden, Sneddon, Devlin, Brown, Holliday, Eastham, Musgrave.
Att: 1,215

Second Round
Mar 8 v Blackpool (h) 2-2
Currie, Devlin
A.J.Jones; Holliday, Ashe, Bodle, Ryden, Sneddon, Devlin, Currie, Cocker, Eastham, Musgrave.
Att: 12,500
Second Round Replay
Mar 15 v Blackpool (h) 1-2
B.Jones
White; Mellor, Langstreth, Moran, Holliday, Bodle, Devlin, T.B.Jones, Watkinson, Smith, Musgrave.
Att: 8,700

Friendlies
Feb 15 v East Fife (h) 4-1
Cocker 2, Musgrave, Sneddon
White; Langstreth, Ashe, Bodle, Ryden, Sneddon, Devlin, Currie, Cocker, Eastham, Musgrave.
Att: 9,750
(Official opening of floodlights)
Feb 22 v Third Lanark (h) 1-0
Devlin
White; Holliday, Ashe, Bodle, Ryden, Sneddon, Devlin, Currie, Watkinson, Eastham, Musgrave.
Att: 10,000

Benefit Match for Dennis Smith, Thomas Butler & Richard Webster
Mar 29 v All Stars XI (h) 3-2
Brydon, Butler, Neal
Lomas(Wigan Athletic); Mellor, Galbraith, Moran, Cadden, Smith, Butler(Wigan Athletic), Neal(Bolton Wanderers), Brydon, Place, Hubbick.
Att: 7,000
Apr 8 v Clyde (h) 0-0
A.J.Jones; Holliday, Ashe, Bodle, Ryden, Sneddon, Devlin, Cocker, Brydon, Eastham, Musgrave.
Att: 6,200

1954-55
Lancashire Senior Cup
First Round
Nov 1 v Everton (h) 3-2
Cocker 3
McQueen; Ferguson, Ashe, Hunter, Ryden, Stones, Devlin, Cocker, Holliday, Wright, Henderson.
Att: 8,000

Second Round
Mar 31 v Oldham Athletic (h) 1-3
Ferguson (pen)
A.J.Jones; Ferguson, Harrower, Holliday, Ryden, Sneddon, Devlin, Cocker, Brydon, Scott, Henderson.
Att: 4,200

Friendlies
Oct 18 v St.Mirren (h) 2-2
Stewart 2
A.J.Jones; Ashe, Bodle, Hunter, Ryden, Sneddon, Devlin, Cocker, Stewart, Wright, Scott.
Att: 8,000
Nov 15 v Blackburn Rovers (h) 2-2
Scott, Stewart
A.J.Jones; Pirie, Ashe, Hunter, Ryden, Holliday, Devlin, Cocker, Brydon, Wright, Scott.
Att: 17,634
(Record Att at Peel Park)
Oct 29 v Tottenham Hotspur (h) 0-0
A.J.Jones; Pirie, Ashe, Holliday, Ryden, Bodle, Devlin, Cocker, Stewart, Wright, Scott.
Att: 6,286
(Abandoned after 52 minutes due to a waterlogged pitch)
Feb 21 v East Fife (h) 2-2
Stewart, Harrower
A.J.Jones(McQueen); Ashe, Harrower, Hunter, Ryden, Bodle, McKeown(Heggie), Cocker, Stewart, Wright, Scott.
Att: 2,339
Mar 7 v Alloa Athletic (h) 4-1
Heggie 3, Bodle
A.J.Jones; Ashe, Harrower, Hunter, Ryden, Bodle, McKeown, Wright, Heggie, Currie (Sneddon), Scott.
Att: 3,200
Mar 21 v Third Lanark (h) 1-3
Heggie
McQueen; Ashe, Holliday, Hunter, Ryden, Sneddon, Brydon, Wright(Cocker), Heggie, Bodle, Henderson.
Att: 3,400

1955-56
Lancashire Senior Cup
First Round
Oct 17 v Chester (h) 2-3

Dick, Stewart
McQueen; Ashe, Harrower, Cocker, Ryden, Sneddon, Scott, Wright, Stewart, Dick, McCredie.
Att: 3,700

Friendlies

Oct 31 v Fulham (h) 2-0
Stewart 2
McQueen; Ashe, McCredie, Hunter, Harrower, Sneddon, Cocker, Wright, Stewart, Dick, Scott.
Att: 5,350

Oct 7 v Bury (h) 2-1
Dick, Cocker
McQueen; Ashe, McCredie, Hunter, Harrower, Sneddon, Cocker, Turner, Stewart, Dick, Scott.
Att: 4,870

1956-57

Lancashire Senior Cup

First Round

Feb 26 v Manchester United (h) 3-0
Scott 2, Garrity
McInnes; McNichol, Ashe, Hunter, Harrower, Dick, Scott, Sowden, Stewart, Garrity, J.Anders.
Att: 3,700

Second Round

Apr 1 v Chester (h) 0-1
Marshall; Pirie, McCredie, Hughes, Stones, Sneddon, Wright, Cozens, Cocker, Garrity, Mason.
Att: 2,700

Friendlies

Oct 1 v Port Vale (h) 0-1
McQueen; McNichol, Ashe, Harrower, Stones, Sneddon, Scott, Turner(Sowden), Stewart, Dick, McCredie.
Att: 5,389

Nov 5 v Burnley (h) 2-0
Sowden, Dick
McQueen; McNichol, Harrower, Hunter, Stones, Sneddon, Scott, Sowden, Stewart, Dick, Millar.
Att: 10,282

Feb 18 v Doncaster Rovers (h) 3-3
Sowden, Cocker, Garrity
McInnes; McNichol, Ashe, Hunter, Harrower, Dick, Scott, Sowden, Cocker, Garrity, J.Anders.
Att: 2,927

1957-58
Lancashire Senior Cup
First Round
Feb 10 v Chester (h) 3-0
Stewart (pen), Byrom, Tighe
McInnes; McNichol, Harrower, Hunter, Kelly, Tighe, Scott, Sowden, Stewart, Dick, Byrom.
Att: 2,260
Second Round
Apr 1 v Preston North End (h) 2-3
Garrity, Sowden
Nicholson; Pirie, Kelly, Tighe, Ralston, Nightingale, Scott, Sowden, Garrity, Stinson, Byrom.
Att: 2,308

1958-59
Lancashire Senior Cup
First Round
Oct 28 v Burnley (a) 1-4
Dick
McInnes; McNichol, Lord, Tighe, Stones, Hunter, H.Anders, Mulkerrin, Stewart, Dick, J.Anders.

Friendlies
Oct 20 v Dumbarton (a) 1-1
Scott
McInnes; McNichol, Harrower, Tighe, Ralston, Dick, H.Anders, Scott, Stewart, Garrity, J.Anders.
Att: 6,000
Nov 3 v Dumbarton (h) 2-0
Stinson, Tighe
McInnes; McNichol, Lord, Tighe, Stones, Hunter(McCreadie), Gibson, Stinson, Garrity, Dick, Byrom.
Att: 2,472

Abandoned League Match
Jan 17 v Swindon Town (h) 1-0
Tighe
McInnes; McNichol, Lord, Tighe, Stones, Hamilton, H.Anders, Scott, Mulkerrin, Stinson, J.Anders.
Att: 5,579
(Abandoned after 36 minutes due to an icy pitch)

1959-60

Lancashire Senior Cup

First Round

Oct 28 v Rochdale (h) 0-1

McInnes; Garrity, Lord, Tighe, Jack, Sneddon, Bades, Keeley, McCreadie, Blackwood, Ness.

1960-61

Lancashire Cup

First Round

Oct 25 v Bury (a) 0-1

McInnes; Forrester, Lord, Sneddon, Harrower, Hamilton, Bennett, Swindells, Entwistle, Marshall, Duff.

Abandoned League Match

Aug 28 v York City (h) 1-2

Hudson

McInnes; Forrester, Harrower, Smith, Stones, Hamilton, Bennett, Swindells, Hudson, Tighe, Devine.

Att: 2,904

(Abandoned after 83 minutes due to a thunderstorm)

1961-62

Lancashire Senior Cup

First Round

Oct 16 v Bury (a) 1-0

Pickup

Smith; Forrester, Walton, Gordon, Wilson, Cuddihey, Irving, Milner, Pickup, Ferguson, Mulvey.

Second Round

Accrington Stanley were due to play Burnley at Peel Park on the 7 March 1961. The match was never played.

Friendlies

Aug 10 v Stockport County (a) 0-6

A.Smith; Pickup, Walton, Wilson(W.H.Smith), Richardson, Hamilton(Cuddihey), Bennett, Ferguson, Hudson, Sturrock, Devine.

Aug 12 v Stockport County (h) 0-1

A.Smith; Forrester, Walton, Wilson, Richardson, Hamilton, Devine(Bennett), Ferguson, Hudson, Sturrock, Mulvey(Devine).

Att: 1,477

SUBSCRIBERS

Presentation Copies

1 Accrington Stanley Football Club

2 The Football League • 3 The Football Association

4 Mike Jackman
5 Garth Dykes
6 Ann E Whitchelo
7 W H & A Jackman
8 J A Harris
9 D Ashcroft
10 Frank Clayton
11 V J Studholme
12 John G Thacker
13 Catherine Laycock
14 Mavis Jones
15 Dean Halliwell
16 Jack Brydon
17 Brian Gastall JP
18 Henry Baldwin
19 Raymond Jarzembski
20 Mrs Joan Barton
21 William Joseph Taylor
22 Mrs Debra Phillips
23 Mark Sumner
24 Geoffrey G Hall
25 Stephen Hardman
26 Stanley Sanderson
27 Terence Ross Slinger
28 Joseph Addison
29 Anthony Ireland
30 Ann Plachta
31 Alan Duxbury
32 Marion Mahoney
33 Alan Duckworth
34 Gordon Mason
35 Allan Mason
36 Graham Stirzaker
37 Anthony Mackle
38 Anthony Adrian Clements
39 D J Prior
40 Bryan Haworth
41 David Lord
42 Ian Tattersall
43 A J Mason
44 K Bassinder
45 Richard Yates
46 Andrew James Camm
47 Dave Hooley
48 Stephen Purslow
49 Richard Ashworth
50 Derek Holden
51 Anthony Foley
52 Paul Wallace Smith
53 Mr Leslie Busson
54 Peter Thomas Jordan
55 Peter Thomas Jordan
56 Peter Thomas Jordan
57 Ray Grimshaw
58 Keith Digby
59 Gerald Conroy
60 Harold Harrison
61 Kenneth Chamberlain
62 John S Kenyon
63 Norman Renton
64 Peter Vipham
65 Errick Peterson
66 Terry Wilson
67 Jonathan Charles Bond
68 John Anson
69 Dr Lance Cavannagh
70 Ernest Smith
71 B F Heyes
72 Jeff Bannister
73 G A Pratt
74 Cyril Wood
75 M L Taylor
76 Jack Hilton
77 Miss Sarah Jayne Parke
78 Alan Cook
79 Michael Pelc
80 John Honeyman
81 Stephen Wolfenden
82 Michael McDonough
83 Christian Pountain
84 David Heys
85 B H Standish
86 Brian Spridgens
87 Brian H Hobbs
88 Raymond Shaw
89 John Motson
90 George Bordessa
91 Julian Mann
92 Terry Tighe
93 Tony Hayhurst
94 James Dunn
95 Kenneth Marchant
96 Andrew C Whitham
97 Bernard Haworth
98 David Sullivan
99 K P Wood
100 Tony Hindle (Baxenden)
101 Harry Kay
102 David Coulson
103 Duncan Watt
104 D Bumstead
105 James Anders
106 W McInnes
107 W McInnes
108 W McInnes
109 Paul Gilligan
110 Roy K Shoesmith
111 David Earnshaw
112 D T Bryant
113 P Cogle
114 Ian Willott
115 Wayne Porter
116 Mike Young
117 Lars-Olof Wendler
118 John Treleven
119 J A B Townsend
120 Stewart Fell
121 John Clancy
122 David Keats
123 P J Cooke
124 James A Hodgson
125 John Hacking
126 Charles Sneddon
127 Alan Warrington
128 John K Smith
129 Phillip Hart
130 Andrew Wood
131 Alan McCabe
132 May Butterworth
133 D W Keeley
134 Ian Farrell
135 W D Phillips
136 David Downs
137 Veronica Young
138 Marie Toth
139 John S Alty
140 Terence N Styring
141 J Lesley Crossley
142 A Bolton
143 J A Borwick
144 D N Wike
145 Alan Gosling
146 Fred Yardley
147 John Berry
148 Roger Rothwell
149 Ken Jefferson
150 Philip Edmund Rose
151 Doreen Smith
152 Derek Howard
153 Eric Butterfield
154 Phil Hollow
155 Jonny Stokkeland
156 Lesley Harrison
157 Stephen Charles Pilkington
158 Mark Ollett
159 James Aspin
160 Keith Hindle
161 Stephen W Davies
162 W H Hargreaves
163 Roger Haydock
164 Leonard Jaques
165 P H Whitehead
166 Alan Wheatley
167 Moira & Frederick Furness
168 Douglas Lamming
169 J M Moore
170 Frank Grande
171 P A Robinson
172 John H Schofield
173 Howard Forrest
174 A N Davis
175 Dave Hillam
176 A F Pearson Jnr
177 David Moore
178 Norman Whittaker
179 Gary Wynne
180 John Lathan
181 J S Conway
182 Leonard Herbert
183 Dave Harrison
184 S Burt
185 Philip Leather
186 J A Pyrda

187 Sports Marketing
188 Dennis Wood
189 J Ringrose
190 Fred Beale
191 Fred Lee
192 David W Marsh
193 C J Morton
194 David J Godfrey
195 Gordon Small
196 Andrew Roberts
197 David A Barnett
198 Richard D N Wells
199 Donald Noble
200 Douglas Bidgood
201 M Woods
202 H Berry
203 Richard Shore
204 Christopher J Barnes
205 David Butterworth
206 Göran Schönhult
207 Roberto J Gamble
208 Terry Frost
209 Peter Pickup
210 Stephen Lee
211 Maurice Curtin
212 Alan D Lund
213 C Clements
214 John Norman
215 Geoffrey Wright
216 Trond Isaksen
217 Bernard O'Shea
218 J Musgrove
219 M P Waters
220 Colin Jose
221 John Stanley Bassinder
222 Walter Pearson
223 John Draper
224 Mrs A Holmes
225 Mrs A Holmes
226 L A Zammit
227 Ryan Fisher
228 J S Pyke
229 Riccardo Rossi
230 Christer Svensson
231 Geir Juva
232 Andrew Wallace
233 David A Howgate
234 Peter Frankland
235 Nicholas Brown
236 John Chambers
237 David Gregg
238 J Killelea
239 Mrs Joan Rath
240 Ian Maxwell
241 Rampton Hospital Library
242 Michael Hardman
243 G H Dady
244 Peter Hargreaves
245 Victor Herbert Allonby
246 Brian Stott
247 Roy Sproule
248 David Stark
249 Andrew James Holden
250 Andrew James Holden
251 J Gardiner
252 D K Whalley
253 Glenis Thomas (Edwards)
254 V Anders
255 John Horn
256 Phil O'Dell
257 Christine Lamb
258 J D M Whitaker
259 Timothy D Davies
260 Peter J Davies
261 T D Culshaw
262 P Marks
263 Paul H Bannister
264 Michael Briggs
265 Jim Walker
266 Miss Linda J Washington
267 Ian Petrie
268 Maurice Golesworthy
269 Peter Irving
270 Roger Shilton
271 Derek Wheatcroft
272 C Timbrell
273 Ray Hill
274 Mike Purkiss
275 George Wellock
276 Dereck Taylor
277 Ben Turner
278 David Whitworth
279 James E Snowden
280 Donald Ashwood
281 Angus W Rodger
282 Eric N Hayton
283 John van den Elsen
284 Paul Clarke
285 C Cresswell
286 S A Roberts
287 Derek Hyde
288 Peter A Lee
289 G D Painter
290 A Young
291 L Burgess
292 Patricia Arthur
293 Souris Lamplighters FC PEI
294 Colin Cameron
295 David Lumb
296 Roger Lundberg
297 Martin Simons
298 M Swart
299 S P Tomlin
300 Mario Sirianni
301 Christopher Minchin
302 Q C M Olsthoorn
303 Harry Thompson
304 Harald Lohr
305 Anders Johansson
306 Kåre M Torgrimsen
307 Andrew Tweddell
308 A H Atkins
309 R G Woolman
310 Richard Lane
311 David Helliwell
312 A P J M Otten
313 Edna A Riley
314 Christopher E C Hooker(Canada)
315 Michael Edroff
316 M R Pearce
317 Paul Vibert
318 Brian Tabner
319 Derry Good
320 B R Phillips
321 John Marshall
322 Michael Joyce
323 William Bentley
324 David Johnson
325 Paul Jerome
326 Ivan Ponting
327 D Hutt
328 Henry S Taylor
329 Lewis Bramley
330 Edward V Phillips
331 M C Savage
332 E Kautonen
333 Diamant Yozef
334 Terry Surridge
335 Gerald Hill
336 Dave Smith
337 Stanley A Robinson
338 Roger Wash
339 Hyndburn District Library, Accrington
340 Hyndburn District Library, Accrington
341 Geoff Hindle
342 Gilbert Monnereau
343 Ian Griffiths
344 Alan Hindley
345 David Crawford
346 Michael McConkey
347 Stephen Morris
348 Graham R Parkinson
349 Graham R Parkinson
350 Graham R Parkinson
351 Theodoros Mantzouranis
352 John Fitzhugh
353 Norman Green
354 A J Booth
355 David Pease
356 James Hall
357 Dave Green
358 Robert H Wallbank
359 John W Twissell
360 O F R Whittaker
361 James Angus Grayson
362 Dave Windross
363 Surapot Saengchote
364 Eric Heesom
365 M J Cheadle
366 Richard A Jones
367 Stuart Gray
368 J Gedzielewski
369 T W Stevenson
370 Aslak Bekhus
371 Duncan Pierce
372 Andrew Anderson
373 John Watson
374 Richard Stocken
375 David J Simmons
376 Kelly Louise Jones
377 Roger Leather
378 David S Allen
379 Ian Weller
380 Andrew Carruthers
381 Philip Carruthers
382 Ian Harraden
383 J Partridge
384 D Horn
385 J P Wolstenholme (Houston, Texas)
386 Harry Jones
387 Marjorie Litt
388 Alison & Jim Lakin
389 Nigel & Craig Dykes
390 Angela & Ray Burton
391 Jim Creasy
392 Mike Davage
393 Peter Windle
394 Betta Sox Limited
395 R H Bubb